MASTER[ING]
AutoCA[D]
George Omura

ISBN: 0-7821-4015-7
1,392 pages
$49.99

Written by best-selling author George Omura, this fully revised edition leads users through common tasks, paves the way for intermediate skills, and delves into more advanced topics. The book's step-by-step tutorials allow users to get started using the current release of AutoCAD, the most popular computer-aided drawing software. The CD includes general-purpose utilities, symbols libraries, demos, all the drawing exercises in the book, and full-color slides of related projects.

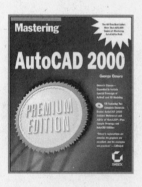

MASTERING™ AutoCAD®
2000 PREMIUM EDITION
George Omura

ISBN 0-7821-2499-2
1,664 pages
$59.99

The bestselling and most comprehensive AutoCAD book just got better. In this Premium Edition, you will get the solid foundation of *Mastering AutoCAD 2000* plus an additional 200 pages on the most important advanced topics including VBA programming, Internet distribution and security, and 3D modeling. Written by bestselling AutoCAD author George Omura, readers will obtain advanced and practical techniques and learn from Omura's involvement with the architecturally amazing San Francisco Public Library project. The CD offers general-purpose utilities for better productivity with Auto-CAD, symbols libraries, demos, all of the drawing exercises in the book, and much more.

AutoCAD® 2002
Complete

SYBEX®

San Francisco ► London

Associate Publisher: Dan Brodnitz

Acquisitions and Developmental Editor: Bonnie Bills

Compilation Editor: Scott Onstott

Editor: Tiffany Taylor

Production Editor: Leslie E.H. Light

Book Designer: Maureen Forys, Happenstance Type-o-Rama

Electronic Publishing Specialist: Franz Baumhackl

Proofreaders: Laurie O'Connell and Nancy Riddiough

Indexer: Ted Laux

Cover Designer: Design Site

Cover Photographer: Jeffery Coolidge/ImageBank

Library of Congress Card Number: 2001096974

ISBN: 0-7821-2967-6

ACKNOWLEDGMENTS

T his book is the work of many, both inside and outside Sybex including the publishing team members Dan Bronitz and Bonnie Bills, and the editorial/production team of Leslie Light, Tiffany Taylor, and Franz Baumhackl.

Scott Onstott deserves particular thanks for making sure all of the material in this book was up-to-date, organized, and flowed together in a cohesive manner.

Finally, our thanks to those contributors who agreed to have their work excerpted into *AutoCAD 2002 Complete*: Marion Cottingham, David Frey, George Omura, and Dietmar Rudolph.

CONTENTS AT A GLANCE

Introduction   xxiii

Part I   **Getting Started**   **1**

Chapter 1   Starting Up AutoCAD 2000   3
            Adapted from *AutoCAD 2000 Visual Jumpstart*

Chapter 2   Understanding How Commands Work   25
            Adapted from *AutoCAD 2000 Visual Jumpstart*

Chapter 3   Creating Your First Drawing   37
            Adapted from *Mastering AutoCAD 2002*

Part II   **Basic Drafting**   **89**

Chapter 4   Basic Commands to Get Started   91
            Adapted from *AutoCAD 2002 No Experience Required*

Chapter 5   Gaining Drawing Strategies   113
            Adapted from *AutoCAD 2002 No Experience Required*

Chapter 6   Putting Text into a Drawing   159
            Adapted from *AutoCAD 2000 Visual Jumpstart*

Chapter 7   Creating Hatch Patterns   173
            Adapted from *Mastering AutoCAD 2002*

Chapter 8   Using Dimensions   193
            Adapted from *Mastering AutoCAD 2002*

Chapter 9   Grouping Objects into Blocks   251
            Adapted from *AutoCAD 2002 No Experience Required*

Chapter 10 Storing and Linking Data with Graphics   303
            Adapted from *Mastering AutoCAD 2002*

Part III   **3D Modeling**   **357**

Chapter 11 Using Advanced 3D Features   359
            Adapted from *Mastering AutoCAD 2000 Premium Edition*

Chapter 12   Mastering 3D Solids   429
              Adapted from Mastering AutoCAD 2000 Premium Edition

Chapter 13   Using AutoCAD with VIZ   497
              Adapted from Mastering 3D Studio VIZ 3

Part IV   Customization and Programming   557

Chapter 14   Introduction to Customization   559
              Adapted from Mastering AutoCAD 2000 Premium Edition

Chapter 15   Integrating AutoCAD into Your Projects
              and Organization   611
              Adapted from Mastering AutoCAD 2000 Premium Edition

Chapter 16   Developing a Simple VBA Application   657
              Adapted from Mastering AutoCAD VBA

Chapter 17   Creating VBA Macros   683
              Adapted from Mastering AutoCAD VBA

Chapter 18   Quick Tour of the IDE   707
              Adapted from Mastering AutoCAD VBA

Chapter 19   VBA Programming Concepts   731
              Adapted from Mastering AutoCAD VBA

Chapter 20   Understanding the AutoCAD Database   785
              Adapted from Mastering AutoCAD 2000 Objects

Chapter 21   Accessing the Drawing Database   801
              Adapted from Mastering AutoCAD 2000 Objects

Chapter 22   Data Types in a Drawing Database   843
              Adapted from Mastering AutoCAD 2000 Objects

Appendix A   3D Rendering in AutoCAD   867
              Adapted from Mastering AutoCAD 2000 Premium Edition

              Index   *923*

CONTENTS

Introduction   xxiii

Part I ▸ Getting Started   1

Chapter 1 ▫ Starting Up AutoCAD 2000   3

Using the Startup Dialog Box   4
  Opening an Existing Drawing   4
  Starting a New Drawing from Scratch   6
  Using a Template to Start a New Drawing   7
  Using a Wizard to Start a New Drawing   9
How the Screen Is Organized—a Quick Tour and Setup Guide   11
  Locating the Title Bar and Pull-Down Menus   12
  Bringing Up Toolbars and Docking Them   13
  The Drawing Area—Setting the Background Color   15
  Scrollbars—How to Turn Them Off   17
  The Command Window—Setting the Number of Lines of Text   17
  The Status Bar—Setting the Buttons to On or Off   18
  The UCS Icon—Turning It Off   19
  The Crosshair—Setting Its Size   20
Saving Drawing Files   21
  Saving a New Drawing File   21
  Saving an Existing Drawing File   22
  Giving an Existing Drawing File a New Name   22
What's Next?   23

Chapter 2 ▫ Understanding How Commands Work   25

Starting Commands   26
  Using Toolbar Icon Buttons to Start Commands   26
  Starting a Command from a Toolbar Flyout   28
  Using Pull-Down Menus to Start Commands   29
  Using the Keyboard to Start Commands   30
Executing Commands   31
  Working with the Command Prompt   31
  How the Cursor Changes in the Course of a Command   32

Ending Commands   33
   Using the Enter Key to End a Command   34
   Right-Clicking to End a Command   34
What's Next?   35

Chapter 3 □ Creating Your First Drawing   37

Getting to Know the Draw Toolbar   38
   Starting Your First Drawing   42
Specifying Distances with Coordinates   48
   Specifying Polar Coordinates   48
   Specifying Relative Cartesian Coordinates   50
Interpreting the Cursor Modes and Understanding Prompts   53
   Choosing Command Options   55
Selecting Objects   59
   Selecting Objects in AutoCAD   60
   Selecting Objects before the Command: Noun/Verb   68
   Restrictions on Noun/Verb Object Selection   72
Editing with Grips   72
   Stretching Lines Using Grips   73
   Moving and Rotating with Grips   75
Getting Help   78
   Using the Search Tab   80
   Using Context-Sensitive Help   82
   Additional Sources for Help   82
Displaying Data in a Text Window   83
Displaying the Properties of an Object   84
If You Want to Experiment...   86
What's Next?   87

Part I I ▸ Basic Drafting   89

Chapter 4 □ Basic Commands to Get Started   91

The Line Command   92
Drawing a Box   95
   Using Relative Cartesian Coordinates   95
   Using Relative Polar Coordinates   97
   The Offset Command   97
   The Fillet Command   100

Completing the Box   102
   Offsetting Lines to Mark an Opening   102
   Extending Lines   104
   Trimming Lines   105
If You Would Like More Practice...   109
What's Next?   110

Chapter 5 □ Gaining Drawing Strategies   **113**

Laying Out the Walls   114
   The Exterior Wall Lines   115
   The Interior Walls   118
   Cutting Openings in the Walls   126
Creating Doors   133
   Drawing Swinging Doors   133
   Copying Objects   141
   Mirroring Objects   143
   Finishing the Swinging Doors   145
   Drawing a Sliding Glass Door   147
If You Would Like More Practice...   155
   An Alternate Sliding Glass Door   155
   An Addition to the Cabin   156
What's Next?   157

Chapter 6 □ Putting Text into a Drawing   **159**

Setting Up a Text Style   160
   Creating a New Text Style   160
   Making an Existing Text Style Current   162
Using Single-Line Text   162
   Putting Single-Line Text into a Drawing   162
   Using a New Justification Point   164
   Changing the Wording of Single-Line Text   165
   Changing Any Aspect of Single-Line Text   166
Using Multiline Text   168
What's Next?   171

Chapter 7 □ Creating Hatch Patterns   **173**

Using Hatch Patterns in Your Drawings   174
   Placing a Hatch in a Specific Area   174

Positioning Hatch Patterns Accurately 176
Changing the Hatch Area 179
Modifying a Hatch Pattern 181
Understanding the Boundary Hatch Options 183
Using the Advanced Hatch Options 184
Tips for Using the Boundary Hatch 187
Space Planning and Hatch Patterns 188
What's Next? 191

Chapter 8 □ Using Dimensions   **193**

Understanding the Components of a Dimension 194
Creating a Dimension Style 195
Setting Up the Primary Unit Style 197
Setting the Height for Dimension Text 199
Setting the Location and Orientation of Dimension Text 200
Choosing an Arrow Style and Setting the Dimension Scale 201
Setting Up Alternate Units 204
Setting the Current Dimension Style 206
Modifying a Dimension Style 206
Drawing Linear Dimensions 208
Finding the Dimension Toolbar 208
Placing Horizontal and Vertical Dimensions 209
Continuing a Dimension 210
Drawing Dimensions from a Common Base Extension Line 211
Editing Dimensions 213
Appending Data to Dimension Text 213
Locating the Definition Points 216
Making Minor Adjustments to Dimensions Using Grips 216
Changing Style Settings of Individual Dimensions 218
Editing Dimensions and Other Objects Together 224
Using True Associative Dimensions 227
Adding a String of Dimensions with a Single Operation 231
Removing the Alternate Dimensions 232
Using Osnap While Dimensioning 233
Dimensioning Nonorthogonal Objects 234
Dimensioning Nonorthogonal Linear Distances 236
Dimensioning Radii, Diameters, and Arcs 237
Adding a Note with an Arrow 240
Exploring the Leader Options 241

Skewing Dimension Lines   244
Applying Ordinate Dimensions   245
Adding Tolerance Notation   247
What's Next?   249

Chapter 9 □ Grouping Objects into Blocks   251

Making a Block for a Door   252
   Inserting the Door Block   256
Finding Blocks in a Drawing   264
   Using Grips to Detect a Block   264
   Using the List Command to Detect a Block 264
   Using the Properties Dialog Box to Detect a Block   266
Creating a Window Block   267
Inserting the Window Block   271
   Rotating a Block during Insertion   271
   Using Guidelines When Inserting a Block   274
   Using Tracking to Insert a Block   276
   Using Blips with Point Filters to Insert Blocks   277
   Finishing the Windows   280
Revising a Block   283
Sharing Information Between Drawings   286
   Dragging and Dropping Between Two Open Drawings   286
   Using AutoCAD's Design Center   289
   Other Ways to Share Information Between Drawings   296
If You Want More Practice...   299
What's Next?   300

Chapter 10 □ Storing and Linking Data with Graphics   303

Creating Attributes   304
   Adding Attributes to Blocks   305
   Adding Attribute Specifications   308
   Inserting Blocks Containing Attributes   312
Editing Attributes   316
   Editing Attribute Values One at a Time   316
   Editing Attribute Text Formats and Properties   318
   Making Global Changes to Attribute Values 319
   Making Invisible Attributes Visible   322
   Making Global Format and Property Changes to Attributes   323
   Redefining Blocks Containing Attributes   326

Extracting and Exporting Attribute Information   327
  Using Extracted Attribute Data with Other Programs   333
Accessing External Databases   333
  Setting Up Your System for Database Access   335
  Opening a Database from AutoCAD   340
  Finding a Record in the Database   341
  Adding a Row to a Database Table   344
Linking Objects to a Database   345
  Creating a Link   345
  Locating Database Records through Drawing Objects   349
  Finding and Selecting Graphics through the Database   350
  Adding Labels with Links   351
  Adding Linked Labels   353
  Hiding Labels   354
  Editing Links   354
  Where to Go from Here   356
What's Next?   356

Part III ▸ 3D Modeling   357

Chapter 11 ▫ Using Advanced 3D Features   359

Mastering the User Coordinate System   360
  Defining a UCS   361
  Saving a UCS   365
  Working in a UCS   366
  Using Viewports to Aid in 3D Drawing   371
  Controlling the UCS   377
Creating Complex 3D Surfaces   385
  Laying Out a 3D Form   385
  Using a 3D Polyline   388
  Creating a Curved 3D Surface   389
  Adjusting the Settings That Control Meshes   397
Other Surface-Drawing Tools   398
  Using Two Objects to Define a Surface   398
  Extruding an Object along a Straight Line   401
  Extruding a Circular Surface   403
Editing a Mesh   405
  Other Mesh-Editing Options   407

Moving Objects in 3D Space   408
   Aligning Objects in 3D Space   408
   Rotating an Object in 3D Space   410
Viewing Your Model in Perspective   411
   Turning on a Perspective View   416
   Using Some Visual Aids   417
   Adjusting the Camera   418
   Using Clipping Planes to Hide Parts of Your View   423
   Getting a Simple Animation of Your View   427
What's Next?   427

Chapter 12 □ Mastering 3D Solids   **429**

Understanding Solid Modeling   430
Creating Solid Forms   433
   Displaying the Solids Toolbar   434
   Creating Primitives   434
   Turning a 2D Polyline into a 3D Solid   436
   Joining Primitives   440
Creating Complex Primitives   445
   Tapering an Extrusion   445
   Extruding on a Curved Path   447
   Revolving a Polyline   450
Editing Solids   454
   Splitting a Solid into Two Pieces   454
   Rounding Corners with the Fillet Tool   456
   Chamfering Corners with the Chamfer Tool   458
   Using the Solids Editing Tools   459
Enhancing the 2D Drawing Process   475
   Drawing Standard Top, Front, and Right-Side Views   475
   Creating an Isometric View   481
   Creating Hidden-Line Views   482
   Adding Dimensions and Notes in Paper Space   485
   Drawing a Cross-Section   487
   Using 3D Solid Operations on 2D Drawings   488
Finding the Properties of a Solid   491
   Finding a Model's Mass Properties   491
Taking Advantage of Stereolithography   492
If You Want to Experiment...   493
What's Next?   495

Chapter 13 ▫ Using AutoCAD with VIZ   497

Creating Topography with Splines . . . 498
   Updating Changes from an AutoCAD File . . . 502
   Exploring Terrain Options . . . 504
Setting up an AutoCAD Plan for VIZ . . . 508
Importing AutoCAD Plans into VIZ . . . 514
   Creating a Floor with Openings . . . 522
Exploring the File Link Manager . . . 528
   Editing Linked AutoCAD Files . . . 530
   Understanding the File Link Manager Options . . . 532
   Understanding File Link Settings . . . 534
Adding Stairs . . . 540
   Tracing over Imported Lines . . . 540
   Adjusting Stair Parameters . . . 542
   Creating a Circular Stair . . . 543
   Finishing the Stair . . . 545
   Adding the Stair Walls . . . 547
Importing a Truss . . . 552
What's Next? . . . 556

Part IV ▶ Customization and Programming 557

Chapter 14 ▫ Introduction to Customization   559

Enhancements Straight from the Source . . . 560
   Opening the Express Toolbars . . . 561
   Tools for Managing Layers . . . 562
   Tools for Editing Text . . . 566
   Express Block Tools . . . 575
   Express Standard Tools . . . 575
   Tools in the Express Pull-Down Menu . . . 588
Utilities Available from Other Sources . . . 601
Putting AutoLISP to Work . . . 601
Creating Keyboard Macros with AutoLISP . . . 602
Using Third-Party Software . . . 605
   Custom-Tailoring AutoCAD . . . 606
   Third-Party Product Information on the World Wide Web . . . 607
   Autodesk's Own Offerings . . . 607

Getting the Latest Information from Online Services   607

If You Want to Experiment...   608

What's Next?   609

Chapter 15 □ **Integrating AutoCAD into Your Projects and Organization**   **611**

Customizing Toolbars   612

   Taking a Closer Look at the Toolbars Dialog Box   612

   Creating Your Own Toolbar   614

Customizing Toolbar Tools   618

   Creating a Custom Button   618

   Creating a Custom Icon   620

   Setting the Properties of Flyouts   622

   Editing Existing Buttons   624

Adding Your Own Pull-Down Menu   625

   Creating Your First Pull-Down Menu   626

   Loading a Menu   626

   How the Pull-Down Menu Works   629

Understanding the Diesel Macro Language   636

   Using Diesel in a Menu   638

   Using Diesel as a Menu Option Label   639

Creating Custom Linetypes   642

   Viewing Available Linetypes   642

   Creating a New Linetype   644

   Creating Complex Linetypes   647

Creating Hatch Patterns   649

If You Want to Experiment...   653

What's Next?   655

Chapter 16 □ **Developing a Simple VBA Application**   **657**

Advantages of Using VBA with AutoCAD   658

The AutoCAD VBA Environment   659

   Creating UserForm Modules   661

   Puttering Around in the Toolbox   662

Developing Your First Application   668

   Creating the GUI   668

   Setting Captions in the Properties Window   671

The VBA Code Window   673
Running Your Application   678
Saving Your Application   679
Returning to AutoCAD   680
What's Next?   681

Chapter 17 □ Creating VBA Macros   683

What Is a Macro?   684
   ThisDrawing Object   684
   Standard Modules   685
Creating a Macro to Add Text to a Drawing   687
   Using the IDE's Editing Features to Enter Code   687
   Saving a Macro   694
   Running a Macro   696
Using VBA's Date and Time Functions   698
   Updating Your DrawText Macro   698
Loading VBA Project Files   699
   Loading a Project Manually   700
   Loading a Project Each Time a Drawing Object Is Opened   701
   Loading a Project When AutoCAD Starts Up   701
   Canceling the Loading of a Project at Startup   703
Starting an Application from a Macro   703
What's Next?   705

Chapter 18 □ Quick Tour of the IDE   707

VBA IDE Components   708
   Exploring the Menu Bar   709
   Setting Your IDE Options   710
   The IDE's Toolbars   715
Printing UserForms   721
Overview of the Code Commands   723
   Commands for Editing Code   723
   Commands for Debugging Code   724
   Commands for Running Code   725
Getting Help   725
   Context-Sensitive Help   728
What's Next?   729

Chapter 19 □ VBA Programming Concepts 731

How Code Instructs the Computer   732
   Statements and Expressions   732
All about Variables   733
   Declaring Variables Using the Dim Statement   735
   To Declare or Not to Declare?   736
Handling Arrays of Variables   738
   Creating an Array   738
   Accessing Array Elements   739
All About Constants   740
   Declaring Symbolic Constants   741
   Viewing Built-in Constants in the Object Browser 742
Scope of Constants and Variables   746
   Public vs. Private   747
   Scope at the Procedure Level   747
   UserForm and Module-Level Scope   747
   Static Statements and the Static Keyword   748
Defining Your Own Types   752
Using Conditions to Control Code Execution   753
   If...Then... Block   753
   If...Then...Else...   755
   Select Case Statement   756
Using Loops to Repeat Code   757
   Repeating Code a Set Number of Times   757
Repeating Code an Unknown Number of Times   759
Overview of Objects, Properties, Methods, and Events   760
   All about Objects   760
   AutoCAD Drawing Objects   762
   The Microsoft Forms Object Model   764
   All about Properties   767
   All about Methods   773
   All about Events   774
Comparing VBA Programming Constructs   775
   Macros   775
   Procedures   776
Setting the Tab Order for Controls   779
   Functions   781
   Parameters and Arguments   781

Programs	782
Applications	782
What's Next?	783

Chapter 20 □ Understanding the AutoCAD Database   785

What's in a Drawing?	786
AutoCAD Drawings or AutoCAD Models?	787
Of Objects and Containers	787
Symbol Tables	788
Understanding Dictionaries	789
Combining Entities into Blocks	790
Non-objects in the Drawing Database	791
Identifying Objects	792
Linking Objects	793
Implicit Links	793
Embedding Objects	794
About Classes and Hierarchies	794
Object Properties	796
Defined versus Calculated Properties	797
Missing Properties	798
Does This Book Completely Document the AutoCAD Drawing Database?	798
Which Objects Are Covered?	799
What's Next?	799

Chapter 21 □ Accessing the Drawing Database   801

The Serialized Way—DXF	803
Some Myths about DXF	804
Some Criticisms of DXF	804
Serializing Drawing Data	805
ASCII and Binary DXF	806
Differences between ASCII and Binary DXF	808
The Structure of a DXF File	808
Objects in DXF	810
AutoLISP—DXF by Another Name	812
Database Access from AutoLISP	813
Getting Entity Names	815
Retrieving Entities with AutoLISP	816
Dictionary Access in AutoLISP	818

Modifying and Making Objects in AutoLISP   820
Reading and Writing Drawing Settings   822
The Same Data with Names—ActiveX Automation   823
Accessing the AutoCAD Database   824
Of Collections, Objects, and Interfaces   825
Accessing Entities via ActiveX Automation   826
Creating Entities via ActiveX Automation   828
Working with Dictionaries in ActiveX Automation   828
Custom Objects in ActiveX Automation   829
Non-objects in ActiveX Automation   830
The Object-Oriented Way—ObjectARX   830
Accessing the AutoCAD Database   831
Opening and Closing Objects in a Database   832
Iterating through Containers   834
Entity Handling in ObjectDBX   836
Working with Dictionaries in ObjectDBX   838
Database Settings and Result Buffers   839
Other Ways to Access the Drawing Database   839
What's Next?   841

Chapter 22 ▫ Data Types in a Drawing Database   843

Integers in the Drawing Database   844
Signed 16-Bit Integer   845
Signed 32-Bit Integer   847
Signed 8-Bit Integer   847
Disguised Integers   848
Enumerations As Integers   849
Group Codes   849
Colors and Lineweights   850
Booleans as Integers   850
Real Numbers in the Drawing Database   852
Length Units   854
Angle Units   854
Date and Time Values   854
Strings in the Drawing Database   855
Character Sets   855
Character Range   856
Handles in the Drawing Database   857
Object Pointers   857

Points in the Drawing Database 858
   Points, Coordinates, and Point Lists 858
   Points, Vectors, and Offsets 859
   Coordinate Systems 860
   Entity Coordinates 861
   The Arbitrary Axis Algorithm 862
Binary Data in the Drawing Database 864
What's Next? 865

Appendix A □ 3D Rendering in AutoCAD **867**

Things to Do Before You Start 868
Creating a Quick Study Rendering 868
   Simulating the Sunlight Angle 870
   Adding Shadows 875
   Adding Materials 879
   Adjusting the Materials' Appearance 883
Adding a Background Scene 886
Effects with Lighting 888
   Simulating the Interior Lighting of an Office Building 889
   Simulating a Night Scene with Spotlights 892
   Controlling Lights with Scenes 895
Adding Reflections and Detail with Ray Tracing 900
   Assigning a Mirror Attribute to Glass 901
   Getting a Sharp, Accurate Shadow with Ray Tracing 903
Creating and Adjusting Texture Maps 904
Adding Landscaping and People 910
Other Rendering Output Options 915
   Rendering to the Render Window 915
   Rendering Directly to a File 917
Improving Your Image and Editing 918
Smoothing Out the Rough Edges 920
If You Want to Experiment... 921

Index *923*

INTRODUCTION

A utoCAD 2002 Complete is a one-of-a-kind computer book—valuable both for the breadth of its content and for its low price. This thousand page compilation of information from some of Sybex's very best books provides comprehensive coverage of AutoCAD 2002. This book, unique in the computer book world, was created with several goals in mind:

- ▸ To offer a thorough guide covering all the important user-level features of AutoCAD 2002 at an affordable price

- ▸ To acquaint you with some of our best authors, their writing styles and teaching skills, and the level of expertise they bring to their books—so that you can easily find a match for your interests and needs as you delve deeper into AutoCAD 2002

AutoCAD 2002 Complete is designed to provide you with all the essential information you'll need to get the most from AutoCAD 2002. At the same time, *AutoCAD 2002 Complete* will invite you to explore the even greater depths and wider coverage of material in the original books.

If you have read other computer "how to" books, you have seen that there are many possible approaches to effectively using the technology. The books from which this one was compiled represent a range of teaching approaches used by Sybex and Sybex authors. From the quick, concise *AutoCAD 2002 Visual Jumpstart* to the wide-ranging, thoroughly detailed *Mastering AutoCAD, Premium Edition* style, you will be able to choose which approach and which level of expertise works best for you. You will also see what these books have in common: a commitment to clarity, accuracy, and practicality.

In these pages, you will find ample evidence of the high quality of Sybex's authors. Unlike publishers who produce "books by committee," Sybex authors are encouraged to write in their individual voices, voices which reflect their own experience with the software at hand and with the evolution of today's personal computers, so you know you are getting the benefit of their direct experience. Nearly every book represented here is the work of a single writer or a pair of close collaborators. Similarly, all of the chapters here are based on the individual experience of the authors, their first-hand testing of pre-release software, and their subsequent expertise with the final product.

In adapting the various source materials for inclusion in *AutoCAD 2002 Complete*, the compilation editor preserved these individual voices and perspectives. Chapters were edited to minimize duplication, omit coverage of non-essential information, update technological issues, and cross-reference material so you can easily follow a topic across chapters. Some sections may have been edited for length in order to include as much updated, relevant, and important information as possible.

Who Can Benefit From This Book?

AutoCAD 2002 Complete is designed to meet the needs of a wide range of computer users working with the world's most popular computer aided design software. AutoCAD 2002 provides an extraordinarily rich environment, with some elements that everyone uses, as well as features that may be essential to some users but of no interest to others. Therefore, while you could read this book from beginning to end, all of you may not need to read every chapter. The contents and the index will guide you to the subjects you're looking for.

Beginners   Even if you have only a little familiarity with computers and their basic terminology, this book will start you working with AutoCAD 2002. You'll find step-by-step instructions for all the operations involved in getting started and in basic drafting, along with clear explanations of essential concepts. You'll want to start at the very beginning of this book, Part I, which covers the basics.

Intermediate Users   Chances are you already know how to do routine tasks in AutoCAD and have a headstart when in comes to AutoCAD 2002. You are comfortable with AutoCAD and day-to-day basic drafting. You also know that there is always more to learn about working more effectively, and you want to get up to speed on the new AutoCAD 2002 features. You may also want to start creating 3D models. Throughout this book, you'll find instructions for just about anything you want to do. Nearly every chapter has nuggets of knowledge from which you can benefit.

Power Users   Maybe you're a hardcore AutoCAD fiend looking to take advantage of AutoCAD 2002's expanded capabilities, or the unofficial CAD guru of your office. There's plenty for you here, too, particularly in the chapters from the Mastering books.

This book is for people using AutoCAD 2002 in any environment. You may be a SOHO (small office and home office) user, working with a stand-alone computer or a simple peer-to-peer network with no administrators or CAD Managers to rely on. In that case, you'll find plenty of information about customizing AutoCAD and learning how to automate tasks. Or you may be working with a larger company and simply want to gain a deeper understanding of advanced features as your office migrates to AutoCAD 2002.

How This Book Is Organized

Here's a look at what *AutoCAD 2002 Complete* covers in each part:

Part I: Getting Started   Here's where you'll find the information you need to get started with AutoCAD, including detailed descriptions of all the key commands and drawing setup features.

Part II: Basic Drafting   Once you've mastered the basics, this part will let you dig deep into AutoCAD's capabilities and perform sophisticated tasks that will transform your drafting process.

Part III: 3D Modeling   If you find the third dimension an exciting extension of traditional 2D drafting, you'll love the creative techniques for 3D modeling revealed in this part.

Part IV: Customization and Programming   When it's time for you to learn how to automate repetitive tasks, or to create time saving programs to use with AutoCAD, you'll want to use this part of the book as a handy reference and constant companion.

Appendix   If you plan to use AutoCAD to create color output of your 3D models, this appendix on Rendering will be an invaluable resource.

NOTE
You can download files for this book from Sybex's website at http://www .sybex.com. Search for "AutoCAD 2002 Complete" to locate the files.

A Few Typographic Conventions

When an AutoCAD operation requires a series of choices from menus or dialog boxes, the ➤ symbol is used to guide you through the instructions, like this: "Select Programs ➤ Accessories ➤ System Tools ➤ System

Information." The items the ➤ symbol separates may be menu names, toolbar icons, check boxes, or other elements of the AutoCAD interface—any place you can make a selection.

This typeface is used to identify Internet URLs and HTML code, and **boldface type** is used whenever you need to type something into a text box.

You'll find these types of special notes throughout the book:

TIP

You'll see a lot of these Tips—quicker and smarter ways to accomplish a task, which the authors have based on many hours spent testing and using Auto-CAD 2002.

NOTE

You'll see Notes too. They usually represent alternate ways of accomplishing a task or some additional information that needs to be highlighted.

WARNING

In a few places, you'll see a Warning like this one. There are not too many because it's hard to do irrevocable things in AutoCAD unless you work at it. But when you see a Warning, do pay attention to it.

YOU'LL ALSO SEE SIDEBAR BOXES LIKE THIS

These sections provide added explanations of special topics that are referred to in the surrounding discussions, but that you may want to explore separately in greater detail.

For More Information

See the Sybex website, www.sybex.com, to learn more about all the books contributed to *AutoCAD 2002 Complete*. On the site's Catalog page, you'll find links to any book you're interested in. Also, be sure to check out the Sybex site for late-breaking developments about AutoCAD itself.

PART i
GETTING STARTED

Chapter 1

STARTING UP AutoCAD 2000

Once you have clicked the AutoCAD 2000 icon on your desktop or selected AutoCAD 2000 from the Start menu, AutoCAD begins to start up. In this chapter, I will explain how to use the Startup dialog box, take you on a quick tour of the Graphical User Interface (GUI), and show you how to save your drawing. I recommend that you read this chapter first, unless you are already familiar with the information presented here.

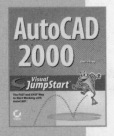

Adapted from *AutoCAD 2000 Visual Jumpstart*
by David Frey
ISBN 0-7821-2777-0   272 pages $19.99

Using the Startup Dialog Box

When AutoCAD starts, the Startup dialog box appears in the middle of your screen. It offers you several ways to begin your drawing session. You can open a drawing already stored on disk or you can create a new one, either entirely from scratch, based on a template, or with the help of a wizard. (A *wizard* is a short routine that leads you through a series of steps to accomplish a task.) The following section covers each of these options in turn.

Opening an Existing Drawing

The Open a Drawing option is used to open a drawing that has already been saved to your hard disk, a floppy disk or removable Zip disk, or a network system.

1. When the Startup dialog box opens, the button for the method you (or another user) *last* used to start AutoCAD is selected (in this case, Start from Scratch). Instead, click the Open a Drawing button.

TIP

When you hold the cursor on a button without clicking, a *ToolTip* appears that identifies the button. A ToolTip is the small text box that appears on the screen to help you identify toolbar and dialog box buttons.

2. The middle of the dialog box now displays a list of drawings that have been opened recently. Highlight one of the names in the list to see a preview image of that drawing.

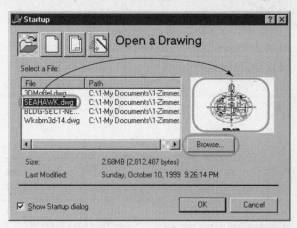

3. If the drawing you want is not in the list, click the Browse button to choose a drawing from the Sample folder, or navigate to another drawing that has been made available on your file system by another user.

4. In the Select File dialog box, navigate to the correct folder and open it. Then, find your drawing in the list and highlight it. A preview image of that drawing is displayed.

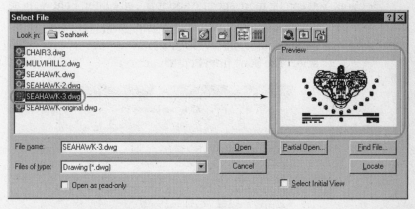

5. Click the Open button.

6. Your drawing will be opened in AutoCAD, ready to work on.

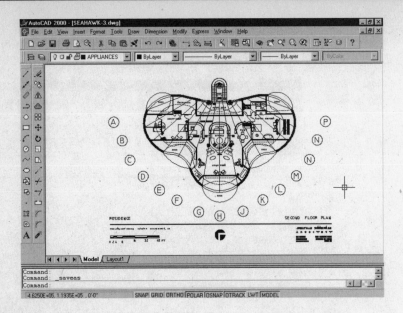

Starting a New Drawing from Scratch

The Start from Scratch option creates a blank drawing using AutoCAD's default settings, similar to the blank sheet when you start a new file with a word-processing application. (A *default setting* is a preset value that will be used unless a setting has been changed [customized].) If you just want to start drawing but aren't sure how big a sheet you will need, use this option. You can be more specific about the size later. Follow these steps:

1. On the Startup screen, ignore whatever startup method was selected previously (Open a Drawing in this example) and select the Start from Scratch button.

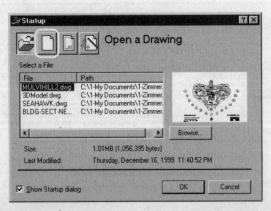

2. In the Default Settings area, you can choose between English and Metric measurements. Click the OK button. AutoCAD will bring up a blank drawing.

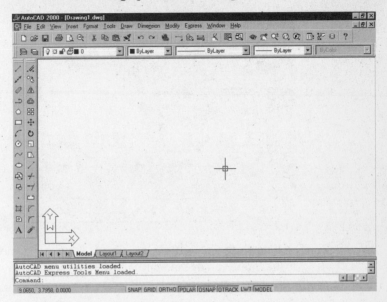

We will take a tour of the screen in the next section.

TIP

If you click the Cancel button in the Startup dialog box, AutoCAD will always start up as if you had clicked the Start from Scratch button, regardless of which of the four upper buttons is depressed in the dialog box.

Using a Template to Start a New Drawing

If you want to use a pre-drawn border and title block at a specific sheet size for your new drawing, use the Template option.

TIP

You can create your own template drawing and include it in the list of templates that come with AutoCAD. A *template drawing* is used as a pattern for new drawings. Most template files are kept in the AutoCAD 2000\Template folder, but if you know of additional locations where they might be stored, use the Browse button to navigate to a different folder. The ability to create template drawings is great if you find yourself using the same borders or text all the time.

1. On the Startup screen, ignore whatever startup method was selected previously (Start from Scratch in this example) and click the Template option.

2. Scroll down the list of template files and highlight one that you are interested in. An image preview of that template will be displayed.

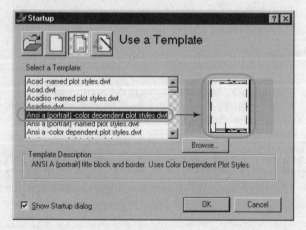

3. Click OK. A new drawing comes up based on the chosen template.

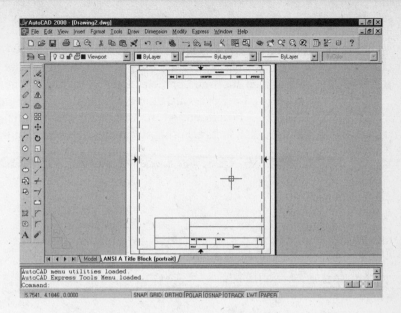

Using a Wizard to Start a New Drawing

Two wizards are available to help you set up parameters for a new drawing: Quick, which has two criteria, and Advanced, with five. Let's work through the steps of the Quick Setup Wizard:

1. On the Startup screen, ignore whatever startup method was selected previously (Use a Template in this example) and instead click the Use a Wizard button.

2. Highlight Quick Setup and click OK.

3. Click on a unit of measurement, and then click Next. A *unit of measurement* is the kind of quantity used for a distance, such as inch, foot, mile, or meter. Decimal units can represent any length. Twelve decimal units could be 12 inches, 12 yards, 12 miles, 12 meters, and so on. Architectural units are specifically feet and inches. For this example, use decimal units.

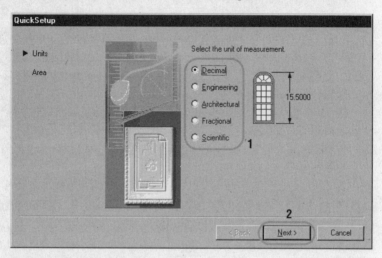

4. Enter a Width of 12 and a Length of 9 for your drawing sheet. Click Finish.

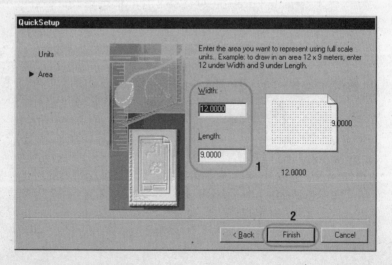

5. A new drawing comes up. It has the units and area that you set with the wizard.

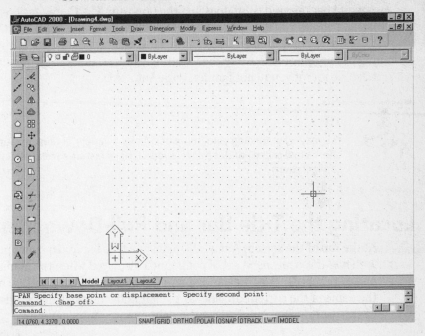

NOTE

Once AutoCAD is running, you can access the Startup dialog box by clicking File ➤ New on the pull-down menus. It's the same dialog box that opened when you started AutoCAD, except that the Open a Drawing button is not available.

HOW THE SCREEN IS ORGANIZED— A QUICK TOUR AND SETUP GUIDE

This section will take you on a quick tour of the Graphical User Interface (GUI) and show you how to set up each component to match the monitor screens shown in this chapter. A GUI is the way the monitor screen looks when AutoCAD is running. It has various parts—toolbars, menus, the drawing area, and so on. The drawing area is the large, blank portion of the AutoCAD screen where you create your drawing. The best background color for the drawing area depends on the lighting in your room and the colors you use for the lines in your drawing. A black background works well in a brightly lit room and highlights brighter colors like green and yellow. A white background color does just the opposite. The Color Options dialog box allows you to control the color of all parts of the AutoCAD GUI. I'll show you how to make some of the most basic types of customizations. It's purely optional to make these setting changes, but you should at least take the tour if you're not familiar with AutoCAD.

TIP

You may want to keep your setup as it is for a variety of reasons. AutoCAD offers a tool called Profiles that lets you save and restore several screen setup configurations.

Locating the Title Bar and Pull-Down Menus

At the top of the screen, AutoCAD displays a title bar and a menu bar with *pull-down menus* (a set of commands displayed when the menu name is clicked). The title bar displays the name of the application and the name of the current drawing at the left end, and the three window control buttons for AutoCAD at the right end.

Below the title bar, you'll find the menu bar. It contains the pull-down menus. Some of these menus contain only AutoCAD commands, and others are used in most Windows applications but have some AutoCAD commands on them. We'll start with an AutoCAD-specific menu, Draw.

1. Click the Draw menu.

2. On the Draw menu, choose Point. A *cascading menu* appears; this is a submenu that flies out from a pull-down menu when an item on it is clicked. A small arrow to the right of a menu item indicates that clicking the item will display a cascading menu with further options.

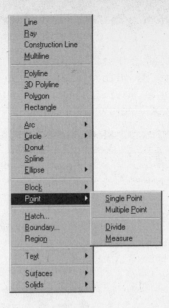

3. Press the Esc key twice to remove the menus, or click a blank part of the screen that's outside the drawing area.

TIP

When you have a menu pulled down, if you click the drawing area, a selection window begins. If you click a toolbar, a command begins. (A *toolbar* is a grouping of icons, or small pictures, that represent related commands. On the Toolbar menu, those toolbars currently visible on the screen have a checkmark next to them.) If you click the Command window, the cursor becomes a text cursor. You must click a blank area of the screen to remove the menus without making something else happen.

Bringing Up Toolbars and Docking Them

You probably have some toolbars already on your screen. Deciding which toolbars to display—that is, which tools you want to have at your fingertips—is an essential part of customizing your workspace. To give you some practice, let's bring other toolbars onto the screen and dock them. A *docked* toolbar's location has been temporarily fixed outside the drawing area, but near its edge. Toolbars on the drawing area have title bars and are called *floating* toolbars. You will also un-dock toolbars in this exercise:

1. The toolbar that is just under the menu bar is the Standard toolbar. Move the cursor onto the toolbar and place it over one of the icons. The icons become buttons, and a ToolTip appears, identifying the command.

2. Right-click any of the buttons. A menu appears with a list of available toolbars.

3. Click Inquiry on the Toolbar menu. The Inquiry toolbar appears. It has commands that help you get information about your drawing.

4. Click the title bar of the Inquiry toolbar, hold down the mouse button, and drag the toolbar to the right side of the drawing area.

5. When the rectangle changes its shape, release the mouse button. The toolbar will be *docked* on the right side of the screen.

6. Move the cursor to the double bars at the top of the docked Inquiry toolbar, hold down the left mouse button, and drag the toolbar onto the screen.

7. Release the mouse button. The toolbar regains its title bar.

8. Click the toolbar's Close button. The toolbar is removed from the screen.

The Drawing Area—
Setting the Background Color

The large open area in the middle of the screen where you construct your drawing is called the *drawing area*. You can control its background color using the Options dialog box.

1. Open the Options dialog box from the Tools menu.

2. In the Options dialog box, click the Display tab.

3. On the Display tab, click the Colors button.

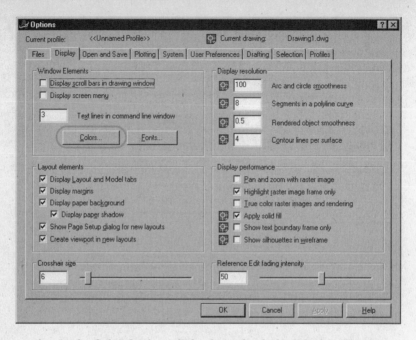

4. In the Color Options dialog box, check the Window Element drop-down list to be sure Model Tab Background is displayed. If it's not, open the list and choose it.

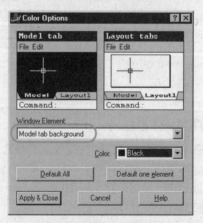

5. Open the Color drop-down list and choose White.

6. Click the Apply & Close button.

7. In the Options dialog box, click OK.

Scrollbars—How to Turn Them Off

A *scrollbar* is a strip with arrow buttons and a slider on the side of a draw-ing. You use it to slide the current drawing around on the screen. The scrollbars on the right and bottom of the drawing area aren't necessary, because AutoCAD provides tools that do the same thing a better way.

These scrollbars also take up space that could be used for the drawing area. Of course, if you are comfortable with them and prefer to use them, leave them on the screen. To remove the scrollbars, follow these steps:

1. Open the Options dialog box from the Tools menu.

2. In the Options dialog box, click the Display tab.

3. On the Display tab, uncheck the Display Scroll Bars in Draw-ing Window check box.

4. Click Apply, and then click OK.

The Command Window—
Setting the Number of Lines of Text

In the Command window, AutoCAD gives you instructions and feedback as it executes commands for you. It is helpful to have at least three lines of text displayed here.

1. Check your Command window for the number of lines of text displayed. If you already have three lines, go on to the next section.

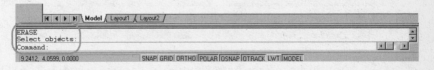

2. To change the number of lines, choose Tools ➤ Options to open the Options dialog box.

3. In the Options dialog box, click the Display tab.

4. On the Display tab, change the Text Lines in Command Line Window text box setting to 3.

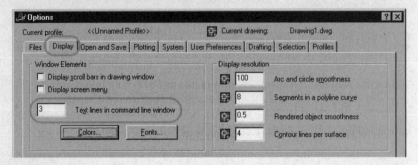

5. Click Apply, and then Click OK.

The Status Bar—
Setting the Buttons to On or Off

At the very bottom of the screen, you'll see a coordinate display and a set of buttons. To turn the buttons on or off, follow these steps:

1. Move the crosshair on the screen and keep your eye on the coordinate display. It displays the position of the crosshair in an *x, y, z coordinate*. These three numbers, separated by commas, specify the location of a point in 3D space.

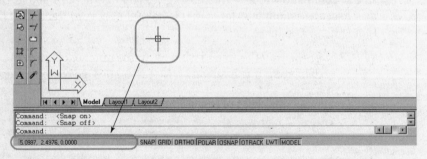

2. Click the Snap button until it looks pressed in; this is the On position. When the button is in the out position, it is Off.

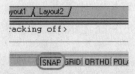

3. Click any buttons on the status bar necessary to set the Model button on the far right to On and the rest of the buttons to Off.

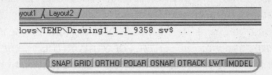

The UCS Icon—Turning It Off

The icon in the lower left of the drawing area is called the User Coordinate System (UCS) icon.

The orientation of the UCS tells you the current directions of the *x and y axes,* which are the two directions—left/right and up/down—that define the plane you draw on in AutoCAD. You won't need to know much about this feature for this chapter, but let's look at it so you'll know how to hide the icon if you prefer:

1. Open the View pull-down menu.

2. Click Display, and then click UCS Icon.

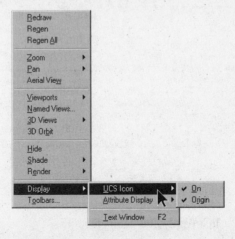

3. Click On to remove the checkmark and turn off the UCS icon.

The Crosshair—Setting Its Size

The *crosshair cursor* is the form of the cursor that AutoCAD uses for drawing lines. It consists of intersecting vertical and horizontal lines. Their intersection is the current location of the cursor. By making the crosshair lines long, you have the advantage of being able to line up objects vertically and horizontally on the screen. For clarity in this chapter, however, I have set the lines of the crosshair to be short. You may want them to extend to the edges of the drawing area on your own screen.

1. Click Tools ➤ Options to open the Options dialog box.

2. In the Options dialog box, click the Display tab.

3. On the Display tab, drag the sliding handle for the Crosshair Size to the right or left. The text box will read the percentage of the screen across which the crosshairs will extend. For the chapter, the size is set to 6%.

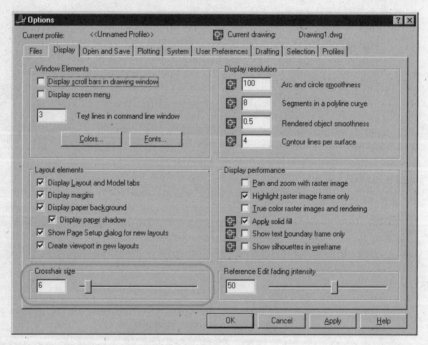

4. Click Apply and then click OK.

This completes the tour of the AutoCAD graphical user interface.

SAVING DRAWING FILES

When you end a drawing session, you can save your work in several ways.
These options are illustrated in this section.

Saving a New Drawing File

When you finish working on a new drawing that has not yet been saved,
the drawing will need to be named and stored in a folder.

1. Click the Save button on the Standard toolbar.

2. In the Save Drawing As dialog box, navigate to the folder
    where you want to save the new drawing. Open that folder.

3. In the File Name text box, type in the drawing's name.

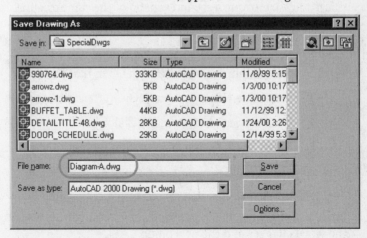

4. Click the Save button.

5. Back in the main AutoCAD window, check the title bar to be sure it includes the new name of the drawing.

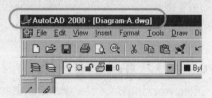

Saving an Existing Drawing File

When you finish working on an existing drawing that has already been named and located in a folder, all you need to do to save your changes is to click the Save button.

Giving an Existing Drawing File a New Name

If you have changed an existing drawing and want to save it separately from the original drawing, you can save it with a new name. You might do this if you are creating a second version of the same original drawing.

1. Open the File pull-down menu and click Save As.

2. In the Save Drawing As dialog box, navigate to the folder that will contain the new drawing. Open that folder.

3. In the File Name text box, type in the drawing's new name.

4. Click the Save button in the dialog box.

5. Check the Title Bar to be sure it includes the new name of the drawing.

You'll find that the old version of the drawing still exists in its unsaved version with the original name, and you have a new second drawing with the saved changes and the new name.

WHAT'S NEXT?

This chapter introduced you to the AutoCAD GUI. It also illustrated how to start up AutoCAD, adjust some of the default settings of the GUI, and save drawing files in various ways. The next chapter is an overview of the procedures for executing commands in AutoCAD.

Part i

Chapter 2

UNDERSTANDING HOW COMMANDS WORK

In AutoCAD, a large number of commands are at your disposal. You will learn the basic commands in this chapter and, over time, become familiar with others. This chapter is meant to be used as a reference, to help you get a general idea of how commands work.

Adapted from *AutoCAD 2000 Visual Jumpstart*
by David Frey
ISBN 0-7821-2777-0   272 pages $19.99

STARTING COMMANDS

A *command* is a contained action taken by AutoCAD, such as making a circle or erasing a line. Each command discussed in this book can be started in several ways. We will mostly use toolbars and pull-down menus to start commands, but in this chapter we will also look at how to initiate and execute commands from the keyboard.

Using Toolbar Icon Buttons to Start Commands

The toolbars have icons for the most-used commands. An icon changes into a button when you roll the pointer cursor over it, and you can then click it to start the command. Using the toolbars is often the quickest way to start commands, so you should note whether the command you want is on a toolbar that is currently on the screen:

1. Move the cursor to the toolbar that contains the icon of the command you wish to start, and hold the *pointer arrow* (the form the AutoCAD cursor takes when it is not in the drawing area) on the icon until a ToolTip appears and identifies the icon. At the same time, the icon now looks like it's on a button.

2. Click and release the left mouse button while keeping the pointer on the button.

NOTE

For the rest of this chapter, we will refer to the toolbar icon button as the button for a command.

When the command starts:

3. A dialog box may appear on the screen, depending on the command you choose.

NOTE

Dialog boxes usually contain several options for completing a command.

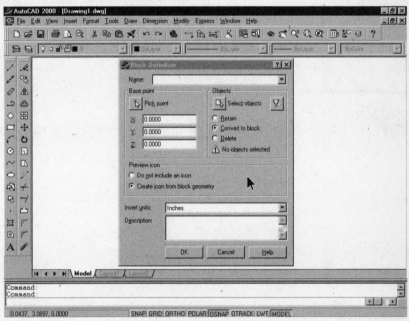

Or:

4. The Command window may change and prompt you to take the next step in the command. (A *prompt* is the information or choices on the Command line that AutoCAD requests from you.)

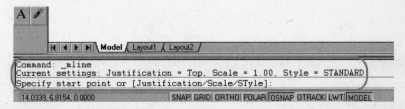

Starting a Command from a Toolbar Flyout

Some command buttons are on *toolbar flyouts*—subtoolbars that are accessed from a button on the regular toolbars. You can open the flyout to access all the command buttons on it:

1. Move the pointer cursor to any button that has a flyout. These buttons have a black arrow below and to the right of the button icon.

2. Place the pointer arrow on the button and hold down the left mouse button. The flyout will open.

NOTE

Some of the toolbar flyouts can be opened and docked like regular toolbars.

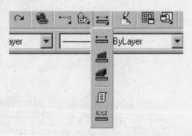

3. Keep holding down the left mouse button and move the pointer cursor down the flyout. Stop it on the button you want. A ToolTip will identify the button.

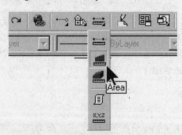

TIP

Once a command from a flyout is used, its button replaces the flyout button that was on the original toolbar. You can then just click the top flyout button to execute that command without having to reopen the flyout.

4. Release the button, and the command begins.

Using Pull-Down Menus to Start Commands

The pull-down menus contain most of the commands you will need to use in AutoCAD:

NOTE

Almost all the commands on the toolbars can be found on the pull-down menus.

1. Move the cursor to the pull-down menu bar and rest the pointer on the menu title you want to open. The selected menu title will look like it's on a button. Click on the menu. The menu opens.

2. Move the pointer down the menu to the command you wish to start.

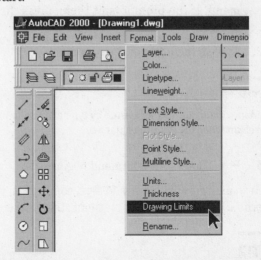

TIP

Commands on the pull-down menus that have an ellipsis (...) are executed using dialog boxes. The others use the command line. If you need a refresher, see Chapter 1.

3. Click the menu item. The menu disappears, and the command begins.

NOTE

In this chapter and throughout the book, *click* means to click and release the left mouse button. When you need to click the right mouse button, I will say *right-click*.

Using the Keyboard to Start Commands

Many users consider the keyboard the fastest way to start and run commands:

1. Look at the Command window and be sure the Command *prompt* (text that says Command:) is on the bottom line of the Command window. It tells you that no commands are currently running, and it's waiting for you to enter the next command. If the prompt isn't there, press the Esc key until it appears.

2. Type in the name of the command.

TIP

Many commands can be started by typing in one or two letters, like O for Offset, and then pressing the Enter key.

3. Press Enter. The command begins.

With so many available ways to start commands, you will need to find the method, or combination of methods, that best serves you.

TIP

Some commands can be started by holding down the Ctrl key while pressing a letter key, such as Ctrl+P for Plot. Such a key combination is called a *hotkey*.

EXECUTING COMMANDS

Once a command has been started, several actions may be required to complete the execution of the command. As you finish one stage of the command and begin the next, the Command window will prompt you for what you need to do next, and the cursor will often change its form.

Working with the Command Prompt

The lines in the Command window give you the information you need to execute a command. They are as follows.

NOTE
You may have to enter data, click buttons in a dialog box, pick points on the screen, or all three, in the course of a command.

▶ The display of the Command prompt (Command:) on the bottom line of the Command window is AutoCAD's signal to you that no commands are running. It means you can now start a command.

▶ Once a command is started, the command's name is usually—but not always—displayed on one of the three command lines. The bottom line prompts you to take an action.

TIP
In the Command window, the command that's been started usually has an underscore (_) before its name.

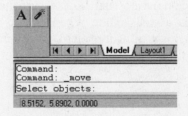

NOTE
You can use the Options dialog box to set the number of lines displayed in the Command window. See Chapter 1 for instructions.

▶ Sometimes the bottom line prompts you to make choices. You can choose a command option by entering its capitalized letters.

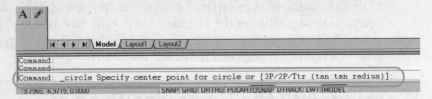

▶ Sometimes the bottom line prompts you to enter data.

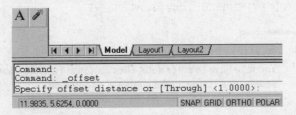

▶ When a command has finished executing, you'll see `Command:` again on the bottom line.

How the Cursor Changes in the Course of a Command

The AutoCAD cursor may take on several forms in the course of a command's being executed. Each form gives you a clue about what you need to do at the time:

▶ When no command is running, the cursor has a pickbox superimposed on the crosshair. A *pickbox* is the form of the cursor that looks like a small square. When the cursor is a pickbox by itself, AutoCAD is waiting for you to select items in the drawing or—if you are finished selecting—to press Enter.

NOTE
You can adjust the length of the crosshairs. See Chapter 1.

▶ When you are prompted to select items on the screen, the pick-box appears by itself.

▶ The crosshair by itself indicates that you need to pick reference points in the drawing.

▶ When you move the cursor (in any of its forms) off the drawing area, it changes to the standard selection pointer.

TIP

The cursor will also change to a pointer when it moves onto a dialog box, menu, or toolbar that is on the drawing area.

ENDING COMMANDS

Some commands automatically end when they have done their work. Others will continue to be active until you end them yourself. For example, the Circle command ends once one circle is drawn. On the other hand, the Line command continues running until you end it, because it assumes you will want to draw multiple line segments that are connected to each other. You must tell AutoCAD to end the Line command. You can use three tools to end commands: You can press the Enter key, right-click, or press Esc.

TIP

When a command ends, Command: is displayed in the bottom line of text in the Command window.

Using the Enter Key to End a Command

Pressing the Enter key will do different things at different times in the execution of a command. It is particularly useful for ending commands:

1. When you have finished using a command, but it hasn't ended, a prompt for further action will still be on the bottom line of the Command window.

2. Press the Enter key. The command ends, and the Command: prompt returns.

Right-Clicking to End a Command

Right-clicking the mouse performs several functions, including that of ending a command:

1. When you have finished using a command, but it hasn't ended, a prompt for further action will still be on the bottom line of the Command window.

2. Right-click. A shortcut menu appears on the screen near the cursor; the shortcut menu offers several options for the current command.

TIP

You can set the right-click function to do exactly what pressing Enter does. Choose Tools ➢ Options, click the User Preferences tab, and click the Right-Click Customization button. Then, change the settings to your preference.

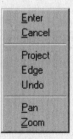

3. Click Enter on the shortcut menu. The command ends and the Command: prompt returns.

TIP

Pressing the Esc key once or twice will cancel a command at any point in the course of its execution.

TIP

You can restart the command that just ended by pressing Enter, or by right-clicking, and then clicking the top item on the shortcut menu.

WHAT'S NEXT?

This chapter has provided a general summary of how commands work in AutoCAD. I hope it will make learning the commands less of an ordeal and more of an adventure for you. In the next chapter, you will put this knowledge to work and create your first drawing.

Part i

Chapter 3

CREATING YOUR FIRST DRAWING

This chapter examines some of AutoCAD's basic functions. You will get a chance to practice with the drawing editor by building a simple drawing to use in later exercises. You'll learn how to give input to AutoCAD, interpret prompts, and get help when you need it. This chapter also covers the use of coordinate systems to give AutoCAD exact measurements for objects. You'll see how to select objects you've drawn and how to specify base points for moving and copying.

If you're not a beginning AutoCAD user, you might want to move on to the more complex material in Chapter 4. You can use the files supplied on the companion website of this book to continue the tutorials at that point.

Adapted from *Mastering™ AutoCAD® 2002*
by George Omura
ISBN 0-7821-4015-7   1,392 pages $49.99

Getting to Know the Draw Toolbar

Your first task in learning how to draw in AutoCAD is simply to draw a line. But before you begin drawing, take a moment to familiarize yourself with the toolbar you'll be using more than any other to create objects with AutoCAD: the Draw toolbar.

1. Start AutoCAD just as you did in Chapter 1, by choosing Start ➤ Programs ➤ AutoCAD 2002 ➤ AutoCAD 2002.

2. When the AutoCAD 2002 Today dialog box appears, click the Close button. You'll learn more about this dialog box later in this chapter and in Chapter 4.

3. In the AutoCAD window, move the arrow cursor to the top icon in the Draw toolbar, which is the vertical toolbar at the far left of the AutoCAD window, and rest it there so that the ToolTip appears.

4. Slowly move the arrow cursor downward over the other tools in the Draw toolbar, and read each ToolTip.

In most cases, you'll be able to guess what each tool does by looking at its icon. The icon with an arc, for instance, indicates that the tool draws arcs; the one with the ellipse shows that the tool draws ellipses; and so on. For further clarification, the ToolTip gives you the name of the tool. In addition, the status bar at the bottom of the AutoCAD window gives you information about a tool. For example, if you point to the Arc icon just below the Rectangle icon, the status bar reads Creates an Arc. It also shows you the actual AutoCAD command name: Arc. You type this command in the Command window to invoke the Arc tool. You also use this word if you are writing a macro or creating your own custom tools.

Table 3.1 will aid you in navigating the two main toolbars, Draw and Modify. You'll get experience with many of AutoCAD's tools as you work through this book.

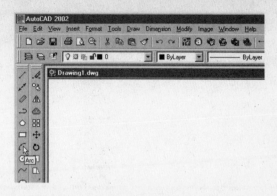

TABLE 3.1 The Options on the Draw and Modify Toolbars

DRAW		MODIFY	
ICON	TOOL	ICON	TOOL
	Line		Erase
	Construction Line (Xline)		Copy Object
	Multiline (Mline)		Mirror
	Polyline (Pline)		Offset
	Polygon		Array
	Rectangle		Move
	Arc		Rotate
	Circle		Scale
	Spline		Stretch
	Ellipse		Lengthen
	Ellipse Arc (new since 2000)		Trim
	Insert Block		Extend
	Make Block		Break at Point (new since 2000)
	Point		Break

TABLE 3.1 CONTINUED The Options on the Draw and Modify Toolbars

DRAW		MODIFY	
ICON	TOOL	ICON	TOOL
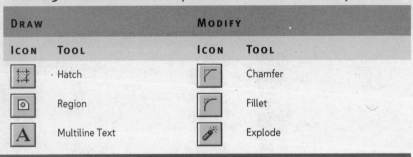	Hatch		Chamfer
	Region		Fillet
	Multiline Text		Explode

Clicking a tool issues a command. Some tools allow clicking and dragging, which opens a flyout. A flyout offers further options for that tool. You can identify flyout tools by a small triangle located in the lower-right corner of the tool.

1. Click and drag the Zoom Window tool on the Standard toolbar. A flyout appears with an additional set of tools. These tools allow you to adjust your view in various ways.

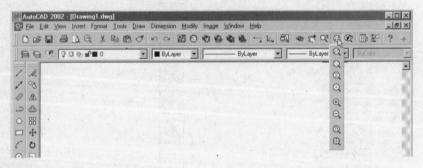

2. Move the cursor down the flyout to the last tool, until the ToolTip reads *Zoom Extents*; let go of the mouse button. Notice that the icon representing the Zoom Windows tool now changes and becomes the icon from the flyout that represents Zoom Extents.

By selecting the Zoom Extents tool, you've also issued the Zoom Extents command. This command adjusts the view of the drawing so that it fills the drawing area. Because there is currently nothing in the drawing, the view doesn't change. You'll use Zoom Extents in Chapter 4 and see how it behaves when the drawing contains objects.

3. For now, you'll want to keep the Zoom Window tool visible in the Standard toolbar, so click and drag the Zoom Extents tool, and then select Zoom Window from the top of the flyout. Press the Escape key to cancel the Zoom Window command. You'll get a chance to use Zoom Window in Chapter 4.

By making the most recently selected option on a flyout the default option for the toolbar tool, AutoCAD gives you quick access to frequently used commands. A word of caution, however: This feature can confuse the first-time AutoCAD user. Also, the grouping of options on the flyout menus is not always self-explanatory—even to a veteran AutoCAD user.

TIP

If you find you are working a lot with one particular flyout, you can easily open a version of the flyout as a floating toolbar, so that all the flyout options are readily available with a single click. For example, the Zoom flyout you just used can be opened as a toolbar by right-clicking any toolbar and then selecting Zoom from the right-click menu.

WORKING WITH TOOLBARS

As you work through the exercises, this book will show you the tools to choose, along with the toolbar or flyout that contains the tool. Don't be alarmed, however, if the toolbars you see in the examples don't look exactly like those on your screen. To save page space, I have oriented the toolbars and flyouts horizontally for the illustrations; the ones on your screen may be oriented vertically, like the Draw and Modify toolbars to the left of the AutoCAD window.

Although the shape of your toolbars and flyouts may differ from the ones you see in this book, the contents are the same. So when you see a graphic showing a tool, focus on the tool icon itself with its ToolTip name, along with the name of the toolbar in which it is shown.

Starting Your First Drawing

You will begin your own drawing by creating a door that will be used in later exercises. First, though, you must learn how to tell AutoCAD what you want and, even more important, to understand what AutoCAD wants from you.

TIP

In this chapter, you'll see instructions for both English measurement and metric users. In general, I give the instructions for English measurement first, followed by the metric instructions. You won't be dealing with inches or centimeters yet, however. You're just getting to know the AutoCAD system.

1. Choose File ➤ Close to close the current file. Click No in the Save Changes dialog box. Notice that the toolbars disappear and the AutoCAD drawing window appears blank when no drawings are open.

2. Choose File ➤ New. The AutoCAD 2002 Today dialog box appears, with the Create Drawings tab selected in the My Drawings portion.

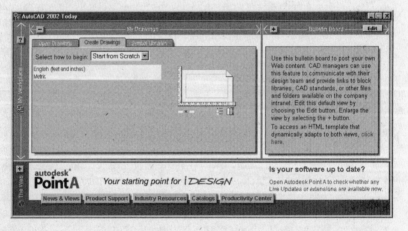

3. Click the Select How to Begin drop-down list and select Wizards. Two new options appear below the drop-down list: Quick Setup and Advanced Setup.

4. Click the Quick Setup option. The Units dialog box appears.

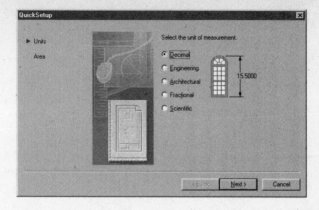

5. For now, you'll use the default decimal units, as indicated by the radio buttons. You'll learn more about these options in the next chapter. Click Next in the Units dialog box. The Area dialog box appears.

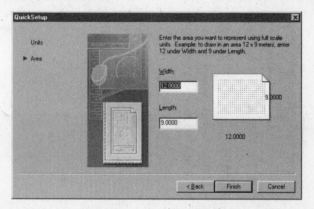

6. If the Width text box doesn't already show 12, double-click it and enter **12**. Metric users should enter **40**.

7. Press the Tab key to move to the next text box and enter **9**. Metric users should enter **30**.

8. Click Finish. A new drawing file appears in the AutoCAD window.

9. Choose View ➤ Zoom ➤ All from the menu bar. Doing so ensures that your display covers the entire area you specified in steps 6 and 7.

10. To give your new file a unique name, choose File ➤ Save As.

11. At the Save Drawing As dialog box, type **Door**. As you type, the name appears in the File Name text box.

12. Double-click the Sample folder shown in the main file list of the dialog box. By doing this, you open the Sample subdirectory.

13. Click Save. You now have a file called Door.dwg, located in the Sample subdirectory of your AutoCAD2002 directory. Of course, your drawing doesn't contain anything yet. You'll take care of that next.

The new file shows a drawing area roughly 12 inches wide by 9 inches high. Metric users will have a file that shows an area roughly 40 mm wide by 30 mm high. This area is your workspace, although you're not limited to it in any way. No visual clues indicate the size of the area. To check the area size for yourself, move the crosshair cursor to the upper-right corner of the screen and observe the value shown in the coordinate readout. This is the standard AutoCAD default drawing area for new drawings.

To begin a drawing, follow these steps:

1. Click the Line tool on the Draw toolbar, or type **L** and press Enter.

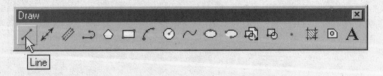

You've just issued the Line command. AutoCAD responds in two ways. First, you see the message

    Specify first point:

in the Command prompt, asking you to select a point to begin your line. Also, the cursor has changed its appearance; it no longer has a square in the crosshairs. This is a clue telling you to pick a point to start a line.

TIP

Throughout this book, you'll be given the option to use the keyboard shortcuts for commands. For example, in step 1, you were given the option to type **L** and press Enter in the Command window to start the Line command.

2. Using the left mouse-button, select a point on the screen near the center. As you select the point, AutoCAD changes the prompt to

```
Specify next point or [Undo]:
```

Now as you move the mouse around, notice a line with one end fixed on the point you just selected, and the other end following the cursor (see the top image of Figure 3.1). This action is called *rubber-banding*.

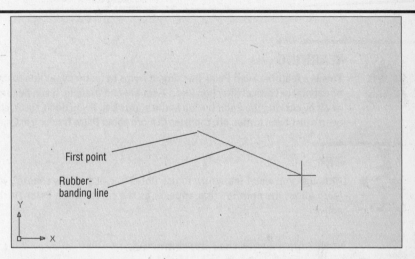

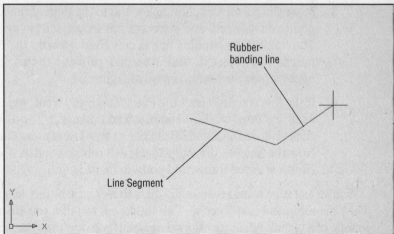

FIGURE 3.1: Two rubber-banding lines

If you move the cursor to a location directly to the left or right of the point you clicked on, you'll see a dotted horizontal line appear, along with a message that appears at the cursor. This action also occurs when you point directly up or down. In fact, your cursor will seem to jump to a horizontal or vertical position.

Polar: 2.7083 < 0°

WARNING

This is a feature called Polar Tracking. It helps to restrict your line to an exact horizontal or vertical direction like a T-square and triangle. It can be turned on or off by clicking the Polar button in the status bar. If you don't see it, chances are it's just been turned off. You'll learn more about Polar Tracking in Chapter 4.

TIP

Although you won't learn how to use Polar Tracking in this chapter, you will learn about the notation that appears by the cursor when Polar Tracking is active.

Now continue with the Line command:

3. Move the cursor to a point below and to the right of the first point you selected, and press the left mouse button again. The first rubber-banding line is now fixed between the two points you selected, and a second rubber-banding line appears (see the bottom image of Figure 3.1).

4. If the line you drew isn't the exact length you want, you can back up during the Line command and change it. To do this, click Undo in the Standard toolbar, or type **U** and press Enter. Now the line you drew previously will rubber-band as if you hadn't selected the second point to fix its length.

You've just drawn, and then undrawn, a line of an arbitrary length. The Line command is still active. Two things tell you that you are in the middle of a command, as mentioned earlier. If you don't see the word Command in the bottom line of the Command window, you know a command is still active. Also, the cursor will be the plain crosshair without the box at its intersection.

TIP

From now on, I will refer to the crosshair cursor without the small box as the *point selection mode* of the cursor. If you look ahead to Figure 3.7, you'll see all the different modes of the drawing cursor.

GETTING OUT OF TROUBLE

Beginners and experts alike are bound to make a few mistakes. Before you get too far into the tutorial, here are some powerful yet easy-to-use tools to help you recover from accidents.

Backspace (←)   If you make a typing error, you can use the Backspace key to back up to your error, and then retype your command or response. Backspace is located in the upper-right corner of the main keyboard area.

Escape (Esc)   This is perhaps the single most important key on your keyboard. When you need to quickly exit a command or dialog box without making changes, just press the Esc key in the upper-left corner of your keyboard. In prior versions of AutoCAD, you had to press Esc twice in some instances. Beginning with AutoCAD 2000, you only need to press Esc once, though it won't hurt to press it twice.

Tip: Use the Esc key before editing with grips or issuing commands through the keyboard.

U+Enter   If you accidentally change something in the drawing and want to reverse that change, click the Undo tool in the Standard toolbar (the left-pointing curved arrow). You can also type **U** and press Enter at the Command prompt. Each time you do this, AutoCAD will undo one operation in reverse order, so the last command performed will be undone first, then the next-to-last command, and so on. The prompt displays the name of the command being undone, and the drawing reverts to its state prior to that command. If you need to, you can undo everything back to the beginning of an editing session.

Redo+Enter   If you accidentally Undo one too many commands, you can redo the last undone command by clicking the Redo tool (the right-pointing curved arrow) in the Standard toolbar. Or type **Redo** and press Enter. Unfortunately, Redo only restores one command, and it can only be invoked immediately after an Undo.

Part i

Specifying Distances with Coordinates

Next, you will continue with the Line command to draw a plan view (an overhead view) of a door, to no particular scale. Later, you will resize the drawing to use in future exercises. The door will be 3.0 units long and 0.15 units thick. For metric users, the door will be 9 units long and 0.5 units thick. To specify these exact distances in AutoCAD, you can use either relative polar coordinates or Cartesian coordinates.

WARNING

The English and metric distances are not equivalent in the exercises of this chapter. For example, 3 units in the English-based drawing are not equal to 9 metric units. These distances are arbitrary and based on how they will appear in the figures of this chapter.

Specifying Polar Coordinates

To enter the exact distance of 3 (or 9 metric) units to the right of the last point you selected, do the following:

1. Type **@3<0**. Metric users should type **@9<0**. As you type, the letters appear at the Command prompt.

2. Press Enter. A line appears, starting from the first point you picked and ending 3 units to the right of it (see Figure 3.2). You have just entered a relative polar coordinate.

The at sign (@) you entered tells AutoCAD that the distance you are specifying is from the last point you selected. The 3 (or 9 metric) is the distance, and the less-than symbol (<) tells AutoCAD that you are designating the angle at which the line is to be drawn. The last part is the value for the angle, which in this case is 0. This is how to use polar coordinates to communicate distances and directions to AutoCAD.

TIP

If you are accustomed to a different method for describing directions, you can set AutoCAD to use a vertical direction or downward direction as 0°. See Chapter 4 for details.

Angles are given based on the system shown in Figure 3.3, where 0° is a horizontal direction from left to right, 90° is straight up, 180° is horizontal from right to left, and so on. You can specify degrees, minutes, and seconds of arc if you want to be that exact. We'll discuss angle formats in more detail in Chapter 4.

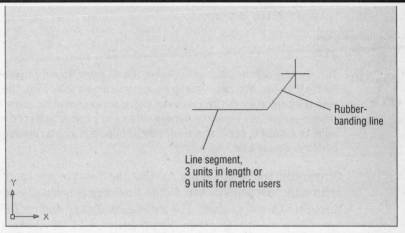

FIGURE 3.2: Notice that the rubber-banding line now starts from the last point selected. This tells you that you can continue to add more line segments.

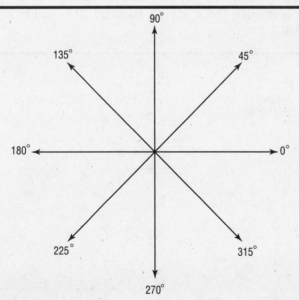

FIGURE 3.3: AutoCAD's default system for specifying angles

Specifying Relative Cartesian Coordinates

For the next line segment, let's try another method of specifying exact distances:

1. Enter **@0,0.15** and press Enter. Metric users should enter **@0,0.5** and press Enter. A short line appears above the endpoint of the last line.

TIP

This section indicates that metric users should enter **@0,0.5** and press Enter for the distance. You can also enter **0,.5** (zero comma point five). The leading zero is included for clarity. European metric users should be aware that the comma is used as a separator between the *x* and *y* components of the coordinate. In AutoCAD, commas are not used for decimal points; you must use a period to denote a decimal point.

Once again, the @ tells AutoCAD that the distance you specify is from the last point picked. But in this example, you give the distance in x and y values. The x distance, 0, is given first, followed by a comma, and then the y distance, 0.15. This is how to specify distances in relative Cartesian coordinates.

2. Enter **@-3,0** and press Enter. Metric users should enter **@-9,0** and press Enter. The result is a drawing that looks like Figure 3.4.

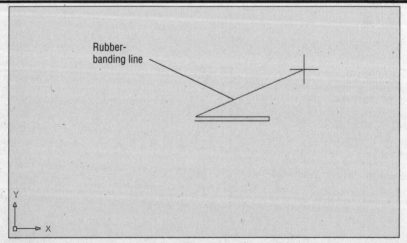

Rubber-
banding line

FIGURE 3.4: These three sides of the door were drawn using the Line tool. Points are specified using either relative Cartesian or polar coordinates.

WARNING

The distance you entered in step 2 was also in x, y values, but here you used a negative value to specify the x distance. Positive values in the Cartesian coordinate system are from left to right and from bottom to top (see Figure 3.5). (You may remember this from your high school geometry class!) If you want to draw a line from right to left, you must designate a negative x value.

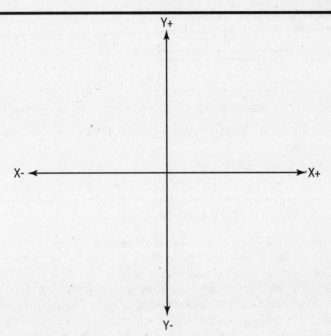

FIGURE 3.5: Positive and negative Cartesian coordinate directions

TIP

To finish drawing a series of lines without closing them, you can press Esc or the spacebar.

3. Now type **C** and press Enter. This C stands for the Close command. It closes a sequence of line segments. A line connecting the first and last points of a sequence of lines is drawn (see Figure 3.6), and the Line command terminates.

The rubber-banding line also disappears, telling you that AutoCAD has finished drawing line segments. You can also use the rubber-banding line to indicate direction while simultaneously entering the distance through the keyboard. See the sidebar "A Fast Way to Enter Distances" in this chapter.

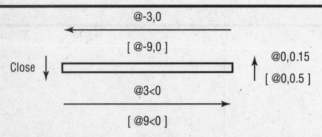

FIGURE 3.6: Distance and direction input for the door. Distances for metric users are shown in brackets.

A FAST WAY TO ENTER DISTANCES

A third method for entering distances is to simply point in a direction with a rubber-banding line and then enter the distance through the keyboard. For example, to draw a line 3 units long from left to right, click the Line tool from the Draw toolbar, click a start point, and then move the cursor so the rubber-banding line points to the right at some arbitrary distance. While holding the cursor in the direction you want, type **3** and press Enter. The rubber-banding line becomes a fixed line 3 units long.

Using this method, called the Direct Distance method, along with the Ortho mode or Polar Snap described in Chapter 4, can be a fast way to draw objects of specific lengths. Use the standard Cartesian or polar coordinate methods when you need to enter exact distances at angles other than those that are exactly horizontal or vertical.

CLEANING UP THE SCREEN

On some systems, the AutoCAD Blipmode setting may be turned on. This setting causes tiny cross-shaped markers called *blips* to appear where you've selected points. These blips can help you keep track of the points you've selected on the screen. You can also enter **R** and press Enter.

Blips aren't actually part of your drawing and do not print. Still, they can interfere with your work. To clear the screen of blips, click the Redraw tool in the toolbar (it looks like a pencil point drawing an arc) or type **R** and press Enter. The screen quickly redraws the objects, clearing the screen of the blips. You can also choose View ➤ Redraw View to accomplish the same thing. Redraw can also clear up other display problems.

Another command, Regen, does the same thing as Redraw, but it also updates the drawing display database—which means it takes a bit longer to restore the drawing. Regen updates certain types of changes that occur in a drawing.

To turn Blipmode on and off, type **blipmode** and press Enter at the Command prompt and then enter **on** or **off** and press Enter.

INTERPRETING THE CURSOR MODES AND UNDERSTANDING PROMPTS

The key to working with AutoCAD successfully is understanding the way it interacts with you. This section will help you become familiar with some of the ways AutoCAD prompts you for input. Understanding the format of the messages in the Command window and recognizing other events on the screen will help you learn the program more easily.

As the Command window aids you with messages, the cursor also gives you clues about what to do. Figure 3.7 illustrates the various modes of the cursor and gives a brief description of the role of each mode. Take a moment to study this figure.

The Standard cursor tells you that AutoCAD is waiting for instructions. You can also edit objects using grips when you see this cursor. The Point Selection cursor appears whenever AutoCAD expects point input. It can also appear in conjunction with a rubber-banding line. You can either click a point or enter a coordinate through the keyboard. The Object Selection cursor tells you that you must select objects—either by clicking them or by using any of the object selection options available. The Osnap (object snap) marker appears along with the Point Selection cursor when you invoke an Osnap. Osnaps let you accurately select specific points on an object, such as endpoints or midpoints. The tracking vector appears when you use the Polar Tracking or Object Snap Tracking feature. Polar Tracking aids you in drawing orthogonal lines, and Object Snap Tracking helps you align points in space relative to the geometry of existing objects. Object Snap Tracking works in conjunction with Osnap.

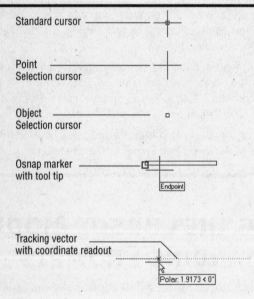

Standard cursor

Point
Selection cursor

Object
Selection cursor

Osnap marker
with tool tip

Endpoint

Tracking vector
with coordinate readout

Polar: 1.9173 < 0°

FIGURE 3.7: The drawing cursor's modes

TIP

If you are an experienced AutoCAD user and prefer to use the old-style crosshair cursor that crosses the entire screen, use the Pointer tab of the Preferences dialog box (Tools ➣ Preferences) to set the cursor size. Set the Percent of Screen Size option near the bottom of the dialog box to 100. The cursor then appears as it did in prior versions of AutoCAD. As the option name implies, you can set the cursor size to any percentage of the screen you want. The default is 6%.

Choosing Command Options

Many commands in AutoCAD offer several options, which are often presented to you in the Command window in the form of a prompt. This section uses the Arc command to illustrate the format of AutoCAD's prompts.

Usually, in a floor-plan drawing in the U.S., an arc is drawn to indicate the direction of a door swing. Figure 3.8 shows some of the other standard symbols used in architectural-style drawings.

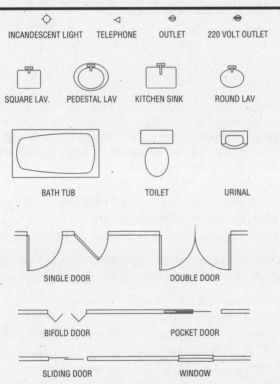

FIGURE 3.8: Samples of standard symbols used in architectural drawings

Next, you'll draw the arc for the door you started in the previous exercise:

1. Click the Arc tool in the Draw toolbar. The prompt Specify start point of arc or [Center]: appears, and the cursor changes to point selection mode.

Let's examine this Specify start point of arc or [Center]: prompt. The start point contains two options. The default option is stated in the main part of the prompt. In this case, the default option is to specify the start point of the arc. If other options are available, they will appear within brackets. In the Arc command, you see the word Center within brackets, telling you that if you prefer, you can start your arc by selecting a center point instead of a start point. If multiple options are available, they appear within the brackets and are separated by slashes (/). The default is the option AutoCAD assumes you intend to use unless you tell it otherwise.

2. Type **C** and press Enter to select the Center option. The prompt Specify center point of arc: appears. Notice that you only had to type **C** and not the entire word **Center**.

TIP

When you see a set of options in the Command window, note their capitalization. If you choose to respond to prompts using the keyboard, these capitalized letters are all you need to enter to select that option. In some cases, the first two letters are capitalized to differentiate two options that begin with the same letter, such as LAyer and LType.

3. Pick a point representing the center of the arc near the upper-left corner of the door (see the first image of Figure 3.9). The prompt Specify start point of arc: appears.

4. Type **@3<0**. Metric users should type **@9<0**. The prompt Specify end point of arc or [Angle/chord Length]: appears.

5. Move the mouse and a temporary arc appears, originating from a point 3 units to the right of the center point you selected and rotating about that center, as in the middle image of Figure 3.9. (Metric users will see the temporary arc originating 9 units to the right of the center point.)

As the prompt indicates, you now have three options. You can enter an angle, a chord length, or the endpoint of the arc. The prompt default picks the arc's endpoint. Again, the cursor is in a point selection mode, telling you it is waiting for point input. To select this default option, you only need to pick a point on the screen indicating where you want the endpoint.

6. Move the cursor so that it points in a vertical direction from the center of the arc. You'll see the Polar Tracking vector snap to a vertical position.

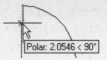

7. Click any location with the Polar Tracking vector in the vertical position. The arc is now fixed in place, as in the bottom image of Figure 3.9.

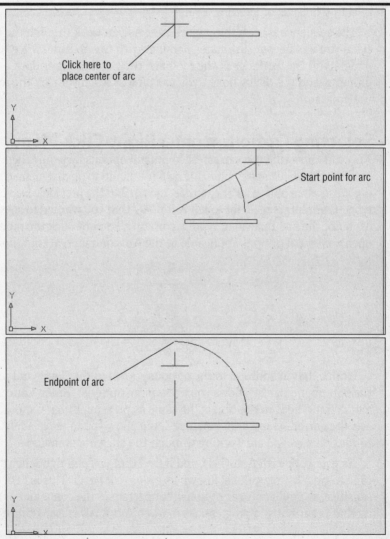

FIGURE 3.9: Using the Arc command

This exercise has given you some practice working with AutoCAD's Command window prompts and entering keyboard commands—skills you will need when you start to use some of the more advanced AutoCAD functions.

As you can see, AutoCAD has a distinct structure in its prompt messages. You first issue a command, which in turn offers options in the form of a prompt. Depending on the option you select, you get another set of options or you are prompted to take some action, such as picking a point, selecting objects, or entering a value.

The sequence is something like a tree. As you work through the exercises, you will become intimately familiar with this routine. Once you understand the workings of the toolbars, the Command window prompts, and the dialog boxes, you can almost teach yourself the rest of the program.

Selecting Options from a Right-Click Menu

Now you know that you can select command options by typing them. You can also right-click at any time during a command to open a menu containing those same options. For example, in step 2 in the previous exercise, you typed **C** and pressed Enter to tell AutoCAD that you wanted to select the center of the arc. Instead of typing, you can also right-click the mouse to open a menu of options applicable to the Arc command at that time.

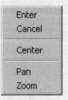

Notice that in addition to the options shown in the Command prompt, the pop-up menu also shows you a few more options: Enter, Cancel, Pan, and Zoom. The Enter option is the same as pressing Enter. Cancel cancels the current command. Pan and Zoom allow you to make adjustments to your view as you are working through the current command.

As you work with AutoCAD, you'll find that you can right-click at any time to get a list of options, known as a *shortcut menu*. This list is context sensitive, so you'll only see options that pertain to the command or activity that is currently in progress. Also, when AutoCAD is expecting a point, an object selection, or a numeric value, right-clicking does not display a shortcut menu. Instead, AutoCAD reacts to a right-click as if you pressed Enter.

Be aware that the location of your cursor when you right-click determines the contents of the shortcut list. You've already seen that you can right-click a toolbar to get a list of other toolbars. A right-click in the Command window displays a list of operations you can apply to the Command line, such as repeating one of the last five commands you've used or copying the most recent history of command activity to the clipboard.

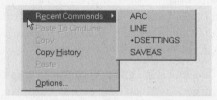

A right-click in the drawing area when no command is active gives you a set of basic options for editing your file, like Cut, Paste, Undo, Repeat the last command, Pan, and Zoom, to name a few.

If you're ever in doubt about what to do in AutoCAD, you can right-click any time to see a list of options. For now, let's move on to the topic of selecting objects.

If you're a veteran AutoCAD user and you prefer to have the right-click always react as if you pressed Enter (as in versions prior to AutoCAD 14) instead of opening the shortcut menu, you can configure AutoCAD to do just that. Be aware, however, that the tutorials in this book assume that AutoCAD is configured for the right-click shortcut menu.

SELECTING OBJECTS

AutoCAD provides many options for selecting objects. This section has two parts: The first part deals with object selection methods unique to AutoCAD, and the second part deals with the more common selection method used in most popular graphic programs: the Noun/Verb method. Because these two methods play a major role in working with AutoCAD, it's a good idea to familiarize yourself with them early on.

Selecting Objects in AutoCAD

Many AutoCAD commands prompt you to Select objects:. Along with this prompt, the cursor changes from crosshairs to a small square (look back at Figure 3.7). Whenever you see the Select objects: prompt and the square cursor, you have several options while making your selection. Often, as you select objects on the screen, you will change your mind about a selection or accidentally pick an object you do not want. Let's look at most of the selection options available in AutoCAD and learn what to do when you make the wrong selection.

Before you continue, you'll turn off two features that, although extremely useful, can be confusing to new users. These features are called Running Osnaps and Osnap Tracking. You'll get a chance to explore these features in depth later in this book.

1. Check to see if either Running Osnaps or Osnap Tracking is turned on. To do this, look at the buttons labeled Osnap and Otrack in the status bar at the bottom of the AutoCAD window. If they are turned on, they look like they are pressed in.

2. To turn off Running Osnaps or Osnap Tracking, click the button labeled Osnap or Otrack in the status bar at the bottom of the AutoCAD window. When turned off, they will look like they are not pressed.

Now let's go ahead and see how to select an object in AutoCAD.

1. Choose Move from the Modify toolbar.

2. At the Select objects: prompt, click on each of the two horizontal lines that form the door. Whenever AutoCAD wants you to select objects, the cursor turns into the small square pickbox. This tells you that you are in Object Selection mode. As you pick an object, it is highlighted, as shown in Figure 3.10.

TIP

Highlighting means an object changes from a solid image to one composed of dots. When you see an object highlighted on the screen, you know that you have chosen that object to be acted upon by your next or current command.

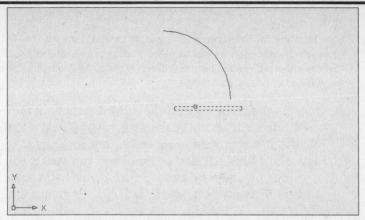

FIGURE 3.10: Selecting the lines of the door and seeing them highlighted

3. After making your selections, you may decide to deselect some items. Click Undo in the Standard toolbar, or enter **U** and press Enter from the keyboard.

Notice that one line is no longer highlighted. The Undo option deselects objects, one at a time, in reverse order of selection.

4. There is another way to deselect objects: Hold down the Shift key and click the remaining highlighted line. It reverts to a solid line, showing you that it is no longer selected for editing.

By now you have deselected both lines. Let's try using another method for selecting groups of objects:

5. Another option for selecting objects is to window them. Type **W** and press Enter. The cursor changes to a Point Selection cursor, and the prompt changes to

`Specify First corner:`

6. Click a point below and to the left of the rectangle representing the door. As you move your cursor across the screen, the window appears and stretches across the drawing area.

7. Once the window completely encloses the door but not the arc, click this location; the entire door is highlighted. This window selects only objects that are completely enclosed by the window, as shown in Figure 3.11.

TIP

Don't confuse the selection window you are creating here with the Zoom window, which simply defines an area of the drawing you want to enlarge. Remember that the window option works differently under the Zoom command than it does for other editing commands.

8. Now that you have selected the entire door but not the arc, press Enter to tell AutoCAD that you have finished selecting objects. It is important to remember to press Enter as soon as you have finished selecting the objects you want to edit. A new prompt, Specify base point or displacement:, appears. The cursor changes to its Point Selection mode.

Now you have seen how the selection process works in AutoCAD—but you're in the middle of the Move command. The next section discusses the prompt that's now on your screen and describes how to enter base points and displacement distances.

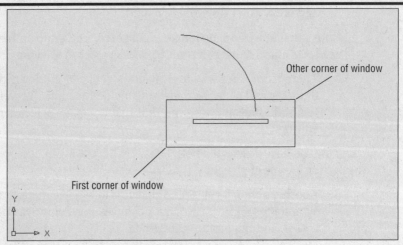

FIGURE 3.11: Selecting the door within a window

Providing Base Points

When you move or copy objects, AutoCAD prompts you for a base point, which is a difficult concept to grasp. AutoCAD must be told specifically from where and to where the move occurs. The *base point* is the exact location from which you determine the distance and direction of the move. Once the base point is determined, you can tell AutoCAD where to move the object in relation to that point.

1. To select a base point, hold down the Shift key and right-click. A menu appears, displaying the Object Snap (Osnap) options.

WARNING

When right-clicking the mouse, make sure the cursor is within the AutoCAD drawing area; otherwise, you will not get the results described in this book.

2. Choose Intersection from the Osnap menu. The Osnap menu disappears.

3. Move the cursor to the lower-right corner of the door. Notice that as you approach the corner, a small x-shaped graphic called an *Osnap marker* appears on the corner.

4. After the x-shaped marker appears, hold the mouse motionless for a second or two. A ToolTip appears, telling you the current Osnap point AutoCAD has selected.

5. Click the left mouse button to select the intersection indicated by the Osnap marker. Whenever you see the Osnap marker at the point you wish to select, you don't have to point exactly at the location with your cursor; just left-click the mouse, and the exact Osnap point is selected (see Figure 3.12). In this case, you selected the exact intersection of two lines.

6. At the `Specify second point of displacement or <use first point as displacement>:` prompt, hold down the Shift key and right-click again. You'll use the Endpoint Osnap option this time, but instead of clicking the option with the mouse, type **E**.

7. Pick the lower-right end of the arc you drew earlier. (Remember that you only need to move your cursor close to the endpoint until the Osnap marker appears.) The door moves so that the corner of the door connects exactly with the endpoint of the arc (see Figure 3.13).

As you can see, the Osnap options allow you to select specific points on an object. You used Endpoint and Intersect in this exercise, but other options are available. Chapter 4 discusses some of the other Osnap options. You may have also noticed that the Osnap marker is different for each of the options you used. You'll learn more about Osnaps in Chapter 4. Now, let's continue with our look at point selection.

TIP

You might have noticed the statement Use first point as displacement in the prompt in step 6. It means that if you press Enter instead of clicking a point, the object will move a distance based on the coordinates of the point you selected as a base point. For example, if the point you click for the base point is at coordinate 2,4, the object will move 2 units in the x-axis and 4 in the y-axis.

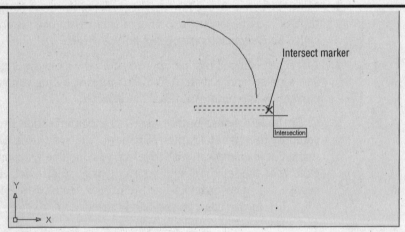

FIGURE 3.12: Using the Osnap cursor

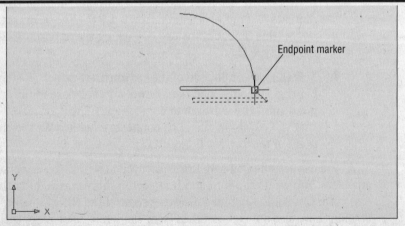

FIGURE 3.13: The rectangle in its new position after using the Endpoint Osnap

If you want to specify an exact distance and direction by typing a value, select any point on the screen as a base point. Or you can just type @ and press Enter at the base point prompt; then, enter the second point's location in relative coordinates. Remember that @ means the last point selected. In this next exercise, you'll move the entire door an exact distance of 1 unit in a 45° angle. Metric users will move the door 3 units in a 45° angle. Follow these steps:

1. Click the Move tool from the Modify toolbar.

2. Type **P** and press Enter. The set of objects you selected in the previous command is highlighted. P is a selection option that selects the previously selected set of objects.

3. You're still in Object Selection mode, so click the arc to include it in the set of selected objects. The entire door, including the arc, is highlighted.

4. Press Enter to tell AutoCAD that you have finished your selection. The cursor changes to Point Selection mode.

5. At the Base point or displacement: prompt, choose a point on the screen between the door and the left side of the screen (see Figure 3.14).

6. Move the cursor around slowly and notice that the door moves as if the base point you selected were attached to the door. The door moves with the cursor, at a fixed distance from it. This action demonstrates how the base point relates to the objects you select.

7. Type **@1<45** and press Enter. (Metric users should type **@3<45** and press Enter.) The door moves to a new location on the screen at a distance of 1 unit (or 3 for metric users) from its previous location and at an angle of 45°.

TIP

If AutoCAD is waiting for a command, you can repeat the last command used by pressing the spacebar or by pressing the Enter key. You can also right-click in the drawing area and select the option at the top of the list. If you right-click the Command window, a shortcut menu offers the most recent commands.

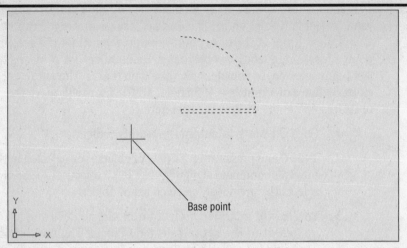

FIGURE 3.14: The highlighted door and the base point just to the left of the door. Note that the base point does not need to be on the object that you are moving.

This exercise illustrates that the base point does not have to be on the object you are manipulating; it can be virtually anywhere on your drawing. You also saw how to reselect a group of objects that were selected previously, without having to duplicate the selection process.

OTHER SELECTION OPTIONS

There are several other selection options you haven't tried yet. You'll see how these options work in exercises later in this book. Or, if you are adventurous, try them now on your own. To use these options, type their keyboard abbreviations (shown in brackets in the following list) at any Select object: prompt.

All [all+Enter] Selects all the objects in a drawing except those in frozen or locked layers.

Crossing [c+Enter] Similar to the Select Window option but selects anything that crosses through the window you define.

Crossing Polygon [cp+Enter] Acts exactly like WPolygon (described in a moment) but, like the Select Crossing option, selects anything that crosses through a polygon boundary.

CONTINUED ➠

Fence [f+Enter]   Selects objects that are crossed over by a temporary line called a *fence*. This operation is like crossing out the objects you want to select with a line. When you invoke this option, you can then pick points, as when you are drawing a series of line segments. When you are done drawing the fence, press Enter and then go on to select other objects, or press Enter again to finish your selection.

Last [l+Enter]   Selects the last object you entered.

Multiple [m+Enter]   Lets you select several objects first, before AutoCAD highlights them. In a very large file, picking objects individually can cause AutoCAD to pause after each pick while it locates and highlights each object. The Multiple option can speed things up by letting you first pick all the objects quickly, and then highlight them all by pressing Enter. This option has no menu equivalent.

Previous [p+Enter]   Selects the last object or set of objects that was edited or changed.

Window [w+Enter]   Forces a standard selection window. This option is useful when your drawing area is too crowded to use the Autoselect feature to place a window around a set of objects (see the Auto entry in this sidebar). It prevents you from accidentally selecting an object with a single pick when you are placing your window.

Window Polygon [wp+Enter]   Lets you select objects by enclosing them in an irregularly shaped polygon boundary. When you use this option, you see the prompt First polygon point:. You then pick points to define the polygon boundary. As you pick points, the prompt Undo/<Endpoint of line>: appears. Select as many points as you need to define the boundary. You can undo boundary line segments as you go by clicking the Undo tool on the Standard toolbar, or by pressing the U key. With the boundary defined, press Enter. The bounded objects are highlighted and the Select object prompt returns, allowing you to use more selection options.

CONTINUED ➡

The following two selection options are also available, but are seldom used. They are intended for use in creating custom menu options or custom toolbar tools.

Auto [au+Enter]   Forces the standard automatic window or crossing window when a point is picked and no object is found (see "Using Autoselect" later in this chapter). A standard window is produced when you pick the two window corners from left to right. A crossing window is produced when you pick the two corners from right to left. Once this option is selected, it remains active for the duration of the current command. Auto is intended for use on systems where the Automatic Selection feature has been turned off.

Single [si+Enter]   Forces the current command to select only a single object. If you use this option, you can pick a single object; then the current command acts on that object as if you had pressed Enter immediately after selecting the object. This option has no menu equivalent.

Selecting Objects before the Command: Noun/Verb

Nearly all graphics programs today have tacitly acknowledged the Noun/Verb method for selecting objects. This method requires you to select objects before you issue a command to edit them. The next set of exercises shows you how to use the Noun/Verb method in AutoCAD.

You have seen that when AutoCAD is waiting for a command, it displays the crosshair cursor with the small square. This square is actually a pickbox superimposed on the cursor. It tells you that you can select objects, even while the Command prompt appears at the bottom of the screen and no command is currently active. The square momentarily disappears when you are in a command that asks you to select points.

Now try moving objects by first selecting them and then using the Move command:

1.   Press the Esc key twice to make sure AutoCAD isn't in the middle of a command you may have accidentally issued. Click the arc. The arc is highlighted, and you may also see squares

appear at its endpoints and its midpoint. These squares are called *grips*. (You may know them as *workpoints* from other graphics programs.) You'll get a chance to work with them a bit later.

2. Choose Move from the Modify toolbar. The cursor changes to Point Selection mode. Notice that the grips on the arc disappear, but the arc is still selected.

3. At the `Base point:` prompt, pick any point on the screen. The prompt `To point:` appears.

4. Type `@1<0` and press Enter. Metric users should type `@3<0` and press Enter. The arc moves to a new location 1 unit (3 units for metric users) to the right.

WARNING

If you find that this exercise does not work as described, chances are the Noun/Verb setting has been turned off on your copy of AutoCAD. To turn on the Noun/Verb setting, do the following: Choose Tools ➤ Options ➤ Selection tab and, in the Selection Modes group, turn on the Noun/Verb selection option. Click OK when you're finished.

In this exercise, you picked the arc *before* issuing the Move command. Then, when you clicked the Move tool, you didn't see the `Select object:` prompt. Instead, AutoCAD assumed you wanted to move the arc that you had selected and went directly to the `Base point:` prompt.

Using Autoselect

Next, you will move the rest of the door in the same direction using the Autoselect feature:

1. Pick a point just above and to the left of the rectangle representing the door. Be sure not to pick the door itself. A window appears that you can drag across the screen as you move the cursor. If you move the cursor to the left of the last point selected, the window appears dotted (see the top image of Figure 3.15). If you move the cursor to the right of that point, it appears solid (see the bottom image of Figure 3.15).

2. Pick a point below and to the right of the door, so that the door is completely enclosed by the window, as shown in the bottom image of Figure 3.15. The door is highlighted (and

again, you may see small squares appear at the line's end-points and midpoints).

3. Click the Move tool again. Just as in the last exercise, the Base point: prompt appears.

4. Pick any point on the screen; then, enter **@1<0** and press Enter. Metric users should enter **@3<0** and press Enter. The door joins with the arc.

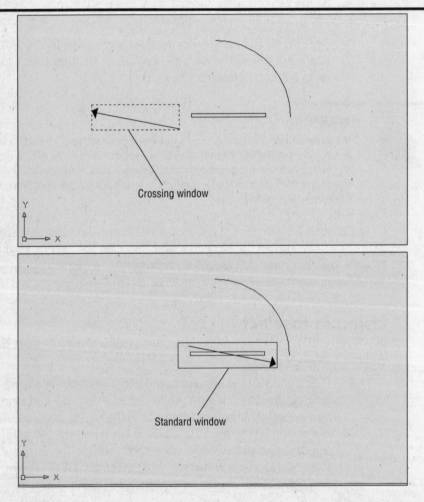

FIGURE 3.15: The dotted window (top image) indicates a crossing selection; the solid window (bottom image) indicates a standard selection window.

The two different windows you have just seen—the solid one and the dotted one—represent a standard window and a crossing window. If you use a standard window, anything that is completely contained within the window is selected. If you use a crossing window, anything that crosses through the window is selected. These two types of windows start automatically when you click any blank portion of the drawing area with a Standard cursor or Point Selection cursor; hence the name Autoselect.

Next, you will select objects with an automatic crossing window:

1. Pick a point below and to the right of the door. As you move the cursor left, the crossing (dotted) window appears.

2. Select the next point so that the window encloses the door and part of the arc (see Figure 3.16). The entire door, including the arc, is highlighted.

3. Click the Move tool.

4. Pick any point on the screen; then, enter **@1<180** and press Enter. Metric users should type **@3<180** and press Enter. The door moves back to its original location.

You'll find that in most cases, the Autoselect standard and crossing windows are all you need when selecting objects. They really save you time, so you'll want to become familiar with these features.

Before continuing, you need to choose File ➢ Save to save the Door file. You won't want to save the changes you make in the next section, so saving now stores the current condition of the file on your hard disk for safekeeping.

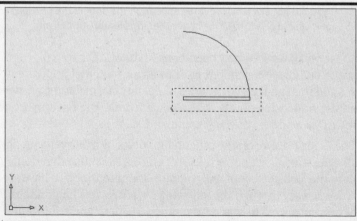

FIGURE 3.16: The door enclosed by a crossing window

Restrictions on Noun/Verb Object Selection

If you prefer to work with the Noun/Verb selection feature, you should know that its use is limited to the following subset of AutoCAD commands, listed here in alphabetical order:

Array	Copy	Hatch	Rotate
Block	Dview	List	Scale
Change	Erase	Mirror	Stretch
Chprop	Explode	Move	Wblock

For all other modifying or construction-oriented commands, the Noun/Verb selection method is inappropriate, because for those commands you must select more than one set of objects. But you do not need to remember this list; you'll know right away if a command accepts the Noun/Verb selection method. Commands that don't accept the Noun/Verb selection method clear the selection and then display a `Select object:` prompt.

EDITING WITH GRIPS

Earlier, when you selected the door, little squares appeared at the endpoints and midpoints of the lines and arcs. These squares are called *grips*. Grips can be used to make direct changes to the shape of objects, or to quickly move and copy them.

WARNING

If you did not see small squares appear on the door in the previous exercise, your version of AutoCAD may have the Grips feature turned off.

So far, you have seen how operations in AutoCAD have a discrete beginning and ending. For example, to draw an arc, you first issue the Arc command and then go through a series of operations, including answering prompts and picking points. When you are done, you have an arc, and AutoCAD is ready for the next command.

The Grips feature, on the other hand, plays by a different set of rules. Grips offer a small yet powerful set of editing functions that don't conform to the lockstep command/prompt/input routine you have seen so far. As you work through the following exercises, it is helpful to think of grips as a subset of the standard method of operation within AutoCAD.

To practice using the Grips feature, you'll make some temporary modifications to the door drawing.

Stretching Lines Using Grips

In this exercise, you'll stretch one corner of the door by grabbing the grip points of two lines. Follow these steps:

1. Press the Esc key to make sure you're not in the middle of a command. Click a point below and to the left of the door to start a selection window.

2. Click above and to the right of the rectangular part of the door to select it.

3. Place the cursor on the lower-left corner grip of the rectangle, *but don't press the pick button yet*. Notice that the cursor jumps to the grip point.

4. Move the cursor to another grip point. Notice again how the cursor jumps to it. When placed on a grip, the cursor moves to the exact center of the grip point. This means, for example, that if the cursor is placed on an endpoint grip, it is on the exact endpoint of the object.

5. Move the cursor to the upper-left corner grip of the rectangle and click it. The grip becomes a solid color, and is now a *hot grip*. The prompt displays the following message:

   ```
   **STRETCH**
   Specify stretch point or [Base point/Copy/Undo/eXit]:
   ```

   This prompt tells you that the Stretch mode is active. Notice the options shown in the prompt. As you move the cursor, the corner follows and the lines of the rectangle stretch (see the top image in Figure 3.17).

TIP

When you select a grip by clicking it, it turns a solid color (typically red) and is known as a *hot grip*. You can control the size and color of grips using the Grips dialog box.

6. Move the cursor upward toward the top end of the arc and click that point. The rectangle deforms, with the corner placed at your pick point (see the bottom image in Figure 3.17).

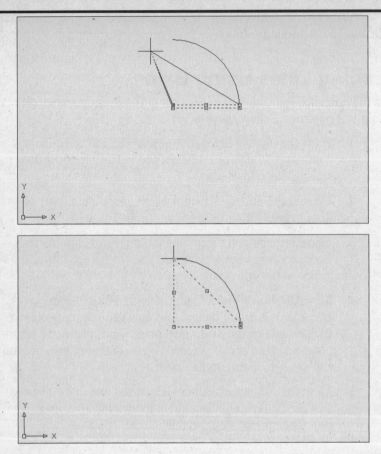

FIGURE 3.17: Stretching lines using hot grips. The top image shows the rectangle's corner being stretched upward. The bottom image shows the new location of the corner at the top of the arc.

TIP

When you click the corner grip point, AutoCAD selects the overlapping grips of two lines. When you stretch the corner away from its original location, the endpoints of both lines follow.

Here you saw that a command called STRETCH is issued simply by clicking a grip point. As you will see, a handful of other hot grip commands are also available.

1. Notice that the grips are still active. Click the grip point that you moved before to make it a hot grip again.

2. Right-click the mouse. A list of grip edit options appears.

3. Select Base Point from the list, and then click a point to the right of the hot grip. Now, as you move the cursor, the hot grip moves relative to the cursor.

4. Right-click again, and then select the Copy option from the list, enter **@1<-30**, and press Enter. (Metric users should enter **@3<-30** and press Enter.) Instead of moving the hot grip and changing the lines, AutoCAD copies the two lines, with their endpoints 1 unit (or 3 units for metric users) below and to the right of the first set of endpoints.

5. Pick another point just below the last. More copies are made.

6. Press Enter or type **X** and press Enter to exit Stretch mode. You can also right-click again and select Exit from the short-cut menu.

In this exercise, you saw that you can select a base point other than the hot grip. You also saw how you can specify relative coordinates to move or copy a hot grip. Finally, you saw that with grips selected on an object, a right-click of the mouse opens a shortcut menu showing grip edit options.

Moving and Rotating with Grips

As you've just learned, the Grips feature offers an alternative method of editing your drawings. You've already seen how you can stretch end-points, but you can do much more with grips. The next exercise demon-strates some other options. You will start by undoing the modifications you made in the last exercise:

1. Click the Undo tool in the Standard toolbar, or type **U** and press Enter. The copies of the stretched lines disappear.

2. Press Enter again. The deformed door snaps back to its orig-inal form.

TIP

Pressing Enter at the Command prompt causes AutoCAD to repeat the last com-mand entered — in this case, U.

3. Select the entire door by first clicking a blank area below and to the right of the door.

4. Move the cursor to a location above and to the left of the rectangular portion of the door, and click. Because you went from right to left, you created a crossing window. Recall that the crossing window selects anything enclosed in and crossing through the window.

5. Click the lower-left grip of the rectangle to turn it into a hot grip. Just as before, as you move your cursor, the corner stretches.

6. Right-click the mouse. In the grip edit shortcut menu, select Move. The Command window displays the following:

```
**MOVE**
<Move to point>/Base point/Copy/Undo/eXit:
```

Now, as you move the cursor, the entire door moves with it.

7. Position the door near the center of the screen and click there. The door moves to the center of the screen. Notice that the Command prompt returns, yet the door remains highlighted, telling you that it is still selected for the next operation.

8. Click the lower-left grip again, and right-click the mouse. This time, select Rotate from the list. The Command window displays the following:

```
**ROTATE** <Rotation angle>/Base
point/copy/Undo/Reference/eXit:
```

As you move the cursor, the door rotates about the grip point.

9. Position the cursor so that the door rotates approximately 180° (see Figure 3.18). While holding down the Shift key, press the mouse/pick button. A copy of the door appears in the new rotated position, leaving the original door in place.

10. Press Enter to exit Grip Edit mode.

TIP

You've seen how the Move command is duplicated in a modified way as a hot grip command. Other hot grip commands (Stretch, Rotate, Scale, and Mirror) also have similar counterparts in the standard set of AutoCAD commands.

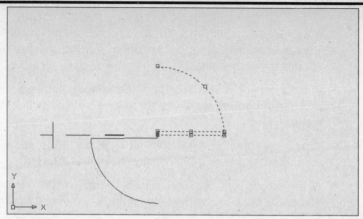

FIGURE 3.18: Rotating and copying the door using a hot grip. Notice that more than one object is being affected by the grip edit, even though only one grip is hot.

After you've completed any operation using grips, the objects are still highlighted with their grips still active. To clear the grip selection, press the Esc key.

In this exercise, you saw how hot grip options appear in a shortcut menu. Several other options are available in that list, including Exit, Base Point, Copy, and Undo. You can also make adjustments to an object's properties using the Properties option.

You can access many of these grip edit options by pressing the spacebar or Enter while a grip is selected. With each press, the next option becomes active. The options then repeat if you continue to press Enter. The Shift key acts as a shortcut to the Copy option. You only have to use it once; each time you click a point thereafter, a copy is made.

A QUICK SUMMARY OF THE GRIPS FEATURE

The exercises in this chapter using hot grips include only a few of the grips options. Here is a summary of the grips feature:

▶ Clicking endpoint grips causes those endpoints to stretch.

▶ Clicking midpoint grips of lines causes the entire line to move.

▶ If two objects meet end to end and you click their overlapping grips, both grips are selected simultaneously.

CONTINUED ➡

▶ You can select multiple grips by holding down the Shift key and clicking the desired grips.

▶ When a hot grip is selected, the Stretch, Move, Rotate, Scale, and Mirror options are available to you; just right-click the mouse.

▶ You can cycle through the Stretch, Move, Rotate, Scale, and Mirror options by pressing Enter while a hot grip is selected.

▶ All the hot grip options allow you to make copies of the selected objects by either using the Copy option or holding down the Shift key while selecting points.

▶ All the hot grip options allow you to select a base point other than the originally selected hot grip.

GETTING HELP

Eventually, you will find yourself somewhere without documentation and you will have a question about an AutoCAD feature. AutoCAD provides an online help facility that gives you information on nearly any topic related to AutoCAD. Here's how to find help:

1. Choose Help ➢ Help from the menu bar. A Help window appears.

2. If it isn't already selected, click the Contents tab. This window shows a table of contents. Four more tabs labeled Index, Search, Favorites, and Ask Me offer assistance in finding specific topics.

TIP
You can also press F1 to open the AutoCAD Help window.

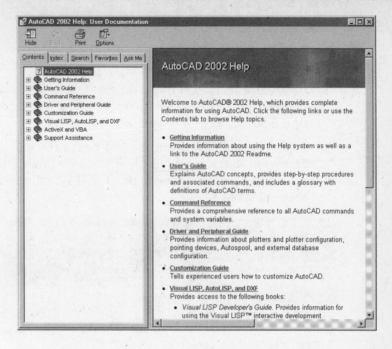

3. Scan down the screen until you see the topic Command References; double-click it. The list expands to show more topics.

4. Double-click the item labeled C Commands. The Help window expands to show a list of command names that start with the letter C.

5. Scroll down the list and click the word *Copy*. A description of the Copy command appears in the panel to the right.

6. Click the line that reads Display All Hidden Text on This Page. The panel expands to give more details about the Copy command. You can close the expanded view by scrolling down the panel and selecting Collapse All Hidden Text on This Page.

In addition, the Concepts, Procedures, and Reference tabs along the top of the right-hand panel offer more detailed information on the use of the selected item.

Using the Search Tab

If you want to find information about a topic based on a keyword, you can use the Search tab of the Help dialog box.

1. Click the Search tab. If this is the first time you've selected the Search tab, you may see a message telling you that Auto-CAD is setting up an index for searches.

2. Type the word **Change** in the text box at the top of the Search tab and then click List Topics or press Enter. The list box displays all of the items in the Help system that contain the word *Change*.

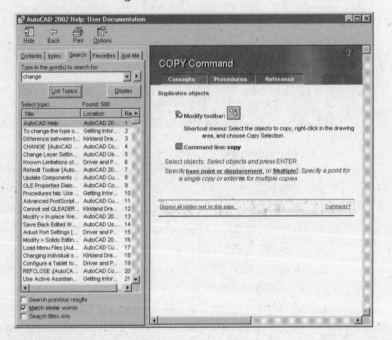

This list is a bit overwhelming. You can use Boolean AND, OR, NEAR, and NOT in conjunction with other keywords to help filter your searches, just as in a typical search engine that you might use in your web browser. Once you've found a topic you want, select it from the Select Topic list and then click the Display button to make the right-hand panel display information related to the topic.

Another interesting tool in the Help dialog box is the Ask Me tab. This tab lets you ask "natural language" questions. Try the following steps to see how it works:

1. Click the Ask Me tab.

2. In the top text box, enter **How do I zoom into my view**. The list below the text box changes to show several items that relate to adjusting views in AutoCAD.

3. Click the item entitled Magnify a View (Zoom). The right panel changes to display a description of how the Zoom command works.

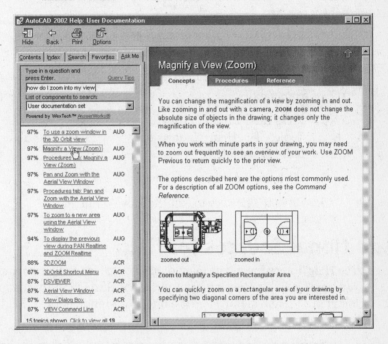

You'll notice a three-letter acronym to the right of each item listed in the Ask Me tab. These tell you the document source for the listed option. For example, the Magnify a View (Zoom) item is listed in the AutoCAD User Guide or AUG. Other items show ACR for AutoCAD Command Reference. You can also limit the query to specific document sources by selecting a source from the List of Components to Search list box.

If you scroll down to the bottom of the Ask Me list, you'll find a Search the Web For: option. This option does just what it says. If you don't find a satisfactory answer in the AutoCAD help system, you can select this option to open a search web page in the right-hand panel. (Make sure you are connected to the Internet if you use this option.)

The Index tab lets you locate specific topics in the AutoCAD Help system by entering a word in a list box. The Favorites tab lets you store locations in the Help system that you refer to frequently.

Using Context-Sensitive Help

AutoCAD also provides *context-sensitive help* to give you information related to the command you are currently using. To see how this works, try the following:

1. Close or minimize the Help window and return to the Auto-CAD window.

2. Click the Move tool in the Modify toolbar to start the Move command.

3. Press the F1 function key, or choose Help ➤ AutoCAD Help Topics. The Help window appears, with a description of the Move command.

4. Click the Close button or press the Esc key.

5. Press the Esc key to exit the Move command.

Additional Sources for Help

The Help Topics tool is the main online source for reference material, but you can also find answers to your questions through the other options found in the Help menu. Here is a brief description of the other Help menu options:

Active Assistance   A pop-up window that offers immediate feedback on the command you are using. If you are a first-time user, this option may be helpful, but some users find it annoying. If you want to turn it off, right-click the Active Assistant icon in the System tray (in the lower-right corner of the Windows desktop) and select Exit.

Developer Help   Information specifically for developers. This would include anyone interested in customizing AutoCAD.

Product Support on PointA   Opens the PointA website using your default web browser. At PointA, you can get the latest information about AutoCAD and related software.

Support Assistance   A series of answers to frequently asked questions. This unique support tool can be updated through the Autodesk website.

What's New   An overview of the new features found in Auto-CAD 2002. If you're an experienced AutoCAD user and just want to know about the new features in AutoCAD 2002, this is a good place to start.

Learning Assistance   Offers new users some quick tutorials that show you how to use AutoCAD to accomplish particular tasks.

Autodesk User Group International   Information on the Autodesk User Group International, an organization devoted to sharing information among users of Autodesk products worldwide.

About   Information about the version of AutoCAD you are using.

DISPLAYING DATA IN A TEXT WINDOW

You may have noticed that as you work in AutoCAD, the activity displayed in the Command window scrolls up. Sometimes it is helpful to view information that has scrolled past the view shown in the Command window. For example, you can review the command activity from your session to check input values or to recall other data entry information. Try the following exercise to see how the Text window works:

1. Choose Tools ➢ Inquiry ➢ List. This command offers information about objects in your drawing.

2. At the Select objects: prompt, click one of the arcs and press Enter. Information about the arc is displayed in the AutoCAD Text window (see Figure 3.19). Toward the bottom is the list of the arc's properties. Don't worry if the meaning of some listed properties isn't obvious yet. As you work through this book, you'll learn what the different properties of an object mean.

3. Press F2. The AutoCAD Text window closes.

TIP

The F2 function key offers a quick way to switch between the drawing editor and the Text window.

The scroll bar to the right of the Text window lets you scroll to earlier events. You can even set the number of lines AutoCAD retains in the Text window using the Options dialog box, or you can have AutoCAD record the Text window information in a text file.

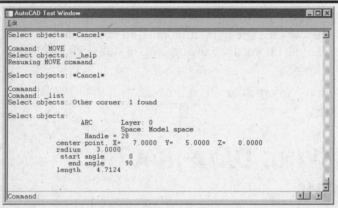

FIGURE 3.19: The AutoCAD text screen showing the data displayed by the List tool

When you have more than one document open, the Text window will display a listing for the drawing that is currently active.

DISPLAYING THE PROPERTIES OF AN OBJECT

While we're on the subject of displaying information, you'll want to know about the Properties dialog box. In the last exercise, you saw how the List command showed some information regarding the properties of an object, such as the location of an arc's center and endpoints. You can also double-click an object to display a Properties dialog box that shows similar information. (In fact, you may accidentally bring up the Properties dialog box from time to time!) To see what this dialog box is for, try the following exercise:

1. Double-click an arc in the drawing. The properties for that arc appear in a dialog box,

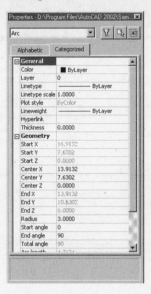

Don't worry if many of the items in this dialog box are undecipherable. For now, just be aware that this dialog box appears whenever you double-click on an object and that it displays the object's properties. It also allows you to modify many of the properties listed.

2. Close the Properties dialog box.

3. You are done with the door drawing, so choose File ➤ Close.

4. In the Save Changes dialog box, click the No button. (You've already saved this file just as you want it, so you do not need to save it again.)

TIP

You can also open the Properties dialog box by clicking an object, right-clicking, and then selecting Properties from the shortcut menu.

IF YOU WANT TO EXPERIMENT...

To try drawing the latch shown in Figure 3.20, follow these steps:

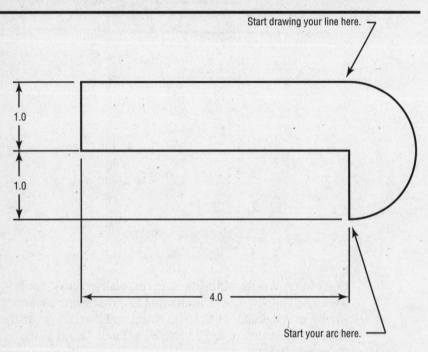

FIGURE 3.20: Try drawing this latch. Dimensions are provided for your reference.

1. Start AutoCAD, open a new file, and name it Latch.

2. When you get to the drawing editor, use the Line command to draw the straight portions of the latch. Start a line as indicated in the figure; then, enter relative coordinates from the keyboard. For example, for the first line segment, enter **@4<180** and press Enter to draw a line segment 4 units long from right to left.

3. Draw an arc for the curved part. To do this, click the Arc tool from the Draw toolbar.

4. Use the Endpoint Osnap to pick the endpoint indicated in the figure to start your arc.

5. Type **E** and press Enter to issue the End option of the Arc command.

6. Using the Endpoint Osnap again, click the endpoint above where you started your line. A rubber-banding line and a temporary arc appear.

7. Type **D** and press Enter to issue the Direction option for the Arc command.

8. Position your cursor so the ghosted arc looks like the one in the figure, and then press the mouse/pick button to draw in the arc.

WHAT'S NEXT?

This chapter has examined basic functions. You have created your first drawing and learned how to interpret prompts on the Command line. In the next chapter, you will learn how to use AutoCAD's basic tools in greater detail. You will gain experience with more drawing practice, and you will learn how to work with scale.

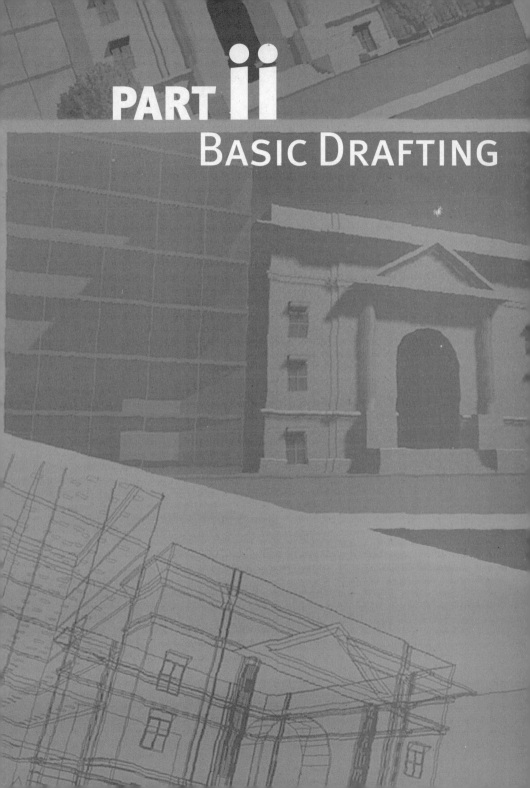

PART II
BASIC DRAFTING

Chapter 4
BASIC COMMANDS
TO GET STARTED

N ow that you have taken a quick tour of the AutoCAD screen, you are ready to begin drawing. In this chapter you will be introduced to the most basic commands used in drawing with AutoCAD. To get you started, I will guide you through the process of drawing a box (see Figure 4.1).

Adapted from *AutoCAD® 2002 No Experience Required®*
by David Frey
ISBN 0-7821-4016-5   688 pages $29.99

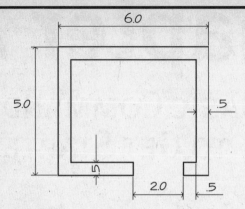

FIGURE 4.1: The box to be drawn

You need to use only five or six commands to draw the box. First, you'll become familiar with the Line command and how to make lines a specific length. Then we'll go over the strategy for completing the box.

THE LINE COMMAND

In traditional architectural drafting, lines were often drawn to extend slightly past their endpoints (Figure 4.2). This is no longer done in CAD except for special effects.

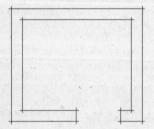

FIGURE 4.2: Box drawn with overlapping lines

The *Line command* draws a line between locations on existing lines, between geometric figures, or between two points that you can choose anywhere within the drawing area. These points can be designated by clicking them on the screen, by entering the *x* and *y* coordinates for each point in the Command window, or by entering distances and angles at the command line. After the first segment of a line is drawn, you have the option of ending the command or drawing another line segment from the end of the first one. You can continue to draw adjoining line segments for as long as you like. Let's see how it works.

1. Click File ➤ New. In the Create New Drawing dialog box, be sure English is selected, then click the Start from Scratch button and click OK to start a new drawing.

2. Glance down at the Status bar at the bottom of your screen. All buttons except Model should be Off—that is, in an *unpressed* state. If any are pressed in, click them to turn them off.

3. Be sure that the Draw and Modify toolbars have been docked on the left side of the drawing area, as in Figure 4.3.

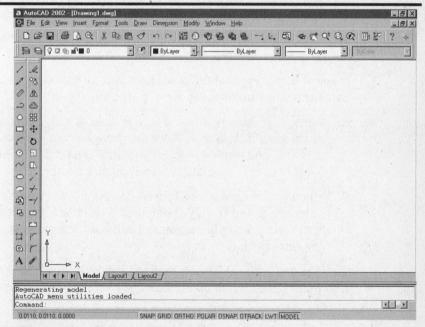

FIGURE 4.3: The Draw and Modify toolbars docked on the left side of the drawing area, and all status bar buttons except Model turned off

4. Click the Line button at the top of the Draw toolbar.

Part ii

TIP
You can also start the Line command by choosing Draw ➤ Line on the Menu bar, or by typing **L** and pressing the Enter key.

Look at the bottom of the Command window and see how the Command: prompt has changed.

The prompt now tells you that the Line command has been started (Command: _line) and that AutoCAD is waiting for you to designate the first point of the line (Specify first point:).

5. Move the cursor onto the drawing area and, using the left mouse button, click a random point to start a line.

6. Move the cursor away from the point you clicked and notice how a line segment appears that stretches like a rubber band from the point you just picked to the cursor. The line changes length and direction as you move the cursor.

7. Look at the Command window again and notice that the prompt has changed.

It now is telling you that AutoCAD is waiting for you to designate the next point (Specify next point or [Undo]:).

8. Continue picking points and adding lines as you move the cursor around the screen. After the third segment is drawn, the Command window repeats the Specify next point or [Close/Undo]: prompt each time you pick another point.

9. When you've drawn six or seven line segments, press the Enter key to end the Line command. The cursor separates from the last drawn line segment. Look at the Command window once again.

The Command: prompt has returned to the bottom line. This tells you there is no command running.

In this exercise, you used the left mouse button to select the Line button from the Draw toolbar and also to pick several points in the drawing area to make the line segments. Then you pressed Enter on the keyboard to end the Line command.

DRAWING A BOX

Now that you have the basics down, the following exercises will take you through the steps to draw the four lines that form the outline of the box using both relative Cartesian and polar coordinate systems.

Using Relative Cartesian Coordinates

To begin drawing the box, start with a new drawing.

1. Choose File ➤ Close. You will be prompted to save your last drawing: Click No.

2. Choose File ➤ New.

3. In the Create New Drawing dialog box, click Start from Scratch, select English, and then click OK.

4. Select the Line button from the top of the Draw toolbar.

5. At the Specify First point: prompt in the Command window, type **3,3** and press Enter. This is an absolute Cartesian coordinate and will be the first point.

6. Type **@6,0** and press Enter.

7. Type **@0,5** and press Enter.

8. Type **@-6,0** and press Enter.

9. Type **c** and press Enter. The letter *c* stands for *close*. Entering this letter after drawing several lines closes the shape by making the next line segment extend from the last point specified to the first point (see Figure 4.4). It also ends the Line command. Notice that in the Command window the prompt is Command:, signifying that AutoCAD is ready for a new command.

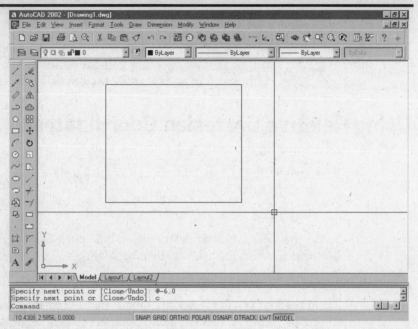

FIGURE 4.4: The first four lines of the box

Erasing Lines

To prepare to draw the box again, use the Erase command to erase the four lines you just drew.

1. Click Modify ➤ Erase. Notice how the cursor changes from the crosshair to a little square, called the *pickbox*. When you see it on the screen, it's a sign that AutoCAD is ready for you to select objects on the screen. Also notice that the Command window is prompting you to select objects.

2. Place the pickbox on one of the lines and click. The line changes into a dashed line. This is called *ghosting* or *highlighting*.

3. Do the same thing with the rest of the lines.

4. Press Enter. The objects are erased, and the Erase command ends.

Using Relative Polar Coordinates

Now draw the box again using the polar method by following these steps:

1. Start the Line command. (Choose the Line button from the Draw toolbar.)

2. Type **3,3** and press Enter to start the box at the same point.

3. Type **@6<0** and press Enter.

4. Type **@5<90** and press Enter.

5. Type **@6<180** and press Enter.

6. Type **c** and press Enter to close the box and end the Line command. Your box will once again resemble the box in Figure 4.4.

You can see from this simple exercise that either method can be used to draw a simple shape. In situations where the shapes you are drawing are more complex and the amount of available information about the shapes varies from segment to segment, one of the two relative coordinate systems will generally turn out to be more appropriate.

The Offset Command

The next task is to create the lines that represent the inside walls of the box. Because they are all equidistant from the lines you have already drawn, the Offset command is the appropriate command to use. You will offset the existing lines 0.5 units to the inside.

The Offset command has three steps:

▶ Setting the offset distance

▶ Picking the object to offset

▶ Indicating the offset direction

Here's how it works:

1. Be sure the prompt line in the Command window reads Command:. If it doesn't, press the Esc key until it does. Then, click the Offset button on the Modify toolbar. The prompt changes to Specify offset distance or Through <1.0000>:. This is a confusing prompt, but it will become clear soon. For now, let's specify an offset distance through the keyboard.

Part ii

TIP

You can also start the Offset command by choosing Modify ➤ Offset from the pull-down menus or typing **o** and pressing Enter.

WARNING

As important as it is to keep an eye on the Command window, some of the prompts may not make sense to you until you get used to them.

2. Type **.5** for a distance and press Enter. Now you move to the second stage of the command.

Note that the cursor changes to a pickbox, and the prompt changes to say `Select object to offset or <exit>:`.

3. Place the pickbox on one of the lines and click. The selected line ghosts, the cursor changes back to the crosshair, and the prompt changes to `Specify point on side to offset:`. AutoCAD is telling you that to determine the direction of the offset, you must specify a point on one side of the line or the other. You make the choice by picking anywhere in the drawing area, on the side of the line where you want the offset to occur.

4. Pick a point somewhere inside the box. The offset takes place, and the new line is exactly 0.5 units to the inside of the chosen line (see Figure 4.5). Notice that the pickbox comes back on. The Offset command is still running, and you can offset more lines the same distance.

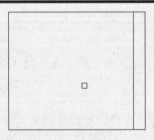

FIGURE 4.5: The first line is offset.

You have three more lines to offset.

NOTE
You can cancel a command at any time by pressing Esc.

5. Click another line, and then click inside the box again. The second line is offset.

6. Click a third line and click inside the box. Then, click the fourth line and click again inside the box (Figure 4.6).

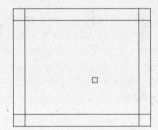

FIGURE 4.6: Four lines have been offset.

NOTE
The offset distance stays set at the last distance you specify—0.5, in this case—until you change it.

7. Press Enter to end the Offset command.

This command is similar to the Line command in that it keeps running until it is stopped. After the first offset, the prompts switch between Select object to offset or <exit>: and Specify point on side to offset: until you press Enter to end the command.

The inside lines are now drawn, but to complete the box, you need to clean up the intersecting corners. To handle this task efficiently, you will use the fillet tool.

SPECIFYING DISTANCES FOR THE OFFSET COMMAND

The prompt you see in the Command window after starting the Off-set command is Specify offset distance or [Through] <1.0000>:. This prompt is actually describing several options for setting the offset distance:

▶ Enter a distance at the keyboard.

▶ Pick two points on the screen to establish the offset distance as the distance between those two points.

▶ Press Enter to accept the offset distance that is displayed in the prompt in the angle brackets.

▶ Type **t** and press Enter to use the Through option. When you select this option, you are prompted to select the line to offset. Then, you are prompted to pick a point. The line will be offset to that point. When you pick the next line to offset, you then pick a new point to locate the position of the new line. The Through option allows each line to be offset a different distance.

As you get used to using Offset, you will find uses for each of these options.

The Fillet Command

The Fillet command allows you to round off a corner formed by two lines. You control the radius of the curve, so if you set the curve's radius to zero, the lines will form a sharp corner. This way, you can clean up corners like those formed by the lines inside the box.

1. At the Command: prompt, click the Fillet button on the Modify toolbar.

TIP

You can also start the Fillet command by selecting Modify ➢ Fillet from the menu bar, or by typing **f** and pressing Enter.

Notice the Command window:

```
Command: _fillet
Current settings: Mode = TRIM, Radius = 0.5000
Select first object or [Polyline/Radius/Trim]:
```

The default fillet radius is 0.5 units, but you want to use a radius of 0 units.

2. Type **r** and press Enter and then type **0** and press Enter to change the radius to 0.

3. Move the cursor—now a pickbox—to the box and click two intersecting lines as shown in Figure 4.7. The intersecting lines will both be trimmed to make a sharp corner (Figure 4.8). The Fillet command automatically ends.

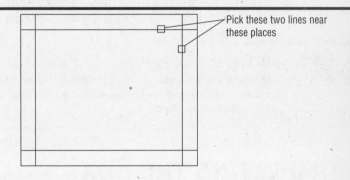

Pick these two lines near these places

FIGURE 4.7: Pick two lines to execute the Fillet command.

FIGURE 4.8: The first cleaned-up corner

4. Press Enter to restart the command and fillet two more lines in a similar fashion.

NOTE

Once a command has ended, you can restart it by pressing Enter or by right-clicking and then picking the Repeat command option at the top of the short-cut menu that appears.

5. Continue restarting the command and filleting the lines for each corner until all the corners are cleaned up.

NOTE

If you make a mistake and pick the wrong part of a line or the wrong line, press Esc to end the command and then type u and press Enter. Doing so will undo the effect of the last command.

COMPLETING THE BOX

The final step in completing the box (Figure 4.1) is to make an opening in the bottom wall. From the diagram, you can see that the opening is 2 units wide and set off from the right inside corner by 0.5 units. To make this opening, you will use the Offset command twice, changing the offset distance for each offset, to create marks for the opening.

Offsetting Lines to Mark an Opening

Follow these steps to establish the precise position of the opening:

1. At the Command: prompt, start the Offset command, either from the Modify toolbar or the Modify menu. Notice the Command window. The default distance is now set at 0.5, the offset distance you previously set to offset the outside lines of the box to make the inside lines. You want to use this distance again. Press Enter to accept this preset distance.

2. Pick the inside vertical line on the right, and then pick a point to the left of this line. The line is offset to make a new line 0.5 units to its left (see Figure 4.9).

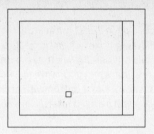

FIGURE 4.9: Offsetting the first line of the opening

3. Press Enter to end the Offset command. Press it again to restart the command, allowing you to reset the offset distance.

4. Enter **2** as the new offset distance and press Enter.

5. Click the new line and then pick a point to the left. Press Enter to end the Offset command (see Figure 4.10).

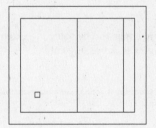

FIGURE 4.10: Offsetting the second line of the opening

You now have two new lines indicating where the opening will be. You can use these lines to form the opening using the Extend and Trim commands.

TIP

The buttons you have been clicking in this chapter are also referred to as *icons* and *tools*. When they are in dialog boxes or on the status bar, they look like buttons to push that have icons on them. When they are on the toolbars, they look like icons—little pictures. But when you move the Pointer Arrow cursor onto one, it takes on the appearance of a button with an icon on it. All three terms—*button*, *icon*, and *tool*—will be used interchangeably.

Extending Lines

The Extend command is used to lengthen (extend) lines to meet other lines or geometric figures (called *boundary edges*). The execution of the Extend command may be a little tricky at first until you see how it works. Once you understand it, however, it will become automatic. The command has two steps: First you will pick the boundary edge or edges, and second you will pick the lines you wish to extend to meet those boundary edges. After selecting the boundary edges, you must press Enter before you begin selecting lines to extend.

1. To begin the Extend command, click the Extend button on the Modify toolbar. Notice the Command window.

NOTE

You can also start the Extend command by selecting Extend from the Modify pull-down menu or by typing **ex** and pressing Enter.

```
Current settings: Projection=UCS Edge=None
Select boundary edges ...
Select objects:
```

2. The bottom line says to Select objects:, but in this case, you need to observe the other two lines of text in order to know that AutoCAD is prompting you to select boundary edges.

3. Pick the very bottom horizontal line and press Enter.

TIP

The Select Objects: prompt would be more useful if it said, "Select objects and press Enter when finished selecting objects." But it doesn't. You have to train yourself to press Enter when you are finished selecting objects in order to get out of selection mode and move on to the next step in the command.

4. Pick the two new vertical lines created by the Offset command. Be sure to place the pickbox somewhere on the lower half of each line, or AutoCAD will ignore your picks. The lines are extended to the boundary edge line. Press Enter to end the Extend command (see Figure 4.11).

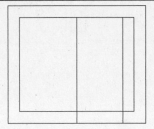

FIGURE 4.11: The lines are extended to the boundary edge.

Trimming Lines

The final step is to trim away the horizontal lines to complete the opening. To do this, you will use the Trim command. As with the Extend command, trimming involves two steps. The first one is to select reference lines—in this case, they're called *cutting edges* because they determine the edge or edges to which a line is trimmed.

1. Click the Trim button on the Modify toolbar to start the Trim command.

NOTE

You can also start the Trim command by picking Trim from the Modify pull-down menu or by typing **tr** and pressing Enter.

Notice the Command window. Similar to the Extend command, the bottom line prompts you to select objects, but the second line up tells you to select cutting edges.

2. Pick the two vertical offset lines that were just extended as your cutting edges (see Figure 4.12). Press Enter.

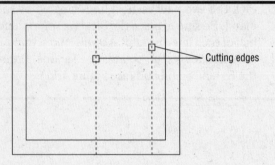

FIGURE 4.12: Lines selected to be cutting edges

3. Pick the two horizontal lines across the opening somewhere between the cutting edge lines (Figure 4.13).

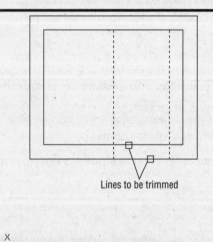

FIGURE 4.13: Lines selected to be trimmed

The opening is trimmed away (Figure 4.14).

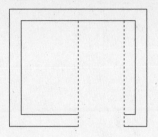

FIGURE 4.14: Wall lines are trimmed to make the opening.

NOTE

If you trim the wrong line or wrong part of a line, you can click the Undo button on the Standard toolbar. This action will undo the last trim without canceling the Trim command, and you can try again.

Now let's remove the extra part of our trimming guide lines.

1. Press Enter twice—once to end the Trim command and again to restart it. Doing so will allow you to pick new cutting edges for another trim operation.

2. Pick the two upper horizontal lines in the lower wall as your cutting edges, shown in Figure 4.15, and press Enter.

3. Pick the two vertical lines that extend above the new opening. Be sure to pick them above the opening (see Figure 4.16). The lines are trimmed away and the opening is complete (see Figure 4.17). Press Enter to end the Trim command.

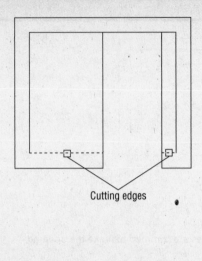

FIGURE 4.15: Lines picked to be cutting edges

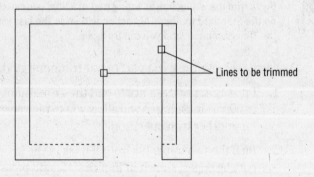

FIGURE 4.16: Lines picked to be trimmed

Congratulations! You have just covered all the tools in this chapter. As you will see in later sections of the book, these skills will be very useful as you learn how to work on drawings for actual projects. A valuable exercise at this time would be to draw this box two or three more times, until you can do it without the instructions.

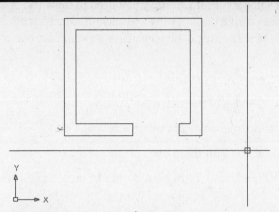

FIGURE 4.17: The completed trim

You can exit AutoCAD now without saving this drawing. To do so, choose File ➢ Exit. When the dialog box comes up asking if you want to save changes, click No.

IF YOU WOULD LIKE MORE PRACTICE...

Draw the object shown in Figure 4.18.

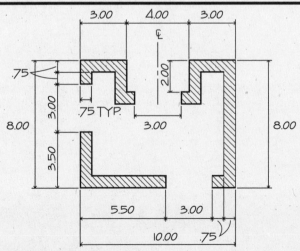

FIGURE 4.18: Practice drawing

You can use the same tools and strategy you used to draw the box. Choose File ➤ New to start a new drawing and click the Start from Scratch button in the Create New Drawing dialog box. Here's a summary of the steps to follow:

▶ Ignore the three openings at first.

▶ Draw the outside edge of the shape.

▶ Offset the outside lines to create the inside wall.

▶ Fillet the corners to clean them up.

▶ Use Offset, Extend, and Trim commands to create the three openings.

What's Next?

In this chapter, you have learned to use the most common drawing commands in AutoCAD. In the next chapter you will develop an actual floor plan for a small cabin. You will gain a feel for drawing strategies and learn how to solve common drawing problems.

Chapter 5
GAINING DRAWING STRATEGIES

Assuming that you have worked your way through the first few chapters, you can now successfully draw a box. From here on, you will develop a floor plan for a cabin. The focus in this chapter is on gaining a feel for the strategy of drawing in AutoCAD, and on how to solve drawing problems that may come up in the course of laying out the floor plan. Working your way through this chapter, your activities will include making the walls, cutting doorway openings, and drawing the doors (Figure 5.1).

Adapted from *AutoCAD® 2002 No Experience Required®* by David Frey

ISBN 0-7821-4016-5   688 pages $29.99

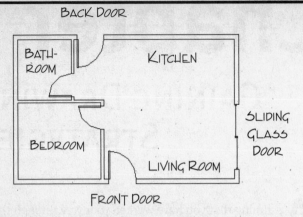

FIGURE 5.1: The basic floor plan of the cabin

Each of the exercises in this chapter will present opportunities to practice using commands you already know from previous chapters and to learn a few new ones. The most important goal is to begin to use strategic thinking as you develop methods for creating new elements of the floor plan.

LAYING OUT THE WALLS

For most floor plans, the walls come first. The first lesson of this chapter is to understand that you will not be putting very many new lines in the drawing, at least not as many as you might expect. Most new objects in this chapter will be created from items already in your drawing. In fact, no new lines will be drawn to make walls. All new walls will be generated from the four exterior wall lines.

You will need to create an inside wall line for the exterior walls (because the wall has thickness) and then make the three new interior walls (Figure 5.2). The wall thickness will be 4" for interior walls and 6" for exterior walls, because exterior walls have an additional layer or two of weather protection, such as shingles or stucco. Finally, you will need to cut five openings in these walls (interior and exterior) for the doorways.

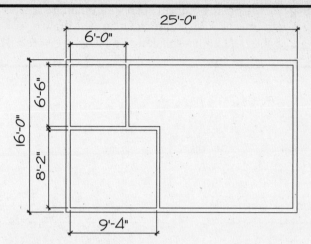

FIGURE 5.2: The wall dimensions

The Exterior Wall Lines

The first step is to offset the existing four wall lines to the inside to make the inside wall lines for the exterior walls. Then you will need to fillet them to clean up their corners.

TIP

Buildings are usually—but not always—dimensioned to the outside edge of exterior walls and to the centerline of interior walls. Wood frame buildings are dimensioned to the outside edges of their frames, and to the centerlines of the interior walls.

1. If AutoCAD is already running, select File ➤ Open. In the Select File dialog box, navigate to the folder you have designated as your training folder and select Cabin01.dwg. This file is available on the companion website. Click Open.

   If you are starting up AutoCAD, the Startup dialog box will appear. Be sure the Open a Drawing button is selected, and then look for the Cabin03 drawing in the Select a File list box. This box keeps a list of the most recently opened .dwg files. Highlight your .dwg file and click OK. If you don't find your file in the list, click the Browse button. The Select File dialog box will open. Find and open your training folder, select your drawing file, and click Open. The drawing should consist of four lines making a rectangle (Figure 5.3).

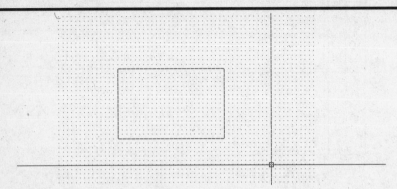

FIGURE 5.3: The cabin drawing

2. On the status bar, click the Grid and Snap buttons to turn them off. Then, start the Offset command by clicking the Offset button on the Modify toolbar.

NOTE
You can also start the Offset command by typing **o** and pressing Enter, or by selecting Modify ➢ Offset from the drop-down menus.

3. At the `Offset distance:` prompt, type **6** and press Enter.

NOTE
Remember: You do not have to enter the inch sign ("), but you are required to enter the foot sign (').

4. At the `Select object to offset:` prompt, click one of the four lines.

5. Click in a blank area inside the rectangle. The first line is off-set 6" to the inside. The Offset command is still running and the `Select object to offset:` prompt is still in effect.

6. Select another outside wall line and click in a blank area on the inside again. Continue doing this until you have offset all

four outside wall lines to the inside at the set distance of 6". Press Enter to end the Offset command (Figure 5.4). Now you will clean up the corners with the Fillet command.

FIGURE 5.4: All four lines are now offset 6" to the inside.

7. Start the Fillet command by clicking the Fillet button on the Modify toolbar.

8. Look at the Command window to see whether the radius is set to zero. If it is, go on to step 9. Otherwise, type **r** and press Enter and then type **0** and press Enter to set the Fillet radius to zero.

9. Click any two lines that form an inside corner. Be sure to click the part of the lines you want to remain after the fillet is completed. Both lines will be trimmed to make an inside corner (Figure 5.5). The Fillet command automatically ends after each fillet.

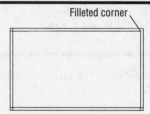

Filleted corner

FIGURE 5.5: The first corner is filleted.

10. Press Enter to restart the Fillet command.

TIP
You can restart the most recently used command by pressing Enter at the Command: prompt, or by right-clicking and selecting the top item on the shortcut menu that appears.

11. Pick two more lines to fillet, and then press Enter to restart the Fillet command. Continue doing this until all four corners have been cleaned up. After the last fillet, the Fillet command will end automatically.

CHARACTERISTICS THAT OFFSET AND FILLET HAVE IN COMMON

▶ Both are found on the Modify toolbar and on the Modify drop-down menu.

▶ Both have a default distance setting—offset distance and fillet radius—that can be accepted or reset.

▶ Both require you to select object(s).

CHARACTERISTICS THAT ARE DIFFERENT IN OFFSET AND FILLET

▶ You select one object with Offset and two with Fillet.

▶ Offset keeps running until you stop it. Fillet ends after each fillet operation, so you must restart Fillet to use it again.

You will find several uses for Offset and Fillet in the subsequent sections of this chapter.

The Interior Walls

Create the interior wall lines by offsetting the exterior wall lines.

1. At the Command: prompt, start the Offset command by typing **O** and pressing Enter (the letter o, not the number 0) or by selecting Offset from the Modify toolbar.

2. At the `Offset distance:` prompt, type **9'4** and press Enter. Leave no space between the foot sign (') and the 4.

NOTE

AutoCAD requires that you enter a distance containing feet and inches in a particular format: no space between the foot sign (') and the inches, and a hyphen (-) between the inches and the fraction. So if you were entering a distance of 6'-4 3/4", you would type 6'4-3/4. The measurement will be displayed in the normal way, 6'-4 3/4", but it must be entered in the format that has no spaces.

3. Click the inside line of the left exterior wall (Figure 5.6).

Select this line to offset

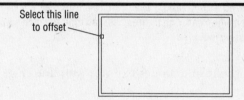

FIGURE 5.6: Selecting the wall line to offset

4. Click in a blank area to the right of the selected line. The line is offset 9'-4" to the right.

5. Press Enter twice. The Offset command is now restarted, and you can reset the offset distance.

TIP

In the Offset command, your opportunity to change the offset distance comes right after you start the command. So if the Offset command is already running, and you need to change the offset distance, you must stop and then restart the command. You can easily do this by pressing Enter twice.

6. Type **4** and press Enter to reset the offset distance.

7. Click the new line that was just offset, and then click in a blank area to the right of that line. You have created a vertical interior wall (Figure 5.7). Press Enter twice to stop and restart the Offset command.

8. Type **6.5'** and press Enter to set the distance for offsetting the next wall.

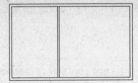

FIGURE 5.7: The first interior wall

NOTE

With Architectural units set, you can still enter distances in decimal form for feet and inches, and AutoCAD will translate them into their appropriate form. Thus, 6'-6" can be entered as 6.5', and 4 1/2" can be entered as 4.5 without the inch sign. Remember, when entering figures, you can omit the inch sign ("), but the foot sign (') must be included.

9. Pick a point on the inside, upper exterior wall line (Figure 5.8).

Select this line to offset

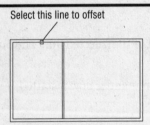

FIGURE 5.8: Selecting another wall line to offset

10. Click in a blank area below the line selected. The inside exterior wall line is offset to make a new interior wall line. Press Enter twice to stop and restart the Offset command.

11. Type **4** and press Enter. Click the new line and click again below it. A second wall line is made, and you now have two interior walls. Press Enter to end the Offset command.

These interior wall lines form the bedroom and one side of the bathroom. Their intersections with each other and with the exterior walls need to be cleaned up. If you take the time to do this now, it will be easier to make the last interior wall and, thereby, complete the bathroom. Refer back to Figures 5.1 and 5.2 to see where we're headed.

Cleaning Up Wall Lines

Earlier, you used the Fillet command to clean up the inside corners of the exterior walls. You can use that command again to clean up some of the interior walls, but you will have to use the Trim command to do the rest of them. You'll see why as you progress through the next set of steps.

1. It will be easier to pick the wall lines if you make the draw-ing larger on the screen. Type **Z** and press Enter, and then type **E** and press Enter. Press Enter, and then type **.6x** and press Enter. The drawing is bigger. You've just used two options of the Zoom command: First, you zoomed to *Extents* to fill the screen with your drawing. Then you zoomed to a scale (.6x) to make the drawing 0.6 the size it had been after zooming to Extents. This is a change in magnification on the view only—the building is still 25 feet long by 16 feet wide.

2. Pick the Fillet button from the Modify toolbar to start the Fillet command and, after checking the Command window to be sure the radius is still set to zero, click two of the wall lines as shown in Figure 5.9a. The lines will be filleted, and the results will look like Figure 5.9b.

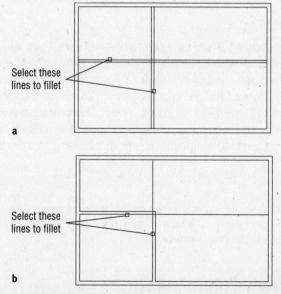

FIGURE 5.9: Selecting the first two lines to fillet (a), and the result of the fillet (b)

3. Press Enter to restart the Fillet command. Select the two lines as shown in Figure 5.10a. The results are shown in Figure 5.10b.

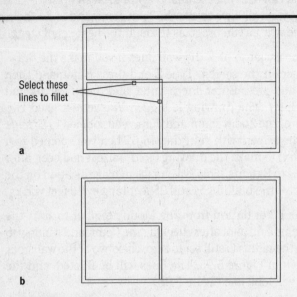

Select these
lines to fillet

a

b

FIGURE 5.10: Selecting the second two lines to fillet (a), and the result of the second fillet (b)

The two new interior walls are now the right length, but you will have to clean up the area where they form T intersections with the exterior walls. The Fillet command won't work in T intersections because too much of one of the wall lines is trimmed away. You'll have to use the Trim command in T intersection cases. The Fillet command does a specific kind of trim and is easy and quick to execute, but its uses are limited (for the most part) to single intersections between two lines.

TIP
The best rule for choosing between Fillet and Trim is the following: If you need to clean up a single intersection between two lines, use the Fillet command. For other cases, use the Trim command.

Using the Zoom Command
To do this trim, you need to have a closer view of the T intersections. Use the Zoom command to get a better look.

1. Type **z** and press Enter. Move the crosshair cursor to a point slightly above and to the left of the upper T intersection (Figure 5.11) and click in a blank area outside the floor plan.

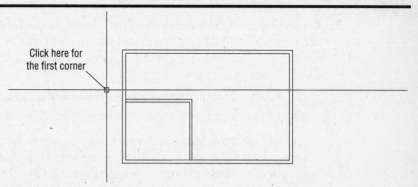

Click here for
the first corner

FIGURE 5.11: Positioning the cursor for the first click of the Zoom command

2. Move the cursor down and to the right, and notice a rectangle with solid lines being drawn. Keep moving the cursor down and to the right until the rectangle encloses the upper T intersection (Figure 5.12). When the rectangle fully encloses the T intersection, click again. The view changes to a closer view of the intersection of the interior and exterior wall. The rectangle you've just created is called a *zoom window*. The part of the drawing enclosed by the zoom window becomes the view on the screen. This is one of several zoom options for changing the magnification of the view. Other zoom options are introduced later in this chapter.

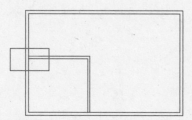

FIGURE 5.12: Using the Zoom Window option: positioning the rectangle

NOTE

When you start the Zoom command by typing **z** and pressing Enter and then pick a point on the screen, a zoom window begins.

3. On the Modify toolbar, click the Trim button. In the Command window, notice the second and third lines of text. You are being prompted to select cutting edges or objects to use as limits for the lines you want to trim.

4. Select the two interior wall lines and press Enter. The prompt changes, now asking you to select the lines to be trimmed.

5. Select the inside exterior wall line at the T intersection, between the two intersections with the interior wall lines that you have just picked as cutting edges (Figure 5.13a). The exterior wall line is trimmed at the T intersection (Figure 5.13b). Press Enter to end the Trim command.

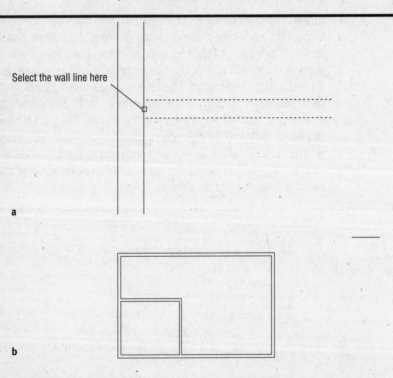

Select the wall line here

a

b

FIGURE 5.13: Selecting a line to be trimmed (a), and the result of the Trim command (b)

NOTE

In the Trim command, when picking lines to be trimmed, click the part of the line that needs to be trimmed away. In the Fillet command, select the part of the line that you want to keep.

6. Return to a view of the whole drawing by typing **z** and pressing Enter and then **p** and pressing Enter. This is the Zoom command's Previous option, which restores the view that was active before the last use of the Zoom command.

7. Repeat this procedure to trim the lower T intersection. Follow these steps:

   A. Type **z** and press Enter and click two points to make a rectangular zoom window around the intersection.

   B. Start the Trim command by choosing Modify ➢ Trim, select the interior walls as cutting edges, and press Enter.

   C. Select the inside exterior wall line between the cutting edges.

   D. Press Enter to end the Trim command.

   E. Zoom previous by typing **z** and pressing Enter and typing **p** and pressing Enter.

Figure 5.14 shows the results.

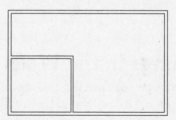

FIGURE 5.14: The second trim is completed.

You need to create one more interior wall to complete the bathroom.

Finishing the Interior Walls

You will use the same method to create the last bathroom wall that you used to make the first two interior walls. Briefly, this is how it's done:

1. Offset the upper-inside line of the left exterior wall 6' to the right, and then offset this new line 4" to the right.

2. Use the zoom window to zoom into the bathroom area.

3. Use the Trim command to trim away the short portion of the intersected wall lines between the two new wall lines.

4. Use Zoom previous to restore the full view.

The results should look like Figure 5.15. You used Offset, Fillet, Trim, and a couple of zooms to create the interior walls. The next task is to create five doorway openings in these walls. If you need to end the drawing session before completing the chapter, click File ➤ Save As, and then change the name of this drawing to Cabin02a.dwg and click Save. Then, you can exit AutoCAD.

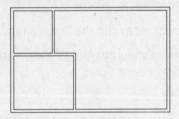

FIGURE 5.15: The completed interior walls

Cutting Openings in the Walls

Of the five doorway openings needed, two are on interior and three are on exterior walls (Figure 5.16). Four of them will be for swinging doors, and one will be for a sliding glass door.

You begin by establishing the location of the *jambs*, or sides, of an opening. One jamb for each swinging door opening will be located 6" away from an inside wall corner. This location allows the door to be positioned next to a wall and out of the way when swung open. When the jambs are established, you will trim away the wall lines between the edges. The commands used in this exercise are Offset, Extend, and Trim. You'll make openings for the 3'-0" exterior doorways first.

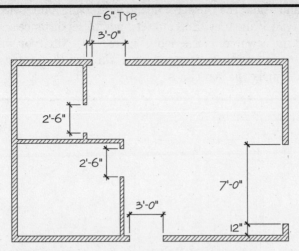

FIGURE 5.16: The drawing with doorway openings

The Exterior Openings

The exterior openings are on the front and back walls of the cabin and have one side set 6" in from an inside corner.

1. Click the Offset button on the Modify toolbar to start the Offset command, and then type **6** and press Enter to set the distance.

2. Click one of the two lines indicated in Figure 5.17, and then click in a blank area to the right of the line that you selected. Now do the same thing to the second wall line. You have to offset one line at a time because of the way the Offset command works.

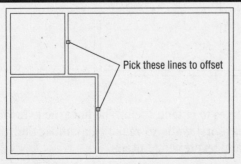

FIGURE 5.17: Lines to offset for 3'-0" openings

Part ii

3. End and restart the Offset command by pressing Enter twice; then type **3'** and press Enter to set a new offset distance and offset the new lines to the right (Figure 5.18). Next, you will need to extend these four new lines through the external walls to make the jamb lines.

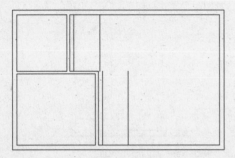

FIGURE 5.18: Offset lines for 3'-0" openings

4. Be sure to end the Offset command by pressing Enter. Type **ex** and press Enter to start the Extend command. Select the upper and lower horizontal outside, external wall lines as boundary edges for the Extend command, and press Enter.

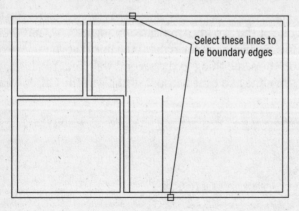

Select these lines to be boundary edges

5. Click the four lines to extend them. The lines are extended through the external walls to make the jambs. End the Extend command by pressing Enter.

Part ii

TIP

The lines to be extended must be picked on the half nearest the boundary's edge, or they will be extended to the opposite boundary edge.

To complete the openings, you will first trim away the excess part of the jamb lines and then the wall lines between the jamb lines. You'll do a *compound* trim to clean up the wall and jamb lines in one cycle of the command.

6. Type **tr** and press Enter to start the Trim command. Select the three lines at each opening as shown in Figure 5.19. Then press Enter to tell AutoCAD you are finished selecting objects to serve as cutting edges.

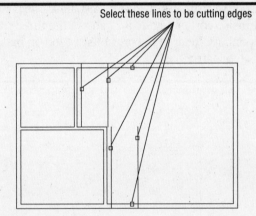

Select these lines to be cutting edges

FIGURE 5.19: Selecting the cutting edges

7. Pick the four wall lines between the jamb lines, and then pick the jamb lines—the lines you just extended to the outside exterior walls. Each time you pick a line, it is trimmed. Press Enter to end the command. Your drawing should look like Figure 5.20.

TIP

When picking lines to be trimmed, remember to pick the lines on the portion to be trimmed away.

The two interior openings can be constructed using the same procedure.

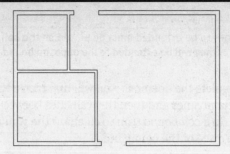

FIGURE 5.20: The finished 3'-0" openings

The Interior Openings

These doorways are 2'-6" wide and also have one jamb set in 6" from the nearest inside corner. Figure 5.21 shows the three stages of fabricating these openings. Refer to the previous section on making openings for step-by-step instructions.

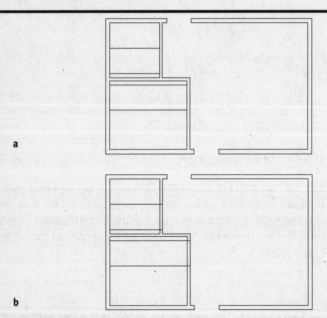

a

b

FIGURE 5.21: Creating the interior openings: the offset lines that locate the jamb lines (a), the extended lines that form the jamb lines (b), and the completed openings after trimming (c)

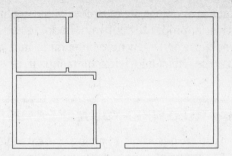

c

FIGURE 5.21 CONTINUED

Part ii

Construct the 7'-0" exterior opening using the same commands and technique.

The 7'-0" Opening

Notice the opening on the right side of the building has one jamb set 12" in from the inside corner. This will be the sliding glass door.

You've done this before, so here's a summary of the steps:

1. Offset a wall line 12".

2. Offset the new line 7'-0".

3. Extend both new lines through the wall.

4. Trim the new lines and the wall lines to complete the opening.

Save this drawing now as Cabin02b.dwg. This completes the openings.

As you gain more control over the commands you used here, you will be able to anticipate how much of a task can be done for each use of a command. Each opening required offsetting, extending, and trimming. You constructed these openings by drawing two at a time except for the last one, thereby using each of the three commands three times. It is possible to do all the openings using each command only once. This way, you would do all the offsetting, then all the extending, and finally, all the trimming. In cutting these openings, however, the arrangement of the offset lines determined how many cycles of the Trim command were most efficient to use. If lines being trimmed and used as cutting edges cross each other, the trimming is complicated. For these five openings, the most efficient procedure would be to use each command twice.

Now that the openings are complete, you can place doors and door swings in their appropriate doorways. In doing this, you'll be introduced to two new objects and a few new commands, and you will have an opportunity to use the Offset and Trim commands in new, strategic ways.

WHAT TO DO WHEN YOU MAKE A MISTAKE

When you are offsetting, trimming, and extending lines, it's easy to pick the wrong line. Here are some tips on how to correct these errors and get back on track.

▶ You can always cancel any command by pressing the Esc key until you see the Command: prompt in the Command window. Then, click the Undo button on the Standard toolbar to undo the results of the last command.

▶ Errors made with the Offset command include setting the wrong distance, picking the wrong line to offset, or picking the wrong side to offset toward. If the distance is correct, you can continue offsetting, end the command when you have the results you want, and then erase the lines that were offset wrong. Otherwise, press Esc and undo your previous offset.

▶ Errors made with the Trim and Extend commands can sometimes be corrected on the fly so you don't have to end the command, because each of these commands has an Undo option. If you pick a line and it doesn't trim or extend the right way, you can undo that last action without stopping the command, and then continue trimming or extending. The Undo option used while the command is running can be activated in three ways: click the Undo button on the Standard toolbar; type **u** and press Enter; or right-click and pick Undo from the shortcut menu that appears. Each of these methods will undo the last trim or extend, and you can try again without having to restart the command. Each time you activate the Undo option *from within the command*, another trim or extend is undone.

▶ The Line command also has the same Undo option as the Trim and Extend commands. You can undo the last segment drawn (or the last several segments) and redraw them.

CREATING DOORS

In a floor plan, a rectangle or a line for the door and an arc showing the path of the door swing usually indicates a door. The door's position varies, but it's most often shown at 90° from the closed position (Figure 5.22). The best rule I have come across is to display them in such a way that others working with your floor plan will be able to see how far, and in what direction, the door will swing open.

FIGURE 5.22: Possible ways to illustrate doors

The cabin has five openings. Four of them need swinging doors, which open 90°. The fifth is a sliding glass door. Drawing the sliding glass door will require a different approach.

Drawing Swinging Doors

The swinging doors are of two widths: 3' for exterior and 2'-6" for interior (refer to Figure 5.1). In general, doorway openings leading to the outside are wider than interior doors, with bathroom and closet doors usually being the narrowest. For the cabin, you'll use two sizes of swinging doors. You will draw one door of each size, and then copy them to the other openings as required. Start with the front door at the bottom of the floor plan. To get a closer view of the front door opening, use the Zoom Window command.

1. Before you begin drawing, check the status bar at the bottom of the screen and make sure only the Model button at the far right is pressed in. All other buttons should be in the Off position—that is, up. If any are pressed in, click them once to turn them off.

2. Click Tools ➤ Drafting Settings to bring up the Drafting Settings dialog box. Click the Object Snap tab to activate it, if it's not already on top.

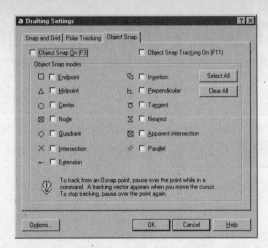

Be sure all check boxes are unchecked. If any boxes have checks in them, click the Clear All button to uncheck them. Then, click OK to close the dialog box.

3. At the Command: prompt, move the cursor to the Standard toolbar and click the Zoom Window button. Doing so has the same effect as typing **z** and pressing Enter, as you did earlier in this chapter.

4. Pick two points to form a window around the front doorway opening. The view changes, and you now have a close-up view of the opening. You'll draw the door in a closed position and then rotate it open.

5. To draw the door, click the Rectangle button on the Draw toolbar.

TIP

You can also start the Rectangle command by picking Rectangle from the Draw drop-down menu, or by typing **rec** and pressing Enter in the Command window.

Notice the Command window prompt. Several options appear in brackets, but the default option Specify first corner point (before the brackets) is the one you want. You form the rectangle like the zoom window—by picking two points to represent opposite corners of the rectangle. In its closed position, the door will fit exactly between the jambs, with its upper corners coinciding with the upper endpoints of the jambs. To make the first corner of the rectangle coincide with the upper endpoint of the left jamb exactly, you will use an Object Snap to assist you. *Object Snaps* (or *Osnaps*) allow you to pick specific points on objects like endpoints, midpoints, the center of a circle, and so on.

NOTE

Osnap is a nickname for *Object Snap*. The two terms are used interchangeably.

6. Move the cursor onto the Temporary Tracking Point button on the Standard toolbar and hold down the left mouse button. The Object Snap flyout opens and you see all the Object Snap tools.

7. Holding down the left mouse button, drag the cursor down the flyout to the Endpoint button, and release the mouse button. The prompt line now displays the addition of **_endp of**. This is a signal to you that the Endpoint Object Snap has been activated.

8. Move the cursor near the upper end of the left jamb line. When the cursor gets very close to a line, a colored square appears at the nearest endpoint. It shows you which endpoint in the drawing is closest to the position of the crosshair cursor at that moment.

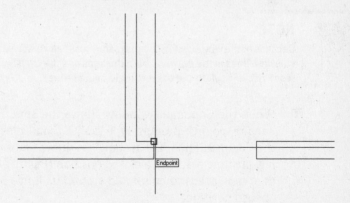

9. Move the cursor until the square is positioned on the upper end of the left jamb line, as shown above, and then click that point. The first corner of the rectangle now is located

Part ii

at that point. Move the cursor to the right and slightly down to see the rectangle being formed (Figure 5.23a). To locate the opposite corner, let's use relative Cartesian coordinates.

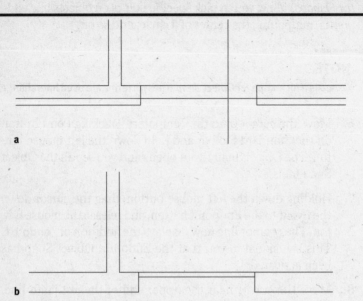

FIGURE 5.23: The rectangle after picking the first corner (a), and the completed door in a closed position (b)

NOTE

Because of the way AutoCAD displays the crosshair cursor, when its lines coincide with lines in the drawing, both the lines and the crosshair disappear. As a result, it's difficult to see the rectangle being formed.

10. When the Command window shows the Specify other corner point: prompt, type **@3',-1.5** and press Enter in the Command line. The rectangle is drawn across the opening, creating a door in a closed position (Figure 5.23b). The door now needs to be rotated around its hinge point to an opened position.

NOTE

You could have used the Rectangle command to lay out the first four wall lines of the cabin. Then you could have offset all four lines in one step to complete the exterior walls, and the corners would have been automatically filleted. It would have been faster than the method we used, but a rectangle's lines are all one object. In order to offset them to make the interior walls, they would have to be separated into individual lines using the Explode command.

Rotating the Door

This rotation will be through an arc of 90° in the counter-clockwise direction, making it a rotation of +90. By default, counter-clockwise rotations are positive and clockwise rotations are negative. You'll use the Rotate command to rotate the door.

1. Pick the Rotate button from the Modify toolbar. You'll see a prompt to select objects. Click the door and press Enter.

TIP

You can also start the Rotate command by clicking Modify ➤ Rotate on the pull-down menus or by typing **ro** and pressing Enter.

NOTE

Note that when you select the door, one pick selects all four lines. Rectangles are made of a special line called a *polyline* that connects all segments into one object.

You will be prompted for a base point. You need to indicate a point around which the door will be rotated. To keep the door placed correctly, pick the hinge point for the base point. The hinge point for this opening is the upper endpoint of the left jamb line.

2. Return to the Standard toolbar and select the Endpoint Osnap button. Endpoint Osnap has replaced the Tracking button because it was the last Osnap button selected from the flyout toolbar.

3. Move the cursor near the upper-left corner of the door. When the colored square is displayed at that corner, left-click to locate the base point.

Part ii

4. Check the status bar to be sure the Ortho button is not pressed in. If it is, click it to turn Ortho off. When the Ortho button is on, the cursor is forced to move in a vertical or horizontal direction. This restriction is very useful at times; but, in this instance, it would keep you from being able to see the door rotate.

5. Move the cursor away from the hinge point and see how the door rotates as the cursor moves (Figure 5.24). If the door swings properly, you are reassured that you correctly selected the base point. The prompt reads `Specify rotation angle or [reference]`, asking you to enter an angle.

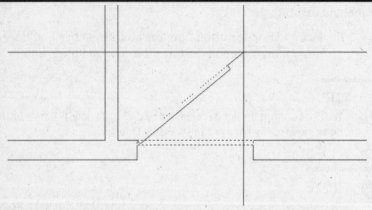

FIGURE 5.24: The door rotating with movement of the cursor

6. Type **90** and press Enter. The door is rotated 90° to an open position.

To finish this door, you need to add the door's swing. You'll use the Arc command to do this.

Drawing the Door Swing

The *swing* shows the path that the outer edge of a door takes when it swings from closed to fully open. Including a swing with the door in a floor plan helps to resolve clearance issues. The swings are drawn with the Arc command, in this case using the Endpoint Osnap.

TIP

You can start abbreviated versions of the Arc command from the Draw toolbar, or by typing **a** and pressing Enter.

1. From the Draw menu, select Arc. The Arc menu is displayed. An arc for this door swing needs to be drawn from the upper end of the right jamb line through a rotation of 90°. So, you know the start point of the arc, the center of rotation, and the angle through which the rotation occurs. The center point of the arc is the hinge point of the door.

THE OPTIONS OF THE ARC COMMAND

The position and size of an arc can be specified by a combination of its components, some of which are starting point, ending point, angle, center point, and radius. The Arc command gives you 11 options, each of which uses three components. With a little study of the geometric information available to you on the drawing, you can choose the option that best fits the situation.

When you use the Draw drop-down menu to select the Arc command, 10 options are displayed with their three components and an 11th option is used to continue the last arc drawn. For that reason, this is the best way to start the Arc command when you are first learning it.

When you start the Arc command by using the Arc button on the Draw toolbar or by typing **a** and pressing Enter, you get an abbreviated form of the command in the Command window. All 11 command options can be accessed through this prompt, but you have to select various options along the way.

2. From the Arc menu, select Start, Center, Angle. The Command prompt now reads: arc Specify start point of arc or [Center]:. The default option is Specify start point of arc. You also have the option to start with the center point, but you would have to type **c** and press Enter before picking a point to be the center point.

3. Activate the Endpoint Osnap and pick the upper endpoint of the right jamb line.

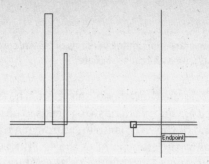

The prompt changes to read: Specify second point of arc or [Center/End]: _c Specify center point of arc.

This prompt may be confusing at first. It gives you three options: Second Point, Center, and End. (Center and End are in brackets.) Because you have previously chosen the Start, Center, Angle option, AutoCAD automatically chooses Center for you. That is the last part of the prompt.

4. Activate the Endpoint Osnap again and select the hinge point. The arc is now visible, and its endpoint follows the cursor's movement (Figure 5.25a). The prompt displays a different set of options, and then ends the Included angle option.

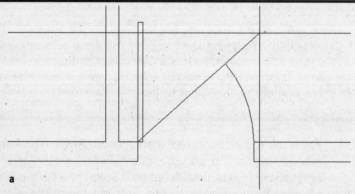

a

FIGURE 5.25: Drawing the arc: the ending point of the arc follows the cursor's movements (a), and the completed arc (b)

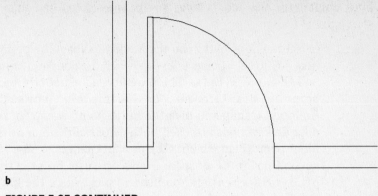

b

FIGURE 5.25 CONTINUED

5. Type **90** and press Enter. The arc is completed and the Arc command ends (Figure 5.25b).

The front door is completed. Because the back door is the same size, you can save time by copying this door to the other opening. Let's see how to do that.

Copying Objects

The Copy command makes a copy of the objects you select. This copy can be located either by a point you pick or by relative coordinates that you enter from the keyboard. For AutoCAD to position these copied objects, you must designate two points: a base point, which serves as a point of reference for where the copy move starts; and then a second point, which serves as the ending point for the Copy command. The copy is moved the same distance and direction from its original that the second point is moved from the first point. When you know the actual distance and direction to move the copy, the base point isn't critical because you will specify the second point with relative polar or Cartesian coordinates. But in this situation, you don't know the exact distance or angle to move a copy of the front door to the back door opening, so you need to choose a base point for the copy carefully.

In copying this new door and its swing to the back door opening of the cabin, you need to find a point somewhere on the existing door or swing that can be located precisely on a point at the back door opening. You can choose from two such points: the hinge point or the start point of the door swing. Let's use the hinge point. You usually know where the hinge point of the new door belongs, so this is easier to locate than the start point of the arc.

1. Select the Copy button on the Modify toolbar. The prompt asks you to select objects to copy. Pick the door and swing, and then press Enter. The prompt reads `Specify base point or displacement, or [Multiple]:`. Activate the Endpoint Osnap and pick the hinge point. A copy of the door and swing is attached to the crosshair cursor at the hinge point (Figure 5.26). The prompt changes to `Specify second point of displacement or <use first point of displacement>:`. You need to pick where the hinge point of the copied door will be located at the back door opening. To do this, you need to change the view back to what it was before you zoomed in to the doorway opening.

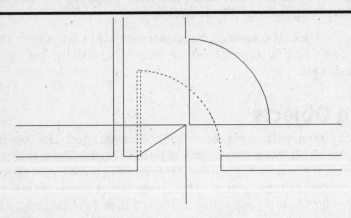

FIGURE 5.26: The copy of the door and swing attached to the crosshair cursor

TIP
You can also start the Copy command from the drop-down menus by picking Modify ➢ Copy, or from the keyboard by typing **cp** and pressing Enter.

2. From the Standard toolbar, click the Zoom Previous button. The full view of the cabin is restored. Move the crosshair cursor with the door in tow up to the vicinity of the back door opening. The back door should swing to the inside and be against the wall when open, so the hinge point for this opening will be at the lower end of the left jamb line.

3. Activate the Endpoint Osnap and pick the lower end of the left jamb line on the back door opening. The copy of the door and swing is placed in the opening (Figure 5.27) and, by looking at the Command window, you can see that the Copy command has ended.

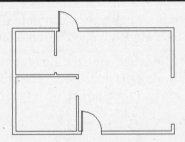

FIGURE 5.27: The door is copied to the back door opening.

NOTE

The Copy command ends when you pick or specify the second point of the move, unless you're copying the same object to multiple places.

The door is oriented the wrong way, but you'll fix that next.

When you copy doors from one opening to another, often the orientation may not match. The best strategy is to use the hinge point as a point of reference and place it where it needs to go, as you have just done. Then, you can flip and/or rotate the door so that it sits and swings the right way. The flipping of an object is known as *mirroring*.

NOTE

You were able to use the Zoom command while you were in the middle of using the Copy command. Most of the display commands—Zoom, Pan, and so on— can be used this way. This technique is called using a command *transparently.*

Mirroring Objects

You have located the door in the opening, but it needs to be flipped so that it swings to the inside of the cabin. To do this, you'll use the Mirror command.

The Mirror command allows you to flip objects around an axis called the *mirror line*. You define this imaginary line by designating two points to be the endpoints of the line. Strategic selection of the mirror line ensures the accuracy of the mirroring action, so it's critical to visualize where the proper line lies. Sometimes you will have to draw a guideline in order to designate one or both of the endpoints.

1. Choose the Zoom Window icon from the Standard toolbar and create a window around the back door and its opening.

2. Pick the Mirror button on the Modify toolbar. Select the back door and swing and press Enter. The prompt line changes to read Specify first point of mirror line:.

TIP

You can also find the Mirror command on the Modify drop-down menu or start it by typing **mi** and pressing Enter.

3. Activate the Endpoint Osnap, and then pick the hinge point of the door. The prompt changes to read Specify second point of mirror line:, and you will see the mirrored image of the door and the swing moving as you move the cursor around the drawing area. You are rotating the mirror line about the hinge point as you move the cursor. As the mirror line moves, the location of the mirrored image moves (Figure 5.28).

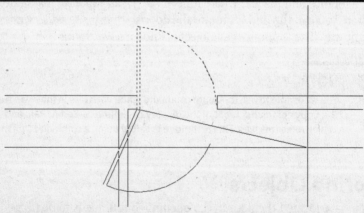

FIGURE 5.28: The mirror image moves as the mirror line moves.

4. Hold the crosshair cursor directly to the right of the first point picked, along the inside wall line. The mirror image appears to be where you want the door to be.

5. Activate the Endpoint Osnap again and pick the lower end of the right jamb line. The mirror image disappears and the prompt changes to read Delete source objects? [Yes/No] <N>:. You have two choices. You can keep both doors by pressing Enter and accepting the default (No). Or, you can discard the original one by typing **y** (for yes) in the Command line and pressing Enter.

6. Type **y** and press Enter. The flipped door is displayed, and the original one is deleted. The Mirror command ends. Like the Copy command, the Mirror command ends automatically after one mirroring operation.

It may take some practice to become proficient at visualizing and designating the mirror line, but once you are accustomed to it, you will have learned to use a very powerful tool. Because many building layouts have some symmetry, wise use of the Mirror command can save you a lot of drawing time.

You have two more swinging doors to place in the floor plan.

Finishing the Swinging Doors

You can't copy the existing doors and swings to the interior openings because the sizes don't conform, but you can use the same procedure to draw one door and swing, and then copy it to the other opening.

NOTE
You could have used the Stretch command to lengthen the door, but that's an advanced Modify command. Besides, the arc would have to be modified to a larger radius. It's easier to just draw another door and swing to a different size.

1. Click the Zoom Previous button on the Standard toolbar. Then, click the Zoom Window button next to the Zoom Previous button, and make a zoom window to magnify the view of the interior door openings. Be sure to make the zoom window large enough to leave some room for the new doors to be drawn.

Part ii

2. Follow the same procedure to draw the door and swing in the lower opening. Here is a summary of the steps:

   A. Use the Rectangle command and Endpoint Osnap to draw the door from the hinge point to a point @1.5,-2'6.

   B. Rotate the door around the hinge point to an open position. You will have to use a rotation angle of −90°.

   C. Use the Start, Center, Angle option of the Arc command to draw the door swing, starting at the upper-left corner of the door and using Endpoint Osnap for the two picks.

NOTE

The Start, Center, Angle option—as well as a few others—of the Arc command requires that you choose the start point for the arc in such a way that the arc is drawn in a counter-clockwise direction. If you progress in a clockwise direction, use a negative number for the angle.

3. Use the Copy command to copy this door and swing to the other interior opening. The base point will be the hinge point, and the second point will be the left end of the lower jamb line in the upper opening. Use the Endpoint Osnap for both picks.

4. Use the Mirror command to flip this copy of the door and swing up. The mirror line will be different from the one you used for the back door. The geometrical arrangement at the back opening required that the door and its swing be flipped across the opening. In this case, the door and its swing must flip in a direction parallel to the opening. For this opening, the mirror line is the lower jamb line itself, so pick each end of this line (using Endpoint Osnap) to establish the mirror line.

5. Use the Zoom Previous button to see the four swinging doors in place (Figure 5.29).

The last door to draw is the sliding glass door. This kind of door requires an entirely different strategy, but you'll use commands familiar to you by now.

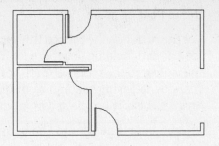

FIGURE 5.29: The four swinging doors in place

Drawing a Sliding Glass Door

Sliding glass doors are usually drawn to show their glass panels within the door frames.

To draw the sliding door, you will apply the Line, Offset, and Trim commands to the 7-foot opening you made earlier.

1. Pick the Zoom Window button on the Standard toolbar and make a zoom window closely around the 7' opening. In making the zoom window, pick one point just above and to the left of the upper doorjamb and below and to the right of the lower jamb. This will make the opening as large as possible while including everything you will need in the view.

2. You will use several Osnaps for this procedure, so it will be convenient to have the Osnap Flyout toolbar more immediately available. Here's how:

   A. Right-click on any button on any of the toolbars on your screen. The Toolbar menu appears.

B. Click Object Snap on the menu. The menu closes, and the Object Snap toolbar is displayed in the drawing area. It is in floating mode.

C. Put the cursor on the colored title bar of the Object Snap toolbar and, holding down the left mouse button, drag the toolbar to the right side of the drawing area. Dock it there by releasing the mouse button. Now all Object Snaps can easily be selected as needed.

3. Offset each jamb line 2" into the doorway opening (Figure 5.30).

FIGURE 5.30: Jamb lines offset 2" into the doorway opening

4. Type **l** and press Enter to start the Line command. Pick the Midpoint Osnap button from the Object Snap toolbar, and then place the cursor near the midpoint of the upper door-jamb line. Notice how a colored triangle appears when your cursor is in the vicinity of the midpoint. Each Osnap has a symbol with a distinctive shape. When the triangle appears at the midpoint of the jamb line, left-click. Click the Midpoint Osnap button again, move the cursor to the bottom jamb line, and, when the triangle appears at that midpoint, click again. Press Enter to end the Line command.

5. Start the Offset command, type **1.5,** and press Enter to set the offset distance. Pick the newly drawn line, and then pick

a point anywhere to the right side. While the Offset command is still running, pick the original line again and pick another point in a blank area somewhere to the left side of the doorway opening (Figure 5.31). Press Enter to end the Offset command.

FIGURE 5.31: Offset vertical line between jambs

NOTE

A line *offset* from itself—that is, a copy of the selected line—is automatically made at a specified perpendicular distance from the selected line.

6. Check the status bar to see if Ortho is on. If it isn't, click it to activate it. Type **l** and press Enter to start the Line command. Click the Midpoint Osnap button and move the cursor near the midpoint of the left vertical line. When the colored triangle appears at the midpoint of this leftmost line, click. Hold the cursor out directly to the right of the point you just selected to draw a horizontal line through the three vertical lines. When the cursor is about two feet to the right of the three vertical lines, pick a point to set the endpoint of this guideline. Press Enter to end the Line command (Figure 5.32).

FIGURE 5.32: Horizontal guideline drawn through vertical lines

7. Type **o** and press Enter to start the Offset command. Type **1** and press Enter to set the offset distance. Pick this new line, and then pick a point in a blank area anywhere above the line. Pick the original line again and then pick anywhere below it. The new line has been offset 1" above and below itself (Figure 5.33). Now you have placed all the lines necessary to create the sliding glass door frames in the opening. You still need to trim some of these lines back and erase others. Press Enter to end the Offset command.

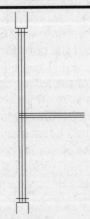

FIGURE 5.33: Offset horizontal guideline

8. Start the Trim command by typing **tr** and pressing Enter. When you are prompted to select cutting edges, pick the two horizontal lines that you just created with the Offset command. Press Enter.

9. Trim the two outside vertical lines by picking them as shown in Figure 5.34a. The result is shown in Figure 5.34b.

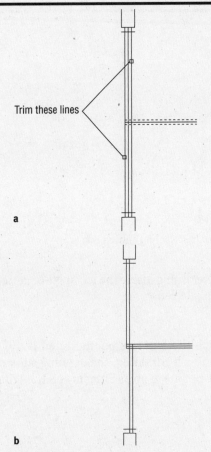

FIGURE 5.34: Picking the vertical lines to trim (a), and the result (b)

10. Press **Enter** twice to stop and restart the Trim command. When you are prompted to select cutting edges, use a special window called a *crossing window* to select all the lines visible

in the drawing. A crossing window will select everything within the window or crossing it. Here's how to do it:

A. Pick a point above and to the right of the opening.

B. Move the cursor to a point below and to the left of the opening, forming a window with dashed lines (Figure 5.35).

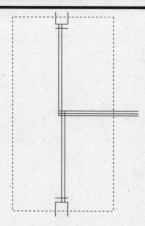

FIGURE 55.35: The crossing window for selecting cutting edges

C. Pick that point. Everything inside the rectangle or crossing an edge of it is selected.

D. Press Enter.

11. To trim the lines, pick them at the points noted in Figure 5.36a. When you finish trimming, the opening should look like Figure 5.36b. Be sure to press Enter to end the Trim command.

NOTE

If all lines don't trim the way you expect them to, you may have to change the setting for the Edgemode variable. It's easy. Cancel the trim operation and undo any trims you've made to the sliding glass door. Type **edgemode** and press Enter, and then type **o** and press Enter. Now, start the Trim command and continue trimming.

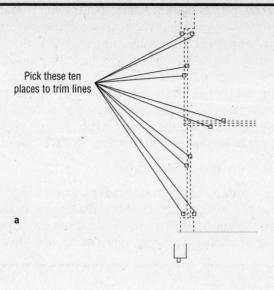

Pick these ten
places to trim lines

a

b

FIGURE 5.36: Lines to trim (a), and the result (b)

12. Start the Erase command and erase the remaining horizontal guideline.

   To finish the sliding glass doors, you need to draw in two lines to represent the glass panes for each door panel. Each pane of glass is centered inside its frame, so the line representing the pane will run between the midpoints of the inside edge of each frame section.

13. Type **l** and press Enter to start the Line command. Pick the Midpoint button on the Object Snap toolbar.

14. For each of the two sliding door frames, put the cursor near the midpoint of the inside line of the frame section nearest the jamb. When the colored triangle appears there, click. Select the Perpendicular Osnap button from the Object Snap toolbar and move the cursor to the other frame section of that door panel. When you get near the horizontal line that represents both the inside edge of one frame section and the back edge of the frame section next to it, the colored Perpendicular Osnap symbol will appear on that line. When it does, select that point.

15. Press Enter to end the Line command.

16. Press Enter to restart the Line command and repeat the procedure described in step 14 for the other door panel, being sure to start the line at the frame section nearest the other jamb. The finished opening should look like Figure 5.37a.

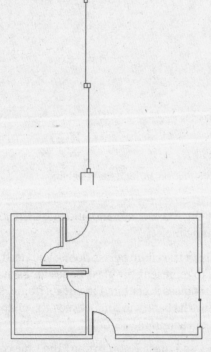

a

b
FIGURE 5.37: The finished sliding glass doors (a), and the floor plan with all doors finished (b)

17. Use the Zoom Previous button to see the full floor plan with all doors (Figure 5.37b).

18. Save this drawing as Cabin02c.

This completes the doors for the floor plan. The focus here has been on walls and doors, and the strategies for drawing them. As a result, you now have a basic floor plan for the cabin.

The overall drawing strategy that has been emphasized in this chapter is using objects already in the drawing to create new ones. You started out with four lines that formed the outside wall lines. By offsetting, filleting, extending, and trimming, you drew all the walls and openings without drawing any new lines. For the swinging doors, you made two rectangles and two arcs. Then, by copying, rotating, and mirroring, you formed the other two swinging doors. For the sliding glass door, you drew two new lines and then used Offset, Trim, and Erase to finish the door. So, you used four lines and created six new objects to complete the walls and doors. This is a pretty good start in learning to use AutoCAD wisely.

By working with the tools and strategies in this chapter, you now should have an idea of an approach to drawing many objects.

IF YOU WOULD LIKE MORE PRACTICE...

If you would like to practice the skills you have learned so far, here are a couple of extra exercises.

An Alternate Sliding Glass Door

Here is a simplified version of the sliding glass door of the cabin. It doesn't include any representation of the panes of glass and their frames.

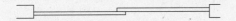

To draw it, use a technique similar to the one described in the previous section. Copy the jambs for the 7' opening to the right and draw this door between them.

An Addition to the Cabin

This addition is connected to the cabin by a sidewalk and consists of a remodeled two-car garage in which one car slot has been converted into a storage area and an office (Figure 5.38). Use the same commands and strategies you have been using up to now to draw this layout adjacent to the cabin. Save this exercise as Cabin02b-addon.dwg.

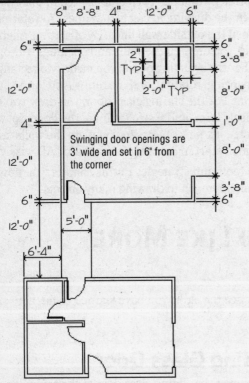

FIGURE 5.38: The garage addition

Refer back to this chapter for specific commands. Here is the general procedure:

1. Draw the two lines that represent the walkway between the two buildings.

2. Draw the outside exterior wall line.

3. Use Offset, Fillet, and Trim to create the rest of the walls and wall lines.

4. Use Offset, Extend, and Trim to create the openings.

5. Use Rectangle and Arc to create a swinging door.

6. Use Copy, Rotate, and Mirror to put in the rest of the doors.

7. Use Offset, Line, and Copy to draw the storage partitions.

WHAT'S NEXT?

In this chapter you have drawn the floor plan for a small cabin. You have begun to think strategically in regard to using drawing tools. You have been exposed to common problems that occur when drawing, and have come up with practical solutions. In the next chapter, you will learn the skills to put text into a drawing.

Part ii

Chapter 6

PUTTING TEXT INTO A DRAWING

When you work with text in a drawing, you use skills in three areas: setting up a text style, putting text in the drawing, and modifying text that has already been placed in a drawing. (A *text style* is a named group of settings that control the appearance of text in your drawing.) AutoCAD has two kinds of text: single-line text and multiline text. They both use the same text styles, but you place them in the drawing differently and modify them using similar but somewhat different methods.

Adapted from *AutoCAD® 2000 Visual Jumpstart* by David Frey

ISBN 0-7821-2777-0   272 pages $19.99

SETTING UP A TEXT STYLE

A text style consists of a name for the style, a font, and various settings for the size and orientation of the text. (A *font* is a collection of letters, characters, and punctuation marks that share common features of design and appearance.) Once you have several text styles to choose from, you use a style by making it current, or *active*.

TIP

If you need several sizes of the same font, does each one require a separate style? No. If you set up a text style so that the height of the text is set to 0, you can use the same text style to make text with various heights.

Creating a New Text Style

Each new AutoCAD drawing comes with a Standard text style. When you create a new text style, you make a copy of the Standard style and rename it, and then make any necessary changes to the aspects of the new style.

NOTE

You can certainly use the Standard text style as is, but the text font that it uses is quite primitive: All letters consist of only straight lines.

1. On the pull-down menus, choose Format ➤ Text Style to bring up the Text Style dialog box.

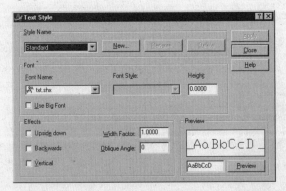

2. In the Style Name area, click the New button to bring up the New Text Style dialog box.

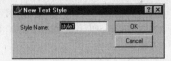

3. Enter a new text style name—you probably won't prefer to use the default Style1 name—and click OK.

4. Back in the Text Style dialog box, the new text style name will replace Standard in the Style Name drop-down list. In the Font area, click in the Font Name drop-down list to open it.

NOTE

The Style Name drop-down list displays all the text styles that have been defined in the current drawing.

5. Scroll the list to find the font you wish to assign to this new text style. Click it to select it and to close the list.

NOTE

When you select a font, its appearance is previewed in the Preview area of the Text Style dialog box. If you make changes to other text settings, they are also reflected in the Preview area.

6. For most AutoCAD text uses, you may also need to make changes to the following settings:

Font Style For some fonts, you will have choices of bold, italic, and so on.

Height This value specifies the height of the uppercase characters.

NOTE

If you leave the Height set to 0, you will be prompted for the text height when you place text in the drawing.

Width Factor A number greater than 1 gives you wider letters; less than 1 results in thinner letters.

Part ii

Oblique Angle Enter an angle to slant letters away from vertical.

7. When you have made all your desired setting changes, click Apply to save the setting changes to the new text style. Then, click Close.

Making an Existing Text Style Current

When you follow the steps in the previous section to create a new text style, it becomes the *current text style*—the text style that is active in your drawing. New text put into a drawing is made in the current style. You can use the Text Style dialog box to change the current style from one text style to another.

1. Choose Format ➤ Text Style to bring up the Text Style dialog box.

2. Click the drop-down list in the Style Name area to open it.

3. Click the style that you wish to make current.

4. Click the Close button.

USING SINGLE-LINE TEXT

For single letters, words, or short sentences and notes, AutoCAD offers single-line text. Each line of text, whether it consists of one letter or several words, behaves as a single item. You can make multiple lines of text with single-line text, but the text won't word-wrap at a predefined margin, as it will with AutoCAD's multiline text. *Word-wrap* is a feature of most word-processing programs, in which words are automatically placed on the next line down when a line exceeds a set length.

Putting Single-Line Text into a Drawing

To use single-line text, you start by specifying a point in the drawing to begin the text and deciding whether the text will be placed with an orientation other than horizontal.

1. Choose Draw ➤ Text ➤ Single Line Text. In the Command window, you will see the name of the current text style and its height, and you will be prompted to pick a point or select one of two options: Style or Justify.

NOTE

The Style option allows you to change the current style. The Justify option is discussed in the next section.

```
Command: _dtext
Current text style:  "NOTES"  Text height:  1'-0"
Specify start point of text or [Justify/Style]:
1.5687E+03, 1.6315E+03 , 0'-0"            SNAP GRID ORTHO POLAR 0
```

2. Pick a point in the drawing to serve as the lower-left corner of a new line of text. The Command window now gives you the options of accepting the default angle of rotation of the text (0.00) or entering a different angle. Press Enter to accept the default of no rotation.

TIP

Use the Rotation option when you want your text to follow a sloping line.

3. A text prompt appears in your drawing at the point you picked in the previous step. Type your new text. The prompt stays to the right of the new text.

NOTE

With single-line text, the new text appears in your drawing as you type it.

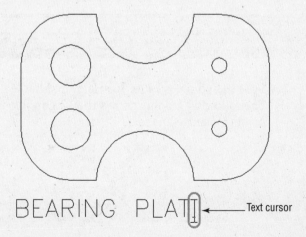

BEARING PLAT← Text cursor

Part ii

4. When you're finished, press Enter. The text cursor jumps one line down and sits at the beginning of a new line of text.

5. Press Enter a second time to end the Single Line Text command, or type in a second line of text and then press Enter twice.

TIP

When you're using single-line text, pressing Enter twice will end the command.

Using a New Justification Point

If you want your single-line text to be centered inside a circle, for example, use the Justification option to change the *text justification point*. This point is associated with a line of single-line text and is used to locate that text in the drawing. Each line of text has 12 possible justification points.

1. After starting the Single Line Text command, type **j** and press Enter. The Command window displays all the justification options.

NOTE

The 12 justification points each define the position of the insertion point relative to the text. TL, for example, places the insertion point at the top-left of the text area.

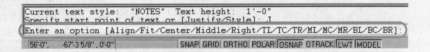

```
Current text style:  "NOTES"  Text height:  1'-0"
Specify start point of text or [Justify/Style]: J
Enter an option [Align/Fit/Center/Middle/Right/TL/TC/TR/ML/MC/MR/BL/BC/BR]:
56'-0",    -67'-3 5/8", 0'-0"         SNAP GRID ORTHO POLAR OSNAP OTRACK LWT MODEL
```

2. Type **m** and press Enter to select the Middle justification. The following graphic shows the 12 possible justification points for single-line text.

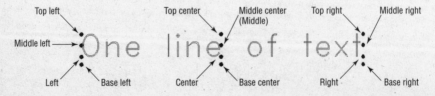

3. Choose Center Osnap from the Object Snap flyout on the Standard toolbar.

4. Click on the circle.

5. Press Enter for the Rotation option.

6. Type in the letter or word to be centered in the circle.

7. Press Enter twice. The text is centered, and the Single Line Text command ends.

NOTE

The text won't appear centered until you press Enter the second time and end the command.

Changing the Wording of Single-Line Text

When you need to make changes in the wording of single-line text in your drawing, you have a handy tool at your disposal.

1. Choose Modify ➤ Text on the pull-down menus.

2. Click on the line of text you wish to change. The Edit Text dialog box comes up and displays the text you selected. The text is highlighted.

3. Make any changes necessary and click OK. The text is modified in your drawing, and you are prompted to select another line of text for editing.

NOTE
The Modify Text command keeps running until you end it.

4. Repeat steps 2 and 3 to modify more text, or press Enter to end the command.

NOTE
This method can be used to modify only one line of text at a time.

Changing Any Aspect of Single-Line Text

If you need to change a property of single-line text other than its wording, use the Properties window.

1. Click the line of text that you wish to modify. A grip will appear at its justification point.

NOTE
This method for modifying text can be used for more than one line of text at a time.

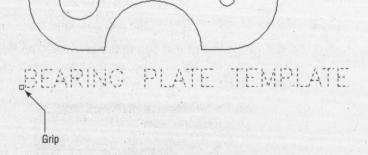

Grip

2. Click the Properties button on the Standard toolbar.

3. In the Properties window, note the list of text properties and their current values after the list of General properties. *Text properties* are various characteristics that define the appearance of text, such as height, font, width factor, and so on. The text style settings define the properties.

NOTE

If you select multiple lines of single-line text for modification, the Properties window will display only those property values that all the selected lines have in common.

4. Click the Text property that you wish to change.

TIP

You can use the Properties window to modify the wording of the text, but if that is all you wish to do, it's easier and quicker to use the Modify Text method described in the previous section.

5. Click again on the current value for that property and make the necessary change.

6. Close the Properties window by clicking the X in its upper-right corner.

7. Press the Esc key twice to remove the grip from the modified text.

USING MULTILINE TEXT

For notes and paragraphs of text, use multiline text (or *mtext*, for short). This text is placed in your drawing using the Multiline Text command. The icon for this command is at the bottom of the Draw toolbar.

When you use this command, you are first prompted to pick two points to create a controlling rectangle. In mtext, a *controlling rectangle* encompasses the text. You create it at the beginning of the *Mtext* command, and its width is the line width for the mtext. Its height will change depending on how much text is used.

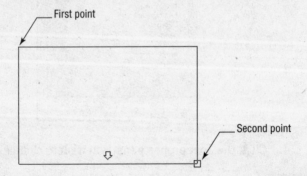

Then the Multiline Text Editor comes up. It has four tabs of settings, several buttons, and a large blank area where you will enter your text.

TIP

Click the Help button in the Multiline Text Editor to find out about all the tabs and other buttons.

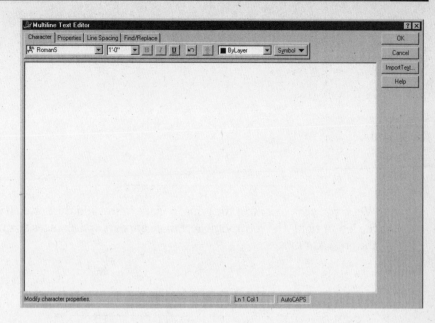

Use the Multiline Text Editor like a word processor when you enter your text. When you finish typing and click OK, AutoCAD will place the text in your drawing.

TIP

Don't worry about the height of the controlling rectangle limiting the amount of text you can enter. If you type more text than can fit in the rectangle, the rectangle just drops down (or up, depending on the justification point) to accommodate it.

You can easily modify the line length of mtext using grips. When you click on a letter, all the text is selected. It is ghosted, and grips appear at each of the four corners of the body of mtext.

NOTE

A body of mtext behaves like a single object.

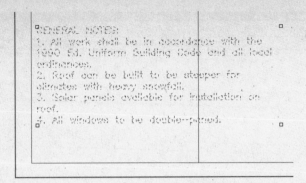

When you click on one of the grips to make it hot, and then stretch it to the left or right, the controlling rectangle appears and changes shape as the crosshair moves.

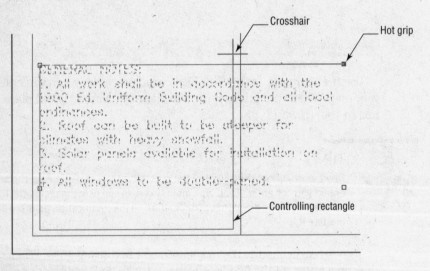

NOTE

You can also use the grips to move the paragraph to a new location without changing its line length.

This action results in a change in the line length for all the text. The body of text is thereby resized.

Other features of multiline text include the following:

▶ Individual letters or words can have different properties (height, color, and so on) than the main body of text.

▶ The Properties window and the Modify Text command, discussed in previous sections of this chapter, can both be used to modify mtext. When modifying mtext, you use the same Multiline Text Editor that you used to first enter the text.

▶ Special characters like the symbols for diameter and degrees can be inserted into mtext.

▶ Mtext can be converted into single-line text.

▶ Whole documents made with a word-processing program can be imported into AutoCAD as mtext.

WHAT'S NEXT?

This chapter demonstrated the basic procedures for setting up a new text style and working with single-line text and gave a brief description of Auto-CAD's Multiline Text feature. In the next chapter, you will learn how to create and modify hatch patterns.

Part ii

Chapter 7

CREATING HATCH PATTERNS

I n this chapter, you'll see how you can enhance the appearance of your drawings by adding hatch patterns. Hatch patterns can be used to fill in walls on a floor plan using a technique called *poche*. This technique makes the walls stand out more and makes the plan easier to read. Hatch patterns can also be used to indicate materials, as you'll learn in this chapter.

Adapted from *Mastering™ AutoCAD® 2002*
by George Omura
ISBN 0-7821-4015-7   1,392 pages $49.99

USING HATCH PATTERNS IN YOUR DRAWINGS

To help communicate your ideas to others, you will want to add graphic elements that represent types of materials, special regions, or textures. AutoCAD provides *hatch patterns* for quickly placing a texture over an area of your drawing. In this section, you will add a hatch pattern to the floor of the studio apartment unit, thereby instantly enhancing the appearance of one drawing. In the process, you'll learn how to quickly update all the units in the overall floor plan to reflect the changes in the unit.

Placing a Hatch in a Specific Area

It's always a good idea to provide a separate layer for hatch patterns. By doing so, you can turn them off if you need to.

In the following exercise, you will add a hatch pattern representing floor tile. Doing so will give you the opportunity to learn the different methods of creating and controlling hatch patterns.

1. Open the Unit file from the companion website.

2. Zoom in to the bathroom and kitchen area.

3. Create a new layer called Flr-pat.

4. Make Flr-pat the current layer.

Once you've set up the layer for the hatch pattern, you can place the pattern in the drawing.

1. Click the Hatch tool on the Draw toolbar or type **H** and press Enter. Hatch is also located in the Draw pull-down menu.

   The Boundary Hatch dialog box appears.

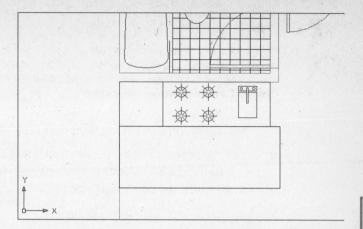

2. Under Type, open the pop-up list and select User-Defined. The User-Defined option lets you define a simple crosshatch pattern by specifying the line spacing of the hatch and whether it is a single- or double-hatch pattern. The Angle and Spacing input boxes become available, so you can enter values.

3. Double-click the Spacing input box near the bottom and enter **6** (metric users should enter **15**). This value tells AutoCAD you want the hatch's line spacing to be 6 inches or 15 cm. Leave the Angle value at 0 because you want the pattern to be aligned with the bathroom.

4. Click the check box labeled Double (just to the right of the Spacing input box). This option tells AutoCAD you want the hatch pattern to run both vertically and horizontally. Also notice that the Swatch button offers a sample view of your hatch pattern.

5. Click the Pick Points button. The dialog box momentarily disappears, allowing you to pick a point inside the area you want hatched.

6. Click a point anywhere inside the bathroom floor area, below the toilet. Notice that a highlighted outline appears in the bathroom. This is the boundary AutoCAD has selected to enclose the hatch pattern. It outlines everything, including the door swing arc.

TIP

If you have text in the hatch boundary, AutoCAD will avoid hatching over it, unless you select the Ignore option in the Boundary Style options of the Advanced Hatch settings. See "Using the Advanced Hatch Options" in this chapter for more on the Ignore setting.

7. Press Enter to return to the Boundary Hatch dialog box.

8. Click the Preview button in the lower-left corner of the dialog box. The hatch pattern appears everywhere on the floor except where the door swing occurs.

9. Right-click to return to the dialog box.

10. Click the Pick Points button again, pick a point inside the door swing, and press Enter.

11. Click Preview again. The hatch pattern now covers the entire floor area.

12. Right-click to return to the dialog box.

13. Click the OK button to place the hatch pattern in the drawing.

The Boundary Hatch dialog box lets you first define the boundary within which you want to place a hatch pattern. You do this by simply clicking a location inside the boundary area, as in step 6. AutoCAD finds the actual boundary for you. Many options give you control over how a hatch boundary is selected. If you want to find out more, look at "Understanding the Boundary Hatch Options" later in this chapter.

TIP

Say you want to add a hatch pattern that you have previously inserted in another part of the drawing. You may think that you have to guess at its scale and rotation angle. But with the Inherit Properties option in the Boundary Hatch dialog box, you can select a previously inserted hatch pattern as a prototype for the current hatch pattern. However, this feature does not work with exploded hatch patterns.

Positioning Hatch Patterns Accurately

In the last exercise, you placed the hatch pattern in the bathroom without regard for the location of the lines that make up the pattern. In most cases, however, you will want to have accurate control over where the lines of the pattern are placed.

Part ii

TIP

You can also click the Swatch button to browse through a graphical representation of the predefined hatch patterns.

Hatch patterns use the same origin as the snap origin. By default, this
origin is the same as the drawing origin, 0,0. You can change the snap origin (and thus the hatch pattern origin) by using the Snapbase system variable. The following exercise guides you through the process of placing a
hatch pattern accurately, using the example of adding floor tile to the
kitchenette.

1. Pan your view so that you can see the area below the kitchenette. Using the Rectangle tool in the Draw toolbar, draw
   the 3'0" × 8'0" outline of the floor tile area, as shown in
   Figure 7.1. Metric users should create a rectangle that is 91
   cm × 228 cm. You may also use a closed polyline.

TIP

If you know the coordinates of the new snap origin, you can enter them in the
Drawing Aids dialog box under the X Base and Y Base input boxes instead of
using the Snapbase system variable.

2. At the Command prompt, type **Snapbase** and press Enter.

3. At the Enter new value for Snapbase <0'-0",0'-0">:
   prompt, use the Endpoint Osnap and click the lower-left corner of the area you just defined (see Figure 7.1).

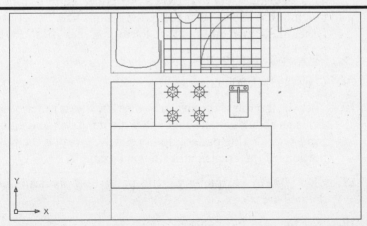

FIGURE 7.1: The area below the kitchen showing the outline of the floor tile area

4. Click the Hatch tool in the Draw toolbar.

5. In the Boundary Hatch dialog box, make sure that Predefined is selected in the Type pull-down list.

6. Click the button labeled with the ellipses (...) just to the right of the Pattern drop-down list. The Hatch Pattern Palette dialog box appears.

TIP

If you know the name of the pattern you want, you can select it from the Pattern drop-down list in the Boundary Hatch dialog box.

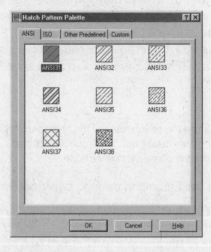

7. This dialog box lets you select a predefined pattern from a graphic that shows what the pattern looks like. Select the Other Predefined tab, and then locate and click AR-PARQ1.

8. Click OK to exit the dialog box.

9. Click the Pick Points button.

10. Click the interior of the area to be tiled, and press Enter. Metric users should double-click the Scale input box and enter **2.54** to scale this pattern appropriately to match the proportions of the English measurement example.

11. Click OK. A parquet-style tile pattern appears in the defined area.

12. Save the Unit file, but keep it open.

TIP

You can use the Solid predefined hatch pattern at the top of the list to create solid fills. It is a vast improvement over the Solid command that early versions of AutoCAD used for solid fills.

Notice that each tile is shown whole; none of the tiles is cut off, as in the bathroom example. This is the case because you first used the Snapbase system variable to set the origin for the hatch pattern. You can now move the Snapbase setting back to the 0,0 setting and not affect the hatch pattern.

TIP

Predefined patterns with an *AR* prefix are architectural patterns that are drawn to full scale. In general, you will want to leave their scale settings at 1. You can adjust the scale after you have placed the hatch pattern using the Properties tool, as described later in this chapter.

TIP

If you are a veteran AutoCAD user, you may hesitate to use many hatch patterns in an already crowded drawing. In the past, hatch patterns were memory hogs. You'll be happy to know that beginning with AutoCAD 2000, hatch patterns are much more memory efficient. AutoCAD 2000 also introduced a solid fill hatch pattern, which uses less memory than cross-hatching.

Changing the Hatch Area

You may have noticed the Associative option in the Boundary Hatch dialog box. When this option is checked, AutoCAD creates an associative hatch pattern. *Associative* hatches will adjust their shapes to any changes in their associated boundary; hence the name. The following exercise demonstrates how this works.

Suppose you want to enlarge the tiled area of the kitchen by one tile. Here's how it's done.

1. Return to the Unit file (Window ➢ \directory path\Unit .dwg); then click the outline border of the hatch pattern you created earlier. Notice the grips that appear around the hatch pattern area.

TIP

You may need to zoom in closer to the pattern area or use the object selection cycling feature to select the hatch boundary.

2. Shift+click the grip in the lower-left corner of the hatch area.

TIP

If the boundary of the hatch pattern consists of line segments, you can use a crossing window or polygon-crossing window to select the corner grips of the hatch pattern.

3. With the lower-left grip highlighted, Shift+click the lower-right grip.

4. Click the lower-right grip again, but don't Shift+click this time.

5. Enter @12<–90 (@30<–90 for metric users) to widen the hatch pattern by 1 foot. The hatch pattern adjusts to the new size of the hatch boundary.

6. Press the Esc key twice to clear any grip selections.

7. Save the Unit file to disk and exit the file.

The Associative feature of hatch patterns can save time when you need to make modifications to your drawing. But you should be aware of its limitations. A hatch pattern can lose its associativity several ways:

▶ Erasing or exploding a hatch boundary

▶ Erasing or exploding a block that forms part of the boundary

▶ Moving a hatch pattern away from its boundary

▶ Moving a hatch boundary away from the hatch pattern

These situations frequently arise when you edit an unfamiliar drawing. Often, boundary objects are placed on a layer that is off or frozen, so the boundary objects are not visible. Or, the hatch pattern may be on a layer that is turned off, and you proceed to edit the file, not knowing that a hatch pattern exists. When you encounter such a file, take a moment to check for hatch boundaries so you can deal with them properly.

Modifying a Hatch Pattern

Like everything else in a project, a hatch pattern may eventually need to be changed in some way. Hatch patterns are like blocks in that they act like single objects. You can explode a hatch pattern to edit its individual lines. The Properties tool in the Object Properties toolbar offers most of the settings you'll need to make changes to your hatch patterns.

1. Return to the Unit drawing by choosing Window ➣ \directory path\Unit.dwg.

2. Press the Esc key to clear any grip selections that may be active from earlier exercises.

3. Double-click the hatch pattern in the kitchen. The Hatch Edit dialog box appears. It is the same as the Boundary Hatch dialog box with a few options grayed out.

TIP

When you double-click on a hatch pattern, you don't get the typical Properties dialog box. In AutoCAD 2002, double-clicking on complex objects such as text, blocks, attributes, and hatch patterns opens a dialog box that allows you to edit the object in a more direct way. You can still access the Properties dialog box for any object by right-clicking the object and then selecting Properties from the shortcut menu.

4. Click the ellipsis button to the right of the Pattern drop-down list. The Hatch Pattern Palette dialog box appears, with the Other Predefined tab already selected.

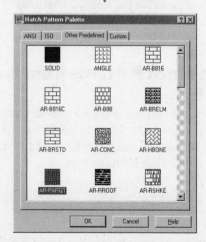

Part ii

5. Locate and double-click the pattern named AR-BRSTD. The Hatch Pattern Palette dialog box disappears, and you see the AR-BRSTD hatch pattern in the Pattern drop-down list.

6. Click OK to accept the change to the hatch pattern. The AR-BRSTD pattern appears in place of the original parquet pattern.

7. You want to keep the old pattern in your drawing, so exit the Unit file without saving it.

In this exercise, you were able to change the hatch just by double-clicking it. Although you only changed the pattern type, other options are available to you. You can, for example, modify a predefined pattern to a user-defined one by selecting User Defined from the Type listing in the Hatch Edit dialog box. You can then enter angle and spacing values for your hatch pattern in the spaces provided in the Hatch Edit dialog box.

The other items listed in the Hatch Edit dialog box duplicate some of the options in the Boundary Hatch dialog box. They let you modify the individual properties of the selected hatch pattern. The next section, "Understanding the Boundary Hatch Options," describes these other properties in detail.

TIP

If you create and edit hatch patterns frequently, you will find the Modify II toolbar useful. It contains an Edit Hatch tool that gives you ready access to the Hatch Edit dialog box. To open the Modify II toolbar, right-click any toolbar, and then click the Modify II check box in the Toolbars dialog box that appears.

Editing Hatch Patterns from the Properties Dialog Box

If you prefer, you can still use the older method to edit a hatch pattern. To use the Properties dialog box, click a pattern, right-click, and select Properties. The Properties dialog box appears and displays a Pattern category, which offers a Pattern Name option.

When you click this option, an ellipsis button appears, allowing you to open the Hatch Pattern Palette, just as in step 4 of the previous exercise. You can then select a new pattern from the dialog box. The Type option in the Properties dialog box lets you change the type of hatch pattern from Predefined to User Defined.

UNDERSTANDING THE BOUNDARY HATCH OPTIONS

The Boundary Hatch dialog box offers many other options that you didn't explore in the previous exercises. For example, instead of selecting the area to be hatched by clicking a point, you can select the actual objects that bound the area you wish to hatch using the Select Objects button. The Swatch button opens the Hatch Pattern Palette dialog box, which lets you select a predefined hatch pattern from a graphic window.

The Hatch Pattern Palette dialog box offers several tabs that further divide the types of hatch patterns into four different categories: ANSI, ISO, Other Predefined, and Custom. The Custom tab is empty until you create your own set of custom hatch patterns.

Other options in the right-hand column of the Boundary Hatch dialog box include Remove Islands, View Selections, and Inherit Properties.

Remove Islands   Lets you remove an area within a hatch pattern boundary that has been removed from the hatch pattern. An example of this is the toilet seat in the bathroom. This option is available only when you select a hatch area using the Pick Points option and an island has been detected.

View Selections   Temporarily closes the dialog box and then highlights the objects that have been selected as the hatch boundary by AutoCAD.

Inherit Properties   Lets you select a hatch pattern from an existing one in the drawing. This option is helpful when you want to apply a hatch pattern that is already used, but you do not know its name or its scale, rotation, or other properties.

At the very bottom of the column of options is the Composition button group. This option lets you determine whether the hatch pattern being inserted is associative or nonassociative. As discussed earlier, an associative hatch pattern automatically changes to fill its boundary whenever that boundary is stretched or edited.

Using the Advanced Hatch Options

AutoCAD's Boundary Hatch command has a fair amount of intelligence. As you saw in an earlier exercise, it was able to detect not only the outline of the floor area, but also the outline of the toilet seat that represents an island within the pattern area. If you prefer, you can control how AutoCAD treats these island conditions and other situations by selecting options available when you click the Advanced tab in the Boundary Hatch dialog box.

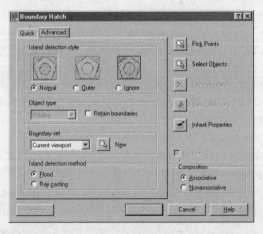

In addition to controlling the Island Detection feature of hatch patterns, the Advanced tab lets you fine-tune other aspects of hatch pattern creation.

Island Detection Style

The Island Detection Style button group at the top of the dialog box controls how nested boundaries affect the hatch pattern. The graphics in this button group show examples of the effect of the selected option. The Island Detection Style options include the following:

Normal   Causes the hatch pattern to alternate between nested boundaries. The outer boundary is hatched; if there is a closed object within the boundary, it is not hatched. If another closed object *is* inside the first closed object, *that* object is hatched. This is the default setting.

Outer   Applies the hatch pattern to an area defined by the outermost boundary and by any boundaries nested within the outermost boundary. Any boundaries nested within the nested boundaries are ignored.

Ignore   Supplies the hatch pattern to the entire area within the outermost boundary, ignoring any nested boundaries.

Object Type

The Boundary Hatch command can also create an outline of the hatch area using one of two objects: 2D regions, which are like 2D planes, or polyline outlines. Boundary Hatch actually creates such a polyline boundary temporarily, to establish the hatch area. These boundaries are automatically removed after the hatch pattern is inserted. If you want to retain the boundaries in the drawing, make sure the Retain Boundaries check box is checked. Retaining the boundary can be useful in situations where you know you will be hatching the area more than once, or if you are hatching a fairly complex area.

TIP

Retaining a hatch boundary is useful if you want to know the hatched area's dimensions in square inches or feet, because you can find the area of a closed polyline using the List command. The Boundary command creates a polyline outline or region within a selected area. It works much like the Boundary Hatch command but does not add a hatch pattern.

Part ii

Boundary Set Options

The Boundary Hatch feature is view-dependent; that is, it locates boundaries based on what is visible in the current view. If the current view contains a lot of graphic data, AutoCAD can have difficulty finding a boundary, or it may be very slow in finding a boundary. If you run into this problem, or if you want to single out a specific object for a point selection boundary, you can further limit the area that AutoCAD uses to locate hatch boundaries by using the Boundary Set options:

New   Lets you select the objects from which you want AutoCAD to determine the hatch boundary, instead of searching the entire view. The screen clears and lets you select objects. This option discards previous boundary sets. It is useful for hatching areas in a drawing that may contain many objects that you do not want to include in the hatch boundary.

Current Viewport   Tells you that AutoCAD will use all of the current view to determine the hatch boundary. Once you select a set of objects using the New button, you also see Existing Set as an option in this drop-down list. You can then use this drop-down list to choose the entire view or the objects you select for the hatch boundary.

The Boundary Set options are designed to give you more control over the way a point selection boundary is created. These options have no effect when you use the Select Objects button to select specific objects for the hatch boundary.

Island Detection Method

You may have noticed that the Boundary Hatch command did not place a hatch pattern on the toilet seat. This is the case because the Island Detection feature was turned on. The toilet seat is like an island within the hatch area. The Island Detection Method radio buttons let you control whether islands such as the toilet seat are detected. The Flood option detects islands and hatches around them. The Ray Casting option determines the boundary outline by first looking for the nearest object to your pick point, and then tracing along that object in a counterclockwise direction.

Tips for Using the Boundary Hatch

Here are a few tips on using the Boundary Hatch feature:

▶ Watch out for boundary areas that are part of a very large block. AutoCAD examines the entire block when defining boundaries. This process can take time if the block is quite large. Use the Boundary Set option to focus in on the set of objects you want AutoCAD to use for your hatch boundary.

▶ The Boundary Hatch feature is view-dependent; that is, it locates boundaries based on what is visible in the current view. To ensure that AutoCAD finds every detail, zoom in to the area to be hatched.

▶ If the area to be hatched will be very large yet will require fine detail, first outline the hatch area using a polyline. Then use the Select Objects option in the Boundary Hatch dialog box to select the polyline boundary manually, instead of depending on Boundary Hatch to find the boundary for you.

▶ Consider turning off layers that might interfere with AutoCAD's ability to find a boundary. For example, in the previous exercise, you could have turned off the Door layer and then used Pick Points to locate the boundary of the hatch pattern.

▶ Boundary Hatch works on nested blocks as long as the nested block entities are parallel to the current UCS and are uniformly scaled in the x- and y-axes.

HOW TO QUICKLY MATCH A HATCH PATTERN AND OTHER PROPERTIES

Another tool to help you edit hatch patterns is Match Properties, which is similar to the Format Painter in the Microsoft Office suite. This tool lets you change an existing hatch pattern to match another existing hatch pattern. Here's how to use it.

1. Click the Match Properties tool in the Standard toolbar.

2. Click the source hatch pattern you want to copy.

3. Click the target hatch pattern you want to change.

CONTINUED ➡

The target pattern changes to match the source pattern.

The Match Properties tool transfers other properties as well, such as layer, color, and line-type settings. You can select the properties that are transferred by opening the Property Settings dialog box.

To open this dialog box, type **S** and press Enter after selecting the object in step 2, or right-click and select Settings from the shortcut menu. You can then select the properties you wish to transfer from the options shown. All the properties are selected by default. Note that text and dimension style settings can also be transferred.

Space Planning and Hatch Patterns

Suppose you are working on a plan within which you are constantly repositioning equipment and furniture, or you are in the process of designing the floor covering. You may be a little hesitant to place a hatch pattern on the floor because you don't want to have to rehatch the area each time you move a piece of equipment or change the flooring. You have two options in this situation: You can use the Boundary Hatch's associative capabilities to include the furnishings in the boundary set, or you can use the Display Order feature.

Using Associative Hatch

Associative hatch is the most straightforward method. Make sure the Associative option is checked in the Boundary Hatch dialog box and include your equipment or furniture in the boundary set. You can do this by using the Select Objects option in the dialog box.

Once the pattern is in place, you can move the furnishings in your drawing, and the hatch pattern automatically adjusts to their new location. One drawback, however, is that AutoCAD attempts to hatch the interior of your furnishings if they cross over the outer boundary of the hatch pattern. Also, if any boundary objects are erased or exploded, the hatch pattern no longer follows the location of your furnishings. To avoid these problems, you can use the method described in the next section.

Overlapping Objects with Display Order

The second method for masking hatch patterns requires the use of the Display Order feature. This feature lets you determine how objects overlap each other. In the space-planning example, you can create furniture using a solid hatch to indicate horizontal surfaces (see Figure 7.2). Then, you can place the furniture "on top" of the floor covering pattern, and the pattern will be covered and hidden by the furniture. Here's how you would do that.

1. Draw the equipment outline and make sure the outline is a closed polygon.

2. Use the Hatch tool described earlier in this chapter to place a solid hatch pattern inside the equipment outline.

3. Choose Tools ➤ Display Order ➤ Send to Back.

4. At the Select Object prompt, select the solid hatch pattern, and then press Enter to confirm your selection.

5. Turn the outline and solid hatch into a block or use the Group command to group them together.

6. Choose Tools ➤ Display Order ➤ Bring to Front, and select the equipment. When you are done, the equipment will "cover" the floor hatch pattern (see Figure 7.2).

Part ii

Draw an outline of the furniture or equipment, then use the Make Hatch tool in the Draw toolbar to fill the outline with a Solid hatch pattern.

Choose Tools > Display Order > Send to Back and select the hatch pattern to place it "behind" the outline.

Place the drawing of the equipment on the floor pattern then choose Tools > Display Order > Send to Back and select the floor pattern.

The equipment will appear to sit on top of the floor pattern.

FIGURE 7.2: Using Display Order to create an overlapping effect over a hatch pattern

WARNING

When you use the Display Order options, all the Object Sort Method options in the User Preferences tab of the Options dialog box are turned on. This condition can increase regeneration and redraw times.

After you've taken these steps, you can place the equipment over a hatched floor pattern, and the equipment will appear to rest on top of the pattern. If you create a floor pattern *after* you've created the equipment, use Tools ➤ Display Order ➤ Send to Back to move the pattern to the back of the display order. You can also change the display order of objects relative to other objects.

The Display Order options are all part of the Draworder command. As an alternative to using the dialog box, you can type in **Draworder** and press Enter at the Command prompt, and then enter an option from the Draworder prompt:

```
Enter object ordering option
[Above object/Under object/Front/Back] <Back>:
```

For example, the equivalent of Tools ➤ Display Order ➤ Send to Back is typing **Draworder**, pressing Enter, typing **B,** and pressing Enter again.

TIP

If you need to "white out" an area of a hatch pattern to make text more read-able, you can use a solid hatch along with the Display Order option to block out areas behind text.

You've completed the exercises in this chapter so you can exit Auto-CAD without saving these changes.

WHAT'S NEXT?

In this chapter you have learned how to work with hatch patterns in drawings. In the next chapter, you will learn the components of dimension styles. You will place accurate dimensions without having to take measurements. In addition, you will learn time-saving features that allow you to resize objects and have their associated dimensions update automatically.

Chapter 8
Using Dimensions

Before you determine the dimensions of a project, your design is in flux and many questions may be unanswered. Once you begin dimensioning, you will begin to see if things fit or work together. Dimensioning can be crucial to how well a design works and how quickly it develops. The dimensions answer questions about code conformance if you are an architect; they answer questions about tolerances, fit, and interference if you are involved in mechanical applications. Once you and your design team have reached a design on a schematic level, communicating even tentative dimensions to others on the team can accelerate design development. Dimensions represent a point from which you can further develop your ideas.

Adapted from *Mastering™ AutoCAD® 2002* by George Omura

ISBN 0-7821-4015-7   1,392 pages $49.99

With AutoCAD, you can easily add tentative or final dimensions to any drawing. AutoCAD gives you an accurate dimension without your having to take measurements. You simply pick the two points to be dimensioned and the dimension line location, and AutoCAD does the rest. AutoCAD's *associative dimensioning* capability automatically updates dimensions whenever the size or shape of the dimensioned object is changed. These dimensioning features can save you valuable time and reduce the number of dimensional errors in your drawings.

UNDERSTANDING THE COMPONENTS OF A DIMENSION

Before you get started with the exercises in this chapter, it will help you to know the names of the different parts of a dimension. Figure 8.1 shows a sample of a dimension with the different parts labeled. The *dimension line* is the line that represents the distance being dimensioned. It is the line with the arrows on either end. The *extension lines* are the lines that originate from the object being dimensioned. They show you the exact location from which the dimension is taken. The *dimension text* is the actual dimension value, usually shown inside or above the dimension line.

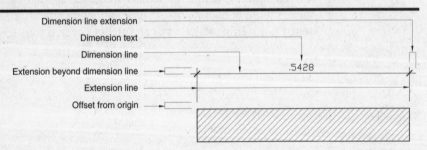

FIGURE 8.1: The components of a dimension

Another component of a dimension line is the *dimension line extension*. This is the part of the dimension line that extends beyond the extension line. Dimension line extensions are usually used only on architectural dimensions. The extension lines usually extend beyond the dimension lines in all types of dimensions. The extension line *offset from origin* is the distance from the beginning of the extension line to the object being dimensioned.

You can control each of these components by creating or editing *dimension styles*. Dimension styles are the settings that determine the look of your dimensions. You can store multiple styles within a single drawing. Your first exercise in this chapter will show you how to create a dimension style.

CREATING A DIMENSION STYLE

Dimension styles are similar to text styles. They determine the look of your dimensions as well as the size of dimensioning features, such as the dimension text and arrows. You might set up a dimension style to have special types of arrows, for instance, or to position the dimension text above or in line with the dimension line. Dimension styles also make your work easier by allowing you to store and duplicate your most common dimension settings.

AutoCAD gives you one of two default dimension styles called *ISO-25* or *Standard*, depending on whether you use the metric or English measurement system. You will probably add many other styles to suit the type of drawings you are creating. You can also create variations of a general style for those situations that call for only minor changes in the dimension's appearance.

In this first section, you'll learn how to set up your own dimension style based on the Standard dimension style (see Figure 8.2). For metric users, the settings will be different but the overall methods will be the same.

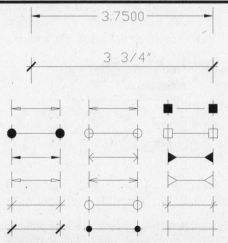

FIGURE 8.2: AutoCAD's Standard dimension style compared with an architectural-style dimension

Part ii

1. Open the 09a-unit.dwg file on the companion website and rename it Unit.dwg.

2. Issue Zoom All to display the entire floor plan.

3. Choose Format ➤ Dimension Style, or type **D** and press Enter at the Command prompt. The Dimension Style Manager dialog box appears.

4. Select Standard from the Styles list box. Metric users should select ISO-25.

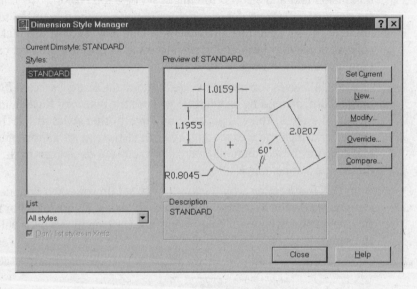

5. Click New. The New Dimension Style dialog box appears.

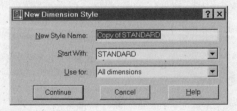

6. With the Copy of Standard or ISO-25 name highlighted in the New Style Name input box, enter **My Architectural**.

7. Click Continue. The detailed New Dimension Style dialog box appears.

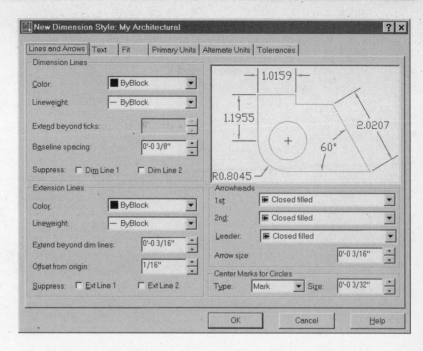

You've just created a dimension style called My Architectural, but at this point it is identical to the Standard style on which it is based. Nothing has happened to the Standard style; it is still available if you need to use it.

Setting Up the Primary Unit Style

Now you need to set up your new dimension style so that it conforms to the U.S. architectural style of dimensioning. Let's start by changing the unit style for the dimension text. Just as you changed the overall unit style of AutoCAD to a feet-and-inches style for your toilet and tub drawing, you must do the same for your dimension styles. Setting the overall unit style does not automatically set the dimension unit style.

1. In the New Dimension Style dialog box, click the Primary Units tab. The options for the Primary Units style appear.

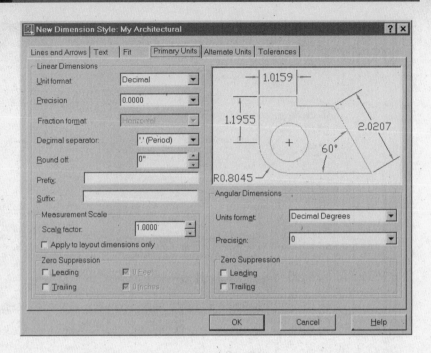

2. In the Linear Dimensions group, open the Unit Format drop-down list and choose Architectural. Notice that this drop-down list contains the same unit styles as the main Units dialog box (Format ➤ Units). Metric users can skip this option.

TIP

You might notice the Decimal Separator option a few settings below the Unit Format option. The Decimal Separator option lets you choose between a period and a comma for decimal points. Metric users will often use the comma for a decimal point, whereas U.S. users will use a period. This option doesn't have any meaning for feet-and-inch measurements, so it is dimmed when the Architectural unit format is selected.

3. Select 0'-0 1/4" from the Precision option, just below the Unit Format list. Metric users should select 0.00. The Precision

option allows you to set the level of precision that is displayed in the dimension text. It doesn't limit the precision of Auto-CAD's drawing database. This value is only used to limit the display of dimension text values.

TIP

Every dimension style setting has an equivalent system variable.

4. Just below the Precision option, open the Fraction Format drop-down list and select Diagonal. Notice what happens to the graphic at right in the dialog box. The fractional dimensions change to show you how your dimension text will look. Metric users can skip this step, because it isn't available when the Decimal unit format is selected.

5. In the Zero Suppression check box group in the lower-left corner, click 0 Inches to turn off this check box. If you leave it turned on, indications of 0 inches will be omitted from the dimension text. (In architectural drawings, 0 inches are shown as in this dimension: 12'-0".) Metric users can ignore this option.

If you use the English measurement system, you have set up My Architectural's dimension unit style to show dimensions in feet and inches, the standard method for U.S. construction documents. Metric users have just changed the precision value and kept the Decimal unit system.

Setting the Height for Dimension Text

Along with the unit style, you will want to adjust the size of the dimension text. The Text tab of the New Dimension Style dialog box lets you set a variety of text options, including text location relative to the dimension line, style, and height.

1. Click the Text tab to display the text options.

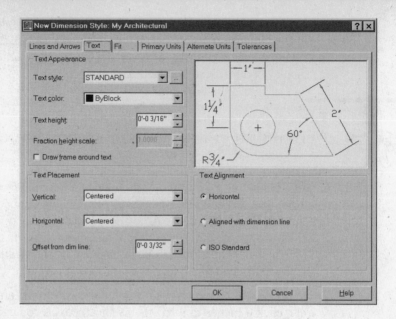

2. Highlight the contents of the Text Height input box.

3. Type **1/8** and press Enter to make the text height 1/8" high. Metric users should enter **0.3** and press Enter for the text height.

You specify the text height by its final plot size. You then specify an overall dimension scale factor that affects the sizing of all of the dimensioning settings such as text and arrows.

If you want to use a specific text style for your dimensions, select a text style in the Text Style drop-down list in the Text tab. If the style you select happens to have a height specification greater than 0, then that height will override any text height settings you may enter here in the Text tab.

Setting the Location and Orientation of Dimension Text

AutoCAD's default setting for the placement of dimension text puts the text in line with the dimension line, as shown in the example at the top of Figure 8.2. However, you want the new Architectural style to put the text above the dimension line, as is done in the center of Figure 8.2. To do that, you will use the Text Placement and Text Alignment options in the Text tab of the New Dimension Style dialog box.

1. In the Text Alignment group, click the Aligned With Dimension Line radio button.

2. In the Text Placement group, open the drop-down list labeled Vertical and select Above. Notice how the appearance of the sample image changes to show you how your new settings will look.

3. Again in the Text Placement group, change the Offset from Dim Line value to 1/16. This setting controls the size of the gap between the dimension line and the dimension text.

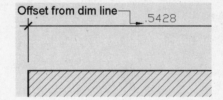

Each time you change a setting, you get immediate feedback on how your changes will affect your dimension style by watching the graphic.

TIP

Metric users may not need to change these settings, depending on your preference for dimension styles.

Choosing an Arrow Style and Setting the Dimension Scale

Next, you'll specify a different type of arrow for your new dimension style. For linear dimension in architectural drawings, a diagonal line or *tick mark* is typically used, rather than an arrow.

In addition, you'll set the scale for the graphical components of the dimension, such as the arrows and text. Text must be scaled up in size in order to appear at the proper size in the final output of the drawing. Dimensions, too, must be scaled so they look correct when the drawing is plotted. The arrows are controlled by settings in the Lines and Arrows tab, and the overall scale of the dimension style is set in the Fit tab.

1. Choose the Lines and Arrows tab. You see the options for controlling the arrow style and dimension line extensions.

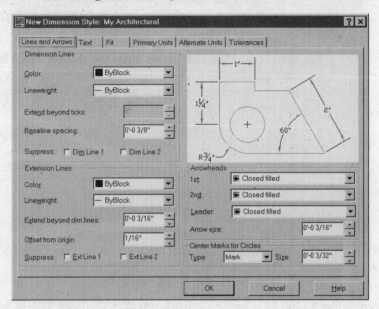

2. In the Arrowheads group, open the drop-down list labeled 1st and choose Architectural Tick. The graphic next to the arrowhead name shows you what the arrowhead looks like.

3. In the Arrowheads group, change the Arrow Size setting to **1/8**. Metric users should enter **.3**.

4. In the Dimension Lines group, highlight the value in the Extend beyond Ticks input box, and then enter **1/16**. (Metric users should enter **0.15**.) This setting causes the dimension lines to extend past the tick arrows. This is a standard graphic practice used for dimensioning linear dimensions in architectural plans.

5. In the Extension Lines group, change the Extend beyond Dim Lines setting to **1/8**. Metric users should change it to **.3**. This setting determines the distance the extension line extends past the dimension line.

6. Again in the Extension Lines group, change the Offset from Origin setting to **1/8**. Metric users should change it to **.3**.

This option sets the distance from the point being dimensioned to the beginning of the dimension extension line.

7. Click the Fit tab of the New Dimension Style dialog box to display the options for overall dimension scale and miscellaneous settings.

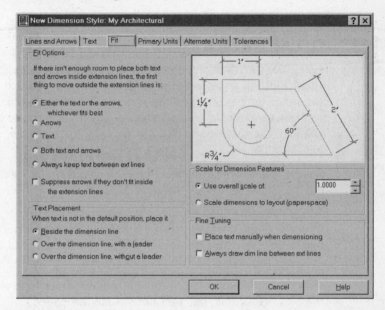

8. In the Scale for Dimension Features group, select the Use Overall Scale Of radio button.

9. Double-click the list box just to the right of the Use Overall Scale Of radio button, and then enter **48**. This is the scale factor for a 1/4" scale drawing. Metric users should enter **50**.

All the values that you enter for the various options in the New Dimension Style dialog box will be multiplied by this value to obtain the final size of the dimension components. For example, the text height you entered earlier, 1/4", will be multiplied by 48 for a dimension text height of 6". For metric users, the text height of 0.3 will be multiplied by 50 for a text height of 15 cm.

TIP

If you use the Scale Dimensions to Layout (Paperspace) option in the Scale for Dimension Features group of the Fit tab, AutoCAD uses the layout viewport scale to size the dimension components.

FITTING TEXT AND ARROWS IN TIGHT PLACES

Every now and then, you'll need to dimension a small gap or a small width of an object that won't allow dimension text to fit within the dimension. The Fit tab offers a few other settings that control how dimensions act when the extension lines are too close. The Text Placement group offers three options to place the text in tight situations:

Beside the Dimension Line   Places text next to the extension line but close to the dimension line. You'll see how this option affects your dimension later.

Over the Dimension Line, with a Leader   Places the dimension text farther away from the dimension line and includes an arrow or leader from the dimension line to the text.

Over the Dimension Line, without a Leader   Does the same as the previous setting, but does not include the leader.

The options in the Fit Options group let you control how text and arrows are placed when there isn't enough room for both of them between the extension lines.

Setting Up Alternate Units

You can use the Alternate Units tab of the New Dimension Style dialog box to set up AutoCAD to display a second dimension in centimeters or millimeters. Likewise, if you are a metric user, you can set up a second dimension to display feet and inches. In most situations, you won't need to use these alternate units, but for these exercises you'll use them for the benefit of AutoCAD users in all parts of the world.

Take the following steps to add alternate units to your dimension style:

TIP

If you decide later that you do not want the alternate units to be displayed, you can turn them off by returning to this dialog box and removing the check mark in the Display Alternate Units check box.

1. In the New Dimension Style dialog box, select the Alternate Units tab.

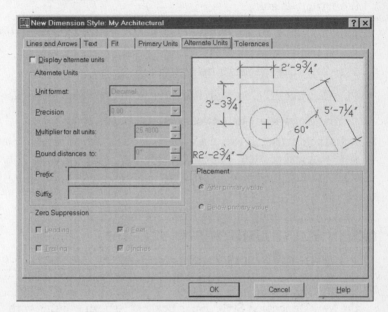

2. Click the Display Alternate Units check box. The options in the tab become available for your input.

3. Select the appropriate option from the Unit Format drop-down list. U.S. users should select Decimal to show metric alternate units. Metric users should select Architectural.

4. Select 0.00 from the Precision drop-down list. Metric users should select 1/4".

5. Enter a scale factor for your alternate dimension in the Multiplier for Alt Units input box. For U.S. users, the default value is 25.4. This value converts feet-and-inch dimensions to millimeters. In the metric examples, you've been using centimeters, so change this setting to **2.54**. Metric users should enter **0.3937** to convert centimeters to feet and inches.

6. In the Placement group, select the Below Primary Value option.

7. Click OK to exit the New Dimension Style dialog box. The Dimension Style Manager dialog box reappears.

Setting the Current Dimension Style

Before you can begin to use your new dimension style, you must make it the current default.

1. Click My Architectural in the Styles list box in the Dimension Style Manager dialog box.

2. Click the Set Current button.

3. Click Close to exit the Dimension Style Manager dialog box.

You're now ready to use your new dimension style.

In the next set of exercises, you will be using the My Architectural style you just created. To switch to another style, open the Dimension Style Manager dialog box again, select the style you want from the Styles list, and click Set Current, just as you did in the previous exercise.

Modifying a Dimension Style

To modify an existing dimension style, open the Dimension Style Manager dialog box, highlight the style you want to edit, and then click Modify. The Modify Dimension Style dialog box appears, which is virtually identical to the New Dimension Style dialog box you've been working with. You can then make changes to the different components of the selected dimension style. When you've finished making changes and closed both dialog boxes, all of the dimensions associated with the edited style will update automatically in your drawing. For example, if you decide you need to change the dimension scale of a style, you can open the Modify Dimension Style dialog box and change the Scale value in the Fit tab. In prior versions of AutoCAD, you had to use the Update option and manually select each dimension that required the new setting. This section introduces you to the various settings that let you set the appearance of a dimension style.

TIP

If your application is strictly architectural, you may want to make these same dimension style changes to the Acad.dwt template file or create a set of template files specifically for architectural drawings of differing scales.

USING GRIDS IN ARCHITECTURAL DIMENSIONS

Common, if not essential, elements in architectural drawings are the building grids. These are the center lines of the main structural components, which are usually the columns and structural walls of the building. Grids are labeled similarly to map grids, with numeric labels going horizontally and alphabetical labels going vertically. A circle or hexagon is used at the end of the grid to label it. The grids are the first items dimensioned; all other building components are dimensioned from the grid lines. The San Francisco Main Library made ample use of grids, incorporating both major and minor grid systems. There, a hexagon was used to label the grids.

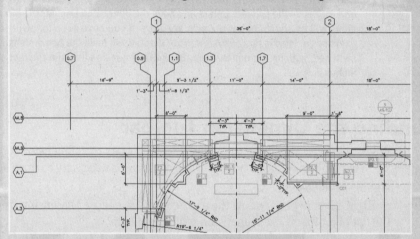

Because the structural components of a building are usually the first parts put in place, they play a crucial role in locating other components of the building during the construction process. When producing floor plans, the grid is usually the first thing an architect draws, mimicking to some degree the construction process. All other elements of the plan are then drawn in relation to that grid.

While working in AutoCAD, you can use a grid to start building your drawing. Once the grid is in place, you can use the Offset tool to locate walls or other building components. Using AutoCAD's tracking feature, you can easily align drawing elements to grid lines.

DRAWING LINEAR DIMENSIONS

The most common type of dimension you'll be using is the *linear dimension*. The linear dimension is an orthogonal dimension measuring the width and length of an object. AutoCAD offers three dimensioning tools for this purpose: Linear (Dimlinear), Continue (Dimcont), and Baseline (Dimbase). These options are readily accessible from the Dimension toolbar or the Dimension pull-down menu.

NOTE

In the following exercise, you'll see figures displaying dimensions with feet and inches as the primary unit style above the dimension line. Metric dimensions will be shown below the primary units. If you have been following the exercises using the metric system, your display will have the two dimensions switched, with metric dimensions above the dimension line and the feet and inches below.

Finding the Dimension Toolbar

Before you apply any dimension, you'll want to open the Dimension toolbar. This toolbar contains nearly all the commands necessary to draw and edit your dimensions.

Right-click any toolbar. At the shortcut menu, choose Dimension from the list of toolbars. The Dimension toolbar appears.

The Dimension commands are also available from the Dimension pull-down menu. Now you're ready to begin dimensioning.

TIP

To help keep your screen organized, you may want to dock the Dimension toolbar to the right side of the AutoCAD window. Note that you will lose the Style drop-down list if you dock the toolbar.

Placing Horizontal and Vertical Dimensions

Let's start by looking at the basic dimensioning tool, Linear Dimension. The Linear Dimension button (the Dimlinear command) on the Dimension toolbar accommodates both the horizontal and vertical dimensions.

In this exercise, you'll add a vertical dimension to the right side of the Unit plan.

1. To start either a vertical or horizontal dimension, click Linear Dimension on the Dimension toolbar, or enter **Dli** and press Enter at the Command prompt. You can also choose Dimension ➤ Linear from the pull-down menu.

2. The Specify first extension line origin or <select object>: prompt asks you for the first point of the distance to be dimensioned. An extension line is the line that connects the object being dimensioned to the dimension line. Use the Endpoint Osnap override and pick the upper-right corner of the entry, as shown in Figure 8.3.

TIP

Notice that the prompt in step 2 gives you the option of pressing Enter to select an object. If you do this, you are prompted to pick the object you wish to dimension, rather than the actual distance to be dimensioned. This method is discussed later in this chapter.

3. At the Specify second extension line origin: prompt, pick the lower-right corner of the living room, as shown in Figure 8.3.

4. In the next prompt, Specify dimension line location or [Mtext/Text/Angle/Horizontal/Vertical/Rotated]:, the dimension line is the line indicating the direction of the dimension and containing the arrows or tick marks. Move your cursor from left to right, and a temporary dimension appears that allows you to visually select a dimension line location.

TIP

In step 4, you have the option to append information to the dimension's text or change the dimension text altogether. You'll see how later in this chapter.

5. Enter **@4"<0** and press Enter to tell AutoCAD you want the dimension line to be 4" to the right of the last point you selected. Metric users should enter **@122<0** and press Enter. (You could pick a point using your cursor, but doing so doesn't let you place the dimension line as accurately.) After you've done this, the dimension is placed in the drawing, as shown in Figure 8.3.

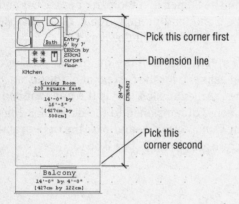

FIGURE 8.3: The dimension line added to the Unit drawing

Continuing a Dimension

You will often want to enter a group of dimensions strung together in a line. For example, you may want to continue dimensioning the balcony and have the continued dimension aligned with the dimension you just entered. To do this, use the Continue option found in both the Dimension toolbar and the Dimension pull-down menu.

1. Click the Continue Dimension option on the Dimension toolbar, or enter **Dco** and press Enter. You can also choose Dimension ➤ Continue from the pull-down menu.

2. At the `Specify a second extension line origin or [Undo/Select] <Select>:` prompt, pick the upper-right corner of the balcony.

3. Pick the right end of the rail on the balcony.

4. Press Enter twice to exit the command.

TIP

If you find that you've selected the wrong location for a continued dimension, you can click the Undo tool or type **U** and press Enter to back up your dimension.

The Continue Dimension option adds a dimension from where you left off. The last drawn extension line is used as the first extension line for the continued dimension. AutoCAD keeps adding dimensions as you continue to pick points, until you press Enter.

You probably noticed that the 5" dimension is placed away from the dimension line with a leader line pointing to it. This is the result of the 5" dimension's not having enough space to fit between the dimension extension lines. You'll learn about dimension style settings that can remedy this problem. For now, let's continue with adding dimensions to the plan.

Continuing a Dimension from a Previous Dimension

If you need to continue a string of dimensions from an older linear dimension, instead of the most recently added one, press Enter at the Specify a second extension line origin or (<select>/Undo): prompt you saw in step 2 of the previous exercise. Then, at the Select continued dimension: prompt, click the extension line from which you wish to continue.

Drawing Dimensions from a Common Base Extension Line

Another method for dimensioning objects is to have several dimensions originate from the same extension line. To accommodate this technique, AutoCAD provides the Baseline option on the Dimension toolbar or Dimension pull-down menu. To see how this works, you will start another dimension—this time a horizontal one—across the top of the plan.

1. Click Linear Dimension on the Dimension toolbar. Or, just as you did for the vertical dimension, you can type **Dli** and press Enter to start the horizontal dimension. This option is also on the Dimension pull-down menu.

2. At the Specify first extension line origin or <select object>: prompt, use the Endpoint Osnap to pick the upper-left corner of the bathroom.

Part ii

3. At the Specify second extension line origin: prompt, pick the upper-right corner of the bathroom.

4. At the Specify dimension line location or[Mtext/ Text/Angle/Horizontal/Vertical/Rotated]: prompt, pick a point above the Unit plan. If you need to, pan your view downward to fit the dimension in.

TIP

Because you usually pick exact locations on your drawing as you dimension, you may want to turn on Running Osnaps to avoid the extra step of selecting Osnaps from the Osnap shortcut menu.

Now you're all set to draw another dimension continuing from the first extension line of the dimension you just drew.

5. Click the Baseline Dimension option on the Dimension toolbar. Or you can type **Dba** and press Enter at the Command prompt to start a baseline dimension.

6. At the Specify second extension line origin or [Undo/Select] <Select>: prompt, click the upper-right corner of the entry, as shown in Figure 8.4.

7. Press Enter twice to exit the Baseline Dimension command.

8. Pan your view down so it looks similar to Figure 8.4.

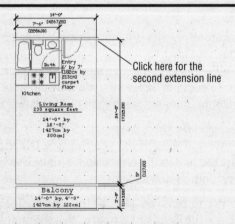

FIGURE 8.4: The overall width dimension

In this example, you see that the Baseline Dimension option is similar to the Continue Dimension option, except that the Baseline Dimension option allows you to use the first extension line of the previous dimension as the base for a second dimension.

Continuing from an Older Dimension

You may have noticed in step 7 of the previous exercise that you had to press Enter twice to exit the command. As with the Continue Dimension option, you can draw the baseline dimension from an older dimension by pressing Enter at the Specify a second extension line origin [Undo/Select] <select>: prompt. You then get the Select base dimension: prompt, at which you can either select another dimension or press Enter again to exit the command.

EDITING DIMENSIONS

As you begin to add more dimensions to your drawings, you will find that AutoCAD will occasionally place a dimension text or line in an inappropriate location, or you may need to make a modification to the dimension text. In this section, you'll take an in-depth look at how dimensions can be modified to suit those special circumstances that always crop up.

Appending Data to Dimension Text

So far in this chapter, you've been accepting the default dimension text. You can append information to the default dimension value, or change it entirely if you need to. At the point when you see the temporary dimension dragging with your cursor, enter **T** and press Enter. Then, by using the less-than (<) and greater-than (>) symbols, you can add text either before or after the default dimension or replace the symbols entirely to replace the default text. The Properties button on the Object Properties toolbar lets you modify the existing dimension text in a similar way. Let's see how this works by changing an existing dimension's text in your drawing.

1. Choose Modify ➤ Object ➤ Text ➤ Edit or type **ED** and press Enter.

2. Click the last horizontal dimension you added to the drawing at the top of the screen.

3. Press and press Enter. The Multiline Text Editor dialog box appears.

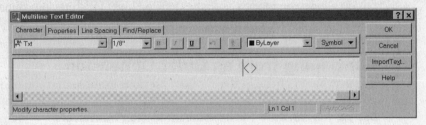

4. Click the Contents input box, move the cursor to the left of the <> sign, and then type **to face of stud**.

5. Click OK. The dimension changes to read "14'-0" to face of stud". The text you entered is appended below the dimension text.

6. Because you don't really need the new appended text for the tutorial, click the Undo button in the Standard toolbar to remove the appended text.

TIP

Place your appended text in front of the <> symbols if you want to add text to the beginning of the dimension text. You can also replace the dimension text entirely by replacing the <> sign is in the Contents input box with new text. If you want to restore a dimension that has been modified, delete everything in the Contents input box, including space. Or include a space to leave the dimension text blank.

TIP

In this exercise, you were able to edit only a single dimension. To append text to several dimensions at once, you need to use the Dimension Edit tool. See the "Making Changes to Multiple Dimensions" sidebar in this chapter for more on this command.

You can also have AutoCAD automatically add a dimension suffix or prefix to all dimensions, instead of just a chosen few, by using the Suffix or Prefix option in the Primary Units tab of the Dimension Style dialog box.

MAKING CHANGES TO MULTIPLE DIMENSIONS

The Dimension Edit tool offers a quick way to edit existing dimensions. It gives you the ability to edit more than one dimension's text at one time. One common use for the Dimension Edit tool might be to change a string of dimensions to read "Equal", instead of showing the actual dimensioned distance. The following example shows an alternative to the Properties tool for appending text to a dimension:

1. Click the Dimension Edit tool in the Dimension toolbar, or type **Ded** and press Enter.

2. At this prompt

   ```
   Enter type of dimension Edit
   [Home/New/Rotate/Oblique]<Home>:
   ```

   type **N** and press Enter to use the New option. The Multiline Text Editor appears, showing the <> brackets in the text box.

3. Click the space either before or after the <> brackets, and then enter the text you want to append to the dimension. Or you can replace the brackets entirely to replace the dimension with your text.

4. Click OK.

5. At the Select objects: prompt, pick the dimensions you wish to edit. The Select objects: prompt remains, allowing you to select several dimensions.

6. Press Enter to finish your selection. The dimension changes to include your new text or to replace the existing dimension text.

The Dimension Edit tool is useful in editing dimension text, but you can also use this command to make graphical changes to the text. Here is a list of the other Dimension Edit tool options:

Home   Moves the dimension text to its standard default position and angle.

Rotate   Allows you to rotate the dimension text to a new angle.

Oblique   Skews the dimension extension lines to a new angle. See the "Skewing Dimension Lines" section later in this chapter.

Part ii

Locating the Definition Points

AutoCAD provides the associative dimensioning capability to automatically update dimension text when a drawing is edited. You use objects called *definition points* to determine how edited dimensions are updated.

The definition points are located at the same points you pick when you determine the dimension location. For example, the definition points for linear dimensions are the extension line origin and the intersection of the extension line/dimension line. The definition points for a circle diameter are the points used to pick the circle and the opposite side of the circle. The definition points for a radius are the points used to pick the circle, plus the center of the circle.

Definition points are actually point objects. They are very difficult to see because they are usually covered by the feature they define. You can, however, see them indirectly by using grips. The definition points of a dimension are the same as the dimension's grip points. You can see them simply by clicking a dimension. Try the following:

1. Make sure the Grips feature is turned on.

2. Click the longest of the three vertical dimensions you drew in the earlier exercise. You will see the grips of the dimension.

TIP

AutoCAD 2002 treats dimensions as fully associative. This means that dimensions are updated automatically whenever an object associated with the dimension is modified. See "Using True Associative Dimensions" later in this chapter.

Making Minor Adjustments to Dimensions Using Grips

The definition points, whose locations you can see through their grips, are located on their own unique layer called Defpoints. Definition points are displayed regardless of whether the Defpoints layer is on or off. To give you an idea of how these definition points work, try the following exercises, which show you how to directly manipulate the definition points:

1. With the grips visible, click the grip near the dimension text.

TIP

Because the Defpoints layer has the unique feature of being visible even when turned off, you can use it as a layer for laying out your drawing. While Defpoints is turned off, you can still see objects assigned to it, but the objects won't plot.

2. Move the cursor around. Notice that when you move the cursor vertically, the text moves along the dimension line. When you move the cursor horizontally, the dimension line and text move together, keeping their parallel orientation to the dimensioned floor plan.

TIP

Here the entire dimension line, including the text, moves. In a later exercise, you'll see how you can move the dimension text independently of the dimension line.

3. Enter **@9"<0** and press Enter. Metric users should enter **@275<0** and press Enter. The dimension line, text, and dimension extensions move to the new location to the right of the text (see Figure 8.5).

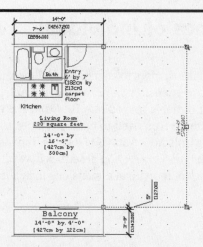

FIGURE 8.5: Moving the dimension line using its grip

Part ii

TIP

If you need to move several dimension lines at once, select them all at the Command prompt; and then Shift+click one set of dimension-line grips from each dimension. Once you've selected the grips, click one of the hot grips again. You can then move all the dimension lines at once.

In step 3 of the last exercise, you saw that you can specify an exact distance for the dimension line's new location by entering a relative polar coordinate. Cartesian coordinates work just as well. You can even use object snaps to relocate dimension lines. Next, try moving the dimension line back using the Perpendicular Osnap:

1. Click the grip at the bottom of the dimension line you just edited.

2. Shift+right-click and choose Perpendicular from the Osnap shortcut menu.

3. Place the cursor on the vertical dimension line that dimensions the balcony and click it.

The selected dimension line moves to align with the other vertical dimension, back to its original location.

Changing Style Settings of Individual Dimensions

In some cases, you will have to make changes to an individual dimension's style setting in order to edit that dimension. For example, if you try to move the text of a typical linear dimension, you may find that the text and dimension lines are inseparable. You need to make a change to the dimension style setting that controls how AutoCAD locates dimension text in relation to the dimension line. This section describes how you can make changes to the style settings of individual dimensions to facilitate changes in the dimension.

TIP

If you need to change the dimension style of a dimension to match that of another, you can use the Match Properties tool.

Moving a Fixed Dimension Text

Earlier in this chapter, you saw how the dimension text is attached to the dimension line so that when the text is moved, the dimension line follows. You may encounter situations when you want to move the text independently of the dimension line. The following exercise shows you how you can separate dimension text from its dimension line. In the process, you'll learn how you can make a change to a single dimension's style settings. Then, you'll use grips to move the dimension text away from the dimension line.

1. Press the Esc key twice to cancel the grip selection from the previous exercise.

2. Zoom into the 24' dimension so you have a view similar to Figure 8.6.

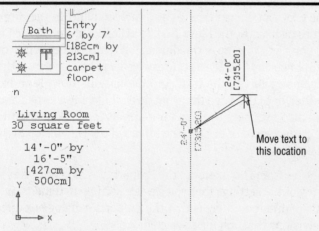

FIGURE 8.6: Selecting and then moving the 24-foot dimension

3. Click the 24'-0 " dimension to expose its grips.

4. Click the Properties tool in the Standard toolbar.

5. Scroll down the list of properties until you see an option called Fit; click the plus sign to the left of the Fit option. A new set of options appears below it.

6. Scroll down the list further until you see the Keep Dim Line with Text option to the right of the Text Movement listing, and then click this option.

7. Click the arrow that appears next to it to open the drop-down list; then, select the Move Text, Add Leader option.

8. Close the Properties dialog box.

Let's see the effect of the changes you just made.

9. Click the grip of the 24'-0 " dimension text and move it up and to the right. Click again to place the text in a new location, as shown in Figure 8.6.

10. Review the changes you made, and then click the Undo button to return to the previous state before you moved the dimension text. Moving the text in step 1 demonstrates that the text is no longer tied to the dimension line. In the Properties dialog box, the Move Text, Add Leader option in the Fit options lets you move the dimension text independently of the dimension line. It also causes a leader to be drawn from the dimension line to the text. Another option, Move Text, No Leader, does the same thing but doesn't include a leader. You can also set these options for a dimension style using the Text Placement options in the Fit tab of the Dimension Style dialog box.

As you can see from this exercise, the Properties dialog box gives you access to many of the settings that you saw for setting up dimension styles. The main difference here is that the Properties dialog box affects only the dimensions that you have selected.

In the previous exercise, you changed the format setting of a single dimension *after* it was placed. These settings can be made a standard part of your Architectural dimension style by using the Modify button in the Dimension Style Manager dialog box.

You need to make one more change to the drawing's dimension to set up for the next exercise.

1. Pan your view downward so you can see the 5" dimension clearly. Click the 5 " dimension and move it into a position in line with the dimension text.

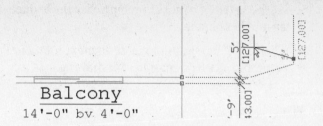

2. Choose ➤ View ➤ Zoom All, and then choose File ➤ Save to save this file in its current state.

In this short exercise, you were able to move the 5" dimension without making any changes to its properties. AutoCAD automatically selects the appropriate Text movement setting if the text is too large to fit between the dimension extension lines. In the case of the 5" dimension text, AutoCAD automatically chose the Move Text, Add Leader setting when the dimension was placed in the drawing.

TIP

If you have multiple dimension styles and you want to change an existing dimension to the current dimension style, use the Dimension Update tool. Click the Dimension Update tool on the Dimension toolbar, or choose Dimension Update from the pull-down menu. Then, select the dimensions you want to change. Press Enter when you've finished selecting dimensions. The selected dimensions will be converted to the current style.

Rotating a Dimension Text

Once in a while, a dimension text works better if it is kept in a horizontal orientation, even if the dimension itself is not horizontal. If you find you need to rotate dimension text, here's the way to do it:

1. Click the Undo button twice in the toolbar or type **U** and press Enter to return the 5" dimension to its original location.

2. Click the Dimension Edit tool in the Dimension toolbar.

3. At the `Enter type of dimension editing [Home/New/ Rotate/Oblique] <Home>:` prompt, enter **R** and press Enter.

4. At the `Enter text angle:` prompt, type **45** and press Enter to rotate the text to a 45° angle.

5. At the Select objects: prompt, click the 5" dimension text again. Press Enter.

6. Click the Undo button to undo the text rotation. You won't want to save this change to your drawing.

TIP

You can also choose Dimension ➢ Align Text ➢ Angle, select the dimension text, and then enter an angle. A 0° angle will cause the dimension text to return to its default angle.

The Dimension Text Edit tool (Dimtedit command) also allows you to align the dimension text to either the left or right side of the dimension line. It is similar to the Alignment option in the Multiline Text Editor that controls text justification.

As you have seen in this section, the Grips feature is especially well suited to editing dimensions. With grips, you can stretch, move, copy, rotate, mirror, and scale dimensions.

MODIFYING THE DIMENSION STYLE SETTINGS USING OVERRIDE

In the "Moving a Fixed Dimension Text" section, you used the Properties button on the toolbar to facilitate the moving of the dimension text. You can also use the Dimension ➢ Override option (Dimoverride command) to accomplish the same thing. The Override option allows you to make changes to an individual dimension's style settings. Here's an example showing how to use the Override option in place of the Properties button in the first exercise of the "Moving a Fixed Dimension Text" section.

1. Press the Esc key twice to make sure you are not in the middle of a command. Choose Dimension ➢ Override from the pulldown menu.

2. At the next prompt

       Enter dimension variable name to override or
       [Clear overrides]:

   type **Dimfit** and press Enter.

CONTINUED ➡

3. At the Current value <3>: prompt, type **4** and press Enter. This command has the same effect as selecting Move Text, Add Leader from the Fit option of the Properties dialog box.

4. The Enter dimension variable to override… prompt appears again, allowing you to enter another dimension variable. Press Enter to move to the next step.

5. At the Select objects: prompt, select the dimension you want to change. You can select a group of dimensions if you want to change several dimensions at once. Press Enter when you have finished with your selection. The dimension settings will change for the selected dimensions.

As you can see from this example, the Dimoverride command requires that you know exactly which dimension variable to edit in order to make the desired modification. In this case, setting the Dimfit variable to 4 lets you move the dimension text independently of the dimension line.

Understanding the Dimension Text Edit Tool

One dimension text-editing tool you haven't used yet is the Dimension Text Edit tool. Although it may sound as though this tool allows you to edit dimension text, its purpose is to allow you to quickly position dimension text to the left, right, or center of the dimension line. To use it, choose Dimension Text Edit from the toolbar, and then click the dimension text you want to move. You'll see the prompt

```
Click on a dimension and the Select dimension: Specify new
location for

dimension text or [Left/Right/Center/Home/Angle]:
```

You can then enter the letter of the option you want. For example, if you enter **L** and press Enter, the dimension text moves to the left side of the dimension line.

Editing Dimensions and Other Objects Together

Certainly it's helpful to be able to edit a dimension directly using its grips. But the key feature of AutoCAD's dimensions is their ability to *automatically* adjust themselves to changes in the drawing. As long as you include the dimension's definition points when you select objects to edit, the dimensions themselves will automatically update to reflect the change in your drawing.

To see how this feature works, try moving the living room closer to the bathroom wall. You can move a group of lines and vertices using the Stretch command and the Crossing option:

1. Click the Stretch tool in the Modify palette, or type **S** and press Enter and then **C** and press Enter. You will see the following prompt:

    ```
    At the Select objects to stretch by crossing-window or -
    polygon...
    Select objects: C
    Specify first corner:
    ```

2. Pick a crossing window, as illustrated in Figure 8.7. Press Enter to confirm your selection.

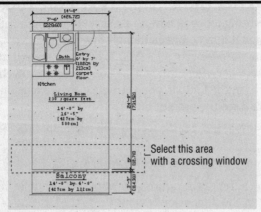

Select this area with a crossing window

FIGURE 8.7: The Stretch crossing window

3. At the Specify base point of displacement: prompt, pick any point on the screen.

4. At the Specify second point of displacement: prompt, enter **@2'<90** to move the wall 2' in a 90° direction. The wall moves, and the dimension text changes to reflect the new dimension.

TIP

In some situations, you may find that a crossing window selects objects other than those you want to stretch. This frequently occurs when many objects are close together at the location of a vertex you want to stretch. To be more selective about the vertices you move and their corresponding objects, use a standard window instead of a crossing window to select the vertices. Then, pick the individual objects whose vertices you wish to move.

When you selected the crossing window corners, you included the definition points of both vertical dimensions. Doing so allowed you to move the dimension extension lines along with the wall, thereby updating the dimensions automatically.

UNDERSTANDING THE STRETCH COMMAND

The tool you used for moving the wall and the dimension line extensions is the Stretch command. This is one of the most useful yet least understood commands offered by AutoCAD. Think of the Stretch command as a vertex mover: Its sole purpose is to move the vertices (or endpoints) of objects.

The Stretch command actually requires you to do two things: select the objects you want to edit, and then select the vertices you wish to move. The crossing window and the Cpolygon window are convenient ways of killing two birds with one stone, because they select objects and vertices in one operation. But when you want to be more selective, you can click objects and window vertices instead. For example, consider the exercise in this chapter where you moved a wall with the Stretch command. To move the walls but not the dimension-line extensions, take the following steps:

1. Click the Stretch tool on the Modify toolbar or click Stretch on the Modify pull-down menu. You can also type **S** and press Enter.

CONTINUED ➡

2. At the Select objects: prompt, enter **W** and press Enter (Window) or **WP** and press Enter (Window Polygon).

3. Window the vertices you wish to move. Because the Window and Window Polygon selection options select objects completely enclosed within the window, most of the items you want to stretch will already be selected.

4. Click the vertical walls to include them in the set of objects to be edited.

5. Press Enter to finish your selection.

6. Indicate the base point and second point for the stretch.

You could also use the Remove Selection option and click the dimensions to deselect them in the previous exercise. Then, when you enter the base and second points, the walls move but the dimensions stay in place.

Stretch will stretch only the vertices included in the last window, crossing window, crossing polygon, or window polygon. Thus, if you had attempted to window another part of your drawing in the wall-moving exercise, nothing would have moved. Before Stretch will do anything, objects need to be highlighted (selected) and their endpoints windowed.

The Stretch command is especially well suited to editing dimensioned objects. When you use it with the Crossing Polygon (CP) or Window Polygon (WP) selection options, you have substantial control over what is edited.

You can also use the Mirror, Rotate, and Stretch commands with dimensions. The polar arrays also work, and Extend and Trim can be used with linear dimensions.

When editing dimensioned objects, be sure to select the dimension associated with the object being edited. As you select objects, using the Crossing (C) or Crossing Polygon (CP) selection option helps you include the dimensions.

TIP

If a hatch pattern or solid fill completely covers a dimension, you can use the Draworder command to have AutoCAD draw the dimension over the hatch or solid fill.

Using True Associative Dimensions

You've seen how you can edit dimensions by manipulating their definition points. For versions prior to 2002, if you want to edit dimensions together with the objects, you need to use a crossing window, because the dimension is not fully associated with the object it is dimensioning. AutoCAD uses the dimension's definition point to simulate what is known as *associative dimensioning*. If you prefer, you can also fully associate a dimension with an object so that you need only change the object and the dimension will follow.

To use this feature, called True Associative Dimensioning, you'll need to turn it on in the Options dialog box. Here's how it's done:

1. Choose Tools ➤ Options; then, click the User Preferences tab.

2. Go to the Associative Dimensioning group and turn on the Associate New Dimensions with Objects option.

3. Click OK.

From now on, any dimension you place will be associated with the object you are dimensioning. Try the following exercise to see how it works:

1. Choose File ➤ New and create a new blank file from the Acad.dwt template.

2. Click the Rectangle tool from the Draw toolbar; then, draw a rectangle roughly 12 units wide by 1 unit high.

3. Use the Zoom Window tool in the Standard toolbar to get a good view of your drawing so far.

4. Choose Dimension ➤ Linear, turn on the Object Snap mode, and then dimension the top of the rectangle.

```
|←———————————— 12.0000 ————————————→|
```

Part ii

5. Click the rectangle to select it; then, click the grip in the upper-right corner of the rectangle.

6. Move the grip to the right and upward and then click. The rectangle corner moves, and the dimension moves with it.

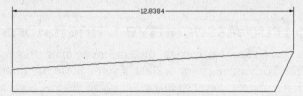

In this case, you only had to change the shape of the rectangle, and the dimension followed the change. The dimension in this example is fully associated with the rectangle.

Associative dimensioning also works with external references and blocks. As a result, you can dimension an Xref, edit the source Xref file, and have the dimensions update in the current file. Such changes are not completely automatic; you need to issue the Dimregen command to have dimensions updated to the new Xref configuration.

You can use Associative Dimensioning on objects within blocks, and if the block is edited, those dimensions will update automatically. But be aware that non-uniform scaling of a block—that is, scaling along one axis and not the other—will not affect an associative dimension.

In AutoCAD 2002, you can dimension a model space object in paper space, and the paper space dimension will be associated with the model space object. As a result, even though the paper space dimension will not be visible in model space, the paper space dimension will reflect changes made to objects in model space. In some instances, you may need to use the Dimregen command to refresh paper space dimensions.

Associating Dimensions with Objects

Now, suppose you have a drawing from an older version of AutoCAD and you want to create an association between an existing dimension and an object. The next exercise will show you how this is done. You'll use the Unit plan to associate one of the dimensions you've already created with a line representing a wall.

1. Close the rectangle drawing file. You don't have to save it.

2. Back in the Unit drawing, zoom in to the balcony area so your view looks similar to Figure 8.8.

3. Choose Dimension ➤ Reassociate Dimensions. You may also type **Dimreassociate** and press Enter at the Command prompt.

4. At the Select dimension to reassociate… Select Object: prompt, select the vertical dimension that dimensions the balcony (see Figure 8.8), and then press Enter.

5. At the Specify first extension line origin or [Select object] <next>: prompt, you'll see an X appear at the top definition point of the dimension.

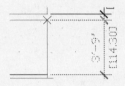

6. Press Enter to tell AutoCAD to go to the next extension line origin. You'll see an X appear at the bottom definition point of the dimension.

7. Use the Endpoint Osnap and click the end of the line representing the rail of the unit (see Figure 8.8).

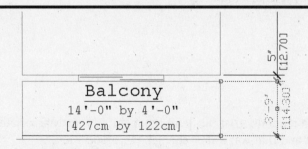

FIGURE 8.8: Reassociating a dimension to an object

Part ii

You now have the dimension associated with the endpoint of the line representing the rail of the balcony. Try moving the rail to see what happens.

8. Use the Move tool in the Modify toolbar to move the balcony rail downward, as shown in Figure 8.9. The dimension follows the line.

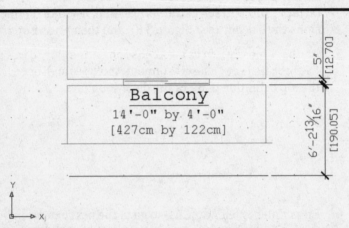

FIGURE 8.09: The reassociated dimension follows the rail as it is moved.

In step 5, you saw an X appear at the location of a dimension definition point. If the definition point is already associated with an object, the X will appear with a box around it.

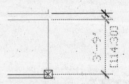

The box is a reminder that the definition point is already associated with an object and that you will be changing its association.

Also in step 5, you have the option to select an object. This option allows you to associate the dimension with an entire object instead of just one endpoint. If you type **S** and press Enter at that prompt in step 5, you can then select the object that you want to have associated with the dimension.

The dimension will change so that its definition points coincide with the endpoints of the object. The dimension will remain in its original orientation. For example, a vertical dimension will remain vertical even if you associate the dimension with a horizontal line. In this situation, the dimension dutifully dimensions the endpoints of the line but will show a distance of zero.

TIP

You can remove a dimension's association with an object by using the Dimdisassociate command. Type **Dimdisassociate** and press Enter at the Command prompt, select the dimension(s), and then press Enter.

Adding a String of Dimensions with a Single Operation

AutoCAD 2002 offers a method for creating a string of dimensions using a single operation. The Qdim command lets you select a set of objects instead of having to select points. The following exercise demonstrates how the Qdim command works.

1. If you haven't done so already, zoom out so you have an overall view of the Unit floor plan.

2. Choose Dimension ➢ Qdim or click Quick Dimension on the Dimension toolbar.

3. At the Select geometry to dimension: prompt, place a selection window around the entire left-side wall of the unit.

4. Press Enter to finish your selection. The following prompt appears:

   ```
   Specify dimension line position, or
   [Continuous/Staggered/Baseline/Ordinate/Radius/Diameter/
   datumPoint/Edit] <Continuous>:
   ```

5. Click a point to the left of the wall to place the dimension. A string of dimensions appears, displaying all the dimensions for the wall.

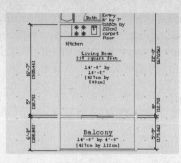

6. When you have finished reviewing the results of this exercise, exit the file without saving it.

The prompt in step 4 indicates several types of dimensions you can choose from. For example, if you want the dimensions to originate from a single baseline, you can enter **B** and press Enter in step 5 to select the Baseline option.

The Qdim command can be a time-saver when you want to dimension a wall quickly. It may not work in all situations, but if the object you're dimensioning is fairly simple, it may be all you need.

TIP

In this exercise, you used a simple window to select the wall. For more complex shapes, try using a crossing polygon selection window.

Removing the Alternate Dimensions

In the beginning of this chapter, you set up the My Architectural dimension style to include an alternate dimension. You can remove those alternate dimensions by turning off the alternate dimension features. Here's how it's done:

1. Choose Dimension ➤ Style or enter **D** and press Enter.

2. In the Dimension Style Manager dialog box, select the style that uses the alternate units. In the Styles list box, choose Modify.

3. Select the Alternate Units tab.

4. Click the Display Alternate Units check box to remove the check mark.

5. Click OK, and then click Close in the Dimension Style Manager dialog box.

The dimensions that use the style you just edited change to remove the alternate dimensions. You can also perform the reverse operation and add alternate dimensions to an existing set of dimensions. Follow the steps shown here, but instead of removing the check mark in step 4, add the check mark and make the appropriate setting changes to the rest of the Alternate Units tab.

Using Osnap While Dimensioning

WARNING

Setting a Running Osnap mode has a drawback: When your drawing gets crowded, you may end up picking the wrong point by accident. However, you can easily toggle off the Running Osnap mode by clicking the OSNAP label in the status bar.

You may find that when you pick intersections and endpoints frequently, as during dimensioning, it is a bit inconvenient to use the Osnap shortcut menu. In situations where you know you will be using certain Osnaps frequently, you can use Running Osnaps. You can do so in the following two ways:

▶ Choose Tools ➤ Drafting Settings. In the Object Snap tab of the Drafting Settings dialog box, make sure the Object Snap On check box is checked and then select the desired default Osnap mode. You can pick more than one mode—for example, Intersection, Endpoint, and Midpoint—so that whichever geometry you happen to be nearest will be the point selected.

▶ Type **-osnap** and press Enter at the Command prompt and then enter the name of the Osnap modes you want to use. If you want to use more than one mode, enter their names separated by commas; for example:

```
endpoint,midpoint,intersect
```

Once you've designated your Running Osnaps, the next time you are prompted to select a point, the selected Osnap modes are automatically activated. You can still override the default settings using the Osnap shortcut menu (Shift+right-click). You can toggle the Running Osnaps on or off by clicking the OSNAP label in the status bar or by pressing F3.

Part ii

The toggle feature is especially helpful in crowded drawings where you may accidentally select an Osnap location while panning or zooming or selecting points for other operations.

DIMENSIONING NONORTHOGONAL OBJECTS

So far, you've been reading about how to work with linear dimensions. You can also dimension nonorthogonal objects, such as circles, arcs, triangles, and trapezoids. In this section, you will practice dimensioning nonorthogonal objects by drawing an elevation of a window in the set of plans for your studio apartment building. You'll start by setting up the drawing and then drawing the window itself:

1.   Create a new file called Window.

2.   In the Create New Drawing Wizard, click the Start from Scratch icon at the top. Click the English radio button if you are using feet and inches; otherwise, click the Metric radio button. This step is important because depending on which option you select, AutoCAD will set up the drawing with different dimension style defaults. AutoCAD will create a style called ISO-25 as the default style for metric users.

3.   Set the file up as an architectural drawing at a scale of 3"=1'-0" on an 8 1/2" × 11" sheet. Metric users set up an A4 sheet at a scale of 1:4.

4.   If you are using the English measurement system, start by setting the dimension scale to 4. Normally, you would use the Dimension Style Manager dialog box to set the dimension scale. A shortcut to do this is to type **Dimscale**, press Enter, type **4**, and press Enter again. Doing so changes the scale factor of the current dimension style to 4. Metric users can use the default setting.

5.   English system users should set two more options. Type **Dimtih**, press Enter, type **O**, and press Enter again to turn off the setting that forces the dimension text to be horizontal. Next, type **Dimtad**, press Enter, type **1**, and press Enter again to turn on the text-above-dimension feature. You'll want these two settings to match the appearance of text in

the metric ISO-25 style. Again, metric users do not have to change these settings.

Now you are ready to start drawing the window.

WARNING

In the figures shown for the following exercises, you'll see both English and metric dimensions for the benefit of users of both systems. Your view will contain only the measurement in the system you've chosen in the previous exercise.

1. Click Polygon on the Draw toolbar, or type **Pol** and press Enter.

2. At the Enter number of sides: prompt, type **6** and press Enter.

3. At the Specify center of polygon or [Edge]: prompt, pick the center of the polygon at coordinate 22,18. Metric users use 59,42 for the center coordinate.

TIP

You can turn on the Snap mode to help you locate points for this exercise.

4. Type **C** and press Enter at the Enter an option [Inscribe in circle/circumscribeabout circle] <I>: prompt to select the Circumscribe option. This option tells AutoCAD to place the polygon outside the temporary circle used to define the polygon.

5. At the Specify radius of circle: prompt, you will see the hexagon drag along with the cursor. You can pick a point with your mouse to determine its size.

6. Enter **8** and press Enter to get an exact size for the hexagon. Metric users enter **20.32** and press Enter.

7. Draw a circle with a radius of 7" using 22,18 as its center. Metric users draw a circle with a radius of 17.78 using 59.42 for the center location. Your drawing will look like Figure 8.10.

Part ii

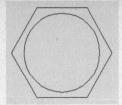

FIGURE 8.10: The window frame

Dimensioning Nonorthogonal Linear Distances

Now you will dimension the window. The unusual shape of the window prevents you from using the horizontal or vertical dimensions you've used already. However, the Dimension ➤ Aligned option will allow you to dimension at an angle:

1. Click the Aligned Dimension tool on the Dimension toolbar. You can also enter **Dal** and press Enter to start the aligned dimension or select Dimension ➤ Aligned.

2. At the Specify first extension line origin or <select object>: prompt, press Enter. You could have picked extension line origins as you did in earlier examples, but using Enter shows you firsthand how the Select option works.

3. At the Select object to dimension: prompt, pick the upper-right face of the hexagon near coordinate 2'-5",1'-10" (75,55 for metric users). As the prompt indicates, you can also pick an arc or circle for this type of dimension.

4. At the Specify dimension line location or [Mtext/ Text/Angle]: prompt, pick a point near coordinate 34,26 (90,60 for metric users).

TIP

Just as with linear dimensions, you can enter **T** and press Enter at step 4 to enter alternate text for the dimension.

Next, you will dimension a face of the hexagon. Instead of its actual length, however, you will dimension a distance at a specified angle—the distance from the center of the face:

1. Click the Linear Dimension tool on the Dimension toolbar.

2. At the `Specify first extension line origin or <select> object:` prompt, press Enter.

3. At the `Select object to dimension:` prompt, pick the lower-right face of the hexagon near coordinate 30,16 (77,33 for metric users).

4. At the `Specify dimension line location or [Mtext/ Text/Angle/Horizontal/Vertical/Rotated]:` prompt, type **R** and press Enter to select the rotated option.

5. At the `Dimension line angle <0>:` prompt, enter **30** and press Enter.

6. At the `Dimension line location:` prompt, pick a point near coordinate 35,8 (88,12 for metric users). Your drawing will look like Figure 8.11.

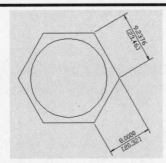

FIGURE 8.11: A linear dimension using the Rotated option

Dimensioning Radii, Diameters, and Arcs

To dimension circular objects, you use another set of options from the Draw ➤ Dimensioning menu:

1. Click the Angular Dimension tool on the Dimension toolbar. Or you can enter **Dan** and press Enter or choose Dimension ➤ Angular from the pull-down menu to start the angular dimension.

2. At the Select arc, circle, line, or <Specify vertex>: prompt, pick the upper-left face of the hexagon near coordinate 15,22 (44,57 for metric users).

3. At the Select second line: prompt, pick the first three faces at coordinate 21,26 (54,62 for metric users).

4. At the Specify dimension arc line location or [Mtext/ Text/Angle]: prompt, notice that as you move the cursor around the upper-left corner of the hexagon, the dimension changes, as shown in the first three images of Figure 8.12.

5. Pick a point near coordinate 21,23 (49,50 for metric users). The dimension is fixed in the drawing (see the bottom image of Figure 8.12).

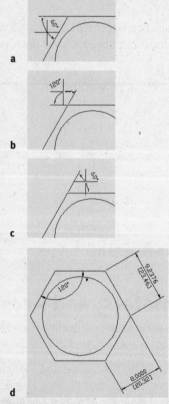

a

b

c

d

FIGURE 8.12: The angular dimension added to the window frame

TIP

If you need to make subtle adjustments to the dimension line or text location, you can do so using grips, after you have placed the angular dimension.

Now try the Diameter option, which shows the diameter of a circle:

1. Click the Diameter Dimension tool on the Dimension tool-bar. Or you can enter **Ddi** and press Enter at the Command prompt.

2. At the Select arc or circle: prompt, pick the circle.

3. At the Specify dimension line location or [Mtext/ Text/Angle]: prompt, you will see the diameter dimension drag along the circle as you move the cursor. If you move the cursor outside the circle, the dimension will display on the outside.

TIP

If the dimension text can't fit within the circle, AutoCAD gives you the option to place the dimension text outside the circle as you drag the temporary dimension to a horizontal position.

4. Place the cursor inside the circle so that the dimension arrow points in a horizontal direction.

5. With the text centered, click the mouse.

The Radius Dimension tool on the Dimension toolbar gives you a radius dimension just as the diameter dimension provides a circle's diameter.

Figure 8.13 shows a radius dimension on the outside of the circle, but you can place it inside in a manner similar to the diameter dimension. The Center Mark tool on the Dimension toolbar just places a cross mark in the center of the selected arc or circle.

TIP

You can alter the format of diameter dimensions by changing the Dimtix and Dimtofl dimension variable settings. For example, to have two arrows appear across the diameter of the circle, turn on both Dimtix and Dimtofl.

Part ii

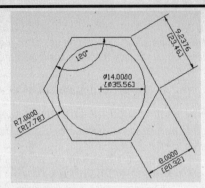

FIGURE 8.13: A radius dimension shown on the outside of the circle

ADDING A NOTE WITH AN ARROW

Finally, there is the Dimension ➤ Leader option, which allows you to add a note with an arrow pointing to the object the note describes.

1. Click the Quick Leader tool on the Dimension toolbar, or enter **Le** and press Enter, or select Dimension ➤ Leader from the pull-down menu.

2. At the Specify first leader point, or [Settings]<Settings>: prompt, pick a point near the top-left edge of the hexagon at coordinate 16,24 (45,59 for metric users).

3. At the Specify next point: prompt, enter **@6<110** and press Enter. Metric users should enter **@15<110** and press Enter.

4. At the Specify next point: prompt, you can continue to pick points just as you would draw lines. For this exercise, however, press Enter to finish drawing leader lines.

TIP

You can also add multiline text at the leader. See the next section, "Exploring the Leader Options."

5. At the Enter first line of annotation text <Mtext>: prompt, type **Window frame** and press Enter as the label for this leader. Your drawing will look like Figure 8.14.

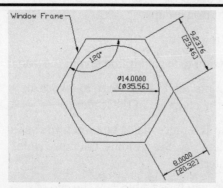

FIGURE 8.14: The leader with a note added

Exploring the Leader Options

The Leader tool is deceptively simple and has numerous options. In step 2 of the previous exercise, you can enter **S** and press Enter to open the Leader Settings dialog box.

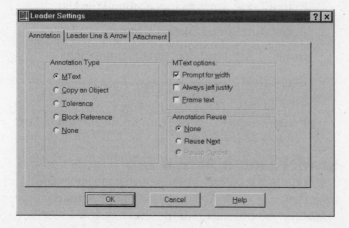

From here, you can have the Leader tool perform any number of functions, depending on the type of leader you want. The following subsection lists the options and their functions.

Annotation Tab

The options in the Annotation tab let you control the type of annotation that is attached to the leader. AutoCAD uses the MText option by default, which places a multiline text object at the end of the leader. Here are the other options organized by button groups:

Annotation Type Button Group

MText   Select this option to use multiline text in the leader.

Copy an Object   Prompts you to select text, tolerance, or blocks to be copied to the endpoint of the leader.

Tolerance   Opens the Tolerance dialog box when you've finished drawing the leader lines. See "Adding Tolerance Notation" later in this chapter.

Block Reference   Lets you insert a block at the end of the leader.

None   Ends the leader without adding a note.

MText Options Button Group

Prompt for Width   Asks you to select a width for multiline text.

Always Left Justify   Left justifies multiline text.

Frame Text   Draws a frame around the text.

Annotation Reuse Button Group

None   Always prompts you for annotation.

Reuse Next   Reuses the annotation you enter for the next leader.

Reuse Current   Reuses the current annotation text.

Leader Line & Arrow Tab

The options in the Leader Line & Arrow tab give you control over the leader line and arrow. You can select an arrow that is different from the default, or you can constrain the lines to follow a specific angle:

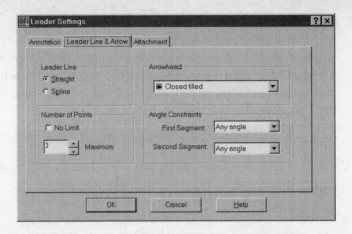

Leader Line Lets you select from either a straight line or spline for your lines. (see Figure 8.15).

Number of Points Lets you constrain the number of points you select before the Command prompts you for the annotation.

Arrowhead Lets you select an arrowhead from a list similar to the one in the Dimension Style dialog box.

Angle Constraints Lets you constrain the angle at which the leader line extends from the arrow and the second point.

Straight option

Spline option

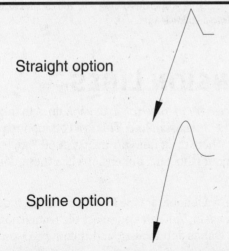

FIGURE 8.15: Straight and spline leader lines

Attachment Tab

The options in the Attachment tab let you control how the leader connects to MText annotation, depending on which side of the leader the annotation appears. The location of the leader endpoint in relation to the note is frequently a focus of drafting standards. These options let you customize your leader to produce results that conform to the standards you work with.

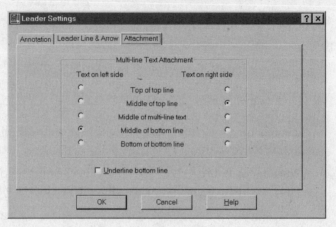

TIP

Just as with other dimensions, and objects in general, you can modify some of the properties of a leader using the Properties dialog box. You can, for example, change a straight leader into a spline leader.

SKEWING DIMENSION LINES

At times, you may find it necessary to force the extension lines to take on an angle other than 90° to the dimension line. This is a common requirement of isometric drawings, where most lines are at 30° or 60° angles instead of 90°. To facilitate nonorthogonal dimensions like these, Auto-CAD offers the Oblique option.

1. Choose Dimension ➤ Oblique, or type **Ded**, press Enter, type **O**, and press Enter again. You can also select the Dimension Edit tool from the Dimension toolbar, and then type **O** and press Enter.

2. At the Select object prompt, pick the aligned dimension at the upper-right of the drawing and press Enter to confirm your selection.

3. At the Enter obliquing angle (Press enter for none): prompt, enter **60** for 60 degrees. The dimension will skew so that the extension lines are at 60°, as shown in Figure 8.16.

4. Exit AutoCAD.

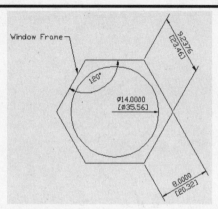

FIGURE 8.16: A dimension using the Oblique option

APPLYING ORDINATE DIMENSIONS

In mechanical drafting, *ordinate dimensions* are used to maintain the accuracy of machined parts by establishing an origin on the part. All major dimensions are described as x-coordinates or y-coordinates of that origin. The origin is usually an easily locatable feature of the part, such as a machined bore or two machined surfaces. Figure 8.17 shows a typical application of ordinate dimensions. In the lower-left corner, note the two dimensions whose leaders are jogged. Also note the origin location in the upper-right corner.

To use AutoCAD's Ordinate Dimension command, perform the following steps:

1. Click Tools ➤ UCS ➤ Origin, or type **UCS**, press Enter, type **Or**, and press Enter again.

2. At the Specify new origin point <0,0,0>: prompt, click the exact location of the origin of your part.

3. Toggle the Ortho mode on.

4. Click the Ordinate Dimension tool on the Dimension tool-bar. You can also type **Dor** and press Enter to start the ordinate dimension.

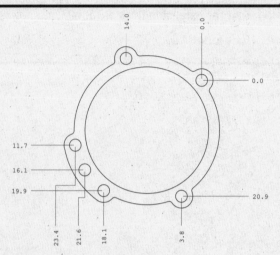

FIGURE 8.17: A drawing using ordinate dimensions

5. At the Select feature location: prompt, click the item you want to dimension.

TIP

The direction of the leader determines whether the dimension will be of the Xdatum or the Ydatum.

6. At the Specify leader endpoint or [Xdatum/Ydatum/Mtext/Text/Angle]: prompt, indicate the length and direction of the leader. Do this by positioning the rubber-banding leader perpendicular to the coordinate direction you want to dimension and then clicking that point.

In steps 1 and 2, you used the UCS feature to establish a second origin in the drawing. The Ordinate Dimension tool then uses that origin to determine the ordinate dimensions.

You may have noticed options in the Command window for the Ordinate Dimension tool. The Xdatum and Ydatum options force the dimension to be of the x or y coordinate no matter what direction the leader takes. The MText option opens the Multiline Text Editor, allowing you to append or replace the ordinate dimension text. The Text option lets you enter the replacement text directly through the Command window.

TIP

As with all other dimensions, you can use grips to make adjustments to the location of ordinate dimensions.

If you turn Ortho mode off, the dimension leader will be drawn with a jog to maintain the orthogonal (look back at Figure 8.17).

ADDING TOLERANCE NOTATION

In mechanical drafting, tolerances are a key part of a drawing's notation. They specify the allowable variation in size and shape that a mechanical part can have. To facilitate tolerance notation, AutoCAD provides the Tolerance command, which offers common ISO tolerance symbols together with a quick way to build a standard *feature control* symbol. Feature control symbols are industry-standard symbols used to specify tolerances. If you are a mechanical engineer or drafter, AutoCAD's tolerance notation options will be a valuable tool. However, a full discussion of tolerances requires a basic understanding of mechanical design and drafting and is beyond the scope of this book.

To use the Tolerance command, choose Tolerance from the Dimension toolbar, type **Tol** and press Enter at the Command prompt, or select Dimension ➤ Tolerance from the drop-down menu.

The Geometric Tolerance dialog box appears.

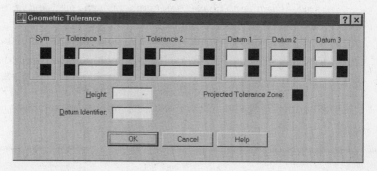

Part II

Here, you enter tolerance and datum values for the feature control symbol. You can enter two tolerance values and three datum values. In addition, you can stack values in a two-tiered fashion.

In the Geometric Tolerance dialog box, if you click a box in any of the Datum groups, or a box in the right side of the Tolerance groups, the Material Condition dialog box appears.

UNDERSTANDING THE POWER OF THE PROPERTIES DIALOG BOX

In this chapter, you've made frequent use of the Properties dialog box. By now, you may have recognized that the Properties dialog box is like a gateway to editing virtually any object. It allows you to edit the general properties of layer, color, and line type assignments. When used with individual objects, it lets you edit properties that are unique to the selected object. For example, through this tool, you are able to change a spline leader with an arrow into one with straight-line segments and no arrow.

If the Properties dialog box does not offer specific options to edit the object, then it offers a button to open a dialog box that will. If you edit a multiline text object with the Properties dialog box, for example, you have the option to open the Multiline Text Editor. The same is true for dimension text.

Beginning with AutoCAD 2000, AutoDesk has made a clear effort to make AutoCAD's interface more consistent. The text-editing tools now edit text of all types—single-line, multiline, and dimension text—so you don't have to remember which command or tool you need for a particular object. Likewise, the Properties dialog box offers a powerful means to edit all types of objects in your drawing.

As you continue with the rest of this book, you may want to experiment with the Properties dialog box as you learn about new objects. In addition to allowing you to edit properties, the Properties dialog box can show you the status of an object, much like the List tool.

WHAT'S NEXT?

In this chapter, you have learned how to effectively create dimension styles and how to dimension drawings. In the next chapter, you will group collections of objects into blocks. You will instance blocks into drawings and learn how to share blocks between drawings.

Chapter 9

GROUPING OBJECTS INTO BLOCKS

Computer drafting gains much of its efficiency from a feature that makes it possible to group a collection of objects into an entity that behaves as one object. AutoCAD calls these grouped objects a *block*. The AutoCAD tools that work specifically with blocks make it possible to:

- ▶ Create a block in your current drawing
- ▶ Repeatedly place copies of a block in precise locations in your drawing
- ▶ Share blocks between drawings
- ▶ Create .dwg files either from blocks or from portions of your current drawing

Adapted from *AutoCAD® 2002 No Experience Required®* by David Frey
ISBN 0-7821-4016-5   688 pages $29.99

In general, objects best suited to becoming part of a block are the components of a building that are repeatedly used in the drawing, such as doors, windows, and fixtures; or drawing symbols, like a North arrow or labels for a section cut line. In your cabin drawing, you will convert the doors with swings into blocks. Then you will create a new block that you will use to place the windows in the drawing. To accomplish these tasks, you will need to learn two new commands: Make Block and Insert Block.

MAKING A BLOCK FOR A DOOR

When making a block, you will create a *block definition*. This invisible entity is stored in the drawing file and consists of:

▶ The block name

▶ An insertion point to help you place the block in the drawing

▶ The objects to be grouped into the block

You will specify each of these in the course of using the Make Block command. When the command is completed, the block definition is stored with the drawing file. Then, you will insert the object (as a block) back into the drawing using the Insert Block command.

Before you create a block, you must consider the layers on which the objects to be blocked reside. When objects on the 0 layer are grouped into a block, they will take on the color and linetype of the layer that is current when the block is inserted. Objects on other layers retain the properties of their original layers, regardless of which color or linetype has been assigned to the current layer. This characteristic distinguishes the 0 layer from all other layers.

As you define a block, you must decide which—if any—of the objects to be included in the block will need to be on the 0 layer before they are blocked. If a block will always be on the same layer, the objects making up the block can remain on that layer. On the other hand, if a block may be inserted on several layers, you will need to move the objects in the block to the 0 layer before you create the block definition, to avoid confusion of colors and linetypes.

NOTE

In complex blocks, the objects that form them may reside on more than one layer.

As you learn to make blocks for the cabin doors, you will also see how layers work in the process of creating block definitions. You'll create a block for the exterior doors first, using the front door, and call it door3_0 to distinguish it from the smaller interior door. For the insertion point, you will need to assign a point on or near the door that will facilitate its placement as a block in your drawing. The hinge point will make the best insertion point.

For this chapter, the Endpoint Osnap should be running most of the time, and Polar tracking should be off. Follow the next five steps to set up your drawing:

1. If you are starting up a new session, start AutoCAD. In the Startup dialog box, click Open a Drawing. In the Select a File list, highlight Cabin06b and click OK. If this .dwg file is not in the list, use the Browse button to navigate to your training folder and select the file. This file is available on the companion website.

2. The Roof layer should be visible in the Layers drop-down list on the Object Properties toolbar. Click the list to open it, and then click Doors to make the Doors layer current. The list will close. Click the drop-down list again; this time, click the sun icons for the Roof and Header layers to freeze them. The suns turn into snowflakes. Click the Doors layer to close the list. The Doors layer is now current, and the Headers and Roof are no longer visible in the drawing (Figure 9.1).

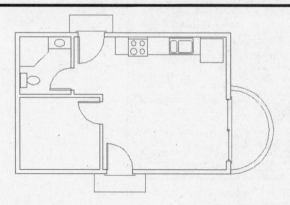

FIGURE 9.1: The floor plan with the Headers and Roof layers frozen

Part ii

NOTE

You are using the Freeze option for layers because you won't need to see the lines on the Roof and Headers layers for a while.

3. Check the status bar and note whether the Osnap button is in the On position. Right-click that button and pick Settings from the shortcut menu that appears.

4. In the Object Snap tab of the Drafting Settings dialog box, be sure the check box next to Endpoint is marked. Also, be sure Object Snap On is checked.

5. Click OK. In the status bar, click Polar off if it is on, and be sure only the Model and Osnap buttons are in the On position.

Now you're ready to make blocks.

1. Click the Make Block button on the Draw toolbar. The Block Definition dialog box comes up (Figure 9.2). Notice the flashing cursor in the text box next to Name. Type **door3_0** but do not press Enter.

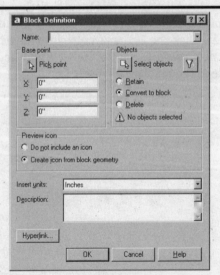

FIGURE 9.2: The Block Definition dialog box

TIP

You can also start the Block command by picking Draw ➤ Block ➤ Make, or by typing **b** and pressing Enter.

2. Click the Pick Point button in the Base Point area. The dialog box momentarily disappears, and you are returned to your drawing.

3. You need to zoom in to the front door area. In your drawing, click the Zoom Window button on the Standard toolbar and make a window around the front door area. The area in the zoom window will fill the screen.

4. Move the cursor to the front door area and position it near the hinge point of the door. When a square appears on the hinge point, click. Doing so selects the insertion point for the door, and the Block Definition dialog box returns.

5. Click the Select Objects button in the Objects area. You are returned to the drawing again. The cursor changes to a pickbox, and the Command window displays the Select objects: prompt.

6. Select the door and swing, and then press Enter. You are returned to the Block Definition dialog box. At the bottom of the Objects area, the count of selected objects is displayed. Just above that are three radio buttons. Click the Delete radio button if it's not already selected.

7. In the middle of the dialog box, be sure Create Icon from Block Geometry is selected. Click OK, and the dialog box disappears. The door and swing disappear (Figure 9.3).

You have now created a block definition called door3_0. Block definitions are stored electronically with the drawing file. You need to insert the door3_0 block (known formally as a *block reference*) into the front door opening to replace the door and swing that were just deleted when the block was created.

Part ii

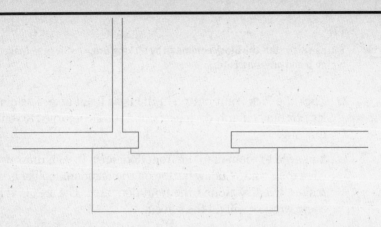

FIGURE 9.3: The front door after creating the door3_0 block and deleting the door and swing

Inserting the Door Block

You will use the Insert command to place the door3_0 block back into the drawing.

1. On the Draw toolbar, click the Insert Block button. The Insert dialog box comes up (Figure 9.4). At the top, the Name drop-down list contains the names of the blocks in the drawing. In this case, there is only one so far—door3_0—so it is on top. Below the Name list are three areas that include the Specify On-screen option. These areas are used for the insertion procedure.

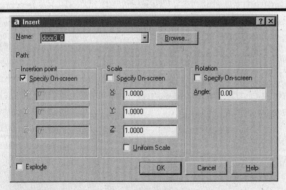

FIGURE 9.4: The Insert dialog box

TIP
You can also start the Insert command by selecting Insert ➢ Block, or by typing **i** and pressing Enter.

2. Be sure the Specify On-screen option is checked for all three areas.

3. Click OK. You are returned to your drawing. The door3_0 block is now attached to the cursor, with the hinge point coinciding with the intersection of the crosshairs (Figure 9.5). The Command window reads `Specify insertion point or[Scale/X/Y/Z/Rotate/PScale/PX/PY/PZ/PRotate]:`.

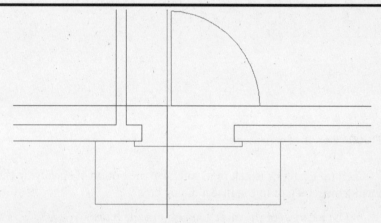

FIGURE 9.5: The door3_0 block attached to the cursor

4. With Endpoint Osnap running, move the cursor toward the upper end of the left jamb line in the front door opening. When a colored square appears at the jamb-line upper endpoint, click. The insertion point has been positioned, and the Command window now displays an additional prompt: `Enter X scale factor, specify opposite corner, or [corner/XYZ]<1>:`.

5. Press Enter to accept the default of 1 for the X scale factor. The prompt changes to: `Y scale factor <use X scale factor> :`.

6. Press Enter again to accept the default for this option. The door3_0 block comes into view; you can see that its insertion point has been placed at the upper end of the left jamb line, and that the block rotates as you move the cursor. Another prompt comes up: Specify rotation angle <0>:. Press Enter again to accept the default of 0. The door3_0 block is placed in the drawing (Figure 9.6).

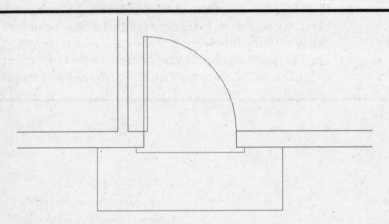

FIGURE 9.6: The final placement

Each time a block is inserted, you have the option of specifying the following on-screen or in the Insert dialog box:

- ▶ The location of the insertion point of the block
- ▶ The X and Y scale factors
- ▶ The Z factor in the dialog box (used in 3D drawings only)
- ▶ A rotation angle

When blocks are inserted, they can be stretched or flipped horizontally (the X scale factor) or vertically (the Y scale factor), or they can be rotated from their original orientation. Because you created the door3_0 block from the door and swing that occupied the front door opening, and the size was the same, inserting this block back into the front door opening required no rotation, so you followed the defaults. When you insert the same block into the back door opening, you will have to change the Y scale factor, because the door will be flipped vertically.

Flipping a Block While Inserting It

The X scale factor controls the block's horizontal size and orientation. The Y scale factor mimics the X scale factor unless you change it. For the next insertion, you will make such a change.

1. Click the Zoom Previous button on the Standard toolbar to zoom back out to a full view of the floor plan.

2. Click the Zoom Window button and make a window around the back door area, including plenty of room inside and outside the opening so that you can see the door3_0 block as it is being inserted. You will be zoomed into a close view of the back door.

3. Use the Erase command to erase the door and swing from the back door opening.

4. Click Insert ➢ Block. In the Insert dialog box, door3_0 should still be in the Name drop-down list.

5. Click OK. You are returned to your drawing, and the door3_0 block is attached to the cursor.

6. Move the cursor to the lower end of the left jamb line. When the colored square appears at that endpoint, click. The insertion point has been placed and the prompt reads Enter X scale factor, specify opposite corner, or [corner/XYZ]<1>:.

7. Press Enter to accept the default X scale factor of 1. The prompt changes to read Specify Y scale factor <use X scale factor:. In order to flip the door down to the inside of the cabin, you need to give the Y scale factor a value of -1.

8. Type **-1** and press Enter. Press Enter again to accept the default rotation angle of 0°. The Insert command ends, and the door3_0 block is placed in the back door opening (Figure 9.7).

NOTE

Nothing has changed about the geometry of the door, but it is now a different kind of object. Before, it was a rectangle and an arc; now it's a block reference made up of a rectangle and an arc.

Part ii

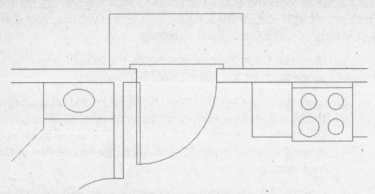

FIGURE 9.7: The door3_0 block after insertion

9. Click the Zoom Previous button on the Object Properties toolbar to zoom back out to a full view of the floor plan.

NOTE

When you're inserting a block, giving a value of -1 to the X or Y scale factor has the effect of flipping the block, much like the Mirror command did in Chapter 5, "Gaining Drawing Strategies," when you first drew the doors. Because you can flip or rotate the door3_0 block as it is inserted, it can be used to place a door and swing in any 3'-0" opening, regardless of its orientation.

Doors are traditionally sorted into four categories, depending on which side the hinges and doorknob are on and which way the door swings open. To be able to use one door block for all openings of the same size, you need to know:

▸ How the door and swing in the block are oriented

▸ Where the hinge point is to be in the next opening

▸ How the block has to be flipped and/or rotated during the insertion process to properly fit in the next doorway opening

Blocking and Inserting the Interior Doors

Because the interior doors are smaller, you will need to make a new block for them. You could insert the door3_0 block with a 5/6 scale factor, but the door thickness would also be reduced by the same factor, and you don't want that.

On the other hand, it's a good idea to have all door blocks oriented the same way, and the bath and bedroom doors are turned relative to the door3_0 block. You'll move and rotate the bathroom door and orient it like the front door.

1. Use Zoom Window to define a window that encloses both the bathroom and bedroom doors. The view will change to a close-up view of the area enclosed in your window.

2. Use the Move command to move the bathroom door to the right, and then use the Rotate command to rotate it -90° (Figure 9.8).

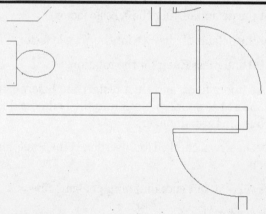

FIGURE 9.8: The bathroom door moved and rotated

3. Repeat a procedure similar to the one you used to make a block out of the front door and swing to make a block out of the bathroom door and swing. Here is a summary of the steps:

    A. Start the Block command (pick the Make Block button on the Draw toolbar).

    B. In the dialog box, type **door2_6** to name the new block. Don't press Enter.

    C. Click the Pick Point button and pick the hinge point of the bathroom door.

    D. Click the Select Objects button and pick the door and swing. Press Enter.

    E. In the Objects area, select the radio button for Delete.

    F. Click OK. The door and swing disappear.

4. Start the Insert command and insert the door2_6 block into the bedroom doorway opening. Follow the steps carefully. Here's a summary of the steps:

    A. Start the Insert command.

    B. Open the Name drop-down list and select door2_6, and then click OK.

    C. Pick the left end of the lower jamb line.

    D. Accept the default of 1 for the X scale factor.

    E. Accept the default of <use X> for the Y scale factor.

    F. Enter **90** and press Enter for the rotation.

5. Erase the bedroom door, and then restart the Insert command and insert the door2_6 block into the bedroom door opening. Here are the parameters:

    ▶ Specify On-screen checked for Insertion Point, Scale, and Rotation

    ▶ Insertion Point: left endpoint of upper jamb line

    ▶ X Scale Factor: -1

    ▶ Y Scale Factor: 1

    ▶ Rotation: 90

6. Zoom Previous (Figure 9.9).

This view looks the same as the view you started with at the beginning of this chapter—see Figure 9.1. Blocks look the same as other objects and can't be detected by viewing only. Their usefulness comes from your being able to use them over and over again in a drawing or many drawings, and in the fact that the block is a grouping of two or more (and sometimes many more) objects together into a single object. The next section will discuss how you can detect a block.

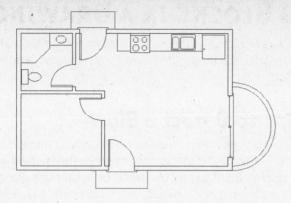

FIGURE 9.9: The floor plan with all swinging doors converted into blocks

THE FATE OF OBJECTS USED TO MAKE A BLOCK

The three radio buttons in the Objects area of the Block Definition dialog box represent the options you have for objects transformed into a block:

Retain   The objects remain unblocked. Use this option if you want to make several similar blocks from the same set of objects.

Convert to Block   The objects become a block reference. Use this option if the first use of the block has geometry identical to that of the set of objects it is replacing.

Delete   The objects are automatically erased after the block has been defined. Use this option if the first use of the block will be at a different scale, orientation, or location from the set of objects it is replacing.

When you made the first door block, you could have used the Convert to Block option because the door3_o block replaced the front door and its swing. I decided not to have you use this option so I could show you the insertion process with default X and Y scale factors and rotation.

Finding Blocks in a Drawing

You can detect blocks in a drawing three ways: with grips, with the List command, or with the Properties button. Each method is detailed in the following sections.

Using Grips to Detect a Block

Grips appear on objects that are selected when no command is started. When you select an object that is not a block in this manner, grips appear at strategic places. But if you select a block, by default only one grip appears, and it's always located at the block's insertion point. As a result, clicking on an object when no command is started is a quick way to see if the object is a block.

1. At the Command: prompt, click one of the door swings. The door and swing ghost, and a colored square appears at the hinge point.

2. Press Esc to clear the grip.

3. Click Tools ➤ Options and then click the Selection tab. The Grips area is in the upper-right corner. Enable Grips within Blocks is unchecked by default. If it is checked, when you click on a block with no command running, grips appear on all objects in the block as if they weren't blocked. Leave this setting unchecked.

4. Click OK to close the Options dialog box.

You may need to know more about a block than just whether something is one. If that is the case, you will need to use the List command.

Using the List Command to Detect a Block

You can also find blocks in a drawing by using the List command.

1. Click Tools ➤ Inquiry ➤ List.

2. Click the bedroom door block and then press Enter. The AutoCAD Text Window temporarily covers the drawing (Figure 9.10). In the text window, you can see the words BLOCK REFERENCE Layer: "Doors", followed by eight lines of text. These nine lines describe the block you selected.

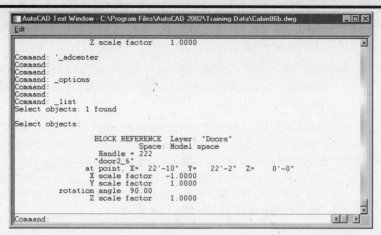

FIGURE 9.10: The AutoCAD text window

NOTE

Each time you use the List command and select an object, the text screen will display information that is tailored to the kind of object selected.

Some of the information stored here about the selected object is as follows:

- ▶ What the object is (Block Reference)
- ▶ The layer the object is on (Doors layer)
- ▶ The name of the block (door2_6)
- ▶ The coordinates of the insertion point in the drawing
- ▶ The X and Y scale factors
- ▶ The rotation angle

3. Press F2. The drawing area returns.

TIP

The F2 key toggles the text screen on and off.

4. Right-click and select Restart List from the top of the short-cut menu that appears.

5. At the Select objects: prompt, click one of the arcs that represent the balcony, and then click one of the wall lines and press Enter.

6. The text screen comes up again, and you see information about the arc that you selected, followed by information about the selected wall line.

7. Press F2, and then slowly press it a few more times. As you switch back and forth between the text screen and the drawing, notice that the last three lines on the text screen are the three lines of text in the Command window of the drawing. The Command window is displaying a strip of text from the text screen, usually the last three lines.

8. Press F2 to display the drawing.

Using the Properties Dialog Box to Detect a Block

When the Properties command is started and only one object is selected, the Properties dialog box will display data specific to the selected object.

1. Click one of the door blocks.

2. Click the Properties button on the Object Properties toolbar. The Properties dialog box appears. If the Categorized tab is not on top, click it.

The data displayed in the dialog box is similar to that displayed when you used the List Command, but in slightly different form (Figure 9.11). At the top of the dialog box, a drop-down list displays the type of object selected—in this case, a Block Reference.

NOTE

Block insertion means the same thing as block reference, and they are both casually called "blocks."

3. Close the Properties dialog box by clicking the X in the upper-right corner. Press Esc to remove the grip on the door block.

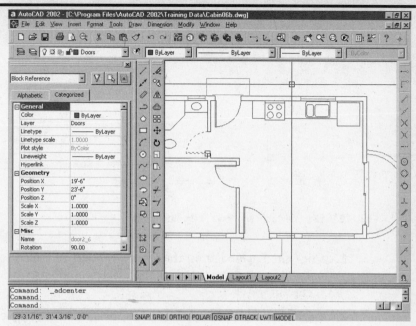

FIGURE 9.11: The Properties dialog box

NOTE

The Properties window may be docked or floating. The window illustrated in Figure 9.11 is in docked mode.

If you are ever working on a drawing that you did not draw, these tools for finding out about objects will be invaluable. The next exercise on working with blocks will involve the placement of windows in the walls of the cabin.

CREATING A WINDOW BLOCK

You can create the windows in the cabin floor plan from one block, even though they are four different sizes (Figure 9.12). You'll create a window block, and then go from room to room to insert the block into the walls.

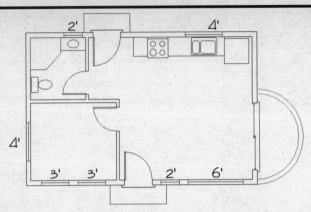

FIGURE 9.12: The cabin windows in the floor plan

1. Click the Layers list on the Object Properties toolbar to open the drop-down list. Click the 0 layer in the list to make it current.

2. Right-click on the Osnap button on the status bar and pick Settings from the shortcut menu. Add check marks to Midpoint and Perpendicular Osnaps. Click OK.

3. Zoom in to a horizontal section of wall where there are no jamb lines or intersections with other walls by clicking the Zoom Window button on the Standard toolbar and picking two points to be opposite corners of the zoom window. Because the widths of the windows in the cabin are multiples of 12", you can insert a block made from a 12"-wide window for each window and apply an X scale factor to the block to make it the right width. The first step is to draw a 12"-wide window inside the wall lines.

4. Start the Line command. Pick the Nearest Osnap button from the Object Snap toolbar or the Osnap flyout on the Standard toolbar. The Nearest Osnap will allow you to start a line on one of the wall lines. It finds the point on the wall line nearest to the point you pick.

5. Move the cursor to the upper wall line, a little to the left of the center of the screen and, with the hourglass symbol still displayed, click. A line begins.

6. Move the cursor to the lower wall line. A colored perpendicular icon will appear directly below the point you previously picked. When it is displayed, click. The line is drawn between the wall lines. Press Enter to end the Line command.

7. Start the Offset command. Type **12** and press Enter to set the offset distance to 12". Pick the line you just drew, and then pick a point to the right of that line. The line is offset 12" to the right. Press Enter to end the Offset command.

8. Start the Line command again. Move the cursor near the midpoint of the line you first drew. When the midpoint symbol appears, click. Move the cursor near the midpoint of the line that was just offset. When the Perpendicular or Midpoint symbol appears, click. Press Enter to end the Line command. Your drawing should look like Figure 9.13.

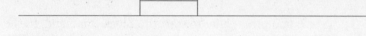

FIGURE 9.13: Completed lines for the window block

The three lines you've drawn will make up a window block. They represent the two jamb lines and the glass (usually called *glazing*). When you insert the block, by varying the X scale factor from 2 to 6, you will be able to create windows 2', 3', 4', and 6' wide.

Before you create the block, you need to decide the best place for the insertion point. For the doors, you chose the hinge point because you always know where it will be in the drawing. Locating a similar strategic point for the window is a little more difficult, but certainly possible. You know the insertion point can't be on the horizontal line representing the glazing, because it will always rest in the middle of the wall, and there is no guideline in the drawing for the middle of the wall. Windows are usually dimensioned to the midpoint of the glazing line rather than to either jamb line, so you don't want the insertion point to be at the endpoint of a jamb line. The insertion point will need to be positioned on a wall line but also lined up with the midpoint of the glazing line.

To locate this point, draw a guideline from the midpoint of the glazing line straight to one of the wall lines.

1. Press Enter to restart the Line command. Move to a point near the midpoint of the glazing line. When the Midpoint symbol appears, click.

2. Move to the bottom wall line. When the Perpendicular symbol appears, click. A guideline is drawn from the midpoint of the glazing line that is perpendicular to the lower wall line (Figure 9.14). The lower endpoint of this line is the location of the window block insertion point. Press Enter to end the Line command. Now you are ready to define the window block.

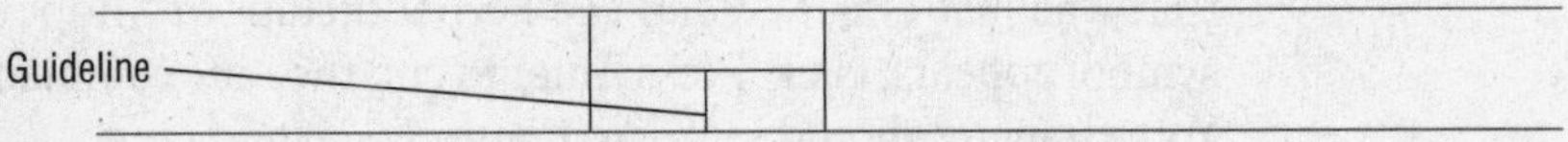

Guideline

FIGURE 9.14: The guideline is completed.

3. Type **b** and press Enter to start the Block command. In the dialog box, type **win-1** for the block name. Click the Pick Point button.

4. Back in the drawing, with Endpoint, Midpoint, and Perpendicular Osnaps running, move the cursor to the lower end of the guideline you just drew. When the Endpoint symbol appears at that location, click.

5. In the dialog box, click the Select Objects button.

6. Back in the drawing, select the two jamb lines and the glazing line, but don't select the guideline whose endpoint locates the insertion point. Press Enter.

7. Back in the dialog box, click the radio button next to Delete. Click OK. The win-1 block has been defined, and the 12" window has been erased.

8. Erase the guideline with the Erase command.

9. Zoom Previous to zoom out to a view of the whole floor plan.

This completes the definition of the block that will represent the windows. The next task is to insert the win-1 block where the windows will be located.

INSERTING THE WINDOW BLOCK

Several factors come into play when you're deciding where to locate windows in a floor plan:

- ▶ The structure of the building
- ▶ The appearance of windows from outside the building
- ▶ The appearance of windows from inside a room
- ▶ The location of fixtures that may interfere with placement
- ▶ The sun angle and climate considerations

For this exercise, you will work on the windows for each room, starting with the bedroom.

Rotating a Block during Insertion

The bedroom has windows on two walls: two 3' windows centered in the front wall 12" apart, and one 4' window centered in the left wall. You'll make the 4' window first.

1. Use a zoom window to zoom in to the bedroom. Click the Polar button on the status bar to turn on Polar tracking. Polar, Osnap, and Model should now be in the On position.

2. Create a new layer by clicking the Layer button and then clicking the New button in the Layer Properties Manager dialog box. Layer1 will appear and be highlighted. Type **Windows** and press Enter to rename Layer1.

3. Click the color square in the Windows row. When the Select Color dialog box comes up, White will be highlighted in the Color text box. Type **30** and press Enter to change the color to a bright orange. (If you don't have 256 colors available, choose any color.) The Select Color dialog box will close.

4. With Windows still highlighted in the Layers Properties Manager dialog box, click the Current button to make the Windows layer current. Click OK. You are returned to your drawing, and Windows is the current layer.

5. Start the Insert command (it's on the Draw toolbar). Open the Name drop-down list in the Insert dialog box. In the list

of blocks, click win-1. Be sure all three of the Specify On-screen check boxes are selected, and then click OK.

6. In your drawing, the 12" window block is attached to the cursor at the insertion point (Figure 9.15). Note that it is still in the same horizontal orientation that it was in when you defined the block. To fit it into the left wall, you will need to rotate it as you insert it.

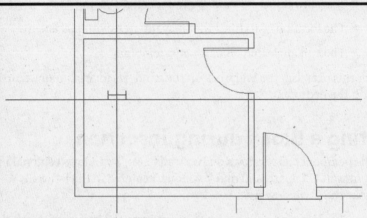

FIGURE 9.15: The win-1 block attached to the cursor

7. Move the cursor near the midpoint of the left inside wall line. When a colored triangle appears at the midpoint of that wall line, click.

8. You will be prompted for an X scale factor. This is a 4' window, so type **4** and press Enter. For the Y scale factor, type **1** and press Enter.

NOTE

The Y scale factor will be 1 for all the win-1 blocks because all walls that have windows are 6" wide—the same width as the win-1 block.

9. You are prompted for the rotation angle. The window block is now 4' wide and rotates with movement of the cursor. Move the cursor so that it's directly to the right of the insertion

point. The Polar tracking lines and ToolTip appear (Figure 9.16a). They will show you how the window will be positioned if the rotation stays at 0°. Obviously, you don't want this positioning.

10. Move the cursor so that it is directly above the insertion point. Another tracking line and ToolTip appear. They shows what position a 90° rotation will result in (Figure 9.16b). The window fits nicely into the wall here.

11. With the tracking line and ToolTip visible, click. The win-1 block is placed in the left wall. The Insert command ends.

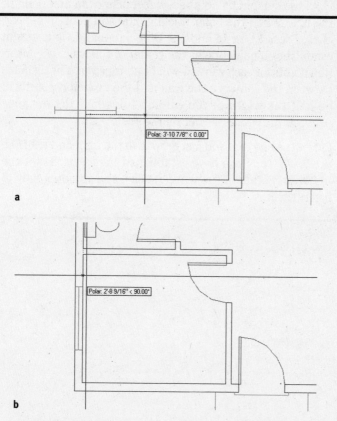

FIGURE 9.16: Rotating the win-1 block 0° (a) and 90° (b)

Using Guidelines When Inserting a Block

The pair of windows in the front wall of the bedroom are 3' wide, 12" apart, and centered horizontally in the bedroom wall (refer to Figure 9.12). You can use a guideline to locate the insertion points for these two windows.

1. Start the Line command and locate the cursor on the inside, horizontal exterior wall line near its midpoint. When the colored triangle appears at the midpoint of this line, click. A line starts.

2. Hold the cursor at a point a few feet below the first point of the line. When the Polar tracking line and ToolTip appear, click. Press Enter to end the Line command. This action establishes a guideline at the center of the wall. The insertion points for each window will be at its center. The distance between the center of the wall and the insertion point will be half the width of the window, plus half the distance between the windows—in other words, 2 feet.

3. Offset the line that you just drew 2' to the right and left (Figure 9.17). Now you have established the locations for the insertion points of the win-1 blocks, and you are ready to insert them.

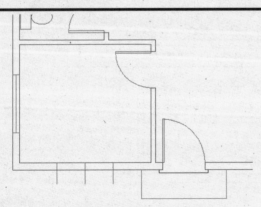

FIGURE 9.17: Guidelines for the pair of window blocks

4. Select the Insert button on the Draw toolbar to start the Insert command. In the Insert dialog box, the win-1 block will still be displayed in the Name drop-down list because it was the last block inserted. Click OK.

5. Back in the drawing, the win-1 block is again attached to the cursor. To locate the insertion point, you can choose the upper endpoint of one of the outer guidelines, or the intersection of this guideline with the exterior outside wall line. Which one would be better? The second choice requires no rotation of the block, so it's easier and faster to use that intersection.

6. Pick the Intersection Osnap button from the Object Snap toolbar and position the cursor on the outside wall (Figure 9.18a). A colored x appears with three dots to its right, along with a ToolTip that says "Extended Intersection." Click. Hold the crosshair cursor on the lower portion of the left-most offset guideline, again without touching any other lines. The x will appear, this time at the intersection of this guideline with the outside wall line and without the three dots. The ToolTip now says "Intersection" (Figure 9.18b). Click again. The insertion point is set at the intersection of the guideline and the outside wall line.

7. Type **3** and press Enter for the X scale factor, and then type **1** and press Enter for the Y scale factor. At the rotation angle prompt, press Enter to accept the default of 0°. The 3' window on the left is inserted in the front wall.

8. Repeat this procedure for the other 3' window.

9. Erase the three guidelines.

Because you chose to locate the insertion point on the lower of the two wall lines, the block needed no rotation.

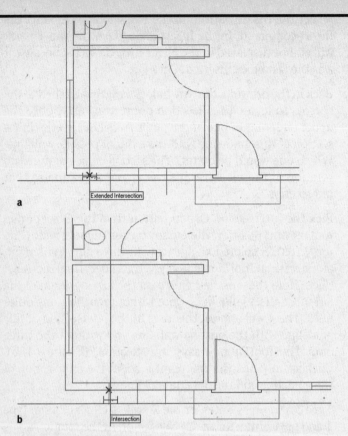

a

Extended Intersection

b

Intersection

FIGURE 9.18: Selecting the first line (a), and the second (b)

Using Tracking to Insert a Block

The next room to work on is the bathroom, which has one small window over the sink.

1. Click the Pan button on the Standard toolbar. The cursor changes to a hand.

2. Position the hand on the wall between the bedroom and bathroom, and then hold down the left mouse button and drag the drawing down. When the bathroom is in the middle of the drawing area, release the mouse button. Press Esc or Enter to cancel the Pan command. You want to create one 2' window,

centered over the sink. This time you'll insert the block without the use of guidelines. Endpoint Osnap should be running.

3. Start the Insert command, be sure win-1 is in the Name drop-down list, and check that all Specify On-screen check boxes are marked. Click OK and, at the `Specify insertion point:` prompt, click the Temporary Tracking Point button on the Object Snap toolbar.

4. Position the crosshair cursor on the line representing the front edge of the sink counter. A colored triangle will appear at the midpoint of that line. When it does, click—you have set a temporary tracking point, and a cross appears at that point.

5. Move the cursor to the lower outside wall line, just in back of the sink. When the colored Perpendicular symbol appears on the line, click. The insertion point has been placed on the inside wall line, centered over the sink.

6. At the X scale factor prompt, type **2** and press Enter. At the Y scale factor prompt, type **1** and press Enter. Press Enter again to accept the default rotation angle of 0°. The 2' window is inserted into the wall behind the sink.

Note that no mark is left at the insertion point location on the wall. You have to wait until the insertion process is over to see if everything has been done correctly. When I walk you through the next insertion, you'll learn how to change a setting so that AutoCAD will leave a mark.

Using Blips with Point Filters to Insert Blocks

You're more than half done with the windows. Just three remain to be inserted: one in the kitchen and two in the living room.

1. Click the Pan button on the Standard toolbar. Position the hand cursor on the back door swing. Hold down the left mouse button and drag the drawing to the left until the kitchen is in the middle of the drawing area. Release the mouse button. Press Esc or Enter to cancel the Real Time Pan.

2. Zoom in to the sink area. Type **blipmode** and press Enter, and then type **on** and press Enter. The Blipmode feature is activated.

3. You need to insert a 4' window in the back wall, centered behind the sink. Start the Insert command. Click OK when the Insert dialog box comes up. The win-1 block appears on the cursor.

4. At the Specify insertion point: prompt, type **.x** and press Enter to activate the point filters. You need to pick the midpoint of the back or front edge of the sink. Because the front edge is more accessible, select it.

NOTE

Point filters allow you to locate a point by picking two points: one having the x coordinate you want, and the other having the y coordinate you want. This feature sounds confusing, but it will become clearer once you use it.

5. Put the target box on the front edge of the sink. When the colored triangle appears on the front edge, click. A small + is placed at the midpoint of the front edge of the sink (Figure 9.19a). It is called a *blip* or a *blipmark*.

6. Position the target box on the inside wall line of the back wall where it's not touching any other lines. Because Endpoint Osnap is running, a colored square should show up at one of the endpoints of this wall line. When it does, click. The + is placed at the endpoint of the wall line and at a position on the wall line directly behind the midpoint of the sink's back edge (Figure 9.19b). This blip assures you that the point filters successfully set the insertion point exactly where you need it.

7. Type **4** and press Enter for the X scale factor. Type **1** and press Enter for the Y scale factor. For the rotation angle, press Enter again to accept the default angle of 0°. The window is placed in the back wall, centered behind the sink.

8. Zoom Previous.

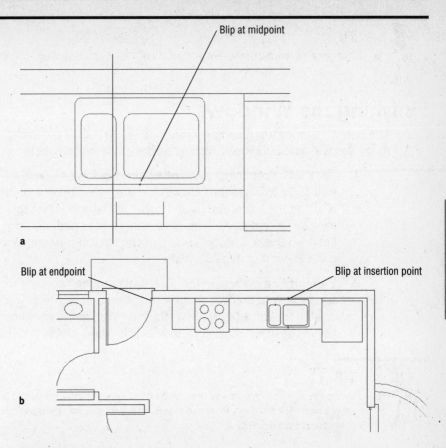

FIGURE 9.19: A blip marks the midpoint of the front edge of the sink (a), and the resulting insertion point location (b)

When Blipmode is on, a + is placed wherever you pick a point in the drawing area, whether you are drawing or selecting objects. These are temporary markers and are not saved with the drawing file, nor do they show up in printouts. As they accumulate, you can delete them by typing **r** and pressing Enter at the Command: prompt, or with any use of the Zoom or Pan commands.

Using blips is up to you. Some people find them irritating and would rather not see them. Others find them useful because they are a record of what you've done, as you just saw when placing an insertion point. Let's leave them visible through the next two sections so you can see how you feel about them.

TIP

You can also redraw the screen and get rid of blips by picking View ➤ Redraw.

Finishing the Windows

The last two windows to insert are both in the front wall of the living room. You will use skills you've already worked with to place them.

1. Use the Pan command to move the drawing down to the front wall of the living room. One window is 6' wide. Its right jamb is 12" to the left of the inside corner of the wall. The other window is circular, 2' in diameter, positioned halfway between the 6' window jamb and the front doorjamb. We don't know that distance yet.

2. Turn off Perpendicular and Midpoint running osnaps. (To review how to do this, go back to the section in which you created the win-1 block.) Start the Insert command and click OK in the Insert dialog box to select the win-1 block.

TIP

To change any object snaps so they aren't running, right-click on Osnap in the status bar, pick Settings from the menu, and uncheck any osnaps that are checked. Then, click OK.

3. Select the Temporary Tracking Point Osnap button. With Endpoint Osnap running, pick the lower-right inside corner of the cabin. The insertion point will be positioned to the left of this corner at a distance of 12" in plus half the width of the 6' window—in other words, 4' from the corner.

4. Hold the crosshair cursor directly to the left of the point you just picked. When the tracking path and ToolTip appear, type **4'** and press Enter. Doing so sets the insertion point 4' to the left of the corner, on the inside wall line. A blip appears there.

5. For the scale factors, type **6** and press Enter, and then type **1** and press Enter.

6. For the rotation angle, hold the cursor directly to the right of the insertion point to see the position of the window at 0°

rotation. Then, hold the cursor directly above the insertion point to see how a 90° rotation would look. Finally, hold the cursor directly to the left for a view of the effect of a 180° rotation. The 180-degree view is the one you want.

7. Type **180** and press Enter. The 6' window is placed in the front wall.

Finally, you need to locate the 2' circular window halfway between the left jamb of the 6' window and the right jamb of the front door opening. Use the Distance command to find out the distance between the two jambs. Then, offset one of the jambs half that distance to establish the location of the insertion point on the wall lines. Of the two jamb lines, you must offset the doorjamb because the window jamb is part of the window block and can't be offset.

1. Type **di** and press Enter to start the Distance command. With Endpoint Osnap running, pick the upper end of the front doorjamb, and then pick the upper end of the left window jamb. In the Command window, the distance is displayed as 3'-10". You need to offset the doorjamb half that distance to locate the insertion point for the 2' window.

2. Start the Offset command. Type **1'-11** and press Enter to set the offset distance.

3. Pick the doorjamb, type **non**, and press Enter. Pick a point to the right of the doorjamb. Press Enter to end the Offset command.

TIP

Typing **non** (none) and pressing Enter cancels any running osnaps for one pick.

4. Start the Insert command. Click OK to accept the win-1 block. Pick the bottom endpoint of the offset jamb line to establish the insertion point.

5. Type **2** and press Enter for the X scale factor. Type **1** and press Enter for the Y scale factor.

6. For the rotation angle, press Enter to accept the default of 0°. The last window is inserted in the front wall, and the Insert command ends. Erase the offset jamb line.

NOTE

Notice how blips have been appearing on and near the wall as you've been working.

7. Type **r** and press Enter to use the Redraw command to refresh the screen. The blips disappear.

8. Type **z**, press Enter, type **e**, and press Enter again to zoom out to the Extents view of the drawing. Doing so changes the view to include all the visible lines. The view fills the drawing area.

NOTE

Zooming to *Extents* is one of the zoom options. It is the bottom button of the Zoom flyout on the Standard toolbar.

9. Type **z**, press Enter, type **.85x**, and press Enter again to zoom out a little from the Extents view, so all objects are set in slightly from the edge of the drawing area (Figure 9.20).

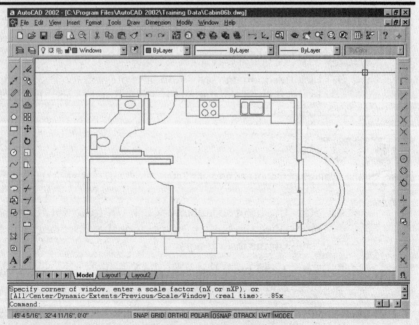

FIGURE 9.20: Zooming to .85× after zooming to Extents

10. Save this drawing as Cabin07a.

You have inserted seven windows into the floor plan, each of them generated from the win-1 block. You created the win-1 block on the 0 layer and then made the Windows layer current, so each window block reference took on the characteristics of the Windows layer when it was inserted.

You can ungroup blocks by using the Explode command. Exploding a block has the effect of reducing the block to the objects that make it up. For the win-1 block, exploding it would reduce it to three lines, all on the 0 layer. If you exploded one of the door blocks, it would be reduced to a rectangle and an arc, with both objects on the Doors layer because these components of the door block were on the Doors layer when the block was defined.

REVISING A BLOCK

If you need to revise a block that has already been inserted several times, you will need to modify one of the block references that you inserted with the X and Y scale factors both set to 1 and the rotation at 0. All the windows were inserted using different X and Y scale factors, so to revise the win-1 block, you'll need to insert that block one more time, this time using default scale factors and rotation. Then, you can make changes to the objects that make up the win-1 block reference. When you're finished with the changes, you can save the changes to the block definition. Doing so redefines the block and updates all associated block references.

Let's say that the client who's building the cabin finds out that double-glazing is required in all windows. You want the windows to show two lines for the glass. You can't make such a change in each window block because blocks can't be modified this way, and you don't want to have to change seven windows separately. If you revise the win-1 block definition, the changes you make in one block reference will be made in all seven windows.

NOTE

Using standard commands, blocks can be moved, rotated, copied, erased, scaled, and exploded. They can't be trimmed, extended, offset, or filleted, and you can't erase or move part of a block. All objects in a block are grouped together and behave as if they were one object.

Part ii

1. Start the Insert command and click OK to accept the win-1 block to be inserted.

2. Pick a point in the middle of the living room to establish the insertion point location.

3. Press Enter three times to accept the defaults for the X and Y scale factors and the rotation angle. The win-1 block is inserted in the living room (Figure 9.21).

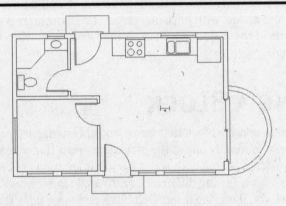

FIGURE 9.21: The win-1 block inserted into the living room

4. Zoom in to a closer view of the window. Click Modify ➤ In-place Xref and Block Edit ➤ Edit reference.

5. Select the new block reference in the middle of the living room. The Reference Edit dialog box comes up. The win-1 block is identified and a preview is displayed.

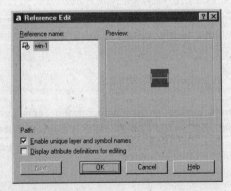

6. Click OK. You are prompted to select nested objects.

7. Select the glazing line in the win-1 block, and then press Enter. The glazing line turns white (or black), and the Refedit toolbar appears.

8. Use the Offset command to offset the glazing line 0.5" up and down. Erase the original horizontal line (Figure 9.22). This window block now has double-glazing.

FIGURE 9.22: The result of the modifications to the win-1 block

9. On the Refedit toolbar, click the right-most button, whose ToolTip says "Save back changes to reference."

10. An AutoCAD warning window appears. Click OK. The glazing lines change back to orange, the Refedit toolbar disappears, and the blips are deleted. The block definition has been revised.

11. Erase this block reference; you don't need it anymore.

12. Zoom Previous to view the entire drawing. All windows in the cabin now have double-glazing.

13. Zoom in to a closer look at the bedroom in order to view some of the modified window block references.

14. This is a good time to turn off the blips if you find them more of a nuisance than an aid. To turn them off, type **blipmode** and press Enter, and then type **off** and press Enter.

15. Zoom Previous to a view of the entire floor plan. Save this drawing as Cabin07b.

SHARING INFORMATION BETWEEN DRAWINGS

Most information in a drawing can be transferred to another drawing. You can do this several ways, depending on the kind of information you need to transfer. Blocks and lines can be dragged from one open drawing to another when both drawings are visible on the screen. Layers, blocks, and other *named objects* can be copied out of a closed drawing into an open one using the Design Center. You'll use these two features as we end this chapter.

NOTE

Named objects are, quite simply, AutoCAD objects with names, like blocks and layers. Lines, circles, and arcs don't have individual names, so they are not named objects.

Dragging and Dropping Between Two Open Drawings

AutoCAD is capable of supporting several drawings open at the same time, just like a word processor. You can control which one is visible, or tile two or more to be visible simultaneously. When more than one drawing is visible at once, you can drag objects from one drawing to another.

NOTE

Like most Windows-based programs, AutoCAD 2002 can have multiple drawing files open in a session. When you open the Window menu, the bottom of the menu contains a list of AutoCAD files currently open. Click the file you want to be the current one.

1. With Cabin07b as the current drawing, click the New button on the Standard toolbar. In the Create New Drawing dialog box, click the Start from Scratch button and click OK.

2. Click Window ➤ Tile Vertically. The new drawing (called Drawing1) appears alongside Cabin07b (Figure 9.23).

Each drawing has a title bar, but only one drawing can be active at a time. At this time, Drawing1 should be active. If it is, its title bar will be dark blue or some other color, and the Cabin07b title bar will be grayed out. If your Cabin07b drawing is active instead, click once in Drawing1.

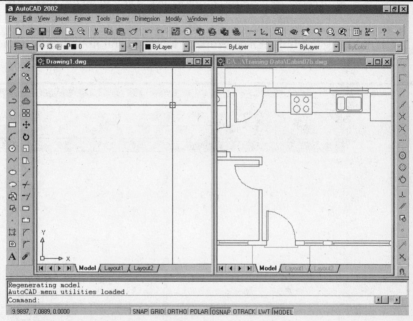

FIGURE 9.23: The user interface with two drawings tiled

3. Click Format ➤ Units. In the Drawing Units dialog box, change the type of units in the Length area to Architectural, and then click OK.

4. Click in the Cabin07b drawing to make it the active drawing.

5. Zoom to Extents, and then use Realtime Zoom to zoom out a little.

6. Use the Layer Control drop down list to turn off the Doors, Fixtures, Steps, and Windows layers, and to make the Walls layer current. The walls and balcony should be the only lines visible.

7. Form a selection window to surround the cabin with its balcony. Grips will appear on all lines.

8. Place the cursor on one of the wall lines at a point where there are no grips, and then click and hold down the left mouse button. Drag the cursor across the drawing to the center of Drawing1, and then release the mouse button. Drawing1 is now active and contains the lines for the walls and balcony.

9. Zoom to Extents in Drawing1. Type **ucsicon**, press Enter, type **off**, and press Enter again (Figure 9.24).

10. Open the Layer Property Manager and note that Drawing1 now has the Walls and Balcony layers.

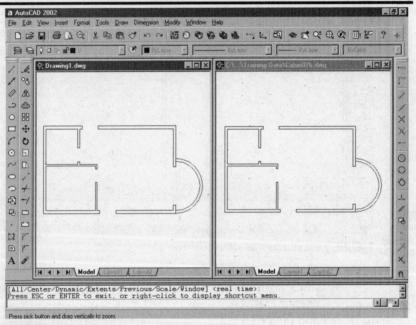

FIGURE 9.24: The result after dragging lines from one drawing to another.

Any visible objects can be dragged in this fashion from one drawing into another, including blocks. If you drag and drop a block, its definition will be copied over to the new drawing, along with all layers used by objects in the block. If you use the right mouse button to make the drag, you get a few options as to how to place the objects in the receiving drawing.

If you don't choose to have both open drawings visible at the same time, you can always use the Copy and Paste tools available on most Windows-based programs. Here's the general procedure:

1. Click the Maximize icon in the upper-right corner of the new drawing. The new drawing will fill the screen.

2. Click Window in the pull-down menu bar. When the menu opens, notice at the bottom that the open drawings are displayed with the active one checked.

3. Click the Cabin07b drawing. It replaces Drawing1 as the active drawing and fills the screen. Turn back on the layers you turned off previously. Leave the Headers and Roof layers frozen.

4. Select objects from this drawing and right-click. In the menu that appears, select Copy or Copy with Base Point. If you choose Copy with Base Point, you will be prompted to specify a base point in the Cabin07b drawing.

5. Click Window in the pull-down menu bar. When the menu opens, click Drawing1 to make it active.

6. Click the Paste button on the Standard toolbar. Pick a point in the drawing to locate the copied objects.

Using AutoCAD's Design Center

The Design Center is a very simple yet powerful tool. Its function is to find named objects (blocks, layers, text styles, and so on) from unopened drawings that you have access to and retrieve them into your current drawing. These drawings may be located on your hard drive, on a network, or on the Internet. Lines, circles, and other unnamed objects cannot be copied unless they are part of a block. At the top of the Design Center window, the buttons on the left are tools for navigating through drives and folders to find the files you need to access; the buttons on the right give you options for viewing the named objects in the window.

DESIGN CENTER OPTIONS

Here's a brief description of the functions of the Design Center buttons, from left to right:

Desktop makes the left window display the regular Windows Explorer–type file tree that can include drive, folder, subfolders, drawing files, and object types.

Open Drawings displays a list of currently open drawings and will show object types.

History displays a list of the last few drawings that were opened, along with their paths. When this list is open, the viewing palette window on the right is temporarily closed.

Tree View Toggle opens or shuts the left window and controls the visibility of the three previous buttons.

Favorites displays the list of favorite files and folders you have previously set up.

Load opens a file selection dialog box where you can navigate to a drawing whose contents you wish to view.

Find opens the Find dialog box where you can search for a particular file.

Up moves up one level in the tree from the highlighted item in the left window.

Preview enables a preview window at the bottom of the right palette window. When you highlight a drawing or block in the palette window, a preview is displayed. The preview window may be resized.

Description enables a previously written description of a block or drawing to be displayed. The description window may be resized.

Views controls how the item in the palette window are displayed. There are four choices. Each click on this button toggles from one type of view to another. When you click the arrow to the right, the list of four options is displayed.

You'll demonstrate the Design Center feature by bringing some layers and a block into Drawing1 from Cabin07b.

1. Close Cabin07b. Do not save changes. Maximize the window for Drawing1 if it is not already maximized.

2. Click the Design Center button on the Standard toolbar. (It's just to the left of the Properties button.) The Design Center appears on the drawing area. It may be docked or floating (Figure 9.25). Your screen may not look exactly like the samples shown here; the tree diagram of file folders on the left half may or may not be visible, and your Design Center may be wider or narrower.

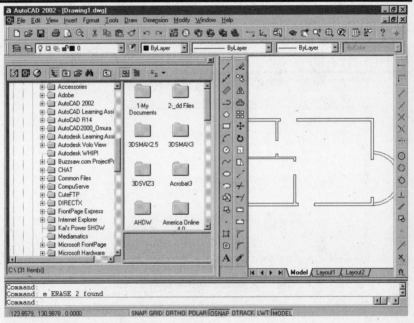

FIGURE 9.25: The Design Center docked

3. Click the Tree View Toggle at the top of the Design Center to close and open the file folder tree diagram. Notice that when it's open, more buttons are visible at the top on the left. The Design Center can be resized horizontally (and vertically as well, if it is floating). Leave the Tree View open.

4. Use the same procedure you would in Windows Explorer to navigate to the AutoCAD 2002 folder, open it, and click your Training Data folder to open it (Figure 9.26a). If yours is stored somewhere else, navigate to its location and click it to

open it. On the right side of the Design Center, the drawings in your Training Data folder are displayed, either in icon or listed form.

5. On the right side, find `Cabin07b` and double-click on it. Now the left side displays a list of your drawings in the Training Data folder with `Cabin07b` highlighted, and the right side shows the types of objects in `Cabin07b` that are available to be copied into the current drawing—in this case, `Drawing1` (Figure 9.26b).

6. Double-click on the Layers symbol. Now the individual layers are displayed in the right side and a list of available types of objects is displayed on the left, under `Cabin07b` (Figure 9.26c).

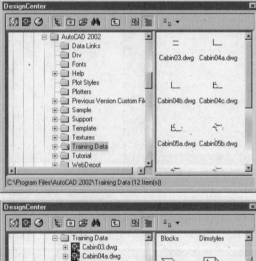

a

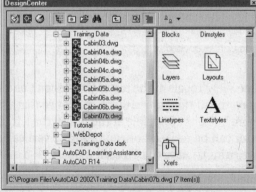

b

FIGURE 9.26: The Design Center displaying folders on the left and files on the right (a), files on the left and types of accessible objects on the right (b), and types of accessible objects on the left and actual accessible layers on the right (c)

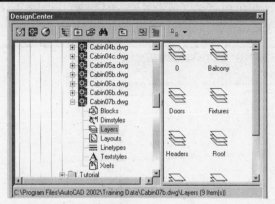

FIGURE 9.26 CONTINUED

c

7. Click the Views button above the right window of the Design Center to change the view of layers displayed below. It's a four-way toggle. Click until you get a view of the layers in a list.

8. Use the Shift+ and Ctrl+ keys to help you select all the layers except 0, Walls, and Balcony.

9. Right-click somewhere on the highlighted layers. Pick Add Layers from the shortcut menu that appears.

10. Open the Layer Control drop-down list on the Object Properties toolbar. It will now display all the layers of the Cabin07b drawing, including those you just transferred.

TIP

If you prefer dragging and dropping, use the left mouse button, click and hold, drag the cursor onto the drawing, and then release.

Now let's see how this process works when you want to get a block from another drawing.

1. On the left side of the Design Center, click Blocks in the list under the Cabin07b drawing. On the right side, the list of blocks in that drawing is displayed (Figure 9.27a).

2. Click on the Preview button at the top of the Design Center, and then click on door3_0. A picture of the block is displayed

in the lower-right corner of the Design Center (Figure 9.27b). The preview picture window can be resized.

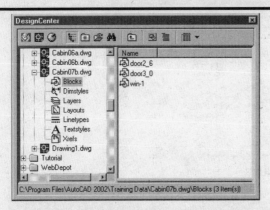

a

b

FIGURE 9.27: The Design Center with Blocks selected (a) and with the door3_0 block selected and Preview on (b)

3. Open the Layer Control list and make Doors the current layer.

4. Dock the Design Center on the left side of the drawing area if it's not already there. Zoom in to the front door area of the drawing (Figure 9.28).

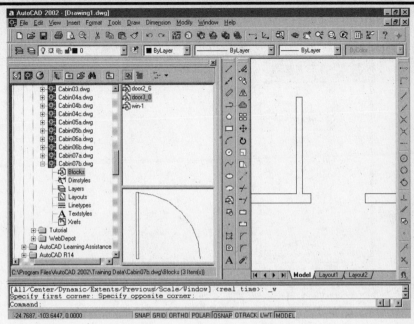

FIGURE 9.28: Zoomed in to the front door area with the Design Center docked

5. In the Design Center, left-click and drag door3_0 from the list to the drawing. As the cursor comes onto the drawing, the door3_0 block appears. Use Endpoint Osnap to locate the block at the opening, as you did earlier in the chapter (Figure 9.29).

6. Click the Close icon in the upper-right corner to close Design Center.

7. Keep Drawing1 open in case you want to use it in the practice exercises at the end of the chapter. Otherwise, close it without saving it.

By doing this insertion, the door3_0 block is now a part of Drawing1 and you can reinsert it in that drawing without using the Design Center.

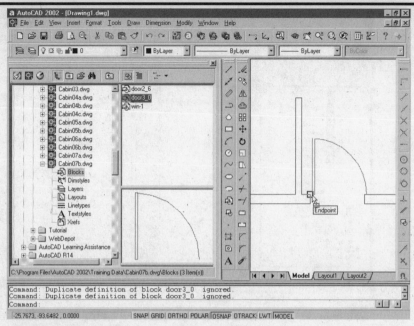

FIGURE 9.29: Dragging the door3_0 block into Drawing1 from the Design Center

Other Ways to Share Information Between Drawings

Two other ways to transfer information between drawings deserve mention. First, you can use the Wblock command to take a portion of a drawing and create a new drawing file from the selected objects. Second, any drawing file (.dwg) can be inserted into any other drawing file (.dwg). I'll summarize the two procedures in the following sections.

Wblocking

To perform a Wblock operation, you create a new file, and then tell Auto-CAD what elements of the current drawing you want in the new file. Let's say you want to create a new .dwg file for the bathroom of the cabin. Here are the steps to accomplish this task:

1. With Cabin07b as the current drawing, type **w** and press Enter. The Write Block dialog box comes up (Figure 9.30).

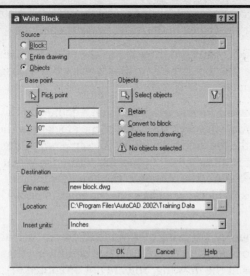

FIGURE 9.30: The Write Block dialog box

2. At the top, in the Source area, select the Objects radio button.

3. In the middle portion, the Base Point and Objects choices are similar to those for creating a block. For the Base Point, the default is 0,0. Click the Pick Point button and, in the drawing, pick a point just below and to the left of the area to be captured. For the Objects, click Select Objects and use a crossing window to select everything near the part of the drawing you want. For the radio button in this area, choose Retain so the selected material is not deleted from the current drawing.

NOTE

When you select with a crossing window here, you'll get more than you need, but you can clean up the new drawing later.

4. In the Destination area, enter a filename for the new drawing and choose a folder in which to save it.

5. The units in the Insert Units drop-down list should be set to Inches, in case the new drawing is used in a drawing that has units other than Architectural.

6. Click OK. The command ends and the selected material is now a new drawing file located in the folder that you specified.

You can use the Wblock command three ways. The other two are shown as radio buttons at the top of the Write Block dialog box. Here's a brief description of them:

Block makes a drawing file out of a block that's defined in the current drawing. You will select the name of the block from the drop-down list at the top, and then follow the same procedure described in steps 4 through 6 of the previous example. When you follow this procedure, the objects in the new drawing are no longer in a block. Wblocking a block has the effect of unblocking it.

Entire Drawing purges a drawing of unwanted objects such as layers that have no objects on them and block definitions that have no references in the drawing. You are not prompted to select anything except the information called for in steps 4 through 6 of the previous example. You can keep the same drawing name or type in a new one.

Inserting a Drawing into a Drawing

When you insert a drawing into another drawing, it comes in as a block. You use the same Insert command that you use to insert blocks, in a slightly different way. For example, say you have hypothetically Wblocked a portion of Cabin07b.dwg and made a new file called Bath.dwg. Now you want to insert Bath into DrawingC.dwg. Use this procedure:

1. Make DrawingC current.

2. Start the Insert command.

3. In the Insert dialog box, click the Browse button, and then navigate to the folder containing Bath.dwg.

4. Open that folder, highlight Bath.dwg, and click Open.

5. The Insert dialog box comes up again, this time with the drawing file that you selected displayed in the name drop-down list. At this point Bath has been converted into a block definition in DrawingC.

6. Set the insertion parameters in the dialog box and click OK.

7. Finish the insertion procedure as if you were inserting a block.

Blocks are transferred between drawings by dragging and dropping or by use of the Design Center. They can also be converted into .dwg files by use of the Wblock command, and inserted back into other .dwg files as blocks by use of the Insert command. They become unblocked when they leave the drawing and reblocked when they enter another drawing.

This chapter has outlined the procedure for setting up and using blocks, the Wblock command, and AutoCAD's Design Center. Blocks follow a set of complex rules, some of which are beyond the scope of this book.

IF YOU WANT MORE PRACTICE...

Here are a couple of suggestions that will give you practice working with blocks, drag-and-drop procedures, and the Design Center:

▶ Use the Design Center to bring the door2_6 and win_1 blocks into Drawing1. Position the win-1 blocks into new locations in the walls of this drawing. Then, open Cabin07b and drag and drop the kitchen and bathroom fixtures into Drawing1.

▶ Make blocks out of any of the fixtures in the bathroom or kitchen. Try to decide on the best location to use for the insertion point of each fixture. Then, insert them back into the Cabin07b drawing in their original locations. Create them on the 0 layer, and then insert them on the Fixtures layer. Here's a list of the fixtures:

1. Shower

2. Bath sink

3. Toilet

4. Oven/Range

5. Kitchen sink

6. Refrigerator

Part ii

▶ If you have access to the sample files that come with AutoCAD 2002, use the Design Center to find the drawing called db_sam.dwg and view the blocks and layers inside it. Freeze the Doors layer in the cabin drawing, and then transfer some of the office furniture and door blocks into the cabin floor plan and see how the cabin might work as a small office.

What's Next?

In this chapter, you have learned how to create and instance blocks into drawings and how to share blocks among multiple drawings. In the next chapter, you will store and link data with graphics through the use of attributes.

Chapter 10

STORING AND LINKING DATA WITH GRAPHICS

*A**ttributes* are unique to computer-aided design and drafting; nothing quite like them exists in traditional drafting. As a result, they are often poorly understood. Attributes enable you to store information as text that you can later extract to use in database managers, spreadsheet programs, and word processors. By using attributes, you can keep track of virtually any object in a drawing, or maintain textual information within the drawing that can be queried.

Adapted from *Mastering™ AutoCAD® 2002* by George Omura

ISBN 0-7821-4015-7   1,392 pages $49.99

Keeping track of objects is just one way of using attributes. You can also use them in place of text objects in situations where you must enter the same text, with minor modifications, in many places in your drawing. For example, if you are drawing a schedule that contains several columns of information, you can use attributes to help simplify your data entry.

In this chapter, you will use attributes for one of their more common functions: maintaining lists of parts. In this case, the parts are doors. This chapter will also describe how to import these attributes into a database management program. As you go through these exercises, think about the ways attributes can help you in your particular application.

CREATING ATTRIBUTES

Attributes depend on blocks. You might think of an attribute as a tag attached to a block, where the tag contains information about the block. For example, you could have included an attribute definition with the door drawing you created in Chapter 3. If you had, then every time you subsequently inserted the door, you would have been prompted for a value associated with that door. The value could be a number, a height or width value, a name, or any type of text information you want. When you insert the block, you are prompted for an attribute value. Once you enter a value, it is stored as part of the block within the drawing database. This value can be displayed as text attached to the door, or it can be made invisible. The value can be changed at any time. You can even specify what the prompts say in asking you for the attribute value.

However, suppose you don't have the attribute information when you design the door. As an alternative, you can add the attribute to a *symbol* that is later placed by the door when you know enough about the design to specify what type of door goes where. The standard door type symbol suits this purpose nicely because it is an object that can be set up and used as a block independent of the actual door block.

TIP
A door type symbol is a graphic code used to indicate special characteristics of the associated door. The code refers to a note on another drawing or in a set of written specifications.

In the following exercises, you will create a door type symbol with attributes for the different values normally assigned to doors: size, thickness, fire rating, material, and construction.

Adding Attributes to Blocks

In this exercise, you will create a door type symbol, which is commonly used to describe the size, thickness, and other characteristics of any given door in an architectural drawing. The symbol is usually a circle, hexagon, or diamond, with a number in it. The number is usually cross-referenced to a schedule that lists all the door types and their characteristics.

Although in this exercise you will be creating a new file containing attribute definitions, you can also include such definitions in blocks you create using the Make Block tool (the Block command) or in files you create using the Wblock command. Just create the attribute definitions as shown here, and then include them with the Block or Wblock selections.

1. Create a new file and call it S-door (for symbol-door). The symbol will fit in the default limits of the drawing, so you don't have to change the limits setting.

TIP

Because this is a new drawing, the circle is automatically placed on Layer 0. Remember that objects in a block that are on Layer 0 take on the color and line-type assignment of the layer on which the block is inserted.

2. Draw a circle with a radius of 0.125 (0.3 for metric users) and with its center at coordinate 7,5.

3. Zoom in to the circle so it is about the same size as shown in Figure 10.1.

Part ii

FIGURE 10.1: The attribute inserted in the circle and the second attribute added

4. If the circle looks like an octagon, Choose View ➤ Regen, or type **Re** and press Enter to regenerate your drawing.

5. Choose Draw ➤ Block ➤ Define Attributes, or type **At** and press Enter. The Attribute Definition dialog box appears.

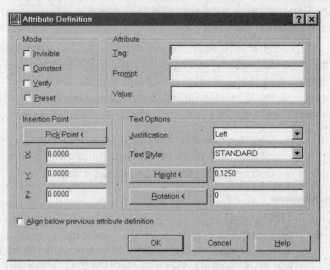

6. Click the input box labeled Tag in the Attribute group. Enter **d-type**.

TIP

The attribute tag is equivalent to a field name in a database; it can be up to 31 characters long but cannot contain spaces. If you plan to use the attribute data in a database program, check that program's manuals for other restrictions on field names.

7. Press the Tab key or click the input box labeled Prompt, and enter **Door type**. Here, you enter the text for the prompt that will appear when you insert the block containing this attribute. Often the prompt is the same as the tag, but it can be anything you like. Unlike the tag, the prompt can include spaces.

TIP

Use a prompt that gives explicit instructions so the user will know exactly what is expected. Consider including an example within the prompt. (Enclose the example in brackets to imitate the way AutoCAD prompts often display defaults.)

8. Click the input box labeled Value. This is where you enter a default value for the door type prompt. Enter a hyphen (-).

TIP

If an attribute is to contain a number that will later be used for making sorts in a database, use a default value such as 000 to indicate the number of digits required. The zeros may also serve to remind the user that values less than 100 must be preceded by a leading zero, as in 099.

9. Click the Justification pull-down list and highlight Middle. This option allows you to center the attribute on the circle's center. You'll notice several other options in the Text Options group. Because attributes appear as text, you can apply the same settings to them as you would to single-line text.

10. Double-click the input box next to the Height < button and enter **0.125**. (Metric users should enter **0.3**.) This setting makes the attribute text 0.125 inches (0.3 cm) high.

11. Check the box labeled Verify in the Mode group. This option instructs AutoCAD to verify any answers you give to the attribute prompts at insertion time. (You'll see later in this chapter how Verify works.)

12. Click the button labeled Pick Point < in the Insertion Point group. The dialog box closes momentarily to let you pick a location for the attribute.

13. Using the Center Osnap, pick the center of the circle. You need to place the cursor on the circle's circumference, not in the circle's center, to obtain the center using the Osnap. The Attribute Definition dialog box reappears.

14. Click OK. The attribute definition appears at the center of the circle (see Figure 10.1).

Part ii

You have just created your first attribute definition. The attribute definition displays its tag in all uppercase letters to help you identify it. When you later insert this file into another drawing, the tag turns into the value you assign to it when it is inserted. If you only want one attribute, you can stop here and save the file. The next section shows how you can quickly add several more attributes to your drawing.

Adding Attribute Specifications

Next, you will add a few more attribute definitions; but instead of using the Attribute Definition dialog box, you will make an arrayed copy of the first attribute, and then edit the attribute definition copies. This method can save you time when you want to create several attribute definitions that have similar characteristics. By making copies and editing them, you'll also get a chance to see firsthand how to make changes to an attribute definition.

1. Click Array on the Modify toolbar, or type **Ar** and press Enter.

2. In the Array dialog box, select the Rectangular Array radio button in the upper-left corner.

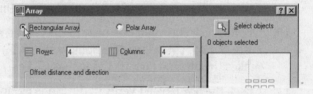

3. Click the Select Objects button, and select the attribute definition you just created. Press Enter to confirm your selection.

4. In the Rows input box, enter 7. In the Columns input box, enter **1**.

5. Enter **−0.18** in the Row Offset input box (**−0.432** for metric users) and **0** in the Column Offset input box. The row offset value is approximately 1.5 times the height of the attribute text height. The minus sign in the Row offset value causes the array to be drawn downward.

6. Click the OK button.

7. Issue a Zoom Extents or use the Zoom Realtime tool to view all the attributes.

Now you are ready to modify the copies of the attribute definitions.

1. Press the Esc key to clear any selections or commands, and click the attribute definition just below the original.

2. Right-click and select Properties from the shortcut menu.

TIP

You can double-click on an attribute definition to change its Tag, Prompt, or default value in the Edit Attribute Definition dialog box. However, this dialog box doesn't let you change an attribute definition's visibility mode.

3. Make sure the Categorized tab is selected, and scroll down the list of properties until you see the Invisible option in the Misc category.

4. Double-click the No setting to the right of the Invisible option. The setting changes to Yes.

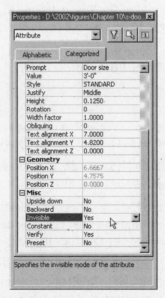

5. Scroll back up the list of properties and locate the Tag option in the Text category.

Part ii

6. Highlight the Tag value to the right, and type **D-SIZE** and press Enter. The attribute changes to reflect the change in the tag value.

7. While still in the Text category, highlight the Prompt value and type **Door size** and press Enter.

8. In the Value field, type **3'-0"** and press Enter. Metric users should type **90** and press Enter.

TIP

Make sure you press Enter after entering a new value for the properties in the Properties dialog box. Doing so confirms your new entry.

You've just learned how to edit an attribute definition. Now go ahead and make changes to the other attribute definitions.

1. Press the Esc key to clear the selection of the attribute you've been editing, and then click the next attribute down so you can display its properties in the Properties dialog box.

2. Continue to edit this and the rest of the attribute definition properties using the attribute settings listed in Table 10.1. To do this, repeat steps 4 through 9 for each attribute definition, replacing the Tag, Prompt, and Default Value with those shown in Table 10.1. Also, make sure all but the original attributes have the Invisible option turned on.

3. When you've finished editing the attribute definition properties, close the Properties dialog box.

4. After you have modified all the attributes, use the Draw ➢ Block ➢ Base option to change the base point of this drawing to the center of the circle. Use the Center Osnap to get the exact center.

5. You have finished creating your door type symbol with attributes. Save the S-door file.

TABLE 10.1: Attributes for the Door Type Symbol

TAG	PROMPT	DEFAULT VALUE
D-number	Door number	-
D-thick	Door thickness	-
D-rate	Fire rating	-
D-matrl	Door material	-
D-const	Door construction	-

Make sure the Invisible option is checked.

When you later insert a file or block containing attributes, the attribute prompts will appear in the order that their associated definitions were created. If the order of the prompts at insertion time is important, you can control it by editing the attribute definitions so their creation order corresponds to the desired prompt order. You can also control the order using the Block Attribute Manager, which you'll look at later.

UNDERSTANDING ATTRIBUTE DEFINITION MODES

In the Attribute Definition dialog box, you saw several choices in the Mode group, and you've used two of these modes to see what they do. You won't use any of the other modes in this tutorial, so here is a list describing all the modes for your reference:

Invisible   Controls whether the attribute is shown as part of the drawing.

CONTINUED ➡

Constant   Creates an attribute that does not prompt you to enter a value. Instead, the attribute simply has a constant, or fixed, value you give it during creation. The Constant mode is used in situations where you know you will assign a fixed value to an object. Once they are set in a block, constant values cannot be changed using the standard set of attribute editing commands.

Verify   Causes AutoCAD to review the attribute values you enter at insertion time and ask you if they are correct.

Preset   Causes AutoCAD to assign the default value to an attribute automatically when its block is inserted. This action saves time because a preset attribute will not prompt you for a value. Unlike the Constant mode, a Preset attribute can be edited.

You can have all four modes on, all four off, or any combination of modes. With the exception of the Invisible mode, none of these modes can be altered once the attribute becomes part of a block. Later, this chapter will discuss how to make an invisible attribute visible.

Inserting Blocks Containing Attributes

In the last section, you created a door type symbol at the desired size for the actual plotted symbol. This means that whenever you insert that symbol, you have to specify an X and Y scale factor appropriate to the scale of your drawing. Doing so allows you to use the same symbol in any drawing, regardless of its scale. (You could have several door type symbols, one for each scale you anticipate using, but this would be inefficient.)

1. Open the 10a-plan.dwg file from the companion website. Metric users can use the file named 06b-plan-metric.dwg from the website.

2. Turn on the Attribute Dialog mode by typing **Attdia**, pressing Enter, typing **1**, and pressing Enter again at the Command prompt. Doing so allows you to enter attribute values through a dialog box in the next exercise.

3. Choose View ➤ Named View to restore the view named First.

4. Be sure the Ceiling and Flr-Pat layers are off. Normally in a floor plan, the door headers are not visible, and they will interfere with the placement of the door reference symbol.

5. Click the Insert Block tool or type **I** and press Enter to open the Insert dialog box.

6. In the Insert dialog box, click the Browse button.

7. Locate the S-door file in the file list and double-click it.

8. In the Scale button group, make sure the Uniform Scale check box is selected; then enter **96** in the X input box. Metric users should enter **100** in the X input box.

9. Click OK.

You created the S-door file at the actual plotted size, so in step 8, you needed to scale it up by the drawing scale factor to make it the appropriate size for this drawing. Now you're ready to place the file in your drawing and enter the attribute values for the symbol.

1. AutoCAD is waiting for you to select a location for the symbol. To place the symbol, click in the doorway of the lower-left unit, near coordinate 41'-3",72'-4". Metric users should use coordinate 1256,2202. When you've clicked the location, the Enter Attributes dialog box appears.

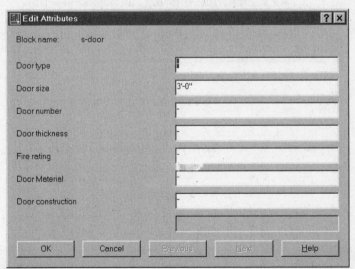

2. In the Door Type input box, enter **A**. Note that this prompt is the prompt you created. Note also that the default value is the hyphen you specified.

TIP

Attribute data is case sensitive, so any text you enter in all capital letters will be stored in all capital letters.

3. In the Door Number input box, change the hyphen to **116**. Continue to change the values for each input box, as shown in Table 10.2.

4. When you've finished, the symbol appears. The only attribute you can see is the one you selected to be visible: the door type.

TIP

If the symbol does not appear, go back to the S-door.dwg file and make sure you have set the base point to the center of the circle.

5. Add the rest of the door type symbols for the apartment entry doors by copying or arraying the door symbol you just inserted. You can use the previously saved views to help you get around the drawing quickly. Don't worry that the attribute values won't be appropriate for each unit. You'll see how to edit the attributes in the next section.

TABLE 10.2: Attribute Values for the Typical Studio Entry Door

PROMPT	VALUE
Door type	A
Door number	(Same as the room number)
Door thickness	1 3/4"
Fire rating	20 min.
Door material	Wood
Door construction	Solid core

As a review exercise, you'll now create another file for the apartment number symbol (shown in Figure 10.2). This will be a rectangular box with the room number that you will place in each studio apartment.

1. Save the plan file and then open a new file called S-apart (for the apartment number symbol).

2. Create an attribute definition and give it the tag name **R-number**, the prompt **Room number**, a default value of **000**, and a text height of **0.125** inches.

3. Use the Base command (Draw ➤ Block ➤ Base) to set the base point of this drawing in the lower-left corner of the rectangle.

4. Save and close S-apart.

5. Open the plan file again and insert the S-apart drawing you just created (using an X scale factor of 96) into the lower-left unit. Give this attribute the value **116**.

6. Copy or array the room number symbol so that there is one symbol in each of the units. You'll learn how to modify the attributes to reflect their proper values in the following section, "Editing Attributes." Figure 10.3 shows what the view should look like once you've entered the door symbols and apartment numbers.

FIGURE 10.2: The apartment number symbol

Part ii

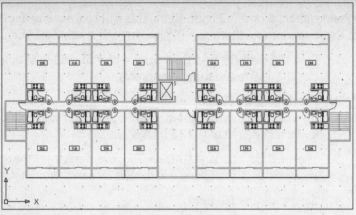

FIGURE 10.3: An overall view of the plan with door symbols and apartment numbers added

Editing Attributes

Because drawings are usually in flux even after actual construction or manufacturing begins, you will eventually have to edit previously entered attributes. In the example of the apartment building, many things can change before the final set of drawings is completed.

Attributes can be edited individually or *globally*—you can edit several occurrences of a particular attribute tag all at one time. In this section, you will make changes to the attributes you have entered so far, using both individual and global editing techniques, and you will practice editing invisible attributes.

TIP

If you prefer to access editing windows using a toolbar, the Modify II toolbar in AutoCAD 2002 offers tools for the Enhanced Attribute Editor and the Block Attribute Manager discussed in this section.

Editing Attribute Values One at a Time

AutoCAD offers an easy way to edit attributes one at a time through a dialog box. The following exercise demonstrates this feature.

1. Use the View ➤ Named View option to restore the First view.

2. Double-click the apartment number attribute in the unit just to the right of the first unit in the lower-left corner. You can also choose Modify ➤ Object ➤ Attribute ➤ Single, and then select the attribute. The Enhanced Attribute Editor appears.

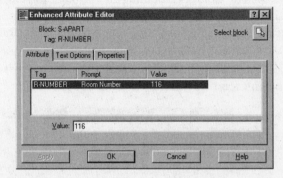

3. Change the value in the Value input box to **112** and then click OK to make the change.

4. Do this for each room number, using Figure 10.4 to assign room numbers.

TIP

If you're a veteran AutoCAD user, you can still use the Ddatte (type **Ate** and press Enter) command to open the Edit Attributes dialog box. This dialog box is useful for reviewing attributes as well as editing them, because it displays both visible and invisible attributes.

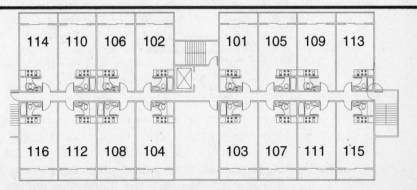

FIGURE 10.4: Apartment numbers for one floor of the studio apartment building

Editing Attribute Text Formats and Properties

You may have noticed that the Enhanced Attribute Editor in the last exercise offered three tabs: Attribute, Text Options, and Properties. When you double-click on a block containing an attribute, you are automatically presented with the Attribute tab of the Enhanced Attribute Editor. You can use the other two tabs to control the size, font, color, and other properties of the selected attribute.

The Text Options tab lets you alter the attribute text style, justification, height, rotation width factor, and oblique angle.

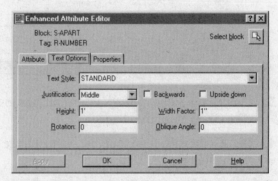

The Properties tab lets you alter the attributes layer, color, line weight (effective only on AutoCAD fonts), and plot style assignments.

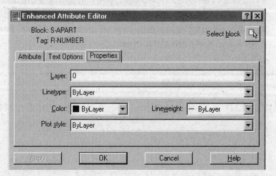

In the previous exercise, you edited a block containing just a single attribute. If you happen to double-click on a block containing multiple attributes, such as the S-DOOR block, the Attribute tab of the Enhanced Attribute Editor will display all the attributes, whether or not they are visible, as shown in Figure 10.5. You can then edit the value, formats, and properties of the individual attributes by highlighting the attribute in the Attribute tab and using the other tabs to make changes. The changes you make will affect only the attribute you've highlighted in the Attribute tab.

TIP

If you want to change the location of individual attributes in a block, you can move them using grips. Click the block to expose the grips and then click the grip connected to the attribute. Or, if you've selected several blocks, Shift+click the attribute grips; then move the attributes to their new location. They will still be attached to their associated blocks.

The Enhanced Attribute Editor lets you change attribute values, formats, and properties one block at a time, but, as you'll see in the next section, you can also make changes to several attributes at once.

Part ii

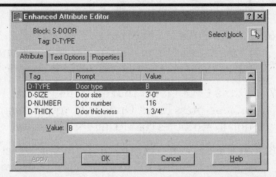

FIGURE 10.5: The Enhanced Attribute Editor showing the contents of a block that contains several attributes.

Making Global Changes to Attribute Values

Sometimes you'll want to change the value of several attributes in a file to be the same value. You can use the Edit Attribute Globally option to make any global changes to attribute values.

Suppose you decide you want to change all the entry doors to a type designated as B, rather than A. Perhaps door type A was an input error, or type B happens to be better suited for an entry door. The following exercise demonstrates how this is done.

1. Use the View Control dialog box (View ➣ Named View) to restore the view named Fourth. Pan your view down so you can see the door reference symbol for all the rooms in this view of the drawing.

2. Choose Modify ➤ Object ➤ Attribute ➤ Global, or type **Attedit** and press Enter at the Command prompt.

3. At the Edit Attributes one at a time? [Yes/No]<Y>: prompt, enter **N** and press Enter for No. You will see the message Performing global editing of attribute values, which tells you that you are in the Global Edit mode.

4. At the Edit only attributes visible on screen? [Yes/No] <Y>: prompt, press Enter. As you can see from this prompt, you have the option to edit all attributes, including those out of the view area. You'll get a chance to work with this option later in the chapter.

5. At the Enter block name specification <*>: prompt, press Enter. Optionally, you can enter a block name to narrow the selection to specific blocks.

6. At the Enter attribute tag specification <*>: prompt, press Enter. Optionally, you can enter an attribute tag name to narrow your selection to specific tags.

7. At the Enter attribute value specification <*>: prompt, press Enter. Optionally, you can narrow your selection to attributes containing specific values.

8. At the Select Attributes: prompt, select the door type symbols for units 103 to 115. You can use a window to select the attributes if you prefer.

9. At the Enter string to Change: prompt, enter **A** and press Enter.

10. At the Enter new String: prompt, enter **B** and press Enter. The door type symbols all change to the new value.

In step 8 above, you are asked to select the attributes to be edited. AutoCAD limits the changes to those attributes you select. If you know you need to change every single attribute in your drawing, you can do so by answering the series of prompts in a slightly different way, as in the following exercise:

1. Try the same procedure again, but this time enter **N** at the Edit only attributes visible on screen? prompt (step 4 in the previous exercise). The message Drawing must be regenerated afterwards appears. The AutoCAD Text window appears.

2. Once again, you are prompted for the block name, the tag, and the value (steps 5, 6, and 7 in the previous exercise). Respond to these prompts as you did before. Once you have done that, you get the message `128 attributes selected`. This tells you the number of attributes that fit the specifications you just entered.

3. At the `Enter string to change:` prompt, enter **A** and press Enter to indicate that you want to change the rest of the A attribute values.

4. At the `Enter new string:` prompt, enter **B** and press Enter. A series of Bs appears, indicating the number of strings that were replaced.

WARNING

If the Regenauto command is off, you must regenerate the drawing to see the change.

You may have noticed in the last exercise that the `Select Attribute:` prompt is skipped and you go directly to the `Enter string to change:` prompt. AutoCAD assumes that you want it to edit every attribute in the drawing, so it doesn't bother asking you to select specific attributes.

USING SPACES IN ATTRIBUTE VALUES

At times, you may want the default value to begin with a blank space. This enables you to specify text strings more easily when you edit the attribute. For example, you may have an attribute value that reads 3334333. If you want to change the first 3 in this string of numbers, you have to specify 3334 when prompted for the string to change. If you start with a space, as in _3334333 (I'm only using an underline here to represent the space; it doesn't mean you type an underline character), you can isolate the first 3 from the rest by specifying _3 as the string to change (again, type a space instead of the underline).

You must enter a backslash character (\) before the space in the default value to tell AutoCAD to interpret the space literally, rather than as a press of the spacebar (which is equivalent to pressing Enter).

Making Invisible Attributes Visible

Invisible attributes, such as those in the door reference symbol, can be edited globally using the tools just described. You may, however, want to be a bit more selective about which invisible attribute you want to modify. Or you may simply want to make them temporarily visible for other editing purposes. This section describes how you can make invisible attributes visible.

1. Enter **Attdisp** and press Enter.

TIP

You can also use the View menu to change the display characteristics of attributes. Choose View ➢ Display ➢ Attribute Display, and then click the desired option on the cascading menu.

2. At the Enter attribute visibility setting [Normal/ON/OFF] <Normal>: prompt, enter **ON**. Your drawing will look like Figure 10.6. If Regenauto is turned off, you may have to issue the Regen command. At this point, you could edit the invisible attributes individually, as in the first attribute-editing exercise. For now, set the attribute display back to normal.

3. Enter **Attdisp** and press Enter again; at the Enter attribute visibility setting [Normal/ON/OFF] <ON>: prompt, enter **N** for normal.

TIP

You've seen the results of the On and Normal options. The Off option makes all attributes invisible, regardless of the mode used when they were created.

Because the attributes were not intended to be visible, they appear to overlap each other and cover other parts of the drawing when they are made visible. Just remember to turn them back off when you are done reviewing them.

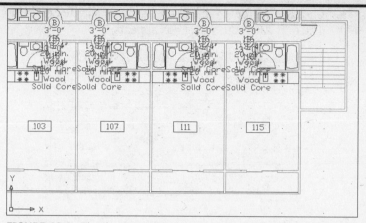

FIGURE 10.6: The drawing with all the attributes visible (door type symbols are so close together that they overlap)

Making Global Format and Property Changes to Attributes

While we're on the subject of global editing, you'll want to know how to make global changes to the format and properties of attributes. Earlier in this section, you saw how you can make format changes to individual attributes using the Enhanced Attribute Editor. The Block Attribute Manager can be invoked to perform global changes too, as the following exercise demonstrates:

1. Choose Modify ➤ Object ➤ Attribute ➤ Block Attribute Manager. The Block Attribute Manager dialog box appears.

2. Select S-APART from the Block drop-down list at the top of the dialog box. This list displays all the blocks that contain attributes. The only attribute you've defined for the selected block is displayed in the list box below it.

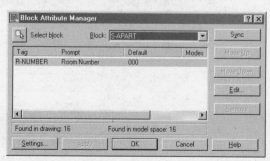

3. Click the attribute value in the list and click the Edit button. The Edit Attribute dialog box appears.

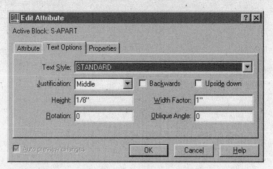

TIP

If only one attribute appears in the attribute list box, you don't have to select it before clicking the Edit button.

The Edit Attribute dialog box is nearly identical to the Enhanced Attribute Editor you saw earlier in this section.

4. Click the Properties tab, select Red from the Color drop-down list, and click OK.

5. Click OK to exit the dialog box.

The Edit Attribute dialog box you saw in the last exercise offers a slightly different set of options from those of the Enhanced Attribute Editor. In the Attribute tab of the Edit Attribute dialog box, you have the option to change some of the mode settings for the attribute, such as visibility and the Verify and Preset modes. You can also change the tag, prompt, and default values.

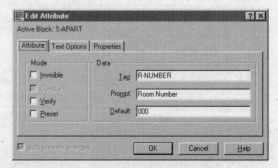

You may recall that the Attribute tab of the Enhanced Attribute Editor allows you to change the attribute value but none of the other attribute properties.

Other Block Attribute Manager Options

A few other options in the Block Attribute Manager dialog box weren't covered in the exercises. Here's a rundown of the Settings, Move Up, Move Down, and Remove options.

> **Settings**   Lets you control which attribute properties are displayed in the list box of the Block Attribute Manager dialog box. When you click this button, the Settings dialog box appears.

> You can then select the properties to be displayed. The Emphasize Duplicate Tags option highlights duplicate tag names by showing them in red. The Apply Changes to Existing References option forces any changes you make to the attribute properties to be applied to existing attributes. If this setting is turned off, you have to use the Sync button to update existing attributes, and the changes you make to attribute properties are applied only to new attributes added after the change. You can also enter **Attsync** at the Command prompt to synchronize older attributes.

> **Move Up and Move Down**   Move a selected attribute up and down the list of attributes in the list box. If you move an item down the list, the item will change its position when viewed using the Ddatte command or when viewing the

attribute's properties in the Enhanced Attribute editor. Of course, this action only has effect on blocks containing multiple attributes.

Remove   Removes the selected attribute from the block, so make sure you really mean it when you select this option.

Redefining Blocks Containing Attributes

Finally, you should be aware that attributes act differently from other objects when included in redefined blocks. Normally, blocks that have been redefined change their configuration to reflect the new block definition. But if a redefined block contains attributes, the attributes will maintain their old properties, including their position in relation to other objects in the block. As a result, the old attribute position, style, and so on do not change even though you may have changed them in the new definition.

Fortunately, AutoCAD offers a tool specifically designed to let you update blocks with attributes. The following steps describe how you would go about updating attribute blocks:

1. Before you use the command to redefine an attribute block, you must first create the objects and attribute definitions that will make up the new replacement attribute block. The simplest way to do this is to explode a copy of the attribute block you wish to update. Doing so ensures that you have the same attribute definitions in the updated block.

2. Make your changes to the exploded attribute block.

WARNING

Before you explode the attribute block copy, be sure that it is at a 1-to-1 scale. This is important, because if you don't use the original size of the block, you could end up with all your new attribute blocks at the wrong size. Also be sure you use some marker device, such as a line, to locate the insertion point of the attribute block before you explode it. Doing so will help you locate and maintain the original insertion point for the redefined block.

3. Type **Attredef** and press Enter.

4. At the Enter name of block you wish to redefine: prompt, enter the appropriate name.

5. At the Select objects for new block: prompt, select all the objects, including the attribute definitions, you want to include in the revised attribute block.

6. At the Insertion base point of new block: prompt, pick the same location used for the original block.

Once you pick the insertion point, AutoCAD takes a few seconds to update the blocks. The amount of time will vary depending on the complexity of the block and the number of times the block occurs in the drawing. If you include a new attribute definition with your new block, it too will be added to all the updated blocks, with its default value. Attribute definitions that are deleted from your new definition will be removed from all the updated blocks.

COMMON USES FOR ATTRIBUTES

Attributes are an easy way to combine editable text with graphic symbols without resorting to groups or separate text and graphic elements. One of the more common uses of attributes is in column grid symbols. Attributes are well suited for this purpose because they maintain their location in relation to the circle or hexagon shape usually used for grid symbols, and they can be easily edited.

Part ii

EXTRACTING AND EXPORTING ATTRIBUTE INFORMATION

Once you have entered the attributes into your drawing, you can extract the information contained in the attributes and use it to generate reports or to analyze the attribute data in other programs. You may, for example, want to keep track of the number and type of doors in your drawing through a database manager. Doing so is especially useful if you have a project such as a large hotel that contains thousands of doors.

When you extract Attribute data, AutoCAD creates a text file. You can choose to have the file exported in either comma-delimited or tab-delimited format. If you have Microsoft Excel or Access installed, you will also have the option to export the attribute data in a format compatible with these programs.

1. Go back to the plan file and choose Tools ➤ Attribute Extraction. The Attribute Extraction — Select Drawing dialog box appears.

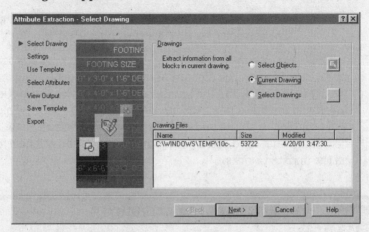

In this dialog box, you have the option to select specific blocks for the attribute data extraction. You may also select other drawings besides the current one. The default is to select the entire current drawing. The name of the selected drawing files appears in the list box at the bottom of the dialog box.

2. Click Next. The Attribute Extraction — Settings dialog box appears. In this dialog box, you can choose to have attribute data from Xrefs and nested blocks extracted.

3. Click Next again. The Attribute Extraction — User Template dialog box appears. This dialog box allows you to import settings from an external file. Right now, it's not likely that you have any saved settings available, but in a later page of this Attribute Extraction Wizard, you will have a chance to save the options you select as a template file that you can import in later Attribute Extraction sessions.

4. Click Next again. The Attribute Extraction — Select Attributes dialog box appears.

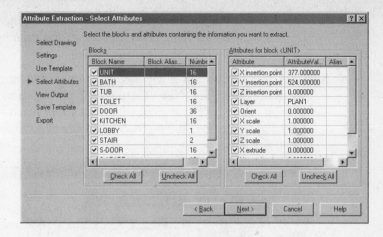

Selecting What to Extract

Take a moment to study this dialog box. It is the heart of the extraction process. Here you select the blocks that contain attributes as well as the specific attributes you want to extract. Notice that in the left list box, all the blocks in the drawing are displayed—not just the ones that contain attributes. The Attribute for Block list box to the right displays attribute and block properties.

You can obtain some helpful information about your drawing just by looking at this dialog box. For example, you can find out how many copies of a particular block occur in the drawing by looking at the right column of the Blocks list box.

You can also add an alternate name in the Block Alias column to help better describe the block. An Alias option is also available in the Attribute for Block list box.

Let's continue by selecting specific information for the extraction.

1. Click the Uncheck All button at the bottom of the Blocks list. Notice that the boxes to the left of the list box become unchecked.

2. Scroll down to the bottom of the Blocks list box and check the S-DOOR block name. Notice that the attribute list changes to show values for the selected block.

3. Click the Uncheck All button at the bottom of the Attribute list.

4. Scroll down to the bottom of the Attribute list and check all the attribute names. Remember that the attribute names are all prefixed with *D-*.

5. Click the Next button at the bottom of the dialog box. The Attribute Extraction – View Output dialog box appears, displaying a listing of the attribute data that you selected in the previous dialog box. You see each attribute in order as you scroll down the list.

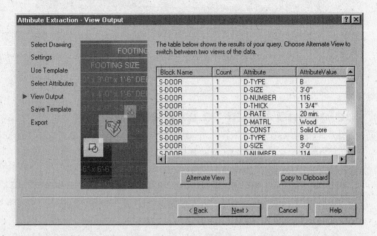

6. Click the Alternate View button. The list changes so that the attribute values are shown in a row and column matrix with each block listed as a row and the attributes of the block listed in columns. You can use the horizontal scroll bar at the bottom of the list to view all the columns.

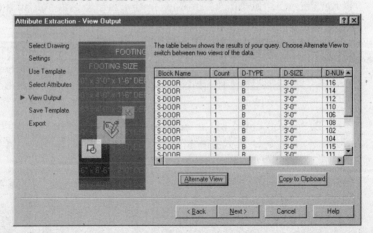

This alternate offers a clearer view of the data. Notice that every door is listed. When any attribute data differs in each block, the Attribute Extraction Wizard dutifully shows the data for each occurrence of the block. But suppose all the attribute data is the same for each block. The Attribute Extraction Wizard will then consolidate the data into a more compact form. Try the following to see how this works:

1. Click the Back button to return to the Attribute Extraction – Select Attributes dialog box.

2. Go to the bottom of the Attribute list and remove the check next to the D-NUMBER attribute. This is the only attribute that changes for each instance of the S-DOOR block, and you are no longer extracting it.

3. Click the Next button. You return to the Attribute Extraction – View Output dialog box. Now you see only a single listing for the S-DOOR block. But this time, a new column called Count has been added.

Because all the data is the same for each selected attribute, the Attribute Extraction Wizard lists the block name once and then tells you the number of times the block appears in the drawing under the Count column.

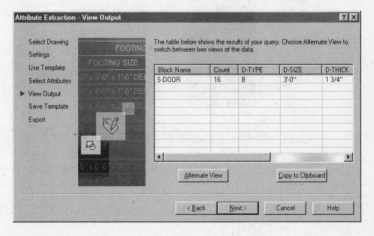

As you can see from the exercises so far, you can use the Attribute Extraction Wizard to quickly view attribute and block data without performing the entire extraction process. You can also copy the data to the Clipboard to save the data "on the fly."

Saving the Attribute Data to a File

Now let's go ahead and complete the extraction process. First go back and restore the D-NUMBER attribute so you can get a complete listing of the S-DOOR data.

1. Click the Back button.

2. In the Attribute for Block list, make sure the D-NUMBER attribute is checked, and click Next.

3. Click Next again at the Attribute Extraction — View Output dialog box, and you'll see the Attribute Extraction — Save Template dialog box. You may recall that earlier you had the option to recall a template file. This is where you can save a template file for subsequent recall.

4. Click Next. The Attribute Extraction — Export dialog box appears.

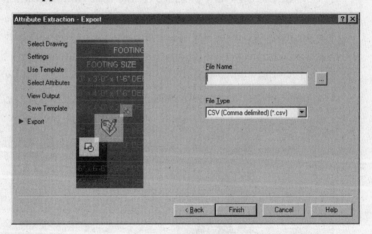

This is where you specify the filename and type of file you want to extract.

5. Click the File Type drop-down list and select Tab Delimited File (*.txt).

6. Click the ellipsis (...) button to the right of the File Name input box; then, in the Save As dialog box, Enter **Planattribute**.

7. Using the Save In drop-down list, locate the directory where you are storing your sample files for the exercises in this book, and click Save.

8. At the Attribute Extraction – Export dialog box, click Finish. You return to your drawing.

You now have a file called Planattribute.txt that contains the data you saw earlier in the Attribute Extraction – View Output dialog box. That data can be imported into any program that will accept a tab-delimited data file, including database, spreadsheet, and word processing programs.

Using Extracted Attribute Data with Other Programs

In step 5 of the previous exercise, you also had the option to save the file in a CSV or comma-delimited format. This format is common to many of the Microsoft Office products. If you have Microsoft Excel or Access, you will also have the option to export files to the native formats of these programs.

ACCESSING EXTERNAL DATABASES

You can access an external database from within AutoCAD through the dbConnect Manager, a tool that lets you read and manipulate data from external database files. You can also use dbConnect Manager to link parts of your drawing to an external database.

There are numerous reasons for doing this. The most obvious is to keep inventory on parts of your drawing. If you are an interior designer doing office planning, you can link inventory data from a database to your drawing, with a resulting decrease in the size of your drawing file. If you are a facilities manager, you can track the movement of people and facilities using AutoCAD linked to a database file.

This section will avoid the more complex programming issues of database management systems, and it does not discuss the SQL language, which you can use to query and edit your database files through dbConnect. Still, you should be able to make good use of the dbConnect Manager with the information provided here. You'll also be departing from the studio apartment example to make use of an office plan example that has already been created by Autodesk.

AUTOCAD AND YOUR DATABASE

These exercises assume that you are somewhat familiar with data-bases. For example, these exercises will refer frequently to something called a *table*. A table is an SQL term referring to the row-and-column data structure of a typical database file. Other terms I'll use are *rows*, which are the records in a database, and *columns*, which refer to the database fields. Finally, it is very important that you follow the instructions in these beginning exercises carefully. If anything is missed in the beginning, later exercises will not work properly.

AutoCAD uses Windows Open Database Connectivity (ODBC) to help link drawings to databases. ODBC is an interface that lets diverse programs connect to a variety of different types of databases. It serves as a translator between the program, which in this case is AutoCAD, and the database file you want your program to "talk to." Before ODBC can do its translating, you need to install a driver that allows ODBC to communicate with the particular database type you want to work with. The following drivers are already included with Windows ODBC:

▶ Microsoft Access

▶ dBase

▶ Microsoft Excel

▶ Microsoft Fox Pro

▶ Oracle

▶ Paradox

▶ Microsoft SQL Server

▶ Text files

▶ Microsoft Visual Fox Pro

If your database type is not listed here, you'll need to obtain an ODBC driver for it. Also, you may need to configure the ODBC driver before you can connect your database to AutoCAD. You can do this through the ODBC Data Source Administrator in Windows Control Panel.

Setting Up Your System for Database Access

The dbConnect Manager doesn't create new database files. You must use existing files or create them in the database program yourself before you use this tool. In addition, you will need to set up a Data Link file that will direct AutoCAD to the database file you want to work with. You can create a Data Link file through the Microsoft Data Link dialog box, which also lets you manage Data Link files. Once you've created and set up a Data Link file, you can begin to access and link databases to AutoCAD drawings.

In the first set of exercises that follow, you'll learn how to create a new Data Link file that tells AutoCAD where to look for database information. Then, for the rest of the tutorial, you will use a Microsoft Access file from the companion website. The file, called db-mastersample.mdb, is located on the Sybex.com website.

The db-mastersample.mdb file contains three tables: Computer, Employee, and Inventory. The contents of the Employee table are shown in Figure 10.7.

EMP_ID	LAST_NAME	FIRST_NAME	DEPT	TITLE	ROOM	EXT
1000	Meredith	Dave	Sales	V.P.	101	8600
1001	Williams	Janice	Sales	Western Region Mgr.	102	8601
1003	Smith	Jill	Sales	Central Region Mgr.	104	8603
1004	Nelson	Kirk	Sales	Canadian Sales Mgr.	109	8640
1005	Clark	Karl	Sales	Educational Sales Mgr.	106	8605
1006	Wilson	Cindy	Accounting	Accountant	109	8606
1007	Ortega	Emilio	Accounting	Accountant	109	8607
1008	Benson	Adam	Accounting	Accountant	109	8608
1009	Rogers	Kevin	Accounting	Accountant	109	8609
1011	Thompson	Frank	Engineering	Mechanical Engineer	123	8611
1012	Simpson	Paul	Engineering	Mechanical Engineer	124	8612
1013	Debrine	Todd	Engineering	Design Engineer	125	8613
1014	Frazier	Heather	Engineering	Application Engineer	126	8614
1016	Taylor	Patrick	Engineering	Software Engineer	128	8616
1017	Chang	Yuan	Engineering	Software Engineer	129	8617
1018	Dempsy	Phil	Engineering	Application Engineer	112	8618
1019	Kahn	Jenny	Engineering	Programmer	113	8619
1020	Moore	George	Engineering	Programmer	114	8620
1021	Price	Mark	Engineering	Software Engineer	115	8621
1022	Quinn	Scott	Engineering	Software Engineer	116	8622
1023	Sanchez	Maria	Engineering	Mechanical Engineer	117	8623
1024	Ross	Ted	Engineering	Application Engineer	118	8624
1025	Saunders	Terry	Engineering	Software Engineer	119	8625
1026	Fong	Albert	Engineering	Programmer	120	8626

FIGURE 10.7: The contents of the Employee table from the db-mastersample .mdb file

Part ii

Creating a Data Link File

A Data Link file is like a switchboard that connects applications to database files. The application can be anything that requires Data Link files for database connections, not just AutoCAD. You can have as many Data Link files as you need for your application, and as you'll see, you'll be able to access all of them from the AutoCAD dbConnect Manager.

1. Using Windows Explorer, locate the Data Links folder under the main AutoCAD folder. Typically, this would be C:\Program Files\AutoCAD 2002\Data Links.

2. Right-click a blank area in the folder listing, and choose New ➤ Text Document. A new file appears, called New Text Document.txt.

3. Rename this file My Acad Data Link.UDL. You will see a warning message that the file may become unusable. Click Yes.

You've just created a Data Link file. You may have noticed one other UDL file in the Data Link folder. These are sample files provided by Autodesk that allow you to explore AutoCAD's dbConnect feature on your own.

TIP

You can also create a new Data Link file directly in AutoCAD by doing the following: Choose Tools ➤ dbConnect. Next, choose dbConnect ➤ Data Source ➤ Configure. The Configure a Data Source dialog box appears. Enter a name for your Data Link file in the Data Source name text box and click OK. The Data Link Properties dialog box appears, with the Provider tab selected. Select Microsoft OLE DB Provider for ODBC drivers from the list, click Next, and then proceed to step 2 in the next exercise. The new Data Link file is created in the AutoCAD 2002\Data Links folder.

Configuring Data Links

Next, you'll configure your new Data Link file to locate the sample database files.

1. With the Data Link folder open, double-click My Acad Data Link.UDL. The Data Link Properties dialog box appears.

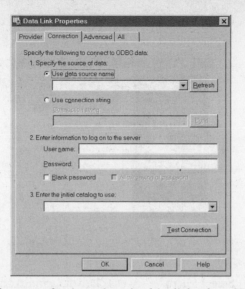

You have two basic options in this dialog box. You can connect to a database through the Data Source Name (DSN) setting that is controlled through the ODBC Data Source Administrator in Windows Control Panel, or you can create a link to a database directly from this dialog box. In this exercise, you'll use the Build option to create a database directly through this dialog box.

2. Click the Use Connection String radio button.

3. Click the Build button next to the Connection String input box. The Select Data Source dialog box appears.

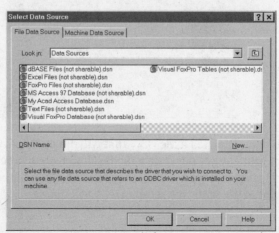

4. Click New next to the DSN Name input box. The Create New Data Source Wizard appears.

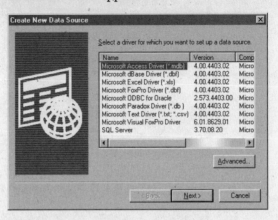

5. Select Microsoft Access Driver (*.mdb) and click Next.

6. On the next page, click the Browse button.

7. In the Save As dialog box, enter **My Acad Access Database** and click Save. The previous dialog box reappears.

8. Click Next, and then click Finish in the last dialog box. The ODBC Microsoft Access Setup dialog box appears.

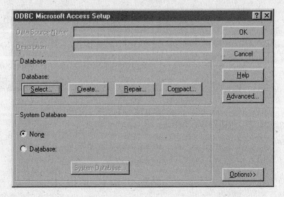

You've just created a file DSN that will direct AutoCAD to the database of your choice. But once a file DSN is created, it needs to be configured. This is where you indicate the exact location of the database file you want to use with this setup.

1. Click the Select button in the Database group. The Select Database dialog box appears. This is a standard file dialog box.

2. Locate db-mastersample.mdb and select it.

3. Click OK in the ODBC Microsoft Access Setup dialog box. The Select Data Source dialog box reappears.

4. Select My Acad Access Database.dsn from the list and click OK.

5. Click OK in the ODBC Microsoft Access Setup dialog box.

6. Click Test Connection in the Data Link Properties dialog box. You should see a message telling you that the test succeeded. Click OK and then click OK again in the Data Link Properties dialog box.

TIP

You can also create a new Data Link file or edit an existing one by choosing dbConnect ➤ Data Sources ➤ Configure after you have clicked the dbConnect tool. The Configure a Data Source dialog box appears and asks for a data source name. Enter a new name or select the name of an existing Data Link file from the Data Link list box. Enter a name and then click OK. The Data Link Properties dialog box appears, and you can set up the Data Link file.

Most of the steps you took in this exercise are the same steps you would take to create a file DSN through the ODBC Data Source Administrator in Windows Control Panel. The Build button is a convenient way to access the ODBC Data Source Administrator through the Data Link Properties dialog box.

TIP

AutoCAD is set up to look in the AutoCAD 2002\Data Links folder for Data Link files. You can direct AutoCAD to look in a different folder by changing settings in the Files tab of the Options dialog box. Look for the Data Source Location listing and edit its value.

Part ii

Opening a Database from AutoCAD

Now you're ready to access your database files directly from AutoCAD. In the following exercise, you'll take the first step by making a connection between a database table and AutoCAD.

1. Open the dbSample.dwg file from the companion website.

2. Choose Tools ➤ dbConnect. You can also type **dbc** and press Enter or press Ctrl+6.

    The dbConnect window appears.

3. Right-click My Acad Data Link and select Connect from the shortcut menu. The directory listing of the tables in the Access database file appears below My Acad Data Link.

4. Click the Employee listing and then click the Edit Table tool in the dbConnect window, or right-click the Employee listing and select Edit Table. (You can also double-click the Employee listing.)

    The Data View dialog box appears. Your view of the data may be wider than the one shown here.

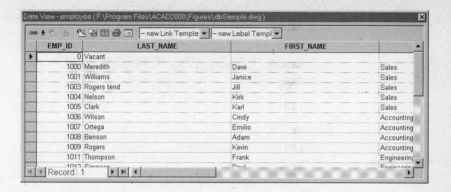

EMP_ID	LAST_NAME	FIRST_NAME	
0	Vacant		
1000	Meredith	Dave	Sales
1001	Williams	Janice	Sales
1003	Rogers tend	Jill	Sales
1004	Nelson	Kirk	Sales
1005	Clark	Karl	Sales
1006	Wilson	Cindy	Accounting
1007	Ortega	Emilio	Accounting
1008	Benson	Adam	Accounting
1009	Rogers	Kevin	Accounting
1011	Thompson	Frank	Engineering
1012	Simpson	Paul	Engineering

TIP

If you right-click the label at the top of each field in the Data View dialog box, a shortcut menu lets you sort the table by values in the field, control alignment of the field values, and perform simple find or replace functions. You can also resize the column widths by clicking and dragging the borders between the column headings.

You are now connected to the Employee table of the db-Mastersample .mdb database.

Take a moment to look at the dbConnect window. (You may need to move the Data View dialog box out of the way to do so.) At the top is a set of buttons that duplicate the options you saw in step 4 in the shortcut menu. Also notice that you now have two more options in the menu bar: dbConnect and Data View. Most of the options in these two pull-down menus are duplicated in other parts of the dbConnect and Data View windows.

You've already seen that dbConnect's Edit Table tool opens the Data View dialog box to allow you to edit a database table. The View tool opens a view of the database, without allowing you to edit anything. You'll learn about the functions of the New Link and New Label template options later in this chapter.

Finding a Record in the Database

Now that you are connected to the database, suppose you want to find the record for a specific individual. You might already know that the individual you're looking for is in the Accounting department.

1. Click the Query icon in the Data View toolbar. The New Query dialog box appears.

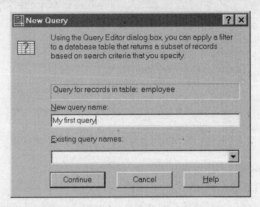

2. Type **My first query** in the New Query Name input box. You can save queries under different names in case you need to repeat a query later.

3. Click Continue. The Query Editor dialog box appears.

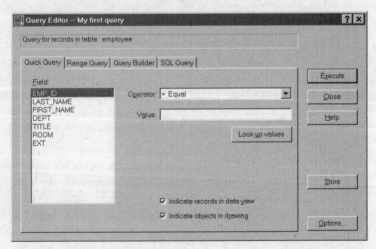

The Query Editor dialog box lets you set the criteria for your query. As you can see from the numerous tabs, you can use several methods to query the database. Try using the Quick Query method, which is the tab already selected.

4. Highlight DEPT in the Field list box.

5. Click the Look Up Values button just below the Value input box. A listing of the DEPT categories appears.

6. Select Accounting from the list and click OK.

7. Click Store. Doing so saves the current query under the name that you entered in the New Query dialog box. The name My First Query appears in the dbConnect window, just under the drawing name.

8. Click Execute. The Data View dialog box changes to show only the Accounting department records.

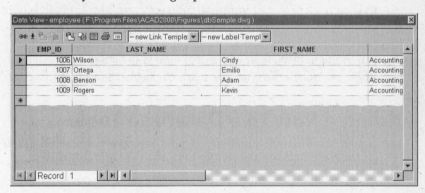

9. After reviewing the results of this exercise, right-click the Employee listing in the dbConnect window and select Edit Table to restore the view of the entire table.

You've just seen how you can locate and view a set of records in a database. If you want to edit any of those records, simply highlight the field of a record you want to change, and then enter a new value. If you open the Data View window using the View option in the dbConnect window, you are locked out of making changes to your database. In some cases, the View option is the only option available to access a database. You may be limited to the View option if the database is locked or if the ODBC driver for a database does not allow editing.

You used the Store option to store your query. Once you've stored a query, you can quickly re-execute it from the dbConnect window. To do that, right-click the query name and select Execute. You can also make modifications to a stored query. Right-click the query name in the dbConnect window and select Edit Query from the shortcut menu. The Query Editor dialog box appears, allowing you to make changes and re-execute your query.

Other options in the shortcut menu allow you to rename the query or delete it altogether.

TIP

You can also launch a new query from the dbConnect window. Right-click the database filename and select New Query. You'll see the New Query dialog box. You can then proceed with your query, just as you did in this exercise.

The ability to access databases in this way can help you connect Auto-CAD graphic data with database information. For example, you may want to keep track of tenant information in your studio apartment building. As you will see later, you can actually link graphics to database records so you can quickly access data regarding a particular tenant. Another application might be generating a bill of materials for a mechanical project, where records in the database relate to parts in a mechanical assembly.

Adding a Row to a Database Table

Now let's get back to our office example. Suppose you have a new employee who needs to be set up in an office. The first thing you need to do is add his or her name to the database. Here's how it's done.

1. In the Data View dialog box, right-click any button to the far left of the table and select New Record from the shortcut menu. A blank row appears, and the cursor appears in the first field of the row for entering data.

2. Enter the following data in the blank row. To add an item, click the appropriate field, and then enter the new data. After you type in the new data, press the Tab key to move to the next field.

EMP_ID: **2000**

LAST_NAME: **Ryan**

FIRST_NAME: **Roma**

DEPT: **Creative Resources**

TITLE: **Producer/Lyricist**

ROOM: **122**

EXT: **8888**

3. Press Enter after entering the last entry. You've just added a new record to the database.

KEEPING YOUR WINDOWS ORGANIZED

If you plan to work with a database for an extended period of time, you will find it easier to work with the dbConnect and Data View windows by docking them in your AutoCAD windows.

First, maximize the AutoCAD window to fill your entire screen. Next, right-click the title bar of either dialog box and make sure that Allow Docking is checked in the shortcut menu. Move both dialog boxes into the AutoCAD window. You can place dbConnect on either side of the window and Data View at the bottom. Although this arrangement will reduce the size of your AutoCAD drawing window, it will help you keep the dbConnect and Data View windows out of your way but easy to get to.

Part ii

LINKING OBJECTS TO A DATABASE

So far, you've looked at ways you can access and edit an external database file. You can also link specific drawing objects to elements in a database. But before you can link your drawing to data, you must create a *link template*. Link templates let you set up different sets of links to a database. For example, you can set up a link template that associates all the phones in your AutoCAD drawing with specific records in your database file. Another link template can link the room numbers in your drawing to the LAST_NAME records in your database file.

This section will show you how to create a link to the database by linking your new employee to one of the vacant rooms.

Creating a Link

In the following set of exercises, you will link an AutoCAD object to the record you just added to the Employee database table. The first step is to set up a link template.

1. Close the Data View dialog box.

2. Highlight the Employee table listing in the dbConnect window, and then click the New Link Template tool in the dbConnect toolbar. You can also right-click the Employee listing and select New Link Template from the shortcut menu.

The New Link Template dialog box appears.

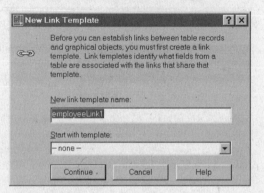

3. Notice that its format is similar to the New Query dialog box. You can enter a name for your link template in the New Link Template Name input box.

4. Enter **Room Number** for the name and click Continue. The Link Template dialog box appears.

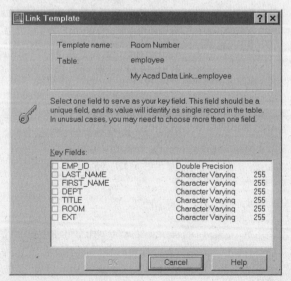

The Link Template dialog box lets you select a field to act as your key field. You can select more than one field for your key field.

TIP

A *key field* is any field whose values uniquely identify that table. For example, the set of values of the Employee ID is unique to this table. You can further improve uniqueness by including another field, like the room numbers. The choice of fields is somewhat arbitrary, but you should select fields that will not change frequently.

5. Click LAST_NAME and ROOM; then click OK. The Room Number template appears in the dbConnect window.

You've just created a link template. You'll see your link template listed in the dbConnect window under the drawing name. If you need to edit this link template, you can do so by right-clicking its name and selecting Edit or by just double-clicking the template. Right now, you'll continue to add a link between your drawing and the database.

You are ready to add a link to room 122. The first step is to set up your AutoCAD drawing so you can easily access the rooms you will be linking to. Then you will locate the record that is associated with room 122 in the Data View dialog box.

1. Zoom in to the set of rooms in the lower-right corner of the plan so your view looks like Figure 10.8.

2. Click the Employee listing in the dbConnect window and click the Edit Table tool in the dbConnect toolbar. The Data View dialog box appears. Notice that Room Number appears in the list box in the toolbar. This tells you which link template you are using. If you have more than one link template, you can select the link template you want to use from this list box.

3. Scroll down the records to locate the record you added in the previous exercise. You can also use the New Query option to isolate the record, or you can quickly go to the end of the records by clicking the end-of-table navigation arrow at the bottom of the dialog box.

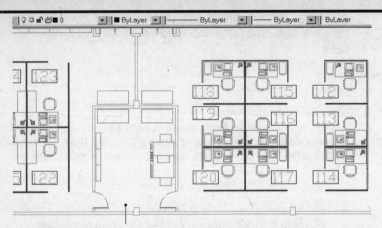

FIGURE 10.8: The view of the drawing showing the rooms to the right of 122

4. Once you've found the record, click any field of the record.

5. Click the Link and Label Settings tool in the toolbar and make sure the Create Link option is selected. This option determines what type of link AutoCAD will create.

6. Click the Link! tool in the toolbar. The Data View dialog box disappears, and you see the selection cursor in the AutoCAD window.

7. Click the room number 122 and the phone in the upper-left corner of the room; then press Enter to finish your selection. The Data View dialog box returns. Now you see that the record is highlighted in yellow, indicating that it is linked to an object in the current drawing.

8. In the Data View dialog box, link the records for rooms 116 and 114 to the same room numbers in the drawing. Remember to first select the record you want to link, click the Link! tool, and then select the room number you want to link to. Room 116 is assigned to employee number 1022, and room number 114 is assigned to employee 1020.

Now you have a link established between the records for rooms 122, 116, and 114 in the database and their room numbers in your drawing. Next you'll learn how you can use those links to locate objects in the drawing or records in your database.

Locating Database Records through Drawing Objects

Now that you've got database links established, you can begin to use them. In the following exercise, you'll see how you can locate a database record by selecting an object in your drawing:

1. Go to the top of the table by clicking the first-record button at the bottom of the Data View dialog box.

2. Click the View Linked Record in Table button in the Data View toolbar. The dialog box disappears.

3. Click the telephone in the upper-left corner of room 122, and then click room numbers 114 and 116.

4. Press Enter when you've completed your selections. The Data View dialog box appears again with the records for employees 1020, 1022, and 2000 highlighted.

As you can see from step 3, you can select several objects. AutoCAD isolates all the records that are linked to the selected objects. You can go a step further and have AutoCAD display only the records associated with the linked objects.

1. Right-click the Room Number link template in the dbConnect window, and choose Link Select. The Link Select dialog box appears.

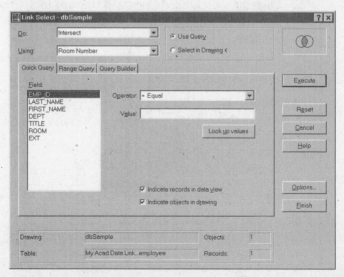

Part ii

2. Click the Select in Drawing < radio button near the top of the dialog box.

3. Click the Select button. The dialog box disappears to allow you to select objects in the drawing.

4. Select room number 116 and press Enter. The Link Select dialog box reappears.

5. Click Finish. The Data View dialog box now displays only the record linked to the room number you selected.

The Link Select dialog box offers many more features that allow you to locate data either within your drawing or in your database.

Finding and Selecting Graphics through the Database

You've just seen how you can use links to locate records in a database. Links can also help you find and select objects in a drawing that are linked to a database. The next exercise shows, in a simplified way, how this works.

1. Click the Employee listing in the dbConnect window, and click the Edit Table tool to open the entire table.

2. In the Data View dialog box, select the record for employee 2000. You can use the Last Record button to take you there.

3. Click the View Linked Objects in Drawing tool in the toolbar. The display shifts to center the linked object in the AutoCAD window.

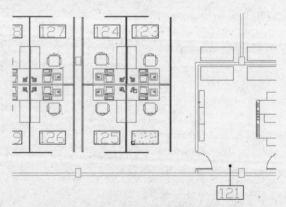

4. Move the Data View dialog box out of the way temporarily so you can view your drawing. Notice that the room number 122 and the telephone are highlighted and their grips are exposed.

Once these steps have been taken, you can use the Previous Object Selection option to select those objects that were highlighted in step 3.

In this example, you only selected objects in one office. However, you can create a record called Vacant, and then link all the vacant offices to this one record. When a new employee is hired, you can then quickly locate all the vacant rooms in the floor plan to place the new employee. If you continue to link each database record with rooms in the drawing, you can then later locate a person's room through the same process.

Adding Labels with Links

Database links can help you add labels to a drawing by using the data from a database table for the label text. The following exercise will show how you can add the employee name and telephone extension number to the sample drawing:

1. In the Data View dialog box, click the Link and Label Settings tool in the toolbar and make sure that the Create Freestanding Labels option is selected. When you do this, the tool to the left changes to the Create Freestanding Label tool.

2. Click the button to the right of employee number 2000 to select that record.

3. Click the Create Freestanding Label tool in the toolbar. The New Label Template dialog box appears.

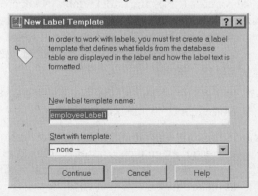

Part ii

4. Enter the name **Employee Names** and click Continue. The Label Template dialog box appears. Notice that it looks quite similar to the Multiline Text Editor.

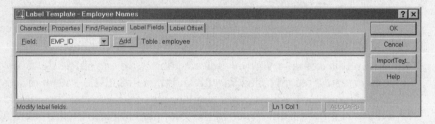

5. Click the Character tab and highlight the text in the text box.

6. Click the Text Height drop-down list and enter **6**.

7. Click the Label Fields tab.

8. Select Last Name from the Field drop-down list and click Add. The LAST_NAME entry appears in the text box.

9. Select Title from the Field drop-down list and click Add again. The TITLE entry appears in the text box.

10. Click OK. The dialog box disappears, and the Point Selection cursor appears in the AutoCAD window.

11. Click a clear location in room 122. The last name and title of employee 2000 appear as text in the drawing. Notice that these are the actual field values from the record you selected in step 2 and the fields you selected in steps 8 and 9.

Notice that now you have a listing in the dbConnect window called Employee Names. This is the Label template you created in steps 4 through 10. Next, you'll add a few more employee name labels to the floor plan. First you'll turn on the AutoView Linked Objects in Drawing tool so you can pan to the selected room number automatically. Then you'll add the new labels.

1. In the Data View dialog box, click the AutoView Linked Objects in Drawing tool.

2. In the Data View dialog box, click the button to the far left of the record for employee number 1020. Your view of the drawing pans to the link in room 114 that is already established in the drawing.

3. Click the Create Freestanding Label tool.

4. In the drawing, click a clear space in room 114 to place the label.

5. In the Data View dialog box, select the record for employee number 1022, and then click the Create Freestanding Label tool.

6. In the drawing, click a free space in room 116 to place a label there.

Each label you add is linked to its corresponding record in the database. Notice that the label template appears just below the link template in the dbConnect window. This tells you that the label template is dependent on the link template.

If you want to create labels based on different field data, you can create other label templates that include different sets of field values.

Adding Linked Labels

Now, suppose you want to label all the links in the drawing automatically. For example, suppose you want to show the telephone extension number for each link. In the next exercise, you'll create a new label template for the telephone extension field of the database table.

1. In the dbConnect window, highlight the Employee listing; then click the New Label Template tool or right-click and select New Label Template from the shortcut menu.

2. In the New Label Template dialog box, enter **Extension** in the input box, and then click Continue.

3. In the Label Template dialog box, select the Character tab.

4. Highlight the value in the Font Height drop-down list and enter **8**.

5. Select the Label Fields tab and select Ext from the Field drop-down list.

6. Click Add and then OK to exit the dialog box.

You now have a label template for the telephone extension numbers. This label template is also dependent on the link template you created earlier in this set of exercises. You can use this template to automatically add phone extension labels to the drawing.

1. In the Data View dialog box, make sure the Extension label template appears in the Label Template drop-down list.

2. Click the Link and Label Settings tool and select Create Attached Labels.

3. Select the record for employee number 1020 and click the Create Attached Label tool. Extension number labels appear on each item that is linked to the record. The labels are placed on top of the objects they are linked to.

4. Click the extension label that is on top of the employee name; use its grip to move it away from the name. Doing so shows you that the labels can be adjusted to a new position once they are placed.

5. Repeat steps 3 and 4 for employee numbers 1022 and 2000.

Each label you add with the Create Attached Label tool is linked to its associated record in the database.

Hiding Labels

You can edit the label in your drawing as you would any other multiline text object. Another characteristic of database labels is that you can control their visibility.

1. Right-click the Extension label template listed in the db-Connect window and select Hide Labels. The labels associated with the extension label template disappear.

2. Right-click the link template again and click Show Labels. The label reappears.

If you want to delete all the labels associated with a label template, right-click the label template's name in the dbConnect window and select Delete Labels from the shortcut menu. Once you've done this, you can delete the label template as well by right-clicking the label template name and selecting Delete.

Editing Links

People and databases are always changing, so you need a way to update the links between your database and objects in your drawing. AutoCAD offers the Link Manager for this purpose.

Suppose you want to delete the link between the room number 116 in your drawing and the record for employee 1022.

1. Choose dbConnect ➤ Links ➤ Link Manager.

2. Click the room number 116 in your drawing. The Link Manager dialog box appears.

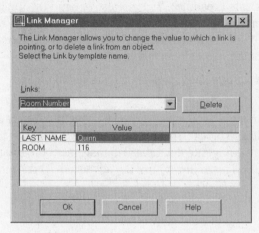

3. Click the Delete button.

4. Click OK. The link is removed and the linked label disappears.

You can also delete all the links associated with a link table by choosing dbConnect ➤ Links ➤ Delete Links. A dialog box appears, displaying a list of link tables.

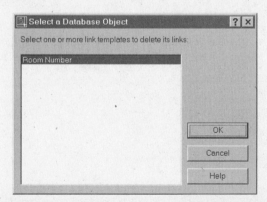

Select the link table whose links you want to delete, and click OK.

Where to Go from Here

You've seen how you can access a database and link your drawing to it. This chapter can help you find the information you will need to develop your own database needs.

If you understand SQL, you can take advantage of it to perform more sophisticated searches. You can also expand the functionality of the dbConnect Manager. For more detailed information about dbConnect and SQL, refer to the *AutoCAD SQL Extension* reference manual.

WHAT'S NEXT?

In this chapter, you have learned what attributes are and how to attach attributes to blocks. In addition, you have seen how to import attributes from a drawing into a database management program. In the next chapter, you will learn how to use the advanced 3D features of AutoCAD.

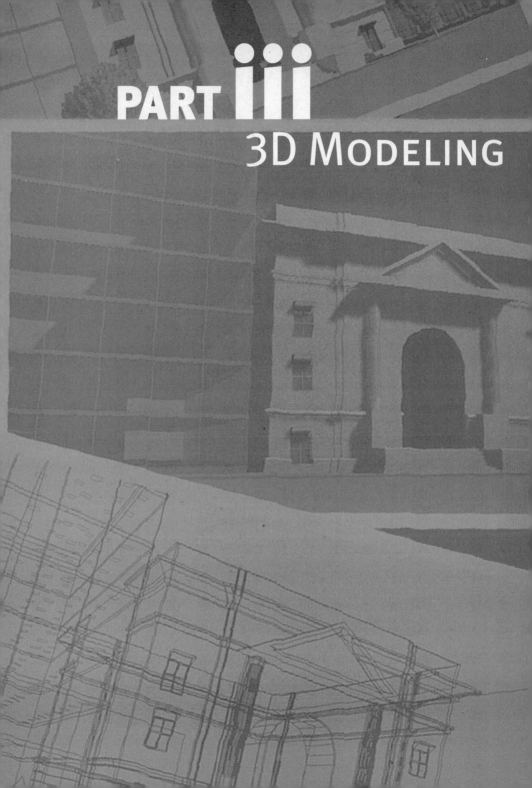

PART iii

3D MODELING

Chapter 11

Using Advanced 3D Features

AutoCAD's extended set of tools for working with 3D drawings lets you create 3D objects with few limitations on shape and orientation. This chapter focuses on the use of these tools, which help you easily generate 3D forms and view them in both the Perspective and Orthogonal modes.

Adapted from *Mastering™ AutoCAD® 2000 Premium Edition* by George Omura
ISBN 0-7821-2499-2   1,664 pages $59.99

MASTERING THE USER COORDINATE SYSTEM

The User Coordinate System (UCS) allows you to define a custom coordinate system in 2D and 3D space. In fact, you've been using a special UCS called the World Coordinate System (WCS) all along.

By now you are familiar with the L-shaped icon in the lower-left corner of the AutoCAD screen, containing the letters W, X, and Y. The W indicates that you are currently in the WCS; the X and Y indicate the positive directions of the x- and y-axes. WCS is a global system of reference from which you can define other User Coordinate Systems.

It may help to think of these AutoCAD User Coordinate Systems as different drawing surfaces, or two-dimensional planes. You can have several UCSs at any given time. By setting up these different UCSs, you are able to draw as you would in the WCS in 2D, yet draw a 3D image. Suppose you want to draw a house in 3D with doors and windows on each of its sides. You can set up a UCS for each of the sides; then you can move from UCS to UCS to add your doors and windows (see Figure 11.1). Within each of these UCSs, you draw your doors and windows as you would in a typical 2D drawing. You can even insert elevation views of doors and windows that you have created in other drawings.

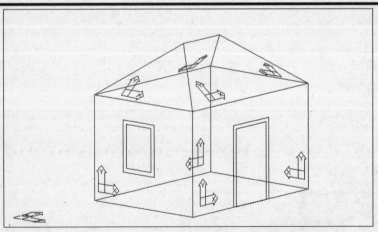

FIGURE 11.1: Different User Coordinate Systems in a 3D drawing

In this chapter, you will be experimenting with a number of different views and UCSs. All the commands you will use are available both at the Command line and via the menu bar. In addition, a number of the UCS commands can be accessed from the UCS toolbar.

Defining a UCS

In the first set of exercises, you will draw a chair. In drawing this chair, you will be exposed to the use of the UCS, as well as to some of the other 3D capabilities available in AutoCAD.

Begin the chair by drawing the seat and seat back.

1. Start AutoCAD and create a new file called Barcelon.

2. Set up your drawing as an architectural drawing with a scale of 1"=1'-0" on an 8 1/2" × 11" sheet. Set the upper-right corner of the limits to 132 × 102. If you're a metric user, you'll be drawing the chair at a scale of 1 to 10 on an A4 sheet. Your work area should be 297 × 210, which is the equivalent of a 297cm by 210cm area.

TIP

If you are a metric user and you prefer to work in millimeters, you can set the upper-right corner of the limits to 2970,2100. Then, when the book specifies a length or coordinate, multiply the specified value by 10. For example, 50cm becomes 500mm. Coordinate 50,50 becomes 500,500. Your scale factor would also change to 100.

Part iii

3. Choose View ➤ Zoom ➤ All or type **Z**, press Enter, type **A**, and press Enter again.

4. To draw the seat of the chair, click the Rectangle tool on the Draw toolbar. Draw a rectangle measuring 20" in the x-axis and 30" in the y-axis. Position the rectangle so the lower-left corner is at the coordinate 2'-0",2' -0" (see the top image of Figure 11.2). Metric users should draw a rectangle that is 50cm by 76cm with its lower-left corner at coordinate 50,50.

5. To draw the back of the chair, draw another rectangle 17" in the x-axis and 30" in the y-axis, just to the right of the previous rectangle (see the top image of Figure 11.2). Metric users should make this rectangle 43cm by 76cm.

40 × 760

650 × 50

6. Choose View ➤ 3D Views ➤ SW Isometric to see a 3D view from the lower-left of the rectangles, as shown in the bottom image of Figure 11.2.

7. Select the two rectangles, and then click the Properties tool on the Standard toolbar.

8. In the Properties dialog box, enter **3** in the Thickness setting and click OK. This setting gives the seat and back a thickness of 3". Metric users should make the thickness 7.6cm.

9. Close the Properties dialog box.

10. Zoom out a bit and give yourself some room to work.

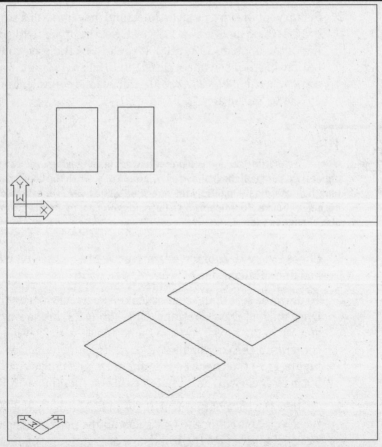

FIGURE 11.2: The chair seat (top) and back (bottom) in the Plan and Isometric views

Notice that the UCS icon appears in the same plane as the current coordinate system. The icon will help you keep track of which coordinate system you are in. Now you can see the chair components as 3D objects.

Next, you will define a UCS that is aligned with one side of the seat.

1. Right-click any toolbar, and at the pop-up menu, select UCS. The UCS toolbar appears.

2. Click the Display UCS Dialog tool in the UCS toolbar.

The UCS dialog box appears.

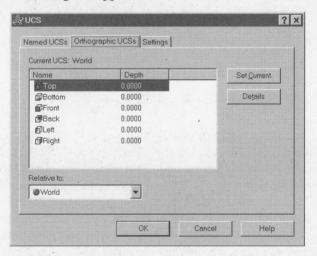

3. Select the Orthographic UCSs tab to view a set of predefined UCSs.

4. Select Front in the list box. Figure 11.3 shows the orientation of the Front UCS.

5. Click the Set Current button to make the Front UCS the current one.

6. Click OK to close the dialog box.

Part iii

The Orthographic UCSs tab offers a set of predefined UCSs for each of the six standard orthographic projection planes. Figure 11.3 shows these UCSs in relation to the World Coordinate System. You can also access these orthographic UCSs from the Tools ➤ Orthographic UCS cascading menu, or from the UCS dialog box.

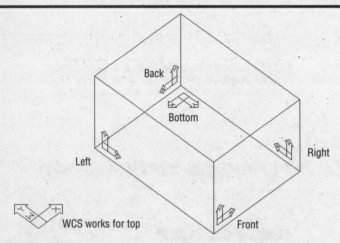

FIGURE 11.3: The six predefined UCS orientations

Because a good part of 3D work involves drawing in these orthographic planes, AutoCAD supplies these ready-made UCS orientations for quick access. But you aren't limited to these six orientations by any means. If you're familiar with mechanical drafting, you'll see that the orthographic UCSs correspond to the typical orthographic projections used in mechanical drafting. If you're an architect, the Front, Left, Back, and Right UCSs correspond to the south, west, north, and east elevations of a building. Before you continue building the chair model, you'll want to move the UCS to the surface on which you will be working. Right now, the UCS has its origin located in the same place as the WCS origin. You can move a UCS so that its origin is anywhere in the drawing where it's needed.

1. Click the Origin UCS tool in the UCS toolbar.

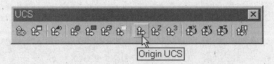

2. Use the Endpoint Osnap and click the bottom-front corner of the chair seat, as shown in Figure 11.4. The UCS icon moves to indicate its new origin's location.

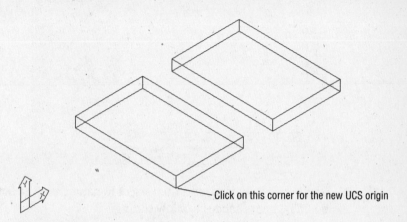

Click on this corner for the new UCS origin

FIGURE 11.4: Setting up a UCS

The operation you just performed created a new UCS based on the Front UCS you selected from the UCS dialog box. Now, as you move your cursor, you'll see that the origin of the UCS icon corresponds to a 0,0 coordinate. Although you have a new UCS, the WCS still exists, and you can always return to it when you need to.

Saving a UCS

Once you've gone through the work of creating a UCS, you may want to save it, especially if you think you'll want to come back to it later on. Here's how to save a UCS.

1. Click Display UCS Dialog on the UCS toolbar. You can also choose Tools ➢ Named UCS. The UCS dialog box appears.

2. Make sure the Named UCSs tab is selected, and then highlight the Unnamed option in the Current UCS list box.

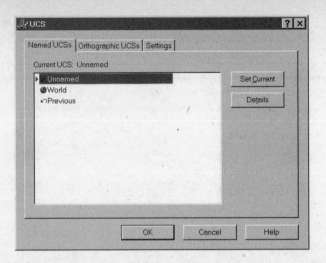

3. Right-click Unnamed, and then select Rename from the list box. The item changes to allow editing.

4. Type **3DSW** and press Enter for the name of your new UCS.

5. Click OK to exit the dialog box.

Your UCS is now saved under the name of 3DSW. You'll be able to recall it from the UCS dialog box, or from other methods that you'll learn about later in this chapter.

Working in a UCS

Next, you will arrange the seat and back and draw the legs of the chair. Your UCS is oriented so that you can easily adjust the chair components to their proper orientation. As you work through the next exercise, notice that while you are manipulating 3D objects, you are really using the same tools you've used to edit 2D objects.

1. Click the seat back to expose its grips.

2. Click the bottom grip, as shown in the first image of Figure 11.5.

3. Right-click the mouse to open the Grip Edit pop-up menu.

4. Select Rotate from the menu. Notice how the seat back now rotates with the movement of the cursor. Take a moment to play with this rotation; it may take a while to grow accustomed

to it. Because this is an Isometric view, you can get an optical illusion effect.

5. Type **80** and press Enter to rotate the seat back 80°. Your view will look like the second image of Figure 11.5.

6. Click the bottom grip shown in the second image of Figure 11.5.

7. Right-click the mouse again and select Move.

8. Using the Endpoint Osnap, click the top corner of the chair seat, as shown in the second image of Figure 11.5, to join the chair back to the seat.

9. Click both the chair seat and back; then, click the bottom-corner grip of the seat, as shown in the third image of Figure 11.5.

10. Right-click the mouse; then, at the Grip Edit pop-up menu, click Rotate.

11. Enter **−10** and press Enter to rotate both the seat and back minus 10 degrees. Press the Esc key twice to clear the grips. Your chair will look like Figure 11.6.

The new UCS orientation enabled you to use the grips to adjust the chair seat and back. All of the grip rotation in the previous exercise was confined to the plane of the new UCS. Mirroring and scaling will also occur in relation to the current UCS.

Part iii

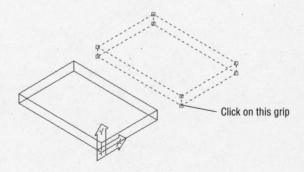

Click on this grip

FIGURE 11.5: Moving the components of the chair into place

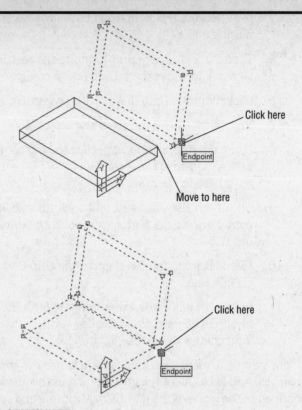

Click here

Endpoint

Move to here

Click here

Endpoint

FIGURE 11.5 CONTINUED

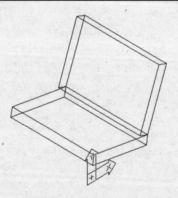

FIGURE 11.6: The chair, after rotating and moving the components into place

Now, to finish the chair seat and back, add a 3D Face to their top and bottom surfaces.

1. To help you visualize what's going on as you add the 3D Face, turn on the Hidden Shade mode by choosing View ➤ Shade ➤ Hidden. Or, if you have the Shade toolbar open, you can click the Hidden tool.

2. Click the 3D Face button on the Surfaces toolbar, or choose Draw ➤ Surfaces ➤ 3D Face, to draw a surface over the top sides of the chair seat and back. Start the 3D Face in the left-most corner of the seat and work in a counterclockwise fashion.

NOTE

To display the Surfaces toolbar, right-click any toolbar, and then choose Surfaces from the Toolbars dialog box.

3. Add the 3D Faces to the bottom of the chair seat and to the chair back, as shown in Figure 11.7.

4. When you've finished adding the 3D Faces, turn off the Hidden Shade mode. Choose View ➤ Shade ➤ 2D Wireframe.

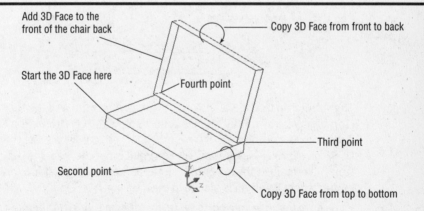

Add 3D Face to the front of the chair back

Copy 3D Face from front to back

Start the 3D Face here

Fourth point

Third point

Second point

Copy 3D Face from top to bottom

FIGURE 11.7: The 3D view of your drawing so far, showing where to pick points for the 3D Faces

Normally, when you're picking points for 3D Faces, it doesn't matter where you begin selecting points. But for the purpose of this chapter, you selected points for the seat's 3D Face starting at the left-most corner and

Part iii

working in a counterclockwise fashion. The way you create the chair seat will influence the action of some UCS command options that you'll use later in this chapter.

CONTROLLING THE UCS ICON

If the UCS icon is not behaving as described in the exercises of this chapter, then chances are that its settings have been altered. You can control the behavior of the UCS icon through the UCS dialog box. To access the UCS dialog box, choose Tools ➤ Named UCS. You can also click the Display UCS Dialog tool on the UCS II or UCS toolbar. Once you've opened the dialog box, click the Settings tab.

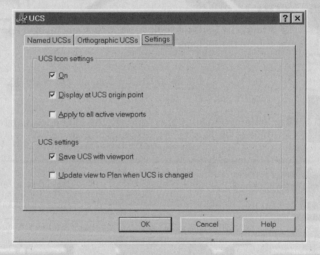

The settings in the UCS Icon Settings group affect the way the UCS icon behaves. Normally, the On and Display at UCS Origin Point check boxes are checked. If On is not checked, you won't see the UCS Icon at all. If Display at UCS Origin Point is not checked, the UCS icon will remain in the lower-left corner of the drawing window, no matter where its origin is placed in the drawing.

If you have multiple viewports set up in a drawing, you can set these two options independently for each viewport. The third option, Apply to All Active Viewports, forces the first two settings to apply in all viewports.

CONTINUED ➡

Two more options appear in the UCS Settings group. If you have multiple viewports open, the Save UCS with Viewport option allows AutoCAD to maintain a separate UCS for each viewport. The Update View to Plan When UCS Is Changed option forces the display to show a plan view of the current UCS. This means that if you change a UCS orientation, AutoCAD will automatically show a plan view of the new UCS orientation.

Using Viewports to Aid in 3D Drawing

In this section, you will use *tiled* viewports to see your 3D model from several sides at the same time. Doing so is helpful in both creating and editing 3D drawings because it allows you to refer to different portions of the drawing without having to change views. Tiled viewports are created directly in model space.

1. Select View ➤ Viewports ➤ Named Viewports. The Viewports dialog box appears.

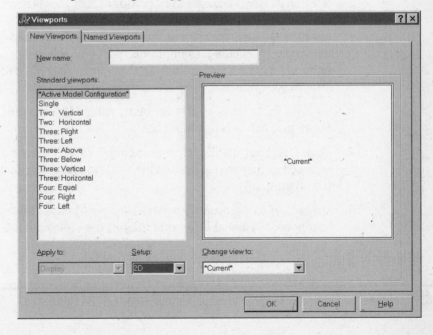

2. Make sure the New Viewports tab is selected, and then click Three: Right from the Standard Viewports list on the left. The window on the right changes to display a sample of the viewport configuration. It shows three rectangles, which represent the viewports, arranged with two on the left and a larger one to the right. Notice that each rectangle is labeled as Current. This label tells you that the current view will be placed in each viewport.

3. Open the Setup drop-down list at the bottom of the dialog box and select 3D. Now notice that the labels in the viewport sample change to indicate Top, Front, and SE Isometric. This is close to the arrangement that you'll want, but you need to make one more adjustment. The viewport to the right, SE Isometric, shows the backside of the chair. You want an SW Isometric view in this window.

4. Click the SE Isometric viewport sample. Notice that the sample viewport border thickens to indicate that it is selected.

5. Open the Change View To drop-down list just below the sample viewports and select SW Isometric. The label in the selected viewport changes to let you know that the view will now contain the SW Isometric view. Notice that the list contains the standard four isometric views and the six orthogonal views. By clicking a sample viewport and selecting an option from the Change View To drop-down list, you can arrange your viewport views in nearly any way you want.

6. To keep this viewport arrangement, enter **My Viewport Setup** in the New Name input box.

7. Click OK. Your display changes to show three viewports arranged as they were indicated in the Viewports dialog box (see Figure 11.8).

8. To check to see that your viewport was saved, Choose View ➤ Viewports ➤ Named Viewports to open the Viewports dialog box again.

9. Click the Named Viewports tab. My Viewport Setup is listed in the Named Viewports list box. If you click it, a sample view of your viewport arrangement appears on the right.

10. After you've reviewed the addition to the Named Viewports list, close the dialog box.

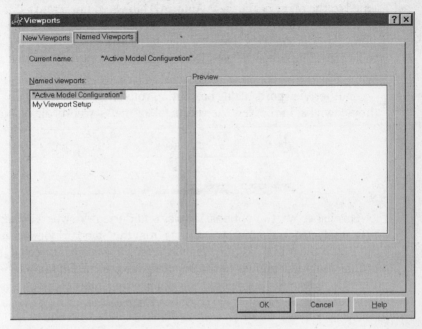

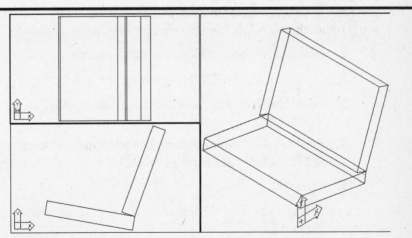

FIGURE 11.8: Three viewports, each displaying a different view

Now take a close look at your viewport setup. Notice that the UCS icon in each of the two orthogonal views in the two left viewports is oriented to the plane of the view. AutoCAD allows you to set up a different UCS for each viewport. The top view uses the WCS because it is in the same plane as the WCS. The side view has its own UCS, which is parallel to its view. The isometric view to the right retains the UCS you saved—the 3DSW UCS.

Another Viewports dialog box option you didn't try is the Apply To drop-down list in the New Viewports tab of the Viewports dialog box.

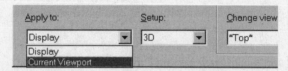

This list shows two options: Display and Current Viewport. When Display is selected, the option you choose from the Standard Viewports list applies to the overall display. When Current Viewport is selected, the option you select applies to the selected viewport in the sample view in the right side of the dialog box. You can use the Current Viewport option to build multiple viewports in custom arrangements.

Adding the Legs

The next items you will add to your chair are the legs. Before you do that, you'll set up the 3DSW UCS in the side view of your chair.

1. Click the lower-left viewport to make it active.

2. Click the Display UCS Dialog tool on the UCS toolbar.

3. Select the Named UCSs tab, and then select 3DSW from the list of UCSs.

4. Click the Set Current button. The triangular marker to the left of the UCS names moves to 3DSW.

5. Click OK.

Now you're ready to draw the legs using the coordinate information shown in Figure 11.9.

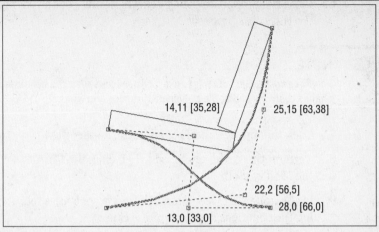

14,11 [35,28]   25,15 [63,38]

22,2 [56,5]

28,0 [66,0]

13,0 [33,0]

FIGURE 11.9: Drawing the legs of the chair. Metric coordinates are shown in brackets.

1. Go to the side view of the chair and move the chair seat and back vertically in the y-axis 8.5" or 21.6cm for metric users. Make sure you select all the lines and 3D Faces for the move. You may have to pan the view down so that the entire chair is displayed.

TIP

If you anticipate moving a group of 3D objects frequently, use the Group command to group objects together. The Group command is especially useful in 3D work, because you can group sets of objects together for easy manipulation, yet you can still edit the individual objects within a group.

2. Draw two curved polylines, as shown in Figure 11.9. You may have to adjust your view so that you can draw the legs more easily. You don't have to be absolutely perfect about placing or shaping these lines.

3. Use the grips of the polylines to adjust their curve, if necessary.

4. Use Modify ➤ Polyline to give the polylines a width of 0.5" (1.27cm for metric users).

5. Use the Properties dialog box to give the polylines a thickness of –2" (minus 2 inches). Metric users should make the thickness –5cm. Notice that as you draw and edit a polyline, it appears in both the Plan and 3D views.

6. Close the Properties dialog box when you are done changing the thickness property.

NOTE

Polylines are the best objects to use for 3D, because you can generate complex shapes easily by giving the polylines thickness and width.

7. Click the top view of the chair in the upper-left viewport.

8. Turn on the Ortho mode, and then click the Mirror tool on the Modify toolbar.

9. In the upper-left viewport, click the two polylines representing the chair legs, and then press Enter.

10. At the First point of mirror line: prompt, use the Midpoint Osnap and select the midpoint of the chair seat, as shown in Figure 11.10.

11. At the second point, pick any location to the right of the point you selected, so that the rubber-banding line is exactly horizontal.

12. Press Enter at the Delete old object: prompt. The legs are mirrored to the opposite side of the chair. Your screen should look similar to Figure 11.10.

NOTE

Notice that the broken-pencil UCS icon has shifted to the viewport in the lower-left corner. This icon tells you that the current UCS is perpendicular to the plane of that view.

Your chair is now complete. Let's finish up by getting a better look at it.

1. Click the viewport to the right showing the isometric view.

2. Open the Viewports dialog box and select the New Viewports tab.

3. Select Single from the Standard Viewports list, and then click OK.

4. Choose View ➤ Hide to get a view of your chair with the lines hidden.

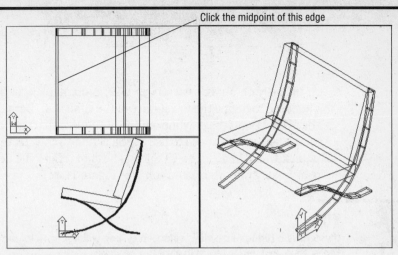

Click the midpoint of this edge

FIGURE 11.10: Mirroring the legs from one side to another

Controlling the UCS

You've seen how you can select a UCS from a set of predefined UCSs. You can frequently use these preset UCSs and make minor adjustments to them to get the exact UCS you want.

You can also define a UCS a number of other ways. For example, you can use the 3D Face of your chair seat as the definition for a UCS. In the following set of exercises, you will get some practice moving your UCS around. Learning how to move effortlessly between UCSs is crucial to your mastering the creation of 3D models, so you'll want to pay special attention to the command options shown in these procedures. These options are accessible from either the Tools ➤ UCS cascading menu or the UCS toolbar.

UCS Based on Object Orientation

You can define a UCS based on the orientation of an object. Doing so is helpful when you want to work on a predefined object to fill in detail on its surface plane.

1. Click the Object UCS tool on the UCS toolbar, or choose Tools ➤ New UCS ➤ Object. You can also type **UCS**, press Enter, type **OB**, and press Enter again.

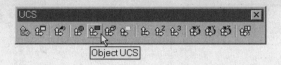

2. At the `Select object to align UCS:` prompt, pick the 3D
   Face used to define the top surface of the chair seat. Because
   the 3D Face and the polyline outline of the seat share a common edge, you may need to use the Selection Cycling feature
   to pick the 3D Face. The UCS icon shifts to reflect the new
   coordinate system's orientation (see Figure 11.11).

TIP

If you have a Hidden-Line view, selection cycling will not work for picking 3D
Faces. Issue a Regen to return to a wireframe view.

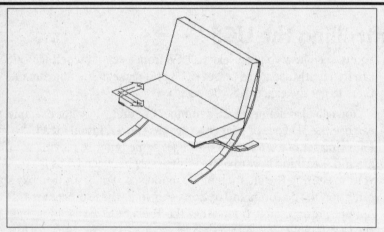

FIGURE 11.11: Using the Object option of the UCS command to locate a UCS

Orientation of the UCS Origin   Remember earlier in the chapter
when you drew the 3D Face for the seat in a specific way? Well, the location of the UCS origin and its orientation depend on how that 3D Face
was created. If you had drawn it other than as instructed, the UCS you
defined using the Object option in the previous exercise would not have
been generated as described.

Table 11.1 describes how an object can determine the orientation of a UCS.

TABLE 11.1:   Effects of Objects on the Orientation of an UCS

OBJECT TYPE	UCS ORIENTATION
Arc	The center of the arc establishes the UCS origin. The x-axis of the UCS passes through the pick point on the arc.
Circle	The center of the circle establishes the UCS origin. The x-axis of the UCS passes through the pick point on the circle.
Dimension	The midpoint of the dimension text establishes the origin of the UCS origin. The x-axis of the UCS is parallel to the x-axis that was active when the dimension was drawn.
Line	The endpoint nearest the pick point establishes the origin of the UCS, and the xz plane of the UCS contains the line.
Point	The point location establishes the UCS origin. The UCS orientation is arbitrary.
2D polyline	The starting point of the polyline establishes the UCS origin. The x-axis is determined by the direction from the first point to the next vertex.
Solid	The first point of the solid establishes the origin of the UCS. The second point of the solid establishes the x-axis.
Trace	The direction of the trace establishes the x-axis of the UCS with the beginning point setting the origin.
3D Face	The first point of the 3D Face establishes the origin. The first and second points establish the x-axis. The plane defined by the 3D Face determines the orientation of the UCS.
Shapes, text, blocks, attributes, and attribute definitions	The insertion point establishes the origin of the UCS. The object's rotation angle establishes the x-axis.

UCS Based on Offset Orientation

Sometimes you may want to work in a UCS that has the same orientation as the current UCS but is offset. For example, you may be making a drawing of a building that has several parallel walls offset with a sawtooth effect (see Figure 11.12). You can easily hop from one UCS to another parallel UCS by using the Origin option.

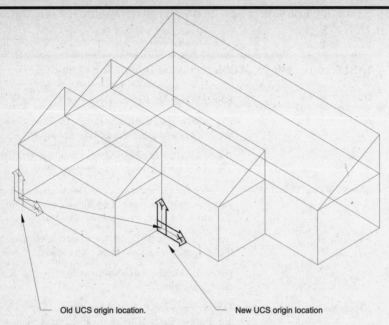

Old UCS origin location.   New UCS origin location

FIGURE 11.12: Using the Origin option to shift the UCS

1. Click the Origin UCS tool on the UCS toolbar, or choose Tools ➤ New UCS ➤ Origin. You can also type **UCS**, press Enter, type **O**, and press Enter again.

2. At the Origin point <0,0,0>: prompt, pick the bottom end of the chair leg, just below the current UCS origin. The UCS icon shifts to the end of the leg, with its origin at the point you picked (see Figure 11.13).

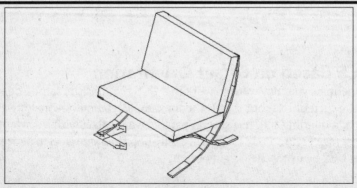

FIGURE 11.13: Moving the origin of the UCS ·

Moving vs. Creating a UCS Origin

The Origin UCS tool creates a new UCS that you can save under its own name. Another option that is very similar to the Origin UCS tool is the Move UCS option on the Tools pull-down menu. At first glance, they seem to do the same thing: create a new UCS by moving an existing UCS's origin. There is a subtle difference between the two, however. The Tools ➤ Move UCS option is intended to move an existing named UCS to a new location. It doesn't create a new one. For example, if you use Move UCS to move the 3DSW UCS you created earlier in this chapter, then when you recall 3DSW, it will appear in its new location. On the other hand, if you use the Origin UCS tool to change the origin of the 3DSW UCS, AutoCAD creates an entirely different UCS and maintains the original location of 3DSW.

The Tools ➤ Move UCS option can also be found on the UCS II toolbar. You'll get a chance to work with the UCS II toolbar in the next section.

UCS Rotated Around an Axis

Now suppose you want to change the orientation of the x-, y-, or z-axis of a UCS. You can accomplish this by using the X, Y, or X Axis Rotate UCS option on the UCS toolbar. Let's try rotating the UCS about the z-axis to see how this works.

1. Click the Z Axis Rotate UCS tool on the UCS toolbar, or choose Tools ➤ New UCS ➤ Z Axis Rotate. You can also type **UCS**, press Enter, type **Z**, and press Enter again. Doing so will allow you to rotate the current UCS around the z-axis.

2. At the Rotation angle about Z axis <0>: prompt, enter **90** for 90°. The UCS icon rotates to reflect the new orientation of the current UCS (see Figure 11.14).

Similarly, the X and Y Axis Rotate UCS options allow you to rotate the UCS about the current x- and y-axis, respectively, just as you did for the z-axis above. The X and Y Axis Rotate UCS tools are very helpful in orienting a UCS to an inclined plane. For example, if you want to work on a plane of a sloped roof of a building, you can first use the Origin UCS tool to align the UCS to the edge of a roof and then use the X Axis Rotate UCS tool to rotate the UCS to the angle of the roof slope, as shown in Figure 11.15.

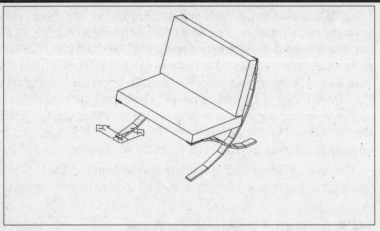

FIGURE 11.14: Rotating the UCS about the z-axis

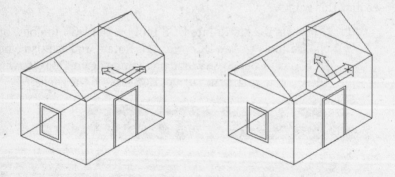

FIGURE 11.15: Moving a UCS to the plane of a sloping roof

Finally, you can skew the UCS using the Z Axis Vector option. This technique is useful when you need to define a UCS based on a z-axis determined by two objects.

1. Click the Z Axis Vector UCS tool on the UCS toolbar, or choose Tools ➤ UCS ➤ Z Axis Vector. You can also type **UCS**, press Enter, type **ZA**, and press Enter again.

2. At the `Origin point <0,0,0>:` prompt, press Enter to accept the default, which is the current UCS origin. You can shift the origin point at this prompt if you like.

3. At the next prompt

   `Point on positive portion of Z-axis <0'-0", 0'- 0", 0'-1">:`

use the Endpoint Osnap override and pick the other chair leg end, as shown in Figure 11.16. The UCS twists to reflect the new z-axis of the UCS.

WARNING

Because your cursor location is in the plane of the current UCS, it is best to pick a point on an object using either the Osnap overrides or the coordinate filters.

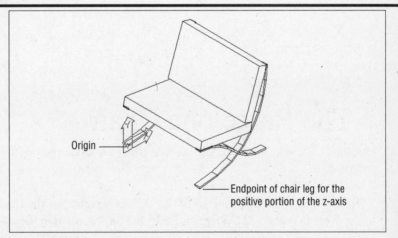

FIGURE 11.16: Picking points for the Z Axis Vector option

Orienting a UCS in the View Plan

Finally, you can define a UCS in the current view plane. Doing so is useful if you want to switch quickly to the current view plane for editing or for adding text to a 3D view.

Part iii

Click the View UCS tool on the UCS toolbar, or choose View ➤ Set UCS ➤ View. You can also type **UCS**, press Enter, type **V**, and press Enter again. The UCS icon changes to show that the UCS is aligned with the current view.

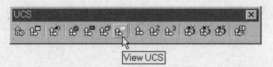

AutoCAD uses the current UCS origin point for the origin of the new UCS. By defining a view as a UCS, you can enter text to label your drawing, just as you would in a technical illustration. Text entered in a plane created in this way appears normal (see Figure 11.17).

The Barcelona Chair

FIGURE 11.17: Adding text to a 3D view using the View option of the UCS command

Now you've finished your tour of the UCS command. Set the UCS back to the World Coordinate System and save the Barcelon.dwg file.

You've explored nearly every option in creating a UCS, except for one. In the next section, you'll learn about the 3 Point option for creating a UCS. The 3 Point option is the most versatile method for creating a UCS, but it is a bit more involved than some of the other UCS options.

TIP

A new feature as of AutoCAD 2000 is the ability to save a UCS with a view. Choose View ➢ Named Views, and then select the Named Views tab of the Views dialog box. Click the New button. In the New View dialog box, enter a name for your new view and make sure the Save UCS with View option is checked. By default, AutoCAD saves the current UCS with the view. You can also choose a UCS to save with a new view using the UCS Name drop-down list.

CREATING COMPLEX 3D SURFACES

In the previous example, you drew a chair composed of objects that were mostly straight lines or curves with a thickness. All the forms in that chair were defined in planes perpendicular to each other. For a 3D model such as this, you can get by using the Orthographic UCSs. At times, however, you will want to draw objects that do not fit so easily into perpendicular or parallel planes. The following exercise demonstrates how you can create more complex forms using some of AutoCAD's other 3D commands.

Laying Out a 3D Form

In this next group of exercises, you will draw a butterfly chair. This chair has no perpendicular or parallel planes to work with, so you will start by setting up some points that you will use for reference only. This is similar in concept to laying out a 2D drawing. You will construct some temporary 3D lines to use for reference. These temporary lines will be your layout. These points will define the major UCSs needed to construct the drawing. As you progress through the drawing construction, notice how the reference points are established to help create the chair.

1. If it isn't open already, open the Barcelon drawing, and then use File ➢ Save As to save the file under the name Btrfly.

2. Choose View ➢ 3D Views ➢ Plan View ➢ World UCS. Then, choose View ➢ Zoom ➢ All to display the overall area of the drawing.

NOTE

You will draw the butterfly chair almost entirely while viewing it in 3D. This approach is useful when you are creating complex shapes.

3. Erase the entire contents of the drawing, and then make sure you are in the WCS by choosing Tools ➤ UCS ➤ World.

4. Click Rectangle on the Draw toolbar. Draw a rectangle 20" square with its first corner at coordinate 36,36. Metric users should draw a rectangle 51cm square, with its first corner at coordinate 81,81.

5. Use the Offset tool to offset the square 4" out, so you have two concentric squares with the outer square measuring 28". Metric users should offset 10cm for an outer square measuring 71cm.

6. Move the larger of the two squares, the 28" square, to the left 2". Metric users should move the larger square 5cm to the left. Your screen should look similar to Figure 11.18.

7. Choose View ➤ 3D Viewpoint ➤ SW Isometric so you see a view from the lower-left side of the rectangles.

8. Zoom out so the rectangles occupy about a third of the drawing area window.

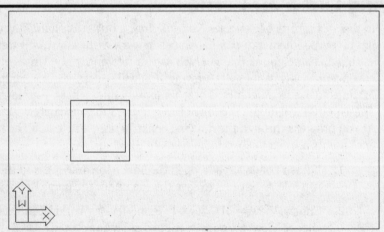

FIGURE 11.18: Setting up a layout for a butterfly chair

Now you need to move the outer rectangle in the z-axis so that its elevation is 30" (76cm for metric users).

1. Click the outer rectangle, and then click one of its grips.

2. Right-click to open the Grip Edit pop-up menu.

3. Select Move, and then enter **@0,0,30** and press Enter. Metric users should enter **@0,0,76** and press Enter. This command tells AutoCAD to move the rectangle a 0 distance in both the x-axis and y-axis, and 30" (or 76cm) in the z-axis.

4. Pan your view downward so it looks similar to Figure 11.19.

5. Use the Line tool to draw lines from the corners of the outer square to the corners of the inner square, as shown in Figure 11.19. Use the Endpoint Osnap to select the exact corners of the squares. This is the layout for your chair—not yet the finished product.

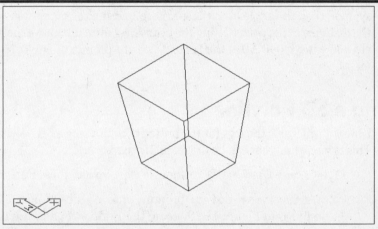

FIGURE 11.19: The finished chair layout

Spherical and Cylindrical Coordinate Formats

In the foregoing exercise, you used relative Cartesian coordinates to locate the second point for the Move command. For commands that accept 3D input, you can also specify displacements by using the *spherical* and *cylindrical coordinate* formats.

The spherical coordinate format lets you specify a distance in 3D space while specifying the angle in terms of degrees from the x-axis of the current UCS and degrees from the xy plane of the current UCS. For example, to specify a distance of 4.5" (11.43cm) at a 30° angle from the x-axis and 45° from the xy plane, enter **@4.5<30<45** (**@11.43<30<45** for metric users). This command refers to the direct distance, followed by a < symbol; then the angle from the x-axis of the current UCS, followed by another < symbol;

and then the angle from the xy plane of the current UCS. To use the spherical coordinate format to move the rectangle in the exercise, enter **@30<0<90** at the Second point: prompt or **@76<0<90** for metric users.

The cylindrical coordinate format, on the other hand, lets you specify a location in terms of a distance in the plane of the current UCS and a distance in the z-axis. You also specify an angle from the x-axis of the current UCS. For example, to locate a point that is a distance of 4.5" (11.43cm) in the plane of the current UCS, at an angle of 30° from the x-axis, and a distance of 3.3" (8.38cm) in the z-axis, enter **@4.5<30,3.3** (**@11.43<30, 8.38** for metric users). This command refers to the distance of the displacement as it relates to the plane of the current UCS, followed by the < symbol; then the angle from the x-axis, followed by a comma; and then the distance in the z-axis. Using the cylindrical format to move the rectangle, you enter **@0<0,30** at the Second point: prompt or **@0<0,76** for metric users.

Using a 3D Polyline

Now you will draw the legs for the butterfly chair using a 3D polyline. This is a polyline that can be drawn in 3D space.

1. Choose Draw ➢ 3D Polyline, or type **3p** and press Enter.

2. At the First point: prompt, pick a series of points, as shown in Figure 11.20, using the Endpoint and Midpoint Osnap.

TIP
This would be a good place to use the Running Osnaps feature.

3. Draw another 3D polyline in the mirror image of the first (see Figure 11.20).

4. Erase the rectangles and connecting lines that make up the frame.

All objects, with the exception of lines, 3D Faces, 3D Meshes, and 3D polylines, are restricted to the plane of your current UCS. The Pline command can only be used to draw polylines in one plane, but the 3DPoly command allows you to create a polyline in three dimensions. Three-dimensional polylines cannot, however, be given thickness or width.

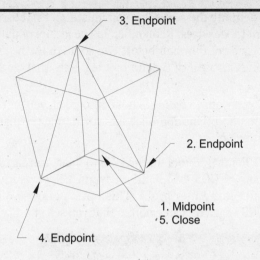

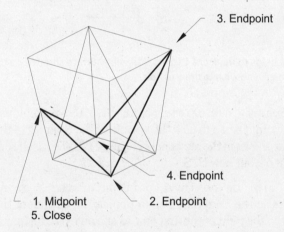

FIGURE 11.20: Using 3D polylines to draw the legs of the butterfly chair

Creating a Curved 3D Surface

Next, you will draw the seat of the chair. The seat of a butterfly chair is usually made of canvas and drapes from the four corners of the chair legs. You will first define the perimeter of the seat using arcs, and then use the Edge Surface tool on the Surfaces toolbar to form the shape of the draped canvas. The Edge Surface tool creates a surface based on four objects defining the edges of that surface. In this example, you will use arcs to define the edges of the seat.

To draw the arcs defining the seat edge, you must first establish the UCSs in the planes of those edges. Remember, in the last example you created a UCS for the side of the chair before you could draw the legs. In the same way, you must create a UCS defining the planes that contain the edges of the seat.

Because the UCS you want to define is not orthogonal, you will need to use the three-point method. This approach lets you define the plane of the UCS based on three points.

1. Click the 3 Point UCS tool on the UCS toolbar. You can also choose Tools ➢ UCS ➢ 3 Point, or type **UCS**, press Enter, type **3**, and press Enter again. This option allows you to define a UCS based on three points that you select.

NOTE

Remember, it helps to think of a UCS as a drawing surface situated on the surface of the object you wish to draw or edit.

2. At the Specify new origin point <0,0,0>: prompt, use the Endpoint Osnap to pick the bottom of the chair leg to the far left, as shown in the top panel of Figure 11.21. This is the origin point of your new UCS.

3. At the Point on positive portion of the X axis: prompt, use the Endpoint Osnap to pick the bottom of the next leg to the right of the first one, as shown in the top panel of Figure 11.21.

4. At the Point on positive - Y portion of the UCS X-Y plane: prompt, pick the top corner of the butterfly chair seat, as shown in the top panel of Figure 11.21. The UCS icon changes to indicate your new UCS.

5. Now that you have defined a UCS, you need to save it so that you can return to it later. Click Display UCS Dialog from the UCS toolbar, or choose Tools ➢ UCS ➢ Named UCS. You can also type **UC** and press Enter. The UCS dialog box appears.

Set up the Front UCS

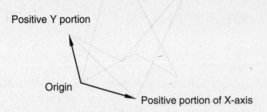

Positive Y portion

Origin

Positive portion of X-axis

Set up the Side UCS

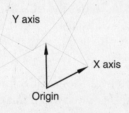

Y axis

X axis

Origin

Set up the Back UCS

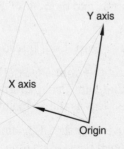

Y axis

X axis

Origin

FIGURE 11.21: Defining and saving three UCSs

6. With the Named UCSs tab selected, right-click the Unnamed item in the list box, and then select Rename.

7. Enter **Front Side** and press Enter.

8. Click OK to exit the UCS dialog box.

NOTE

Remember: Only lines, 3D polylines, and other 3D objects can be drawn in three-dimensional space. All other objects can be drawn only in the current UCS. Therefore, it is necessary to change the UCS in many situations when you are modeling in three dimensions.

You've defined and saved a UCS for the front side of the chair. As you can see from the UCS icon, this UCS is at a non-orthogonal angle to the WCS. Continue by creating UCSs for the other four sides of the butterfly chair.

1. Define a UCS for the side of the chair as shown in the middle image of Figure 11.21. Use the UCS Control dialog box to rename this UCS Left Side, just as you did for Front Side in steps 5 through 8. Remember that you renamed the Unnamed UCS.

2. Repeat these steps again for a UCS for the back of the chair, named Back. Use the bottom image of Figure 11.21 for reference.

3. Open the UCS dialog box again, and in the Named UCSs tab, highlight Front Side.

4. Click the Current button, and then click OK to activate Front Side as the current UCS.

5. Choose Draw ➤ Arc ➤ Start, End, Direction.

6. Draw the arc defining the front edge of the chair (see Figure 11.22). Use the Endpoint Osnap override to pick the top endpoints of the chair legs as the endpoints of the arc.

7. Repeat steps 3 through 6 for the UCS named Side, and then again for the UCS named Back—each time using the top endpoints of the legs for the endpoints of the arc.

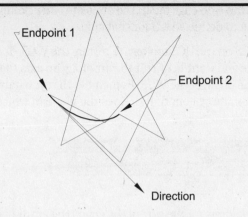

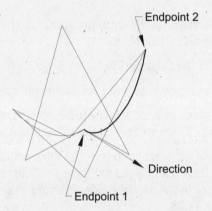

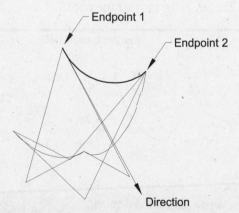

FIGURE 11.22: Drawing the seat edge using arcs

Next, you will mirror the side-edge arc to the opposite side. Doing so will save you from having to define a UCS for that side.

1. Click World UCS on the UCS toolbar. to restore the WCS. You do this because you want to mirror the arc along an axis that is parallel to the plane of the WCS. Remember that you must go to the coordinate system that defines the plane in which you wish to work.

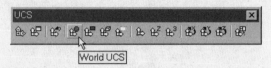

2. Click the arc you drew for the side of the chair (the arc drawn on the Side UCS).

3. Click the midpoint grip of the arc in the Side UCS; then, right-click the mouse and select Mirror.

4. Enter **C** to select the Copy option.

5. Enter **B** to select a new base point for the mirror axis.

6. At the Base point: prompt, use the Intersect Osnap to pick the intersection of the two lines in the Front plane.

7. Use the Intersection override to pick the intersection of the two legs in the Back plane. Refer to Figure 11.23 for help. The arc should mirror to the opposite side, and your chair should look like Figure 11.24.

8. Press the Esc key twice to clear the grips.

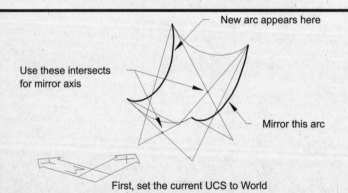

New arc appears here

Use these intersects for mirror axis

Mirror this arc

First, set the current UCS to World

FIGURE 11.23: Mirroring the arc that defines the side of the chair seat

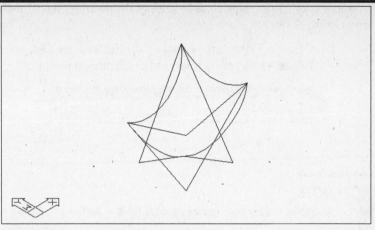

FIGURE 11.24: Your butterfly chair so far

QUICK HOPS TO YOUR UCSS

If you find you're jumping from one saved UCS to another, you'll want to know about the UCS II toolbar. The UCS II toolbar offers a drop-down list that contains all the saved UCSs in a drawing. You can use this list as a quick way to move between UCSs that you've set up, or even between the predefined orthogonal UCSs.

Two other tools on the UCS II toolbar give you access to the UCS dialog box and the Move UCS origin tool, which moves an existing UCS to another location. As with all toolbars, you can open the UCS II toolbar by right-clicking any toolbar and then selecting UCS II from the pop-up menu.

Finally, let's finish this chair by adding the mesh representing the chair seat.

1. Click the Edge Surface tool on the Surfaces toolbar, or enter **Edgesurf** and press Enter at the Command prompt.

NOTE

To display the Surfaces toolbar, choose Tools ➤ Toolbars ➤ Surfaces.

2. At the Select edge 1: prompt, pick the arc on the Front UCS.

3. At the Select edge 2: prompt, pick the next arc on the Side UCS.

WARNING

For the command to work properly, the arcs (or any set of objects) used with the Edge Surface option to define the boundary of a mesh must be connected exactly end-to-end.

4. Continue to pick the other two arcs in succession. (The arcs must be picked in a circular fashion, not crosswise.) A mesh appears, filling the space between the four arcs. Your chair is now complete.

5. Use View ➤ Hide to get a better view of the butterfly chair. You should have a view similar to Figure 11.25.

6. Save this file.

At this point, you've been introduced to a few of the options on the Surfaces toolbar. You'll get a chance to use these later in this chapter. Next, you'll learn how to edit mesh objects like the butterfly chair's seat.

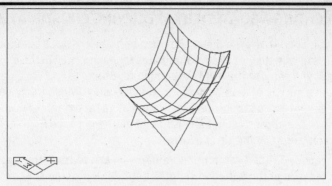

FIGURE 11.25: The completed butterfly chair

Adjusting the Settings That Control Meshes

As you can see, the seat in your butterfly chair is made up of rectangular segments. If you want to increase the number of segments in the mesh (to get a look like that in Figure 11.26), you can change the Surftab1 and Surftab2 system variables. Surftab1 controls the number of segments along edge 1, the first edge you pick in the sequence; and Surftab2 controls the number of segments along edge 2. AutoCAD refers to the direction of edge 1 as m and the direction of edge 2 as n. These two directions can be loosely described as the x- and y-axes of the mesh, with m being the x-axis and n being the y-axis.

In Figure 11.26, the setting for Surftab1 is 24, and for Surftab2 the setting is 12. The default value for both settings is 6. If you would like to try different Surftab settings on the chair mesh, you must erase the existing mesh, change the Surftab settings, and then use the Edge Surface tool again to define the mesh.

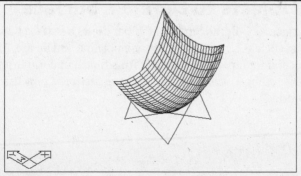

FIGURE 11.26: The butterfly chair with different Surftab settings

CREATING A 3D MESH BY SPECIFYING COORDINATES

If you need to draw a mesh like the one in the previous example, but you want to give exact coordinates for each vertex in the mesh grid, you can use the 3DMesh command. Suppose you have data from a survey of a piece of land; you can use 3DMesh to convert your data into a graphic representation of its topography. Another use of the 3DMesh command is to plot mathematical data to get a graphic representation of a formula.

Because you must enter the coordinate for each vertex in the mesh, 3DMesh is better suited in scripts or AutoLISP programs, where a list of coordinates can be applied automatically to the 3DMesh command in a sequential order.

OTHER SURFACE-DRAWING TOOLS

In the last example, you used the Edge Surface tool to create a 3D surface. Several other 3D surface commands are available that allow you to generate complex surface shapes easily.

TIP

All the objects described in this section, along with the meshes described earlier, are actually composites of 3D Faces. This means that you can explode these 3D objects into their component 3D Faces, which in turn can be edited individually.

Using Two Objects to Define a Surface

The Ruled Surface tool on the Surfaces toolbar draws a surface between two 2D objects, such as a line and an arc or a polyline and an arc. This command is useful for creating extruded forms that transform from one shape to another along a straight path. Let's see firsthand how the Ruled Surface tool works.

1. Open the file called Rulesurf.dwg from the companion website. It looks like the top image of Figure 11.27. This drawing is of a simple half-circle, drawn using a line and an arc. Ignore the diagonal blue line for now.

2. Move the line between the arc endpoints 10 units in the z-axis.

3. You are ready to connect the two objects with a 3D surface. Click the Ruled Surface tool on the Surfaces toolbar, or choose Draw ➤ Surfaces ➤ Ruled Surface.

4. At the Select first defining curve: prompt, place the cursor toward the right end of the arc and click.

5. At the Select second defining curve: prompt, move the cursor toward the right end of the line and click, as shown in the bottom image of Figure 11.27. The surface will appear as shown in Figure 11.28.

NOTE

The position you use to pick the second object will determine how the surface is generated.

Part iii

The location you use to select the two objects for the ruled surface is important. You selected specific locations on the arc and line so that the ruled surface is generated properly. Had you selected the opposite end of the line, for example, your result would look more like Figure 11.29. Notice that the segments defining the surface cross each other. This crossing effect is caused by picking the defining objects near opposite endpoints. The arc was picked near its lower end, and the line was picked toward the top end. At times, you may actually want this effect.

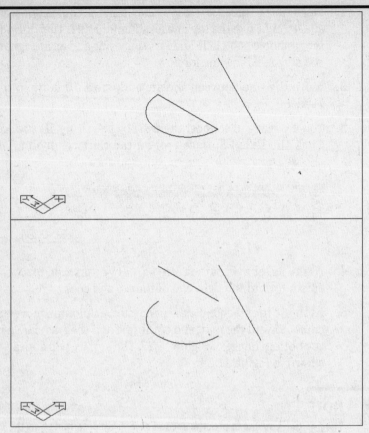

FIGURE 11.27: Drawing two edges for the Ruled Surface option

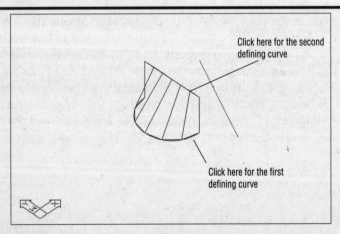

FIGURE 11.28: The Rulesurf surface

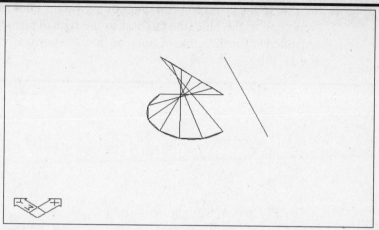

FIGURE 11.29: The ruled surface redrawn by using different points to select the objects

Extruding an Object along a Straight Line

The Tabulated Surface tool also uses two objects to draw a 3D surface, but instead of drawing the surface between the objects, the Tabulated Surface tool extrudes one object in a direction defined by a direction vector. The net result is an extruded shape that is the length and direction of the direction vector. To see what this means firsthand, try the following exercise.

1. While still in the Rulesurf drawing, click the Undo button in the Standard toolbar to undo the ruled surface from the previous exercise.

2. Click the Tabulated Surface tool from the Surface toolbar, or choose Draw ➤ Surfaces ➤ Tabulated Surfaces.

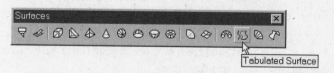

3. At the Path curve: prompt, click the arc.

4. At the Select Direction Vector: prompt, click the lower end of the blue line farthest to the right. The arc is extruded in the direction of the blue line, as shown in Figure 11.30.

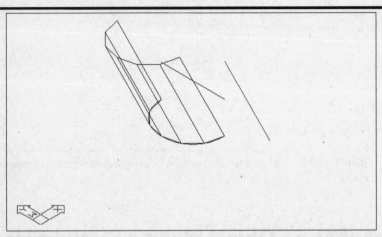

FIGURE 11.30: Extruding an arc using a line to indicate the extrusion direction

The direction vector can be any object, but AutoCAD will only consider the object's two endpoints when extruding the path curve. Just as with the Ruled Surface tool, the point at which you select the direction vector object affects the outcome of the extrusion. If you had selected a location near the top of the blue line, the extrusion would have gone in the opposite direction from the exercise.

Because the direction vector can point in any direction, the Tabulated Surface tool allows you to create an extruded shape that is not restricted to a direction perpendicular to the object being extruded.

The path curve defining the shape of the extrusion can be an arc, circle, line, or polyline. You can use a curve-fitted polyline or a spline polyline to create more complex shapes, as shown in Figure 11.31.

If you want to increase the number of facets in either the Ruled Surface or Tabulated Surface tools, set the Surftab1 system variable to the number of facets you desire.

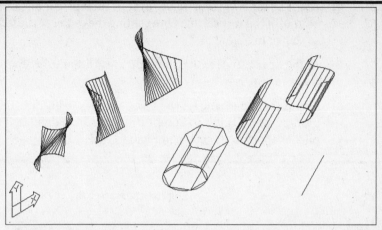

FIGURE 11.31: Some samples of other shapes created using the Ruled Surface and Tabulated Surface tools

Extruding a Circular Surface

The Revolved Surface tool allows you to quickly generate circular extrusions. Typical examples are vases or teacups. The following exercise illustrates how you can use the Revolved Surface tool to draw a pitcher. You'll use an existing drawing that has a profile of the pitcher already drawn.

1. Open the Pitcher.dwg file from the companion website. This file contains a polyline profile of a pitcher as well as a single line representing the center of the pitcher (see Figure 11.32). The profile and line have already been rotated to a position that is perpendicular to the WCS. The grid is turned on so you can better visualize the plane of the WCS.

2. Click the Revolved Surface tool on the Surfaces Toolbar.

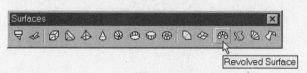

3. At the Select Path Curve: prompt, click the polyline profile, as shown in Figure 11.32.

Part iii

4. At the `Select Axis of Revolution:` prompt, click near the bottom of the vertical line representing the center of the vase, as shown in Figure 11.32.

5. At the `Start angle <0>:` prompt, press Enter to accept the 0 start angle.

6. At the `Included angle (+=ccw, -=cw) <Full circle>:` prompt, press Enter to accept the Full Circle default. The pitcher appears, as shown in Figure 11.33.

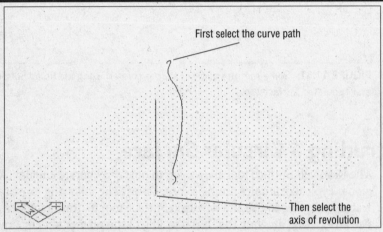

FIGURE 11.32: Drawing a pitcher using the Revolved Surface tool

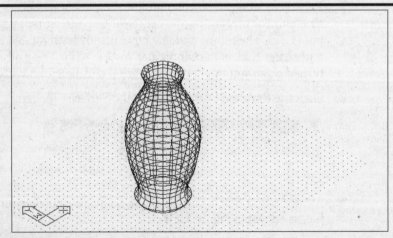

FIGURE 11.33: The completed pitcher

Notice that the pitcher is made up of a faceted mesh, like the mesh that is created by the Edge Surface tool. Just as with the Edge Surface tool, you can set the number of facets in each direction using the Surftab1 and Surftab2 system variable settings. Both Surftab1 and Surftab2 were already set to 24 in the Pitcher.dwg file, so the pitcher shape would appear fairly smooth.

You may have noticed that in steps 5 and 6 of the previous exercise, you have a few options. In step 5, you can specify a start angle. In this case, you accepted the 0 default. Had you entered a different value, **90** for example, then the extrusion would have started in the 90° position relative to the current WCS. In step 6, you have the option of specifying the angle of the extrusion. Had you entered **180**, for example, your result would have been half the pitcher. You can also specify the direction of the extrusion by specifying a negative or positive angle.

EDITING A MESH

Once you've created a mesh surface with either the Edge Surface or Revolved Surface tool, you can make modifications to it. For example, suppose you want to add a spout to the pitcher you created in the previous exercise. You can use grips to adjust the individual points on the mesh to reshape the object. Here, you must take care how you select points. The UCS will become useful for editing meshes, as shown in the following exercise.

1. Zoom into the area shown in the first image of Figure 11.34.

2. Click the pitcher mesh to expose its grips.

3. Shift+click the grips shown in the second image of Figure 11.34.

4. Click the grip shown in the third image of Figure 11.34 and slowly drag the cursor to the left. As you move the cursor, notice how the lip of the pitcher deforms.

5. When you have the shape of a spout, select that point. The spout is fixed in the new position.

You can refine the shape of the spout by carefully adjusting the position of other grip points around the edge of the pitcher. Later, when you render the pitcher, you can apply a smooth shading value so that the sharp edges of the spout are smoothed out.

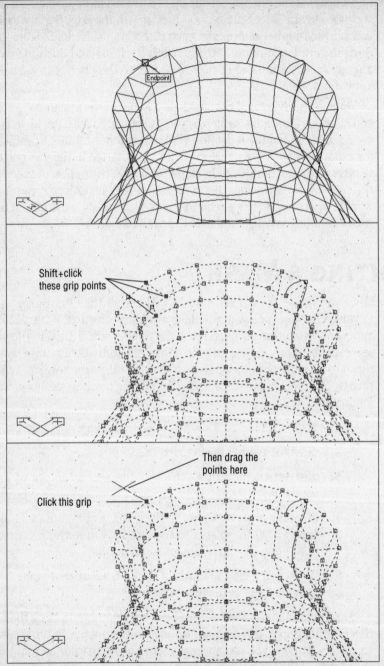

FIGURE 11.34: Adding a spout to the pitcher mesh

This exercise shows how easy it is to make changes to a mesh by moving individual grip locations. You may want to know, however, that when you move mesh grips manually (as opposed to entering coordinates), their motion is restricted to a plane that is perpendicular to the current UCS. You can use this restriction to your advantage. For example, if you want to move the spout downward at a 30° angle, rotate the UCS so it is tipped at a 30° angle in relation to the top of the pitcher. Then edit the mesh grips as you did in the previous exercise.

Another option would be to specify a *relative* coordinate as opposed to selecting a point. By specifying a coordinate, such as **@.5<50**, you do not have to move the UCS. Using this method, however, removes you from the spontaneity of being able to select a point visually.

Other Mesh-Editing Options

You can use Modify ➤ Object ➤ Polyline to edit meshes in a way similar to editing polylines. When you choose this option and pick a mesh, you get the following prompt:

```
Edit vertex/Smooth surface/Desmooth/Mclose/Nclose/Undo/eXit <X>:
```

Here are the descriptions of these options:

Edit Vertex   Allows you to relocate individual vertices in the mesh.

Smooth Surface   This option is similar to the Spline option for polylines. Rather than having the mesh's shape determined by the vertex points, the Smooth Surface option adjusts the mesh, so that mesh vertices act as control points that pull the mesh—much as a spline frame pulls a spline curve.

TIP

You can adjust the amount of pull the vertex points exert on a mesh by using the Smooth Surface option in conjunction with the Surftype system variable.

Desmooth   Reverses the effects of the Smooth Surface option.

Mclose and Nclose   Allow you to close the mesh in either the *m* or *n* direction. When you use either of these options, the prompt line changes (it replaces Mclose or Nclose with Mopen or Nopen) and allows you to open a closed mesh.

The Edit Polyline tool on the Modify II toolbar performs the same function as Modify ➤ Object ➤ Polyline.

MOVING OBJECTS IN 3D SPACE

AutoCAD provides two tools for moving objects in 3D space: Align and 3D Rotate. Both of these commands are found on the Rotate flyout of the Modify toolbar. They help you perform some of the more common moves associated with 3D editing.

Aligning Objects in 3D Space

In mechanical drawing, you often create the parts in 3D and then show an assembly of the parts. The Align command can greatly simplify the assembly process. The following exercise describes how Align works.

1. Choose Modify ➤ 3D Operation ➤ Align, or type **Al** and press Enter.

2. At the Select objects: prompt, select the 3D source object you want to align to another part. (The *source object* is the object you want to move.)

3. At the 1st source point: prompt, pick a point on the source object that is the first point of an alignment axis, such as the center of a hole or the corner of a surface.

4. At the 1st destination point: prompt, pick a point on the destination object to which you want the first source point to move. (The *destination object* is the object with which you want the source object to align.)

5. At the 2nd source point: prompt, pick a point on the source object that is the second point of an alignment axis, such as another center point or other corner of a surface.

6. At the 2nd destination point: prompt, pick a point on the destination object indicating how the first and second source points are to align in relation to the destination object.

7. At the 3rd source point: prompt, you can press Enter if two points are adequate to describe the alignment. Otherwise, pick a third point on the source object that, along with

the first two points, best describes the surface plane you want aligned with the destination object.

8. At the 3rd destination point: prompt, pick a point on the destination object that, along with the previous two destination points, describes the plane with which you want the source object to be aligned. The source object will move into alignment with the destination object.

Figure 11.35 gives some examples of how the Align tool works.

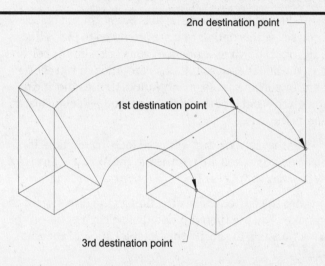

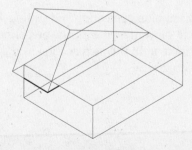

Result

FIGURE 11.35: Aligning two 3D objects

Rotating an Object in 3D Space

If you just want to rotate an object in 3D space, the Modify ➤ 3D Operation ➤ Rotate 3D option on the menu bar can simplify the operation. Once you've selected this option and selected the objects you want to rotate, you get the following prompt:

```
Axis by Entity/Last/View/Xaxis/YAxis/Zaxis/<2points>:
```

This prompt is asking you to describe the axis of rotation. Here are descriptions of the options presented in the prompt:

Entity Allows you to indicate an axis by clicking an object. When you select this option, you are prompted to pick a line, circle, arc, or 2D polyline segment. If you click a line or polyline segment, the line is used as the axis of rotation. If you click a circle, arc, or polyline arc segment, AutoCAD uses the line passing through the center of the circle or arc and perpendicular to its plane as the axis.

Last Uses the last axis that was used for a 3D rotation. If no previous axis exists, you are returned to the `Axis by Entity/Last/View/Xaxis/YAxis/Zaxis/<2points>:` prompt.

View Uses the current view direction as the direction of the rotation axis. You are then prompted to select a point on the view direction axis to specify the exact location of the rotation axis.

Xaxis/Yaxis/Zaxis Uses the standard x-, y-, or z-axis as the direction for the rotation axis. You are then prompted to select points on the x-, y-, or z-axis to locate the rotation axis.

<2points> Uses two points you provide as the endpoints of the rotation axis.

This completes the discussion of creating and editing 3D objects. You might want to experiment on your own with the predefined 3D shapes offered on the Surfaces toolbar. In the next section, you'll discover how you can generate perspective views.

Viewing Your Model in Perspective

So far, your views of 3D drawings have been in *parallel projection*. This means that parallel lines appear parallel on your screen. Although this type of view is helpful while constructing your drawing, you will want to view your drawing in true perspective from time to time, to get a better feel for what your 3D model actually looks like.

AutoCAD provides the 3D Orbit tool to help you get the 3D view you want. You can use the 3D Orbit tool to refine your parallel projection views, but it is also the gateway to perspective views of your model. 3D Orbit has a lot of features and settings. With this in mind, you may want to begin these exercises when you know you have an hour or so to complete them all at one sitting.

1. Open the Setting.dwg file from the companion website. This file contains a simple 3D model of some chairs, a table, and a lamp.

2. Right-click any toolbar and then select 3D Orbit from the pop-up list. Open the View toolbar as well.

To set up your view, use the Camera tool on the View toolbar.

1. Choose the Camera tool on the View menu.

2. At the Specify new camera point: prompt, click the lower-left corner of the drawing, as shown in Figure 11.36.

3. At the Specify new camera target: prompt, click the center of the circle that appears in the middle of the drawing, as shown in Figure 11.36. Your view changes to a side view of the chairs, as shown in Figure 11.37.

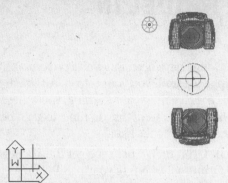

FIGURE 11.36: Selecting the camera and target points

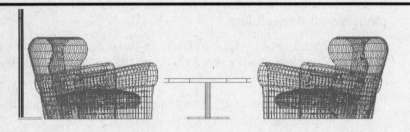

FIGURE 11.37: The side view of the chairs

This new view is from the camera point that you specified in step 2. The view's center is the target point you selected in step 3. Now you're ready to use the 3D Orbit tool. The camera and target points you selected are at the 0 coordinate on the z-axis, so your view is aimed at the bottom of the chairs. That's why the view is oriented toward the top of the screen.

1. Click the 3D Orbit tool on the 3D Orbit toolbar. You can also select 3D Orbit from the Standard toolbar.

You see a circle with four smaller circles at its cardinal points. This circle is called an *arcball*. It helps you control your view, along with the cursor.

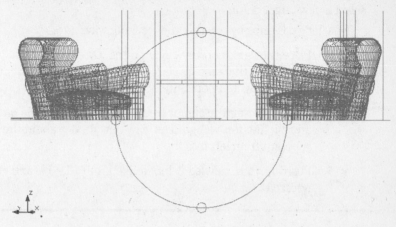

2. Place the cursor on the small circle at the top of the arcball. The cursor changes its appearance to a vertically elongated ellipse.

3. Click and drag the cursor downward from the top circle of the arcball, but don't let go yet. The view follows your cursor and the motion is constrained vertically. When your view is similar to Figure 11.38, release the mouse button.

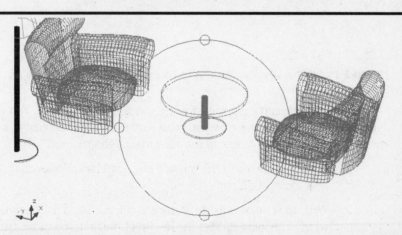

FIGURE 11.38: The view after clicking and dragging the top arcball circle

When you click and drag the circle at the top or bottom of the arcball, your view rotates about the target point you selected in step 3 of the first exercise. You can relocate the rotation point by using the Camera tool to select a new target point.

Now let's continue by rotating the view sideways.

1. Place the cursor on the circle on the left side of the arcball. Notice that this time, the cursor changes to look like a ellipse that is elongated horizontally.

2. Click and drag the cursor to the left from this circle on the arcball, but don't let go. The view now rotates about the target point from left to right.

3. Position your view so it looks like Figure 11.39, and then release the mouse.

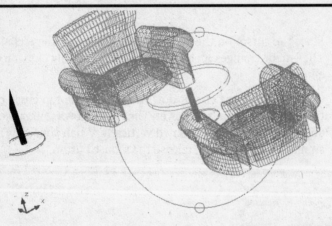

FIGURE 11.39: The view after clicking and dragging the left arcball circle

By now, you should have a feel for the way the arcball works. You click and drag until you get the view you want. But right now, the view is not exactly right. You need to rotate the view to straighten it out.

1. Move the cursor to the outside of the arcball. Notice that it now looks like a circle.

2. With the cursor outside of the arcball, click and drag downward. The view rotates in the direction that you move the cursor.

3. Adjust the view until it looks similar to the one in Figure 11.40.

When the cursor appears as a circle, you can rotate the view in the view plane. Doing so allows you to "straighten" your view once you've moved your viewpoint or camera location.

You've tried nearly all the arcball options. There's one more option that is a combination of the top and side circles.

1. Place the cursor inside the arcball. The cursor now looks like two superimposed ellipses.

2. Click and drag the cursor and move it in a slight circular motion. Notice how the view pivots in all directions about the target point.

3. Return the view to the one shown in Figure 11.40.

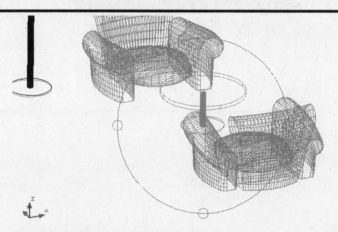

FIGURE 11.40: The view straightened out

This last option gives you a bit more freedom to move the view, although it can be a bit unwieldy.

TIP

You can change the target point, and therefore the point around which your 3D Orbit view rotates, by using the Camera tool on the View toolbar. Click the Camera tool, and then press Enter when you are prompted for a camera location. Then, select the new target location. You can use an object in your drawing as a selection point.

Turning on a Perspective View

The view is still a bit high in the AutoCAD window. You need to move it downward to include more of the lamp and the chair at the top. You're also still viewing your drawing in a parallel projection mode. In the next exercise, you'll switch to a perspective view, and then use the Pan tool to center your view.

1. Right-click and select Projection ➤ Perspective from the pop-up menu. Your view changes to a perspective one. The view is a bit high, so you'll use the 3D Orbit Pan tool to center your view.

2. Right-click and select 3D Pan from the pop-up menu. You can also select Pan from the 3D Orbit toolbar. The arcball disappears and the cursor turns into the familiar Pan cursor.

3. Click and drag the view downward to center the table top in the view. Your view should look like Figure 11.41.

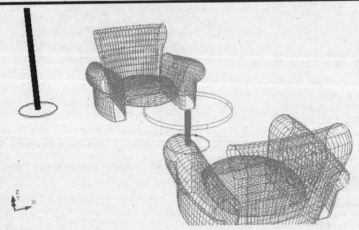

FIGURE 11.41: The perspective view after being panned downward

You saw several things happen in this brief exercise. First, you saw how easy it is to obtain a perspective view. You were also introduced to the 3D Orbit pop-up menu. This menu offers a few options that don't appear on the 3D Orbit toolbar. You also used the 3D Pan tool on the 3D Orbit toolbar.

The 3D Pan tool on the 3D Orbit toolbar works just like the standard Pan tool you've been using all along, but there is a difference. You may have noticed that when you panned your view, the perspective changed as you panned. The effect is similar to that of looking out of a car's side window as you move down the highway. When you pan your view using the 3D Pan tool on the 3D Orbit toolbar, you are moving both the camera viewpoint and the target point together. Doing so maintains your camera and target orientation while moving the overall scene.

Using Some Visual Aids

You're still in 3D Orbit mode, even though you don't see the arcball anymore. This can be a bit confusing. You can use a visual aid to remind yourself that 3D Orbit is still active.

1. Right-click and then select Visual Aids ➤ Compass from the pop-up menu. The 3D Orbit Compass appears.

2. Right-click again and select Visual Aids ➤ Grid. A grid appears at the 0 z-coordinate.

3. To help visualize the forms of the objects in this scene, turn on the shade mode. Right-click and then select Shading Modes ➤ Hidden. Figure 11.42 shows how your view will look after turning on the Compass, Grid, and Hidden Shade mode.

You may have noticed that the options under the Shading Modes cascading menu were the same options available from the Shade Mode toolbar. They're offered in the 3D Orbit pop-up menu for easy access, in case you want to view your model with hidden lines removed.

FIGURE 11.42: The view with the Compass, Grid, and Hidden shade modes turned on

Adjusting the Camera

The 3D Orbit arcball lets you rotate your camera location about the target. You've also seen how the Pan option moves both the target and the camera to view a different part of your 3D model. All of these tools maintain the distance between the target and the camera. In the following set of exercises, you learn how to use the tools that let you fine-tune your camera location and characteristics.

Start by changing the distance between the camera and target.

1. Right-click and then choose More ➤ Adjust distance from the pop-up menu. You can also choose the 3D Adjust Distance tool from the 3D Orbit toolbar.

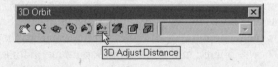

The cursor turns into a double-headed arrow in a perspective view.

2. Click and drag the mouse downward. As you do, the view recedes as if you were backing away from the scene. You are moving the camera away from the target location.

3. Adjust your view so that it looks like Figure 11.43.

FIGURE 11.43: The view after using the 3D Adjust Distance tool

You can adjust the camera distance from the target by clicking and dragging up or down. An upward motion brings the camera closer to the target. A downward motion moves the camera away.

At first glance, the Zoom option on the 3D Orbit toolbar appears to do the same thing as the 3D Adjust Distance option. However, the Zoom option actually has a very different effect on the display. The Zoom option has the effect of enlarging or reducing the size of the image, but it does so by changing the field of view of the camera. It's like using a telephoto lens on a camera. You can zoom in on a scene without actually changing your position relative to the scene.

A telephoto lens does its work by changing its focal length. By increasing its focal length, you get a closer view. By decreasing the focal length, you see more of the scene. If you shorten the focal length a lot, the image begins to distort, like the image in a fish-eye lens. The Zoom option of the 3D Orbit tool works in the same way. Try the following exercise to see firsthand:

1. Right-click and select Orbit from the pop-up menu. The arcball returns.

2. Click the circle on the right side of the arcball and drag the view to the right so you get a side view of both the chairs.

3. Use the Arcball to adjust your view so it looks like Figure 11.44.

Part iii

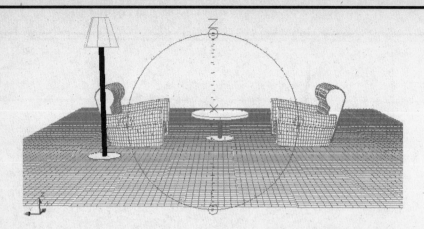

FIGURE 11.44: The side view of the chairs after rotating the view horizontally

Next, you'll temporarily leave the 3D Orbit tool to turn on a layer.

1. Right-click and then select Exit from the pop-up menu to exit the 3D Orbit tool.

2. Use the Layer drop-down list to locate and turn on the Wall layer. You'll see some walls appear in the foreground.

3. Click the 3D Orbit tool in the Standard toolbar and then right-click and select Zoom. You can also select the Zoom tool from the 3D Orbit toolbar.

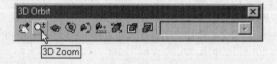

4. Click and drag the mouse slowly downward. As your view moves slowly away, it also begins to distort. The vertical walls start to splay outward more and more as you zoom out, as shown in the first image in Figure 11.45. You also see the 3D Orbit compass distort.

5. Bring your view back to normal by clicking and dragging the mouse upward until you have a view similar to the second image of Figure 11.45.

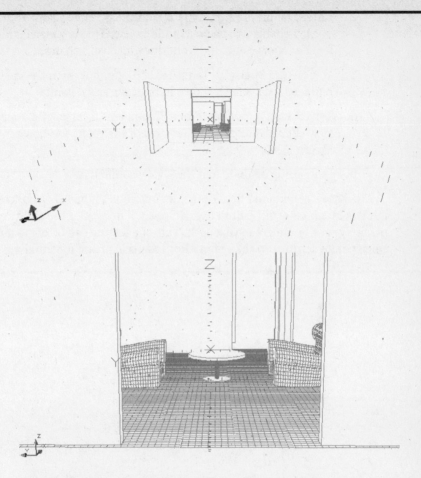

FIGURE 11.45: A view of the walls begins to distort when zooming out.

In this exercise, you turned on the walls of the room and then used the Zoom option to see its effects. As you zoomed back, you were actually changing the field of view, or focal length of the camera, to that of a wide-angle lens. You can control the focal length in a more precise way by using another command outside the 3D Orbit tool—the Dview command. The following exercise will show you how you can precisely set the focal length of the camera:

    1. Right-click and then choose Exit from the pop-up menu.

2. Enter **Dv**, press Enter, type **Z**, and press Enter again. Your display changes to show a crude house. This is a visual aid for the Dview command; your drawing hasn't changed.

3. You see the Specify lens length: prompt, with the current lens focal length shown in brackets as a default.

4. Type **35** and press Enter for a 35-mm lens focal length. Your view changes to offer a wider view of the room, as shown in Figure 11.46.

5. Press Enter again to exit the Dview command.

The Dview command offers the same functions as the 3D Orbit tool, but it is much more difficult to use. However, it does offer the ability to precisely set the camera focal length. This one feature can be of great use when you're setting up views of interior spaces in an architectural model.

FIGURE 11.46: The view of the room after setting the camera focal length to 35mm

Now, suppose you want to move the target of your view upward slightly to encompass more of the back of the room. You can accomplish this by rotating the camera. Here's how it's done.

1. Click the 3D Orbit tool from the Standard toolbar. Right-click and select More ➢ Swivel Camera. You can also click the 3D Swivel tool in the 3D Orbit toolbar. The cursor changes to a camera icon with a curved arrow.

2. Click and drag the mouse upward to view more of the back wall of the room so that it looks similar to Figure 11.47.

FIGURE 11.47: The room after swiveling the camera upward

Using Clipping Planes to Hide Parts of Your View

The walls in the foreground obscure the current view of the interior of the room. Although this may be an accurate view of your model, you may want to remove parts of your model that obstruct your view in the foreground. To do this, you can use clipping planes.

1. While in the 3D Orbit mode, right-click, and then select More ➤ Adjust Clipping Planes. The Adjust Clipping Planes dialog box appears. It shows your model as though you were looking at it from above.

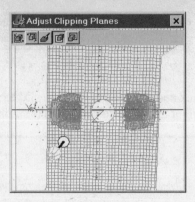

Also notice that the view of the room in the AutoCAD window changes. You see more of the room, and the chairs appear to be sliced in half.

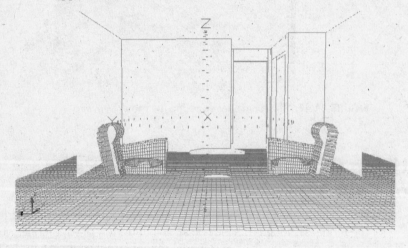

2. Right-click in the Adjust Clipping Planes dialog box. The pop-up menu that appears offers several options.

3. Make sure the Adjust Front Clipping option is checked; then, click the screen to close the pop-up menu. This option allows you to adjust the front clipping plane. You can also press the Adjust Front Clipping button on the dialog box toolbar.

4. Place the cursor over the horizontal line in the middle of the dialog box, and then click and drag downward. The line moves downward. This line represents the location of the front clipping plane in relation to the objects in the drawing. Notice what happens to your view in the main part of the AutoCAD window as you move the clipping plane. The chairs become whole again, and the lamp appears. Move the cursor up and down to see the effect.

5. Move the clipping plane downward until it is just past the lamp toward the bottom of the dialog box.

6. Close the Adjust Clipping Planes dialog box. Your view should now show more of the room, as shown in Figure 11.48.

Part iii

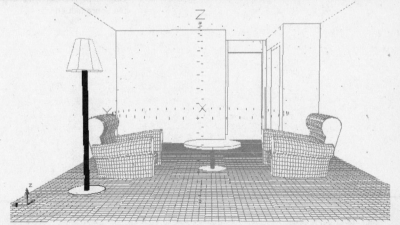

FIGURE 11.48: The interior view of the room with the front clipping plane turned on

The front clipping plane is turned on as soon as you open the Adjust Clipping Planes dialog box. You can then adjust the clipping plane by moving in the dialog box. In addition, you can turn on and adjust a back clipping plane to hide objects in the back of your scene, as shown in Figure 11.49. To do this, you turn on the back clipping plane; then adjust it just as you did the front clipping plane. Two buttons control these functions in the Adjust Clipping Planes dialog box: Adjust Back Clipping lets you adjust the location of the back clipping plane, and Back Clipping On/Off turns the back clipping plane on or off.

A third option, the Create Slice button, lets you move both the back and front clipping planes in unison. All of these options are also on the Adjust Clipping Planes pop-up menu.

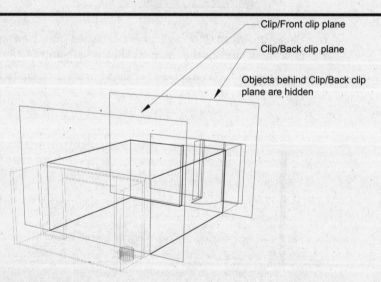

FIGURE 11.49: Effects of the clipping planes

Getting a Simple Animation of Your View

The last 3D Orbit option you'll learn about is one that is perhaps more fun than practical. You can get a simple animated view of your model that rotates your view about the target point. Try this exercise to see how it works.

1. To make this animation a bit more interesting, turn on the Gouraud shading mode. While in 3D Orbit mode, right-click and then select Shading Modes ➤ Gouraud Shaded.

2. Right-click again; then, select More Continuous Orbit. You can also select 3D Continuous Orbit from the 3D Orbit toolbar.

3. Click and drag to the left just a short distance. Your view begins to spin in a clockwise direction. The distance you click and drag controls the speed of the spin.

4. Click anywhere to stop the rotation; then click and drag to the right. This time the model spins in a counterclockwise direction.

5. Click again to stop the spinning.

6. After you've reviewed the results of this exercise, close the Setting.dwg file without saving it.

The 3D Continuous Orbit option is better suited to viewing single objects rather than the interior of a room, but this exercise shows what can be done with this option.

This concludes your tour of the 3D Orbit tool. You've used nearly every option available in this tool. With this knowledge, you should be able to set up practically any view you want. You covered a lot of ground here, so you may want to review this section before you work in 3D again.

WHAT'S NEXT?

In this chapter, you have learned how to generate 3D objects using several different techniques. You now have experience viewing 3D models in both perspective and orthogonal modes. In the next chapter, you will learn how to add materials and lighting to the 3D scene. You'll render the scene and output a rendered image.

Part iii

Chapter 12

MASTERING 3D SOLIDS

S o far, you have been creating 3D models according to a
method called *surface modeling:* As you drew, you used 3D
Faces to give your models form and the appearance of solidity.
But you can use another method use to create 3D computer
models: *solid modeling.*

Adapted from *Mastering™ AutoCAD® 2000
Premium Edition* by George Omura
ISBN 0-7821-2499-2   1,664 pages $59.99

With surface models, drawing a simple cube requires several steps; with solids, you can create a cube with one command. Having created a solid model, you can assign materials to it and have the computer find physical properties of the model, such as weight and center of mass. It is easier to create models by using solid modeling, and the technique offers many advantages, especially in mechanical design and engineering.

Solid modeling was once thought to require more computational power than most personal computers could offer, but with today's powerful microcomputer hardware, solid modeling is well within the reach of most PC users. AutoCAD offers built-in solid modeling functions, which you will explore in this chapter.

Understanding Solid Modeling

Solid modeling is a way of defining 3D objects as solid forms rather than as wireframes with surfaces attached. When you create a 3D model using solid modeling, you start with the basic forms of your model—cubes, cones, and cylinders, for instance. These basic solids are called *primitives.* Then, using more of these primitives, you begin to add to or subtract from your basic forms. For example, to create a model of a tube, you first create two solid cylinders, one smaller in diameter than the other. Then you align the two cylinders so they are concentric and tell AutoCAD to subtract the smaller cylinder from the larger one. The larger of the two cylinders then becomes a tube whose inside diameter is that of the smaller cylinder, as shown in Figure 12.1.

Several primitives are available for modeling solids in AutoCAD (see Figure 12.2).

These shapes—box, wedge, cone, cylinder, sphere, and donut (or *torus*)—can be joined in one of four ways to produce secondary shapes. The first three, demonstrated in Figure 12.3 using a cube and a cylinder as examples, are called *Boolean operations.* (The name comes from the nineteenth-century mathematician George Boole.) The three joining methods are as follows:

Intersection   Uses only the intersecting region of two objects to define a solid shape

Subtraction   Uses one object to cut out a shape in another

Union   Joins two primitives so they act as one object

Create two cylinder primitives,
one for the outside diameter
and one for the inside diameter.

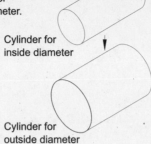

Cylinder for
inside diameter

Cylinder for
outside diameter

Superimpose the cylinder
for the inside diameter onto
the cylinder for the outside
diameter.

Use the Subtract command
to subtract the inside
diameter cylinder from
the outside diameter cylinder.

FIGURE 12.1: Creating a tube using solid modeling

A fourth option, *interference*, lets you find exactly where two or more solids coincide in space—similar to the results of a union. The main difference between interference and union is that interference allows you to keep the original solid shapes, whereas union discards the original solids, leaving the form represented by their intersection. With interference, you can have AutoCAD either show you the shape of the coincident space or create a solid based on the coincident space's shape.

Joined primitives are called *composite solids*. You can join primitives to primitives, composite solids to primitives, and composite solids to other composite solids.

Part iii

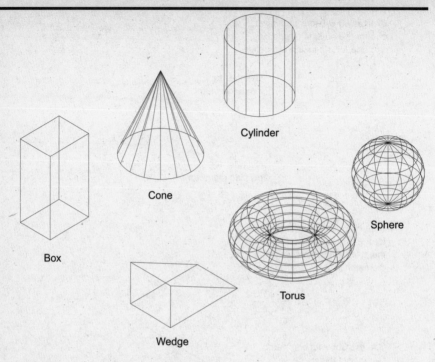

FIGURE 12.2: The solids primitives

Now let's take a look at how these concepts let you create models in AutoCAD.

NOTE

To simplify the exercises in this chapter, all the instructions in the exercises are unitless; that is, they don't specify inches or centimeters. This way, users of both the metric and English measurement systems will be able to use the exercises without having to deal with duplicate information.

A solid box and a solid cylinder are superimposed.

The intersection of the primitives creates a solid cylinder with the ends skewed.

The cylinder subtracted from the box creates a hole in the box.

The union of the two primitives creates a box with two round pegs.

FIGURE 12.3: The intersection, subtraction, and union of a cube and a cylinder

CREATING SOLID FORMS

In this section, you will begin to draw the object shown in Figure 12.4. In the process, you will explore the creation of solid models by creating primitives and then setting up special relationships between them.

FIGURE 12.4: This steel bracket was created and rendered in AutoCAD.

Displaying the Solids Toolbar

All the commands you will use to create the solid primitives, and many of the commands you can use for editing solids, are accessible on the Solids toolbar. Right-click any toolbar and select Solids from the pop-up menu. The Solids toolbar appears.

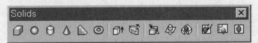

Open the Solids Editing toolbar as well. Now you're ready to begin creating basic solids.

Creating Primitives

Primitives are the basic building blocks of solid modeling. At first, it may seem limiting to have only six primitives to work with, but consider the varied forms you can create with just a few two-dimensional objects. Let's begin by creating the basic mass of your steel bracket. First, prepare your drawing for the exercise.

1. Create a new file called Bracket.

2. Right-click the Snap button on the status bar. In the Drafting Settings dialog box, set the Snap spacing to **0.5** and turn on the Grid and Snap modes.

3. Turn on the dynamic coordinate readout by pressing F6. You'll use the readout to help guide you in selecting points in the exercises that follow.

Now start building the solid model.

1. Click the Box tool on the Solids toolbar, or enter **BOX** and press Enter. You can also choose Draw ➤ Solids ➤ Box.

2. At the Specify corner of box or [CEnter] <0,0,0>: prompt, pick a point at coordinate 3,2.5.

3. At the Specify corner or [Cube/Length]: prompt, enter **@7,4** and press Enter to create a box with a length of 7 and a width of 4.

4. The Specify height: prompt that appears next asks for the height of the box in the z-axis. Enter **1** and press Enter.

You've now drawn your first primitive, a box that is 7 units long by 4 units wide by 1 unit deep. Now, let's change the view so you can see the box more clearly. Use the Vpoint command to shift your view so you are looking at the World Coordinate System (WCS) from the lower left.

5. Open the Viewpoint Presets dialog box (choose View ➤ 3D Views ➤ Select), and then enter **225** in the From X Axis input box and **19.5** in the XY Plane input box.

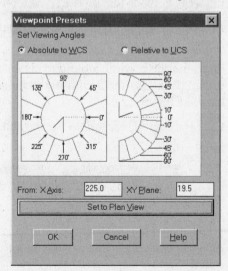

Part iii

6. Click OK, and then adjust your view so it looks similar to Figure 12.5.

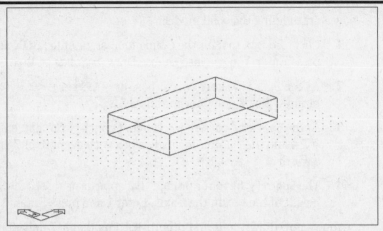

FIGURE 12.5: The first stage of the bracket

Turning a 2D Polyline into a 3D Solid

Now let's add another box to form the lower lip of the bracket. This time, you'll create a box primitive from a polyline.

1. Click the Polyline tool on the Draw toolbar.

2. At the From point: prompt, start the polyline from the coordinate .5,2.5.

3. Continue the polyline around to create a rectangle that is 1 unit in the x-axis and 3 units in the y-axis. Your drawing will look like Figure 12.6.

4. Click the Extrude tool on the Solids toolbar, or type **EXT** and press Enter.

5. At the Select objects: prompt, pick the polyline and press Enter.

6. At the Specify height of extrusion or [Path]: prompt, type **1** and press Enter.

7. At the Specify angle of taper for extrusion <0>: prompt, press Enter to accept the default taper of 0°. (You'll see what the Taper option does in a later exercise.) The polyline now extrudes in the z-axis to form a bar, as shown in Figure 12.7.

8. Type **R** and press Enter to redraw the screen.

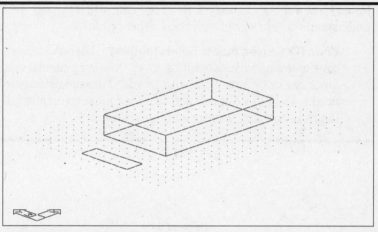

FIGURE 12.6: The polyline drawn in place

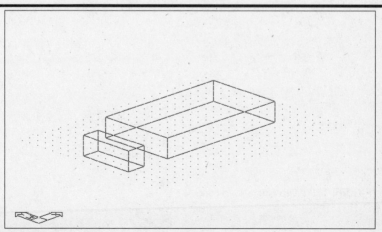

FIGURE 12.7: The converted polyline box

You've now drawn two box primitives using the Box and the Extrude options on the Solids toolbar. Just for variety's sake, this exercise had you create the smaller box by converting a polyline into a solid, but you could just as easily have used the Box option for that as well. The Extrude option converts polylines, circles, and traces into solids. (Regular lines, 3D lines, 3D Faces, and 3D polylines cannot be extruded.)

Other Solids Options

Before you continue, let's examine the commands for primitives that you haven't had a chance to use yet. Refer to Figures 18.8 through 18.11 to understand the terms used with these other primitives.

Cone (Cone icon on the Solids toolbar)   Draws a circular cone or a cone with an elliptical base. Drawing a circular cone is much like drawing a circle, with an added prompt asking for a height. The Ellipse option acts like the Ellipse command (on the Draw toolbar), with an additional prompt for height.

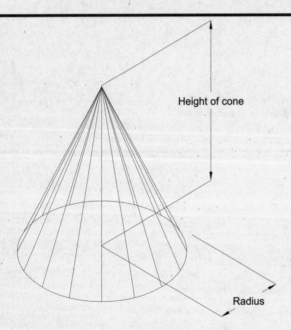

Height of cone

Radius

FIGURE 12.8: Drawing a solid cone

Sphere (Sphere icon on the Solids toolbar)   Acts like the Circle command, but instead of drawing a circle, it draws a sphere.

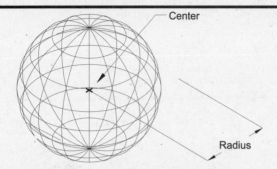

FIGURE 12.9: Drawing a solid sphere

Torus (Torus icon on the Solids toolbar)   Creates a torus (a donut-shaped solid). You are prompted for two diameters or radii, one for the diameter or radius of the torus and another for the diameter or radius of the tube portion of the torus.

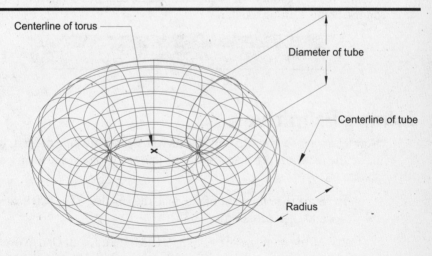

FIGURE 12.10: Drawing a solid torus

Part iii

Wedge (Wedge icon on the Solids toolbar)   Creates a wedge-shaped solid. This command acts much like the Box command you used to draw the bracket. You have the choice of defining the wedge by two corners or by its center and a corner.

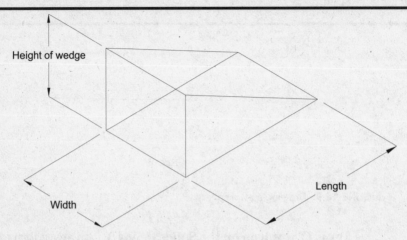

FIGURE 12.11: Drawing a solid wedge

In the following exercises you will be creating and combining solid primitives. The commands required to create complex solids are available on the Solids Editing toolbar.

Joining Primitives

Now let's see how the two box objects you created are joined. First, you'll move the new box into place, and then join the two boxes to form a single solid.

1. Start the Move command, pick the smaller of the two boxes, and then press Enter.

2. At the Base point: prompt, use the Midpoint Osnap override and pick the middle of the back edge of the smaller box, as shown in the top image of Figure 12.12.

3. At the Second point: prompt, pick the middle of the bottom edge of the larger box, as shown in the bottom image of Figure 12.12.

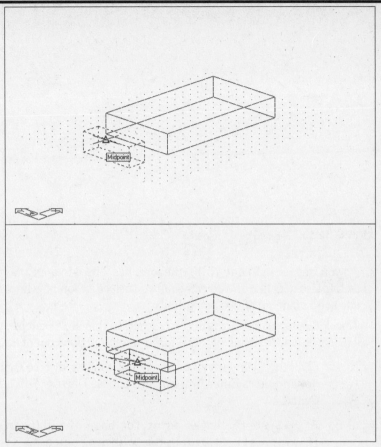

FIGURE 12.12: Moving the smaller box

4. Choose Modify ➤ Solids Editing ➤ Union, or type **Uni** and press Enter. You may also click Union on the Solids Editing toolbar.

5. At the Select objects: prompt, pick both boxes and press Enter. Your drawing now looks like Figure 12.13.

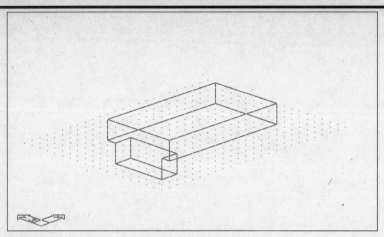

FIGURE 12.13: The two boxes joined

As you can see in Figure 12.13, the form has joined to appear as one object. It also acts like one object when you select it. You now have a composite solid made up of two box primitives.

Now let's place some holes in the bracket. In this next exercise, you will discover how to create negative forms to cut portions out of a solid.

1. Click the Cylinder tool on the Solids toolbar, or type **Cylinder** and press Enter. You can also choose Draw ➣ Solids ➣ Cylinder.

2. At the `Specify center point for base of cylinder or [Elliptical] <0,0,0>:` prompt, pick a point at the coordinate 9,5.5.

3. At the `Specify radius for base of cylinder or [Diameter]:` prompt, enter **.25**.

NOTE

As with the Circle command, you can enter **D** to specify a diameter or enter a radius value directly.

4. At the `Specify height of cylinder or [Center of other end]:` prompt, enter **1.5** and press Enter. The cylinder is drawn.

5. Copy the cylinder two inches in the negative direction of the y-axis, so your drawing looks like Figure 12.14.

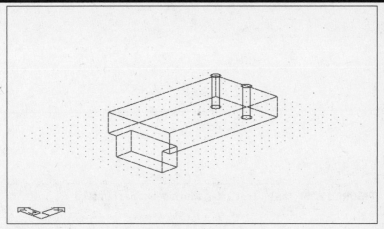

FIGURE 12.14: The cylinders added to the drawing

You now have the cylinder primitive, but you still need to define its relationship to the composite solid you created from the two boxes.

1. Choose Modify ➤ Solids Editing ➤ Subtract, or type **Su** and press Enter. You may also click the Subtract tool on the Solids Editing toolbar.

2. At the Select solids and regions to subtract from... Select objects: prompt, pick the composite solid of the two boxes and press Enter.

3. At the Solids and regions to subtract... Select objects: prompt, pick two of the cylinders and press Enter. The cylinder has now been subtracted from the bracket.

4. To view the solid, choose View ➤ Hide. You'll see a Hidden-Line view of the solid, as shown in Figure 12.15.

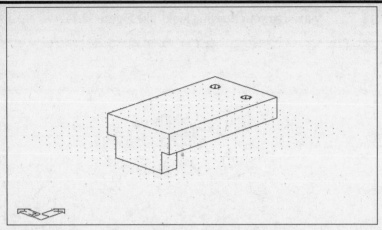

FIGURE 12.15: The bracket so far, with hidden lines removed

Wireframe views, such as the one in step 3, are somewhat difficult to decipher. Until you use the Hide command (step 4), you cannot tell for sure that the subtracted cylinder is in fact a hole. Using the Hide command frequently will help you keep track of what's going on with your solid model.

In step 3 of the previous exercise, you may have noticed that the cylinders changed shape to conform to the depth of the bracket. You'll also recall that you drew the cylinder at a height of 1.5 units, not 1 unit, which is the thickness of the bracket. Having drawn the cylinder taller than needed, you can see that when AutoCAD performed the subtraction, it ignored the portion of the cylinder that doesn't affect the bracket. Auto-CAD always discards the portion of a primitive that isn't used in a Subtract operation.

WHAT ARE ISOLINES?

You may have noticed the message that reads:

```
Current wire frame density:  ISOLINES=4
```

This message tells you the current setting for the Isolines system variable. The Isolines system variable controls the way curved objects, such as cylinders and holes, are displayed. A setting of 4 causes cylinders to be represented by four lines with circles at each

CONTINUED ➡

end. You can see this in the holes that you've created for the bracket model in the previous exercise. You can change the Isolines setting by entering **Isoline** and pressing Enter at the Command prompt. You then enter a value for the number of lines to use to represent surfaces. This setting is also controlled by the Contour Lines Per Surface option in the Display tab of the Options dialog box.

CREATING COMPLEX PRIMITIVES

As you learned earlier, you can convert a polyline into a solid using the Extrude option on the Solids toolbar. This process lets you create more complex primitives. In addition to the simple straight extrusion you've already tried, you can also extrude shapes into curved paths, or you can taper an extrusion.

Tapering an Extrusion

Next, you'll take a look at how you can taper an extrusion to create a fairly complex solid with little effort.

1. Draw a 3 × 3 closed polyline at the top of the current solid. Start at the back-left corner of the bracket at coordinate 3.5,3,1, and then draw the 3 × 3 closed polyline to fit in the top of the composite solid, as shown in Figure 12.16.

WARNING
Remember to use the Close option to create the last side of the box.

2. Click the Fillet tool on the Modify toolbar. At the `Select first object or [Polyline/Radius/Trim]:` prompt, type **R** and press Enter to set the radius of the fillet.

3. At the prompt for the fillet radius, type **.5** and press Enter.

4. At the Command prompt, press Enter to again issue the Fillet command, and then type **P** and press Enter to tell the Fillet command that you want to chamfer a polyline.

5. Click the polyline. The corners become rounded.

6. Click the Extrude button on the Solids toolbar, or enter **Ext** at the Command prompt.

7. At the Select objects: prompt, pick the polyline you just drew and press Enter. (As the prompt indicates, you can pick polylines or circles.)

8. At the Specify height of extrusion or [Path]: prompt, enter **3**.

9. At the Specify angle of taper for extrusion <0>: prompt, enter **4** for 4° of taper. The extruded polyline looks like Figure 12.17.

10. Join the part you just created with the original solid. Choose Modify ➢ Boolean ➢ Union, and then select the extruded part and the rectangular solid just below it.

NOTE

In step 9, you can indicate a taper for the extrusion. Specify a taper in terms of degrees from the z-axis, or enter a negative value to taper the extrusion outward. Press Enter to accept the default, 0°, to extrude the polyline without a taper.

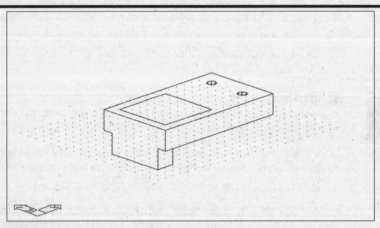

FIGURE 12.16: Drawing the 3 × 3 polyline box

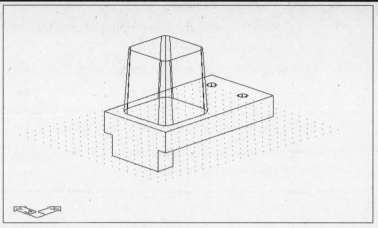

FIGURE 12.17: The extruded polyline

Extruding on a Curved Path

As demonstrated in the following exercise, the Extrude command lets you extrude virtually any polyline shape along a path that is defined by a polyline, arc, or 3D polyline.

1. Choose View ➤ Zoom ➤ Extents and turn off the grid.

2. Choose View ➤ Hide to help you view and select parts of your model in the following steps.

3. Place the User Coordinate System (UCS) on a vertical plane perpendicular to the back of the bracket. Choose Tools ➤ Orthographic UCS ➤ Left.

4. Start a polyline at the point shown in the top image of Figure 12.18. Use the Midpoint Osnap to make sure you select the midpoint of the vertical corner edge. After you locate the first point, enter the following coordinates:

    ```
    @2<180
    @1<270
    @2<180
    ```

    When you are done, your drawing should look like the bottom image of Figure 12.18.

5. Click the Fillet tool on the Modify toolbar, and then type **R** and press Enter to set the fillet radius.

Part iii

6. Enter **.4** for the fillet radius.

7. Press Enter to reissue the Fillet command, and then type **P** and press Enter to select the Polyline option.

8. Click the polyline you drew on the backside of the solid.

9. Choose Tools ➤ New UCS ➤ Y, and then enter **90**. This command rotates the UCS 90 degrees around the y-axis so the UCS is perpendicular to the front face of the solid.

10. Draw a circle with a 0.35-unit radius at the location shown in the second image of Figure 12.18.

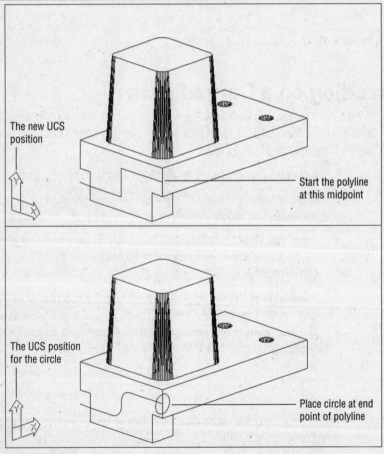

FIGURE 12.18: Setting up your drawing to create a curved extrusion

TIP

The Hidden-Line view of the solid in Figure 12.18 shows a lot of extra facets on the curved portion of the model. You can set up AutoCAD so these extra facets don't appear. Open the Options dialog box and check the Show Silhouettes in Wireframe option on the Display tab.

At this point, you've created the components needed to do the extrusion. Next, you'll finish the extruded shape.

1. Click the Extrude button on the Solids toolbar, click the circle, and then press Enter.

2. At the `Specify height of extrusion or [Path]:` prompt, type **P** and press Enter to enter the Path option.

3. At the `Select extrusion path:` prompt, click the polyline curve. AutoCAD pauses a moment and then generates a solid tube that follows the path. The tube may not look like a tube, because AutoCAD draws extruded solids such as this with a single line showing its profile.

4. Click the Subtract tool on the Solids Editing toolbar or choose Modify ➣ Solids Editing ➣ Subtract, and then select the rectangular solid.

5. Press Enter. At the `Select objects:` prompt, click the curved solid and press Enter. The curved solid is subtracted from the square solid. Your drawing will look like Figure 12.19.

In this exercise, you used a curved polyline for the extrusion path, but you can use any type of 2D or 3D polyline, as well as lines and arcs, for an extrusion path.

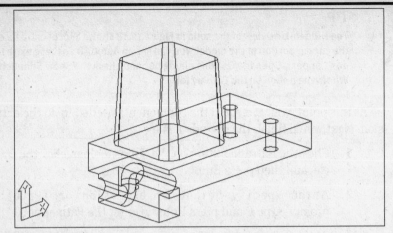

FIGURE 12.19: The solid after subtracting the curve

Revolving a Polyline

When your goal is to draw an object that is circular, the Revolve command on the Solids toolbar is designed to let you create a solid that is revolved, or swept in a circular path. Think of Revolve's action as similar to a lathe that lets you carve a shape from a spinning shaft. In this case, the spinning shaft is a polyline, and rather than carving it, you define the profile and then revolve the profile around an axis.

In the following exercise, you will draw a solid that will form a slot in the tapered solid.

1. Zoom in to the top of the tapered box, so you have a view similar to Figure 12.20.

2. Turn off the Snap mode.

3. Return to the WCS by choosing Tools ➤ New UCS ➤ World.

4. Choose Tools ➤ New UCS ➤ Origin.

5. At the Origin: prompt, use the Midpoint Osnap override and pick the midpoint of the top surface, as shown in Figure 12.20.

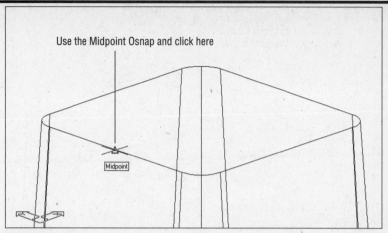

Use the Midpoint Osnap and click here

Midpoint

FIGURE 12.20: An enlarged view of the top of the tapered box and the new UCS location

6. Set the Snap distance to **0.25** and turn on Polar Tracking.

7. Draw a polyline using Polar Tracking with the following polar coordinates:

    ```
    Start at -0.25,0
    0.75<90
    0.75<0
    0.7071<315
    0.5<0
    0.7071<45
    0.75<0
    0.75<270
    ```

8. When you've finished, type **C** and press Enter to close the polyline. AutoCAD will not revolve an open polyline. Your drawing should look like Figure 12.21.

9. Click the Revolve tool on the Solids toolbar, or type **Rev** and press Enter at the Command prompt.

Revolve

10. At the Select objects: prompt, pick the polyline you just drew and press Enter.

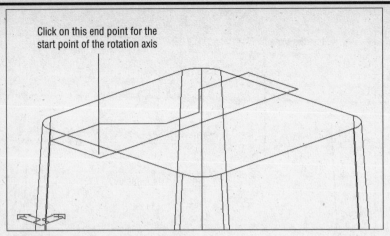

Click on this end point for the
start point of the rotation axis

FIGURE 12.21: Drawing the polyline

11. When you see the next prompt

    `Axis of revolution - Object/X/t/<Start point of axis>:`

    use the Endpoint Osnap override and pick the beginning
    endpoint of the polyline you just drew.

12. Turn on the Ortho mode (press F8) and turn off the Snap
    mode (press F9). Pick a point to the far left of the screen so
    that the rubber-banding line is parallel with the x-axis of the
    current UCS.

13. At the `Angle of revolution <full circle>:` prompt,
    press Enter to sweep the polyline a full 360°. The revolved
    form appears, as shown in Figure 12.22.

You have just created a revolved solid that will be subtracted from the
tapered box to form a slot in the bracket. But before you subtract it, you
need to make a slight change in the orientation of the revolved solid.

1. Choose Modify ➤ 3D Operation ➤ Rotate 3D.

2. At the `Select objects:` prompt, select the revolved solid
   and press Enter.

3. At the prompt

   `Axis by Entity/Last/View/Xaxis/Yaxis/Zaxis/<2point>`

   use the Midpoint Osnap and click the right-side edge of the
   top surface, as shown in Figure 12.23.

FIGURE 12.22: The revolved polyline

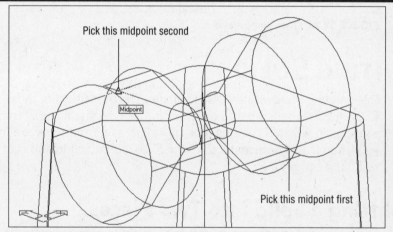

Pick this midpoint second

Midpoint

Pick this midpoint first

FIGURE 12.23: Selecting the points to rotate the revolved solid in 3D space

4. At the 2nd point on axis: prompt, use the Midpoint
   Osnap again and click the opposite side of the top surface,
   as shown in Figure 12.23.

5. At the <Rotation angle>/Reference: prompt, type **5** and
   press Enter. The solid rotates 5°.

6. Click the Subtract tool on the Solids Editing toolbar or
   choose Modify ➤ Solids Editing ➤ Subtract, click the tapered
   box, and then press Enter.

7. At the Select objects: prompt, click the revolved solid and press Enter. Your drawing looks like Figure 12.24.

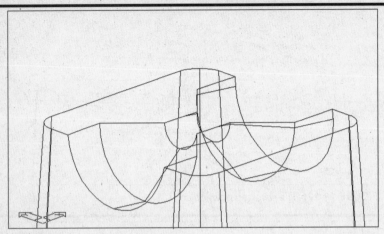

FIGURE 12.24: The composite solid

EDITING SOLIDS

Basic solid forms are fairly easy to create. The refinement of those forms requires some special tools. In this section, you'll learn how to use some familiar 2D editing tools as well as some new tools to edit a solid. You'll also be introduced to the Slice tool, which lets you cut a solid into two pieces.

Splitting a Solid into Two Pieces

Perhaps one of the more common solid editing tools you'll use is the Slice tool. As you might guess from its name, Slice allows you to cut a solid into two pieces. The following exercise demonstrates how it works.

1. Zoom to the previous view and return to the World Coordinate System.

2. Click the Slice tool on the Solids toolbar, or type **Slice** and press Enter.

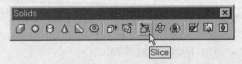

NOTE

In step 3, you could select more than one solid. The Slice command would then slice all the solids through the plane indicated in steps 4 and 5.

3. At the `Select object:` prompt, click the part you've been working on and press Enter.

4. At the prompt

   ```
   Specify first point on slicing plane by [Object/
   Zaxis/View/XY/YZ/ZX/3points] <3points>:
   ```

   type **XY** and press Enter. This command lets you indicate a slice plane parallel to the xy plane.

5. At the `Point on XY plane <0,0,0>:` prompt, type **0,0,.5** and press Enter. This command places the slice plane at the z-coordinate of .5 units. You can use the Midpoint Osnap and pick any vertical edge of the rectangular solid.

NOTE

If you want to delete one side of the sliced solid, you can indicate the side you want to keep by clicking it in step 6, instead of entering **B**.

6. At the `Specify a point on desired side of the plane or [keep Both sides]:` prompt, type **B** and press Enter to keep both sides of the solid. AutoCAD will divide the solid horizontally, one-half inch above the base of the part, as shown in Figure 12.25.

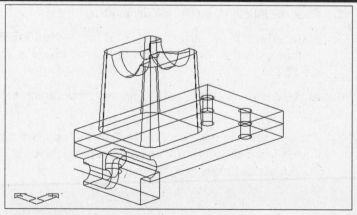

FIGURE 12.25: The solid sliced through the base

Part iii

The Slice Options

Step 4 of the previous exercise included several options that are worth discussing here. Here are descriptions of those options:

Object Lets you select an object to define the slice plane.

Zaxis Lets you select two points defining the z-axis of the slice plane. The two points you pick will be perpendicular to the slice plane.

View Generates a slice plane that is perpendicular to your current view. You are prompted for the coordinate through which the slice plane must pass—usually a point on the object.

3points Is the default, and lets you select three points defining the slice plane. Normally, you would pick points on the solid.

XY/YZ/ZX Pick one of these to determine the slice plane based on the x-, y-, or z-axis. You are prompted to pick a point through which the slice plane must pass.

Rounding Corners with the Fillet Tool

Your bracket has a few sharp corners that you may want to round in order to give the bracket a more realistic appearance. You can use the Construct menu's Fillet and Chamfer commands to add these rounded corners to your solid model.

1. Adjust your view of the model so it looks similar to the top image of Figure 12.26.

2. Click the Fillet tool on the Modify toolbar.

3. At the Select first object or [Polyline/Radius/Trim]: prompt, pick the edge indicated in the top image of Figure 12.26.

4. At the Enter fillet radius: prompt, type **.2** and press Enter.

5. At the Select an edge or [Chain/Radius]: prompt, type **C** and press Enter for the Chain option. Chain lets you select a series of solid edges to be filleted.

6. Select one of the other three edges at the base of the tapered form, and press Enter when you are done.

7. Choose Hide on the Render toolbar, or type **Hide** and press Enter, to get a better look at your model, as shown in the bottom image of Figure 12.26.

As you saw in step 5, Fillet acts a bit differently when you use it on solids. The Chain option lets you select a set of edges, instead of just two adjoining objects.

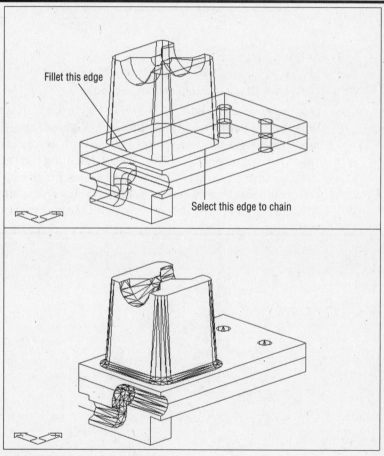

Fillet this edge

Select this edge to chain

FIGURE 12.26: Filleting solids

Part iii

Chamfering Corners with the Chamfer Tool

Now let's try chamfering a corner. To practice using Chamfer, you'll add a countersink to the cylindrical hole you created in the first solid.

1. Type **Regen** and press Enter to return to a Wireframe view of your model.

2. Click the Chamfer tool on the Modify toolbar, or type **Cha**.

3. At this prompt

   ```
   Select first line or
   [Polyline/Distance/Angle/Trim/Method]:
   ```

   pick the edge of the hole, as shown in Figure 12.27. Notice that the top surface of the solid is highlighted, and the prompt changes to Enter surface selection option [Next/OK (current)] <OK>:. The highlighting indicates the base surface, which will be used as a reference in step 5. (You could also type **N** and press Enter to choose the other adjoining surface, the inside of the hole, as the base surface.)

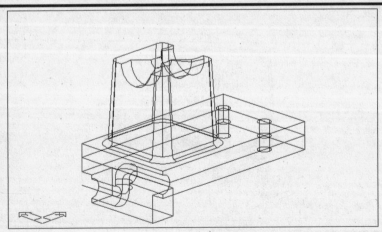

FIGURE 12.27: Picking the edge to chamfer

4. Press Enter to accept the current highlighted face.

5. At the Specify base surface chamfer distance <0.5000>: prompt, type **.125** and press Enter. This command indicates that you want the chamfer to have a width of .125 across the highlighted surface.

6. At the Specify other surface chamfer distance <0.5000>: prompt, type **.2** and press Enter.

7. At the Select an edge or [Loop]: prompt, click the edges of both holes and then press Enter. When it is done, your drawing will look like Figure 12.28.

8. After reviewing the work you've done here, save the Bracket.dwg file.

NOTE

The Loop option in step 7 lets you chamfer the entire circumference of an object. You don't need to use it here because the edge forms a circle. The Loop option is used when you have a rectangular or other polygonal edge you want to chamfer.

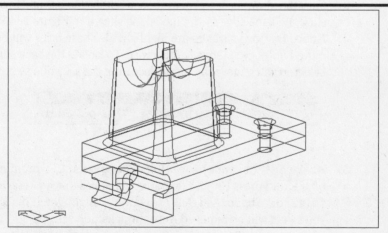

FIGURE 12.28:   The chamfered edges

Using the Solids Editing Tools

You've added some refinements to the bracket model by using some standard AutoCAD editing tools. There is a set of tools specifically geared toward editing solids. You already used the Union and Subtract tools found on the Solids Editing toolbar. In this section, you'll explore some of the other tools available on that toolbar.

To help keep the exercises simple and easy to understand, you'll be using an existing 3D model called Solidedit.dwg. This file will help to demonstrate the Solids Editing tools.

Moving a Surface

The first tool you'll try is the Move tool. The Move tool moves the surface of a solid.

NOTE

You can download files for this book from Sybex's website at http:// www.sybex.com. Search for "AutoCAD 2002 Complete" to locate the files.

1. Open the Solidedit.dwg file. This file is set up with the Hidden Shade mode turned on so you can see the form more easily.

2. Click the Move Faces tool in the Solids Editing toolbar, and then click the back edge of the model, as shown in Figure 12.29. Notice that two surfaces are highlighted. These faces will be moved unless you indicate otherwise. To isolate the back surface, you will remove the top surface from the selection set.

3. At the Select faces or [Undo/Remove/ALL]: prompt, type **R** and press Enter. The prompt changes to read Remove faces or [Undo/Add/ALL]:. Now any highlighted object you select will be removed from the selection set.

4. Click the edge of the top surface, as indicated in Figure 12.29. The top surface is removed from the selection set.

TIP

You can enter **A** at the Remove faces or [Undo/Add/ALL]: prompt to continue to add more surfaces to your selection set.

5. Press Enter to finish your selection.

6. At the Specify a base point or displacement: prompt, click any point near the back face.

7. At the Specify a second point of displacement: prompt, enter **@.6<0** to move the surface 0.6 units to the right.

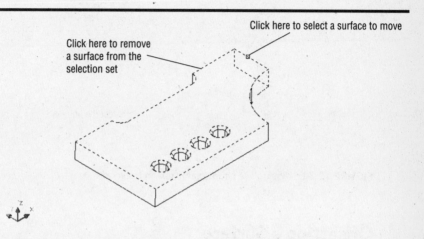

Click here to select a surface to move

Click here to remove a surface from the selection set

FIGURE 12.29: Moving the back surface of the model

Once you've selected the surface you want to move, the Move Faces tool acts just like the Move command. Notice how the curved side of the model extends its curve to meet the new location of the surface. You can see that AutoCAD attempts to maintain the geometry of the model when you make changes to the faces.

Try Move Faces again, but this time, move a set of faces on the interior of the model.

1. Click the Move Faces tool again.

2. Click the countersink hole closest to the foreground, as shown in Figure 12.30. Then click the straight shaft of the hole, as shown in Figure 12.30.

3. Press Enter to finish your selection, and then click any point on the screen.

4. Enter **@1<90**. The hole moves 1 unit in the y-axis.

In some instances, AutoCAD will not be able to move surfaces. This usually occurs when an adjoining surface is too complex.

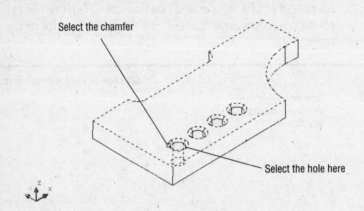

Select the chamfer

Select the hole here

FIGURE 12.30: Moving the countersink hole in the model

Offsetting a Surface

Now suppose you want to decrease the radius of the arc in the right corner of the model, and you also want to thicken the model by the same amount as the decrease in the arc radius. To do this, you can use the Offset Faces tool.

1. Click the Offset Faces tool on the Solids Editing toolbar.

Offset Faces

2. Click the lower edge of the curved surface, as shown in Figure 12.31. Notice that both the curved surface and the bottom of the model are highlighted. You can add or remove surfaces from the selection set as you did in the previous two exercises. Here, you'll just stick with the selection set you have.

3. Press Enter to finish your selection. At the Specify the offset distance: prompt, enter **.5**. The surfaces move to their new location (see Figure 12.32).

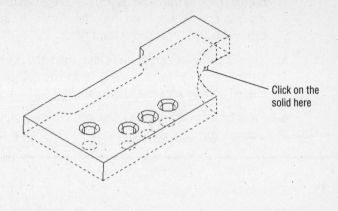

Click on the solid here

FIGURE 12.31: Selecting a surface to offset

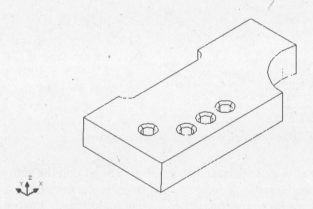

FIGURE 12.32: The model after offsetting the curved and bottom surface

Deleting a Surface

Now suppose you've decided to eliminate the curved part of the model altogether. You can delete a surface using the Delete Faces tool.

1. Click the Delete Faces tool on the Solids Editing toolbar.

Solids Editing

Delete Faces

2. At the `Select faces or [Undo/Remove]:` prompt, click the bottom edge of the curve as you did in the last exercise. You'll need to remove the bottom surface from the selection set; otherwise, this operation won't work.

3. Type **R** and press Enter and then select the back edge of the bottom surface to remove it from the selection set. The curved surface remains highlighted.

4. Press Enter to finish your selection. The curve disappears and a corner forms in its place, as shown in Figure 12.33.

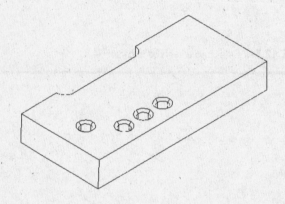

FIGURE 12.33: The model with the curved surface removed

When you attempt to delete surfaces, keep in mind that the surface you delete must be recoverable by other surfaces in the model. For example, you cannot remove the top surface of a cube and expect it to turn into a pyramid. Such a modification would require the sides to change their orientation, which is not allowed in this operation. You can, on the other hand, remove the top of a box with tapered sides. Then, when you remove the top, the sides converge to form a pyramid.

Rotating a Surface

All the surfaces of the model are parallel or perpendicular to each other. Imagine that your design requires two sides to be at an angle. You can change the angle of a surface using the Rotate Faces tool.

1. Click the Rotate Faces tool on the Solids Editing toolbar.

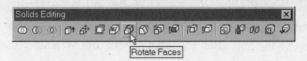

2. At the Select faces or [Undo/Remove]: prompt, select the corner edge in the foreground, as shown in Figure 12.34, and then press Enter. The two surfaces facing you are highlighted.

3. At the Specify an axis point or [Axis by object/ View/Xaxis/Yaxis/Zaxis] <2points>: prompt, use the Endpoint Osnap to select the bottom of the corner, as shown in Figure 12.34.

4. At the Specify the second point on the rotation axis: prompt, use the Endpoint Osnap to select the top of the corner as shown in Figure 12.34. The two points you just selected specify the axis of rotation for the surface rotation.

5. At the Specify a rotation angle or [Reference]: prompt, enter **4**. The two surfaces change their orientation.

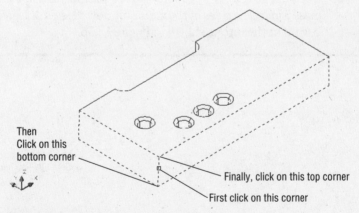

Then
Click on this
bottom corner

Finally, click on this top corner

First click on this corner

FIGURE 12.34: Defining the axis of rotation

Part iii

Tapering Surfaces

In an earlier exercise, you saw how to create a new tapered solid using the Extrude command. But what if you want to taper an existing solid? Here's what you can do to taper an existing 3D solid.

1. Choose the Taper Faces tool from the Solids Editing toolbar.

2. Click the three corners of the model, as indicated in Figure 12.35. You may have to approximate the location of the back corner to select it.

3. Press Enter to finish your selection.

4. At the `Specify the base point:` prompt, use the Endpoint Osnap to click the bottom corner in the foreground of the model, as shown in Figure 12.35.

5. At the `Specify another point along the axis of tapering:` prompt, use the Endpoint Osnap to click the top corner, as shown in Figure 12.35.

6. At the `Specify the taper angle:` prompt, enter **4** and press Enter. The sides of the model are now tapered 4 degrees inward at the top, as shown in Figure 12.36.

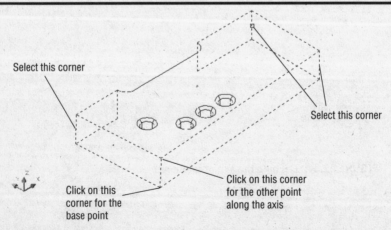

FIGURE 12.35: Selecting the surfaces to taper and indicating the direction of the taper

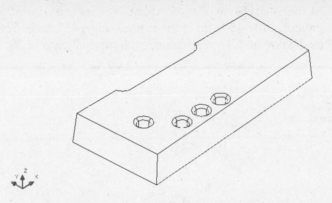

FIGURE 12.36: The model after tapering the sides

Extruding a Surface

You used the Extrude Faces command to create two of the solids in the bracket model. The Extrude command requires a closed polygon as a basis for the extrusion. The Solids Editing toolbar offers the Extrude Faces tool that will extrude a surface of an existing solid. The following exercise demonstrates how it works.

1. Click the Extrude Faces tool on the Solids Editing toolbar.

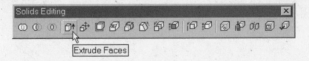

2. Click the bottom edge of the front surface of the model, as shown in Figure 12.37.

3. You don't want to extrude the bottom surface of the model, so type **R** and press Enter; then click the back edge of the highlighted bottom surface, as shown in Figure 12.37.

4. Press Enter. The Specify height of extrusion or [Path]: prompt appears. Notice that this is the same prompt you saw when you used the Extrude command earlier in this chapter.

5. Enter **.5** for an extrusion height of 0.5 units.

6. At the Specify angle of taper for extrusion <0>: prompt, enter **45** to taper the extrusion at a 45° angle. Your model now adds the extrusion, as shown in Figure 12.38.

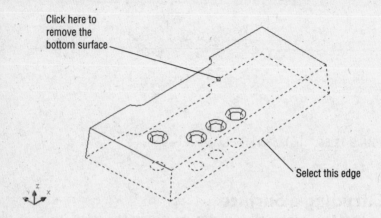

Click here to remove the bottom surface

Select this edge

FIGURE 12.37: Selecting the surfaces for extrusion

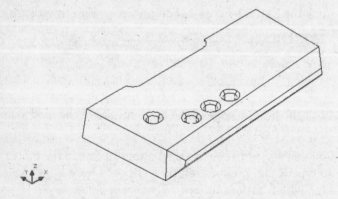

FIGURE 12.38: The model with a surface extruded and tapered

You can extrude multiple surfaces at one time if you need to by selecting more surfaces after step 2. In this exercise, you removed a selected surface in step 3 so that only one surface is extruded.

Other than those features, the Extrude Faces tool works just like the Extrude command.

Turning a Solid into a Shell

In many situations, you'll want your 3D model to be a hollow, rather than solid mass. The Shell tool lets you convert a solid into a shell. Here's an example of how it might be used.

1. Choose the Shell tool from the Solids Editing toolbar.

2. Click the model. The entire model is highlighted. AutoCAD assumes you want to shell the entire object with a few faces completely removed. The Remove faces or [Undo/Add/ALL]: prompt appears and you see the object selection cursor, indicating that you can select objects for removal.

3. Click the top-front corner of the solid, as shown in Figure 12.39, to remove the two surfaces that adjoin that edge.

4. Press Enter to finish your selection.

5. At the Enter the shell offset distance: prompt, enter .1 and press Enter. The solid becomes a shell with a 0.1 wall thickness, as shown in Figure 12.40.

6. After studying the results of the Shell tool, type **U** and press Enter to undo the shell operation in preparation for the next exercise.

The shell thickness is added to the outside surface of the solid, so when you're constructing your solid with the intention of creating a shell, you need to take this into account.

Part iii

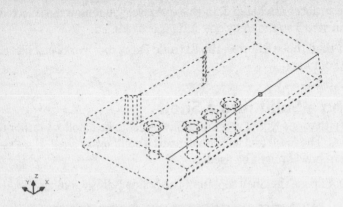

FIGURE 12.39: Selecting the edge to be removed

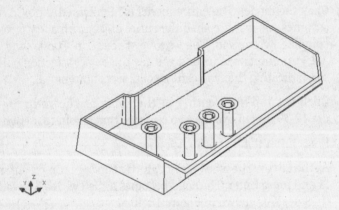

FIGURE 12.40: The solid model after using the Shell tool

Copying Faces and Edges

Sometimes you may want to create a copy of a surface of a solid to analyze its area or to produce another part that mates to that surface. The Copy Faces tool creates a copy of any surface on your model. The copy it produces is a type of object called a *region*. You'll learn more about regions later in this chapter. Right now, let's see how the Copy Faces tool works.

1. Click the Copy Faces tool on the Solids Editing toolbar.

2. Click the front-top edge of the model, the same one shown in Figure 12.40 in the Shell exercise. Two surfaces are highlighted.

3. Press Enter to finish your selection.

4. Click a base point for the copy, and then enter **@10<315**.

5. Choose View ➤ Zoom ➤ Extents or type **Z**, press Enter, type **E**, and press Enter again to view the entire drawing. The copied surfaces appear to the right of the solid.

The copies of the surfaces are opaque and can hide objects behind them when you perform a hidden-line removal (View ➤ Hide).

The Copy Edges tool is similar to Copy Faces. It works in a similar way, but instead of selecting surfaces as in step 2, you select all the edges you want to make copies of. The result is a series of simple lines representing the edges of your model. This tool can be useful if you want to convert a solid into a set of 3D Faces. The Copy Edges tool will create a framework onto which you can add 3D Faces.

USING THE COMMAND LINE FOR SOLIDS EDITING

The Solids Editing tools are actually options of a single AutoCAD command called Solidedit. If you prefer to use the keyboard, here are some tips on using the Solidedit command. When you first enter **Solidedit** at the Command prompt, you see the following prompt:

```
Enter a solids editing option
[Face/Edge/Body/Undo/eXit] <eXit>:
```

CONTINUED ➡

Part iii

You can select the Face, Edge, or Body option to edit the various parts of a solid. The Face option offers the following prompt:

```
[Extrude/Move/Rotate/Offset/Taper/Delete/Copy/coLor/
Undo/eXit] <eXit>:
```

The options from this prompt produce the same results as their counterparts in the Solids Editing toolbar. The Edge option from the first prompt offers the following prompt:

```
Enter an edge editing option [Copy/coLor/Undo/eXit]
<eXit>:
```

The Copy option lets you copy a surface and the coLor option lets you add color to a surface. The Body option from the first prompt offers following prompt:

```
[Imprint/seParate
solids/Shell/cLean/Check/Undo/eXit] <eXit>:
```

These options also perform the same functions as their counterparts on the Solids Editing toolbar. As you work with this command, you can use the Undo option to undo the last Solidedit option you used without exiting the command.

Adding Surface Features

You'll start by inserting an object that will be the source of the imprint. Then you will imprint the main solid model with the object's profile.

NOTE
You can download files for this book from Sybex's website at http://www.sybex.com. Search for "AutoCAD 2002 Complete" to locate the files.

1. Choose Insert ➤ Block.

2. In the Insert dialog box, click Browse, and then locate the Imprint.dwg file and select it.

3. In the Insert dialog box, make sure that the Explode option is checked and uncheck the Specify On-Screen option in the Insertion Point group.

4. Click OK. The block appears in the middle of the solid.

5. Click the Imprint tool.

6. Click the main solid model.

7. Click the imported solid.

8. At the `Delete the source object <N>:` prompt, enter **Y**.

You now have an outline of the intersection between the two solids imprinted on the top surface of your model. To help the imprint stand out, try the following steps to change its color.

1. Click the Color Faces tool on the Solids Editing toolbar.

2. Click the imprint from the last exercise. The imprint and the entire top surface are highlighted.

3. At the `Select faces or [Undo/Remove/ALL]:` prompt, type **R** and press Enter, and then click the outer edge of the top surface to remove it from the selection set.

4. Press Enter. The Select Color dialog box appears.

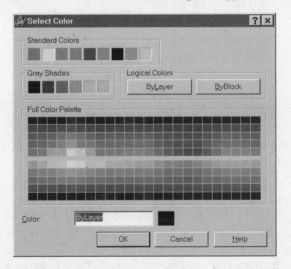

5. Click the red color sample at the top of the dialog box and click OK. The imprint is now red.

6. Press Enter three times to exit the command.

7. To see the full effect of the Color Faces tool, choose View ➢ Shade ➢ Flat Shade. The imprint appears as a solid red area.

If you want to remove an imprint from a surface, use the Clean tool on the Solids Editing toolbar. Click the Clean tool, and then click the imprint you want to remove. If the imprint has a color, then the color will "bleed" out to the surface where the imprint was placed.

Separating a Divided Solid

While in the process of editing solids, you may end up with two separate solid forms that were created from one solid, as shown in Figure 12.41. Even though the two solids appear separated, they act like a single object. In these situations, AutoCAD offers the Separate tool in the Solids Editing toolbar. To use it, just click the Separate tool, and then select the solid that has become separated into two forms.

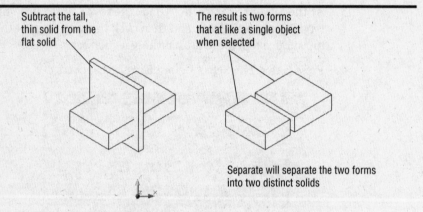

Subtract the tall, thin solid from the flat solid

The result is two forms that at like a single object when selected

Separate will separate the two forms into two distinct solids

FIGURE 12.41: When the tall, thin solid is subtracted from the larger solid, the result is two separate forms, yet they still behave as a single object.

You've seen how each of the Solids Editing tools works through some simple examples. You aren't limited to using these tools in the way shown in this section, and this book cannot anticipate every situation you may encounter as you create your solid models. These examples are intended as an introduction to these tools, so feel free to experiment with them. You can always use the Undo option to backtrack in case you don't get the results you expect.

TIP

You can download files for this book from Sybex's website at http://www .sybex.com. Search for "AutoCAD 2002 Complete" to locate the files. Figure 12.41 is included in the sample figures under the name of Separate.dwg. You can try the Separate tool on this file on your own.

This concludes your tour of the Solids Editing toolbar. Next, you'll learn how to use your 3D solid models to quickly generate 2D working drawings.

ENHANCING THE 2D DRAWING PROCESS

Using solids to model a part—such as the Bracket and the Solidedit examples used in this chapter—may seem a bit exotic, but there are definite advantages to modeling in 3D, even if you want to draw the part in only 2D as a page in a set of manufacturing specs.

The exercises in this section show you how to quickly generate a typical mechanical drawing from your 3D model using paper space and the Solids toolbar. You will also examine techniques for dimensioning and including hidden lines.

TIP

If your application is architecture, and you've created a 3D model of a building using solids, you can use the tools described in this section to generate 2D elevation drawings from your 3D solid model.

Drawing Standard Top, Front, and Right-Side Views

One of the more common types of mechanical drawings is the *orthogonal projection*. This style of drawing shows the top, front, and right-side views of an object. Sometimes a 3D image is also added for clarity. You can derive such a drawing within a few minutes, once you have created your 3D solid model. The first step is to select a sheet title block. The title block consists of a border and an area in the lower-right corner for notes and other drawing information.

Part iii

Setting Up a File with a Title Block

The first step is to create a file using one of AutoCAD's template files designed for mechanical applications.

1. Choose File ➤ New.

2. In the Create New Drawing dialog box, click the Use a Template button.

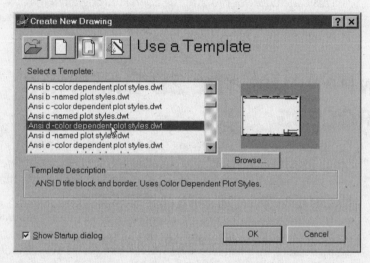

3. From the Select a Template list box, select Ansi d-color dependant plot styles.dwt, and then click OK. A title block appears, along with a viewport to model space.

4. Use File ➤ Save As to save this file as Bracket_title.dwg.

You are now in floating model space. Although it may not be obvious at first glance, the title block is in paper space and an active model space viewport is inside the title block.

WARNING

If for some reason you do not see a list of template files in the Create New Drawing dialog box, you will need to set up AutoCAD to look for these files in the right place. Normally, AutoCAD looks in the \Program Files\AutoCAD 2002\Template directory for template files. Check the Template Drawing File Location list in the Files tab of the Options dialog box.

Importing the 3D Model

The next step is to insert the Bracket solid model into this drawing.
Remember that while you are in a floating model space viewport, anything you do affects model space. So, in the next exercise, you will use
the Insert tool to import the Bracket drawing into the model space of
this new drawing.

1. Choose Insert ➤ Block.

2. In the Insert dialog box, click the File button.

3. At the Select Drawing File dialog box, locate and select the
   Bracket.dwg file and click Open.

4. Back in the Insert dialog box, make sure that the Explode
   check box in the lower-left corner of the dialog box is
   checked. Click the Specify On Screen check box in the Insertion Point group to deselect this option.

5. Click OK. The drawing appears in the viewport.

You need to take one more step before you actually set up the orthogonal views. You want to make the current viewport display a front view of
the bracket. This is easily done with a single menu bar option.

1. Choose View ➤ 3D Views ➤ Front. The Viewport view changes
   to show the front view of the model.

2. Choose View ➤ Zoom ➤ Scale, and then type **1xp** and press
   Enter to give the view a 1-to-1 scale. This command has the
   same effect as setting the Standard Scale property of the
   viewport to a value of 1:1. The view is now in proper scale to
   the title block.

3. Choose View ➤ Paper Space, and then using its grips, resize
   the viewport so it is just large enough to display the model,
   as shown in Figure 12.42. To expose the viewport grip, click
   the inner border of the title block, as shown in Figure 12.42.

4. Move the viewport to a location similar to the one shown in
   Figure 12.42.

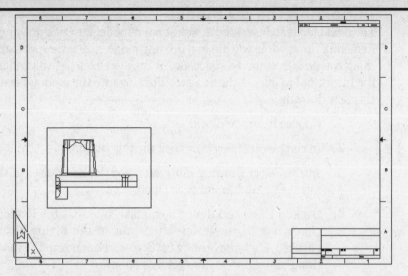

FIGURE 12.42: Resizing the viewport so it is just large enough to contain the view of the bracket

Creating the Orthogonal Views

Now you are ready to create the orthogonal views. The next part will seem simple compared to the steps you had to take to set up the title block and viewport.

1. Click the Setup View tool on the Solids toolbar, or choose Draw ➤ Solids ➤ Setup ➤ View.

2. At the Ucs/Ortho/Auxiliary/Section/<Exit>: prompt, type **O** and press Enter.

3. At the Pick Side of Viewport to Project: prompt, place the cursor on the right side of the viewport so that a Mid-point Osnap marker appears, as shown in the top image of Figure 12.43. A rubber-banding line appears.

4. At the View Center: prompt, click a point to the right of the viewport, at about half the width of the viewport. The right-side view of the bracket appears, as shown in the bottom

image of Figure 12.43. Click again to adjust the horizontal position of the right-side view.

5. Once you're satisfied with the location of the view, press Enter. You don't have to be too precise at this point because you will be able to adjust the view's location later.

6. At the Clip First Corner: prompt, click a location below and to the left of the right-side view, as shown in the continued image of Figure 12.43.

7. At the Clip Other Corner: prompt, click above and to the right of the view, as shown in the continued image of Figure 12.43.

8. At the View Name: prompt, enter **Rightside**. Notice that the Ucs/Ortho/ Auxiliary/Section/<Exit>: prompt appears again. It allows you to set up another view.

At this point, you can exit the Setup View tool by pressing Enter, but you need another view. Continue with the following steps to create the top view.

9. Type **O** and press Enter again, but this time, at the Pick side of Viewport to Project: prompt, click the top edge of the front-view viewport.

10. Follow steps 4 through 8 to create a top view. In step 4, click a point above the viewport instead of to the right.

11. Name this third viewport **Top**.

12. When you return to the Ucs/Ortho/Auxiliary/Section/<Exit>: prompt, press Enter to exit the command.

Each new view you create using the Setup View tool is scaled to match the original view from which it is derived. As you saw from step 3, the view that is generated depends on the side of the viewport you select. If you had picked the bottom of the viewport, a bottom view would be generated, which would look the same as the top view until you use the View ➤ Hide option to see it as a Hidden-Line view.

Part iii

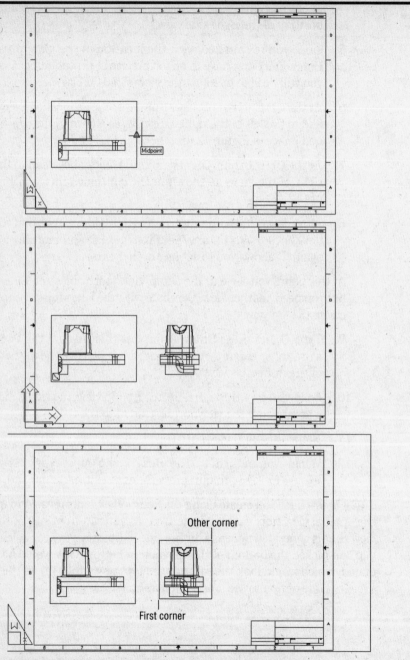

FIGURE 12.43: Adding the Orthogonal views in paper space

Creating an Isometric View

In this section, you will add an Isometric view to your paper space layout at a 1-to-1 scale. You can use the Setup View tool to accomplish this, but you'll need to set up a UCS to which the Setup View tool can refer. The following exercise explains how to set up such a UCS for an Isometric view:

1. Click the Model tab to go to model space.

2. Choose View ➢ 3D Views ➢ SE Isometric to get an Isometric view of the model.

3. Choose Tools ➢ New UCS ➢ View to set the UCS to be parallel to the current view plane.

4. Choose Tools ➢ UCS ➢ Named UCS to open the UCS Control dialog box.

5. Rename the current Unnamed UCS to SEIsometric.

6. Choose View ➢ Paper Space to return to the paper space view of your model.

Notice that even though you changed your view in model space, the paper space viewports maintain the views as you last left them.

Now you're ready to create a viewport showing the same Isometric view you set up in model space.

1. Click the Setup View tool on the Solids toolbar.

2. At the `Ucs/Ortho/Auxiliary/Section/<Exit>:` prompt, type **U** and press Enter.

3. At the `Named/World/?/<Current>:` prompt, press Enter to accept the current UCS.

4. At the `Enter view scale<1.0000>:` prompt, press Enter to accept the scale of 1.

5. At the `View center:` prompt, click a point above and to the right of the original viewport. The Isometric view of the model appears, as shown in Figure 12.44. If you don't like the view's location, you can continue to click points until the view's location is just where you want it.

6. Press Enter when you are satisfied with the view's location.

7. At the Clip First corner: prompt, window the Isometric view to define the viewport border.

8. Name the view **SEIsometric**.

9. Press Enter to exit the Setup View tool.

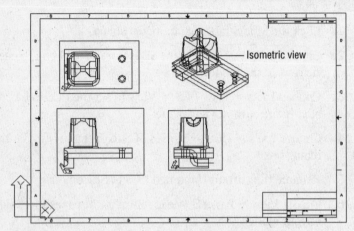

FIGURE 12.44: Adding a viewport for the Isometric view

A lot of steps were involved in creating these views. However, imagine the work involved if you had to create these views manually, and you'll appreciate the power of these few simple tools.

Creating Hidden-Line Views

You aren't quite finished. Typically, orthographic projections, such as the top, front, and right-side views, will show the hidden portions of the model with dashed lines. For example, the holes toward the right end of the bracket would be shown dashed in the front view. You could set up the viewports to do a hidden-line removal at plot time, but doing so would not create the effect you want.

Fortunately, AutoCAD offers the Setup Profile tool to quickly generate a proper Orthographic Projection view of your solid model. Take the following steps to create your first hidden-line view.

1. Go to floating model space by double-clicking the lower-left viewport.

2. Choose Setup Profile from the Solids toolbar, or choose Draw ➤ Solids ➤ Setup ➤ Profile.

3. Click both halves of the solid model, and then press Enter.

4. At the `Display hidden profile lines on separate layer? <Y>:` prompt, press Enter.

5. At the `Project profile lines onto a plane? <Y>:` prompt, press Enter.

6. At the `Delete tangential edges? <Y>:` prompt, press Enter. AutoCAD will work for a moment, and then the Command prompt will appear with no apparent change to the drawing.

You don't see the effects of the Setup Profile tool yet. You'll need to make the solid model invisible to display the work that was done by the Setup Profile tool. You'll also have to make a few layer changes to get the profile views just right.

1. Double-click an area outside the viewport or click the Model button on the status bar to return to paper space.

2. Zoom in to the front view so it fills most of the display area.

3. Turn off Layer 0 (zero). If it is the current layer, you will get a message telling you that you are about to turn off the current layer. Go ahead and click OK. You've just turned off the layer of the solid model, leaving the profile created by the Setup Profile tool. Notice that you only see an image of the front view.

4. Open the Layer Properties Manager (click the Layers tool in the Object Properties toolbar or choose Format ➤ Layer from the menu bar).

5. Select the layer whose name begins with the *PH* prefix.

6. Change its line type to Hidden. You may need to load the hidden-line type.

7. Once you've changed the line type, click OK to exit the Layer Properties Manager dialog box. The front view now displays hidden lines properly with dashed lines, as shown in Figure 12.45.

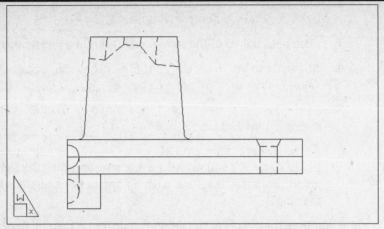

FIGURE 12.45: The front view after using the Setup Profile tool

The Setup Profile tool creates a 2D drawing of your 3D model. This 2D drawing is projected onto an imaginary plane that is parallel to the view from which you selected the model while using the Setup Profile tool. To see this clearly, take a look at your model in model space.

1. Click the Model tab to go to model space.

2. Turn Layer 0 back on. You see the projected 2D view next to the 3D model, as shown in Figure 12.46.

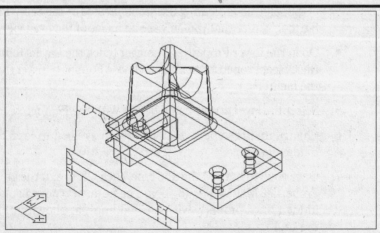

FIGURE 12.46: The projected view next to the 3D solid model

CREATING A 2D PROJECTION FROM YOUR 3D MODEL

Another tool on the Solids toolbar creates 2D drawings of 3D solid models. The Setup Drawing tool does nearly the same thing as the Setup Profile tool, with some differences. First of all, the Setup Drawing tool works only with viewports that are created by the Setup View tool. It automatically turns off the layer on which the solid model resides. So, once it has created a 2D view, you can see the results without having to adjust layer settings. Also, unlike the Setup Profile tool, Setup Drawing leaves the 2D drawing objects as individual objects ready to be edited, instead of turning them into blocks.

Finally, the Setup Drawing tool creates layers whose names offer a better description of their purpose. For example, if you use Setup Drawing to create a 2D drawing of the right-side view, you will get layers entitled Rightside-dim, Rightside-hid, and Rightside-vis. These layer names are derived from the View name from which the 2D drawing is derived. Setup Drawing adds the *-dim*, *-hid*, and *-vis* suffixes to the view names to create the layer names. These suffixes are abbreviations for *dimension*, *hidden*, and *visible*.

Adding Dimensions and Notes in Paper Space

Although I don't recommend adding dimensions in paper space for architectural drawings, it may be a good idea for mechanical drawings like the ones in this chapter. By maintaining the dimensions and notes separate from the actual model, you keep these elements from getting in the way of your work on the solid model. You also avoid the confusion of having to scale the text and dimension features properly to ensure that they will plot at the correct size.

As long as you set up your paper space work area to be equivalent to the final plot size, you can set dimension and text to the sizes you want at plot time. If you want text 1/4" high, you set your text styles to be 1/4" high.

Part iii

To dimension, just make sure you are in paper space (View ≻ Paper Space), and then use the dimension commands in the normal way. However, you do have to be careful of one thing: If your paper space viewports are set to a scale other than 1 to 1, you must set the Annotation Units option in the Dimension Style dialog box to a proper value. The following steps show you how:

1. Choose Dimension ≻ Style.

2. In the Dimension Style Manager dialog box, make sure you have selected the style you want to use, and click Modify.

3. In the Modify Dimension Style dialog box, click the Primary Units tab.

4. In the Scale Factor input box under the Measurement Scale group, enter the value by which you want your paper space dimensions multiplied. For example, if your paper space views are scaled at one-half the actual size of your model, you enter **2** in this box to multiply your dimensions' values by 2.

TIP

To make sure the value you need in step 4 is correct, just determine what scale factor you need for your paper space drawing to get its actual size; that's the value to enter.

5. Click the Apply to Layout Dimensions Only check box. This option ensures that your dimension is scaled only while you are adding dimensions in paper space. Dimensions added in model space are not affected.

6. Click OK to close the Modify Dimension Style dialog box, and then click OK again in the Dimension Style Manager dialog box.

You've completed a lot of steps to get the final drawing, but, compared to having to draw these views by hand, you have undoubtedly saved a great deal of time. In addition, as you will see later in this chapter, you have more than just a 2D drafted image. With this drawing, further refinements are now quite easy.

Drawing a Cross-Section

One element of your drawing is missing: a cross-section. AutoCAD will draw a cross-section through any part of the solid model. In the following exercise, you will draw such a cross-section:

1. Save your drawing so you can return to this stage (in case you don't want to save the results of the following steps).

2. Choose Tools ➢ New UCS ➢ World.

3. Click the Section tool on the Solids toolbar.

4. At the `Select objects:` prompt, click both halves of the solid model and press Enter.

5. At the prompt

```
Section plane by
Object/Last/Zaxis/View/XY/YZ/ZX/<3points>
```

enter **ZX** and press Enter. This command tells AutoCAD you want to cut the solid in the plane defined by the x- and z-axes.

6. At the `Point on ZX plane:` prompt, pick the midpoint of the top-right surface of the solid (see the top image of Figure 12.47). The section cut appears, as shown in the bottom image of Figure 12.47.

The section shown in the bottom image of Figure 12.47 is a type of object called a *region*. In the next section, you'll learn how regions share some characteristics with 3D solids.

Part iii

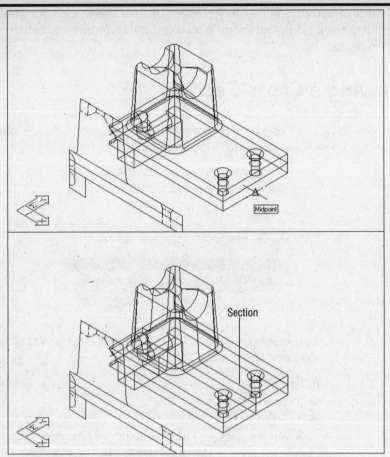

FIGURE 12.47: Selecting the point on the z-x plane to define the section-cut outline

Using 3D Solid Operations on 2D Drawings

You can apply of some of the features described in this chapter to 2D drafting by taking advantage of AutoCAD's *region* object. Regions are two-dimensional objects to which you can apply Boolean operations.

Try the following optional exercise, which demonstrates how two Boolean operations, Union and Subtract, work on 2D objects:

1. If you have been working through the tutorial on 3D solids, save the Bracket drawing now.

2. Open the Region.dwg drawing supplied on the Sybex website. You will see the drawing shown in the top image of Figure 12.48. The objects in this drawing are circles and closed polylines.

3. Click the Region tool on the Draw toolbar, or type **Reg** and press Enter.

4. At the Select objects: prompt, click all the objects in the drawing and press Enter. AutoCAD converts the objects into regions.

5. Move the two circles and the hexagons into the positions illustrated in the bottom image of Figure 12.48. (For this demonstration exercise, you don't have to worry about matching the positions exactly.)

6. Choose Modify ➤ Boolean ➤ Union.

7. At the Select objects: prompt, click the rectangle and the two circles. The circles merge with the rectangle to form one object.

8. Choose Modify ➤ Boolean ➤ Subtract, and then click the newly created region and press Enter.

9. At the next Select objects: prompt, click the two hexagons. Now you have a single, 2D solid object in the shape of a wrench, as shown in the continued image of Figure 12.48.

You can use regions to generate complex surfaces that might include holes or unusual bends (see Figure 12.49). You should keep two things in mind:

▶ Regions act like surfaces; when you remove hidden lines, objects behind the regions are hidden.

▶ You can explode regions to edit them. (You can't do this with solids.) However, exploding a region causes the region to lose its surface-like quality, and objects will no longer hide behind its surface(s).

Part iii

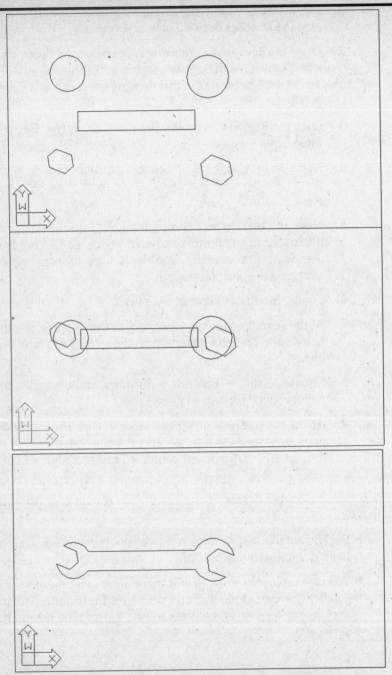

FIGURE 12.48: Working with regions in the Region.dwg file

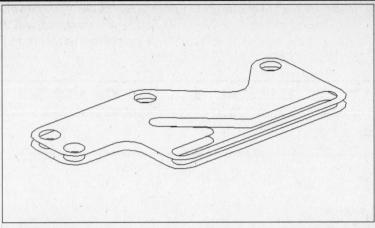

FIGURE 12.49: You can use the regional model to create complex 2D surfaces for use in 3D surface modeling.

FINDING THE PROPERTIES OF A SOLID

All this effort to create a solid model isn't just to create a pretty picture. Once your model is drawn and built, you can obtain information about its physical properties. In the next section, you will look at a few of the commands that let you gather such information.

Finding a Model's Mass Properties

You can find the volume, the moment of inertia, and other physical properties of your model by using the Massprop command. These properties can also be recorded as a file on disk so you can modify your model without worrying about losing track of its original properties.

1. Open the Bracket drawing you worked on through most of this chapter.

2. Click and drag the Distance tool on the Standard toolbar. Select Mass Properties on the flyout, or enter **Massprop**.

3. At the Select objects: prompt, select the two halves of the
    solid model. AutoCAD will calculate for a moment, and then
    it displays a list of the object's properties, as shown in Fig-
    ure 12.50.

```
AutoCAD Text Window                                           _ □ ✕
Edit
Command:  MASSPROP
Select objects: 1 found

 elect objects:  |
 ----------------     SOLIDS      ----------------

Mass:                  35.1657
Volume:                35.1657
Bounding box:      X:  2.9990  --  10.0000
                   Y:  2.5000  --   6.5000
                   Z:  0.4990  --   4.0000
Centroid:          X:  5.5725
                   Y:  4.5055
                   Z:  1.7242
Moments of inertia:  X:  886.9826
                     Y:  1318.5188
                     Z:  1924.6475
Products of inertia:  XY:  882.4382
                      YZ:  272.9676
                      ZX:  317.4906
Radii of gyration:   X:  5.0222
                     Y:  6.1233
                     Z:  7.3980
Press ENTER to continue:
Principal moments and X-Y-Z directions about centroid:
                    I:  61.3669 along [0.9424 -0.0061 -0.3344]
                    J: 121.9476 along [-0.0229 0.9963 -0.0826]
                    K: 126.0628 along [0.3337 0.0855 0.9388]

Write to a file ? <N>:
Command: |                                               ◄ □ ►
```

FIGURE 12.50: The Mass Properties listing derived from the solid model

TAKING ADVANTAGE OF
STEREOLITHOGRAPHY

A discussion of solid modeling wouldn't be complete without mention-
ing *stereolithography*. This is one of the more interesting technological
wonders that has appeared as a by-product of 3D computer modeling.
Stereolithography is a process that generates resin reproductions of 3D
computer solid models. It offers the mechanical designer a method of
rapidly prototyping designs directly from AutoCAD drawings. The

process requires special equipment that will read computer files in a particular format.

AutoCAD supports stereolithography through the Stlout command. This command generates an .stl file, which can be used with *Stereo-lithograph Apparatus (STA)* to generate a model. You must first create a 3D solid model in AutoCAD; then you can proceed with the following steps to create the .stl file.

1. Choose File ➤ Export.

2. In the Export Data dialog box, open the Save as Type drop-down list and select Lithography (*.stl). Click the Save button.

TIP

You can also type **Stlout** and press Enter at the Command prompt to bypass steps 1 and 2.

3. At the Select a single solid for STL output: prompt, select a solid or a set of solids and press Enter. All solids must reside in the positive x-, y-, and z-coordinates of the WCS.

The AutoCAD 3D solids are translated into a set of triangular-faceted meshes in the .stl file. You can use the Facetres system variable to control the fineness of these meshes.

IF YOU WANT TO EXPERIMENT...

This chapter has focused on a mechanical project, but you can, of course, use solids to help simplify the construction of 3D architectural forms. If your interest lies in architecture, try drawing the window in Figure 12.51. (Imagine trying to create this window without the solid-modeling capabilities of AutoCAD!)

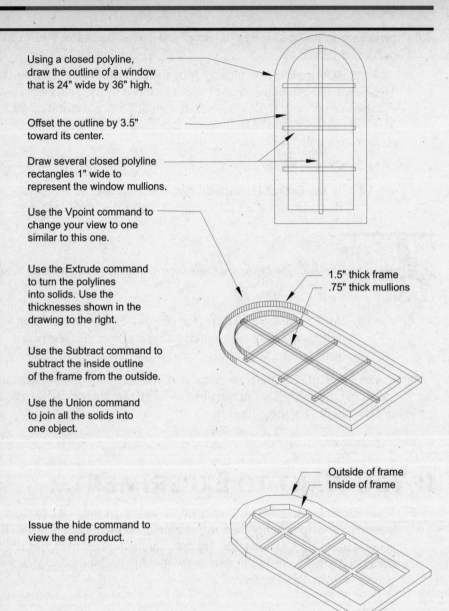

Using a closed polyline, draw the outline of a window that is 24" wide by 36" high.

Offset the outline by 3.5" toward its center.

Draw several closed polyline rectangles 1" wide to represent the window mullions.

Use the Vpoint command to change your view to one similar to this one.

Use the Extrude command to turn the polylines into solids. Use the thicknesses shown in the drawing to the right.

1.5" thick frame
.75" thick mullions

Use the Subtract command to subtract the inside outline of the frame from the outside.

Use the Union command to join all the solids into one object.

Outside of frame
Inside of frame

Issue the hide command to view the end product.

FIGURE 12.51: Drawing a window

Part i

WHAT'S NEXT?

This chapter introduced you to the powerful solid modeling tools in Auto-CAD. The next chapter shows you how to integrate AutoCAD with the even more advanced tools found in 3D Studio VIZ.

Part iii

Chapter 13

USING AUTOCAD WITH VIZ

It is very handy to use AutoCAD with VIZ. You can use Auto-CAD as an aid in creating material maps and to help you analyze photos for VIZ backgrounds. In this section, you'll look at ways that AutoCAD can be used more directly with VIZ to create geometry.

Adapted from *Mastering™ 3D Studio VIZ® 3*
by George Omura
ISBN 0-7821-2775-4   1,152 pages $49.99

AutoCAD is an excellent tool for creating 2D geometry. Much of your work as a designer will require accurate renditions of your designs in the traditional plan and elevation views. Frequently, designs begin as 2D plans anyway, so having the ability to import an AutoCAD drawing is a natural extension of VIZ.

In this section, you'll explore the ways that you can import AutoCAD line drawings as a starting point in the creation of VIZ geometry.

CREATING TOPOGRAPHY WITH SPLINES

A displacement map, which is similar to a bump map, creates a deformed surface based on the light and dark areas of a bitmap image. You could use a displacement map to create terrain by drawing light and dark areas in an image and then using that image as a displacement map, as shown in Figure 13.1.

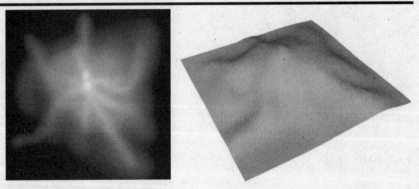

FIGURE 13.1: A bitmap image and the terrain created

This type of terrain modeling is fine for free-form shapes, but if you want an accurate model of terrain based on survey data, you need to use other tools to create your terrain model. In this section, you'll learn how you can quickly create a terrain model from contour lines generated in AutoCAD. You'll also get a look at ways of linking files from AutoCAD to allow you to maintain one data source for both Auto-CAD and VIZ.

1. Start VIZ. Choose Insert ➤ Linked DWG....

2. In the Open dialog box, locate and open the Contour.dwg file. This is an AutoCAD file that contains a series of contour lines, as shown in Figure 13.2. The contour lines are Auto-CAD splines.

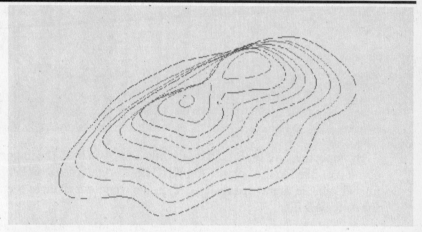

FIGURE 13.2: The Contour.dwg file

3. In the File Link Settings dialog box, click OK.

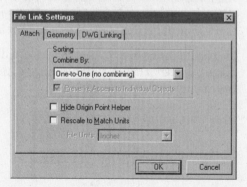

The contours appear in the VIZ Perspective viewport.

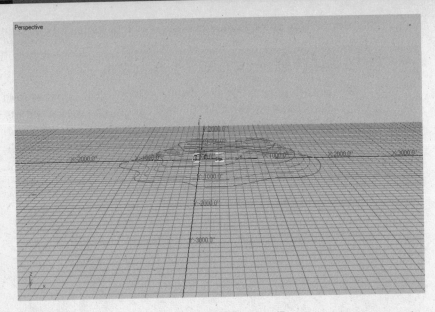

By importing an AutoCAD file as a linked file, you keep the imported geometry linked to the original AutoCAD file. As you'll see a bit later, this link will enable you to update the VIZ design whenever changes occur to the AutoCAD file.

Now let's see how the contours can be turned into a surface model:

1. Click Select by Name to open the Select Object dialog box. Select all of the objects except contour.dwg.01, which is the AutoCAD contour object. VIZ names the objects by their Auto-CAD color numbers. Contour.dwg.01 is an additional object that VIZ creates to identify the origin of the imported drawing.

2. Make sure the Geometry button is selected in the Create tab of the Command Panel, and then choose AEC Extended from the Create tab drop-down list.

3. Click Terrain from the Object Type rollout.

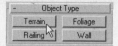

A surface appears over the contour lines.

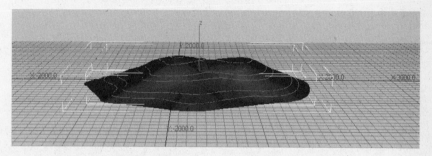

TIP

As an alternative to steps 2 and 3, you can click the Terrain Compound Object tool in the Create AEC tab of the tab panel.

VIZ creates a Terrain object based on the contour lines. You can improve the visibility of the terrain's shape by using the Color by Elevation option.

1. Scroll down to the Color by Elevation rollout and open it.

2. Click the Create Defaults button in the Zones by Base Elevation group.

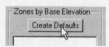

The Terrain object changes to show a series of colored bands.

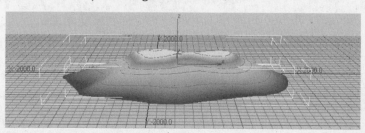

The values in the Zone by Base Elevation group list box tell you the base elevation for each of the colors. You can change the color and the base elevation.

1. Select the item at the top of the list in the list box of the Zones by Base Elevation group.

2. In the Color Zone group, click the Base Color swatch.

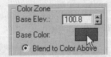

3. In the Color Selector dialog box, click the cyan (blue) color in the Hue/Blackness color selector.

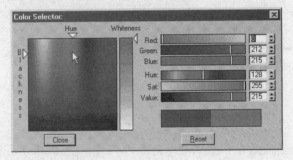

4. Click the Modify Zone button in the Color Zone group. The base of the Terrain object changes to the blue color you selected.

You can also change the vertical location for a color by changing the Base Elev. value in the Color Zone group. This setting doesn't have any effect on the shape of the Terrain object; it only changes the location of the color.

Updating Changes from an AutoCAD File

You imported the AutoCAD contour map using the Insert ➤ Linked DWG option. By using this option, you link your VIZ design to the Contour.dwg file in a way that is similar to Xref files in both VIZ and AutoCAD. Changes in the Contour.dwg file will affect any VIZ file to which it is linked.

Let's suppose that you need to make some corrections to the AutoCAD contour drawing that will affect the Terrain object you've just created. You can change the AutoCAD drawing file, and then update the VIZ design to reflect those changes.

1. Open the Contour.dwg file and make the changes shown in Figure 13.3.

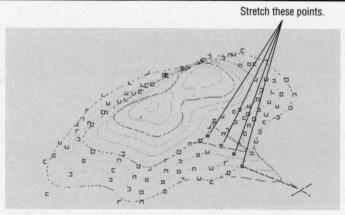

FIGURE 13.3: Stretch these points outward.

2. In VIZ, choose Insert ➤ File Link Manager....

3. In the File Link Manager dialog box, click Contour.dwg in the Linked Files list box.

4. Click the Reload... button.

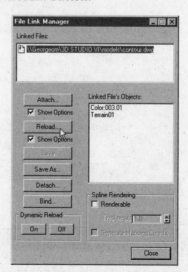

5. In the File Link Settings dialog box, click OK. The file will be reloaded, and the changes will be imported into the current VIZ file.

6. Close the File Link Manager dialog box. The changes are now visible in the Terrain object.

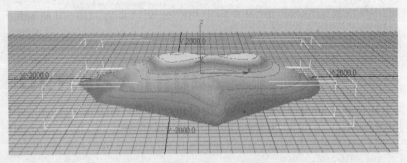

Like Xref files, VIZ designs that are linked to AutoCAD files can be updated to reflect changes that are made to the source AutoCAD file. You'll get a chance to take a closer look at this feature later in this chapter.

Exploring Terrain Options

The Terrain object has quite a few parameters that allow you to make adjustments to the terrain. For example, if you prefer, you can have the terrain appear as a terraced form instead of a smooth one, as shown in Figure 13.4.

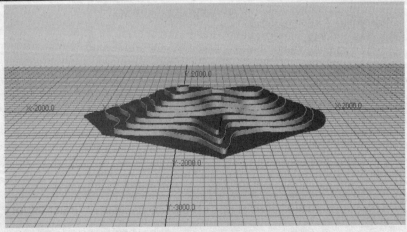

FIGURE 13.4: The Terrain object with the Layered Solid option

NOTE

The Layered Solid option of the Terrain object creates a surface that resembles a traditional site plan model made of foamcore.

You've already seen how a few of the Color by Elevation rollout options work. Here's a rundown of the rest of the Terrain object parameters.

Pick Operand Rollout

These options allow you to add other splines to an existing Terrain object.

The splines used for the Terrain object are referred to as its *operands*. When a Terrain object is created, a reference clone of the selected splines is added as part of the Terrain object. This is the default option in the Pick Operand rollout. When adding more splines, you can choose the type of clone you wish to use instead of the Reference clone. The Override option lets you replace one operand with another.

Parameters Rollout

The Parameters rollout offers settings that control the overall form of the Terrain object. The Operands group lets you selectively delete operands from the terrain.

The Form group gives you control over the way the contour data is formed into a terrain:

Graded Surface   Creates the type of terrain you've seen in previous exercises

Graded Solid   Creates a solid form that encloses the entire terrain, including the underside

Layered Solid   Creates a terraced form

Stitch Border   Improves the formation of terrain where open splines or polylines are used in the contour

Retriangulate   Helps to generate a terrain that follows the contours more closely

The Display group allows you to view the terrain as a surface terrain, contour lines, or both. The Update group lets you control the way that the Terrain object is updated when the operands are edited. Always updates the Terrain object as soon as a contour is modified. The When Rendering option updates when you render the design. You can also use the Update button with this option. The Manually option updates the terrain only when you click the Update button.

Simplification Rollout

VIZ uses the vertices of the original contour polylines to generate the Terrain object. The Simplification Rollout options give you control over the number of vertices used to generate the terrain.

In the Horizontal group, the Use 1/2 of Points and Use 1/4 of Points options both reduce the number of points used from the contour line. These procedures reduce the accuracy of the terrain, but they also reduce

the complexity of the geometry, thereby making the terrain's memory requirements smaller. The Interpolate Points options increase the number of points used. Interpolate Points * 2, for example, doubles the number of vertices used by interpolating new points between the existing points in the contour.

The Vertical group determines whether all of the selected contour lines are used. You can reduce the terrain's complexity by using either the Use 1/2 of Lines or the Use 1/4 of Lines option.

Color by Elevation Rollout

VIZ lets you color the Terrain object by elevation. Doing so lets you visualize the terrain more clearly and helps you identify elevations by color-coding them.

The Maximum Elev. and Minimum Elev. options display the maximum and minimum extents of the terrain, based on the contour data. The Reference Elev. option lets you establish a reference elevation that is used for assigning colors to the terrain. If this value is equal to or less than the lowest contour, VIZ generates five color zones for the terrain, as you saw in an earlier exercise. If the Reference Elev. is greater than the lowest contour, VIZ then treats the lower elevations as water, using the Reference Elev. value as the water level. Water is given a blue color by default.

The Zones by Base Elevation group gives you control over the individual colors for each color zone. As you've seen from the exercise, the Create Defaults button applies the colors to the Terrain object based on the current settings of the rollout. You can also change the color of each zone by selecting the zone elevation from the list box and using the Base Color swatch to select a color.

The Blend to Color Above and Solid to Top of Zone radio buttons let you choose to blend colors between zones or to make each zone one solid color. By default, colors are blended. You can change from blended to solid by selecting the zone elevation from the Zones by Base Elevation list, selecting Solid to Top of Zone, and then clicking the Modify Zones button. The Add Zone and Delete Zone options add and delete zones.

SETTING UP AN AUTOCAD PLAN FOR VIZ

If you're an experienced AutoCAD user, you may find it easier to create at least some of your 3D model in AutoCAD and then import the model to VIZ to refine it. You can also import 2D plans and elevations into VIZ and build your 3D model in VIZ. In this section, you'll explore the ways you can set up an AutoCAD 2D drawing to take advantage of VIZ's modeling tools.

One of the drawbacks to importing fully developed 3D models from AutoCAD is that frequently the surface normals of the AutoCAD model are not all oriented in the same direction. You can use VIZ to adjust the normals to point in the same direction, but doing so takes time. It's usually more efficient in this situation to apply two-sided materials to the offending objects and leave it at that. The use of two-sided materials increases rendering time somewhat, but this disadvantage is often offset by the enormous amount of time it would have taken to adjust misaligned normals.

You can avoid the normals problem altogether by taking a few additional steps while creating your model in AutoCAD. In the next set of exercises, you'll use AutoCAD to prepare a plan for export to VIZ.

1. In AutoCAD, open the Savoye-ground.dwg file from the companion website. This is the ground floor plan of the Villa Savoye designed by Le Corbusier.

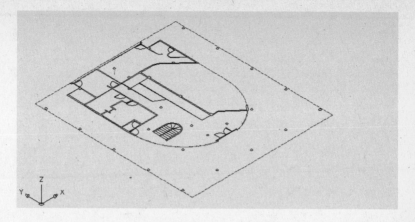

2. Select Wall-viz-EXT from the Layer drop-down list on the Standard toolbar.

3. Use the Zoom Region tool to enlarge your view so it looks similar to Figure 13.5.

4. Choose Draw ➤ Boundary....

5. In the Boundary Creation dialog box, click Pick Points. The dialog box will temporarily disappear to allow you to select points on the screen.

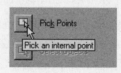

6. Click the points shown in Figure 13.5 and press Enter when you're finished.

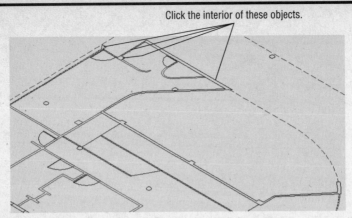

Click the interior of these objects.

FIGURE 13.5: Selecting points inside the exterior walls

A magenta outline of the wall appears, outlining the areas you select. The magenta outline is a continuous polyline, which will become a spline in VIZ. Because Wall-viz-EXT is the current layer, the outline is placed on the Wall-viz-EXT layer. The layer's color is magenta, so the wall acquires the layer's color of magenta.

Next, continue to add the outlines of the exterior walls using the Boundary Creation dialog box.

1. Use the Pan tool to adjust your view to look similar to Figure 13.6.

2. Open the Boundary Creation dialog box again and click the Pick Points button.

3. Select the points indicated in Figure 13.6.

4. Press Enter when you've selected all of the points.

5. Adjust your view as shown in Figure 13.7.

6. Use the Boundary Creation dialog box again to select the areas indicated in Figure 13.7. Press Enter when you're finished.

7. Select Wall-viz-INT from the Layer drop-down list on the Standard toolbar.

8. Use the Boundary Creation dialog box to create outlines of
    the interior walls. When you're finished, the interior walls
    should all appear in the cyan color, which is the color for the
    Wall-viz-INT layer.

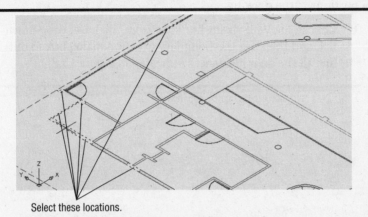

Select these locations.

FIGURE 13.6: Selecting other points for the exterior wall

Select these locations.

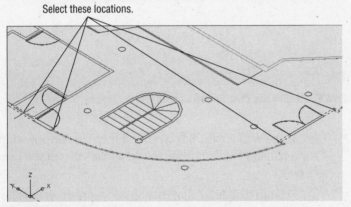

FIGURE 13.7: Select points in the walls near the curved glass.

You want the interior walls to be on a different layer from the exterior
walls so that when the drawing is imported into VIZ, you can apply separate materials to the interior and exterior wall objects. By default, VIZ

converts AutoCAD objects into VIZ objects based on their layers, although you can have VIZ use other criteria for converting objects if you choose.

Go ahead and use the Boundary Creation dialog box to outline the other portions of the drawing.

1. Choose the Wall-viz-int-hdr layer from the Layer drop-down list, and then use the Boundary Creation dialog box to outline all the door headers as indicated in Figure 13.8.

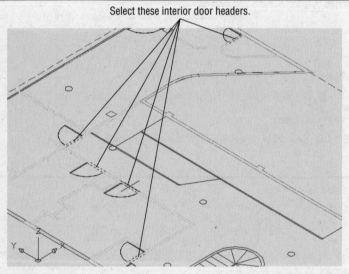

Select these interior door headers.

FIGURE 13.8: Outline the door headers of the interior walls.

2. Choose the Wall-viz-ext-hdr layer, and then use the Boundary Creation dialog box to outline the door headers over the exterior doors.

3. Turn off the Glass layer, and then make the Wall-viz-sill layer current.

4. Use the Boundary Creation dialog box to outline the areas where the windows are indicated in the plan, as shown in Figure 13.9.

Select the window sill areas.

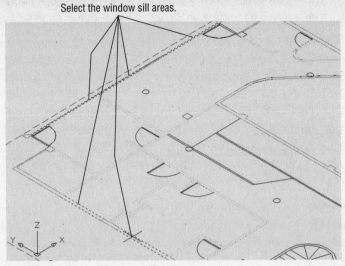

FIGURE 13.9: Outline the window areas.

5. Turn off the Mullion-vert layer, set the current layer to Mullion-horiz, and outline the areas indicated in Figure 13.10.

Select the outline of the curved windows.

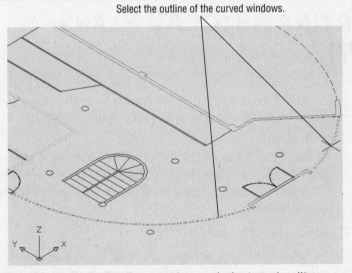

FIGURE 13.10: Outline the areas that are the horizontal mullions.

6. Make sure all the layers are turned back on, and then choose File ➤ Save As and save the file as `MySavoye-ground-viz`.

The main point of these exercises is that you want to segregate the different parts of the drawing so that later, in VIZ, you can control the extruded heights of the separate layers individually. You ensure that you can do so by using layers in AutoCAD to organize the closed polylines that are to be extruded in VIZ.

You use the Boundary Creation dialog box to ensure that the polyline outlines are continuous and closed. You can also just use the Polyline tool on the Draw toolbar to trace over the wall outlines, if you prefer. The Boundary Creation dialog box makes the work a lot easier.

NOTE

Sometimes you will encounter an error message while selecting areas with the Boundary Creation dialog box. This is usually caused by one of two things: Either the area you select is not completely closed, or a single line intrudes into the space you're trying to outline. Also, the entire boundary must be visible on the screen when you attempt to create a new spline. Check for these problems and try Boundary Creation again.

IMPORTING AUTOCAD PLANS INTO VIZ

Now that you've got the plan set up, you can import it into VIZ and make fairly quick work of the conversion to 3D. You've done all the organizing in AutoCAD, so all that is left is to extrude the building parts to their appropriate heights.

1. Open VIZ and choose File ➤ Reset. You don't need to save your changes, so click No at the Do You Want to Save Your Changes? warning and click Yes at the Do You Really Want to Reset? warning.

2. Choose Insert ➤ AutoCAD DWG....

3. In the Select File to Import dialog box, locate and open the `MySavoye-ground-viz.dwg` file. If you haven't done the previous AutoCAD exercises, you can open the `Savoye-ground-viz.dwg` file from the companion website.

4. In the DWG Import dialog box, click Merge Object with Current Design, and then click OK.

5. In the Import AutoCAD DWG File dialog box, make sure the settings are the same as those shown in Figure 13.11.

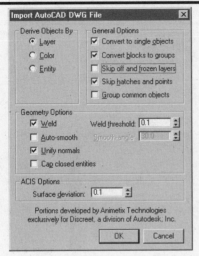

FIGURE 13.11: The Import AutoCAD DWG File dialog box showing the settings needed for this exercise

6. Be sure the Unify Normals check box is checked. This is an important setting because it tells VIZ to align all the normals so that they are pointing outward.

7. Click OK to import the AutoCAD file. The plan appears in the viewport.

The next step is to set up a comfortable view of the model so that you can easily maneuver within it. To make your work a little easier, do the following:

1. Right-click the Perspective label in the upper-left corner of the viewport and select Views ➤ User or enter **U**. Your view changes to an Orthographic Projection view instead of a Perspective view.

2. Choose View ➤ Views ➤ SW to view the design as an Isometric view from the southwest corner.

Part iii

3. Click the Zoom Extents tool to view the plan, and then use the Zoom tool to enlarge it further so it looks similar to Figure 13.12.

4. Click the Grid button at the bottom of the VIZ window to turn off the grid.

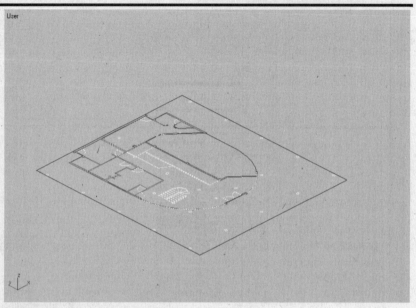

FIGURE 13.12: The view so far

The next step is to begin extruding the walls. The polyline outlines that you created in AutoCAD are converted to closed splines in VIZ, so you need only to select the splines and apply the Extrude modifier.

1. Click the Select by Name tool on the Standard toolbar to open the Select Objects dialog box.

2. Select Wall-viz-INT.01, Wall-viz-EXT.01, and Mullion-vert.01 from the list, and then click Select. Remember that you can select multiple, nonconsecutive items from a list by holding the Ctrl key while you click.

3. Select the Modify tab in the Command panel and click Extrude.

4. In the Parameters rollout, set the Amount input box to **9'6"**. The walls display in the viewport.

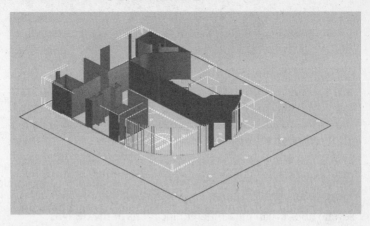

In this exercise, you applied the same modifier to three objects: Wall-viz-INT.01, Wall-viz-EXT.01, and Mullion-vert.01. Whenever you change the Extrude Amount parameter for one object, it changes for the others. The two sets of walls and the vertical mullions were segregated so that you could apply a different material to each of them, but because all these items are the same height, you applied a single modifier to all three of them.

If you decide that you need to give each set of walls its own Extrude modifier, you can do so by clicking one of the walls and then clicking the Make Unique button in the Modifier Stack rollout.

Now, let's continue with the door headers and the walls around the windows:

1. Open the Select Objects dialog box again. Select Wall-viz-ext-hdr, Wall-viz-int-hdr, and Wall-viz-sill.01.

2. Click the Extrude button in the Modify tab, and then change the Amount value in the Parameters to **1'6"**.

3. Click the Select and Move tool, and then right-click it.

4. In the Move Transform Type-in dialog box, change the Z value in the Offset:World group to **96**. The door headers all move to their positions above the doors.

5. Close the dialog box to get a better view of your design.

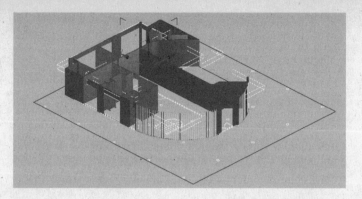

You may have noticed that in step 4 only the Offset:World group showed values. This is the case because you have more than one object selected. The Absolute:World values have no significance for multiple selection because several objects can have different locations in the design.

Also, just as with the walls, you use a single modifier to effect changes to two objects.

Now, take a closer look at the windows. The window headers are in place, but they also need a portion of wall to fill in below the windows. You'll need to copy the window headers and change their Extrude amount.

1. Select the Wall-viz-sill.01 object. You can use the Select Object dialog box to do this, or you can just click one of the window headers toward the back of the building.

2. With the Select and Move tool selected, Shift+click the blue z-axis arrow of the selected header downward to make a clone of the window header object, roughly placing the copy at ground level.

3. In the Clone Options dialog box, make sure the Copy radio button is selected. You can keep the Wall-viz-sill.02 name. Click OK to accept the clone settings.

4. Right-click the Select and Move tool on the Standard tool-bar, and then change the Z value in the Absolute:World group to **0**.

5. Change the Amount value in the Parameters rollout of the Modify tab to **32**.

You now have the walls in place. Because you did some prep work in AutoCAD, the work in VIZ went fairly quickly. Even so, a few items still need to be taken care of. You need to create the horizontal mullions for the curved window.

1. Use the Region Zoom tool to enlarge your view of the plan near the entrance to the right, as shown in Figure 13.13.

2. Select the horizontal mullion outline named Mullion-horiz.01.

3. Click the Extrude button in the Modify tab, and then change the Amount parameter to **2**.

4. Choose Edit ➢ Clone. In the Clone Options dialog box, click OK. The clone is now the selected object.

5. Right-click the Select and Move tool. Change the Z value in the Absolute:World group to **32**.

6. Choose Edit ➢ Clone again. Click OK in the Clone Options dialog box.

7. Right-click the Select and Move tool and change the Z value in the Absolute:World group to **9'''**. The horizontal mullions for the curved window are now in place, as shown in Figure 13.13.

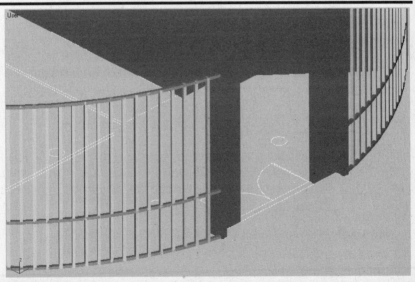

FIGURE 13.13: A close-up view of the entrance and curved window

To finish the ground floor of the Villa, you need to add the glass.

1. Open the Select Object dialog box and select Glass.01.

2. Click the Extrude button in the Modify tab, and then change the Amount parameter to **9'6"**.

The glass appears in only one area, because the Glass object is a single spline and not an outline. The normals of a surface will render the surface visible in only one direction. To compensate for this limitation, you can turn the Glass.01 spline into an outline.

1. In the Command panel, select Editable Spline from the Modifier Stack rollout.

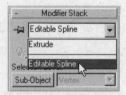

2. Click the Spline button in the Selection rollout.

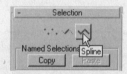

3. Click the Zoom Extent tool to view the entire design.

4. Click the Select Object tool on the Standard toolbar. Place a selection region around the entire building to select the entire Glass.01 spline.

5. Scroll down to the Outline button in the Geometry rollout and enter **0.2** for the Outline value. You won't see any changes at this viewing distance, but the glass is now an outline instead of a single line.

6. Scroll back up to the top of the Command panel. Click the Sub-Object button to exit the Sub-Object level.

7. Select Extrude from the Modifier Stack rollout. The glass now appears in all the appropriate places.

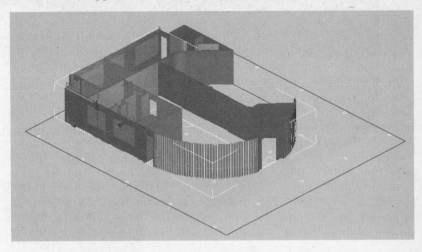

8. Save this file as `Savoye-ground.viz`.

You could have left the glass as a single line. Although doing so makes it difficult to see in a shaded viewport, you can apply a two-sided material to the glass so that it will appear in a finished rendering. A two-sided glass material takes a bit longer to render, but the single-line glass material is a less complex geometry, which makes the file a bit smaller. For this reason, if your model contains lots of curved glass, it may make sense to leave the glass as a single line. Otherwise you may want to convert all the glass in your model to outlines. As you've seen here, that's fairly easy to do in VIZ. It takes a bit more work to accomplish the same result in AutoCAD.

You also may have noticed that in the last exercise you gave the glass a full height of 9'6", even though in many cases the glass filled a height of only 64" or less. You can do this because VIZ takes care of the small details of object intersections. In those places where the glass occurs within a wall, VIZ hides most of the glass; it is displayed only where it appears in an opening, as shown in Figure 13.14. VIZ also takes care of the intersection of the vertical and horizontal mullions.

Part iii

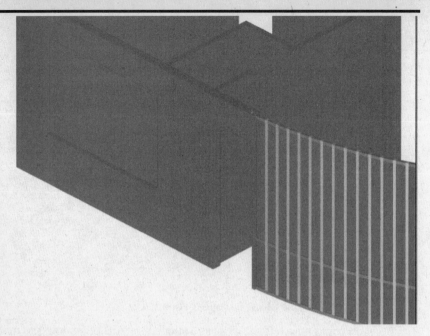

FIGURE 13.14: The window showing the glass

Creating a Floor with Openings

You've seen how the ground floor of the Villa can be set up in AutoCAD to make quick work of the extrusions in VIZ. The second floor and rooftop can be done in the same way, but the floors between the different levels require a slightly different approach.

Both the second floor and roof surface have openings that need some special attention when you're setting up for export to VIZ.

1. Go back to AutoCAD and open the Savoye-second.dwg file from the companion website.

2. Create a layer named VIZ-floor and make it the current layer.

3. Use a polyline to outline the second floor, as shown in Figure 13.15.

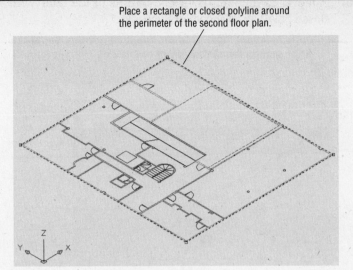

Place a rectangle or closed polyline around the perimeter of the second floor plan.

FIGURE 13.15: Outline the second floor.

4. Turn off all the layers except VIZ-floor, Stair, and Ramp, and then zoom in to the stair, as shown in Figure 13.16.

5. Enlarge the view of the stair. Then, outline the stair with a closed polyline, as shown in Figure 13.16. (In this operation, you're drawing the outline of the stair opening in the floor.)

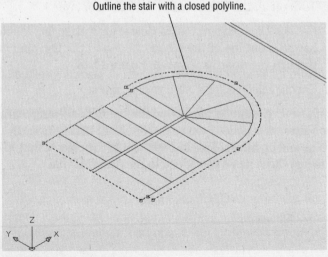

Outline the stair with a closed polyline.

FIGURE 13.16: Outline the stair.

6. Pan over to the ramp. Draw an outline of the ramp with a closed polyline, as shown in Figure 13.17.

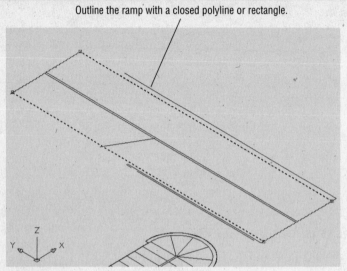

Outline the ramp with a closed polyline or rectangle.

FIGURE 13.17: The outline of the ramp floor opening

You've done all the additional line work required to export the floor of the second story to VIZ. A few more steps are needed to complete the setup for VIZ.

1. Turn off all the layers except the VIZ-floor layer.

2. Use the Zoom Extent tool to view your work so far. You now have the outline of the second floor and the two openings through the floor, as shown in Figure 13.18.

3. Choose File ➤ Save to save your changes.

Basically, you've outlined the second floor and its openings with closed polylines. In addition, you've turned off all the layers except the floor outline and openings. This last step limits the objects that VIZ imports to just those items you added to the AutoCAD file.

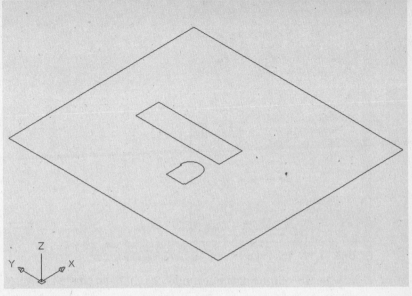

FIGURE 13.18: The outline of the second floor

The next step is to import your work to VIZ.

1. Go back to VIZ and choose File ➤ Reset. (You can reset the file because you've already saved your work.)

2. Choose Insert AutoCAD DWG.... In the Select File to Import dialog box, locate and open the Savoye-second.dwg file you just saved from AutoCAD, or open the Savoye-second-viz.dwg file from the companion website.

3. In the DWG Import dialog box, choose Merge Object with Current Design, and then click OK.

4. In the Import AutoCAD DWG File dialog box, adjust the settings to match those of Figure 13.19, and then click OK.

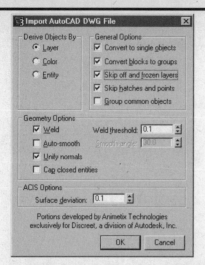

FIGURE 13.19: The Import AutoCAD DWG File dialog box

You see the outline of the second floor that you created in AutoCAD.

The final step is fairly easy. You only need to extrude the spline, and the openings will appear automatically.

1. Click the Select object tool, and then click the floor outline.

2. Select the Modify tab in the Command panel and click the Extrude button.

3. Set the Amount parameter to **18**. You now have the second-story floor, complete with openings.

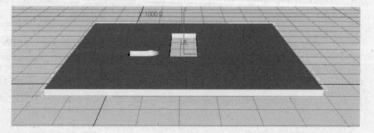

4. If you like, go ahead and save this file as Savoye-second-floor.max for future reference.

VIZ automatically subtracts closed splines that are enclosed by other splines. On the second floor, ramp and stair openings are automatically subtracted from the second floor perimeter.

TIP

As an alternative in AutoCAD, you can convert the closed splines of the stair, ramp, and floor into regions, and then subtract the stair and ramp regions from the floor outline. AutoCAD regions are converted into VIZ surfaces.

You were asked to turn off all the layers in AutoCAD except the Viz-floor layer. Doing so allowed you to limit the objects that were imported from AutoCAD into VIZ. You can go back to the AutoCAD file, turn the wall, header, and other layers back on, and then turn off the VIZ-floor layer. Once you've done that, you can import the other second-story elements into a VIZ file, and then merge the floor and the walls. Of course, you can also turn on all the layers and import all the AutoCAD drawing at once. But importing parts of an AutoCAD file can help simplify your work and keep it manageable.

USING BUILDING ELEVATIONS AND WALL PROFILES FROM AUTOCAD

In the last section, you learned how to convert outlines of a building plan into a floor with openings. You can employ the same procedures for converting building elevations from AutoCAD to VIZ 3D designs. For example, in AutoCAD, you can outline an elevation of the Villa, using concentric rectangles for the second floor outline and the windows. You can then import the outlines to VIZ and extrude them, just as you did with the floor. Doing so will give you the exterior walls of the building that you can rotate into a vertical position.

Using this method, you can even include other detail such as the window mullions. Once you've done this for all four exterior walls, you can join the walls to form the second floor exterior walls, complete with window openings and window detail.

Another great tool for forming building exteriors and interiors is VIZ's Loft tool. Sometimes a simple vertical extrusion won't be enough for walls. You may be working with a design that makes use of strong horizontal elements, such as a wide cornice or exaggerated rustication. You can make quick work of such detail by using the Loft tool. Draw the profile of the wall and the building footprint in AutoCAD.

CONTINUED ➡

Part iii

Make sure each of these items is on a separate layer and is made of polylines. You can then import the AutoCAD file into VIZ and use the Loft Compound Object tool to loft the wall profile along the building footprint. This technique is especially helpful if the building footprint contains lots of curves and corners that would otherwise be difficult to model.

EXPLORING THE FILE LINK MANAGER

Earlier in this chapter, you were introduced to the File Link Manager when you imported topographic contour lines from AutoCAD. In that example, the File Link Manager allowed you to update the VIZ terrain model when a change was made to the AutoCAD .dwg file. You can also use the File Link Manager with floor plans to help maintain design continuity between AutoCAD and VIZ.

Try using the File Link Manager with the second floor of the Villa in the following exercises:

1. Choose File ➢ Reset to reset the file.

2. Choose Insert ➢ File Link Manager....

3. In the File Link Manager dialog box, click Attach....

4. Locate and open the Savoye-second.dwg file you edited in AutoCAD, or use Savoye-second-viz.dwg from the companion website.

5. In the File Link Settings dialog box, click the DWG Linking tab and make sure that the Convert Drawing Layers to Design Layers option is *not* checked.

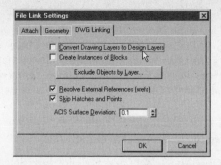

6. Click the Attach tab, and then make sure the Layer option is selected in the Combine By: drop-down list in the Sorting group.

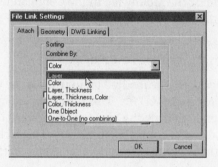

7. Click OK and close the File Link Manager dialog box. The plan displays in the viewport.

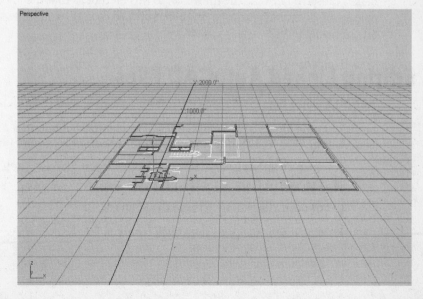

Part iii

TIP

When you turned off the Convert Drawing Layers to Design Layers option in step 5, the Layer option was enabled in step 6. Had you turned on the Convert Drawing Layers to Design Layers option, Layers would not have appeared as an option in the Combine By drop-down list in step 6.

You can now select and extrude objects as you did for the Savoye-ground.dwg file you imported earlier.

1. Open the Select Objects dialog box. Select the Layer:Wall-viz-INT.01 and Layer:Wall-viz-EXT.01 objects.

2. Click the Modify tab in the Command Panel, and then click the Extrude button.

3. Set the Amount parameter to **9'6"**. The interior and exterior walls display in the model.

As you can see, the method for extruding the walls is exactly the same for the linked AutoCAD file. This is due in part to the options you chose earlier when importing the file. You were directed to set up the linked file so that layers were converted to objects. This technique mimics the standard way that VIZ imports non-linked AutoCAD files.

You can also choose to import AutoCAD layers as VIZ layers. You can then control layers as you would in AutoCAD, using the AutoCAD layer names preserved in VIZ. The drawback to this method is that the imported objects are given names based on their AutoCAD colors, which can be a bit confusing in VIZ.

Editing Linked AutoCAD Files

Now let's take a look at one of the key advantages of using the File Link Manager instead of the simpler DWG file import.

1. Go back to AutoCAD and open the Savoye-second.dwg file.

2. Turn on all the layers and use the Stretch command to stretch the wall as shown in Figure 13.20.

3. Choose File ➤ Save to save the changes.

4. Go back to VIZ, and then click Insert ➤ File Link Manager.

5. In the File Link Manager dialog box, select the Savoye-second .dwg listed in the Linked Files list box, and then click the Reload button.

6. In the File Link Settings dialog box, click OK. Close the File Link Manager dialog box.

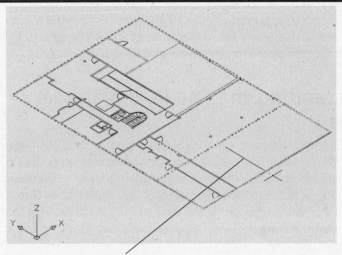

Stretch this wall outward.

FIGURE 13.20: Stretch the wall as shown here.

The VIZ design is updated according to the changes made in the Auto-CAD file.

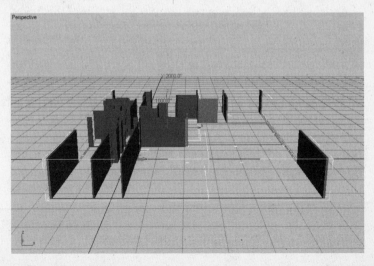

Part iii

You've seen how you can update VIZ designs when changes occur in a linked AutoCAD object. If you add objects in AutoCAD, those objects are also added to the VIZ design. If the new object is added to a layer that already exists, and the objects associated with that layer are attached to a modifier, then the new object is also controlled by the modifier. For example, if you add a rectangle to the AutoCAD drawing on the Wall-viz-EXT layer, the new rectangle will be extruded to the 9'6" height, just like all the other objects on the Wall-viz-EXT layer. New objects that have a thickness or that are extruded within AutoCAD will be ignored by VIZ unless they are placed on a newly created layer.

Understanding the File Link Manager Options

In the previous exercise, you were able to try out a few of the File Link Manager options. The File Link Manager, like so many other VIZ features, offers numerous options to tailor your work to the particular needs of your project. In the limited space of this book, you won't be shown an example of every option available, but you can get started with this feature after reviewing the exercises. Here's a summary of the File Link Manager's options.

Linked Files List Box/Linked Files Objects

The list box at the top of the File Link Manager displays a list of Auto-CAD .dwg and .dxf files that are currently linked to the VIZ design file. An icon next to the filename indicates the status of the linked file:

▶ A paper clip indicates that the source file has not changed and that there are no errors in the link.

▶ A question mark indicates that a file cannot be found.

▶ A red flag indicates that the file has changed since import and that it must be reloaded using the Reload button.

▶ A grayed-out page indicates that a different file has been selected through another path.

▶ A curved arrow indicates that the Dynamic Reload option has been turned on for this file.

The Linked File's Object list box toward the bottom of the dialog box lists the objects found in the selected file.

Attach...

The Attach... button lets you attach an AutoCAD .dwg or .dxf file to the current VIZ design. Files can be attached from versions 12 through 2002 of AutoCAD. If you are using a CAD program other than AutoCAD, you can use the .dxf file format instead of the .dwg format, although many CAD programs today support the .dwg file format directly.

With the Show Options check box selected, you will see the File Link Settings dialog box shown in previous exercises after you've made a file selection with the Attach... option. See the description of the File Link Settings dialog box later in this section.

Reload

As you've seen in previous exercises, this option lets you manually reload a linked AutoCAD file. An abbreviated form of the File Link Settings dialog box appears when you click this button, if you have the Show Options check box checked.

Save/Save As

If you make changes such as object transforms to the linked design in VIZ, you can save those changes to the source AutoCAD file. The application of modifiers will not affect changes to the source file.

Detach

Detach removes a linked file from the current VIZ design. Use this option with caution, because it deletes all the linked objects in the design.

Bind

The Bind option detaches any links to the source AutoCAD file while maintaining the objects in the current VIZ design. The VIZ design then becomes an independent design file and can no longer be affected by the source AutoCAD file.

Dynamic Reload Group

Selecting the On option in the Dynamic Reload group causes VIZ to automatically reload the source AutoCAD file whenever that file is updated. The default Off option tells VIZ to reload the source AutoCAD file only when the Reload button is selected.

Part iii

Spline Rendering Group

You can set up VIZ to render linked splines as tubes by activating the Renderable option in the Spline Rendering group. With this option checked, you can set the thickness for the rendered splines in the Thickness input box. You can also have mapping coordinates applied to the rendered tubes by turning on the Generate Mapping Coord. option.

Understanding File Link Settings

When you import a linked AutoCAD file, you have the option to control the way that file is imported through the File Link Settings dialog box. This dialog box appears by default when you've selected a file for linking, but you can set up VIZ to avoid this dialog box by turning off the Show Options check box in the File Link Manager dialog box.

As you saw in previous exercises, the options selected in the File Link Settings dialog box can make a huge difference in the way the resulting VIZ file is organized. Because AutoCAD and VIZ use entirely different ways to organize data, this dialog box is necessary to make some sense of the way AutoCAD .dwg files are converted to VIZ files. To help in the translation process, VIZ uses a type of compound object called a *VIZblock*. All linked AutoCAD objects are converted to VIZblocks, which are typically collections of AutoCAD objects based on their layer or color assignment.

For example, objects in an AutoCAD file that reside on layer 0 are collected into a single VIZblock. The name of the VIZblock will depend on the settings you choose in the File Link Settings dialog box. In the previous exercise, you chose the Layer option in the File Link Settings dialog box Sorting group. You can further refine the way VIZ combines objects through a combination of layer, thickness, and color, or you can have VIZ import each AutoCAD object as a single object in VIZ.

Organizing Objects by Color

In the first part of this chapter, you imported a contour drawing using the default settings in the File Link Settings dialog box. The default method groups AutoCAD objects by their color. In addition, the Auto-CAD layers are imported into the VIZ file. In this way, imported objects maintain their layer assignments just as they exist in the source AutoCAD file. The objects are converted into VIZblocks and given names based on their color. For example, objects assigned the red color, which is color number 1 in the AutoCAD color naming convention, are given a name beginning with Color:001.01.

If the Preserve Access to Individual Objects option in the Attach tab of the File Link Settings dialog box is turned on, you have access to individual objects in the VIZblock compound object. You can select individual objects by going to the subobject level of the VIZblock and selecting the object name from a list box.

If the Preserve Access to Individual Objects option is turned off, you cannot edit the imported object on a subobject level.

Organizing Objects By Layer

In a recent exercise, you chose a slightly different method for importing the AutoCAD linked file. You were directed to import the Savoye-second.dwg file objects *by layer*. Doing so caused VIZ to collect the AutoCAD objects into VIZblocks according to their layer. The VIZblock names matched the layer names to which the objects were assigned in AutoCAD. The actual layers from the AutoCAD file were not imported. As mentioned in the exercise, this method matches the standard way that VIZ imports AutoCAD files using the Import ➤ AutoCAD DWG option. In order to do this, you had to turn off the Convert Drawing Layers to Design Layers option in the DWG Linking tab of the File Link Settings dialog box.

The Attach Tab Options

Let's take a look at the options in the File Link Settings dialog box, starting with the Attach tab.

Part iii

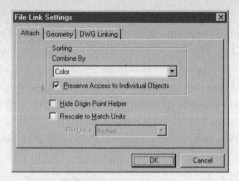

The Sorting group lets you select the method VIZ uses to create the VIZblock objects. The Combine By list box gives you the following options:

Layer   Combines objects according to their layer assignment in AutoCAD.

Color   Combines objects according to their color assignment in AutoCAD. Note that because blocks can contain objects with multiple color assignments, only the color of the block itself is used when converting AutoCAD blocks.

Layer, Thickness   Combines objects in a nested fashion. First objects are converted into VIZblocks according to their layer assignment. Then, within each VIZblock, objects are combined as a subgroup by their thickness.

Layer, Thickness, Color   Combines objects in a way similar to the Layer, Thickness option, with the addition of a color subgroup.

Color, Thickness   Combines objects in a nested fashion by first combining objects of the same color into VIZblocks, and then creating subgroups based on the objects' thickness.

One Object   Converts all the objects of an imported file into a single VIZblock. If the Preserve Access to Individual Objects option is turned on, the VIZblock will allow access to the individual objects on a subobject level. If the Preserve Access to Individual Objects option is turned off, the entire imported file is a single VIZblock.

One-to-One   Converts every AutoCAD object into a linked object in VIZ.

Two other settings in the Attach tab offer control over the orientation and units of the imported file. When VIZ imports a linked file, it creates a User Coordinate System helper. This is an object that marks the origin of the imported file. This helper is also selected immediately upon importing the file. You can hide the User Coordinate System helper by turning on the Hide Origin Point Helper option.

The Rescale to Match Units option, when turned on, lets you determine how units from the imported file are interpreted by VIZ. When Rescale to Match Units is turned on, you can use the File Units drop-down list to select the base unit to which the imported base unit is to be translated. For example, if you wanted to make sure that an AutoCAD drawing's base unit is centimeters, you would check the Rescale to Match Units option, and then select Centimeters from the File Units drop-down list.

Geometry Tab Options

The options in the Geometry tab give you control over the way imported objects are converted into VIZ objects. These options are similar to those found in the Geometry group of the Import AutoCAD DWG File dialog box that you see when you use the Import ➤ AutoCAD DWG option.

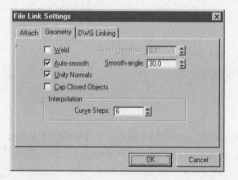

Weld   Determines whether coincident vertices of imported objects are joined, or *welded*, together to form a contiguous object. When Weld is turned on, the Weld Threshold setting is used to determine how close together objects need to be before they are welded.

Auto-smooth   Determines whether to apply smoothing to contiguous surfaces in imported objects. When Auto-smooth is turned on, the Smooth-angle setting is used to determine the minimum angle to which smoothing should be applied.

Part iii

Unify Normals   Attempts to align all the normals of an object so that they point outward from the center of the object.

Cap Closed Objects   Causes VIZ to apply an Extrude modifier to closed objects such as closed polylines or rectangles. In addition, the Cap Start and Cap End extrude modifier options are applied.

The Curve Steps option of the Interpolation group gives you control over the way curves are converted. A low Curve Steps value causes curves to appear as straight segments, whereas higher values generate a more accurate curve.

DWG Linking Tab Options

The options in the DWG Linking tab give you control over the way layers, blocks, AutoCAD Xrefs, hatches, points, and 3D Solids (ACIS Surfaces) are converted.

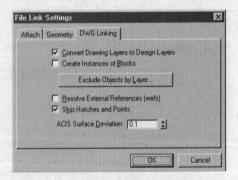

Convert Drawing Layers to Design Layers   Does just what it says. With this option turned on, AutoCAD layers are converted into layers in the VIZ design. Objects are then given names based on the settings in the Attach tab of the File Link Settings dialog box. When this option is turned on, the layer-related options are not available in the Sorting group of the Attach tab. With this option turned off, you can have name objects based on their layer assignments in AutoCAD.

Create Instances of Blocks   Converts multiple copies of Auto-CAD blocks into Instance clones in VIZ. The way these clones are organized depends on the option you select in the Sorting group of the Attach tab. By turning on this option, you cause blocks in VIZ to behave in a way similar to blocks in AutoCAD.

Exclude Objects by Layer   Opens the Select Layers dialog box, where you can select layers to be excluded from the link.

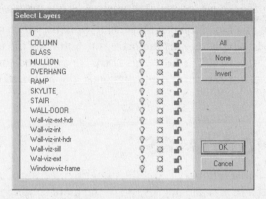

Resolve External References (Xrefs)   Tells VIZ that you want to import AutoCAD Xrefs that are attached to the linked AutoCAD file. You are presented with the Resolve External Reference File dialog box to help you locate the AutoCAD Xref.

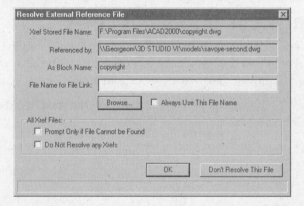

You can turn on the Prompt Only If File Cannot Be Found option in the Resolve External Reference File dialog box if you want this dialog box to appear only when VIZ cannot find an Xref. The imported Xref becomes a single block that is a component of a VIZblock.

Skip Hatches and Points   Does just what it says. With this option turned on, AutoCAD Hatch and Point objects are ignored by VIZ.

Part iii

ACIS Surface Deviation Gives you control over the way VIZ translates AutoCAD 3D Solids into VIZ objects. Smaller values produce more accurate translations but increase file size.

The File Link Manager offers many options, which makes it a good alternative to simply directly importing an AutoCAD file using the Insert ➤ AutoCAD DWG... or AutoCAD DXF... option. You can always use the Bind option to sever the link and make the imported data a stand-alone VIZ file.

Adding Stairs

VIZ offers a number of Architecture/Engineering/Construction (AEC) tools that can make quick work of the more common building design functions. You've already seen how walls, doors, foliage, and terrain work. In this last section, you'll use a few of the AEC stair tools to build one flight of stairs in the Villa design. In general, the stair tools are pretty straightforward.

Tracing over Imported Lines

To practice adding stairs, you'll use the ground-floor file that you created earlier in this chapter. The imported stair plan in the Savoye-ground.viz file will provide the framework for your stair.

1. Open the Savoye-Ground.viz file you created earlier in this chapter.

2. Open the Select Object dialog box and click All.

3. Ctrl+click the Stair.01 item in the list to remove it from the selection, and then click Select.

4. Click the Display tab in the Command panel and click Selected Off.

5. Click the Zoom Extents tool to view the stair.

6. Right-click the Snap button at the bottom of the VIZ window and make sure Endpoint is selected in the Grind and Snap Settings dialog box. Close the dialog box.

7. Click the Snap button to turn on the Snap mode.

You'll create the stair in three sections: the two straight runs and the circular portion. Because the straight runs are identical, you will create one and copy it to the other side.

To create the first stair run, do the following:

1. Click the Create tab in the Command panel.

2. With the Geometry button selected, select Stairs from the drop-down list.

3. Click Stairs from the Object Type rollout.

4. With the Snap mode turned on, click and drag from the corner shown in Figure 13.21.

5. Drag the cursor to the second location shown in Figure 13.21, and then let go of the mouse button.

6. Click the third location shown in Figure 13.21.

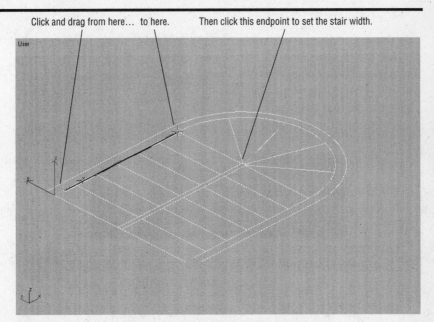

FIGURE 13.21: Click and drag from the corner, as shown here.

7. Move the mouse upward to set the height, and then click OK. You will set the exact height in the next exercise, so you don't have to worry about the look of the stair for now.

You've established the stair in the design. Now you can make some adjustments to its parameters so that the stair dimensions are appropriate to the Villa dimensions.

Adjusting Stair Parameters

The total distance from the ground floor to the second floor is 11 feet, or 114 inches. Thus each of the 18 steps is 7.333 inches high. There is a bit of a trick to setting stair heights with the Stair tools. You must first tell VIZ the number of steps, and then work on the overall height and the height of the risers.

1. In the Create tab of the Command panel, scroll down to the Rise group of the Parameters rollout.

2. Set the Riser Ct setting to **7**, and then click the Pin Riser Count button to the left of the setting. Doing so locks the riser setting to 7.

Notice that now the Overall and Riser Ht settings are both available, whereas the Riser Ct setting is grayed out. Also note that one pin is always down.

3. Set the Riser Ht value to **7.333**. The Overall setting automatically adjusts to the height of 51.331 inches.

4. Scroll up to the Layout group and change the length to **76**.

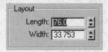

5. Scroll up to the Type group and click the Closed radio button.

VIZ will draw a set of stairs with one less riser than indicated in the Riser Ct parameter. VIZ leaves off the top riser of the stair because the stair length parameter measures the stair from the nosing of the first stair tread to the nosing of the top stair tread. Thus the top stair tread is left out of the length calculation.

When setting up the stair height, it's easiest to start by first setting the number of stair risers. The trick is to use the Pin Riser Count button to lock the riser number. You can then easily adjust the height by adjusting either the overall or riser height.

TIP

Here's another method that works: Pin the riser count, and then set the overall height. Next, pin the overall height and then set either the riser count or riser height.

Creating a Circular Stair

You now have the first part of the stair ready. The circular portion is next.

1. Click the Min/Max toggle to view all four viewports.

2. Click the Zoom Extents All tool to enlarge the view of the stairs in all the viewports.

3. In the Top viewport, move the straight stair to the left to give yourself some room to create the circular portion of the stair, as shown in Figure 13.22.

Now you are ready to use the Spiral Stair tool.

1. Turn off the Snap mode.

2. Scroll to the top of the Command panel and click the Spiral Stair option.

3. In the Top viewport, click and drag the center of the circular portion of the stair plan as shown in Figure 13.22.

4. Drag the mouse to set the radius of the stair to the width of the stair and release the mouse, as shown in Figure 13.22.

5. Move the mouse upward and click to set the height of the stair. Once again you can click any height, because you'll adjust the height accurately in the Command panel.

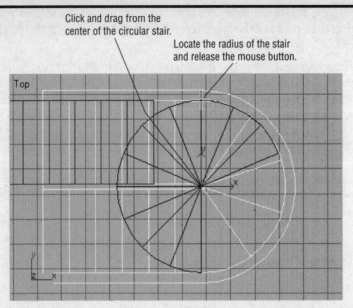

FIGURE 13.22: Selecting points to place the circular portion of the stair

The circular portion has a few problems. It's turning the wrong way, and it extends beyond the 180° arc of the stair in the plan. The following steps will quickly take care of these problems.

1. Click Closed in the Type group to match the straight portion of the stairs.

2. Scroll down to the Layout group and click the CW (clockwise) radio button.

3. In the Rise group, change the Riser Ct value to **6**, and then click the Pin Riser Count button.

4. Set the Riser Ht value to **7.333**.

5. In the Layout group, set the Revs value to **0.602**.

6. Use the Select and Rotate tool to rotate the circular stair in the Top viewport so that it is oriented correctly in the plan.

7. Use the Select and Move tool to move the circular stair vertically in the Left viewport so that it is aligned with the top of the straight stairs.

At this point, you only need to align the circular stair in the vertical axis. You'll move the stair components into position once all of them are constructed and in the proper orientation.

Finishing the Stair

Now make the clone of the straight stair and move the clone into position.

1. Click the Zoom Extents All tool to get a clear view of your work so far.

2. Click the straight stair in the Left viewport, and then Shift+click and drag the y-axis upward so that the bottom of the straight stair aligns with the top of the circular stair, as shown in Figure 13.23.

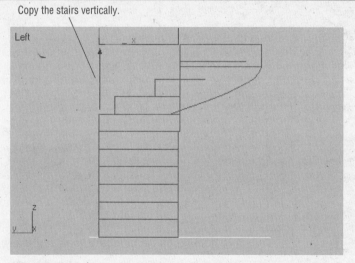

FIGURE 13.23: Copy the straight stair run vertically.

3. In the Clone Options dialog box, click OK.

4. Right-click the Top viewport, and then click the Select and Rotate tool.

5. Select the Center pivot option from the Pivot flyout on the Standard toolbar.

6. Click and drag the z-axis of the cloned stair upward in the Top viewport to rotate the stair 180 degrees.

7. Move the cloned stair downward to align with the circular stair, as shown in Figure 13.24.

Move the clone downward to align with the other end of the circular stair.

FIGURE 13.24: Move the clone into position.

8. Move the two straight stairs to the left so they are connected to the circular stair, as shown in Figure 13.25.

You don't have to worry about being absolutely accurate when placing the stair components together. When you consider construction methods, a ⅛" tolerance for locating building components is about as accurate as you can expect, and for most rendering and modeling purposes, positioning objects visually is usually good enough.

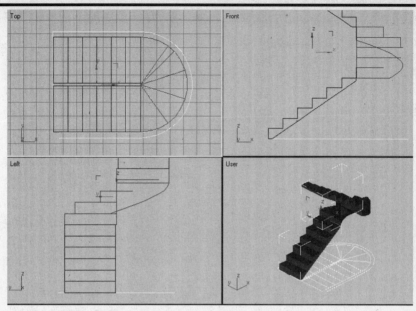

FIGURE 13.25: The straight stairs moved into position next to the circular stair

Adding the Stair Walls

You now have some stairs from the ground floor to the second floor. You still need the walls that surround the stairs. Start by drawing a line that forms the inside edge of the wall.

1. Right-click the Perspective viewport, and then click the Min/Max viewport toggle to enlarge it.

2. Right-click the User label in the upper-left corner of the viewport and select Wireframe. This option allows you to easily select points on the stair.

3. Use the Arc Rotate tool to rotate the view so it looks similar to Figure 13.26.

4. Click the Create tab, and then click the Shapes button and select Line.

5. Turn the Snap mode back on, and then click the points indicated in Figure 13.26. Remember that you can press the Backspace key if you select a point by accident.

Select the points indicated by the Xs starting at the bottom of the stairs.

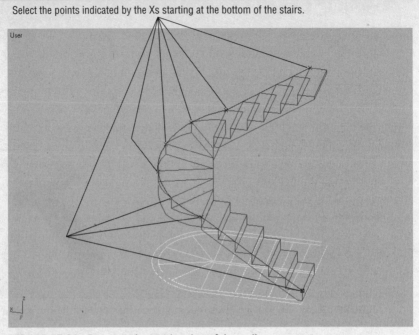

FIGURE 13.26: Drawing the inside edge of the wall

You've set up a path, but the curved portion of the path needs to be smoothed out to form a curve. You'll employ a simple method to change the vertices at the curved portion of the path.

1. Click the Modify tab, and then click the Vertex option in the Selection rollout.

2. Turn off the Snap mode, because it may interfere with the following steps.

3. Use the Select Object tool to right-click one of the vertices in the curved portion of the stairs, as shown in Figure 13.27.

4. Select Smooth from the right-click menu.

5. Repeat steps 3 and 4 for each of the vertices in the curved part of the stair, as indicated in Figure 13.27.

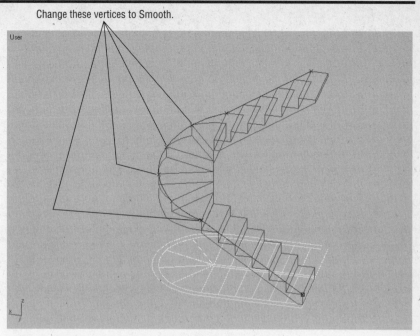

FIGURE 13.27: Change these vertices into smooth vertices.

6. Click the Spline button in the Selection rollout.

7. Click the spline you just created.

8. Scroll down to the Outline parameter and set its value to **6**. You see the line turn into an outline.

9. Scroll up to the Modifier rollout, and then click Extrude.

10. Change the Amount parameter to **50**.

11. Move the wall downward in the z-axis about 7 inches so the bottom of the wall aligns with the bottom of the stair.

12. Click the Zoom Extent tool to get a complete view of the stair, as shown in Figure 13.28.

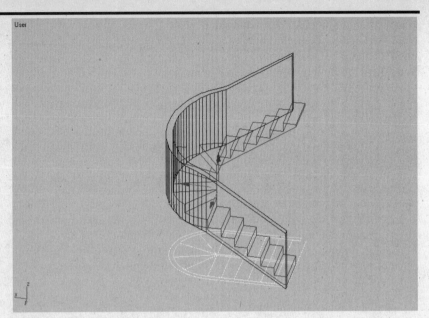

FIGURE 13.28: The stair so far

The wall needs to be extended by one stair step at the top of the stairs. You can go back to the spline vertex subobject level to make this modification.

1. Zoom in to the top stair so your view looks similar to that of Figure 13.29.

2. Choose Line from the Modifier Stack drop-down list.

3. Click the Vertex button in the Selection rollout.

4. Click the Select and Move tool and place a rectangular selection region around the two end vertices indicated in Figure 13.29.

5. Click and drag the blue axis corner mark of the Transform gizmo to move the vertices into the position shown in Figure 13.30.

   By using the corner marks of the Transform gizmo, you can restrict the motion to the two axes indicated by the corner mark while in a Perspective viewport.

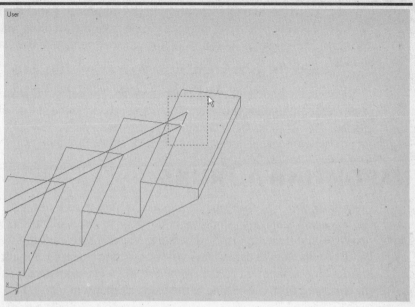

FIGURE 13.29: Select these two vertices.

Click and drag this corner mark to adjust the location of the end vertices.

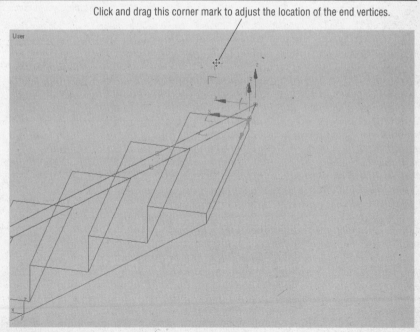

FIGURE 13.30: Move the vertices into this position.

Part iii

6. Click the Sub-Object button in the Command Panel to exit the subobject level. Select Extrude from the Modifier Stack drop-down list to return to the extruded version of the wall.

7. Click the Zoom Extent button to get a view of the stairs.

You've made one flight of stairs for the Villa. The second flight is the same as the first, so for the second floor you can clone the stairs you just created.

IMPORTING A TRUSS

Frequently, you'll be called upon to include a truss in your design. If it's a flat truss, you can draw a side view of the truss in AutoCAD using closed polylines, and then import the drawing to VIZ and extrude it in a way similar to the floor of the earlier Savoye-second.dwg example. If the truss line drawing is imported as a single object, VIZ will automatically subtract the truss web from the outline of the truss, as shown in Figure 13.31.

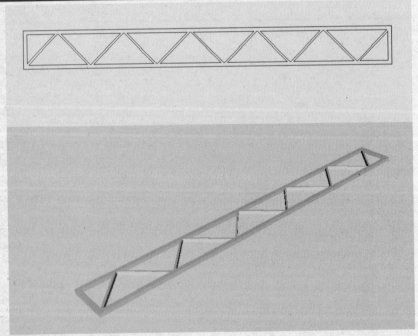

FIGURE 13.31: An AutoCAD drawing of a truss at the top and the resulting VIZ design below

Tubular trusses can be created easily from engineering 3D line dia-grams. Figure 13.32 shows an AutoCAD diagram of a truss whose com-ponents are to be made of tubular steel. The different diameters are represented by different layers in this model.

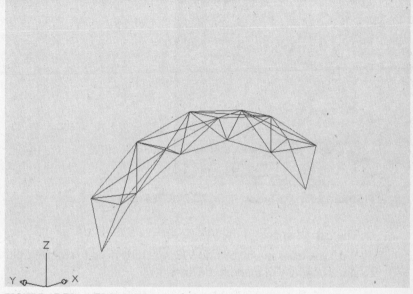

FIGURE 13.32: A 3D line diagram of a truss in AutoCAD

The following exercise will show you how the model can be turned into a renderable truss in VIZ:

1. Choose File ➤ Reset to reset VIZ.

2. Choose Insert ➤ AutoCAD DWG…, and then select and open the Truss.dwg file from the companion website.

3. In the DWG Import dialog box, click OK.

4. Make sure the Import AutoCAD DWG File dialog box settings are the same as those shown in Figure 13.33, and then click OK.

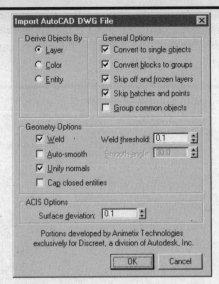

FIGURE 13.33: The Import AutoCAD DWG File settings

The truss displays in the VIZ viewport.

With the truss imported into VIZ, you only need to change a parameter to alter the way VIZ renders the lines.

1. Select one of the blue struts of the truss.

2. Click the Modify tab of the Command panel.

3. Open the General rollout, turn on the Renderable option in the Rendering group, and change the Thickness to **4**.

4. Select one of the magenta lines in the Perspective viewport.

5. In the Command panel, click on the Renderable option and change the Thickness value to **6**.

6. Do a quick rendering of the truss. You see that the rendered view converts the line work into tubes. Figure 13.34 shows a rendering of the truss from a different angle.

TIP

You can use the File Link Manager to import linked AutoCAD drawings and still use the General rollout parameters to create the truss shown in the previous exercise.

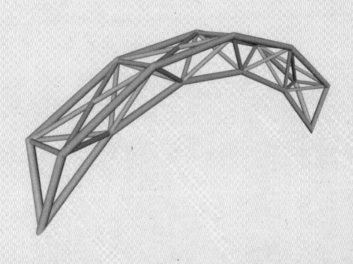

FIGURE 13.34: The rendered truss

Without much work in VIZ, you can create a reasonable-looking truss. You just need to remember to place the different-diameter truss members on different layers.

You can also make quick work of window mullions using this method. Typically, mullions are square, but if they are to be viewed from a distance, you can use single lines for mullions and set up the General parameters to have them render as tubes. From a distance, you won't really be able to tell that they are tubes. Another obvious use of this method is to create guardrails.

What's Next?

In the next chapter, you will begin learning how to customize AutoCAD.
You will see how to manage keyboard macros, AutoLISP code, VBA projects, and other third-party software.

PART IV
CUSTOMIZATION
AND PROGRAMMING

Chapter 14

INTRODUCTION TO CUSTOMIZATION

AutoCAD offers a wealth of features that you can use to improve your productivity. But even with these aids to efficiency, there are always situations that can use further automation. In this chapter, you'll be introduced to the different ways AutoCAD can be customized and enhanced with add-on utilities.

Adapted from *Mastering™ AutoCAD® 2000 Premium Edition* by George Omura
ISBN 0-7821-2499-2   1,664 pages $59.99

First, you'll discover how the AutoCAD Express tools can help boost your productivity. Many of these utilities were created using the programming tools that are available to anyone, namely AutoLISP and VBA.

NOTE The Express tools are now only available for sale as a separate extension to AutoCAD 2002. You can order and download the Express tools from http://estore.autodesk.com.

By doing so, you'll be prepared to take advantage of the many utilities available from user groups and online services. Finally, you'll finish the chapter by taking a look at how third-party applications and the Internet can enhance AutoCAD's role in your workplace.

TIP You can download files for this book from Sybex's website at http://www.sybex.com. Search for "AutoCAD 2002 Complete" to locate the files.

Enhancements Straight from the Source

If you've followed the tutorials in this book, you've already used a few add-on programs that come with AutoCAD, perhaps without even being aware that they were not part of the core AutoCAD program. This section will introduce you to the AutoCAD Express tools: a set of AutoLISP (Autodesk's version of the list processing programming language also known as Common LISP), AutoCAD Runtime eXtension (ARX), and Microsoft's Visual Basic for Applications (VBA) tools that showcase these powerful customization environments. The best part about the Express tools is that you don't have to know a thing about programming to take advantage of them.

There are so many of these Express tools that this chapter can't provide step-by-step instructions for all of them. Instead, you will get a detailed look at some of the more complicated tools and read shorter descriptions for other tools.

Opening the Express Toolbars

If you don't have the Express toolbars on your screen, here's how to open them.

1. Right-click any toolbar, and then select Customize at the bottom of the pop-up menu. The Toolbars dialog box appears.

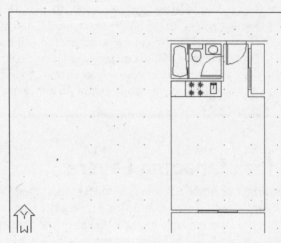

2. Open the Menu Group drop-down list at the bottom of the dialog box and select Express. The Toolbars list box changes to show a listing of toolbars available from the Express menu group.

3. Click the check box to the left of each item in the list.

4. Click Close to close the Toolbars dialog box.

You now have all the Express toolbars on your screen. If you don't want to have them all on your screen, just keep one of them open; when you want to open any of the other Express toolbars, right-click the remaining Express toolbar and select the other toolbars you want to open from the pop-up menu.

Now let's take a look at the Express Layer toolbar.

LOADING THE EXPRESS TOOLS

If you installed AutoCAD using the Typical Installation option, you may not have installed the AutoCAD Express tools yet. Fortunately, you can install these utilities separately without having to reinstall the entire program.

Proceed as if you are installing AutoCAD for the first time. When the Setup Choices dialog box opens, click the Add button to add new components to the current system. You will see an item called Express in the Custom Components dialog box that appears next. Check the Bonus check box, and then proceed with the installation. When Setup is finished, open AutoCAD and load the Express menu.

Tools for Managing Layers

In a survey of AutoCAD users, Autodesk discovered that one of the most frequently used features in AutoCAD was the Layer command. As a result, the layer controls in AutoCAD have been greatly improved. Still, there is room for some improvement. The Express Layer tools include some shortcuts to controlling layer settings as well as one major layer enhancement called the Layer Manager.

TIP

All the bonus tools discussed in this section have keyboard command equivalents. Check the status bar when you're selecting these tools from the toolbar or pull-down menu for the keyboard command name.

Saving and Recalling Layer Settings

The Layer Manager lets you save layer settings. Doing so can be crucial when you are editing a file that serves multiple uses, such as a floor plan and reflected ceiling plan. You can, for example, turn layers on and off to set up the drawing for a reflected ceiling Plan view, and then save the layer settings. Later, when you need to modify the ceiling information, you can recall the layer setting to view the ceiling data. The following steps show you how the Layer Manager works.

1. In AutoCAD, open the 14a-unit.dwg file from the companion website. Open the Layer Properties Manager dialog box

and turn on all the layers except the Notes and Flr-pat layers. Your drawing should look similar to the top image of Figure 14.1.

2. Click the Layer Manager tool in the Express Layer Tools toolbar.

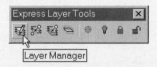

The Layer Manager dialog box appears.

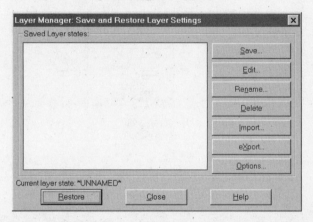

3. Click the Save button. The Layer State Name dialog box appears.

4. Enter **blank floor plan**, and then click OK. The Layer Manager dialog box reappears. Notice that the name you entered for the layer state appears in the list box.

5. Click the Close button.

6. Open the Layer Properties Manager dialog box again, turn on the Flr-pat and Notes layers, and turn off the Ceiling layer. Your drawing will look like the bottom image of Figure 14.1.

7. Click the Layer Manager tool again.

8. Click BLANK FLOOR PLAN in the list, and then click Restore.

9. Click Close. Your drawing reverts to the previous view with the Notes and Flr-pat layers turned off and the Ceiling layer on.

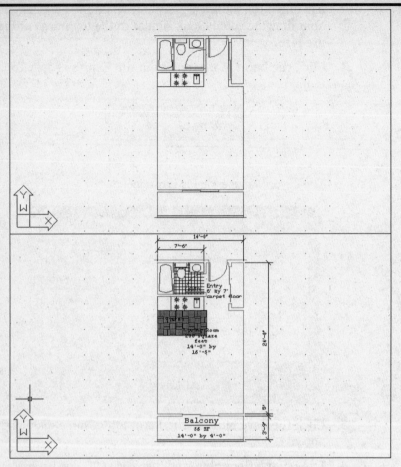

FIGURE 14.1: The view of the Unit.dwg file, before and after changing layer settings

The layer states are saved with the file so you can retrieve them at a later date. As you can see from the Layer Manager dialog box, you have a few other options. Here is a list of those options and what they do:

Edit Opens the Layer Properties Manager dialog box to let you edit the settings for a layer state. Highlight the layer state in the list, and then choose Edit.

Rename Lets you rename an existing layer setting.

Delete Deletes a layer state from the list.

Import Imports a set of layer states that have been exported using the Export option of this dialog box.

Export Saves a set of layer states as a file. By default, the file is given the name of the current file with the .lay filename extension. You can import the layer state file into other files.

Options Lets you control which layer options are saved as part of the layer state. When you click Options, you see the Layer Manager: Restore Options dialog box. This dialog box consists of a set of check boxes. You check the options you want to have saved by the Layer Manager. By default, all the layer options are saved. The options offered in the Layer Manager: Restore Options dialog box are: ON/OFF status, Thaw/Freeze status, Thaw/Freeze in Current Viewport status, Lock/Unlocked status, Color status, Linetype status, Lineweight status, Plot status, and Plot Style status.

Changing the Layer Assignment of Objects

In addition to the Layer Manager, the Express Layer toolbar offers two tools that change the layer assignments of objects. The Match Objects Layer tool is similar to the Match Properties tool, but it is streamlined to operate only on layer assignments. After choosing this tool, you first select the object or objects you wish to change, and then you select an object whose layer you wish to match.

The Change to Current Layer tool changes an object's layer assignment to the current layer. This tool has long existed as an AutoLISP utility, and you'll find that you'll get a lot of use from it.

Controlling Layer Settings through Objects

The remaining set of Express Layer tools lets you make layer settings by selecting objects in the drawing. The tools in this set are simple to use: Just click the tool, and then select an object. These tools are so helpful, you may want to consider docking them permanently in your AutoCAD window. The following list describes what each tool does:

Isolate Objects Layer Turns off all the layers except for the layer of the selected object.

Freeze Object Layer Freezes the layer of the selected objects.

Part iv

Turn Objects Layer Off Turns off the layer of the selected object.

Lock Objects Layer Locks the layer of the selected object. A locked layer is one that is visible but cannot be edited.

Unlock Object Layer Unlocks the layer of the selected object.

Deleting a Layer While Preserving Its Contents

Every now and then, you will inherit an AutoCAD file from some other office or individual and you'll want to convert its layering system to one more suited to the way you work. This process usually involves renaming and deleting layers. The Layer Merge Express tool is a great aid in this effort.

Layer Merge can be found by choosing Express ➤ Layers ➤ Layer Merge. It works by first moving all the objects from one layer to another existing layer. You can either select objects to indicate the layer you want, or you can type in the layer names. Once the objects are moved, Layer Merge deletes the empty layer. Another related tool is Layer Delete (Express ➤ Layers ➤ Layer Delete). This tool completely deletes a layer and its contents.

Tools for Editing Text

It seems that you can never have enough text-editing features. Even in the realm of word processors, innumerable tools let you set fonts, paragraphs, tabs, and tables. Some programs even check your grammar. Although you're not trying to write the great American novel in Auto-CAD, you are interested in getting your text in the right location, at the right size, with some degree of style. Doing so often means using a mixture of text and graphics editing tools. Here are some additional tools that will help ease your way through otherwise difficult editing tasks.

Masking Text Backgrounds

One problem AutoCAD users frequently face is how to get text to appear clearly when it is placed over a hatch pattern or other graphic. The Hatch command will hatch around existing text, leaving a clear space behind it. But what about those situations where you must add text *after* a hatch pattern has been created? Or, what about instances where you need to mask behind text that is placed over non-hatch objects, such as dimension leaders or raster images?

The Text Mask tool addresses this problem by masking the area behind text with a special masking object called a *Wipeout*. Wipeout is not a standard AutoCAD object; it is a new object created through AutoCAD's programming interface.

Try the following exercise on the 14a-unit.dwg file to see firsthand how it works.

1. In the Unit file, make sure the Flr-pat and Notes layers are turned on.

2. Adjust your view so you see the kitchen area as it appears in the top image of Figure 14.2. Notice that the Kitchen label is obscured by the floor's hatch pattern.

3. Choose the Text Mask tool from the Express Text Tools toolbar.

You'll see the following message:

```
Current settings: Offset factor = 0.3500, Mask type =
Wipeout
Select text objects to mask or [Masktype/Offset]:
```

4. Here you can enter the amount of space you want around the text as a percentage of the text height, or you can select a different type of object for the mask.

5. Select the *Kitchen* text and click the *Living Room* text. When you're done selecting text, press Enter. You'll see the message

```
Masking text with a Wipeout
Wipeout created.
1 text items have been masked with a Wipeout.
```

The text appears on a clear background, as shown in the bottom image of Figure 14.2.

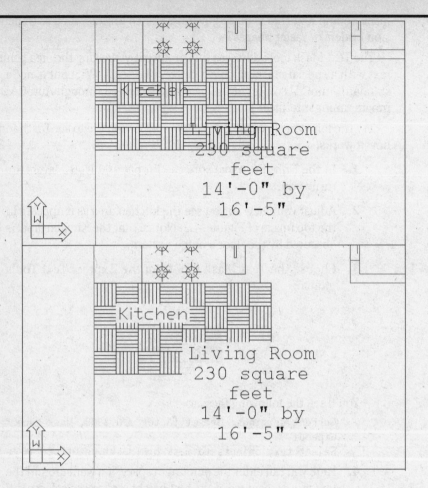

FIGURE 14.2: Creating a mask behind text

If you prefer to use a 3D Face or Solid to hide the background of text, you can do so by entering **M** at the prompt in step 3. You see the following prompt asking you to select a mask type:

```
Specify entity type to use for mask [Wipeout/3dface/Solid]
<Wipeout>:
```

Enter the mask type at this prompt, and you'll return to the previous prompt.

If you want more room around the text, you can enter **O** at the prompt in step 3. You can then enter a value for the margin around the text.

The Wipeout object has its own little quirks that you will want to know about. To get a bit more familiar with Wipeout objects, try the following exercise.

1. Click the *Kitchen* text. Notice that both the text and the Wipeout object are selected.

2. Click Move on the Modify toolbar.

3. Move the text and Wipeout object to the right about 12 inches (30cm for metric users). The text seems to disappear.

4. Type **Re** and press Enter to issue a Regen. The text appears once again.

The text and Wipeout objects are linked so that if you select the text, you automatically select the Wipeout object. Also, the display order of the two objects gets mixed up when you move them, so you need to issue a Regen command to restore the text's visibility. You can also edit or erase the Wipeout object. There is a description of how to edit Wipeout objects in the "Express Standard Tools" section later in this chapter.

If you want to delete the Wipeout background, use the Express ➢ Text ➢ Unmask Text option. This option prompts you to select an object. You then select the masked text, and the Wipeout background disappears.

Next, you'll look at ways to globally change text objects.

Finding and Replacing Text

Although the Find and Replace tool isn't really an Express tool, it is an example of a former Express tool that has been moved into the main part of the AutoCAD program. This is one tool that users had been requesting for a long time.

Find and Replace works like any other find and replace tool in a word-processing program. A few options work specifically with AutoCAD. Here's how it works.

1. Click the Find and Replace tool on the Standard toolbar.

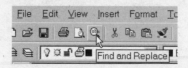

The Find and Replace dialog box appears.

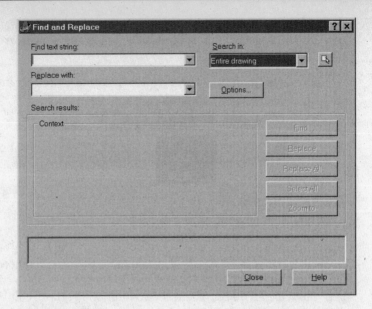

2. Enter the text you want to locate in the Find Text String input box.

3. Enter the replacement text in the Replace With input box.

4. Click Find. When AutoCAD finds the word, it appears in the Context window, along with any other text next to the word.

5. If you have any doubts, click the Zoom To button to display the text in the AutoCAD drawing area.

6. When you're certain this is the text you want to change, click Replace.

If you want to replace all the occurrences of a word in the drawing, click Replace All. You can also limit your find and replace operation to a specific area of your drawing by clicking the Select Object button in the upper-right corner of the Find and Replace dialog box.

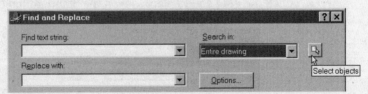

When you click the Select Objects button, the Find and Replace dialog box disappears temporarily to allow you to select a set of objects or a region of your drawing. Find and Replace will then limit its search to those objects or the region you select.

You can further control the types of objects that Find and Replace looks for by clicking the Options button. This button opens the Find and Replace Options dialog box.

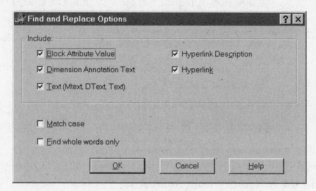

With this dialog box, you can refine your search by limiting it to blocks, dimension text, standard text, or hyperlink text. You can also determine whether to match case or find whole words only.

Adding Linked Text Documents

One of the more frustrating and time-consuming aspects of drafting is editing lengthy notes. General notes and specifications change frequently in the life of a project, so editing notes can be a large part of what you do in AutoCAD. Frequently, notes are written by someone else, perhaps a specification writer, who doesn't work directly with the drawings.

You can improve the efficiency of note editing by using Object Linking and Embedding (OLE) to cut and paste notes into your drawing. That way, you or the specification writer can edit the note and it will be automatically updated in drawings that contain pasted copies of the note. OLE-linked text documents have some drawbacks. However, the biggest problem is that you have little control over the text size and font.

To make note editing easier, AutoCAD supplies the Remote Text object. This special object is linked to an external text document. Like an OLE object, a Remote Text object will automatically update its contents whenever its source document changes. To use Remote Text objects, take the following steps:

1. Choose Express ➤ Text ➤ Remote Text or type **Rtext** and press Enter at the Command prompt.

2. At the `Enter an option [Style/Height/Rotation/File/Diesel] <File>:` prompt, press Enter. The Select Text File dialog box appears. This is a typical file dialog box that lets you locate and select a file for import.

3. Select a file and click Open.

4. At the `Specify start point of RText:` prompt, position the text in the drawing.

5. At the `Enter an option [Style/Height/Rotation/Edit]:` prompt, enter **H**, and then enter the height for the text.

As you can see from the prompt in step 5, you can specify the style, height, and rotation for the imported text. You also have the option to edit the text from within AutoCAD.

Because the Remote Text object is linked to the original document you selected in step 3, whenever that original document is edited, the Remote Text object in your drawing will be updated automatically, in a way similar to Xrefs.

Automatically Updating Drawing Information Labels

Another way to use Remote Text is to add labels containing the drawing's general information, such as the name of the file, the date it was last edited, and the person who did the editing. This information is usually placed in the corner of the drawing for reference so that a print of a drawing can be easily associated with a drawing file.

Remote Text can be used to keep track of this information. Even if the name of the file or its location on the hard drive changes, Remote Text will automatically update labels displaying this information. Here's an example of how to set up Remote Text to do this.

1. Choose Express ➤ Text ➤ Remote Text or type **Rtext** and press Enter at the Command prompt.

2. At the `Enter an option [Style/Height/Rotation/File/ Diesel] <File>:` prompt, enter **D** to select the Diesel option. The Edit Rtext dialog box appears.

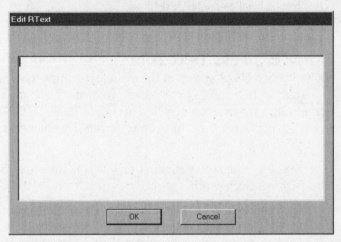

3. Enter the following text: **Drawing name and location: $(getvar, "dwgprefix")$(getvar, "dwgname")**.

4. Click OK. The text string appears as a rectangle in the drawing next to your cursor.

5. Click a location for the text (usually the lower-left corner of a drawing title block). The text displays the drawing location and name.

6. At the `Enter an option [Style/Height/Rotation/Edit]:` prompt, type **R** and press Enter, and then enter **90** to rotate the text 90 degrees.

This example uses the Diesel option of the Remote Text tool. Diesel is one of many macro programming languages AutoCAD supports. The text `$(getvar, "Dwgprefix")$(getvar, "Dwgname")` is the Diesel code that extracts the current drawing location and name from the file. This code is translated into the actual directory listing and filename of the current drawing. This is how Remote Text reads the Dwgprefix and Dwgname system variables of the file. If the file is moved to another location or if it is renamed, Remote Text reads the Dwgprefix and Dwgname system variables and updates the label containing this code.

TIP

You can type **Dwgprefix** or **Dwgname** at the Command prompt to see the information that Remote Text is reading.

Other Express Text Tools

You've learned about several of the main text-editing tools in the Express Text Tools toolbar and Express pull-down menu. There are several more text-editing tools that you may find useful. By now, you should feel comfortable in exploring these tools on your own. The following is a brief description to get you started:

Text Fit   Lets you visually stretch or compress text to fit within a given width.

ArcAlignedText   Creates text that follows the curve of an arc. If the arc is stretched or changed, the text follows the arc's shape. This is one of the more interesting bonus text-editing tools offering a wide range of settings presented in a neat little dialog box.

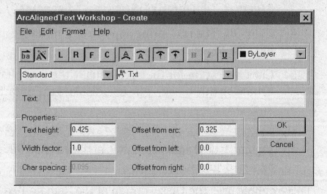

Explode Text   Converts the individual characters in a text object into polylines. Beware! This tool can take some time to work.

TIP

If you want text to follow a curved path, take a look at the Txtpath.1sp utility from this chapter's source book. It draws text on a spline curve to follow virtually any contour you want.

Express Block Tools

Every now and then, you run into a situation where you want to use objects within a block to trim or extend to, or perhaps you may want to copy a part of a block to another part of your drawing. Here are six tools that will let you do these things. They're fairly simple to use, so the following descriptions should be enough to get you started:

Copy Nested Entities   Lets you copy single objects within a block. You are only allowed to select objects individually—one click at a time. The copied objects will be placed on the current layer.

Trim to Block Entities   Lets you trim to objects in a block. It works just like the standard Trim command, with the exception that you must select the objects to trim to individually.

Extend to Block Entities   Lets you extend to objects in a block. It also works like its standard counterpart, with the exception that you must select the objects you wish to extend to individually.

List Xref/Block Entities   Displays basic information about an Xref or block.

Global Attribute Edit   On the Express Block Tools toolbar, simplifies the global editing of attribute text.

Explode Attributes to Text   On the Express Block Tools toolbar, explodes blocks containing attributes so that the attribute values are converted into plain single-line text.

TIP

The Extended Clip tool, described later in this chapter, allows you to hide portions of a block that you do not want to display.

Express Standard Tools

The Express Standard toolbar seems to be the answer to most AutoCAD users' wish lists. As with many of the Express tools discussed so far, these tools have been floating around in the AutoCAD user community as AutoLISP utilities. However, some are completely new. This section starts with a look at one tool that has been on my wish list for quite some time.

Multiple Entity Stretch

The Stretch command has always been limited by the fact that you can select only one set of vertices. The Multiple Entity Stretch tool removes that limitation and makes stretching multiple objects a simpler task. Here's how it works:

1. Click the Multiple Entity Stretch tool on the Express Standard toolbar.

You'll see the following message:

```
Define crossing windows or crossing polygons...
CP(crossing polygon)/<Crossing First point>:
```

2. Start to place crossing windows around the vertices you want to stretch. You can also enter **Cp** and proceed to place crossing polygons around the vertices.

3. When you are done selecting vertices, press Enter.

4. Select a base point and second point to move the vertices.

Streamlined Move Copy Rotate

The Move Copy Rotate tool combines these three functions into one tool. It's like a streamlined Grip Edit tool without the grips. Here's how it works.

1. Click the Move Copy Rotate tool or select Express ➤ Modify ➤ Move Copy Rotate.

2. Select the objects you want to edit, and then press Enter.

3. Click a base point.

4. At the [Move/Copy/Rotate/Scale/Base/Undo]<eXit>: prompt, enter the option you want to use; for example, type **C**. You can also right-click and select Copy from the pop-up menu. The object or objects you selected in step 2 now fol-

low your cursor.

5. Click a location for your copy. You can continue to select more points to create multiple copies.

6. When you are finished making copies, press Enter. The [Move/Copy/Rotate/Scale/Base/Undo]<eXit>: prompt returns, allowing you to make further edits.

7. Press Enter to exit the Move Copy Rotate tool.

The Move Copy Rotate tool acts like the Move or Copy command up until step 4. From step 4 on, you can do any number of operations on the selected objects as listed in the prompt.

Quick Multiple Trims with Extended Trim

The Extended Trim tool is actually best described by its title in the Express pull-down menu: Cookie Cutter Trim. It is capable of trimming a set of objects to a closed shape, such as a circle or closed polyline. You can, for example, use it to cut out a star shape in a crosshatch pattern. You can also trim multiple objects to a line or arc. To use it, do the following:

1. Choose Extended Trim on the Express Standard toolbar, or select Express ➤ Modify ➤ Cookie Cutter Trim.

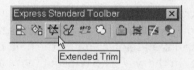

2. Select an object to be the trim boundary—that is, the object to which you want to trim.

3. Click the side of the selected object that you want trimmed.

Extended Trim allows you to select only a single object to trim to, but it trims multiple objects quickly and with fewer clicks of the mouse.

Editing Multiple Polylines with Multiple Pedit

If you only want to change the properties of polylines, you may want to use the Multiple Pedit tool.

Part iv

The Multiple Pedit tool works exactly like the standard Pedit command (found by choosing Modify ➤ Object ➤ Polyline), with two exceptions: It does not offer the Edit Vertex option, and you are not limited to a single polyline. As a result, you can select multiple polylines to change their width, curvature, or open/close status. Multiple Pedit also lets you easily convert multiple lines and arcs into polylines.

Perhaps one of the most common uses for the Multiple Pedit tool is to change the width of a set of lines, arcs, and polylines. If you include lines and arcs in a selection set with this tool, they are converted into polylines and the specified width is applied.

Masking Areas with Wipeout

Wipeout creates an object called a Wipeout, which acts like a mask. If you read the previous section on the Text Mask tool, you've gotten a glimpse at how Wipeout works, because the Text Mask tool uses the Wipeout object. The following exercise demonstrates how to use the Wipeout tool in another application.

Imagine that you've set up a paper space layout showing an enlarged view of one of the units of the studio apartment building. You want to show dimensions and notes around the unit, but there are too many other objects in the way. The Wipeout tool can be a great help in this situation. Here's how.

1. Open the 19wipe.dwg file. This is one of the sample files on the companion website. When you open this file, you will be in paper space.

2. While still in paper space, zoom in to the typical Unit plan so your view looks similar to Figure 14.3.

3. Create a layer called Wipeout and make it current.

4. Switch to floating model space by double-clicking inside the Model Space viewport or by clicking the PAPER button in the status bar.

5. Draw the closed polyline shown in Figure 14.3. You don't have to be exact about the shape; you can adjust it later.

6. Click Wipeout on the Express Standard toolbar.

7. At the Wipeout Frame/New <New>: prompt, press Enter to accept the default New option.

8. At the Select a polyline: prompt, select the polyline you just drew.

9. At the Erase polyline? Yes/No <No>: prompt, enter **Y** to erase the polyline. The area enclosed by the polyline is masked out.

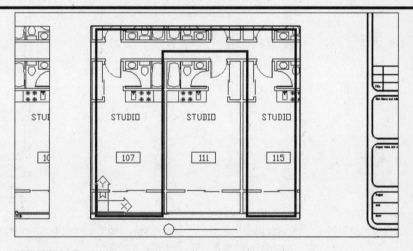

FIGURE 14.3: Adding a polyline to the enlarged Unit plan

The Wipeout object has a border that can be turned on and off. When it's visible, you can click the Wipeout border and use its corner grips to reshape the area that it covers. You can also erase, move, or copy the Wipeout object using its border. In the example of the Unit plan, you will want to hide the Wipeout border. Take the following steps to turn off the Wipeout border's visibility:

1. Click the Wipeout button on the Express Standard toolbar.

2. At the Frame/New <New>: prompt, type **F** and press Enter.

Part iv

3. At the OFF/ON <ON>: prompt, type **OFF** and press Enter. The
   frame disappears.

When the frame is off, you cannot edit the Wipeout object. Of course,
you can turn it back on using the Frame option you used in step 2 of the
previous exercise. (By the way, if you need to edit the Text Mask tool
described earlier in this chapter, you use the Frame option described in
the previous exercise to turn on the Text Mask border.)

With the Wipeout object in place and its border turned off, you can
add dimensions and notes around the image without having the adjoining graphics interfere with the visibility of your notes. Figure 14.4 shows
the Unit plan with the dimensions inserted from the individual Unit
plan file.

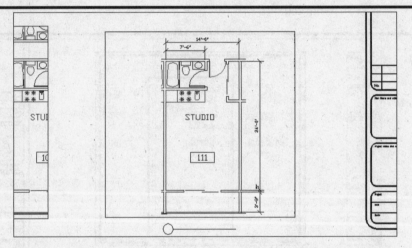

FIGURE 14.4: The Unit plan with dimensions added and the viewport border
adjusted to hide the graphics beyond the Wipeout object

There is one more point to address here. If you switch to paper space
and zoom out to view the entire paper space drawing, you'll notice that
the Wipeout object appears in the overall plan at the top of the screen
(see Figure 14.5). Fortunately, you can freeze the Wipeout layer in the
viewport with the Overall view to hide the Wipeout object.

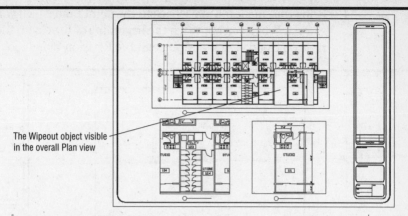

The Wipeout object visible
in the overall Plan view

FIGURE 14.5: The Wipeout object as it appears in the overall Plan view

Drawing Revision Clouds

A *revision cloud* is a cloud-like outline drawn around parts of a drawing that have been revised. Revision clouds are used to alert the viewer to any changes that have occurred in the design of a project since the drawings were last issued. Revision clouds are fairly common in most types of technical drawings, including architectural, civil, and mechanical drawings.

As simple as they might appear, revision clouds are difficult to draw using the standard tools offered by AutoCAD. But now a single tool makes them easy to draw. Try using the Revision Cloud tool on the 19wipe.dwg file by following these steps.

1. If you haven't already done so, switch your drawing to paper space.

2. Click the Revision Cloud tool. Click a point near the right side of the viewport that shows a view of the Unit plan, as shown in Figure 14.6.

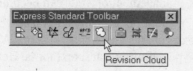

3. Move the cursor in a counterclockwise direction to encircle the Unit plan view. As you move the cursor, the cloud is drawn.

4. Bring the cursor full circle back to the point from which you started. When you approach the beginning of the cloud, the revision cloud closes, and you exit the Revision Cloud tool.

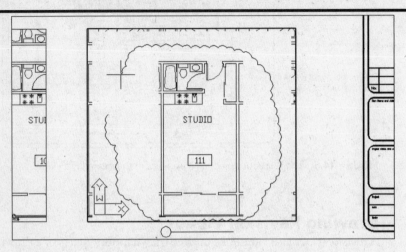

FIGURE 14.6: Drawing a revision cloud

If you need to change the size of the arcs in the revision cloud, you can do so in step 2 by entering **A**. You can then enter an arc length. Also note that you must draw the cloud in a counterclockwise direction; otherwise, the arcs of the cloud will point in the wrong direction.

Keeping Your Xref Files Together with Pack 'n Go

The Xref feature of AutoCAD has helped streamline the production of large architectural projects. But Xrefs also introduce one major problem: When it comes time to send the AutoCAD files to other consultants, you have to figure out which files are external references for other files. In a large project, management of Xrefs can become a major headache.

The Pack 'n Go utility is designed to help you manage Xrefs, as well as most other external resources that an AutoCAD drawing may depend on, such as linetype definitions and text fonts. Here's how it works.

1. Click the Pack 'n Go tool on the Express Standard toolbar.

The Pack & Go dialog box appears.

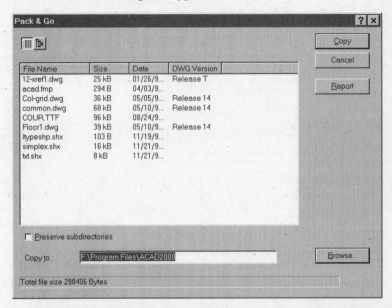

This dialog box shows all external references and resources the current file is using. It also allows you to move all these resources into one location, such as a directory you've set up to collect a set of files to send to a client or consultant.

2. To choose a location for the copies of your files, click the Browse button in the lower-right corner of the dialog box. A Browse for Folder dialog box lets you locate and select a folder in which to place your copies.

3. Click Copy to copy all the drawing files and resources to the selected directory.

In addition to the files and resources, Pack 'n Go generates three script files designed to convert the drawing files into any format from Release 12 to Release 14.

Part iv

Another helpful feature of the Pack 'n Go tool is the report generator. If you click the Report button in the Pack & Go dialog box, a Report dialog box opens, providing a written description of the current file and its resources.

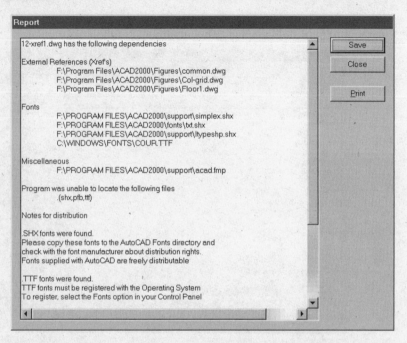

You can save this report as a text file by clicking the Save button. Such a report can be used as a Readme file when you're sending drawings to clients or consultants.

Creating Custom Hatch Patterns with Super Hatch

AutoCAD offers a large variety of hatch patterns from its Boundary Hatch dialog box. But sometimes none of those patterns will fulfill your needs. This is where the Super Hatch tool comes in. With Super Hatch, you can create virtually any hatch pattern you want. You can use objects in your drawing as a basis for a hatch pattern, or you can import bitmap images and use them to form a hatch pattern, like tiled wallpaper in the Windows background. The following exercise shows you how to use Super Hatch.

1. Open the sample file `Superhatch.dwg` from the companion website. You'll see a block of the Sybex logo on the left side of the screen and a rectangular area to the right. In this exercise, you'll turn that logo into a hatch pattern.

2. Click the Super Hatch tool.

The SuperHatch dialog box appears.

3. Click the Select Existing button. The SuperHatch dialog box disappears.

4. Click the arrow. It becomes highlighted, and a magenta rectangle appears encircling the arrow.

5. At this point, you can indicate the area you want repeated in your pattern. The default is the extents of the image as indicated by the magenta rectangle.

6. Click the two points shown in Figure 14.7 to indicate the area that you want repeated. The rectangle changes to reflect the new area. You can repeat the area selection until you get exactly the area you want.

7. Press Enter to move on to the next step.

8. Click the interior of the rectangle to indicate the area you want to hatch. If you have multiple hatch areas, you can continue to select them at this step.

9. Press Enter to finish your selection of hatch areas. The logo appears repeated as a pattern within the rectangle as shown in Figure 14.8.

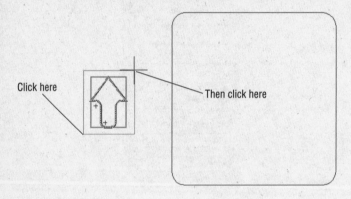

FIGURE 14.7: Selecting the area to be repeated

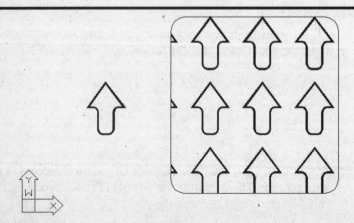

FIGURE 1414.8: The hatch pattern

The object you select using the Select Existing option of the Super-Hatch dialog box must be a block. You can modify that block and the changes will appear in the hatch pattern, as shown in Figure 14.9.

As you can see from the SuperHatch dialog box, you can incorporate Xrefs, blocks, and even image files. Each of these options prompts you to insert the object before you convert it into a hatch pattern. You use the usual insertion method for the type of object you select. For example, if you choose the Block option, you are prompted for an insertion point, the X and Y scale factors, and a rotation angle. For image files, you see the same Image dialog box that you see when you insert an image file, offering the options for insertion point, scale, and rotation. Figure 14.10 shows a sample hatch pattern with an image file used instead of an AutoCAD block.

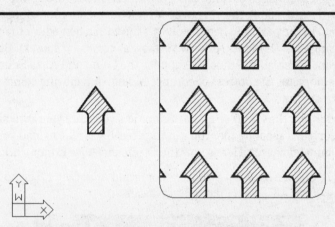

FIGURE 14.9: The hatch pattern after the block is modified

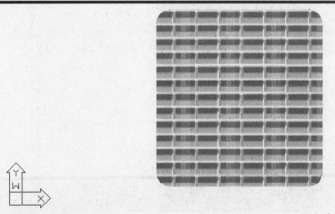

FIGURE 14.10: A hatch pattern using a bitmap image

Tools in the Express Pull-Down Menu

Most of the Express tools discussed so far are available as options in the Express pull-down menu. There are some additional options in the pull-down menu that you won't see in any of the toolbars. You won't want to miss these additional tools; they can greatly enhance your productivity on any type of project.

Controlling Shortcuts with the Command Alias Editor

Throughout this book, you've been learning about the keyboard shortcuts to the commands of AutoCAD. All of these shortcuts are stored in a file called Acad.pgp in the \Program Files\AutoCAD 2000\Support\ directory. In the past, you had to edit this file with a text editor to modify these command shortcuts (otherwise know as *command aliases*). But to make your life simpler, Autodesk supplies the Command Alias Editor, which automates the process of editing, adding, or removing command aliases from AutoCAD.

In addition, the Command Alias Editor lets you store your own alias definitions in a separate file. You can then recall your file to load your own command aliases. Here's how the Command Alias Editor works.

1. Choose Express ➤ Tools ➤ Command Alias Editor. The Auto-CAD Alias Editor dialog box appears.

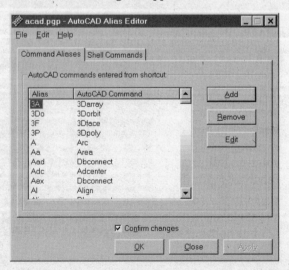

2. As you can see from the button options, you can add a new alias or delete or edit an existing alias. If you click the Add button, you see the New Command Alias dialog box.

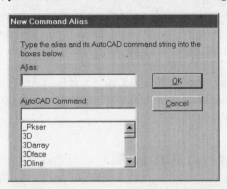

In this dialog box, you enter the desired alias in the Alias input box, and then select the command from the list box. You can also enter a command or macro name, such as Wipeout, in the input box. When you click the Edit option in the AutoCAD Alias Editor dialog box, you see a dialog box identical to this one with the input boxes already filled in.

3. When you are done creating or editing an alias, click OK. The AutoCAD Alias Editor dialog box reappears.

4. Click OK to exit the dialog box. You see a warning message.

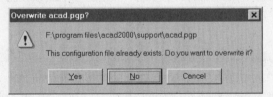

This message tells you that you are about to overwrite the Acad.pgp file.

5. Click No to leave the Acad.pgp file untouched. The Save As dialog box then appears. In the Save As dialog box, enter an alternate filename, such as **Myalias.pgp**, to store your personal set of command aliases.

Part iv

6. Once you've entered a name and saved your settings, a message appears telling you that your new settings have taken effect. Click OK to return to AutoCAD.

If you're a veteran AutoCAD user, you may have become accustomed to your own set of command aliases. If so, you may want to leave the original Acad.pgp file alone and create your own .pgp file as suggested in step 5. Then, whenever you use AutoCAD, you can open the AutoCAD Alias Editor, choose File ➤ Open, and load your personal .pgp file. From then on, the aliases in your file will supersede those of the standard Acad.pgp file.

Full Screen AutoCAD

AutoCAD users can't seem to get enough drawing space. The Full Screen AutoCAD tool is for those AutoCAD users who are never satisfied with the amount of drawing area their screen may provide.

When you choose Express ➤ Tools ➤ Full Screen AutoCAD, the AutoCAD drawing area is pushed to the maximum area available. The AutoCAD title bar is hidden, as is the menu bar. You can access the menu bar by pushing the cursor to the top of the screen until you see a diskette icon, and then clicking and dragging. The menu bar momentarily appears, allowing you to select an option.

To return to the normal AutoCAD window, point to the top edge of the screen until you see the diskette icon, and then click and hold to display the menu bar. Choose Express ➤ Tools ➤ Full Screen AutoCAD to return to the standard AutoCAD view.

Clipping a Raster Image, Xref, or Block to a Curved Shape with Extended Clip

You may have seen how you can clip portions of an Xref or raster image so that only a portion of the object is visible. One limitation of the Raster Clip option is that you can only clip areas defined by straight lines. You cannot, for example, clip an area defined by a circle or ellipse.

The Extended Clip tool is designed for those instances where you absolutely need to clip a raster image or block to a curved area. The following steps show you how it works:

1. Create a clip boundary using a curved polyline or circle.

2. Choose Express ➤ Modify ➤ Extended Clip.

3. Click the boundary.

4. Click the Xref, block, or image you wish to clip.

5. At the Enter max error distance for resolution of arcs <7/16">: prompt, press Enter. The Xref, block, or image clips to the selected boundary.

6. You can erase the boundary you created in step 1 or keep it for future reference.

Extended Clip really doesn't clip to the boundary you created, but instead approximates that boundary by creating a true clip boundary with a series of very short line segments. In fact, the prompt in step 5 lets you specify the maximum allowable distance between the straight-line segments it generates and the curve of the boundary you create (see Figure 14.11).

Once you've created a boundary using Extended Clip, you can edit the properties of the boundary using Modify ➤ Clip ➤ Xref for Xrefs and blocks, or Modify ➤ Clip ➤ Image for raster images.

FIGURE 14.11: Extended Clip allows you to set the maximum distance between your clip boundary and the one it generates.

Part iv

Creating a Custom Linetype with Make Linetype

Most of the time, the linetypes provided by AutoCAD are adequate. But if you're looking for that perfect linetype, you can use the Make Linetype tool to make your own. Here's how it works.

1. Open the Customltype.dwg sample file. The sample drawing is made up of simple lines with no polylines, arcs, or circles. When you create your own linetype prototype, make sure the lines are all aligned. Draw a single line and break it to form the segments of the linetype (see Figure 14.12). Also make sure it is drawn to the actual plotted size.

2. Choose Express ➤ Tools ➤ Make Linetype. The MKLTYPE dialog box appears.

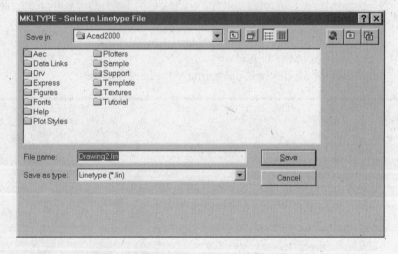

3. Enter **myltype** in the File Name input box, select a location for the file, and click OK.

4. At the Enter a linetype name: prompt, enter **MyLinetype**, or any name you want to use to describe the linetype. The name must be a single word.

5. At the Enter linetype description: prompt, enter a description for your linetype. This can be a sentence that best describes your linetype.

6. At the `Specify starting point for line definition:` prompt, pick one endpoint of the sample linetype.

7. At the `Specify ending point for line definition:` prompt, pick a point just past the opposite end of the sample linetype. Pick a point past the endpoint of the sample to indicate the gap between the end of the first segment of the linetype and the beginning of the repeating portion, as shown in Figure 14.12.

8. At the `Select objects:` prompt, select the sample linetype lines. When you're done, press Enter. You now have a custom linetype.

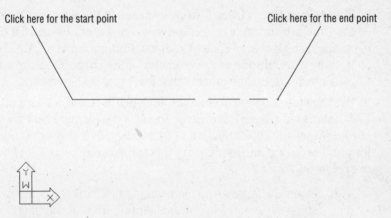

Click here for the start point

Click here for the end point

FIGURE 14.12: Creating a custom linetype using the Make Linetype tool

To load your custom linetype, use the Linetype Manager dialog box (Format ➤ Linetype) to locate your linetype file and load the linetype. You can also get to the Linetype Manager by clicking the Linetype drop-down list in the Properties toolbar and selecting Other.

If you send your file to someone else, make sure you include your custom linetype files with the drawing file. Otherwise, anything drawn using your custom linetype will appear as a continuous line, and your recipient will get an error message saying that AutoCAD cannot find your linetype file.

The Make Linetype tool creates a single linetype file for each linetype you create. The linetype file is a simple ASCII text file. If you end up making several linetypes, you can combine your linetype files into one file using a simple text editor like Windows Notepad. Don't use Windows WordPad or Microsoft Word because those programs will introduce special codes into the linetype file.

Creating Custom Shapes as an Alternative to Blocks

Shapes are a special type of AutoCAD object that are similar to blocks. They are usually simple symbols made up of lines and arcs. Shapes take up less memory and can be displayed faster, but they are much less flexible than blocks, and they are not very accurate. You cannot use Object Snaps to snap to specific parts of a shape, nor can you explode shapes. They are best suited for symbols or as components in complex linetypes.

Shapes have always been difficult to create. In the past, you could not create a shape by drawing it. You had to create something called a *shape definition* using a special code. A shape definition is just an ASCII file containing a description of the geometry of the shape. Creating such a file was a tedious, arcane process that few users bothered with.

With the introduction of complex linetypes in recent versions of AutoCAD, interest in shapes has revived. To make it easier for users to create shapes, AutoCAD 2002 offers a tool that will create a shape definition file for you based on a line drawing. Try this simple exercise to learn how you can create and use a shape.

1. Open the Makeshape.dwg sample file. This file contains a simple drawing of an upward pointing arrow. It contains lines and arcs.

2. Select Express ➤ Tools ➤ Make Shape. The MKSHAPE dialog box appears. This is a typical file dialog box allowing you to specify a name and location for your shape definition file.

3. Enter **Arrow** in the File Name input box.

4. Click OK to create your file.

5. At the Enter the name of the shape: prompt, enter **Arrow**.

6. At the Enter resolution <128>: prompt, enter **512**. Shapes are defined with a square matrix of points. All the endpoints of lines and arcs must be on a point within that matrix. At this prompt, you can define the density of that

matrix. A higher density will give you a better-looking shape, but you don't want to get carried away with this setting.

7. At the Specify insertion base point: prompt, select the tip of the arrow, as shown in Figure 14.13. This will be the insertion point of your shape, which is similar to the insertion point of a block.

8. At the Select objects: prompt, select the entire arrow. Press Enter.

You'll see a series of messages telling you what AutoCAD is doing. The last message will tell you whether AutoCAD was successful in creating the shape file, and it will tell you the location and name of the new shape file:

```
Compilation successful. Output file F:\Program
Files\ACAD2000\Figures\arrow.shx contains 309 bytes.
```

Click here for the insertion base point

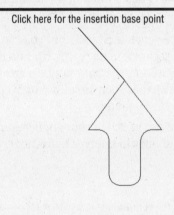

FIGURE 14.13: Creating a shape from an existing drawing

To see how your shape came out, try the following steps. In this exercise, you'll learn how to load and insert a shape.

1. Type **Load** and press Enter at the Command prompt. The Select Shape File dialog box appears. This is a typical file dialog box.

2. Locate the file Arrow.shx, and click Open to load it.

3. Type **Shape** and press Enter.

4. At the Enter shape name or [?]: prompt, type **Arrow** and press Enter. You'll see the arrow follow the cursor as you move it across the drawing area.

NOTE

If you've forgotten the name of a shape you are loading, you can enter **?** to get a listing of available shapes.

5. At the Specify insertion point: prompt, click to the right of the original arrow.

6. At the Specify height: prompt, press Enter to accept the default of 1.

7. At the Specify rotation angle: prompt, enter **45**. The arrow appears at a 45° angle.

In many ways, a shape acts like a block, but you cannot snap to any of its points. It is also less accurate in its representation than a block, although for some applications, this may not be a great concern. Finally, you cannot use complex shapes such as splines or 3D objects for your shape. You can use only lines and arcs.

Still, you may find shapes useful in your application. As mentioned earlier, you can include shapes in linetype definitions.

NOTE

If you plan to send a file containing shapes to someone else, be sure to include the shape file with the drawing file. See the section on the Pack 'n Go Express tool to learn how you can quickly put together a "package" of drawings and their support files.

Filleting Polylines

One of the more frequently used tools is the Fillet tool. It is great for joining endpoints of lines. You can also use the Fillet tool to join the endpoint of a polyline and a line. Unfortunately, Fillet won't join two polyline endpoints. This can be frustrating, especially if you are trying to join a set of polylines to form a single polyline. Polylines must meet exactly end to end before you can join them.

The Express tools come to the rescue with the Polyline Join tool. Polyline Join lets you connect the endpoints of two polylines in a way similar to the Fillet command. You also have the option to connect the endpoints with a line segment. The following exercise demonstrates how Polyline Join works:

1. Open the Pljoin.dwg file.

2. Choose Express ➤ Modify ➤ Polyline Join, or type **Pljoin** and press Enter.

3. At the Select objects: prompt, select the two lines, and then press Enter.

4. At the Enter fuzz distance or [Jointype]: prompt, click two points to define a distance that is roughly the same as the distance between the two endpoints of the polyline, as shown in Figure 14.14. The endpoints of the polylines join.

If you didn't get the results as indicated in step 4, the Polyline Join settings may be set to something other than Fillet. You can change the way Polyline Join works by entering **J** at the prompt in step 4. You then see the following prompt:

```
Enter join type [Fillet/Add/Both]:
```

Enter **F** to make Polyline Join fillet two polylines or enter **A** to make Polyline Join add a line segment between the two polylines. The Both option adds a line segment and fillets the endpoints of polylines.

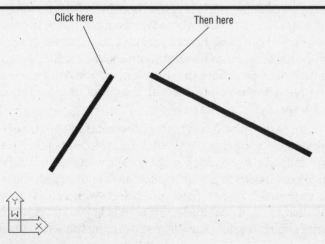

FIGURE 14.14: Filleting a polyline

Using the Anti-Selection Tools

Sometimes it seems that AutoCAD doesn't include enough selection tools. You have used various methods to select groups of objects to build a selection set, a set of objects selected for an operation such as a Move or Copy. The Express Selection tools offer a set of tools that let you create a selection set by subtraction. These tools work by first asking you to select all the objects on a layer, or even the entire drawing. You then select the objects you do *not* want in the selection set. Once you've removed objects from the selection set, you can proceed with whatever command you want to use to edit the selection set. You can use the Previous Selection option at the `Select objects:` prompt to use the selection set you build with the Express Selection tools.

The Express Selection tools work like the standard selection options, only in reverse. Instead of adding objects to the selection set, objects are subtracted from the selection set. Here's a view of the Express Selection tools menu showing the options available.

A tool called Get Selection Set at the top of the menu sets up your selection set based on layers. When you choose Get Selection Set, you are prompted to select an object whose layer contains all the objects you want to select. You can press Enter to create a selection set of all the objects in the drawing. From there, you can use the Exclude Selection option to exclude objects from the selection set. You don't really need to use this option if you want to select all the objects in a drawing except the ones you specify.

If you prefer to type in your selection options at the `Select objects:` prompt, you can do so by entering the standard selection option, preceded by **'EX**. For example, to exclude a set of objects using a window, enter **'EXW**, and then proceed to place a window around the object you want to exclude from the selection set. To exclude objects with a crossing window, enter **'EXC**, and so on. If you're selecting objects before you issue a command, to use grip editing for example, you can enter the selection option without the apostrophe. AutoCAD then selects everything except the selected object.

Dimstyle Export and Dimstyle Import

Most AutoCAD users really need to set up their dimension styles only once, and then make minor alterations for drawing scale. You can set up your dimension styles in a template file and use that template whenever you create new drawings. That way, your dimension styles will already be set up the way you want them.

But frequently, you will receive files that were created by someone else who may not have the same ideas about dimension styles as you do. Normally, this would mean you would have to re-create your favorite settings in a new dimension style. With the Express tools, you can export and import dimension styles at any time, saving you the effort of recreating them. Here's how it works.

1. Open a file from which you wish to export a dimension style.

2. Choose Express ≻ Tools ≻ Dimstyle Export, or enter **Dimex**. The Dimension Style Export dialog box appears.

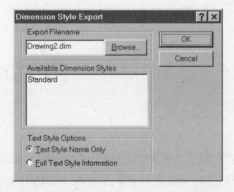

3. Click the Browse button at the top of the dialog box to locate and name a file for storing your dimension style. AutoCAD appends the .dim filename extension.

4. Click Open in the Open dialog box. If the file you specified does not exist, AutoCAD asks you if you want to create it. Click OK to create a new .dim file.

5. Select the name of the dimension style you want to export from the Available Dimension Styles list box.

6. Click the Full Text Style Information radio button to include all the information regarding the associated text style.

7. Click OK. A message appears in the Command window telling you that your dimension style was successfully exported.

To import a style you've exported, take the following steps:

1. Open a file into which you want to import a dimension style.

2. Choose Express ➤ Tools ➤ Dimstyle Import, or type **Dimim** and press Enter. The Dimension Style Import dialog box appears.

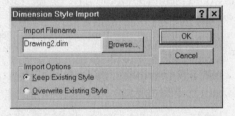

3. Click the Browse button to open the Open dialog box.

4. Locate and select the dimension style file you saved earlier, and then click Open.

5. Click either the Keep Existing Style or Overwrite Existing Style radio button to choose which action to take.

6. Click OK.

Options for Selecting Objects, Attaching Data to Objects, and Updating Polylines

You're less likely to use this last set of options than the others discussed so far, so this section includes a brief description of them without going into too much detail. They're actually fairly easy to use, and you shouldn't have any trouble trying them out:

Selection Tools ➤ Get Selection Set   Lets you create a selection set based on layer and type of object. You can enter either a layer or object type when prompted to do so, or select a representative object from the screen.

Tools ➣ Xdata Attachment   Lets you attach extended data to objects. Extended data is generally used only by AutoLISP, ADS, or ARX applications. You are asked to select the object that will receive the data, and then for an application name that serves as a tag to tell others whom the data belongs to. You can then select a data type. Once this is done, you can enter your data.

Tools ➣ List Entity Xdata   Displays extended data that has been attached to an object.

UTILITIES AVAILABLE FROM OTHER SOURCES

The utilities listed in the previous section are just a few samples of the many utilities available for AutoCAD. Other sources for AutoLISP utilities are the AutoCAD journals *Cadence* and *Cadalyst*. Both offer sections that list utilities written by readers and editorial staff. If you don't already have a subscription to one of these publications and want to know more about them, their contact information follows:

Cadence, published by Miller Freeman Inc., 525 Market Street, Suite 500, San Francisco, CA 94105

URL: http://www.cadence-mag.com

Cadalyst, published by Advanstar Inc., 131W. First St., Duluth, MN 55802-2065

URL: http://www.cadonline.com

PUTTING AUTOLISP TO WORK

Most high-end CAD packages offer a macro or programming language to help users customize their systems. AutoCAD has *AutoLISP*, which is a pared-down version of the popular LISP artificial intelligence language.

Don't let AutoLISP scare you. In many ways, an AutoLISP program is just a set of AutoCAD commands that help you build your own features. The only difference is that you have to follow a different set of rules when using AutoLISP. But this isn't so unusual. After all, you had to learn some basic rules about using AutoCAD commands, too—how to start commands, for instance, and how to use command options.

Part iv

If the thought of using AutoLISP is a little intimidating to you, bear in mind that you don't really need substantial computer knowledge to use this tool. In this section, you will see how you can get AutoLISP to help out in your everyday editing tasks, without having to learn the entire programming language.

OTHER CUSTOMIZATION OPTIONS

If you are serious about customization, you'll want to know about Autodesk's ObjectARX programming environment, which allows Microsoft Visual C++ programmers to develop full applications that work within AutoCAD. ObjectARX lets programmers create new objects within AutoCAD as well as add functionality to existing objects. ObjectARX is beyond the scope of this book; to find out more, contact your AutoCAD dealer or visit Autodesk's website at www.autodesk.com.

If you are familiar with Visual Basic, AutoCAD offers Visual Basic ActiveX Automation as part of its set of customization tools. ActiveX Automation lets you create macros that operate across different applications. It also gives you access to AutoCAD objects through an object-oriented programming environment.

CREATING KEYBOARD MACROS WITH AUTOLISP

You can write some simple AutoLISP programs of your own that create what are called *keyboard macros*. Macros—like script files—are strings of predefined keyboard entries. They are invaluable for shortcuts to commands and options you use frequently. For example, you might find that, while editing a particular drawing, you often use the Break command to break an object at a single point. Here's a way you can turn this operation into a macro.

1. Open the Unit file and, at the Command prompt, enter the following text. Be sure you enter the line exactly as shown here. If you make a mistake while entering this line, you can

use the I-beam cursor or arrow keys to go to the location of your error to fix it:

```
(defun C:breakat () (command "break" pause "f" pause "@"))
```

2. Enter **breakat** at the Command prompt. The Break command starts, and you are prompted to select an object.

3. Click the wall on the right side of the unit.

4. At the Enter First Point: prompt, click a point on the wall where you want to create a break.

5. To see the result of the break, click the wall again. You will see that it has been split into two lines, as shown in Figure 14.15.

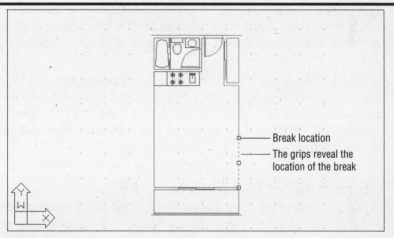

FIGURE 14.15: With the grips exposed, you can see that the wall is split into two lines.

You've just written and run your first AutoLISP macro! Let's take a closer look at this very simple program. It begins with an opening parenthesis, as do all AutoLISP programs, followed by the word defun. Defun is an AutoLISP function that lets you create commands; it is followed by the name you want to give the command (breakat, in this case). The command name is preceded by C:, telling defun to make this command accessible from the Command prompt. If the C: were omitted, you would have to start breakat using parentheses, as in (breakat).

Part iv

After the command name is a set of open and closing parentheses, which enclose what is called the *argument list*. The details aren't important; just be aware that these parentheses must follow the command name.

A list of words follows, enclosed by another set of parentheses. This list starts with the word command. Command is an AutoLISP function that tells AutoLISP that whatever follows should be entered just like regular keyboard input. Only one item in the breakat macro—the word pause—is not part of the keyboard input series. Pause is an AutoLISP function that tells AutoLISP to pause for input. In this particular macro, AutoLISP pauses to let you pick an object to break.

Notice that most of the items in the macro are enclosed in quotation marks. Literal keyboard input must be enclosed in quotation marks in this way. The pause function, on the other hand, does not require quotation marks because it is a proper function, one that AutoLISP can recognize.

Finally, the program closes with two closing parentheses. All parentheses in an AutoLISP program must be in balanced pairs, so these two parentheses close the opening parenthesis at the start of the command function as well as the opening parenthesis back at the beginning of the defun function.

Storing AutoLISP Macros as Files

When you create a program at the Command prompt, as you did with the breakat macro, AutoCAD remembers it only until you exit the current file. Unless you want to re-create this macro the next time you use AutoCAD, you can save it by copying it into an ASCII text file with an .lsp extension, as shown in the following example, where the breakat macro is saved, along with some other macros I use often.

Figure 14.16 shows the contents of a file named Keycad.lsp. This file contains the macro you used previously, along with several others. The other macros are commands that include optional responses. For example, the third item, defun c:corner, would cause AutoCAD to start the Fillet command, enter an **R** to issue the Radius option, and finally enter a **0** for the fillet radius. Table 14.1 shows the command abbreviations and what they do.

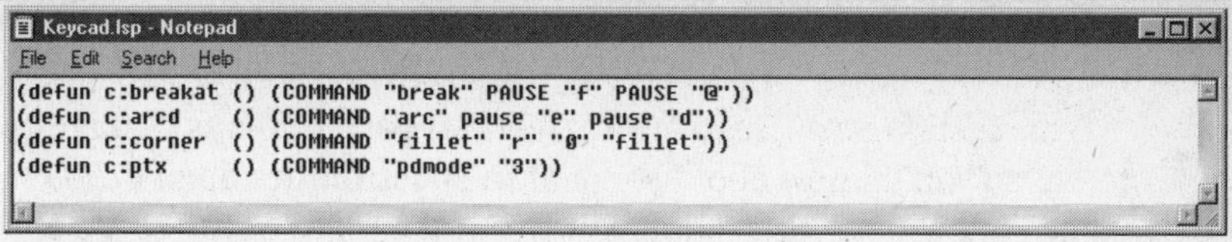

```
Keycad.lsp - Notepad
File  Edit  Search  Help
(defun c:breakat  () (COMMAND "break" PAUSE "f" PAUSE "@"))
(defun c:arcd     () (COMMAND "arc" pause "e" pause "d"))
(defun c:corner   () (COMMAND "fillet" "r" "0" "fillet"))
(defun c:ptx      () (COMMAND "pdmode" "3"))
```

FIGURE 14.16: The contents of Keycad.1sp

TABLE 14.1: The Shortcut Key (Command Abbreviations) Macros Provided by the Keycad.lsp File

ABBREVIATION	COMMAND OR ACTION TAKEN
breakat	Breaks an object at a single point
arcd	Draws an arc using the Start, End, Direction sequence
corner	Sets the fillet radius to 0; then starts the Fillet command
ptx	Sets the point style to be in the shape of an X

Use the Windows Notepad application and copy the listing in Figure 14.16. Give this file the name Keycad.1sp, and be sure you save it as an ASCII file. Then, whenever you want to use these macros, you don't have to load each one individually. Instead, you load the Keycad.1sp file the first time you want to use one of the macros, and they're all available for the rest of the session.

Once the file is loaded, you can use any of the macros contained within it just by entering the macro name. For example, entering **ptx** will set the point style to the shape of an X.

Macros loaded in this manner will be available to you until you exit AutoCAD. Of course, you can have these macros loaded automatically every time you start AutoCAD by including the Keycad.1sp file in the Startup Suite of the Load/Unload Applications dialog box. That way, you don't have to remember to load it in order to use the macros.

USING THIRD-PARTY SOFTWARE

One of the most significant reasons for AutoCAD's popularity is its strong support for third-party software. AutoCAD is like a chameleon; it can change to suit its environment. Out of the box, AutoCAD may not fulfill

Part iv

the needs of some users. But by incorporating one of the over 300 third-party add-ons, you can tailor AutoCAD to suit your specific needs.

This section discusses a few of the third-party add-ons that are popular today, so you'll know about some of the possibilities open to you while using AutoCAD. This section will give you an idea of the scope of third-party software. For more information on the myriad of third-party tools out there, check out the Autodesk website at http://www.autodesk.com.

Custom-Tailoring AutoCAD

The needs of an architect are far different from those of a mechanical designer or a civil engineer. Third-party developers have created some specialized tools that help users of specific types of AutoCAD applications.

Many of these tools come complete with libraries of parts or symbols, AutoLISP, ADS, or ARX programs, and menus—all integrated into a single package. These packages offer added functions to AutoCAD that simplify and speed up the AutoCAD user's work. For example, most AEC (architectural or engineering construction) add-ons offer utilities for drawing walls, inserting doors and windows, and creating schedules. These functions can be performed with the stock AutoCAD package but usually require a certain amount of effort. Certainly, if you have the time, you can create your own system of symbols, AutoLISP programs, and menus, and often this is the best way of molding AutoCAD to your needs. However, when users want a ready-made solution, these add-ons are invaluable.

Specialized third-party add-ons are available for AEC, mechanical, civil engineering, piping, mapping, finite element analysis, numeric control, GIS, and many other applications. They can save you a good deal of frustration and time, especially if you find just the right one for your environment. Like so many things, however, third-party add-ons can't be all things to all people. It is likely that no matter which add-on you purchase, you will find something lacking. When you're considering custom add-ons, make sure the package offers some degree of flexibility, so if you don't like something, you can change it or add to it later.

Check with your AutoCAD dealer for information about third-party add-ons. Most AutoCAD dealers carry the more popular offerings. You might also want to get involved with a user group in your area.

Third-Party Product Information on the World Wide Web

The World Wide Web is another good place to start looking for the third-party add-ons. In particular, you will want to take a look at the Autodesk Resource Guide website at www.autodesk.com/products/autocad/index.htm. You can get there by selecting Help ➤ Autodesk on the Web ➤ Autodesk Developers Resource Guide Homepage. While you're at it, you may want to check out the other options on the Autodesk on the Web cascading menu. It offers links to support, technical bulletins, upgrades, and other valuable information.

Autodesk's Own Offerings

Autodesk also offers a wide variety of add-ons to AutoCAD from simple symbols libraries to full-blown, industry-specific applications. There are offerings for architecture, civil engineering, mechanical drawing, mapping, data management, and 3D Visualization. Check out the Autodesk website for full details.

GETTING THE LATEST INFORMATION FROM ONLINE SERVICES

Many resources are available for the AutoCAD user. Perhaps the most useful resources are today's popular online services and AutoCAD-related newsgroups. If you don't already subscribe to one, you would do well to get a modem and explore the AutoCAD newsgroups, departments, or forums on online services.

To start with, check out the two Internet newsgroups that are devoted to AutoCAD users:

- Alt.cad.autocad

- comp.cad.autocad

Both of these newsgroups offer a forum for you to discuss your AutoCAD questions and problems with other users. Most Internet browsers let you access newsgroups. For example, you can open a News window from

Netscape Communicator by choosing Window ➤ Netscape News. From the Netscape News window, choose File ➤ Add Newsgroup, and then enter the name of the newsgroup into the input box that pops up. From then on, you can read messages, reply to posted messages, or post your questions.

Another online service that offers help to AutoCAD users is America Online (AOL). Although it doesn't offer a direct line to Autodesk, there is a forum for AutoCAD users to exchange ideas and troubleshooting tips. AOL also offers a library of AutoCAD-related utilities. To get to the AutoCAD folder in AOL, choose Go To ➤ Keyword. Then in the Keyword dialog box, enter **CAD** and click GO.

Cadalyst and *Cadence*, the two North American magazines devoted to AutoCAD mentioned earlier, both have their own websites. *Cadalyst* is at http:\\www .cadonline.com; *Cadence* is at http:\\www.cadence.com. Also, check out the Sybex website at http:\\www.sybex.com for the latest information on more great books on AutoCAD. Finally, check out my own site—http:\\www.omura.com—for information concerning this and other books, files, and links to other AutoCAD resources.

IF YOU WANT TO EXPERIMENT...

Try to think of some other keyboard macros that you would like to create. For example, you might try to create a macro that copies and rotates an object at the same time. This operation is a fairly common one that can be performed using the grip edit options, but you can reduce the number of steps needed to copy and rotate by creating a macro. Review the section entitled "Creating Keyboard Macros with AutoLISP" for help.

Here are some hints to get you started:

▶ Use the Copy command to copy an object in place.

▶ Use the same coordinate, like 0,0, for the base point and the second point.

▶ Use the Last Selection option to rotate the last object selected, which happens to be the original object that was copied.

WHAT'S NEXT?

This chapter has introduced you to the many customization options available in AutoCAD. You have seen how to manage keyboard macros, AutoLISP code, VBA projects, and other third-party software. In the next chapter, you will learn how to customize toolbars, menus, linetypes, and hatch patterns.

Part iv

Chapter 15

INTEGRATING AUTOCAD INTO YOUR PROJECTS AND ORGANIZATION

AutoCAD offers a high degree of flexibility and customization, allowing you to tailor the software's look and feel to your requirements. This chapter shows how you can adapt Auto-CAD to fit your particular needs. You will learn how to customize AutoCAD by modifying its menus. You will learn how to create custom macros for commands that your work group uses frequently. You'll look into the inner working of menu files and linetype and hatch-pattern definitions, and you'll learn to create new custom toolbars and tools.

Adapted from *Mastering™ AutoCAD® 2000 Premium Edition* by George Omura
ISBN 0-7821-2499-2   1,664 pages $59.99

CUSTOMIZING TOOLBARS

The most direct way to adapt AutoCAD to your way of working is to customize the toolbars. AutoCAD offers new users an easy route to customization. You can create new toolbars, customize tools, and even create new icons. In this section, you'll discover how easy it is to add features to AutoCAD.

Taking a Closer Look at the Toolbars Dialog Box

Throughout this book, you've used the Toolbars dialog box to open toolbars that are specialized for a particular purpose. The Toolbars dialog box is one of the many entry points to customizing AutoCAD. Let's take a closer look at this dialog box to see what other options it offers besides just opening other toolbars.

1. Right-click the Draw toolbar, and then select Customize. The Toolbars dialog box opens.

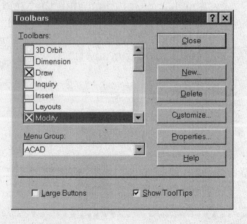

The Toolbars list box shows all the toolbars available in AutoCAD.

2. Scroll the list box up until you see Inquiry. Highlight it and click the Properties button. The Toolbar Properties dialog box appears.

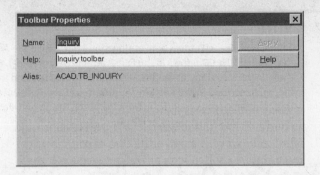

The Name input box controls the title that appears in the toolbar's title bar. The Help input box contains the help message that appears in the status line.

3. Click Close in the Toolbars dialog box to close both dialog boxes.

As you can see from the Toolbar Properties dialog box, you can rename a toolbar and alter its help message, if you choose. Here are brief descriptions of some of the other options in the Toolbars dialog box:

Close   Closes the dialog box.

New   Lets you create a new toolbar.

Delete   Deletes a toolbar from the list.

Customize   Opens the Customize Toolbars dialog box, from which you can click and drag predefined buttons.

Properties   Opens the Toolbar Properties dialog box.

Help   Displays helpful information about the Toolbars dialog box.

Large Buttons   Changes all the tools to a larger format.

Show ToolTips   Controls the display for the ToolTips.

You'll get to use most of these other options in the following sections.

Part iv

NOTE

Typically, AutoCAD stores new toolbars and buttons in the Acad.mns file (see the sidebar "The Windows Menu Files" later in this chapter). You can also store them in your custom menu files. Once you've created and loaded your menu file, as described in the section "Adding Your Own Pull-Down Menu" later in this chapter, choose your menu from the Menu Group pull-down list in the New Toolbar dialog box as described next.

Creating Your Own Toolbar

You may find that instead of using one toolbar or flyout, you are moving from flyout to flyout from a variety of different toolbars. If you keep track of the tools you use most frequently, you can create your own custom toolbar containing your favorite tools. Here's how it's done.

1. Right-click any icon in any toolbar, and then select Customize in the pop-up menu. The Toolbars dialog box opens.

2. Click the New button. The New Toolbar dialog box appears.

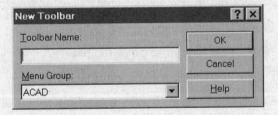

3. Enter **My Toolbar** in the Toolbar Name input box, and then click OK. A small, blank toolbar appears in the AutoCAD window.

    Notice that ACAD appears in the Menu Group list box and My Toolbar now appears in the Toolbars list box. You can now begin to add buttons to your toolbar.

4. Click Customize in the Toolbars dialog box. The Customize Toolbars dialog box appears.

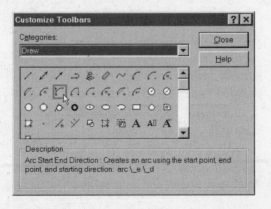

5. Open the Categories pull-down list. Notice that the list contains the main categories of commands.

6. Choose Draw from the list. The list box displays all the tools available for the Draw category. Notice that the dialog box offers several additional arc and circle tools not found in the Draw toolbar.

7. Click the first tool in the top row: the Line tool. You'll see a description of the tool in the Description box at the bottom of the dialog box.

8. Click and drag the Line tool from the Customize Toolbars dialog box into the new toolbar you just created. The Line tool now appears in your toolbar.

9. Click and drag the Arc Start End Direction tool to your new toolbar.

Part iv

10. Exit the Customize Toolbars dialog box and the Toolbars dialog box.

You now have a custom toolbar with two buttons. You can add buttons from different categories if you like; you are not restricted to buttons from one category.

NOTE

If you need to remove a tool from your toolbar, click and drag it out of your toolbar into the blank area of the drawing. Do this while the Customize Toolbars dialog box is open.

AutoCAD treats your custom toolbar just like any other toolbar. It appears when you start AutoCAD and remains until you close it. You can recall it by the same method described in the first exercise.

OPENING TOOLBARS FROM THE COMMAND LINE

You may want to know how to open toolbars using the Command line. Doing so can be especially helpful if you want to create toolbar buttons that open other toolbars.

1. Type **–Toolbar** and press Enter at the Command prompt (don't forget to include the minus sign at the beginning of the Toolbar command).

2. At the Toolbar Name <All>: prompt, enter the name of the toolbar you want to open.

3. At the Show/Hide/Left/Right/Top/Bottom/Float <Show>: prompt, press Enter. The toolbar appears on the screen.

A typical button macro for opening a toolbar might look like this:

```
^c^cToolbar[space]ACAD.Arc[space][space]
```

Here, the [space] is added for clarity. You would press the spacebar in its place. This example shows a macro that opens the Arc toolbar (ACAD.Arc).

As the prompt in step 3 indicates, you can specify the location of the toolbar by left, right, top, or bottom. Float lets you specify the location and number of rows for the toolbar.

CONTINUED →

The following list shows the toolbar names available in the standard AutoCAD system. Use the following names with the Toolbar command:

ACAD.TB_OBJECT_PROPERTIES

ACAD.TB_STANDARD

ACAD.TB_DIMENSION

ACAD.TB_DRAW

ACAD.TB_EXTERNAL_DATABASE

ACAD.TB_INQUIRY

ACAD.TB_INSERT

ACAD.TB_LAYOUTS

ACAD.TB_MODIFY

ACAD.TB_MODIFY_II

ACAD.TB_OBJECT_SNAP

ACAD.TB_3D_ORBIT

ACAD.TB_REFEDIT

ACAD.TB_REFERENCE

ACAD.TB_RENDER

ACAD.TB_SOLIDS

ACAD.TB_SOLIDS2

ACAD.TB_SURFACES

ACAD.TB_UCS

ACAD.TB_UCS2

ACAD.TB_VIEWPOINT

ACAD.TB_VIEWPORTS

ACAD.TB_ZOOM

ACAD.TB_WEB

CONTINUED ➡

Notice that the toolbar names in the Toolbars dialog box do not match those shown in this list. You can find the "true" name of a toolbar by highlighting it in the Toolbars dialog box and then clicking Properties. The toolbar's true name is displayed under Alias.

Customizing Toolbar Tools

Now let's move on to more serious customization. Suppose you want to create an entirely new button with its own functions. For example, you may want to create a set of buttons that will insert your favorite symbols. Or you might want to create a toolbar containing a set of tools that open other toolbars that are normally "put away."

Creating a Custom Button

In the following set of exercises, you'll create a button that inserts a door symbol. You'll add your custom button to the toolbar you just created.

1. Open the Toolbars dialog box again, and then click Customize.

2. Select Custom from the drop-down list. The list box now shows two blank buttons, one for a single command and another for flyouts. (The button for flyouts has a small triangle in the lower-right corner.)

3. Click and drag the single-command blank button to your new toolbar.

4. Right-click the blank button in your new toolbar. The Button Properties dialog box appears. This dialog box lets you define the purpose of your custom button.

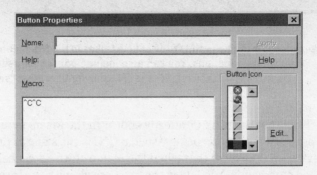

Let's pause for a moment to look at this dialog box. The Name input box lets you enter a name for your button. This name will appear as a ToolTip. You must enter a name before AutoCAD will create the new button definition.

The Help input box just below the name lets you add a help message. This message will appear in the lower-left corner of the AutoCAD window when you point to your button.

The Macro area is the focus of this dialog box. Here, you can enter the keystrokes you want to "play back" when you click on this button.

Finally, to the right, you see a scroll bar that lets you scroll through a set of icons. You'll also see a button labeled Edit. When you highlight an icon in the scroll box and then click Edit, an Icon Editor tool appears, allowing you to edit an existing icon or create a new icon.

Let's go ahead and add a macro and new icon to this button.

1. In the Name input box, enter **Door**. This will be your ToolTip for this button.

2. In the Help input box, enter **Inserts a single door**. This will be the help message for this button.

3. In the Macro input box, enter the following: **^C^C−insert door**.

   Make sure you include the minus sign before the word **insert**. It indicates that you want to use the command-line version of the Insert command.

Part iv

TIP

You can put any valid string of keystrokes in the Macro input box, including AutoLISP functions. You can also include pauses for user input using the backslash (\) character. See the "Pausing for User Input" section later in this chapter.

Note that the two ^Cs already appear in the Macro input box. These represent two Cancels being issued. ^C^C is the same as pressing the Esc key twice; it ensures that when the macro starts, it cancels any unfinished commands. You follow the two Cancels with the Insert command as it is issued from the keyboard.

WARNING

It is important that you enter the exact sequence of keystrokes that follow the command; otherwise your macro may get out of step with the Command prompts. This will take a little practice and some going back and forth between testing your button and editing the macro.

After the Insert command there is a space, and then the name Door appears. This is the same sequence of keystrokes you would enter at the Command line to insert the door drawing. You could go on to include an insertion point, scale factor, and rotation angle in this macro, but these options are better left for the time when the door is actually inserted.

Creating a Custom Icon

You have defined all the essential parts of the button. Now you just need to create a custom icon to go with your door button.

1. In the Icon scroll box, scroll down the list until you see a blank icon.

2. Click the blank icon, and then click Edit. The Button Editor appears.

NOTE

If you prefer, you can use any of the predefined icons in the scroll box. Just click the icon you want to use, and then click Apply.

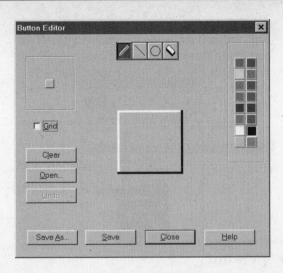

The Button Editor is like a very simple drawing program. Across the top are the tools to draw lines, circles, and points, as well as an eraser. Along the right side, you see a color toolbar from which you can choose colors for your icon button. At upper left, you see a preview of your button. The following list describes the rest of the options:

Grid   Turns a grid on and off in the drawing area. This grid can be an aid in drawing your icon.

Clear   Erases the entire contents of the drawing area.

Open   Opens a .bmp file to import an icon. The .bmp file must be small enough to fit in the 16 × 16 pixel matrix provided for icons (24 × 24 for large-format icons).

Save As   Saves your icon as a .bmp file under a name you enter.

Save   Saves your icon under a name that AutoCAD provides, usually a series of numbers and letters.

Close   Exits the Button Editor.

Help   Displays helpful information about the features of the Button Editor.

Undo   Undoes the last operation you performed.

Now let's continue by creating a new icon.

3. Draw the door icon shown here. Don't worry if it's not perfect; you can always go back and fix it.

4. Click Save, and then click Close.

5. In the Button Properties dialog box, click Apply. You'll see the icon appear in the button in your toolbar.

6. Click the Close button of the Toolbars dialog box.

WARNING

The Door drawing must be in the default directory, or in the Acad search path before the door button will be inserted.

7. Click the Door icon on your new toolbar. The door appears in your drawing, ready to be placed.

You can continue to add more buttons to your toolbar to build a toolbar of symbols. Of course, you're not limited to a symbols library. You can also incorporate your favorite macros or even AutoLISP routines that you may accumulate as you work with AutoCAD. The possibilities are endless.

Setting the Properties of Flyouts

Just as you added a new button to your toolbar, you can also add flyouts. Remember that flyouts are really just another form of a toolbar. This next example shows how you can add a copy of the Zoom toolbar to your custom toolbar, and then make adjustments to the properties of the flyout.

1. Right-click the Door icon in the toolbar you just finished. The Toolbars dialog box opens with My Toolbar already highlighted.

2. Click Customize, and then in the Customize Toolbars dialog box, open the pull-down list and select Custom.

3. Click and drag the flyout button from the list box into the My Toolbar toolbar.

TIP

To delete a button from a toolbar, open the Toolbars dialog box and click Customize. When the Customize Toolbars dialog box appears, click and drag the button you want to delete out of the toolbar and into the drawing area.

You now have a blank flyout to which you can add your own icon. Let's see what options are available for flyout buttons.

4. Close the Customize Toolbars dialog box, and then right-click the new, blank flyout button you just added to your toolbar. The Flyout Properties dialog box appears.

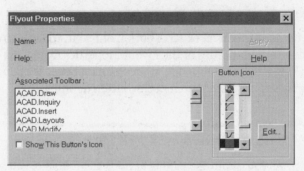

Notice how this dialog box resembles the Button Properties dialog box you used in the previous exercise. But instead of the Macro input box, you see a list of associated toolbars.

5. Scroll down the list of toolbar names until you find ACAD.Zoom. This is a predefined toolbar, although you can use a toolbar you define yourself.

6. Highlight ACAD.Zoom and then enter **My Zoom Flyout** in the Name input box. Enter **My very own flyout** in the Help input box.

7. Locate an icon in the icon scroll box that looks like a magnifying glass, and click it.

8. Click the check box labeled Show This Button's Icon so that a checkmark appears in the box.

9. Click Apply. The flyout button in the My Toolbar toolbar shows the icon you selected.

10. Close the Toolbars dialog box, and then place the arrow cursor on the flyout to display its ToolTip. Notice that your new ToolTip and help message appear.

11. Click and drag the Zoom icon, and then select Zoom In from the flyout. Notice that even though you selected Zoom In, the original Zoom icon remains as the icon for the flyout.

Step 11 demonstrates that you can disable the feature that causes the last flyout to appear as the default on the toolbar. You disabled this feature in step 8 by checking the Show This Button's Icon check box.

Editing Existing Buttons

If you want to edit an existing button or flyout, you can go directly to either the Button Properties or the Flyout Properties dialog box by double-right-clicking a button. Once one of these dialog boxes is open, you can make changes to any component of the button definition.

THE WINDOWS MENU FILES

As you create and modify buttons and toolbars, you see messages momentarily appear in the status line at the bottom of the AutoCAD window. These messages are telling you that AutoCAD is creating new menu files. AutoCAD creates several menu files it uses in the course of an editing session.

Here's a brief rundown of what those different menu files are:

Acad.mnu   The source text file that contains the information required to build the AutoCAD menu. If you are a programmer, you would use this file to do detailed customization of the AutoCAD menu. Here, you can edit the pull-down menus, image tiles, buttons, and so on. Most users won't need to edit this file.

Acad.mnc   AutoCAD's translation of the Acad.mnu file. AutoCAD translates, or *compiles*, the Acad.mnu file so that it can read the menu more quickly.

CONTINUED ➡

Acad.mns   A text file created by AutoCAD containing the source information from the .mnu file plus additional comments. This file is rewritten whenever an .mnu file is loaded. If you make changes or additions to toolbars, you'll want to keep a backup copy of this file to preserve those changes. The Acad.mns file can be used like an Acad.mnu file as a source text file to build the AutoCAD menu.

Acad.mnr   The menu resource file. It is a binary file that contains the bitmap images used for buttons and other graphics.

As you create or edit icon buttons and toolbars, AutoCAD first adds your custom items to the Acad.mns file. It then compiles this file into the Acad.mnc and Acad.mnr files for quicker access to the menus. If you reload the MNU version of your menu, AutoCAD recreates the MNS file, thereby removing any toolbar customization you may have done.

Note that the Acad.mns file is the file you need to copy to other computers to transfer your custom buttons and toolbars. Also, if you create your own pull-down menu files, as in the Mymenu.mnu example in this chapter, AutoCAD creates the source, compiled, and creates the resource files for your custom menu file. You have the option to store new toolbars in your custom menu through the Menu Group pull-down list of the New Toolbar dialog box.

ADDING YOUR OWN PULL-DOWN MENU

In addition to adding buttons and toolbars, AutoCAD lets you add pull-down menu options. This sections looks at how you might add a custom pull-down menu to your AutoCAD environment.

Part iv

Creating Your First Pull-Down Menu

Let's start by trying the following exercise to create a simple pull-down menu file called My Menu:

1. Using a text editor, like the Windows Notepad, create a file called Mymenu.mnu, containing the following lines:

```
***POP1
[My 1st Menu]
[Line]^c^c_line
[-]
[->More]
[Arc-SED]^c^c_arc \_e \_d
[<-Break At]^c^c(defun c:breakat ()+
(command "break" pause "f" pause "@")+
);breakat
[Fillet 0]^c^c_fillet r 0;;
[Point Style X]'pdmode 3
***POP2
[My 2nd Menu]
[door]^c^cInsert door
[Continue Line]^C^CLINE;;
```

2. Save this file; be sure you place it in your \Auto-CAD2000\Support\ directory.

WARNING

Pay special attention to the spaces between letters in the commands described in this chapter. (You need not worry much about whether to type uppercase or lowercase letters.)

Once you've stored the file, you've got your first custom pull-down menu. You may have noticed some familiar items among the lines you entered. The menu contains the Line and Arc commands.

Now let's see how My Menu works in AutoCAD.

Loading a Menu

In the following exercise, you will load and test the menu you just created. The procedure described here for loading menus is the same for all menus, regardless of their source.

1. Choose Tools ➢ Customize Menus. The Menu Customization dialog box appears.

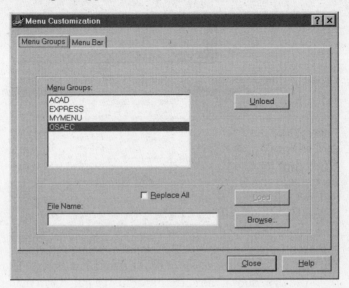

2. Click the Menu Groups tab. Click Browse at the bottom of the dialog box. The Select Menu file dialog box appears.

3. Click the Files of Type drop-down list and select Menu Template (*.mnu).

4. Locate the Mymenu.mnu file, highlight it, and then click Open. You return to the Menu Customization dialog box.

5. Click Load. You see a warning message telling you that you will lose any toolbar customization you have made. This message refers only to the specific menu you are loading. Because you haven't made any toolbar customization changes to your menu, you won't lose anything.

6. Click Yes. The warning dialog box closes, and you see the name of your menu group listed in the Menu Group list box.

7. Click the Menu Bar tab at the top of the dialog box. The dialog box changes to show two lists.

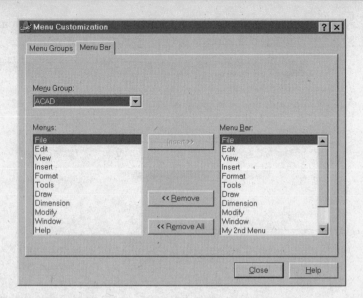

On the left is the name of the current menu group. The list on the right shows the currently available pull-down menus.

8. Click the Menu Group drop-down list and select MYMENU. The names of the pull-down menus in your menu file appear.

9. Highlight Help in the right-hand column. This setting tells AutoCAD you want to add your pull-down menu in front of the Help pull-down menu.

10. Highlight My 1st Menu from the list on the left, and then click the Insert >> button. My 1st Menu moves into the right-hand column and appears in the AutoCAD menu bar.

11. Highlight My 2nd Menu from the list on the left, and then click Insert >> again. My 2nd Menu is copied to the right-hand column and it also appears in the menu bar.

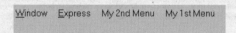

12. Close the Menu Customization dialog box.

13. Draw a line on the screen, and then try the option My 1st
Menu ➤ More ➤ Break At.

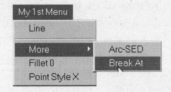

With just an 15-line menu file, you created a menu that contains virtually every tool used to build menus. Now let's take a more detailed look at
how menu files work.

How the Pull-Down Menu Works

Let's take a closer look at the Mymenu.mns file. The first item in the file,
***POP1, identifies the beginning of a pull-down menu. The text just
below the first line is My 1st Menu enclosed in square brackets. This is
the title of the pull-down menu; this text appears in the toolbar. Every
pull-down menu must have this title element.

Following the title, each item in the list starts with a word enclosed in
brackets; these words are the options that actually appear when you open
the pull-down menu. If you were to remove everything else, you would
have the menu as it appears on the screen. The text that follows the item
in brackets conveys instructions to AutoCAD about the option.

Finally, in the My 1st Menu sample, you see ***POP2. This is the beginning of a second pull-down menu. Again, you must follow this line with a
pull-down menu title in square brackets. Below the title, you can add other
menu options.

Calling Commands

Now look at the Line option in the Mymenu.mnu listing. The two Ctrl+C
(^C) elements that follow the square brackets will cancel any command
that is currently operative. The Line command follows, written just as it
would be entered through the keyboard. Two Cancels are issued in case
you are in a command that has two levels, such as the Edit Vertex option
of the Pedit command (Modify ➤ Object ➤ Polyline).

The underscore character (_) that precedes the Line command tells Auto-
CAD that you are using the English-language version of this command. This

feature lets you program non-English versions of AutoCAD using the English-language command names.

You may also notice that there is no space between the second ^C and the Line command. A space in the line would be the same as a carriage return. If there were a space between these two elements, a carriage return would be entered between the last ^C and the Line command, causing the command sequence to misstep. Another way to indicate a carriage return is by using the semicolon, as in the following example:

```
[Continue Line]^C^CLINE;;
```

TIP
When you have many carriage returns in a menu macro, using semicolons instead of spaces can help make your macro more readable.

In this sample menu option, the Line command is issued, and then an additional carriage return is added. The effect of choosing this option is a line that continues from the last line entered into your drawing. The two semicolons following the word Line tell AutoCAD to start the Line command, and then issue carriage returns twice to begin a line from the endpoint of the last line entered. (AutoCAD automatically issues a single carriage return at the end of a menu line. In this case, however, you want two carriage returns, so they must be represented as semicolons.)

Pausing for User Input

Another symbol used in the menu file is the backslash (\); it is used when a pause is required for user input. For example, when you select the Arc-SED option in My 1st Menu, it starts the Arc command and then pauses for your input:

```
[Arc-SED]^c^c_arc \_e \_d
```

NOTE
The underscore character (_) that precedes the command name and option input tells AutoCAD that you are entering the English-language versions of these commands.

The space between ^c^c_arc and the backslash (\) represents the pressing of the spacebar. The backslash indicates a pause to allow you to select the starting endpoint for the arc. Once you have picked a point, the e represents the selection of the Endpoint option under the Arc command. A second backslash allows another point selection. Finally, the _d represents the selection of the Direction option.

If you want the last character in a menu item to be a backslash, you must follow the backslash with a semicolon.

Using the Plus Sign for Long Lines

As you browse through the Acad.mnu file, notice that many of the lines end with a plus sign (+). The length of each line in the menu file is limited to about 80 characters, but you can break a line into two or more lines by adding a plus sign at the end of the line that continues, like this:

```
[<-Break At]^c^c(defun c:breakat ()+
(command "break" pause "f" pause "@")+
);breakat
```

TIP

It's OK to break an AutoLISP program into smaller lines. In fact, it can help you read and understand the program more easily.

This example showed how to include the Break At AutoLISP macro in a menu. Everything in this segment is entered just as it would be with the keyboard. The plus sign indicates the continuation of this long item to the subsequent lines, and the semicolon is used in place of a carriage return.

Creating a Cascading Menu

Look at the More option in the File pull-down menu group; it starts with these characters: ->. This is the way you indicate a menu item that opens a cascading menu. Everything that follows the [->More] menu item will appear in the cascading menu. To indicate the end of the cascading menu, you use the characters <-, as in the [<-Rotate90] menu item farther down. Anything beyond this <- item appears in the main part of the menu. If the last item in a cascading menu is also the last item in the menu group, you must use <-<-, as in [<-<-.XZ].

Part iv

Placing Division Lines and Dimmed Text in Pull-Down Menus

Two symbols are used to place dividing lines in your pull-down menus. One is the *double-hyphen* symbol (--), which divides groups of items in a menu; it will expand to fill the entire width of the pull-down menu with a line of hyphens. The other option is the *tilde* symbol (~). If the tilde precedes a bracketed option name, that option will be dimmed when displayed; when clicked on, it will have no effect. You have probably encountered these dimmed options on various pull-down menus in the programs you use. When you see a dimmed menu item, it usually means that the option is not valid under the current command.

LOADING AUTOLISP MACROS WITH YOUR SUBMENU

As you become a more advanced AutoCAD user, you may find that you want to have many of your own AutoLISP macros load with your menus. This can be accomplished by combining all your AutoLISP macros into a single file. Give this file the same name as your menu file with the .mn1 filename extension. Such a file will be automatically loaded with its menu counterpart. For example, say you have a file called Mymenu.mn1 containing the Break At AutoLISP macro. Whenever you load Mymenu.mns, Mymenu.mn1 is automatically loaded along with it, giving you access to the Break At macro. This is a good way to manage and organize any AutoLISP program code you want to include with a menu.

Adding Help Messages to Pull-Down Menu Items

Earlier in this chapter, you learned how to include a help message with a button. The help message appears in the status bar of AutoCAD window when you highlight an option. You can also include a help message with a pull-down menu item.

First, you must give your pull-down menu file a menu group name. This name helps AutoCAD isolate your file and its help messages from other menus that might be loaded along with yours. To give your menu file a group name, add the following line at the top of the file:

```
***MENUGROUP=MYMENU
```

where *MYMENU* is the name you want for your menu group name.

Next, you have to add an ID name to each menu item that requires a help message. The following example shows how this might be done for the My 1st Menu example you used earlier:

```
***MENUGROUP=MYMENU
***POP1
[My 1st Menu]
ID_1line      [Line]^c^c_line
[-]
[->More]
ID_1arc-sed  [Arc-SED]^c^c_arc \_e \_d
ID_1breakat  [<-Break At]^c^c(defun c:breakat ()+
(command "break" pause "f" pause "@")+
);breakat
ID_1fillet0  [Fillet 0]^c^c_fillet r 0;;
ID_1pointx   [Point Style X]'pdmode 3
***POP2
[My 2nd Menu]
[door]^c^cInsert door
[Continue Line]^C^CLINE;;
```

The ID name starts with the characters *ID* followed by an underscore character (_) and the name for the menu item. Several spaces are added so the menu items align for clarity. Each menu item must have a unique ID name.

Finally, you add a section at the end of your file called ***HELPSTRINGS. For this example, it would look like the following code:

```
***HELPSTRINGS
ID_1line      [Draws a line]
ID_1arc-sed  [Draws an arc with start, end, direction]
ID_1breakat  [Breaks an object at a single point]
ID_1fillet0  [Sets the Fillet radius to zero]
ID_1pointx   [Sets the Point style to an X]
```

Part iv

The menu item ID names are duplicated exactly, followed by several spaces, and then the actual text you want to have appear in the status line, enclosed in brackets. The spaces between the ID and the text are for clarity.

WARNING

The ID names are case sensitive, so make sure they match up in both the HELP-STRINGS section and in the menu section.

Once you've done this and then loaded the menu file, you will see these messages appear in the status bar when the menu options are highlighted. In fact, if you browse your Acad.mnu file, you will see similar ID names. If you prefer, you can use numbers in place of names.

Creating Accelerator Keys

Perhaps one of the more popular methods for customizing AutoCAD has been the keyboard accelerator keys. Accelerator keys are Ctrl or Shift key combinations that invoke commonly used commands or tools in Auto-CAD. The Osnaps are a popular candidate for accelerator keys, as are the display commands.

To add accelerator key definitions to AutoCAD, you need to add some code to your menu file. The following is an example of what you can add to the Mymenu.mnu file to define a set of accelerator keys:

```
***ACCELERATORS
[CONTROL+SHIFT+"E"]endp
[CONTROL+SHIFT+"X"]int
ID_1breakat   [CONTROL+SHIFT+"B"]
```

The ***ACCELERATORS line at the top is the group heading, similar to the ***HELPSTRINGS heading in that it defines the beginning of the section. It is followed by the accelerator descriptions.

The previous example shows two methods for defining an accelerator key. The first two bracketed text items follow the format you've already seen for the pull-down menu. But instead of the menu text in square brackets, you see the keys required to invoke the action that follows the brackets. So in the first line

```
[CONTROL+SHIFT+"E"]endp
```

the CONTROL+SHIFT+"E" tells AutoCAD to enter the Endpoint Osnap (endp) whenever the Ctrl+Shift+E key combination is pressed. Notice that the E is in quotation marks and that all the characters are uppercase. Follow this format for quotation marks and capitalization when you create your own accelerator keys.

A second method is shown in the third line:

```
ID_1breakat   [CONTROL+SHIFT+"B"]
```

Here, ID_1breakat associates a keystroke combination with a menu option, not unlike the way it is used to associate a menu item with a help string. This line tells AutoCAD to issue the Break At macro listed earlier in the menu whenever the Ctrl+Shift+B key combination is pressed.

You can use either Ctrl or Shift individually or together in combination with most keys on your keyboard, including the function keys. You can also assign keys without the Ctrl or Shift options. Note that the function keys and the Esc key are already defined, so take care that you don't redefine them unless you really want to. Table 15.1 contains a brief list of some of the special keys you can define and how you need to specify them in the menu file.

TABLE 15.1:   Key Names to Use in Your Accelerator Key Definitions

Key	Format Used in AutoCAD Menu
Numeric keypad	"NUMPAD0" through "NUMPAD9"
Ins	"INSERT"
Del	"DELETE"
Function keys	"F2" through "F12"
Up arrow	"UP"
Down arrow	"DOWN"
Left arrow	"LEFT"
Right arrow	"RIGHT"

WARNING

Although you can use the F1 and Esc keys for accelerator keys, their use is discouraged because they serve other functions for both Windows and AutoCAD.

Understanding the Diesel Macro Language

If you browse through the Acad.mnu file, you'll see many menu options that contain odd-looking text beginning with a dollar sign ($). In some instances, the dollar sign is used to tell AutoCAD to open a pop-up menu. But in many cases, it is used as part of the Diesel macro language. Diesel is one of many macro languages AutoCAD supports, and it can be used to perform some simple operations. Like AutoLISP, it makes use of parentheses to enclose program code.

You can actually use Diesel at the AutoCAD Command line using a command called Modemacro. The Modemacro command sends information to the status line. Diesel can be used with Modemacro to perform some simple tasks. The following exercise lets you try Diesel for yourself:

1. Type **Modemacro** and press Enter at the Command prompt.

2. At the Enter new value for MODEMACRO, or . for none: prompt, enter **$(/,25,2)**. You'll see the answer to the equation in the far-left side of the status line.

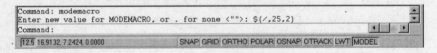

3. To clear the status line, enter **Modemacro**.

The equation you entered in step 2 is referred to as an *expression*. The structure of Diesel expressions is similar to that of AutoLISP. The dollar sign tells AutoCAD that the information that follows is a Diesel expression.

A Diesel expression must include an operator of some sort, followed by the items to be operated on. An *operator* is an instruction to take some specific action such as adding two numbers together or dividing one number by another. Examples of mathematical operators include the plus sign (+) for addition and forward slash (/) for division.

The operator is often referred to as a *function*, and the items to be operated on as the *arguments* to the function or simply the arguments. So, in the expression (/,25,2), the / is the function and 25 and 2 are the arguments. All Diesel expressions, no matter what size, follow this structure and are enclosed by parentheses.

Parentheses are important elements of an expression. All parentheses must be balanced; for each left parenthesis, there must be a right parenthesis.

You can do other things with Diesel besides performing calculations. For example, the Getvar function obtains the drawing prefix and name, which Remote Text can convert into text in the drawing. Try the following to see how Diesel uses Getvar:

1. Type **Modemacro** and press Enter.

2. Type **$(getvar,dwgprefix)** and press Enter. The location of the current drawing appears in the status bar.

3. Press Enter to reissue the Modemacro command, and then type **$(getvar,dwgname)** and press Enter. Now the name of the drawing appears in the status bar.

In this example, the Getvar function extracts the drawing prefix and name and displays it in the status line. Getvar can be used to extract any system variable you want. Virtually all AutoCAD settings are also controlled through system variables. Getvar can be a great tool when you are creating custom menus, because you can use it to "poll" AutoCAD to determine its state. For example, you can find out what command is currently being used. Try the following exercise to see how this technique works:

1. Click the Line tool in the Drawing toolbar.

2. Type **'Modemacro** and press Enter. The apostrophe at the beginning of Modemacro lets you use the command while in another command.

3. Type **$(getvar,cmdnames)** and press Enter. The word line appears in the status bar, indicating that the current command is the Line command.

Diesel can be useful in a menu when you want your menu option to perform a specific task depending on which command is currently active.

Part iv

Using Diesel in a Menu

So far, you've been experimenting with Diesel through the Modemacro command. To use Diesel in a menu requires a slightly different format. You still use the same Diesel format of a dollar sign followed by the expression, but you don't use the Modemacro command to access Diesel. Instead, you use $M=. You can think of $M= as an abbreviation for Modemacro.

Here's a Diesel expression that you can use in a menu:

```
[Blipmode on/off]'Blipmode $M=$(-,1,$(getvar,Blipmode))
```

This menu option turns Blipmode on or off. Blipmode is a feature that displays point selections in the drawing area as tiny crosses. These tiny crosses, or *blips*, do not print and can be cleared from the screen with a redraw. They can be helpful when you need to track your point selections.

In this example, the Blipmode command is invoked, and then the $M= tells AutoCAD that a Diesel expression follows. The expression

```
$(-,1,$(getvar,Blipmode))
```

returns either 1 or a 0, which is applied to the Blipmode command to turn it either on or off. This expression shows that you can nest expressions within each other. The most deeply nested expression is evaluated first, so AutoCAD evaluates

```
$(getvar,Blipmode)
```

to begin with. This expression returns either 1 or 0, depending on whether Blipmode is on or off. Next, AutoCAD evaluates the next level in the expression:

```
$(-,1,getvar_result)
```

where *getvar_result* is either 1 or 0. If *getvar_result* is 1, the expression looks like

```
$(-,1,1)
```

which returns 0. If getvar_result is 0, then the expression looks like

```
$(-,1,0)
```

which returns 1. In either case, the end result is that the Blipmode command is assigned a value that is the opposite of the current Blipmode setting.

Using Diesel as a Menu Option Label

In the previous example, you saw how Diesel can be used in a menu to read the status of a command and then return a numeric value to alter that status. You can also use Diesel as part of the menu option label. The following expression shows the same menu listing you've already seen, with a twist. It includes Diesel code as the menu option label, as follows:

```
[$(eval,"Blipmode =" $(getvar,blipmode))]'BLIPMODE $M=$(-
,1,$(getvar,blipmode))
```

NOTE
When Diesel is used as the menu name, you don't need the $M= code.

Normally, you see the menu name within the square brackets at the beginning of this menu listing, but here you see some Diesel instructions. These instructions tell AutoCAD to display the message Blipmode = 1 or Blipmode = 0 in the menu, depending on the current Blipmode setting.

Here's how it works. You see the familiar $(getvar,blipmode) expression, this time embedded within a different expression. You know that $(getvar,blipmode) returns either 1 or 0, depending on whether Blipmode is on or off. The outer expression

```
$(eval,"Blipmode =" getvar_result)
```

displays *Blipmode* = and then combines this text with *getvar_result*, which, as you've learned, will be either 1 or 0. The eval function evaluates any text that follows it and returns its contents. The end result is the appearance of Blipmode = 1 or Blipmode = 0 in the menu, depending on the status of Blipmode. Here's how the option looks as it appears in a menu.

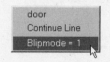

You can get even fancier by using the If Diesel function to set up the Menu option label to read Blipmode On or Blipmode Off. Here's that same menu listing with additional Diesel code to accomplish this:

```
[$(eval,"Blipmode "
$(if,$(getvar,blipmode),"Off","On"))]'BLIPMODE $M=
$(-,1,$(getvar,blipmode))
```

In this example, the simple $(getvar,blipmode) expression is expanded to include the If function. The If function reads the result of $(getvar,blipmode) and then returns Off or On depending on whether $(getvar,blipmode) returns 0 or 1. Here's a simpler look at the expression:

```
$(if, getvar_result, "Off", "On")
```

If getvar_result returns 1, then the If function returns the first of the two options listed after getvar_result, which is Off. If getvar_r esult returns 0, then the If functions returns On. The second of the two options is optional. Here's how the fancier Blipmode option appears in a menu.

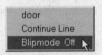

You've really just skimmed the surface of what Diesel can do. To get a more detailed description of how Diesel works, look at the AutoCAD Help Topics dialog box. Choose Help ➢ AutoCAD Help, and then click the Index tab in the Help Topics dialog box. Enter **Diesel** in the input box at the top to see a list of topics that deal with Diesel.

For fun, try adding this Blipmode menu listing to your Mymenu.mnu file under the [Continue Line] option, and then reload the menu file and check the results:

```
[$(eval,"Blipmode "
$(if,$(getvar,blipmode),"Off","On"))]'BLIPMODE $M=
➥ $(-,1,$(getvar,blipmode))
```

Make sure the last line in your menu file is followed by a carriage return.

If you feel you've learned enough to do some work with Diesel, Table 15.2 shows some of the commonly used Diesel functions. Check the AutoCAD Help Topics dialog box for a more detailed list.

TABLE 15.2: A Sample of Diesel Functions. Note That to Indicate True or False, Diesel Uses 1 or 0.

Code	Function	Example	Result	Comments
+	Add	$(+,202,144)	346	
–	Subtract	$(-,202,144)	58	
*	Multiply	$(*,202,144)	29088	
/	Divide	$(/,202,144)	1.4028	
=	Equal to	$(=,202,144)	0	If the numbers are equal, 1 is returned.
<	Less than	$(<,202,144)	0	If the first number is less than the second, 1 is returned.
>	Greater than	$(>,202,144)	1	If the first number is less than the second, 0 is returned.
!	Not equal to	$(!,202,144)	1	If the numbers are equal, 0 is returned.
<=	Less than or equal to	$(+,202,144)	0	If the first number is less than or equal to the second, 1 is returned.
>=	Greater than or equal to	$(+,202,144)	1	If the first number is less than or equal to the second, 0 is returned.
eq	Equal string	$(eq,"Yes","No")	0	If both text strings are the same, 1 is returned.
eval	Evaluate text	$(eval,"Here I Am")	Here I Am	Returns the text in quotes.
getvar	Get system variable value	$(getvar,ltscale)		Current linetype scale
if	If/Then	$(if,1,"Yes","No")	Yes	The second argument is returned if the first argument evaluates to 1. Otherwise, the third argument is returned. The third argument is optional.

CREATING CUSTOM LINETYPES

As your drawing needs expand, you may find that the standard linetypes are not adequate for your application. Fortunately, you can create your own. This section explains how to go about creating your own custom linetypes.

In this section, you'll get an in-depth view of the process of creating linetypes. You'll also learn how to create complex linetypes that cannot be created using the Express Make Linetype tool.

Viewing Available Linetypes

Although AutoCAD provides the linetypes most commonly used in drafting, the dashes and dots may not be spaced the way you would like, or you may want an entirely new linetype.

NOTE

AutoCAD stores the linetypes in a file called Acad.lin, which is in ASCII format. When you create a new linetype, you are actually adding information to this file. Or, if you create a new file containing your own linetype definitions, it, too, will have the extension .lin. You can edit linetypes as described here, or you can edit them directly in these files.

To create a custom linetype, use the Linetype command. Let's see how this handy command works, by first listing the available linetypes.

1. Open a new AutoCAD file.

2. Enter **-Linetype** at the Command prompt. (Don't forget the minus sign at the beginning of the word *Linetype*.)

3. At the ?/Create/Load/Set: prompt, enter **?**.

4. In the File dialog box that appears, locate and double-click ACAD in the listing of available linetype files. You get the list shown in Figure 15.1, which shows the linetypes available in the Acad.lin file along with a simple description of each line. Figure 15.1 shows a few of the standard linetypes and the ISO and complex linetypes.

```
BORDER            Border    __ __ . __ __ . __ __ . __ __ . __ __ .
BORDER2           Border (.5x)  __.__.__.__.__.__.__.__.__.__.__.__
BORDERX2          Border (2x) ____ ____ .    ____ ____ .    ____
CENTER            Center    ____ _ ____ ____ _ ____ ____ _ ____
CENTER2           Center (.5x)  __ _ __ __ _ __ __ _ __ __ _ __

CENTERX2          Center (2x) _____ __ _____ _____ __ ____
DASHDOT           Dash dot  __ . __ . __ . __ . __ . __ . __ .
DASHDOT2          Dash dot (.5x) _.__._.__._.__._.__._.__._.__._.
DASHDOTX2         Dash dot (2x) ____  .   ____  .    ____  .
DASHED            Dashed    __ __ __ __ __ __ __ __ __ __ __ __ __

DASHED2           Dashed (.5x)  _ _ _ _ _ _ _ _ _ _ _ _ _ _ _ _
DASHEDX2          Dashed (2x) ____ ____ ____ ____ ____ ____ ____
DIVIDE            Divide    ____ . . ____ ____ . . ____ . . ____
DIVIDE2           Divide (.5x)  __.._.__.._.__.._.__.._.__.._.
DIVIDEX2          Divide (2x) _____  .  .  _____  _____  .

DOT               Dot . . . . . . . . . . . . . . . . . . . . .
DOT2              Dot (.5x) ................................................
DOTX2             Dot (2x) .   .   .   .   .   .   .   .   .   .
HIDDEN            Hidden    __ __ __ __ __ __ __ __ __ __ __ __
HIDDEN2           Hidden (.5x)  _ _ _ _ _ _ _ _ _ _ _ _ _ _ _ _

HIDDENX2          Hidden (2x) ____ ____ ____ ____ ____ ____ ____
PHANTOM           Phantom   _____ __ __ _____ __ __ _____ __
PHANTOM2          Phantom (.5x) ___ _ _ ___ _ _ ___ _ _ ___
PHANTOMX2         Phantom (2x) _____    _____    _____

ACAD_ISO02W100    ISO dash  __ __ __ __ __ __ __ __ __ __ __ __ __
ACAD_ISO03W100    ISO dash space  __     __     __     __     __
ACAD_ISO04W100    ISO long-dash dot  ____ . ____ . ____ . ____ . .
ACAD_ISO05W100    ISO long-dash double-dot  ____ ..   ____ ..   .
ACAD_ISO06W100    ISO long-dash triple-dot  ____ ...  ____ ...  .
ACAD_ISO07W100    ISO dot . . . . . . . . . . . . . . . . . . . .

ACAD_ISO08W100    ISO long-dash short-dash  ____ __ ____ __ ____ __
ACAD_ISO09W100    ISO long-dash double-short-dash  ____ __ __ ____
ACAD_ISO10W100    ISO dash dot  __ . __ . __ . __ . __ . __ . __ .
ACAD_ISO11W100    ISO double-dash dot  __ __ . __ __ . __ __ . __
ACAD_ISO12W100    ISO dash double-dot  __ . . __ . . __ . . __ .

ACAD_ISO13W100    ISO double-dash double-dot  __ __ . . __ __ . .
ACAD_ISO14W100    ISO dash triple-dot  __ . . . __ . . . __ . . .
ACAD_ISO15W100    ISO double-dash triple-dot  __ __ . . . __ __ .
FENCELINE1        Fenceline circle ----O-----O----O-----O----O---
FENCELINE2        Fenceline square ----[]-----[]----[]-----[]----

TRACKS            Tracks -|-|-|-|-|-|-|-|-|-|-|-|-|-|-|-|-|-|-|-|
BATTING           Batting SSSSSSSSSSSSSSSSSSSSSSSSSSSSSSSSSSSSSSSS
HOT_WATER_SUPPLY  Hot water supply ---- HW ---- HW ---- HW ----
GAS_LINE          Gas line ----GAS----GAS----GAS----GAS----GAS---
ZIGZAG            Zig zag /\/\/\/\/\/\/\/\/\/\/\/\/\/\/\/\/\/\/\/
```

FIGURE 15.1: The lines in this list of standard linetypes were generated with the underscore key (_) and the period (.), and are only rough representations of the actual lines.

Creating a New Linetype

Next, try creating a new linetype.

1. At the ?/Create/Load/Set: prompt, enter **C**.

2. At the Name of linetype to create: prompt, enter **Custom** as the name of your new linetype.

3. Notice that the file dialog box you see next is named Create or Append Linetype File. You need to enter the name of the linetype file you want to create or add to. If you pick the default linetype file, ACAD, your new linetype is added to the Acad.lin file. If you choose to create a new linetype file, Auto-CAD opens a file containing the linetype you create and adds .lin to the filename you supply.

4. Let's assume you want to start a new linetype file. Enter **Newline** in the File Name input box.

NOTE

If you had accepted the default linetype file, ACAD, the prompt in step 5 would say Wait, checking if linetype already defined.... This protects you from inadvertently overwriting an existing linetype you may want to keep.

5. At the Descriptive text: prompt, enter a text description of your linetype. You can use any keyboard character as part of your description, but the actual linetype can be composed only of a series of lines, points, and blank spaces. For this exercise, enter:

   Custom - My own center line _____ _ _____ ~CS

   using the underscore key (_) to simulate the appearance of your line.

6. At the Enter pattern (on next line): prompt, enter the following numbers, known as the *linetype code* (after the a that appears automatically):

   1.0,-.125,.25,-.125

WARNING

If you use the Set option of the –Linetype command to set a new default linetype, you will get that linetype no matter what layer you are on.

7. At the New definition written to file. ?/Create/Load/
Set: prompt, press Enter to exit the –Linetype command.

Remember, once you've created a linetype, you must load it in order to use it.

TIP

You can also open the Acad.lin or other .lin file with Windows Notepad and add the descriptive text and linetype code directly to the end of the file.

The Linetype Code

In step 6 of the previous exercise, you entered a series of numbers separated by commas. This is the linetype code, representing the different lengths of the components that make up the linetype. The separate elements of the linetype code are explained as follows:

▶ The 1.0 following the a is the length of the first part of the line. (The a that begins the linetype definition is a code that is applied to all linetypes.)

▶ The first –.125 is the blank or broken part of the line. The minus sign tells AutoCAD that the line is *not* to be drawn for the specified length, which is 0.125 units in this example.

▶ Next comes the positive value of 0.25. This value tells AutoCAD to draw a line segment 0.25 units long after the blank part of the line.

▶ The last negative value, –.125, again tells AutoCAD to skip drawing the line for the distance of 0.125 units.

This series of numbers represents the one segment that is repeated to form the line (see Figure 15.2). You could also create a very complex linetype that looks like a random broken line, as in Figure 15.3.

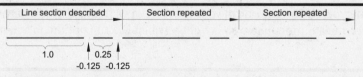

FIGURE 15.2: Linetype description with plotted line

Part iv

FIGURE 15.3: Random broken line

You may be wondering what purpose the a serves at the beginning of the linetype code. A linetype is composed of a series of line segments and points. The a, which is supplied by AutoCAD automatically, is a code that forces the linetype to start and end on a line segment rather than a blank space in the series of lines. At times, AutoCAD stretches the last line segment to force this condition, as shown in Figure 15.4.

Stretched   Stretched

FIGURE 15.4: AutoCAD stretches the beginning and the end of the line as necessary.

NOTE
The values you enter for the line-segment lengths are multiplied by the Ltscale factor, so be sure to enter values for the *plotted* lengths.

As mentioned in the beginning of this section, you can also create linetypes outside AutoCAD by using a word processor or text editor such as Windows Notepad. The standard Acad.lin file looks like Figure 15.1 with the addition of the code used by AutoCAD to determine the line-segment lengths.

Normally, to use a linetype you have created, you have to load it, through either the Layer or the Linetype dialog box (Format ➤ Layers, or Format ➤ Linetype). If you use one of your own linetypes frequently, you may want to create a button macro so it will be available as an option on a menu.

Creating Complex Linetypes

A complex linetype is one that incorporates text or special graphics. For example, if you want to show an underground gas line in a site plan, you normally show a line with an intermittent G. Fences are often shown with an intermittent X (see Figure 15.5).

For the graphics needed to compose complex linetypes, use any of the symbols found in the AutoCAD font files. Just create a text style using these symbol fonts, and then specify the appropriate symbol by using its corresponding letter in the linetype description.

To create a linetype that includes text, use the same linetype code described earlier, with the addition of the necessary font file information in brackets. For example, say you want to create the linetype for the underground gas line. You add the following to your Acad.lin file:

```
*Gas line -- G -- G --
a,1.0,-0.25, ["G", standard, S=.2, R=0, X=-.1, Y=-.1], -0.25
```

The information in the square brackets describes the characteristics of the text. The actual text that you want to appear in the line is surrounded by quotation marks. Next are the text style, scale, rotation angle, X displacement, and Y displacement.

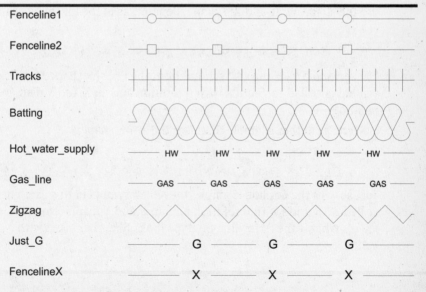

FIGURE 15.5: Samples of complex linetypes

Part iv

WARNING

You cannot use the –Linetype command to define complex linetypes. Instead, you must open the Acad.lin file using a text editor, such as Windows Notepad, and add the linetype information to the end of the file. Make sure you don't duplicate the name of an existing linetype.

You can substitute the rotation angle (the R value) with an A, as in the following example:

```
a,1.0,-0.25, ["G", standard, S=.2 A=0, X=-.1, Y=-.1], -0.25
```

This setting has the effect of keeping the text at the same angle, regardless of the line's direction. Notice that in this sample, the X and Y values are −.1; these values will center the Gs on the line. The scale value of .2 will cause the text to be .2 units high, so −.1 is half the height.

In addition to fonts, you can also specify shapes for linetype definitions. Instead of letters, shapes display symbols. Shapes are stored not as drawings, but as definition files, similar to text-font files. In fact, shape files have the same .shx filename extension as text files and are also defined similarly.

To use a shape in a linetype code, you use the same format as shown previously for text. However, instead of using a letter and style name, you use the shape name and the shape filename, as in the following example:

```
*Capline, ====
a,1.0,-0.25,[CAP,ES.SHX,S=.5,R=0,X=-.1,Y=-.1],-0.25
```

This example uses the CAP symbol from the Es.shx shape file. The symbol is scaled to .5 units with 0 rotation and an X and Y displacement of −.1.

Here is another example that uses the arrow shape:

```
*Arrowline, --|---|---|
a,1.0,-0.25,[ARROW,ARROW.SHX,S=.5,R=0,X=-.1,Y=-.1],-0.25
```

Just as with the Capline example, the ARROW symbol in this example is scaled to .5 units with 0 rotation and an X and Y displacement of −.1. Here's what it the Arrowline linetype looks like when used with a spline.

CREATING HATCH PATTERNS

AutoCAD provides several predefined hatch patterns you can choose from (see Figure 15.6), but you can also create your own. This section demonstrates the basic elements of pattern definition.

Unlike linetypes, hatch patterns cannot be created while you are in an AutoCAD file. The pattern definitions are contained in an external file named Acad.pat. This file can be opened and edited with a text editor that can handle ASCII files, such as the Windows Notepad. Here is one hatch pattern definition from that file:

```
*square,Small aligned squares
0, 0,0, 0,.125, .125,-.125
90, 0,0, 0,.125, .125,-.125
```

You can see some similarities between pattern descriptions and line-type descriptions. They both start with a line of descriptive text, and then give numeric values defining the pattern. However, the numbers in pattern descriptions have a different meaning. This example shows two lines of information. Each line represents a line in the pattern. The first line determines the horizontal line component of the pattern, and the second line represents the vertical component. Figure 15.7 shows the hatch pattern defined in the example.

A pattern is made up of *line groups*. A line group is like a linetype that is arrayed a specified distance to fill the area to be hatched. A line group is defined by a line of code, much as a linetype is defined. In the square pattern, for instance, two lines—one horizontal and one vertical—are used. Each of these lines is duplicated in a fashion that makes the lines appear as boxes when they are combined. Figure 15.8 illustrates this point.

Part iv

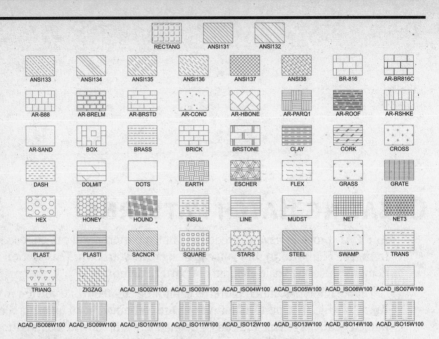

FIGURE 15.6: The standard hatch patterns

FIGURE 15.7: Square pattern

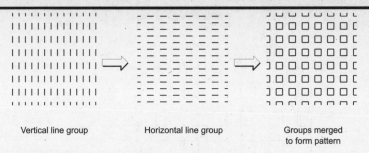

Vertical line group   Horizontal line group   Groups merged
to form pattern

FIGURE 15.8: The individual and combined line groups

Look at the first line in the definition:

```
0, 0,0, 0,.125, .125,-.125
```

This example shows a series of numbers separated by commas; it represents one line group. It actually contains four sets of information, separated by blank spaces:

- The first component is the 0 at the beginning. This value indicates the angle of the line group, as determined by the line's orientation. In this case, it is 0 for a horizontal line that runs from left to right.

- The next component is the origin of the line group, 0,0. This does not mean that the line actually begins at the drawing origin (see Figure 15.9). It gives you a reference point to determine the location of other line groups involved in generating the pattern.

- The next component is 0,.125. It determines the distance for arraying the line and in what direction, as illustrated in Figure 15.10. This value is like a relative coordinate indicating x and y distances for a rectangular array. It is not based on the drawing coordinates, but on a coordinate system relative to the orientation of the line. For a line oriented at a 0° angle, the code 0,.125 indicates a precisely vertical direction. For a line oriented at a 45° angle, the code 0,.125 represents a 135° direction. In this example, the duplication occurs 90° in relation to the line group, because the x value is 0. Figure 15.11 illustrates this point.

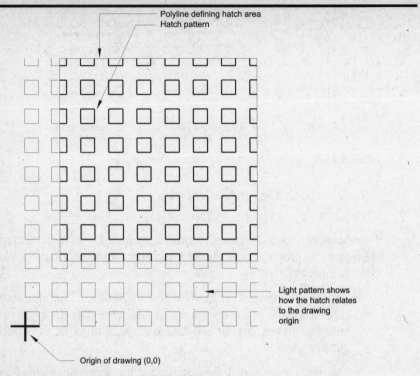

FIGURE 15.9: The origin of the patterns

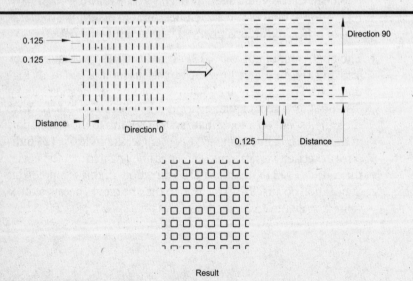

Result

FIGURE 15.10: The distance and direction of duplication

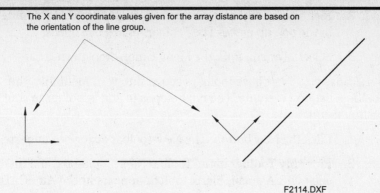

The X and Y coordinate values given for the array distance are based on the orientation of the line group.

F2114.DXF

FIGURE 15.11: How the direction of the line group copy is determined

▶ The last component is the actual description of the line pattern. This value is equivalent to the value given when you create a linetype. Positive values are line segments, and negative values are blank segments. This part of the line-group definition works exactly as in the linetype definitions you studied in the previous section.

This system of defining hatch patterns may seem somewhat limiting, but you can actually do a lot with it. Autodesk managed to come up with 53 patterns—and that was really only scratching the surface.

TIP

If you want to include thick lines in your hatch patterns, you have to "build up" line widths with multiple linetype definitions.

IF YOU WANT TO EXPERIMENT...

In the first part of this chapter, you learned that you can create your own toolbars, and then you went on to learn how to create your own menu. Try adding custom toolbars to the menu you created in the "Adding Your Own Pull-Down Menu section."

1. If you haven't done so already, load the Mymenu.mnu file into the AutoCAD menu bar.

Part iv

2. Right-click a button in any toolbar, and then select Customize in the pop-up menu. The Toolbars dialog box opens.

3. Select Mymenu from the Menu Group drop-down list.

Because you don't have toolbars coded into your menu file, the Toolbars list box is empty. The next step is to add a toolbar to your custom menu.

1. Click the New button. The New Toolbar dialog box appears.

2. Enter **My Toolbar** in the Toolbar Name input box, and then click OK. A small, blank toolbar appears in the AutoCAD window.

3. Click Customize in the Toolbars dialog box. The Customize Toolbars dialog box appears.

4. Open the Categories pull-down list. Notice that the list contains the main categories of commands.

5. Choose Draw from the list. The list box displays all the tools available for the Draw category. Notice that the dialog box offers several additional arc and circle tools not found in the Draw toolbar.

6. Click the first tool in the top row: the Line tool. You'll see a description of the tool in the Description box at the bottom of the dialog box.

7. Click and drag the Line tool from the Customize Toolbars dialog box into the new toolbar you just created. The Line tool now appears in your toolbar.

8. Click and drag the Arc Start End Direction tool to your new toolbar.

9. Exit the Customize Toolbars dialog box and the Toolbars dialog box.

AutoCAD saves your addition in a file called Mymenu.mns, which contains all the code you wrote when you created the Mymenu.mnu file, plus the code needed for the toolbar you added in this last exercise. You can preserve your toolbar additions to your menu file by making a copy of Mymenu.mns and renaming it to Mymenu.mnu.

WHAT'S NEXT?

In this chapter, you have created custom menus and toolbars. In addition, you have seen how to code custom linetypes and hatch patterns. In the next chapter, you will be introduced to the Visual Basic for Applications programming language within AutoCAD. You will how to create a custom graphical user interface for a simple application.

Chapter 16

DEVELOPING A SIMPLE VBA APPLICATION

I n this chapter, you will learn how to create a simple Visual Basic for Applications (VBA) application through a series of tutorials. You will learn how to employ visual tools to create the graphical user interface, and write code to execute simple commands. You will also explore the basics of the Visual Basic environment by using its features to create practical code that you can reuse for repetitive tasks.

Adapted from *Mastering™ AutoCAD® VBA*
by Marion Cottingham
ISBN 0-7821-2871-8   704 pages $49.99

If you consider yourself an intermediate user of AutoCAD VBA and have already written some successful VBA code, you may want to skip this chapter—or even just skim it, depending on your experience. The material covered in Chapter 19, "VBA Programming Concepts," will always be useful to you as a reference.

ADVANTAGES OF USING VBA WITH AUTOCAD

VBA is a programming environment created by Microsoft that is built into applications to automate operations. It provides tools that you can drag and drop to build a Graphical User Interface (GUI), and a programming language that you can use to interact with AutoCAD objects. Using VBA with AutoCAD allows you to customize your AutoCAD application in seemingly unlimited ways. In this chapter, you'll see how simple it is to automate repetitive tasks. With the time saved, you'll be free to concentrate on applying your artistic talents and engineering skills to make your drawings more intricate.

Once you begin writing VBA code, you'll quickly realize just how easy it is to access objects from the AutoCAD and VBA object libraries. You'll soon be able to call on the power of these objects while gaining a deeper insight into AutoCAD's features. As you start to see the benefits that VBA macros and applications can provide, you'll want to spend your extra time customizing even more tasks. Before you know it, you'll have a whole library of reusable macros and applications at your fingertips!

TIP

A *macro* is a group of code statements, usually not very long or complicated, that is useful in automating a repetitive task. In your work at the computer, most likely you've used them already without realizing it.

TIP

An *application* is a program that has been created to perform a specific task. This task can be something very simple, such as prompting the user for their name and password, or something very substantial and complex, such as AutoCAD itself.

Another not-so-obvious advantage of learning AutoCAD VBA is that your skills are transferable to a growing number of other applications that have VBA capability. These applications include all those in the Microsoft Office family of applications, such as Access, Word, and Excel, in addition to Microsoft Visual Basic itself and about 200 other licensees.

VBA interfaces with applications by communicating and controlling objects through the application's object libraries, rather than by having any special connection to the application's inner workings. All you need to know are the names of the objects involved, and you can access their functionality with VBA code. You'll find the object names meaningful and easy to remember, such as ThisDrawing (an object in AutoCAD), ThisDocument (an object in Word), and ThisWorkbook (an object in Excel). As you enter the names of objects in your code, the editing features of VBA's Integrated Development Environment (IDE) offer you drop-down lists of elements particular to the type of object you've entered. You'll see how this works in Chapter 17.

You can use a macro to automate just about anything, but it is probably most productive to start with the tasks you have to do time and time again. Why not think about those boring, uninspiring jobs you hate doing the most, and start with them? These are probably tasks that are time consuming and error prone, so implementing them in macros or applications will not only increase your productivity but lift your spirits by removing some of the tedious tasks that make you yawn just by thinking about them (such as adding all the required bits and pieces of information for starting a new drawing; or perhaps you've found that you regularly draw the same items over and over again).

After you've successfully developed VBA code that works the way you want it to, it's guaranteed to perform correctly and reliably each time you run it. Now *there's* an incentive to learn VBA. So let's begin by examining the interface where you will write your code—the Visual Basic Editor.

THE AUTOCAD VBA ENVIRONMENT

The Visual Basic Editor is the integrated environment in which you develop all your VBA code. As you can see from Figure 16.1, the IDE has its own GUI. Its windows provide all the tools required for creating, editing, debugging, and running your macros and applications. With this much functionality, the IDE is almost a stand-alone application, except

Part iv

that it can only be opened from the AutoCAD window and does not remain open after AutoCAD has been closed.

TIP

The term *VBA Editor* is often used synonymously with the IDE even though the IDE provides more than just editing features.

The VBA IDE can be opened from the AutoCAD window in a variety of ways:

- ► Type **vbaide** next to the Command prompt in the Command line.
- ► Choose Tools ➤ Macro ➤ Visual Basic Editor.
- ► Use the key-combination (shortcut) Alt+F11.

In the examples throughout this chapter, I've used menu commands in instructions. Most commands can also be accessed through a toolbar button or a key combination, so occasionally I give an alternative access method as a reminder that there are other ways to invoke commands. The access method you use is up to your personal preference.

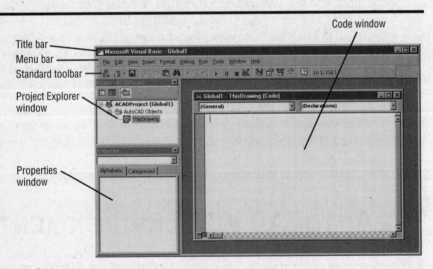

FIGURE 16.1: AutoCAD's VBA environment

Chapter 18 takes you on a guided tour of the IDE and discusses some of its features in more detail.

Creating UserForm Modules

A *module* is just a container for VBA code, and a *UserForm module* is a window (or dialog box) that can be considered a powerful extension to the AutoCAD GUI. You decide what controls to place on your UserForm in order to perform the tasks required by your application. You can place labels and text boxes in which users can enter the information your program needs in order to run. You can use option buttons and check boxes to give users the chance to select the items they require. In fact, just about any control you've seen in the applications running under Windows is available for use in the VBA IDE.

Adding a UserForm Module to Your Application

To add a UserForm module to your application, follow these steps:

1. Start AutoCAD and choose Tools ➢ Macro ➢ Visual Basic Editor. The VBA IDE opens.

2. Choose Insert ➢ UserForm. UserForm1 appears, containing a title bar with a Close button, as shown in Figure 16.2.

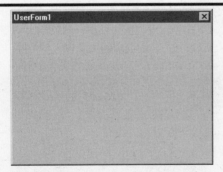

FIGURE 16.2: A brand-new UserForm

A UserForm is the only module that can be viewed from the IDE in two different ways:

- ▶ Graphically, by choosing View ➢ Object to open the UserForm window (see Figure 16.2)

- ▶ With code, by choosing View ➢ Code to open the Code window.

Part iv

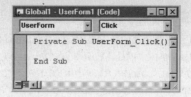

Opening the Code window displays the event procedure that will run if the UserForm is clicked. There are many events to choose from, but double-clicking any control automatically displays the primary event that you'll most likely want to respond to. You'll see how to access the other events later in this chapter, in the section "Coding Event Procedures."

Puttering Around in the Toolbox

VBA provides a set of common controls in a Toolbox window (see Figure 16.3). You can simply drag and drop individual controls onto a User-Form to develop GUI features for your application.

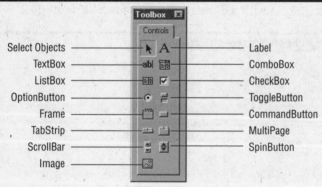

FIGURE 16.3: Controls in the standard Toolbox

If the Toolbox isn't on display, select the Toolbox command from the View menu or click the Toolbox icon at the end of the Standard toolbar. Both of these actions will be available for selection only when a UserForm has been added to a project and is being viewed in its graphical form rather than as a Code window. To view a UserForm graphically, simply choose View ➢ Object.

These controls are all available for you to drag and drop onto your User-Form, making AutoCAD VBA a powerful visual programming system that's extremely efficient at quickly developing the GUI for a project—you can virtually design your whole GUI using only the mouse.

You will recognize most of the controls in the Toolbox because you have already experienced using them in other applications. Following are brief descriptions of what each control does:

Select Objects   Resizes and moves a control after it has been drawn on a UserForm. If you've double-clicked another control to insert multiple instances of it on the UserForm without returning to the Toolbox, you can click the Select Objects control to stop.

Label   Displays text that you've assigned to its Caption property at design time or in code. A Label control is often used to display information or indicate to a user what data should be entered into a TextBox control. The text displayed by the Label control is strictly read-only and cannot be changed by the user during runtime.

TextBox   Allows users to input textual information during runtime. It is common practice to assign the empty string (" ") to this control's Text property to initialize it or to clear out any data that's no longer required.

ComboBox   Combines the functionality of the TextBox control with that of the ListBox control to provide the user with the option of entering text into the TextBox, or clicking the down-arrow button and selecting an item from a drop-down list. When an item is selected from the list, it is automatically displayed in the text box at the top of the ComboBox. You can set the Style property of this control to restrict the user to selecting an item from the ListBox. Doing so eliminates the need to test whether the user has entered a valid value.

ListBox   Enables the user to select one or more items from a list. If there are too many items to be displayed at once, a scroll bar will automatically appear. Even so, this control generally takes up more space than a ComboBox control, which needs only the same amount of space on the UserForm as a TextBox control.

CheckBox   Enables the user to check (select) zero or more boxes from a group of CheckBoxes. This control is often used to indicate whether items are true or false, or to answer yes or no to questions. CheckBoxes are similar in function to OptionButtons, except that they allow more than one item to be selected at the same time.

OptionButton   Used in groups of options to allow selection of one option from the group. When only one group of Option-Buttons is required, it can be placed directly onto the UserForm. When there is more than one group, you use Frame controls to separate groups, to enable one OptionButton per group to be selected. You determine the OptionButton that will be the default selection. If the user selects another OptionButton from the same group, the old one is automatically deselected.

ToggleButton   Toggles between on or off, true or false, and yes or no. When clicked, its appearance changes to match its value; it toggles between a raised button appearance (off) and a pushed-in appearance (on). The Picture property of this control allows you to display a selection of options to the user in a graphical way.

Frame   Allows a UserForm to be divided into areas where you can group other controls, such as OptionButtons and Check-Boxes. The Frame control and the controls inside it then behave collectively as a single entity. When you move the Frame, all the controls inside it move, too; when you disable the Frame, all its controls become disabled. Frames are typically used to create groups of OptionButtons on a UserForm, so that an option from each group can be selected rather than just a single option.

CommandButton   Used when you want something to happen as soon as the button is clicked. It is often used in dialog boxes with the caption OK for users to click when they've finished reading the message displayed to them. This control is useful for running macros by calling the macro in response to the control being clicked.

TabStrip   Contains several pages, each displaying an identical set of controls. Adding a control to any page of the TabStrip control makes it appear on all pages. This control is used to enable viewing of several sets of data containing the same kind of information, one set per page. You provide the code to update the information in the controls according to the tab selected by the user. For example, you could display the name, address, and telephone number of your clients, one client per page.

MultiPage   Similar to the TabStrip control in that it has several pages that can be accessed by clicking their tabs. Each page from the MultiPage control has its own individual set of controls to enable the display of different kinds of information on each page, although the information is typically related in some way. For example, you could display the name and address of a client on the first page, and information about the client's orders on other pages. In such a scheme, you would need to create a Multi-Page control for each client.

ScrollBar   Allows you to place a scroll bar on a UserForm. The scroll bar can be either vertical or horizontal, depending on its width and height. This control provides scrolling for controls that do not have scroll bars added automatically. Appropriate values are set for the control's Min and Max properties to define the limits for the Value property of the ScrollBar. The control's Value property will be set to a value dependent on the position of the slider bar in relation to each end of the scroll bar.

SpinButton   Functions similarly to a ScrollBar control but doesn't have a slider bar. Up- or down-arrow buttons are displayed for the user to click in order to increment or decrement the number assigned to the control's Value property. The Value is typically displayed in another control, such as a TextBox or a Label.

Image   Used to display graphics stored in the major graphical formats, such as bitmaps (`.bmp`), GIFs (`.gif`), JPEGs (`.jpg`), metafiles (`.wmf`), and icons (`.ico`). The image can be cropped, sized, or zoomed as required to fit the control's size. Image controls can be used as fancy command buttons or as toolbar buttons and can even display simple animations.

You can place as many instances of each control as you like onto the same UserForm. Visual Basic gives each instance a default name based on the name of the class it belongs to, appended to a sequential number—this name enables each object to be uniquely identified. Visual Basic also assigns the properties of the control's position and dimensions on the UserForm based on where you've placed it and what size you've made it. All other properties are assigned a default setting.

Placing a Toolbox Control in a UserForm

This tutorial shows you how to drag and drop a TextBox control from the Toolbox onto a UserForm. The same technique is used to place any of the other controls onto a UserForm.

Part iv

1. Click the TextBox icon in the Toolbox and, without pressing the mouse button, move the mouse cursor over the UserForm.

After you click the TextBox icon, the button changes its appearance to look pressed in.

The mouse cursor changes, too, as it moves over the boundary of the UserForm. It becomes a cross alongside the TextBox control's icon.

2. Move the mouse cursor to the position where you want one of the corners of your text box to be, and press the left mouse button. While holding down the mouse button, move the cursor around and watch a rectangle with dashed lines follow the cursor, with one corner anchored at the position you've just selected. This rectangle indicates the size and position for the new text box that will be created when you release the mouse button.

3. Still holding down the mouse button, move the cursor to the corner diagonal to the initial (anchored) one and release the mouse button. The new text box object replaces the dashed rectangle on the screen:

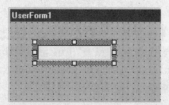

This becomes the new active control, as indicated by the handles and thick border that now appear around the rectangle. These can be used to make further adjustments to the size and position of the text box.

CHANGING THE DIMENSIONS AND POSITION OF A TOOLBOX CONTROL

Click any control on a UserForm to make it the active control. Once active, the control is enclosed by a thick border with eight handles placed around it. You can click and drag these handles to change the position and dimensions of the control, as follows:

▶ If you move the cursor directly over the thick border but not on top of a handle, the cursor changes to a cross with two double-headed arrows to allow you to reposition the whole control without changing its size. Simply click and hold down the mouse button and drag the control to its new position.

▶ If you move the cursor directly over any handle, the cursor changes to a double-headed arrow (shown here). This cursor allows you to drag and drop the handle to change the size of the control while maintaining its position.

Now that you have an understanding of how to place components on your GUI, it's time to use these skills to develop your first simple application—I'm sure you're ready to go.

DEVELOPING YOUR FIRST APPLICATION

For your first application, you'll work with the Metric-Imperial Converter application, which converts metric measurements to imperial, and vice versa. This application uses two text boxes, as shown in Figure 16.4. The interface allows the user to enter imperial measurements in yards into the first text box, and then converts the measurement to metric and displays the results in the second text box. Alternatively, the user can enter metric measurements in meters into the second text box, and the application converts the value to imperial and displays it in the first text box.

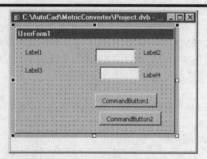

FIGURE 16.4: GUI for the Metric-Imperial Converter application before any properties have been updated

One command button is needed for the user to click in order to tell the application that the measurement has been entered. The second command button allows the user to stop the application.

Creating the GUI

You can create the GUI for the Metric-Imperial Converter application using a single UserForm.

1. Choose Tools ➤ Macro ➤ Visual Basic Editor to open the IDE.

2. Choose Insert ➤ UserForm to create a UserForm. The graphical representation of the UserForm is displayed, along with the Toolbox.

3. Drag and drop a TextBox control from the Toolbox onto the UserForm and place it near the top right. In Figure 16.4, the two empty boxes are TextBox controls.

The Name property of this text box is assigned as TextBox1 by default. The Name property of a control is the first item listed in the control's Properties window, which you'll see in the upcoming section "Setting Captions in the Properties Window." Default names all start with the type of control followed by a number to denote its place in the sequence of controls of the same type. So, the next text box you add will be named TextBox2.

4. Drag and drop a Label control and place it to the left of the TextBox control.

The Name property of this Label control is Label1 by default, which is also the initial value assigned to its Caption property. The Label1 control is used to label the TextBox so that the user knows what its contents represent and can enter appropriate values.

5. Drag and drop a second label and position it to the right of the TextBox control. The Name property of this Label control is Label2 by default.

6. Drag and drop a second text box with two accompanying labels, and place them immediately below the first text box and labels. The default Name properties of these controls are TextBox2, Label3, and Label4.

7. Drag and drop a command button from the Toolbox onto the UserForm, placing it below the second text box. The default Name and Caption properties of this command button are both CommandButton1.

8. Drag and drop a second command button and place it directly below the first. The Name and Caption properties of this command button are—you guessed it—CommandButton2.

9. Now that all the controls required by the GUI have been added to the UserForm, adjust the UserForm's dimensions by dragging and dropping its borders until it is a snug fit for all the controls you've placed inside it. The layout of controls should look similar to the one shown in Figure 16.4.

HOW DEFAULT SETTINGS ARE INITIATED

A lot of the default object settings, such as the color of the title bar and background, are retrieved from the display scheme set in the Microsoft Windows environment of the PC on which the application is running. In the examples throughout this chapter, the Windows Standard display scheme is used. If your PC is set to a different scheme, your GUI will have a similar appearance to some of the other Windows applications that run on your PC. Some default settings, such as those specifying position and dimensions, are determined as you drag and drop controls onto UserForms.

You can find out the display scheme setting for your PC by clicking the Display icon in Control Panel and selecting the Appearance tab in the Display Properties dialog box—the current setting is displayed in the Scheme list box.

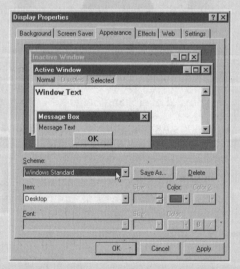

Setting Captions in the Properties Window

The following tutorial shows you how to set the Caption property of User-Form1 in the Metric-Imperial Converter application:

1. If the Properties window is not already open, choose View ➤ Properties Window.

2. The Properties window appears, with property names listed in the left column and their settings listed in the right column. Select the appropriate tab to list the properties in this window alphabetically, as shown in Figure 16.5, or categorically, as shown in Figure 16.6. The list of properties belongs to the object named in the list box at the top (the active object), which is followed by the class the object belongs to.

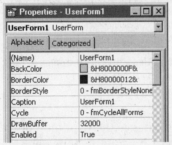

FIGURE 16.5: Properties window Alphabetic tab

FIGURE 16.6: Properties window Categorized tab

3. If the object named at the top of the Properties window is not already UserForm1, select UserForm1 from the drop-down list.

This drop-down list contains all the objects associated with the active UserForm. When UserForm1 is selected, all the properties listed in the window now belong to UserForm1. The graphical representation of UserForm1 becomes the active object and appears with a thick border and eight sizing handles.

4. Scroll the list of properties until the Caption property becomes visible in the left column; select it by double-clicking it. Both the Caption property and the setting UserForm1 are highlighted, and the insertion point (I-beam mouse pointer) blinks at the end of the highlighted text in the settings column on the right.

5. Type **Metric-Imperial Converter**. This text replaces the highlighted setting for the Caption property, and the text in the title bar of UserForm1 is updated as you enter each keystroke.

TIP

Although the Name and Caption properties start with the same default setting, they are two distinct properties. So, the Name property remains set to User-Form1 even after you change the Caption property.

6. Repeat steps 2 through 5 to change the Caption properties of the labels and command buttons to those shown in Table 16.1.

TABLE 16.1 CONTROLS AND THEIR CAPTION PROPERTIES

CONTROL	CAPTION
Label1	Imperial Units
Label2	Yards
Label3	Metric Units
Label4	Metres
CommandButton1	Convert
CommandButton2	Close

TIP

The Properties window can be opened by selecting any graphical object and choosing View ➣ Properties Window, or by right-clicking and selecting Properties from the shortcut menu, or by pressing the F4 function key.

The VBA Code Window

The Code window is where you enter the code that will interact with the user or manipulate AutoCAD objects. When you start a new AutoCAD project, a drawing object is automatically created and made the active document. You can refer to this object in code by its Name property, This-Drawing. When you open the IDE and look in the Project Explorer window, the ThisDrawing object will be the only object listed (shown previously in Figure 16.1).

Every object listed in the Project Explorer window has its own Code window. One way to open the Code window for a particular object is to double-click it from the Project Explorer window. Here is the Code window for ThisDrawing:

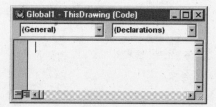

Displaying the Code Window

When double-clicked in the Project Explorer window, all the modules except UserForms will immediately display the Code window. When a UserForm is double-clicked, its graphical representation is displayed in the UserForm window. You must then double-click anywhere inside this UserForm window to display its Code window.

Every Code window has a drop-down list box of objects on the left, and a drop-down list box of procedures on the right. The Object list contains all the objects and controls attached to that module. In the example shown here, all the controls placed on UserForm1 are displayed.

Part iv

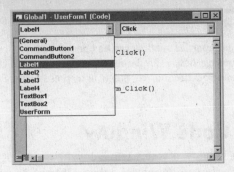

You can tell which UserForm the Code window belongs to by looking at the caption on the title bar. Notice in the preceding example that an object named UserForm appears in the drop-down list. Because a User-Form has its own Code window, there is no need to append a distinguishing number after UserForm when you're referring to it in code in its own Code window. The Procedure list box on the right contains a list of all the procedures (including event procedures) associated with the object named in the Object box.

Coding Event Procedures

The following tutorial shows how to write the code to stop an application in response to the user's clicking the Close button:

1. If the Code window is displayed, choose View ➤ Object to display the graphical representation of UserForm1. Double-click CommandButton2. The Code window appears, containing the skeleton code for the `CommandButton2_Click` event procedure, with the I-beam cursor blinking in the blank line.

2. As shown in Figure 16.7, type
   ```
   Unload Me
   ```

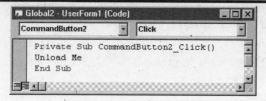

FIGURE 16.7: The Code Window showing the CommandButton2_Click event procedure

Now you're ready to begin coding the response you want given to the user who's entering data into one of the text boxes. When the Metric-Imperial Converter application is run for the first time, both text boxes will be empty. The user enters a measurement into one text box and clicks CommandButton1 to convert the measurement and display the result in the other text box. When CommandButton1 is clicked, the application checks which text box contains the measurement so that it knows which conversion is required. If the user requires another, subsequent conversion and enters another measurement into a text box, the application must clear the other text box of data so that the correct conversion is used. The following steps show you how these actions are coded:

1. Open the Code window and select TextBox1 from the Object list.

2. Select KeyDown from the Procedure list, as shown in Figure 16.8.

FIGURE 16.8: Drop-down list of procedures (events) available for the TextBox class of object

3. In the skeleton TextBox1_KeyDown event procedure, where the Entry cursor is blinking, type

```
TextBox2.Text = ""
```

4. Select TextBox2 from the Object list, and select KeyDown from the Procedure list.

5. In the skeleton TextBox2_KeyDown event procedure, type

```
TextBox1.Text = ""
```

6. Select CommandButton1 from the Object list, and the skeleton (first and last lines) of its Click event procedure will appear.

7. Type the following code inside the skeleton:

```
If TextBox1.Text = "" Then
    TextBox1.Text = TextBox2.Text * 1.0936
Else
    TextBox2.Text = TextBox1.Text * 0.9144
End If
```

That's all the coding necessary for this conversion application. Listing 16.1 provides a numbered listing of all the code, followed by an analysis that describes what each statement does.

TIP

In the listing, the numbers preceding each line of code are not part of the actual code. They are provided to help you follow the discussion in the analysis.

Listing 16.1: Metric-Imperial Conversion Macro

```
1    Private Sub CommandButton1_Click()
2    If TextBox1.Text = "" Then
3        TextBox1.Text = TextBox2.Text * 1.0936
4    Else
5        TextBox2.Text = TextBox1.Text * 0.9144
6    End If
7    End Sub
8
9    Private Sub CommandButton2_Click()
10   End
11   End Sub
12
```

```
13  Private Sub TextBox1_KeyDown(
        ByVal KeyCode As MSForms.ReturnInteger,
        ByVal Shift As Integer)
14  TextBox2.Text = ""
15  End Sub
16
17  Private Sub TextBox2_KeyDown(
        ByVal KeyCode As MSForms.ReturnInteger,
        ByVal Shift As Integer)
18  TextBox1.Text = ""
19  End Sub
```

You'll find the code shown in Listing 16.1 quite straightforward. Let's go through it line by line:

▶ Line 1 is the opening statement and declares the CommandButton1_Click event procedure. The code in this event procedure will be executed when the user clicks the Convert command button. This statement, along with the End Sub statement in Line 7, is provided as a skeleton procedure by the IDE.

▶ Line 2 checks to see if the Text property of TextBox1 is empty, meaning that the user has entered meters into TextBox2; if so, the program executes the statement at Line 3. If TextBox1 isn't empty, it contains yards, and the statement in Line 5 is executed.

▶ Line 3 converts the meters entered into TextBox2 to yards and assigns the results to the Text property of TextBox1. The value of the Text property is displayed in the text box.

TIP

If conditions and Then...Else...End If... conditional structures can be thought of as two separate parts—the If code block and the Else code block.

▶ Line 4 starts the Else part of the If statement. Execution jumps to this point if the condition in the If statement (Line 2) is False. Line 4 also serves as an end marker for the statements in the If code block when the condition is True, in which case execution jumps to the End If statement at Line 6.

▶ Line 5 converts the yards entered into TextBox1 into meters and displays the results in TextBox2.

▶ Line 6 signifies the end of the If statement. Execution jumps to this point from the Else statement (Line 4) if the condition in Line 2 is True.

▶ Line 7 is the End Sub statement, which marks the end of the Command-Button1_Click event procedure.

▶ Line 8 is a blank line inserted to make it easier to see where one event procedure ends and another starts.

▶ Line 9 starts the CommandButton2_Click event procedure. This is the command button that has its Caption property set to Close (see step 6 of "Setting Captions in the Properties Window").

▶ Line 10 contains the End statement that stops executing your application by closing any open files and freeing any memory used by your application during runtime.

▶ Line 13 is the opening statement for the TextBox1_KeyDown event procedure. Unlike the Click event procedures found in Lines 1 and 9, the KeyDown event procedure is passed the integer value representing the ASCII code for the character just entered. This is useful if you want to validate the character input.

▶ Line 14 assigns an empty string to the Text property of TextBox2. The empty string is denoted by two double quote characters (" "). If a new conversion is starting, it doesn't make sense to have any values from the last conversion still displayed in the other text box.

▶ Line 18 clears the Text property of TextBox1 inside the TextBox2_KeyDown event procedure.

Running Your Application

To run your Metric-Imperial Converter application, follow these steps:

1. Ensure that UserForm1's window is open and selected.

2. Choose the Run ➢ Sub/UserForm menu command.

3. Test that your application is working by entering a value into one of the text boxes and clicking the Convert button. Verify that the results are what you expect. Repeat this verification for the other text box.

4. You may want to line up the controls on your UserForm to improve its appearance, as in Figure 16.9.

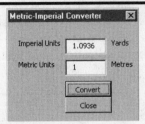

FIGURE 16.9: The finished version of the Metric-Imperial Converter application's GUI with the captions set

Saving Your Application

The IDE has one Save command on the File menu. The exact wording of this command depends on whether you have previously saved your project. Figure 16.10 shows the Save option on the File menu *before* the project has been saved to a file. Figure 16.11 shows how it appears afterward—with the full pathname of the project file.

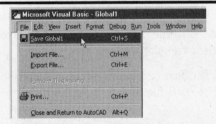

FIGURE 16.10: The File menu option for saving a VBA project that has never before been saved

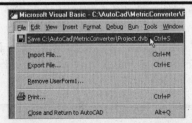

FIGURE 16.11: The File menu option for saving a VBA project that's been saved previously

To save your Metric-Imperial Converter project for the first time, follow these steps:

1. Choose File ➤ Save Global1. The Save As dialog box shown in Figure 16.12 appears. The controls in this dialog box will be familiar to you; they are much the same as those found in the Save As dialog boxes of other applications, including AutoCAD itself.

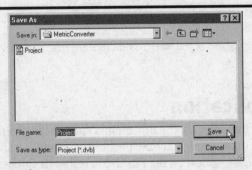

FIGURE 16.12: The Save As dialog box, ready to save your project to the DVB file of your choice

2. Use the controls to create a new directory and click Save. Everything associated with the current project will be saved in a single file with the extension .dvb.

3. Open the File menu. The Save command will now be followed by the full path of the DVB file in which you've just saved your project.

Returning to AutoCAD

You can use two menu commands to display the AutoCAD window, but they serve different purposes:

▶ Choose File ➤ Close and Return to AutoCAD, or use the shortcut Alt+Q. This command unloads the IDE completely before returning to AutoCAD.

▶ Click the View AutoCAD button at the left of the toolbar.

This button hides but does not close the IDE window and makes it accessible from the Taskbar. As you know from other Windows applications, you can much more quickly display a window that's already open by clicking its icon on the Taskbar rather than loading it again from scratch.

WHAT'S NEXT?

This chapter discussed how to create a simple VBA application. You have created a custom user interface and added event procedures to respond to users' actions. The next chapter will teach you how to create VBA macros.

Chapter 17

CREATING VBA MACROS

In this chapter, you'll learn about macros. You'll see how to use them as stand-alone programs for completing simple tasks, as well as for running applications. You'll also gain experience using the editing features of the IDE to help you enter code and to do the typing of code elements for you.

Adapted from *Mastering™ AutoCAD® VBA*
by Marion Cottingham
ISBN 0-7821-2871-8   704 pages $49.99

What Is a Macro?

A *macro* is a block of code statements that perform a particular task. The task might be as simple as displaying a dialog box to remind users to update something on their drawing, or it might be starting up a VBA application. Macros are normally quite short and contain only a few lines of code.

Macros are great relief for those boring repetitive jobs we all have to do from time to time. By creating macros to do these jobs for you, you are left with time free to concentrate on the creative work that's more enjoyable. So macros will not only improve your workflow but also add to your job satisfaction.

Only macros placed inside the ThisDrawing object or a standard module are included in the list of macros available from the AutoCAD window. (Remember, a *module* is just a container for VBA code.) The next two sections describe these two important VBA elements and explain when to use one or the other for your macros.

ThisDrawing Object

The ThisDrawing object contains all the property settings to control the attributes for the active drawing, as well as all the methods and procedures to manipulate the active drawing. For example, the following statement sets the height of the active drawing to 12 units:

```
ThisDrawing.Height = 12
```

And this statement saves the changes to the active drawing:

```
ThisDrawing.Save
```

The drawing object has its own Code window in the IDE, with two items in the Object list—General and AcadDocument (see Figure 17.1).

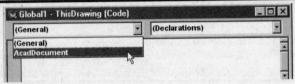

FIGURE 17.1: Code window for the ThisDrawing object

TIP

Macros that directly refer to specific objects in a one-off drawing should be placed in the `ThisDrawing` object, because these macros are dependent on the specific drawing objects' being available at runtime.

Standard Modules

A standard module is where you put macros that aren't associated with any particular UserForm or with the drawing document. Then you can reuse the code from the standard module by including it in various other applications. This is also a good place to put macros that are called from several other modules within the same application, because you avoid any duplication of code.

To insert a standard module into your project from the IDE, you can choose Insert ➤ Module. You can also insert a standard module from the AutoCAD window by following these steps:

1. Choose Tools ➤ Macro ➤ Macros. Figure 17.2 shows the Macros dialog box.

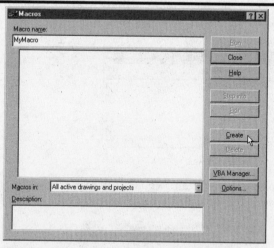

FIGURE 17.2: Macros dialog box in AutoCAD

2. Type the name of your macro into the Macro Name text box. The Create button becomes available for selection.

3. Click the Create button. The Select Project dialog box appears, with the macro's name displayed in the Select... instruction at the top of the dialog box. In the list of projects, Drawing1.dwg is the only item that appears.

4. Select Drawing1.dwg and click OK.

   A standard module is created and given the name Module1. The IDE opens, displaying Module1's Code window as shown in Figure 17.3. The macro appears in the Code window with the first and last lines already in place.

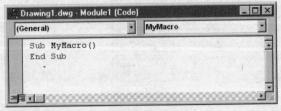

FIGURE 17.3: Code window for Module1

The Project Explorer now contains Module1 in its Modules list for the Drawing1.dwg project, and ThisDrawing in its AutoCAD Objects list.

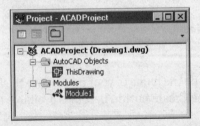

These lists can be expanded and contracted by clicking the little + and − symbols, just as you do in Windows Explorer.

CREATING A MACRO TO ADD TEXT TO A DRAWING

One of the things you do most frequently when you create a drawing is add some text for a title, a label, your name, or simply the date and time the drawing was created. You probably routinely add the same kind of information to every drawing you create, so it would be nice to create a simple macro that does this for you. Let's step through the code for such a macro, and see how to customize it to suit your specific needs.

The code for a macro is entered into a Code window in the IDE. The IDE has some indispensable editing features that you'll find extremely user-friendly, such as the Auto List Members and the Complete Word features. You'll learn how to access and make full use of these features as you enter your macro's code.

Using the IDE's Editing Features to Enter Code

As you work through the steps of creating a macro to add text to a drawing, you'll get a lot of help from the drop-down lists that appear as you enter your code. These lists not only shorten your typing tasks, but they also (and more importantly) provide you with names and keywords appropriate to what you are typing. That means you don't have to memorize lots of programming details, and you're less dependent on the online Help facility.

Listing 17.1 later in this chapter gives the complete macro that you'll create here step by step. The analysis after the listing describes what each line of code does. Let's start at the very beginning and go through all the steps required to code your DrawText macro, making full use of the editing features as you go.

1. Start AutoCAD and choose Tools ➢ Macro ➢ Visual Basic Editor. The VBA IDE appears, with one AutoCAD object

named ThisDrawing listed in the Project Explorer window. If the Project Explorer window is not displayed, choose View ➤ Project Explorer to make it appear.

2. Double-click ThisDrawing. The Code window shown earlier in Figure 17.1 will open, with the Insertion cursor blinking and ready for you to start entering your code.

3. In the Code window, enter the text **Sub DrawText** and press Enter. The IDE appends a pair of parentheses to DrawText and adds an empty line followed by the End Sub statement.

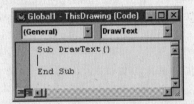

Sub and End Sub are colored according to your foreground setting for keyword text. (You'll see how to change this color in the sidebar "Setting the Colors to Identify Keyword Text in the Code Window.") The Insertion cursor now blinks in the empty line to let you know that the IDE is waiting for you to enter code.

4. In the empty line, type the following, including the single quote (') character at the beginning:

```
'inserts the string "Hello" into the drawing area
```

The single quote denotes that the line is a comment.

5. Press Enter. The comment text changes into the color specified as the foreground color for comment text.

TIP

Comments start with a single quote (') character. These lines are useful for jogging your memory if you ever need to revisit your code, or for clarification for someone else who is giving your code an update. Consider comments your opportunity to document what you've done.

SETTING THE COLORS TO IDENTIFY KEYWORD TEXT IN THE CODE WINDOW

The default color for keyword text in the IDE Code window is blue, but it can be changed to any color you want. Follow these steps:

1. Choose Tools ➤ Options to open the Options dialog box, and select the Editor Format tab.

2. From the Code Colors list, select Keyword Text. The text in the Sample frame changes to the color specified in the Foreground color box. Select your desired color from the drop-down list, and the color of the sample text will be immediately updated.

3. Click OK to finish and return to the Code window.

6. Type the following statement. Be sure to capitalize the T and P in TextPosition, and to end the line with a space:

```
dim TextPosition(0 To 2) as
```

This statement is how you declare an array named Text-Position that can contain three elements. This array passes the position where you want to place the text, to the AddText method (see step 17). The capitalization of the array name in this declaration is maintained throughout the code, wherever this name is used.

Part iv

TIP

Capitalizing the first letter of individual words within a code element name not only enhances the readability of your code but also alerts you to any typing mistakes.

7. When you enter the space after as in your dim statement, the Auto List Members feature of the editor displays the drop-down list of data types available for your array elements, as shown in Figure 17.4.

   If this drop-down list doesn't appear, you'll need to change the editor settings on your PC and try this step again. Alternatively, you can leave the editor settings as they are and choose Edit ➤ Complete Word from the Code window; the same drop-down list will appear.

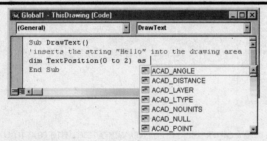

FIGURE 17.4: The Auto List Members editor feature helps you complete the next part of a statement.

8. Continue entering the statement by typing **do**. Watch the list of data types scroll as each character is entered.

9. When the Double entry is highlighted, press Enter. Your do is extended to Double in the Code window. The dim becomes Dim, and its color changes to the Keyword Text color setting, as do To and As Double. The cursor jumps to the start of the next line, where the Insertion cursor blinks in readiness.

10. Type **t** and choose Edit ➤ Complete Word (or use the key-combination Ctrl+spacebar). A drop-down list of possible names, all beginning with *t,* is displayed as shown in Figure 17.5. The TextPosition array name you've just declared appears in this list.

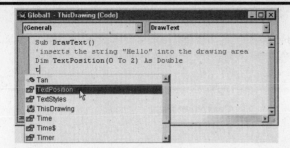

FIGURE 17.5: Selecting TextPosition from the list of possible words displayed by the Complete Word editing feature

11. Double-click TextPosition in the drop-down list. The t you entered is automatically expanded into TextPosition. As an alternative, you can enter **textposition** in its entirety; when you press Enter to move to the next line, the *t* and *p* will change to uppercase to match the array name declaration.

TIP

Use upper- and lowercase when entering names in declarations, but use lowercase when entering the rest of the code. The Visual Basic compiler will change the case of any names entered to match their declarations—that way you'll know if you've entered the name correctly.

12. Finish entering the line by typing **(0)=1.5** and press Enter. Notice that spaces are inserted at each side of the equal character (=). The insertion cursor is positioned at the start of the next line.

13. Repeat steps 10 and 11 to enter the next two lines of code. Complete each line by pressing Enter:

```
TextPosition(1) = 8.5
TextPosition(2) = 0.0
```

Notice that the 0.0 you entered in the second line automatically changes to 0# when you press Enter, and the insertion cursor blinks patiently while it waits on the next line.

TIP

Figure 17.6 defines all the icons that represent the various objects, functions, properties, and methods provided by the Complete Word feature.

This Icon:	Represents a:
	Property
	Default Property
	Method
	Default Method
	Event
	Constant
	Module
	Class
	User Defined Type
	Global
	Library
	Project
	Built-in keywords and types
	Enum

FIGURE 17.6: Meaning of icons next to items in the Complete Word list

TIP

When you enter a decimal fraction with a zero after the decimal point, as in 0.0, the Visual Basic interpreter changes the zero into a hash character (#). This can be disconcerting to new users of Visual Basic. The # is a type-declaration character used to specify that the number is to be treated as a double precision floating-point number (Double type).

14. In the Code window, type **m** and use the key-combination Ctrl+spacebar to display the drop-down list of all words starting with *m* that are possibilities for this statement.

15. Type **o**. ModelSpace appears highlighted in the drop-down list. (The ModelSpace collection of objects provides all the details needed to regenerate model space. Later in this chapter, the analysis after Listing 17.1 describes the ModelSpace collection, so I'll skip the details for now.)

16. Type a period character (.) . The mo is extended to Model-Space followed by a period.

17. Finish the line of code by typing the following:

```
addtext "Hello",textposition,1.8
```

Press Enter. Spaces are inserted as needed and letters capitalized where appropriate. Your finished line of code becomes

```
ModelSpace.AddText "Hello", TextPosition, 1.8
```

That completes your text-insertion macro. Listing 17.1 shows the code in full.

Listing 17.1: Text-Insertion Macro

```
1    Sub DrawText()
2        'inserts the string "Hello" into the drawing area
3        Dim TextPosition(0 To 2) As Double
4        TextPosition(0) = 1.5
5        TextPosition(1) = 8.5
6        TextPosition(2) = 0#
7        ModelSpace.AddText "Hello", TextPosition, 1.8
8    End Sub
```

Here's a line-by-line account of what is happening in the macro:

▶ Line 1 declares the name of the procedure as DrawText. This name allows you to identify it later and run it as a macro (see the next section).

▶ Line 2 contains comment text that is ignored by the Visual Basic interpreter; it is there simply to describe what the procedure does. Comment text always begins with a single quote character (') so that it can be easily identified. Comments provide useful information to whoever is reading the code; I'm sure you'll find your own comments helpful if you ever need to update the code at a later date.

► Line 3 uses the Dim statement to declare an array containing three numbers as the double-precision floating-point type. These numbers will be used to specify the x-, y-, and z-coordinates to be used in positioning the text in 3D inside the Model Space window. Using an array has the advantage of being able to refer to all three numbers using the same name and an index value, as shown in lines 4 through 6.

► Lines 4 through 6 assign values to the three numbers in the TextPosition array. In line 6, the interpreter program automatically replaces the string 0.0 with 0#, so don't think you've made a typo.

► Line 7 calls the AddText method of the ModelSpace collection to add a Text object to this collection, with the Text object's properties assigned to the values of the three arguments specified. The first argument is the text string to be displayed, followed by its position in the Model tab, and then by the height required for the text. If you want to experiment, try changing "Hello" to a string of your choice. (We'll go through an example in the section "Updating Your DrawText Macro.")

► Line 8 ends the DrawText macro.

Now that you've gone to all the trouble of typing your code, it's always best to save your macro before you try to run it—just in case it causes Auto-CAD to stop responding and you have to stop running it. You wouldn't want to start at the beginning again.

Saving a Macro

You already know that AutoCAD uses drawing files with the extension .dwg to save your drawings, and VBA uses project files with the extension .dvb to save all the components of your application from the IDE. These components include all your Visual Basic code, UserForms, and modules. Because the AutoCAD and VBA components are kept in separate files, you must remember to save both files individually. When you open your project again, you must open them individually, too.

I'm sure you're already an expert at saving your drawings by choosing File ➢ Save in the AutoCAD window. To save your DrawText macro in a project file, choose File ➢ Save from the VBA IDE. Because you are saving your macro for the first time, Global1 is appended to the Save menu command.

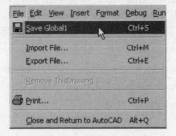

The Save As dialog box shown in Figure 17.7 appears next, with Project already in the File Name box, and Project (*.dvb) in the Save As Type box. You can maneuver your way around your directory system to the folder required, the same way you do in AutoCAD. You can also overtype the default filename Project with any name of your choice.

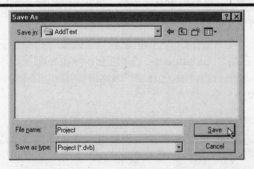

FIGURE 17.7: Using the Save As dialog box to save your VBA macro

In subsequent saves, the full pathname of the Project.dvb file will be appended to the Save menu command.

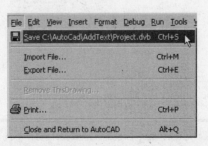

Running a Macro

Throughout the development stage of a project, it's much better to do trial runs from the IDE until you're satisfied that your macro is working the way you want it to. The IDE has many debugging features to help you during these tests, especially when your macros become longer and more complex.

Once your macro is working exactly as planned, it's better to run it straight from AutoCAD without opening the IDE at all. Let's look now at both ways of running a macro.

Running a Macro from the IDE

To run your DrawText macro from the IDE, select the Run Sub/User-Form button from the toolbar.

Running a Macro from AutoCAD

When it is inconvenient to open the IDE just to run your macro, follow these steps to run it from the AutoCAD window:

1. From the AutoCAD menu, choose Tools ➤ Macro ➤ Macros. The Macros dialog box appears, containing a list of all the macros associated with the current ThisDrawing object, as shown in Figure 17.8.

2. Highlight your DrawText macro and click Run to execute it.

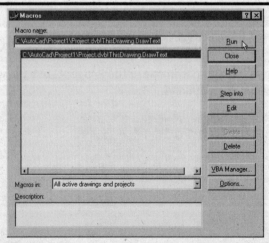

FIGURE 17.8: Macros dialog box listing the macros associated with the current drawing object

TIP

If your macro isn't listed in the Macros dialog box, make sure you have loaded the project file that contains it, and that it has been placed into either `This-Drawing` or `Module#` (where # stands for any number). Procedures placed into UserForm modules are private and are not listed in the Macros dialog box. The section "Loading VBA Project Files" later in this chapter describes how a macro can be loaded manually or automatically.

Returning to AutoCAD

When you return to AutoCAD after running the `DrawText` macro, the text added by the macro is displayed in model space, as shown in Figure 17.9. Your new text will also appear in the Layout1 (see Figure 17.10) and Layout2 tabs. Drawings are designed in model space, and the two Layout tabs are used to plot your drawing to paper space.

FIGURE 17.9: The text has been added to model space by the AddText method.

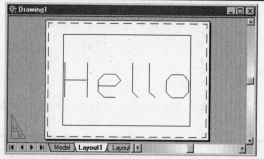

FIGURE 17.10: The AddText method also updates the images in the Layout tabs for the current drawing.

Using VBA's Date and Time Functions

Visual Basic provides numerous functions that you'll find easy to use. This section introduces two of them—Date and Time—that may be useful to include in your DrawText macro. The Date function returns a Variant type containing the string representing the current date, and the Time function returns a Variant type containing a string representing the current time; the content and format of both strings are dependent on your PC's settings.

Updating Your DrawText Macro

Because the Date and Time functions return strings, they can be used wherever any string is required in your code. Try replacing the "Hello" string in line 7 of your DrawText macro with Date, as follows:

```
ModelSpace.AddText Date, TextPosition, 0.75
```

TIP
You don't need to enclose Date in quotes because it is a function name. If you did use quotes, you would end up with the string *Date* in your drawing.

Run your macro again and watch as the current date appears in the Model Space tab of your drawing object.

You can add both the time and date to your drawing by expanding your code statement as follows:

```
ModelSpace.AddText Time & " " & Date, TextPosition, 0.75
```

The ampersand character (&) concatenates strings, so that the last character of one string is joined with the first character of the next string. The string containing one blank character in the middle adds a space in order to visually separate the two strings when they're displayed.

Now that you have created a stand-alone macro, it's time to create a macro for starting up the Metric-Imperial Converter application developed in Chapter 16 (Listing 16.1). This macro can be called from the AutoCAD window. All you need to do is provide the code for showing the UserForm from the application. Before you can call the application, however, it has to be loaded. The next section shows how this is achieved.

LOADING VBA PROJECT FILES

When you open a drawing file from the AutoCAD window, by default no VBA project file is loaded into memory. You'll need to load your project file manually before you can edit or run your macros. This section shows you how to change that.

If you prefer that your macros be loaded automatically, you can set two options in the AutoCAD application so that specific files are loaded in one of two ways:

▸ Every time AutoCAD starts up

▸ Whenever the current AutoCAD application is opened

Loading a Project Manually

Manually loading the project file containing your macro is the best way to load macros that you don't need to run very often. The following steps explain how to do this:

1. From the AutoCAD window, choose Tools ➤ Macro ➤ Load Project. The Open VBA Project dialog box (see Figure 17.11) appears with a list of the project files contained in the current directory.

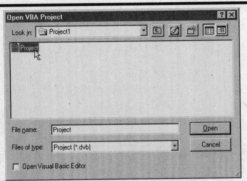

FIGURE 17.11: Selecting a project from the Open VBA Project dialog box

2. Ensure that the Open Visual Basic Editor check box (at the bottom of the dialog box) is checked, select the project containing the required macro, and click Open. If the AutoCAD message shown in Figure 17.12 appears, click Enable Macros to continue. The Code window for ThisDrawing appears, containing the DrawText macro.

TIP

This message box will always appear if its Always Ask Before Opening Projects With Macros check box is selected. If you don't want to see this warning message again, then simply uncheck the box. You can make the warning message appear again by clicking the Options button in the Macros dialog box (Figure 17.8) and selecting the Enable Macro Virus Protection option.

TIP

If you want the IDE to open so that you can edit the macro being loaded, make sure that the Open Visual Basic Editor check box is checked in the bottom-left corner of the Open VBA Project dialog box.

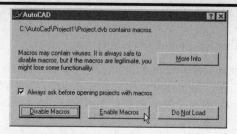

FIGURE 17.12: Message box giving information about macros

Loading a Project Each Time a Drawing Object Is Opened

If you need to run a specific macro just about every time you work with a particular AutoCAD drawing object, consider setting up AutoCAD so that it will automatically load this macro for you every time you open the drawing object. The following steps show you how this is achieved:

1. In AutoCAD, choose Tools ➤ Macro ➤ VBA Manager. The VBA Manager dialog box is displayed.

2. Select the project file to be loaded, and click the Embed button.

3. Close the dialog box and return to the AutoCAD window.

Loading a Project When AutoCAD Starts Up

If a macro is required by most of your AutoCAD drawings, consider setting up AutoCAD so that the project file containing the macro is loaded every time AutoCAD is opened. To load a project file every time AutoCAD starts up, follow these steps:

1. Choose Tools ➤ Load Application from the AutoCAD window. The Load/Unload Applications dialog box is displayed.

2. Click the Contents button in the Startup Suite frame. The Startup Suite dialog box (Figure 17.13) opens, listing all the project files that are automatically loaded when you start AutoCAD. (There were none on my PC.)

3. In the Startup Suite dialog box, click Add to open the Add File to Startup Suite dialog box shown in Figure 17.14.

Part iv

4. Select the project file containing the required macro and click Add. Doing so returns you to the Startup Suite dialog box, which now contains the project file you've just added.

5. Close the Startup Suite dialog box. You return to the Load/Unload Applications dialog box, which now contains the text "Project.dvb was added to the Startup suite" in the frame along the bottom.

6. Click Close to return to the AutoCAD window. Your macro is now available to be run at any time and will always appear in the list displayed in the Macros dialog box.

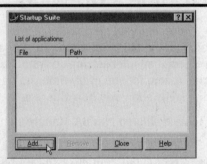

FIGURE 17.13: Startup Suite dialog box

FIGURE 17.14: Adding a file to the elements that run when AutoCAD starts up

Canceling the Loading of a Project at Startup

If a project file always loads when AutoCAD is opened and you decide this is no longer necessary, follow these steps to remove it from the list in the Startup Suite dialog box:

1. In the AutoCAD window, choose Tools ➤ Load Application. The Load/Unload Applications dialog box opens.

2. Click the Contents button in the Startup Suite frame. The Startup Suite dialog box opens, listing all the project files that are automatically loaded when you start AutoCAD.

3. Select the project file you want to remove and click Remove. The name of the project file is no longer listed.

4. Click Close to return to the Load/Unload Applications dialog box.

5. Click Close to return to AutoCAD.

You can now open AutoCAD without the macro being loaded. If you occasionally need to use the macro again, you can always load it manually or add it back into the Startup list.

STARTING AN APPLICATION FROM A MACRO

A VBA application can be run directly from the AutoCAD window without opening the IDE, if you write a macro that will open the UserForm. The following steps show you how to create such a macro to run the Metric-Imperial Converter application developed in Chapter 16:

1. If your Metric-Imperial Converter application isn't loaded, choose Tools ➤ Macro ➤ Load Project in the AutoCAD window. Then, select the project file where the application is stored (see the preceding section, "Loading VBA Project Files").

Part iv

2. Open the IDE and choose View ➤ Project Explorer if the Project Explorer window isn't already displayed. Click Module1. The Code window for Module1 opens.

3. Enter the following code:

```
Sub RunMetricToImperialConverter()
    UserForm1.Show
End Sub
```

Analysis of this code is given after Listing 17.2.

4. Choose File ➤ Close and Return to AutoCAD. The IDE closes, and you are returned to the AutoCAD window.

5. Choose Tools ➤ Macro ➤ Macros. The Macros dialog box appears, containing your macro.

6. Click Run. Your application starts up just as if you had run it from the IDE.

7. Click the command button with the Caption property set to Close. The application's window disappears, and it is unloaded from memory.

Listing 17.2: Application Startup Macro

```
1    Sub RunMetricToImperialConverter()
2        UserForm1.Show
3    End Sub
```

This macro works as follows:

▶ Line 1 starts the procedure RunMetricToImperialConverter.

▶ Line 2 calls the Show method from UserForm1 that displays this UserForm and runs the application until the user clicks the command button with the Close caption.

▶ Line 3 ends the procedure.

What's Next?

This chapter has shown you how to create macros to complete simple tasks. You have learned about the editing features of the VBA IDE and seen how it can save you time when coding. In the next chapter, you will explore the Integrated Development Environment in greater depth and learn more about editing, debugging, and running code.

Chapter 18

QUICK TOUR OF THE IDE

I n this chapter, I'll take you on a quick tour of all the VBA IDE components and some of the features they offer—that way, you'll get an idea about how everything fits together.

Adapted from *Mastering™ AutoCAD® VBA* by Marion Cottingham
ISBN 0-7821-2871-8   704 pages $49.99

VBA IDE COMPONENTS

The VBA IDE contains a collection of powerful commands and tools that you'll find extremely convenient and helpful for creating VBA macros and applications. In this chapter, I've stuck to the components you'll find useful for creating your code. Following are the components from the IDE covered in this chapter:

- ▶ Menu bar

- ▶ Toolbars

- ▶ Toolbox

- ▶ Project Explorer window

- ▶ Object Browser window

- ▶ Code window

- ▶ Properties window

Figure 18.1 illustrates a typical layout of these components in the IDE window. By default, the menu bar is positioned horizontally along the top of the window, immediately below the title bar. The menu bar contains a collection of items, each with its own drop-down list of commands. The Standard toolbar typically sits snugly beneath the menu bar and provides fast access to some of the most-used menu commands. When the menu bar and Standard toolbar are positioned as in Figure 18.1, they are said to be in their *docked* positions.

The menu bar and toolbars can be positioned anywhere on the screen using a drag-and-drop action. In fact, all the IDE windows can be moved by dragging and dropping their title bars, and they can be resized by adjusting their borders. However, when the menu bar and toolbar windows are docked, their title bars are sometimes hidden; so, if you want them repositioned, you'll need to drag them by the two parallel vertical bars on their left-hand sides.

Code window

Menu bar

Standard toolbar

Project Explorer window

Properties window

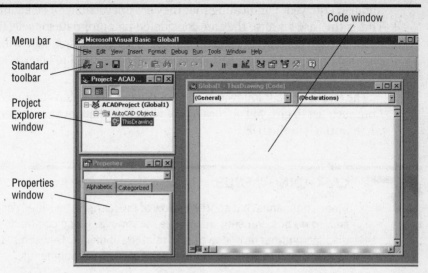

FIGURE 18.1: VBA IDE menu bar and Standard toolbar in their docked positions

Exploring the Menu Bar

The menu bar has 10 drop-down lists of menu commands. They provide access to all the commands available in the IDE. These Windows-style drop-down menus make VBA a powerful, easy-to-learn, easy-to-use visual system that saves you from having to memorize textual commands. Among other things, the commands available from the menu bar allow you to

▶ Save and print files

▶ Use the editing features

▶ Open and close windows in the IDE

▶ Insert forms and modules into your project

▶ Line up controls in forms

▶ Run and debug code

▶ Change settings that alter the appearance and behavior of the IDE

▶ Access the online Help facility

If you take a quick look at all the drop-down lists of menu commands, it won't take long to discover that quite a few of the commands are dimmed ("grayed"), indicating that they are unavailable for selection. This is the case because they are considered inappropriate for selection in the current context. For example, most of the Edit commands will be dimmed unless there is something to edit, so you'll need to open a Code window to make them available.

The examples that follow use a few of the most common commands from each list to give you an idea of the power you have at your fingertips while working in the IDE.

CASCADING MENUS

Menu commands that sport an arrow at the far right are called *cascading menus*. Pausing the mouse cursor over these commands displays another drop-down list of related submenus. For example, several menu commands in the Format group have submenus.

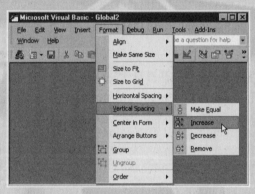

Setting Your IDE Options

The Tools menu commands allow you to access the Visual Basic Editor to create and run macros, set options to customize the features that are available, and set up your project's properties.

When you select Tools ➤ Options, the Options dialog box opens, as shown in Figure 18.2. The options you can set from the Editor and General tabs of the Options dialog box are described in the next two sections. You have already seen how to set the color of the Keyword Text in the Editor Format tab (in the Chapter 17 sidebar "Setting the Colors to Identify Keyword Text in the Code window").

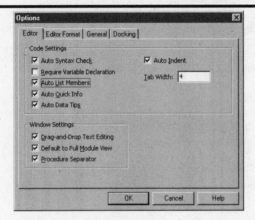

FIGURE 18.2: Editor settings in the Options dialog box

Editor Options

The Editor tab contains the following settings that will help you as you enter your code:

> **Auto Syntax Check**   When this option is enabled (the check box is checked), the Visual Basic interpreter will examine the code for syntax errors line by line as it is entered. If an error is found, the interpreter will change the color of the whole line to the color setting for the Syntax Error Text that has been set in the Editor Format tab. In the following example, you can see that the second line is different in appearance:

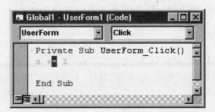

If any particular part of the line can be identified as causing the error, it is highlighted as shown in the previous image, and a message box is displayed with a brief error message.

Clicking the Help button in this message box calls the VBA online Help facility to give a detailed explanation of the cause of the error.

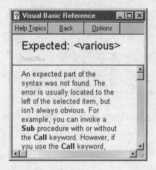

Chapter 17's sidebar "Setting the Colors to Identify Keyword Text in the Code Window" shows how to change the color of syntax error text.

Require Variable Declaration   This option allows you to control whether variables must be declared before you can use them in code without getting an error message. You'll have an opportunity to study this option in Chapter 19, when you read about variables in detail and weigh the pros and cons of enabling this control.

Auto List Members   Enabling this option provides a drop-down list of valid items that can be used to complete the code you have entered so far. For example, Figure 18.3 shows the drop-down list that appears after you enter **ThisDrawing** followed by a full stop character (the period).

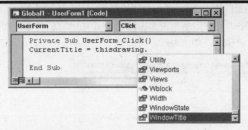

FIGURE 18.3: List of valid code elements that can follow `ThisDrawing`

Auto Quick Info   When this option is turned on, a drop-down list will be displayed if you enter a function name followed by a parenthesis character, as shown in Figure 18.4. The list contains information about the parameters for which you are expected to provide values. The current parameter is always displayed in bold format to keep you informed of how you are progressing through the list.

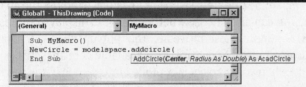

FIGURE 18.4: List of parameters required by the `AddCircle` function

Auto Data Tips   Enabling this option tells the IDE to display the value of the variable currently under the mouse cursor when your application has stopped at a breakpoint or because of an error in the code.

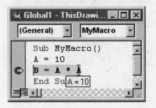

TIP

A *breakpoint* is a statement that you have chosen for the interpreter program to stop at, so that (for example) you can find the current values of variables.

Auto Indent   When this option is turned on and you indent a line of code using the Tab key, the subsequent lines of code will be lined up with the same indent.

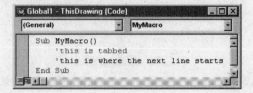

You can also control the number of spaces for the tab, by changing the number in the Editor tab's Tab Width text box (situated just below the Auto Indent check box).

General Options

The options on the General tab of the Options dialog box, shown in Figure 18.5, help you control the grid that is displayed as dots on the User-Form. You can make the grid dots visible or invisible, or adjust the spacing between them. You can also choose whether or not to display ToolTips, the little rectangles containing descriptive text that pop up when you pause the mouse cursor over a button or control. Also available here are settings that determine if and when your project is compiled into p-code if it is run from the IDE. When you start running your code with the Compile On Demand option turned on, only the coding statements visited during a particular run are compiled. When you run your code with Background Compile turned on, statements continue to be compiled while your application waits for you to perform the next interaction.

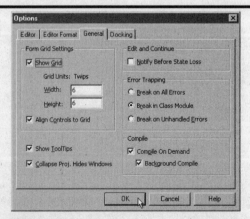

FIGURE 18.5: General settings in the Options dialog box

The IDE's Toolbars

The VBA IDE has four helpful toolbars. You can make them visible (or invisible) by choosing the View ➤ Toolbars command and selecting or deselecting them from the list.

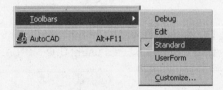

The toolbar buttons provide a fast path to some menu commands. You'll probably find them easier to use after you become accustomed to what menu commands are represented on each toolbar. The following sections briefly describe the buttons on the four toolbars.

Standard Toolbar

The Standard toolbar, shown in Figure 18.6, is also the default toolbar. It is normally placed along the top of the window directly under the menu bar.

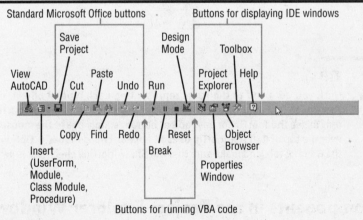

FIGURE 18.6: The Standard toolbar

The Changing Face of the Insert Button   The Insert button has two parts—a button part and a drop-down list. This button is metamorphic, in

Part iv

that it changes its icon and function according to the last type of object inserted. Clicking the icon part of the button will insert the last inserted object type in your project.

Clicking the down-arrow on the button displays a drop-down list of all the objects that can be inserted using this button.

Selecting an item from this list inserts the object into your project, and updates the button's icon and function so that they reflect what you just selected.

In addition, the ToolTip text changes to match the button's new function. For example, after inserting a module into your project, the function of the Insert button changes to

TIP

Until you get used to the icons representing each type of object, use the ToolTips to find out the type of object that will be inserted if you click the button. To see the ToolTip for any toolbar button, simply pause the mouse cursor over the top of it. If the ToolTip doesn't appear, choose Tools ➢ Options, click the General tab, and make sure that the Show ToolTips check box is selected.

Components in the Project Explorer Window

Any macros, programs, or applications you develop in the IDE are all considered a part of the current project and are all stored in a single file with the extension .dvb. You can view all the parts of a project in the Project Explorer window, which displays a hierarchical structure similar to the

Microsoft Windows Explorer window (which I'm sure you're already familiar with). You can view the Project Explorer window by selecting View ≻ Project Explorer or by pressing the Ctrl+R key combination.

Notice the numbers appended to the end of the component names in the Project Explorer window (UserForm1, UserForm2, and so on, Class1 and Class 2). These numbers uniquely identify the components. Because there is only one ThisDrawing component, it doesn't need a number.

Until a project has been saved for the first time, it is given the default filename Global1, which is just a temporary file. Once a file is saved, Global1 is replaced by the new filename.

Edit Toolbar Buttons

The Edit toolbar (Figure 18.7) provides direct access to some of the commands from the Visual Basic Editor's Edit menu and a couple of other commands for handling comments. The icons displayed on the buttons are identical to those shown beside the commands in the Edit menu's drop-down list.

TIP

The Comment Block button is extremely useful during the debugging phase. It allows you to highlight adjacent lines of code and click to add the single quote character (') to the beginning of each selected line, which stops that code from being executed. If you want to execute these lines at any time after debugging, you can reverse the commenting by highlighting the lines again and clicking the Uncomment Block button.

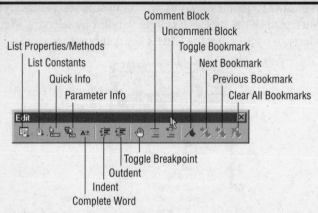

FIGURE 18.7: The Edit toolbar

Debug Toolbar Buttons

The Debug toolbar (Figure 18.8) provides fast access to the commands available from the Debug menu, as well as a few other commands. You'll find this toolbar extremely useful when your code doesn't work as you expected it to.

TIP

Notice that the Toggle Breakpoint button exists in both the Edit and Debug toolbars, giving you two points of quick access to this handy command.

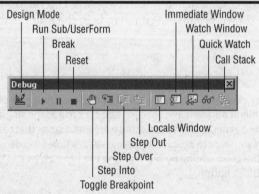

FIGURE 18.8: The Debug toolbar

UserForm Toolbar Buttons

On the UserForm toolbar (Figure 18.9) are buttons that give you an alternate means of accessing some of the commands available on the Format menu. These commands allow you to align, position, and size controls placed on UserForms.

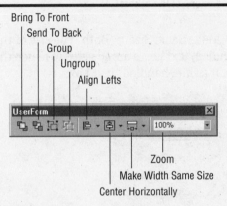

FIGURE 18.9: The UserForm toolbar

The following steps show you how to adjust the size and position of text boxes added to a UserForm:

1. Start a new project, add a UserForm, and place three text boxes on it.

2. Click the topmost text box; then hold down the Shift key while you click the other two text boxes. The handles of all the text boxes appear, indicating they are selected and active.

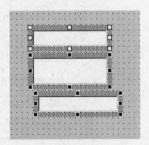

TIP

When several controls are active at the same time, the handles of the first control selected are filled with white to give the control a special status as the dominant control. The handles of the other selected controls are filled with black. The Format menu commands treat the dominant control as a guide for positioning or setting the dimensions of the others.

3. Choose Format ➢ Make Same Size ➢ Both. The size of the selected (black-handled) text boxes are adjusted to match the size of the dominant (white-handled) text box.

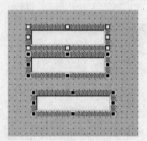

4. With all three text boxes still selected, choose Format ➢ Vertical Spacing ➢ Increase, and then choose this command again. The selected text boxes move down, to increase the space between adjacent pairs by one grid position each time you click the Increase command.

5. Choose Format ➢ Vertical Spacing ➢ Make Equal. The distance between the second and third text boxes is adjusted to be equal to the distance between the first and second boxes.

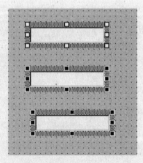

6. With all three text boxes still selected, choose Format ➢ Align ➢ Lefts, or click the Align Lefts toolbar button. The

selected text boxes move horizontally so that their left borders line up with the left border of the dominant text box.

7. Position the cursor over the handle at the bottom-right corner of the top text box so that the cursor turns into a double-headed arrow. Hold down the mouse button and move the cursor until the dashed rectangle is the size required for the text box. Don't release the mouse button yet; notice that the dashed rectangle outline that follows the cursor is displayed at the same relative positions in all three text boxes.

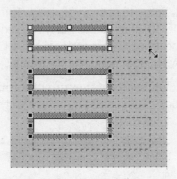

8. Release the mouse button. All the text boxes are resized to fit inside the dashed rectangles.

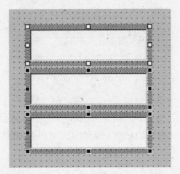

PRINTING USERFORMS

The IDE's Print command uses the default printer that has been designated in the operating system's Control Panel. To print the code from the module currently active in the Visual Basic Editor, follow these steps.

1. From the IDE, select a module and choose File ≻ Print to display the Print – ACADProject dialog box.

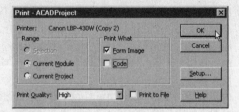

2. Click Setup to open the familiar Print Setup dialog box (Figure 18.10) that you've likely worked with in other Windows applications. These settings are set to values retrieved from the Microsoft Windows operating system environment.

3. Click OK to accept the current settings. The Print Setup dialog box closes, and you return to the Print – ACADProject dialog box.

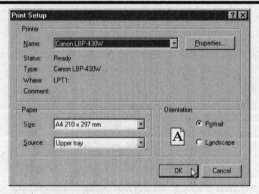

FIGURE 18.10: The Print Setup dialog box displays the name of the default printer and other values retrieved from the Microsoft Windows environment.

4. In the Range frame, the Current Module option button is selected by default. If necessary, select the Form Image check box under Print What and click OK. The code from the active module is sent to the default printer, the ACADProject dialog box closes, and you return to the IDE.

MENU COMMANDS WITH AN ELLIPSIS

Some menu commands end with an ellipsis (...) to let you know that a dialog box will appear when you select that command. An example is the Print... command in the File menu.

Some of these dialog boxes contain information taken straight from the Microsoft Windows environment—so you're ready to roll with these default options.

OVERVIEW OF THE CODE COMMANDS

This section takes a quick look at some of the coding commands available from the Edit, Debug, and Run menus. You'll find that many of these commands are initially hidden. To make them available, a Code window must be open. Let's continue with the three-text-boxes project. Double-click anywhere on UserForm1 to open the Code window for UserForm1, displaying the first and last line for the UserForm_Click event procedure.

Commands for Editing Code

The commands in the Edit menu include indispensable editing tools, some of which you've already used. You experienced their convenience in Chapter 17, when they did your typing for you by completing words and popping up lists so you could choose what to enter next. Also included in the Edit menu are the Undo and Redo, Cut, Copy and Paste, and Find and Replace commands, which are standard in many Windows applications—I'm sure you're familiar with these already. Notice also the Indent and Outdent commands, which allow you to quickly change the left-alignment position of your code lines.

Commands for Debugging Code

The Debug menu commands allow you to run your code line by line while you watch the values of variables change. When you know that sections of your code are correct, then you can set breakpoints to allow your code to run as normal until it encounters a breakpoint, at which point execution stops and you can step through the untested sections of code one statement at a time. In addition, the Compile ACADProject command translates all your code into a format that can be executed by your computer. This translation will make your application run faster, because Visual Basic normally translates the code into intermediate p-code one line at a time as it is required.

Commands for Running Code

The Run menu commands execute your code.

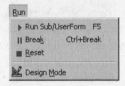

The Run commands evolve dynamically in several ways, according to whatever form or module is active and whether the application is already in Run mode. For example, the Run Sub/UserForm command is available only when a UserForm is open; at other times, the command changes to Run Macro.

As indicated by the icons beside these menu commands, they all have a corresponding toolbar button. Each one also displays a ToolTip when you move your mouse over it. The ToolTip that pops up "evolves" in exactly the same way as the menu command.

If the application is running and stops at a breakpoint or at an error in your code, the Run command changes to let you continue from the breakpoint.

The Reset command, when executed, causes the IDE to tidy up any memory usage and prepares everything so that the application can run again without any interference from values stored during previous runs.

GETTING HELP

The online Help facility is another indispensable feature of the IDE—not only does it offer you a helpful explanation about many topics, but it often gives some sample code, too. You can copy this sample code and run it from the IDE. While you are building your expertise in Visual Basic, it is often useful to see how a method or property is actually put to work in coding statements. You may even be lucky enough to find a sample that you can use as the basis of a macro.

You're probably familiar with using the Help facility in AutoCAD. Well, the IDE's Help works exactly the same way. The following steps show you how to copy and run the sample code for generating a random number from the IDE's Help facility:

1. Open the IDE and choose Help ➤ Microsoft Visual Basic Help. The Help window shown in Figure 18.11 appears.

2. As shown in Figure 18.11, enter the text **randomi** into the box labeled Type In the Keyword to Find. As you type, watch the scrolling list of index entries in the large window. It rolls up to match the string you've entered so far.

   After you type the last letter (**i**), the Randomize Statement topic will be highlighted in the list box.

3. Click the Display button. The Visual Basic Reference window shown in Figure 18.12 appears, containing helpful information about the Randomize statement.

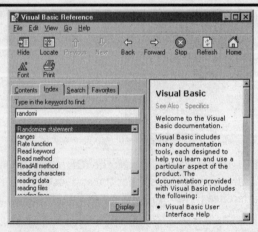

FIGURE 18.11: The Index tab from the IDE's online Help facility

Click the Example link near the top-center of the reference window, and you'll see the sample code shown in the inset of Figure 18.12.

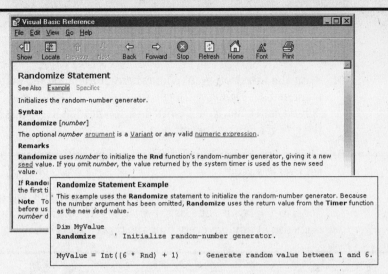

FIGURE 18.12: The inset shows a code example for the Randomize statement after you click the Example link.

4. Right-click anywhere in the Visual Basic Example window to display this pop-up menu:

5. Choose Select All to highlight all the text. Right-click again and choose Copy from the pop-up menu. The content of the Example window is copied to the Clipboard.

6. Open the IDE, choose Insert ➤ Module, and then choose Edit ➤ Paste. The Code window for Module1 opens, and all the text from the Example window is pasted into it.

7. Replace the text above the Dim statement with the name of your procedure; I've called mine RandomNumberGenerator,

as shown in Figure 18.13. Notice I've also used the Edit ➤ Indent command to indent my code.

8. Add End Sub at the end.

9. With the insertion point somewhere in the End Sub statement, choose Debug ➤ Toggle Breakpoint. End Sub is highlighted, and a black circle with an arrowhead in it appears in the gray margin on the left.

10. Choose Run ➤ Run Sub/UserForm and pause the mouse cursor over MyValue.

The code is executed up to the breakpoint, and the pop-up ToolTip displays a value, as shown in Figure 18.13. The value is chosen at random every time the procedure is run.

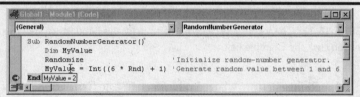

FIGURE 18.13: The procedure name and End Sub statement have been added, shown here with the pop-up ToolTip giving the random value assigned to MyValue.

Context-Sensitive Help

You can get immediate context-sensitive help by making an item in the IDE window active and pressing the F1 function key. Doing so opens the Help page for that topic if there is one. For example, highlight the Visual Basic word Dim and press F1 to open the Help window giving information about the Dim statement.

TIP

If you are a seasoned AutoCAD user, you'll know that the F1 key was originally used to view the full text window in AutoCAD. This functionality was changed to F2 in AutoCAD 2000 and later versions, in order to conform to the Windows pseudo-standard of reserving F1 for viewing the Help facility.

WHAT'S NEXT?

This chapter has introduced you to all the IDE components and how many of their features fit together. The next chapter covers fundamental VBA programming concepts that will give you the knowledge to create your own VBA projects.

Chapter 19

VBA Programming Concepts

This chapter explains the coding concepts and terminology of VBA. If you have previous experience in writing code, some of the material will be familiar to you, so you may want to make your first read a quick one. But I'm sure you'll find it a continuing handy reference as you gain experience. And for you uninitiated, the chapter provides invaluable instruction.

Adapted from *Mastering™ AutoCAD® VBA*
by Marion Cottingham
ISBN 0-7821-2871-8   704 pages $49.99

How Code Instructs the Computer

The Visual Basic compiler partially translates each line of code into p-code whenever you press Enter. It provides instant feedback when it discovers any obvious errors. This translated version of code is saved so that when you run your project, the compiler doesn't have to start from scratch, which saves time.

Using traditional compiled languages, you develop all the code before compiling it into machine language instructions for the PC to execute. Using Visual Basic, there are no longer two distinct steps because some compilation goes on in the background as you develop your code. Before beginning the final compilation step, most syntax errors will have been corrected, and the code will already be in a form that's part of the way there. It just has to undergo the finishing touches in order to become the machine-language instructions your PC can execute.

Statements and Expressions

All the code you write is made up of *statements* that may or may not contain *expressions*. Be sure you understand the difference between a statement and an expression. When the interpreter is translating a statement, any expression contained in the statement is reduced to a value before continuing:

Statements   Any line of code in a VBA application is called a *program statement*. Because statements are partially compiled into p-code, they must be in a form that can be translated by the compiler program. Program statements can contain a mixture of keywords; names that identify variables; objects and their properties and methods; functions, macros, and procedures... and more. You'll find all these terms defined later in this chapter.

Expressions   An expression is any combination of values and symbols that can be reduced to a single value. For example, the statement

```
txtMetricUnits.Text = txtImperialUnits.Text * 0.9144
```

contains an expression on the right of the equal sign (=). A value is retrieved from the TextBox control's Text property and multiplied by the conversion factor, to reduce the right-hand side of the equation to a single numerical value. This value is then assigned to the text box on the left-hand side.

In the statement

```
MetricToImperial = False
```

False is an expression that evaluates to a single numerical value representing False.

ALL ABOUT VARIABLES

A *variable* is a name that's used to refer to a location in memory containing an item of data. Items of data can be anything from strings to whole numbers, from currency to decimal fractions. Figure 19.1 shows the Help window containing all the types of data available and their memory requirements.

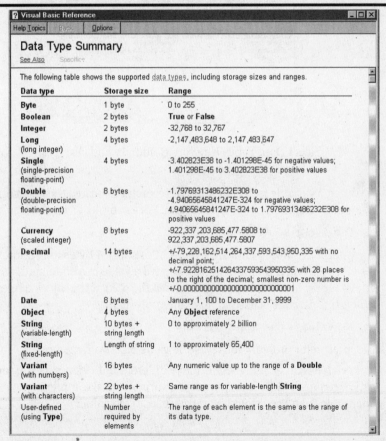

Data Type Summary

See Also   Specifics

The following table shows the supported data types, including storage sizes and ranges.

Data type	Storage size	Range
Byte	1 byte	0 to 255
Boolean	2 bytes	True or False
Integer	2 bytes	-32,768 to 32,767
Long (long integer)	4 bytes	-2,147,483,648 to 2,147,483,647
Single (single-precision floating-point)	4 bytes	-3.402823E38 to -1.401298E-45 for negative values; 1.401298E-45 to 3.402823E38 for positive values
Double (double-precision floating-point)	8 bytes	-1.79769313486232E308 to -4.94065645841247E-324 for negative values; 4.94065645841247E-324 to 1.79769313486232E308 for positive values
Currency (scaled integer)	8 bytes	-922,337,203,685,477.5808 to 922,337,203,685,477.5807
Decimal	14 bytes	+/-79,228,162,514,264,337,593,543,950,335 with no decimal point; +/-7.9228162514264337593543950335 with 28 places to the right of the decimal; smallest non-zero number is +/-0.0000000000000000000000000001
Date	8 bytes	January 1, 100 to December 31, 9999
Object	4 bytes	Any Object reference
String (variable-length)	10 bytes + string length	0 to approximately 2 billion
String (fixed-length)	Length of string	1 to approximately 65,400
Variant (with numbers)	16 bytes	Any numeric value up to the range of a Double
Variant (with characters)	22 bytes + string length	Same range as for variable-length String
User-defined (using Type)	Number required by elements	The range of each element is the same as the range of its data type.

FIGURE 19.1: The Help window containing a summary of data types

Part iv

The Data Type Summary Help window is useful to keep on hand; you'll probably want to look it up a lot until you get used to all the different data types in VBA. The following steps show you how:

1. Open the IDE. Choose Help ➤ Microsoft Visual Basic Help. The Visual Basic Reference dialog box appears with the I-beam cursor blinking in the text box. (If you want another look at this, see Figure 18.11 in Chapter 18.)

2. Type **data types** into the text box. The entries scroll by in the list box below, until the "data types" item appears highlighted.

3. Click Display. The Topics Found dialog box appears.

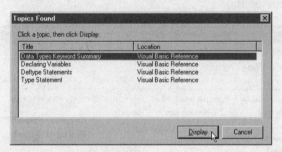

4. Select Data Types Keyword Summary and click Display. The Help window appears.

When a variable is declared, the interpreter allocates the exact amount of memory required by its type of data. For example, given the statement

```
Dim CurValue As Single
```

the interpreter would allocate a block of memory 4 bytes long and initialize it to 0.0. When this variable is assigned a value in a statement, such as CurValue = 5.25, the interpreter stores the 5.25 at this block of memory. When this variable is used in an expression such as

```
NewValue = CurValue * 1.25
```

the interpreter program retrieves the value 5.25 from memory.

Variables can be assigned as many different data values as your application requires while it is running, so variables make applications more adaptable than they would be if they used fixed values.

MEMORY ALLOCATIONS FOR STRING TYPES

In the Help window for Data Type Summary, notice that the String type is allocated memory according to whether it's fixed-length or variable-length. Fixed-length strings are allocated 1 byte of memory for each character; variable-length strings are allocated 1 byte for each character, plus 10 bytes. Strings can be declared as fixed-length by specifying the number of characters; for example, the declaration Dim Name As String * 30 ensures that Name is always exactly 30 characters long. If Name is assigned a string less than 30 characters, trailing spaces are added to make it 30. If Name is assigned a string longer than 30 characters, the string is truncated to 30. Strings that are declared without a specified number of characters are by default variable-length strings.

When VBA encounters a string, it converts each character into a number according to its ASCII representation. The characters in the string "Hello" would be interpreted into five 1-byte numbers in the range 0 to 255. You can see how a string requires a lot more memory than a single integer number.

Declaring Variables Using the *Dim* Statement

You can declare a variable using the Dim statement with or without specifying its type:

```
Dim NewLength
```

```
Dim CurrentRadius as Single
```

If the type is omitted, then by default Visual Basic uses the Variant type and allocates the maximum amount of memory accordingly. The special Variant type has storage space allocated to it that's large enough to store data of any of the other types. Any variables that are not declared or that are declared without specifying their type are assumed to be Variant so that they can be assigned just about anything.

Several variables can be declared in the same Dim statement, separated by commas, even if their types are different. For example:

```
Dim CurrentWidth as Double, NewWidth as Long
```

Part iv

For this reason, every variable that you don't want to end up as a Variant type must have its type specified in the Dim statement, even if it is declared in the same statement as other variables of the same type. In the statement

```
Dim ScalingFactorX, ScalingFactorY As Single
```

the variable ScalingFactorX would be interpreted as being a Variant type. This result differs from some other languages, including C, in which the type is specified only once at the end of a list of variable names of the same type.

IMPORTANT REMINDER: NAMING CONVENTIONS IN VBA CODE

Visual Basic has a few naming conventions that you *must* adhere to when you're naming macros, functions, variables, and constants in code:

► Names must always begin with a letter.

► Names cannot contain spaces, periods, exclamation marks (!), or any of these characters: @ # $ &.

► Names cannot be greater than 255 characters in length.

To Declare or Not to Declare?

As explained, Visual Basic doesn't require variables to be explicitly declared. If you use this default convention, and if a name that appears in code hasn't been declared in the statements translated up to that point, a storage location large enough for a Variant type will be allocated to that name. Whether you want it or not, a new variable is born—and no warning or error messages are given.

You may be tempted not to declare anything and just let Visual Basic do the work for you, but there are two good reasons why you should *not* automatically go down this road:

► Incorrectly spelled variable names are treated as new variables. That means expressions could be evaluated to an erroneous result. Or, if the new variable is a divisor, it could stop execution of your program with a Division By Zero error message box.

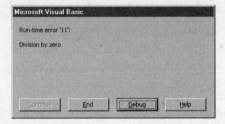

▶ Variables are allocated the maximum amount of memory; even an Integer type variable, which requires 2 bytes if declared, is allocated 16 bytes otherwise. Not only does this allocation blow out the memory requirement of your application very quickly, especially if you are using untyped arrays, but it also increases runtime performance.

To avoid these situations, you can direct the interpreter program to verify that all the variables have been declared *before* they appear in the code, and if not, to give you an error message. This is done using a special Option Explicit statement.

Option Explicit **Statement**

The Option Explicit statement placed in a UserForm or module stipulates to the interpreter program that all variables contained in that User-Form or module must be declared; otherwise the interpreter must create an error and stop the application with the message shown here:

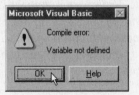

The Option Explicit statement is placed in the General Declarations section of the Code window for a UserForm or module. If you want these statements to be added automatically into the General Declarations

section of all new UserForms and modules in future projects, perform the
following steps:

1. From the Visual Basic Editor, choose Tools ➤ Options. The
   Options dialog box appears.

2. Select the Editor tab. In the list of Code Settings options,
   select the check box for Require Variable Declaration.

3. Click OK to return to the IDE. Now any new UserForm or
   modules you insert into any project in the future will open
   with the Option Explicit statement already in place in the
   General Declarations section of the Code window.

TIP

Any existing UserForms and modules are not affected when you enable the
Require Variable Declaration setting.

Handling Arrays of Variables

Quite often, your VBA code will contain lots of data items that all have the
same type. An efficient way to handle these items is to declare a single
entity called an *array* that allows you to refer to any item using the array's
name and an index that identifies the item's position in the array.

Using an array makes the code much shorter because you don't need
to have variable names for each item. For example, suppose you need to
create 535 lines, all of type LineDetails. Using conventional variables,
you would need to declare each item with a unique name, such as Line1,
Line2... all the way up to Line535, to be able to refer to them in code.
Your program would be extremely lengthy, with 535 declarations and
535 statements to access them. Using an array is the way around this
kind of inefficiency.

Creating an Array

To create an array, you simply declare it by providing its name followed by
the number of elements required, less one, in parentheses. You need to
subtract one because the first element starts at zero. You may also want
to include its type (to avoid the assignment of the default Variant type).
The interpreter allocates your specified number of consecutive memory

locations with enough bytes to hold the values of all the array's elements. For example, in translating the declaration

```
Dim AllLines(535) As LineDetails
```

the interpreter would multiply 536 by the number of bytes required to store a variable of the LineDetails type and allocate that memory to the array. Because an array is really just a group of variables all having the same type, arrays can be declared as any one of the types available for variables.

In terms of processing the array, you need only write the code to process one element and place it inside a loop structure. As described later in this chapter, the For loop is ideal for array processing.

TIP

Individual data items stored in an array are called *elements*.

Accessing Array Elements

You access individual elements in an array using an *index value*. The array name identifies the first memory location, and the index value represents the position in the list of the item required, so it's easy for the interpreter to retrieve the data for any element in the array. The first element in the array by default has an index value of zero, so that the interpreter simply multiplies the index of the array element required, by the amount of memory used to contain one element. The result is added to the starting memory location identified by the array's name.

WARNING

Visual Basic arrays are different from the arraying of objects in AutoCAD, which duplicates objects and lays them out in some formation.

Visual Basic arrays can be declared using several different formats for the dimension. For example:

```
Dim StartPoint(2) as Single        'contains 3 elements
Dim EndPoint(0 to 3) as Single     'contains 4 elements
Dim AllLengths(1 to 5) as Integer  'contains 5 elements
```

In these array declarations, the first elements in StartPoint and EndPoint have an index of zero by default, but the first element in AllLengths has an index of 1 because it has been explicitly declared that way. When you specify a first element that is nonzero, the interpreter takes this into account every time it works out the memory location for the array element required.

Option Base Statement

Some people prefer to have the first element in all their arrays start from 1 rather than 0, because it is more logical to think of 1 as being the first element, 2 the second element, and so on. To ensure that this happens, you can always include the 1 to... clause when you declare an array. Or, you can place the Option Base statement in the General Declarations section of the Code window to specify a new starting value for the default index. The following statement ensures that all arrays declared in the same UserForm or module will automatically have their first element start at 1:

```
Option Base 1
```

Multidimensional Arrays

Most arrays represent a list of values and so have only one dimension, but two-dimensional arrays are also popular for representing things like tables and matrices. For example:

```
Dim AllPoints(10,3) as Single 'contains 11 x 4 elements
```

When this declaration is interpreted, the first dimension is considered to be the number of rows in the table; the second dimension is the number of columns.

Three-dimensional arrays are also quite common:

```
Dim AllData(0 to 4,5,1 to 6) as Double 'contains 5 x 6 x 6
elements
```

In fact, Visual Basic allows up to 60 dimensions.

ALL ABOUT CONSTANTS

A *constant* is a value that remains unchanged as long as the application is running. The values of some constants (such as pi) may never change. Others (such as TaxRates) may change from time to time. Such values should all be declared as constants and given names that can be used throughout the code. The names of constants follow the same naming conventions as variable names.

TIP

Replacing a constant value by a name makes the code not only easier to read and understand, but also easier to maintain. Any change to a constant's value need be updated only once, where the constant is declared and assigned its value. This process saves you the time of looking for instances of a value that you want to change—and prevents possible errors, because you could easily mistype the new value, miss an instance of the original value altogether, or update a value that has nothing to do with the constant.

Constants come in two flavors:

Symbolic Constants   Also known as *user-defined constants*, symbolic constants are those you create with symbolic names and assigned values; they are declared in your code using the Const statement.

Intrinsic Constants   Also known as *built-in constants*, intrinsic constants are an integral part of VBA and its controls for use with objects, methods, and properties.

Declaring Symbolic Constants

Symbolic (or user-defined) constants are declared in a Const statement. The definition of a constant resembles an equation starting with its name, followed by an equal sign, and then its value. The value can be a number, a string, an expression, or another constant. For example:

```
Const MaximumHeight = 150
Const DefaultDoorType = "Federation"
Const MarkUpMultiplier = (100 + 25)/100
Const BestHeight = MaximumHeight - 10
```

You can also specify a constant's type in the Const statement. For example:

```
Const Epsilon as Double = 0.00001
```

If you don't specify the type, VBA uses the one that is the closest match to the constant's value.

Part iv

Several constants can be declared on the same line, separated by commas:

```
Const MaximumSquares = 1000, MinimumSquares = 100
```

Constants with different types can also be declared on the same line, like this:

```
Const MaxHeight as Single=2.5,MaxThickness as Integer=65
```

TIP

If you need to declare a lot of constants, sort them into small logical groups and declare them on consecutive lines, with a few on each line.

Viewing Built-in Constants in the Object Browser

VBA provides lots of built-in (intrinsic) constants that have been predeclared and assigned values; they're ready for you to use without having to declare them. You can see these constants in the Object Browser window (shown in Figure 19.2).

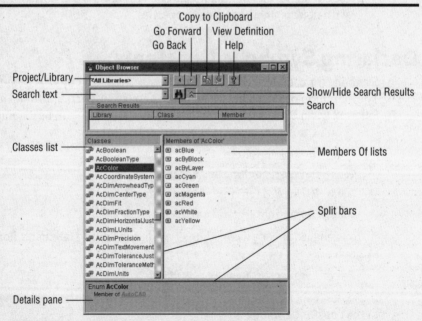

FIGURE 19.2: Object Browser displaying the constants belonging to the enumerated type AcColor

All the libraries listed in the Library box have their own set of constants, qualified by two-letter prefixes that identify the library they belong to. For example, constants from the AutoCAD library are prefixed with the letters ac, those from the MSForms library are prefixed fm, and those from the VBA library are prefixed vb. This naming system enables you to install applications that have VBA capability and know that you won't get heaps of errors because of duplicate declarations of constants. Without this helpful prefix (if constants had only a name appropriate to their represented value), it would be impossible for you to name your own constants with confidence that you weren't duplicating existing ones. In addition, future problems could arise when you updated to new versions of software, should they duplicate one of your names.

TIP

The constants you yourself define are automatically placed in the ACADProject library and will not be listed with a prefix unless you declare them as such.

The following steps show you how to access the intrinsic constants listed in the Object Browser:

1. Open the Visual Basic Editor, and choose Insert ➤ Userform to add a UserForm to your project.

2. If the Object Browser window isn't already on display, choose View ➤ Object Browser.

3. Click the down-arrow button to open the Project/Library list box. A drop-down list of libraries appears.

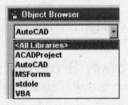

4. Select <All Libraries> from the list. The <All Libraries> item appears in the Project/Library box.

5. Scroll down the Classes list and select fmBorders. Information about the fmBorders item appears in the Details pane at

the bottom of the Object Browser, and its members appear in the Members Of list, as shown in Figure 19.3. The fmBorders item is an Enumerated type, which means it can be assigned only one value from a set of predefined values, using either its name or its value.

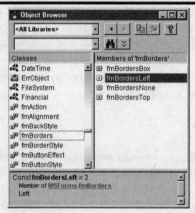

FIGURE 19.3: Constant fmBordersLeft selected from the Members of fmBorders list

6. Click the fmBordersLeft item from the Members Of list. The Details pane now contains information about this constant, including its value of 2 (see Figure 19.3).

7. One by one, click the other members of fmBorders. Notice how the values assigned to each member lie in the range 0 through 3; this sequential nature of values is also a characteristic of all Enumerated types.

Using the Object Browser's Search Engine

The Object Browser window offers a search facility to help you find strings within a library. You enter the string into the search text box directly under the Project/Library box. You can enter any string you like and even use VBA wildcards (see the sidebar "VBA Wildcard Characters").

The drop-down list from the search text box contains up to five of the last strings you searched for since opening the IDE. When you click the

Search button (the binoculars icon), the Object Browser searches the library for every occurrence of the string entered. You can also specify that you want to search for the whole word only, by right-clicking the Search button and selecting Find Whole Word Only from the shortcut menu.

When the search is complete, the list of found items appears in the Search Results pane. It lists the library, class, and member names for each found item.

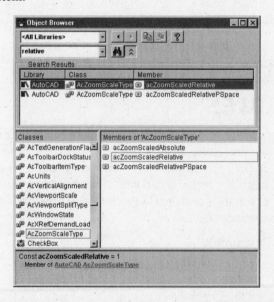

TIP

If a value will never change throughout the runtime of the code, it is best to declare the value as a constant rather than a variable. Doing so will make your code more efficient so it will run faster. When translated, any constant name is replaced by its actual value. As a result, during runtime all the values are already in place; in contrast, the value of a variable has to be retrieved from memory each time its name is encountered.

VBA WILDCARD CHARACTERS

You can include wildcard characters in your search string in the Object Browser. When VBA comes across these characters during the search, it tries to replace the wildcard with a character or a string of characters in an attempt to maximize the number of items it can find. These wildcard characters are available:

?   To replace any single character

*   To replace any number of characters

To replace any single digit

SCOPE OF CONSTANTS AND VARIABLES

The *scope* of a constant or variable refers to whether it can be accessed from one procedure, from all procedures in a module, or from all procedures in the application. The level of scope depends on where the element has been declared and whether it has been declared as public or private. Variables and constants can have three levels of scope, as defined in the sections that follow:

- ▶ Procedure level
- ▶ Private-module (or UserForm) level
- ▶ Public-module level

Public vs. Private

All constants and variables are private by default. You can override the default by declaring them as public, provided that the declaration is inside a standard module rather than in a UserForm or procedure. From the point of view of maintaining the code, it is better to avoid declaring a constant or variable as public if it will be used only by procedures in the same module. This arrangement limits the amount of code that must be checked if the value of that constant or variable is ever updated.

Scope at the Procedure Level

A constant or variable declared *inside* a procedure using the Const or Dim statement is considered local and has a lifetime that lasts only while that procedure is running. When the declaration statement is translated, the interpreter reserves the memory for variables or notes the values of constants. When the end of the procedure is encountered, the interpreter frees the memory reserved for the local variables and no longer remembers the constants' values.

WARNING

Although local variables and constants are restricted to being private, you can't declare them using the Private keyword. If you try to do this, you'll get a run-time error message: "Compile Error – Invalid attribute in Sub or Function."

UserForm and Module-Level Scope

Any constant or variable declaration that is placed *outside* a procedure has UserForm or module-level scope. These declarations are placed in the General Declarations section of the Code window and are private by default.

Any constant or variable declared in a UserForm is restricted to being private. If the declaration is inside a module, the constant or variable is private by default but can be declared using the Public keyword to make it accessible from anywhere in the project.

Part iv

Scope at the Private-Module Level

A module-level constant or variable can be declared as private, in order to limit its accessibility to procedures contained in the same module. For example:

```
Private Const MaximumHeight = 1000
```

Limiting the scope in this way is useful when it comes to maintaining your code. In this example, if you ever want to change the value of the maximum height, you can quickly see where the constant is used in your code. Another benefit is that you can declare another MaximumHeight constant as private in another module, and it can have a different value without causing any adverse effects on other modules.

Scope at the Public-Module Level

A module-based constant or variable can be declared as public, in order for it to be referenced from anywhere in the entire project. For example:

```
Public Const NewRate = 3.5
```

In addition to scope, a variable also has a *lifetime*, which refers to the period of time that it holds onto its value. A variable declared inside a procedure can be accessed only within that procedure; its lifetime will end when it loses its value between calls, unless it is declared as a static variable (see the next section).

Static Statements and the *Static* Keyword

A variable declared using the Static statement is a local variable that retains its memory allocation the whole time the application is running. When a procedure is revisited, the variable is still set to the same value that was last assigned to it.

At the procedure level, the Static keyword preserves the memory values of all a procedure's variables between visits. Listing 19.1 shows the code for a small application that demonstrates the difference between static procedures and static variables. The following exercise demonstrates how the TrueFlag variable keeps its value between runs, whereas the Incremental variable does not.

If you would like to try these procedures, the following steps show you how to develop the GUI needed to run them:

1. Start AutoCAD, open the IDE, and choose Insert ➤ UserForm.

2. Drag and drop two text boxes and two command buttons onto the UserForm, starting from the top, as illustrated in Figure 19.4.

3. Change the Caption properties of the command buttons in the Properties window to **Switch It No 1** and **Switch It No 2**. (You may need to execute View ➤ Properties Window if the Properties Window is not already displayed.)

4. Enter the code shown in Listing 19.1 into the form's code window.

5. Select Run ➤ Run Sub/UserForm.

FIGURE 19.4: The UserForm with two text boxes and two command buttons

6. Repeatedly click the Switch It No 1 button. The static procedure runs with each click. The top text box switches between True and False, and the value in the second text box increases by 5 each time.

7. Repeatedly click the Switch It No 2 button. The SwitchIt2 procedure runs with each click. The top text box switches between True and False, because TrueFlag is declared as a static variable and so retains its previous value. The value in the second text box remains at 5 because the Incremental variable is initialized to 0 every time the SwitchIt2 procedure runs (because the Incremental variable is allocated a fresh memory location each time).

Listing 19.1: Application with *Static* Procedures and Variables

```
1    Private Static Sub SwitchIt1()
2    Dim TrueFlag As Boolean
3    Dim Incremental As Integer
4    TrueFlag = Not TrueFlag
5    TextBox1.Text = TrueFlag
6    Incremental = Incremental + 5
7    TextBox2.Text = Incremental
8    End Sub
9
10   Private Sub SwitchIt2()
11   Static TrueFlag As Boolean
12   Dim Incremental As Integer
13   TrueFlag = Not TrueFlag
14   TextBox1.Text = TrueFlag
15   Incremental = Incremental + 5
16   TextBox2.Text = Incremental
17   End Sub
18
19   Private Sub CommandButton1_Click()
20   SwitchIt1
21   End Sub
22
23   Private Sub CommandButton2_Click()
24   SwitchIt2
25   End Sub
```

Here's how this code works:

▶ Line 1 declares procedure SwitchIt1 using the Static keyword, so that it holds onto all the memory allocated to its variables as long as UserForm1 stays loaded.

▶ Line 2 uses the Dim statement to declare the variable TrueFlag as a Boolean type. This variable will be assigned the default value False.

▶ Line 3 uses the Dim statement to declare the Incremental variable as an Integer type. This variable will be assigned the default value 0.

▶ Line 4 toggles the value of TrueFlag to False if it is True, or to True if it is False.

► Line 5 assigns the value of TrueFlag to the Text property of TextBox1, to display it to the user.

► Line 6 adds 5 to the value stored at the memory location referred to by the Incremental variable.

► Line 7 assigns the value referred to by Incremental to Textbox2's Text property to display it.

► Line 8 ends the static procedure SwitchIt1, but the storage locations allocated to the TrueFlag and Incremental variables are retained intact for the next call to SwitchIt1.

► Line 10 declares SwitchIt2 as a normal, run-of-the-mill procedure, so any variables it contains that are not declared as static variables themselves will lose their values when the procedure finishes executing.

► Line 11 declares the TrueFlag variable using the Static statement so that TrueFlag will hold onto its memory location and value for the whole time the UserForm is loaded.

► Line 12 uses the Dim statement to declare the Incremental variable as an Integer type and sets its value to 0.

► Line 13 toggles the value of TrueFlag from True to False and vice versa.

► Line 14 displays the value of TrueFlag in TextBox1.

► Line 15 adds 5 to the value of Incremental, which has just been set to 0—this has the same effect as assigning a value of 5 to Incremental each time.

► Line 16 displays the value of Incremental in TextBox2.

► Line 17 ends procedure SwitchIt2 and frees the storage location allocated to Incremental.

► Line 19 starts the Click Event procedure of the command button with the caption "Switch It No 1."

► Line 20 calls SwitchIt1 to perform the application's response to the click.

► Line 21 ends the Click event.

► Lines 23 through 25 are similar to lines 19 through 21 but call SwitchIt2 in response to the Switch It No 2 button's being clicked.

TIP

When a UserForm is open, you can unload it by ending the application or by inserting the statement `Unload UserForm1` when `UserForm1` is its name, or more generically as `Unload Me` when it is the active UserForm.

DEFINING YOUR OWN TYPES

You may want to combine a few related items of data together into new types. These are called *user-defined types*. For example, suppose you want to create a type named LineDetails that combines all the details about a line. All you need to do is place the following type definition into the General Declarations section of a UserForm or module:

```
Type LineDetails
    StartPosition(2) As Double
    EndPosition(2) As Double
    Thickness As Double
    Color As Integer
    Length As Double 'read-only
    Angle As Double 'read only
End Type
```

Notice how the declaration starts with Type and finishes with End Type, and that every element within the declaration has its type explicitly defined. These types need to be specified so that the interpreter can calculate the amount of memory required by a new type, by summing the memory requirements of each element. User-defined types can include other user-defined types, provided that they have been previously declared so that Visual Basic can do its memory calculations.

The benefit of having a user-defined type is that related items of data are grouped together in one named variable that can be passed as a procedure argument, rather than your having to pass each item individually. The scope rules that apply to constants and variables also apply to types. See the section "Scope of Constants and Variables" earlier in this chapter.

USING CONDITIONS TO CONTROL CODE EXECUTION

If statements allow you to set conditions that determine whether a block of code is executed. You have just seen the If statement in action in Listing 19.1. VBA offers a variety of If statement structures, which are all described in this section. Also included here is the Select Case statement, which allows the value of one variable or expression to determine which block of statements from a group to execute.

If... Then... **Block**

The If statement allows you to state conditions that must be met before a block of code statements can be executed. The conditional expression is usually some comparison, such as

```
A = 1
B > C
A + B <= C - D
A <> D
```

where > means greater than, <= means less than or equal to, and < > means not equal to. The "Comparison Operators" sidebar lists all the different combinations available. The block of code inside the If statement is executed only if the conditional expression evaluates to True; otherwise, execution jumps to the End If statement, or to the next line if the whole If statement block is contained in a single statement.

When an If statement block contains only one statement, the whole block can be written on a single line, as shown in the following FindMax function:

```
Function FindMax(Length1, Length2)
    If Length1 < Length2 Then Length1 = Length2
    FindMax = Length1
End Function
```

Alternatively, an If statement block with one statement can also be written over several lines, which requires an End If statement to indicate the end. For example, the same FindMax function can be written as

```
Function FindMax(Length1, Length2)
If Length1 < Length2 Then
```

Part iv

```
        Length1 = Length2
    End If
    FindMax = Length1
    End Function
```

Similarly, several coding statements can be placed on separate lines, as in

```
If A = B then
    C = A + 1
    D = A * 2
    E = A - 3
End If
```

Or they can be placed on the same line, separated by colons:

```
If A = B then
    C = A + 1: D = A * 2: E = A - 3
End If
```

Even the whole If statement can be placed on the same line:

```
If A = B then C = A + 1: D = A * 2: E = A - 3
```

Be aware, though, that code containing multiple statement lines is generally harder to read and maintain as compared with single-statement lines.

You can nest If statements inside other If statements, with each one terminated by an End If. For example:

```
If A = B then
    If  A = C then
        D = 3 * A
    End If
End If
```

Placing one If statement inside another If statement without any other coding statements is considered bad programming practice and can be avoided by combining the conditions, as follows:

```
If A = B and A = C then
    D = 3 * A
End if
```

COMPARISON OPERATORS

Comparison operators are used to compare the values of two expressions and provide a True or False result. Here are the operators available in VBA:

=	Equal
>	Greater than
<	Less than
>=	Greater than or equal to
<=	Less than or equal to
<>	Not equal to

If... Then... Else...

The If...Then...Else... statement allows you to have two blocks of statements: one to be executed if the condition is True, and the other to be executed if the condition is False. For example:

```
If A = B then
    C = A
Else
    C = D
End If
```

The following example gives an If...Then...Else... statement that includes some nested If statements:

```
If Number = 1 Then
    Count1 = Count1 + 1
Else
    If Number = 2 Then
        Count2 = Count2 + 1
    Else
        If Number = 3 then
            Count3 = Count3 + 1
        Else
```

```
                CountX = CountX + 1
            End if
        End If
    End If
```

VBA provides an ElseIf clause that is useful for combining an Else clause that's immediately followed by an If statement. For example, the previous If...Then...Else... block can be rewritten as follows:

```
If Number = 1 Then
    Count1 = Count1 + 1
ElseIf Number = 2 Then
    Count2 = Count2 + 1
ElseIf Number = 3 then
    Count3 = Count3 + 1
Else
    CountX = CountX + 1
End If
```

This rewrite avoids the need for so many End If statements and so much statement indenting. The statement in the last Else clause will be executed if the Number variable is not equal to 1, 2, or 3. This version is easier to read and maintain than the first version. However, where the same variable is being tested at every condition, a Select Case statement provides an even better alternative.

Select Case Statement

The Select Case statement provides a way of selecting a block of code to be executed according to the value of an expression given in the first line of this statement. The designated value can be just about anything; in the following statement, the expression is the name of the door style that's currently selected:

```
Select Case CurrentDoorStyle
Case "Tudor"
   Price = 125.00
Case "Victorian"
   Price = 115.00
```

```
Case "Federation"
    Price = 110.00
Case "Colonial"
    Price = 100.00
Case "Leadlight"
    Price = 210.00
Case "Interior2Panel"
    Price = 79.00
Case "Interior4Panel"
    Price = 89.00
Case Else
    Price = 0.00
End Select
```

The value of the variable `CurrentDoorStyle` is a string specifying the current door's style. When the `Select Case` statement is entered, this string is compared with the strings in each `Case` clause until either a match is found or the `Case Else` clause is encountered. The `Price` variable is then set to the price in the statement from the first `Case` clause that evaluates to True.

USING LOOPS TO REPEAT CODE

This section shows you how to execute a block of code repeatedly, for a specified number of times using the `For` loop, or until a certain condition arises using the `While` loop. You'll find these two loops used in many of the coding exercises throughout Chapters 16 through 19. The `For` loop is especially useful when all the objects in a collection need to be accessed, and the `While` loop is especially useful for data input from either a file or the user.

Repeating Code a Set Number of Times

When you want to repeatedly execute a block of statements a specific number of times, use a `For` loop. The `For` loop has the following structure:

```
For Counter = Start to Finish [Step stepsize]
Statements
Next [Counter]
```

where Counter is the variable that keeps tabs on how many times the loop has been executed.

When the For loop is first entered, the Counter variable is initialized to Start. All the statements are then executed until the Next clause. If a step has been specified, it is added to the Counter; otherwise, Counter is incremented by one, which is the default. *Steps* specify how much the counter is incremented and can be positive or negative; negative steps are used when the value assigned to Start is greater than the value assigned to Finish.

When the Counter variable becomes greater than the Finish value (or less than, if you're using negative steps), code execution jumps to the statement after the Next clause.

WARNING

The variable used for the loop counter should never be updated inside the loop. Doing so may lead to a never-ending loop, or the loop may be terminated prematurely.

The For loop is ideal for processing the data values in an array. With an array, the Start and Finish values are replaced by the index value for the first and last elements in the array. For example, to change the color of all the lines stored in the AllLines array to green, use the following code:

```
For Counter = 0 to 534
    AllLines(Counter).Color = acGreen
Next
```

For loops can be nested inside other For loops, which is ideal for processing multidimensional arrays. For example, consider the following three-dimensional array:

```
Dim AllData(0 to 4,5,1 to 6) as Double
```

To initialize all the elements in this array to 0, you'd use the following code:

```
For Index1 = 0 to 4
    For Index2 = 0 to 4
        For Index3 = 1 to 6
            AllData(Index1,Index2,Index3) = 0.0
        Next Index3
    Next Index2
Next Index1
```

TIP

Although it's not a requirement, placing the loop counters after the Next clauses can improve the readability of your code, especially when several For loops are nested inside one another. The loop counters become even more important when there are lots of statements.

There is also a For Each loop that allows you to access each item from a collection of objects or an array. The syntax of the For Each loop is given in the "The Microsoft Forms Object Model" section later in this chapter.

REPEATING CODE AN UNKNOWN NUMBER OF TIMES

When you want to repeat a block of code while some condition evaluates to True (or False), but you don't know the number of times required, you need to include a While loop. The structure of the While loop is as follows:

```
While condition
statements
Wend
```

One of the most common uses of the While loop is to read data from a file when it is not always clear how many data items the file contains.

When the interpreter enters the While loop, it evaluates the condition. If the condition evaluates to True, the statements inside the While loop are executed until the Wend clause is encountered. Then the interpreter jumps back up to the start of the loop and evaluates the condition again. This looping is repeated until the condition becomes False, when execution jumps down to the statement after the Wend clause.

TIP

While loops are the most likely cause of a program's failing to stop, so you must exercise great care to ensure that at least one of the variables in the condition actually changes inside the loop. The best place to update this variable is in the statement preceding the Wend clause.

There is also a Do loop that lets you choose whether the condition is checked at the beginning or the end of the loop.

Overview of Objects, Properties, Methods, and Events

VBA is an object-oriented environment, containing many different classes of objects. Each class has its own set of properties to define the appearance of the objects, and methods to manipulate the objects that are instances of that class.

Some classes, such as Toolbox controls, also have their own set of event procedures that are coded with the application's response to user events. Don't let the substantial number of these objects, properties, methods, and events overwhelm you—a little goes a long way. You only need to know about a few of them to get started.

All about Objects

Everything relating to an object is defined in its class. There are two main groups of AutoCAD objects:

Drawing Objects   Drawing objects represent anything that has been drawn in the Model Space tab of the AutoCAD window (for another look at this window, see Figure 17.9 in Chapter 17). Even when you draw a simple line, AutoCAD creates an object to store all the details needed to regenerate it.

VBA (UserForm) Objects   UserForm objects represent anything that's included in the Graphical User Interface (GUI). So, each time you drag and drop a control from the Toolbox, an object is created that is an instance of that class of control.

Classes of Objects

In the object-oriented paradigm, each type of object and all its properties, methods, and events are encapsulated in a single class that has the same name as the type of object it contains. *Classes* can be thought of as templates for creating as many objects as you need. A class contains the code required to create an instance of that class. For example, when a new object is created, its Name property is assigned the name of the class it is based on, followed by a sequential number to distinguish the new object from any other instances of the same class.

TIP

Objects are said to be *instances* of classes, and their properties, methods, and events are said to be *members* of that class.

Collections of Objects

Related objects are grouped together into *collections*. Collections of objects provide the same benefits as arrays, in that items in the collection can all be referenced using a single name and an index value. A collection differs from an array, however, in that it can contain different types of items. For example, AutoCAD has a ModelSpace collection containing all the objects associated with the Model Space tab. VBA has a Forms collection that contains all the UserForm objects associated with the GUI; UserForms contain objects such as text boxes and command buttons that the user interacts with.

AutoCAD maintains many collections of objects, including the Model-Space, PaperSpace, Documents, Layers, LineTypes, TextStyles, and View-Ports collections. When you insert a UserForm into a project, VBA creates a Controls collection, and any control objects you drag and drop from the Toolbox are automatically added to the Controls collection as you place them on the UserForm.

As already mentioned, objects in a collection—called *members*—need not belong to the same class. You can reference members in several ways; one way is to use an exclamation mark character (!) to associate the object with the collection:

```
UserForm1.Controls!TextBox1.Text = "Hello"
```

If you are an Excel user, you will already be familiar with this notation.

An alternative referencing method is to use an index to identify the member's position within the collection. The *position* is the order in which it was placed on the UserForm:

```
UserForm1.Controls(0).Text = "Text box 1"
```

This statement sets the Text property of the first object placed on User-Form1 to the string "Text box 1". You can also replace the index number with the control's name, if known:

```
UserForm1.Controls.("TextBox1").Text = "Hello"
```

Part iv

Both examples of using indices make use of the fact that the Item method is the default method of any collection and so can be implied. The following statement explicitly uses the Item method and has a numerical index value:

```
UserForm1.Controls.Item(0).Text = "Hello"
```

This statement is said to *fully qualify* the TextBox object. Because the Text property is the default property of a text box, and the Item method is the default method of a collection, and the Controls collection is the default collection of a UserForm, and UserForm1 is the active UserForm, the previous statement can be entered in the Code window belonging to UserForm1 as

```
TextBox1 = "Hello"
```

with the UserForm, the Controls collection, the Item method, and the Text property all being implied.

AutoCAD Drawing Objects

AutoCAD has its own set of drawing objects that help you add the various components needed to construct a drawing. Figure 19.5 shows the hierarchical structure of the AutoCAD object model.

Attaching the Add prefix to a drawing object's name is a common way to create drawing objects. For example, the following statement creates a Circle object:

```
Application.Documents.Item(0).ModelSpace.AddCircle Center,
Radius
```

The Application Object

The AutoCAD Application object sits at the top of the model and represents the current session of the AutoCAD application. As you draw items, their details are stored in objects and added to this Application object. Because only one AutoCAD Application object is allowed per session, the application can be implied when accessing the objects it contains. So, the statement example from the preceding section can be rewritten as

```
Documents.Item(0).ModelSpace.AddCircle Center, Radius
```

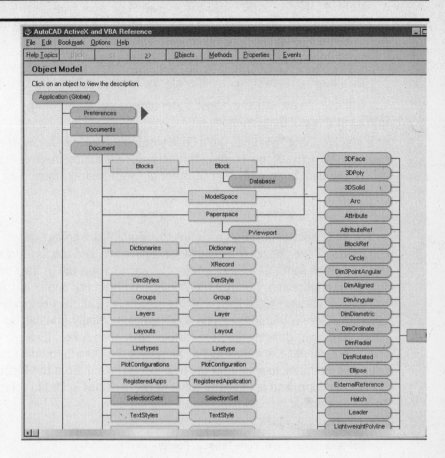

FIGURE 19.5: The AutoCAD object model

The Documents Collection

The AutoCAD Documents collection, which is the next level down from the Application object, allows you to access any document that's currently open in the AutoCAD application. You use the Item method with an index value to denote the Document object's position in the collection.

AutoCAD provides two ways to access the active (or current) document: via the ActiveDocument property (of the Application object), or by using the keyword ThisDrawing. These two methods are illustrated in the following two statements, which are equivalent:

```
ActiveDocument.ModelSpace.AddCircle MyCenter, MyRadius
ThisDrawing.ModelSpace.AddCircle MyCenter, MyRadius
```

You will need to use either of these statements if you are entering code into a UserForm's Code window.

If you are using ThisDrawing's Code window, because only one document can be active at any point in time, the documents themselves can also be implied. So you can rewrite either of the preceding statements as follows:

```
ModelSpace.AddCircle MyCenter, MyRadius
```

The Documents collection includes the ModelSpace collection, which comprises all the objects from the Model Space tab, and the Layouts collection, which contains a Layout object for each Layout tab in the open AutoCAD application. Because the Document object can access any of the collections associated with drawing objects, and all the objects contained in these collections can be accessed individually, you can, in effect, access any drawing object in the currently open AutoCAD application. For example, the following For loop uses the Item method with Count as the index to access all the objects one by one from the Model-Space collection, and assigns the value of the constant acRed to their Color properties:

```
Sub ChangeColor()
For Count = 0 To ModelSpace.Count
    ModelSpace.Item(Count).Color = acRed
Next
End Sub
```

The Microsoft Forms Object Model

AutoCAD's VBA is an object-oriented programming environment that contains a large collection of objects. Figure 19.6 shows the hierarchical structure of the Forms object model.

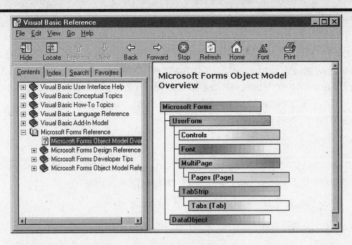

FIGURE 19.6: Microsoft Forms object model

To view the Microsoft Forms object model:

1. Choose Help ➤ Microsoft Visual Basic Help to display the Visual Basic References dialog box.

2. Select the Contents tab and click Microsoft Forms Reference to expand its list.

3. Double-click the Microsoft Forms Object Model Overview item. The Microsoft Forms object model appears in the right pane, as shown in Figure 19.6.

Objects in the Forms object model have sets of properties, events, and methods that help you develop applications with which users can interact.

The Microsoft Forms Collection

The Microsoft Forms collection sits at the top of the model and contains all the UserForm objects from the next level down. A UserForm object, which can be a window or a dialog box, is the main part of the GUI; it acts like a container for the controls the user handles. Each UserForm has properties that are assigned values, allowing it to be maximized, minimized, or closed in the same way as any standard window. Other properties can be assigned text strings and colors to define how they will appear on the screen.

Part iv

The Controls Collection

Each UserForm object has a Controls collection that contains all the Control objects that have been dragged from the Toolbox and positioned on the UserForm. A Control object from the Controls collection can be identified by a number representing the order in which it was placed on the UserForm. For example, a Label control that was the first object placed on UserForm1 can be accessed as

```
UserForm1.Controls(0)
```

This naming system gives you the advantage of being able to access all the controls in a collection using a For loop, as follows:

```
For Each CurrentControl In Controls
    CurrentControl.BackColor = vbBlue
Next
```

The For statement initially accesses the first control from the Controls collection and assigns it to the CurrentControl variable. The next statement (CurrentControl.BackColor = vbBlue) sets its BackColor property to blue. At the Next statement, execution loops back to the beginning of the For statement, and the next control in the collection is assigned to the CurrentControl variable. The looping continues until all the controls in the collection have been set to blue.

The Label control that you used in the Metric-Imperial Converter application in Chapter 16 can also be accessed using the following formats:

```
UserForm1.Controls!Label1
UserForm1.Controls("Label1")
UserForm1.Label1.
```

If you are accessing a control from code entered into the Code window that belongs to the same UserForm as the control, you can refer to the control by name, and the UserForm portion can be implied, like this:

```
Label1
```

TIP
The format I've chosen is to refer to controls by name only. The exception is when the control belongs to a different UserForm, in which case the name of the UserForm also needs to be included.

All about Properties

Each class of object has its own set of properties. These properties are initially set to default values when the object they belong to is first created. *Properties* define how an object appears on the screen, including things such as coloring, dimensions, and position—there is even a Visible property that can be set to False so that the object cannot be seen at all. Values can be assigned to properties at design time in the Properties window from the IDE. You can also assign properties at runtime by assigning values in code. For example, the Properties window for UserForms contains Height and Width entries, and the following statements show how these properties can also be assigned in code:

```
UserForm1.Height = 150
UserForm2.Width = 200
```

DESIGN TIME VS. RUNTIME

All the time you spend puttering around in the IDE developing a project is considered *design time* because you are still designing your project. Anything that happens while your code is actually executing is said to happen in *runtime*. During design time, you will spend your time creating the GUI and developing the code to respond to a user's actions. While creating the GUI you will set properties such as Name, Caption, and Text in the Properties window.

Other kinds of items will require your attention in runtime. For example, you may need to change a property while your application is running, such as making a control visible or invisible; or you may need to give a control such as a text box the focus, so that the Entry cursor appears inside it ready for the user's input.

Changing Properties with Preset Values

Many properties can only be set to one of a limited number of predefined values. These are the Enumerated types. Such properties can be set in the Properties window at design time, or by assigning them the values of predefined constants in code. When you select these properties from the Properties window, a down-arrow button appears in the settings column to indicate that a drop-down list of values is available for you to choose from.

The following steps show you how to change the `StartUpPosition` and `BackColor` properties of `UserForm1`:

1. Select `UserForm1` from the Object list at the top of the Properties window. Select the `StartUpPosition` property. A down-arrow button appears to the right of the settings column to let you know that this property can only be set to one of the predefined values in the drop-down list that appears, as shown in Figure 19.7.

FIGURE 19.7: The Drop-down list for the `StartUpPosition` property

2. Select the CenterScreen setting. The setting appears in the settings column for the `StartUpPosition` property.

TIP

The `StartUpPosition` property is unique to the UserForm class of object and determines the position of the UserForm on the screen.

3. Continuing with `UserForm1` still active, click the `BackColor` property in either tab (Alphabetic or Categorized) of the Properties Window, and click the down-arrow button that appears.

4. A drop-down list with two tabs appears. The System tab (Figure 19.8) contains all the color settings that have been

assigned to Microsoft Windows components by the current Display Scheme in Control Panel. The Palette tab (Figure 19.9) contains the array of colors available in the default palette on your PC.

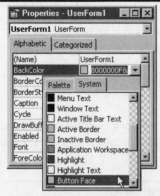

FIGURE 19.8: System tab, containing colors assigned to Windows components according to the Display Scheme in use

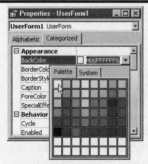

FIGURE 19.9: Palette tab, containing the palette of colors available on your PC

5. Open the Palette tab and click the top-left color square, which is white (see Figure 19.9). The Palette disappears, and the background of the UserForm changes to the color selected.

TIP

Changing the background color of a UserForm does not automatically update the background color of any controls placed on that UserForm. These will need to have their background colors explicitly changed, too. For example, if the User-Form contains any Label controls, only their caption text should be visible now that you've changed the color in step 4. If setting the background property has no effect, make sure the BackStyle property is set to fmBackStyleOpaque.

Changing Properties with Preset Values in Code

When you're assigning properties to the values of Enumerated types in code, a drop-down list containing all the constant names for these values will appear, as shown in Figure 19.10.

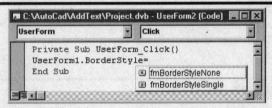

FIGURE 19.10: A drop-down list of Enumerated types

Changing Properties from Dialog Boxes

Some properties display an ellipsis button when selected. Clicking one of these buttons opens a dialog box that is often retrieved from the Microsoft Windows environment under which you're currently running. For example, the following steps show you how to change the Font property for UserForm1:

1. Start a new application, insert a UserForm, and add a Label control. From the Properties window, select Label1 from the Objects list and click the Font property. An ellipsis button appears at the right of the settings column, as shown in Figure 19.11.

FIGURE 19.11: The ellipsis button beside the Font property indicates that a dialog box will be displayed when this is selected.

2. Click the ellipsis button. The Font dialog box appears (Figure 19.12).

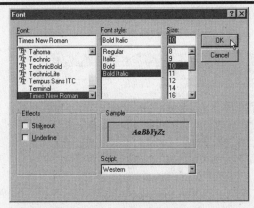

FIGURE 19.12: The Font dialog box

3. Select Times New Roman from the Font list, Bold Italic from the Font Style list, and 10 from the Size list. Click OK. The Font dialog box closes, and the Label1 text appears, written using the new Font property settings.

Now that you've read through the steps for changing properties in the Properties window at design time, let's see how to change them from code so that they are updated while your application is running.

Changing Properties from Dialog Boxes in Code

The following steps show you how to set the Font property in code so that the changes will occur at runtime:

1. Double-click CommandButton1. The Code window opens, displaying the Click event procedure for the CommandButton1 object.

2. Enter the following statement, finishing with a period character (.):

   ```
   commandbutton1.font.
   ```

   The pop-up list of properties belonging to the Font object appears. Compare this list with the items shown in the Font dialog box in Figure 19.12. You'll notice that many of the same options are available, such as Strikethrough, and so on.

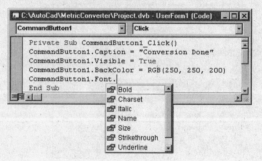

3. Type the remainder of the statement you started at step 2 as follows:

   ```
   commandbutton1.font.name="Arial Black"
   ```

   Choose Run ➤ Run Sub/UserForm to run your program, and click the Convert button. The caption on the command button changes to the new settings.

TIP

When you adjust a property setting in code, the new setting is available only while the application is running—the value assigned in the code will not be associated with that property in the Properties window when you return to Design mode.

All about Methods

A *method* is a procedure that performs some action on the object with which it is associated. Some examples of methods that belong to the AutoCAD drawing object are AddText, AddLine, GetAngle, and Rotate. When called, some methods have parameters to which you assign values by listing arguments in the same order as the parameters are declared. The pop-up text from the Parameter Info editing feature gives you the parameters in the order required. This order allows the interpreter to match up the parameters with the arguments.

The Rotate method has two parameters: BasePoint, which is the center of rotation, and RotationAngle, which is the angle to be rotated. These parameters are listed in a pop-up when you type **Rotate** into the Code window, followed by a space.

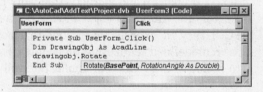

The method's parameters can be passed values using arguments, as follows:

```
DrawingObj.Rotate CenterOfRotation, RotationAngle
```

In this example, the variable CenterOfRotation argument is a three-element array to which you pass the x-, y-, and z-coordinates of a 3D point. The variable RotationAngle argument is passed an angle in radians as required by the Rotate method.

Other methods, such as GetAngle, return a value, so you need to assign the value returned to a variable. For example:

```
ReturnedAngle = ThisDrawing.Utility.GetAngle()
```

TIP

In an assignment statement, the interpreter still requires the parenthesis after the method's name even though no arguments are passed.

TIP

When reading the properties and methods attached to an object, it is often less confusing to read from right to left. For example, the statement ReturnedAngle = ThisDrawing.Utility.GetAngle() can be read as "The variable ReturnedAngle is assigned the value returned by the GetAngle method of the Utility object, which is identified by the Utility property of the active document object named ThisDrawing."

All about Events

UserForms and the controls placed on them from the Toolbox all have their own sets of properties and methods that work in much the same way as those from the AutoCAD object model. Because these objects are part of the GUI, they are expected to respond to a user's actions, so they have their own predefined set of event procedures. For each control, it's up to you to decide what events your application will respond to and what the reaction will be.

The Microsoft Windows operating system continually monitors all the open windows on your PC for any sign of activity (events) from the user, from a program, or from a window. When an activity occurs, a message is sent to the operating system, which passes it around to all the open windows and their controls. Visual Basic automatically processes any relevant messages. If you've written code for a particular event happening to a specific control and the message comes in that the event has occurred, Visual Basic executes the code from that control's event procedure. This style of processing is called *event driven*.

Visual Basic's event-driven model can catch you up sometimes; you must remember that running code from one event can sometimes trigger another event procedure. For example, if you have coded the Change event procedure for a TextBox control and your code assigns a new text string to that text box, your Change event procedure will be invoked, which may cause your program to perform in some unexpected way that could even lead to an abnormal termination.

The set of executable events varies from control to control, but there is a lot of overlap, and often the same event is common to many controls. For example, the Click event is found in UserForms, text boxes, command buttons, option buttons, check boxes, and lots more.

The event procedures have names made up of the control's Name property, then an underscore character (_), followed by the name of the event. Here are a few examples:

```
CommandButton1_Click

OptionButton1_MouseDown

TextBox1_KeyPress
```

TIP

The IDE provides pairs of first and last statements for all event procedures—I refer to these as *skeleton procedures*. All you need to do is decide which user events you want to respond to, and code your response in the appropriate skeleton.

COMPARING VBA PROGRAMMING CONSTRUCTS

This section describes what is meant by each of the terms *macro*, *procedure*, *function*, *program*, and *application*, including the relationships and differences that exist among them.

Macros

A macro is a set of instructions that is executed each time its name or associated shortcut key is used. Macros can be one-liners or they can be quite lengthy and complex—they can even call other macros and run applications.

Macros cannot have parameters, and they cannot return values, but they can be run from the AutoCAD window.

Macros are declared in the same way as normal procedures, using the Sub statement. For example:

```
Sub MyMacro( )
```

If you include any parameters inside the parentheses, for example,

```
Sub MyMacro(CurrentString As String)
```

Visual Basic will treat this block of code as a standard procedure, and it will not appear in the list in the Macros dialog box that's displayed from the AutoCAD window.

Procedures

A procedure contains a set of coding statements that perform a specific task. Visual Basic procedures are a series of statements enclosed between Sub and End Sub statements.

Procedures enable you to split a lengthy piece of code up into smaller more manageable parts, with each part becoming a procedure. It is good programming practice to use procedures when the same task needs to be performed from several different places—to avoid duplicate code.

For example, the Shelf Specification application shown in Figure 19.13 contains a procedure that examines the key pressed by the user to enter data into a text box, checking to see if it is a numeric character. If not, the application cancels the keystroke so that the non-numeric character is not appended to the string in the text box. The procedure is called by the KeyPress event procedures of all three text boxes.

FIGURE 19.13: Shelf Specification UserForm

The following steps show you how to develop the Shelf Specification application:

1. Start a new project and add a UserForm with three labels, three text boxes, and a command button.

2. Set the properties as shown in Table 19.1.

3. Type the CheckNumericKey procedure shown in Listing 19.2 into the General Declarations section of the UserForm. Enter the calls to it into the skeleton Keypress event procedures of the text boxes.

4. Run your application from the Visual Basic Editor window and try entering some letters and numbers. The letters will be cancelled by the CheckNumericKey procedure and won't appear in any of the text boxes. Only when you type numeric characters will the numbers they represent be appended to the text box strings.

TABLE 19.1 Control Properties for Shelf Specification Application

OBJECT	CAPTION
UserForm1	Shelf Specification
Label1	Height
Label2	Width
Label3	Thickness
Command button	Continue

Listing 19.2: *CheckNumericKey* Procedure

```
1   Sub CheckNumericKey(ByRef Keyascii As
    MSForms.ReturnInteger)
2       If Keyascii < 48 Or Keyascii > 57 Then
3           Keyascii = 0
4       End If
5   End Sub
6
```

```
7    Private Sub TextBox1_KeyPress(
         ByVal Keyascii As MSForms.ReturnInteger)
8        CheckNumericKey Keyascii
9    End Sub
10
11   Private Sub TextBox2_KeyPress(
         ByVal Keyascii As MSForms.ReturnInteger)
12       CheckNumericKey Keyascii
13   End Sub
14
15   Private Sub TextBox3_KeyPress(
         ByVal Keyascii As MSForms.ReturnInteger)
16       CheckNumericKey Keyascii
17   End Sub
```

This code works as follows:

▶ Line 1 starts the CheckNumericKey procedure, which has one parameter that expects to be passed the character entered by the user. This procedure cancels any character entered that is outside the range 0 to 9.

▶ Line 2 verifies that the Keyascii character entered by the user is not in the range 48 through 57. The ASCII code for 0 is 48, and the ASCII code for 9 is 57, so the condition is True if a non-numeric key has been pressed.

▶ Line 3 runs when a non-numeric key has been pressed; it sets the Keyascii variable to 0. When 0 is passed back to the calling event procedure, the user input is cancelled.

▶ Line 4 ends the If statement.

▶ Line 5 ends the CheckNumericKey procedure.

▶ Line 6 is a blank line to make the code easier to read.

▶ Line 7 starts the KeyPress event procedure of TextBox1. The KeyPress event procedure has one parameter that is passed the ASCII code of the key pressed by the user while entering data into TextBox1.

▶ Line 8 calls the CheckNumericKey procedure with Keyascii as the argument. If a numeric key has been entered, the Keyascii value returned is appended to the end of the string displayed in the text box. If a non-numeric key has been entered, the Keyascii value returned is 0, and nothing is appended to the string.

▶ Line 9 ends the KeyPress event procedure of TextBox1.

▶ Line 10 is a blank line to make the code easier to read.

▶ Lines 11–13 and 15–17 contain the Keypress event procedures of the other two text boxes, which both call the CheckNumeric-Key procedure in exactly the same way as the KeyPress event procedure of TextBox1.

▶ Line 14 is a blank line to make the code easier to read.

SETTING THE TAB ORDER FOR CONTROLS

When your application is running, you can tab from text box to text box. The tab order is the same as the order in which you added the controls. This section describes how you can change this order—especially if you want to add more controls as an afterthought.

If you have ever had a broken mouse, you may have resorted to pressing the Tab key to move around among controls. The following steps show you how to set the tabs in your application using the TabIndex property, so that users can tab through your controls in a logical order.

1. Start a new application and insert a UserForm containing two text boxes and a command button.

2. Choose Run ➤ Sub/UserForm. UserForm1 opens with the Enter cursor positioned inside the text box at the top.

3. Press the Tab key. The focus is moved to the next control in the Tab sequence, which is the second text box because it

was placed on the UserForm after the first text box. By default, the Tab sequence follows the order in which the controls were placed on the UserForm.

4. Press Tab again. A dotted rectangle appears on the command button to show that it now has the focus. If you press Enter at this moment, the application will react as if you had clicked this command button and will execute the associated event.

TIP

Using the Shift+Tab key combination allows you to go through the Tab sequence backward.

5. Click the Close button to stop the application.

6. Press Tab again; it still works, even though the application isn't running. This time, the control with the focus is displayed just like the active control is displayed—with a thick border and eight handles.

TIP

The order of the controls in the Tab sequence is initially determined by the chronological order in which controls were placed on the UserForm. If you are in Design mode, the Tab key visits all the controls in the sequence as you tab along. But when an application is running, only the controls with which the user interacts are visited by tabbing.

Suppose you need to add another text box between the two that are there already. By default, the Tab key will not visit this new, third text box until it has visited the command button. To change this arrangement, you set the TabIndex property in the Properties window or in the code. The TabIndex property of each control is assigned a number that starts with zero, which represents the control's position in the Tab sequence. If you adjust the TabIndex number of one of the controls, it is slotted into that position in the sequence, and the TabIndex properties of all the other controls are automatically updated accordingly.

Functions

A function is a special kind of procedure that returns a single value, by assigning it to the function's name in the statement immediately before the End Function statement at the close of the function. You can append a type for this value to the end of the function's opening statement, as follows:

```
Function MyMacro(MyValue As Integer) As String
```

If the type is omitted, Visual Basic applies the Variant type.

Parameters and Arguments

A parameter is defined in the declaration of a function or procedure and is assigned a value by the calling statement, which is called an argument.

Parameters

Parameters make a procedure more generic, so it's quite common to have a list of parameters specified in parentheses as the first line (which is where the procedure is declared). Commas separate the parameters in the list, as shown here:

```
Sub ProcessTwoValues(Value1 As Integer, Value2 As Integer)
```

In the procedure call, arguments are used to pass values to these parameters, matching the values with parameters according to their order. For example, the procedure call for the ProcessTwoValues procedure could be as follows:

```
ProcessTwoValues 10, 6
```

where the first argument 10 is passed (or assigned) to the first parameter Value1, and the second argument 6 is passed (or assigned) to Value2.

Arguments

When you call a procedure that has parameters, you allocate values in the way of arguments. These arguments are matched up with the procedure's parameters, and the procedure executes. A procedure can be called in two ways:

```
ProcessTwoValues 4, 3
Call ProcessTwoValues (4, 3)
```

Both ways use the comma character (,) to separate the arguments. If you use the Call statement method, you must enclose the arguments in parentheses.

Programs

A program is a sequence of instructions that can be executed to perform some task. The term program is fairly generic and can encompass macros, procedures, and functions. The sequence of instructions can be in a high-level language such as Visual Basic, or in some other language that can be executed by a computer.

Applications

An application is a program developed to simplify a specific task such as word processing, spreadsheet analysis, or computer-aided drafting. The application is typically much larger than a single procedure, with plenty of facilities to perform various related tasks; the application seldom does just one particular thing.

An application normally has a GUI so that the user can interactively select the features to run. The act of selecting a feature causes one of the application's event procedures to run, which in turn might call a function, a macro, or a procedure that would carry out the user's requests.

WHAT'S NEXT?

This chapter has explained the coding concepts and terminology of VBA. This chapter will serve as a handy reference to you as you continue to gain experience on your own. The next chapter is focused on understanding AutoCAD database objects. Gaining this understanding is critical if you would like to learn how to create more complex forms of automation.

Chapter 20

UNDERSTANDING THE AutoCAD DATABASE

Before you start looking at specific objects in a drawing database, you need to understand the general concept of drawing data. This chapter provides basic information about the internals of AutoCAD's drawing database.

Adapted from *Mastering™ AutoCAD® 2000 Objects*
by Dietmar Rudolph
ISBN 0-7821-2562-X   448 pages $49.99

In the process of presenting this information, I will define a number of terms. Many of them, such as *containers* or *objects*, you already know from daily life. However, they have a special meaning when discussing computer-generated data. And they have an even more specific meaning when discussing a computer-generated drawing. Therefore, it's necessary to define these terms precisely.

NOTE
In books about computer graphics or programming, you'll often find various authors using different terms to describe the same thing. In this chapter, I try to stay with the terminology used in the AutoCAD documentation. For a variety of reasons, mostly historic, this terminology does not always reflect the current industry standard. For example, in AutoCAD an *attribute* is a specific object type; usually, *attribute* is synonymous with the term *property*.

In this chapter, we'll take a look at the general structure of a computer-generated drawing. We'll discuss the data elements saved in a drawing file and how to differentiate them. We'll also examine the internal composition of the drawing data and how the elements of the data correlate. In addition, you will see how objects are identified and linked.

An important question that concerns exchanging drawings between different programs is also a topic in this chapter: Is a drawing database a complete entity? In other words, does the information in an AutoCAD drawing file contain all the data necessary to construct an identical drawing in another program? And a second question arises: Is the documentation of an AutoCAD drawing file, for instance the one in this book, ever complete? This chapter will give you the answers to these questions.

What's in a Drawing?

Before I answer this question, let's start with the basic question: What *is* a drawing? In the pre-CAD era, a drawing was a sheet of paper, Mylar, or papyrus, containing lines in ink or color that formed a visual representation of a real-world or an imaginary object.

A computer-generated "drawing" still describes a real-world or an imaginary object, but it does so by using a mathematical model of the object. The CAD model of a car consists of multiple CAD models, including wheels, tires, and brakes. A tire has a geometrical description, but also has manufacturing properties such as materials and additional functional information such as maximum speed or inflation.

Although you still can output a CAD model onto a sheet of paper, the paper representation is only one of many uses for such a model. In addition, many different visual representations of the model may exist. The paper output may show a front or a side view, may show a detail of the braking system, or may demonstrate what a fully colored production model of the car looks like when caught in a traffic jam.

AutoCAD Drawings or AutoCAD Models?

You may want to say that these fully featured CAD models aren't here yet. Of all AutoCAD drawing files out there, 99.9 percent contain only lines and circles, as did the paper drawings of old.

Although you are correct about the contents of most drawing files, that a drafter used circles to draw a tire doesn't tell you anything about the relationship of lines on the page to the actual tires they represent. An AutoCAD drawing database can contain mathematical models of tires and brakes, just as it can contain lines.

And if you look closely, you'll see that there is no difference between a CAD tire and a CAD line. Both are abstract models of some real-world or abstract object. The CAD tire is an abstract model of a real-world tire. The CAD line is usually an abstract model of the edge of a real-world part.

OF OBJECTS AND CONTAINERS

An AutoCAD drawing is no more than a container for arbitrary abstract models or arbitrary *objects*. This collection of objects is called the *drawing database*.

In many aspects, the drawing database is similar to other databases you already know about or have worked with. Just like the database you use to organize your address book or CD collection, the drawing database contains tables that consist of rows (records) and columns (fields).

Records or objects in the drawing database can be ordinary lines or circles, but it is equally possible, and becoming increasingly probable, that some objects can be cars and tires, walls and doors, books and authors.

AutoCAD places almost no limit on what an object in a drawing database can be. Only if the object is supposed to have a visual representation must it follow a few rules; for instance, an AutoCAD object must have a color property.

Part iv

The creator of an AutoCAD drawing database is free to add arbitrary objects to it. However, the creator is not free to add objects wherever he or she wants. Each object must be placed in one and only one of a number of containers that form the drawing database.

Symbol Tables

Objects that don't have a visual representation but belong to a certain predefined set of object types (or classes) must go into the Symbol Tables container. The Symbol Tables container is made from nine database tables:

- ▶ The dimension style table (`AcDbDimStyleTable`, DIMSTYLE) defines a set of properties to be applied to dimensions, such as the arrow type or text justification.

- ▶ The layer table (`AcDbLayerTable`, LAYER) is for the layer objects that can be used to organize drawing entities.

- ▶ The linetype table (`AcDbLinetypeTable`, LTYPE) contains line styles that define how drawing entities will be displayed or plotted.

- ▶ The table of registered applications (`AcDbRegAppTable`, APPID) contains the names of third-party applications that save extended object data (xdata).

- ▶ The text style table (`AcDbTextStyleTable`, STYLE) defines a set of properties to be applied to text objects, such as the font and the character orientation.

- ▶ The user coordinate system table (`AcDbUCSTable`, UCS) lists Cartesian coordinate systems that a user might activate and work in.

- ▶ The viewport table (`AcDbViewportTable`, VPORT) defines named sets of tiled screen viewports.

- ▶ The view table (`AcDbViewTable`, VIEW) contains the definition of views into a drawing. A user can call such a view for display or plot.

In addition to these symbol tables, the special block table (`AcDbBlockTable`, BLOCK_RECORD) consists of the block containers and all drawing entities.

Like a database table in dBase or Microsoft Access, each symbol table can contain only a specific type of object. The objects within a symbol table are called the *symbol table records*. Symbol table records in a symbol table are always objects of the same class. For example, all records in the layer table are layer record objects. Conversely, layer record objects aren't allowed anywhere outside the layer table.

All the records within a symbol table contain a name field that acts as an identifier or a key to the table record. Again, this is similar to the primary key in a database table. The key value is a string and must be unique inside a symbol table to prevent duplicate data and to maintain data integrity. In this way, it is similar to a Social Security number in a corporation's employee records file. This key field identifier is unique only within one symbol table. Thus, both the layer and the linetype tables can include records whose key fields are STANDARD, but within one symbol table, two records cannot use the same key field value. There is one exception to this one record–one key rule: the AcDbViewportTable is allowed to have duplicate keys.

The case of individual characters within a symbol table key does not matter. Thus, a symbol table can include a Standard key or a STANDARD key, but not both.

In addition to the key field, the records in a symbol table have several other fields. A layer table record, for instance, contains fields to store the color associated with this layer, its linetype, its lock status, and many other properties.

Understanding Dictionaries

Symbol tables or any other database tables that use fixed records are inflexible. All records in a symbol table must look exactly the same. For example, you cannot mix linetype records with layer records in one table.

However, in a drawing database, you have to deal with a number of different types of objects or records. You need to be able to put a circle object and a line object into a common container. Therefore, the drawing database contains a more flexible container for objects than the symbol tables. These containers are called *dictionaries*.

Every dictionary is a container for arbitrary objects, and each object in a dictionary is called a *record*. But unlike a symbol table, a dictionary can contain objects of different types, including other dictionaries. By putting complete dictionaries into another dictionary, you create a hierarchical structure of dictionaries that looks like a tree. At the bottom of this tree is a "root" dictionary, the one that is not contained in any other dictionary.

In an AutoCAD drawing database, every dictionary is either contained in the root dictionary (directly or through a series of intermediate dictionaries), or it is linked to a specific drawing entity (for instance, a circle).

Like a symbol table, within each dictionary each record has a key value. This key value is unique within the dictionary, and, unlike symbol table records, the case of characters is significant. All objects that don't have a visual representation and aren't a symbol table record must go into a dictionary. No objects without visual representation exist outside of dictionaries or symbol tables.

You might be wondering why the distinction is made between symbol tables and dictionaries. There is no technical reason that a symbol table should not be just another dictionary. Symbol tables have been used in the drawing database much longer than dictionaries. Autodesk simply made the decision to differentiate between the two some time ago, and the distinction remains to this day.

Combining Entities into Blocks

Now you've learned where objects *without* a visual representation go. But where do you put those objects that *have* a graphical representation? These objects are called *entities* and are usually those in which most people are interested.

Again, entities go into containers. The containers for objects with graphical representation are called *blocks*. A drawing database can contain any number of blocks. Like dictionaries, blocks have a root container. No, it's not a root block, because blocks don't have a graphical representation and cannot belong to a block. And, no, the block container is not a dictionary. It's a symbol table: the blocks table.

A block container can contain any number of entities—that is, objects that have a visual representation. A block can reference, but not contain, other block objects. By referencing another block, a block displays a transformed graphical representation of the complete contents of the referenced block.

Because each object in a block has a visual representation, a computer program such as AutoCAD can draw an image of the block contents to the screen or to a printout. This is called the *visualization* of the block.

Any block can be visualized. The AutoCAD drawing editor interacts directly with a block called *MODEL_SPACE, adding entities to it, deleting entities, or modifying them. For this reason, the contents of the *MODEL_ SPACE* block are what most people would call the "drawing."

In addition, the AutoCAD layout editor directly interacts with a block called *PAPER_SPACE*. This block references views of the *MODEL_SPACE* block and combines it with other entities. Because this block describes the layout of AutoCAD entities on a printout, other people would call *this* the "drawing."

WARNING

If your application works inside AutoCAD, be aware that activating a different layout *renames* the *PAPER_SPACE* block, exchanging its contents with that of another layout block, *PAPER_SPACE0*.

Technically, there is no difference between these blocks and any other. Even in AutoCAD, commands such as the Contents Explorer can visualize other blocks, and commands such as Refedit directly interact with other blocks.

Any block can contain any object that has a graphical representation. Such objects include lines, arcs, and circles, but likewise there may be cars and tires, walls and doors, books and authors. No key field is associated with the objects in a block container other than the database-global object identifier (discussed later). Thus, a block container is simply a list of objects.

Non-objects in the Drawing Database

So you have entities that have a graphical representation, and you have all the other objects that don't have a graphical representation. Can there be more than that?

Unfortunately, yes. An AutoCAD drawing file contains things that are not database objects. Again, there doesn't seem to be any functional reason for this. If you design a drawing database from scratch, the unspecified things get put into a dictionary, where they belong. And I'm sure Autodesk would put them there automatically as well if the developers had the opportunity to redesign the database from scratch.

The things I'm talking about are a number of settings that AutoCAD saves specifically for each drawing. These settings describe the state AutoCAD should go into after it loads a drawing. Most of these settings define how specific AutoCAD commands should work in each drawing or which defaults they should offer.

The overwhelming number of settings saved in a drawing file is completely irrelevant if you want to evaluate or manipulate an AutoCAD drawing. However, a few settings in a drawing file do have a meaning for the drawing contents. The most important setting is the AutoCAD database version number, because it determines which objects are to be expected in the drawing database. Other settings define if and how AutoCAD will display objects of a specific type: for instance, PDMODE and ATTDISP. If an external program is to completely mimic how AutoCAD would display the drawing, it must be able to recognize these settings.

IDENTIFYING OBJECTS

Every object in an AutoCAD drawing has a unique identifier (some objects, such as symbol table records or dictionary entries, also have a key string, which is unique inside the table or dictionary but not throughout the whole database). This identifier is called the object's *handle*. Objects have a handle independent of whether they have a graphical representation. It's also irrelevant whether the object is included in a symbol table, a dictionary, or a block or whether it is one of these types of containers itself. Handles are unique within a drawing database, so no two objects in the database have the same handle.

For a couple of reasons, there may be additional identifiers, depending on the environment used to access the drawing database. One reason is that some environments (for instance, ObjectARX) allow your application program to access multiple drawings simultaneously—even drawings that are not opened in the AutoCAD drawing editor. You can thus end up with multiple objects from different drawings that share the same handle. Also, ObjectARX allows you to work with temporary, not database-resident, objects. These objects don't have a handle at all. In such environments, objects are usually referenced by an arbitrary, session-dependent *ObjectID*.

A second reason for the existence of additional identifiers is that unique object handles were introduced into the drawing database at a remarkably late stage of AutoCAD's development. Of course, the internal AutoCAD code knew how to distinguish one line from another, probably by means of pointers in the C programming language; but these were not written out to the database files. When AutoCAD introduced entity access through AutoLISP in 1986, AutoLISP needed a way to identify database objects. Because handles weren't invented yet, objects were identified by an additional *entity name*. Like an ObjectID, an entity name is session dependent. It still exists as another identification for objects.

Linking Objects

The only object identification that survives database writes and loads (which means saving a drawing file and reopening it later) is the object handle. Therefore, handles are used to create links between database objects. For instance, if you want to link a brake object to a wheel object, you add the brake object's handle to the wheel object.

If you link the objects, you probably want this link to survive a number of operations. For instance, you might want to keep the link alive even if the brake object gets a new handle. This can happen during filing operations (for example, when you insert or block your design to a different database) or during database reorganization. To keep the link in these situations, you use a special kind of link called a *soft pointer*. In this case, the old handle must be automatically replaced by the new handle.

In addition, you might want to lock the brake object. When you do so, the brake object can be changed, but it can't be deleted as long as the link is active. This kind of link is called a *hard pointer*.

In some sense, this link makes the wheel object own the brake object. It forbids certain actions on the brake object. But the link is only one-directional: No matter what happens to the wheel object, the brake object is not affected. For certain types of links, though, you want the exact opposite. If the wheel object is deleted, you want to delete associated tire or rim objects automatically as well. In such a case, you use a link type called a *soft owner*. Unlike pointership, ownership is an exclusive property, which means that the tire object cannot have an owner other than the wheel object.

A fourth kind of link is called a *hard owner*. This link type combines a *hard pointer* with a *soft owner*. The owned object cannot be deleted as long as the link exists, but is deleted automatically when the owner is erased.

Implicit Links

These four types of links, along with a fifth nonintelligent pointer, allow you to express all the interobject relationships you can imagine. Unfortunately, nothing's ever that easy.

Links to the symbol table do not use handles like the links between containers do. When symbol tables were introduced and linked to drawing entities, handles had yet to be invented.

In most cases (but not all), links from database objects to symbol table records are made using the record's key field value (*symbol name*) instead of the record's handle. One example is the Layer property of drawing entities, which contains the corresponding layer name—that is, the value of the layer record's key string.

Compared with the various link methods listed earlier, links through a symbol name are always hard pointer links. You can't delete a symbol table record if even a single entity references it.

Embedding Objects

Even with close links such as hard pointers, a referencing object and a referenced object are still two objects on their own. Any link includes the risk of breaking. For custom objects, it is sometimes crucial to guarantee nonbreakable links.

For custom applications, it is possible to not only link two objects, but to directly embed one object in another. In this case, the embedded object becomes part of the referencing object, or, in other words, the outer object becomes a container for other objects.

ABOUT CLASSES AND HIERARCHIES

Up to now you have seen that an AutoCAD drawing database consists of a series of containers, each of which contains a certain (usually unlimited) number of objects. These objects can be containers for the objects embedded in them. But what are objects?

In object-oriented design and analysis, an *object* is an instance of a class. A *class* is an abstract definition or template for all the properties and methods owned by their objects. Translated to real life, this means that an object is always "some kind of something." A certain number of classes or object types can be used in a drawing database—for example, AcDbLine, which is the class for simple lines, and AcDbFcf, which is the class for feature control frames, also known as *geometric tolerance annotations*. Every object in the drawing database is an instance of the appropriate class that defines the object's structure and behavior.

Classes underlie a hierarchy in which objects of a class inherit the structure and behavior of all classes higher up in the hierarchy. Usually this hierarchy describes an "is a kind of" relationship between classes. The AcDbLine class, for instance, inherits properties from the AcDbCurve class (which means that every line is a curve and has curve properties, such as a length), which inherits from the AcDbEntity class (which means that every curve is an entity and has entity properties, such as a color), which finally inherits from the AcDbObject class (which means that each entity is an object and has object properties, such as a handle).

All objects in an AutoCAD drawing database are based on AcDbObject. Figure 20.1 shows the class hierarchy in an AutoCAD drawing database.

Database Objects

AcDbObject

Miscellaneous	SymbolTables	SymbolTableRecords
AcDbDictionary	AcDbSymbolTable	AcDbSymbolTableRecord
AcDbDictionaryWithDefault	AcDbAbstractViewTable	AcDbAbstractViewTableRecord
AcDbFilter	AcDbViewportTable	AcDbViewportTableRecord
AcDbLayerFilter	AcDbViewTable	AcDbViewTableRecord
AcDbSpatialFilter	AcDbBlockTable	AcDbBlockTableRecord
AcDbGroup	AcDbDimStyleTable	AcDbDimStyleTableRecord
AcDbIdBuffer	AcDbLayerTable	AcDbLayerTableRecord
AcDbIndex	AcDbLinetypeTable	AcDbLinetypeTableRecord
AcDbLayerIndex	AcDbRegAppTable	AcDbRegAppTableRecord
AcDbSpatialIndex	AcDbTextStyleTable	AcDbTextStyleTableRecord
AcDbLongTransaction	AcDbUCSTable	AcDbUCSTableRecord
AcDbMlineStyle		
AcDbPlaceHolder		
AcDbPlotSettings		
AcDbLayout		
AcDbRasterImageDef		
AcDbRasterImageDefReactor		
AcDbRasterVariables		
AcDbProxyObject		
AcDbXrecord		

Entities
Continued

FIGURE 20.1A: The AutoCAD database class hierarchy

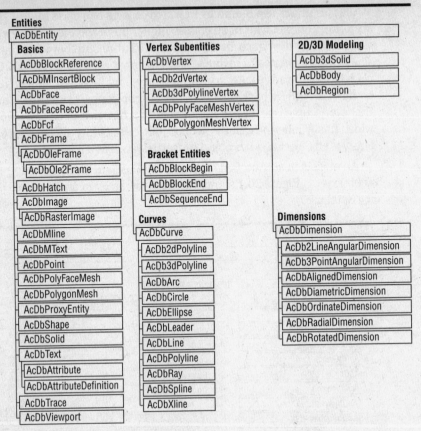

Entities

AcDbEntity

Basics	Vertex Subentities	2D/3D Modeling

Basics

- AcDbBlockReference
- AcDbMInsertBlock
- AcDbFace
- AcDbFaceRecord
- AcDbFcf
- AcDbFrame
- AcDbOleFrame
- AcDbOle2Frame
- AcDbHatch
- AcDbImage
- AcDbRasterImage
- AcDbMline
- AcDbMText
- AcDbPoint
- AcDbPolyFaceMesh
- AcDbPolygonMesh
- AcDbProxyEntity
- AcDbShape
- AcDbSolid
- AcDbText
- AcDbAttribute
- AcDbAttributeDefinition
- AcDbTrace
- AcDbViewport

Vertex Subentities

- AcDbVertex
- AcDb2dVertex
- AcDb3dPolylineVertex
- AcDbPolyFaceMeshVertex
- AcDbPolygonMeshVertex

Bracket Entities

- AcDbBlockBegin
- AcDbBlockEnd
- AcDbSequenceEnd

Curves

- AcDbCurve
- AcDb2dPolyline
- AcDb3dPolyline
- AcDbArc
- AcDbCircle
- AcDbEllipse
- AcDbLeader
- AcDbLine
- AcDbPolyline
- AcDbRay
- AcDbSpline
- AcDbXline

2D/3D Modeling

- AcDb3dSolid
- AcDbBody
- AcDbRegion

Dimensions

- AcDbDimension
- AcDb2LineAngularDimension
- AcDb3PointAngularDimension
- AcDbAlignedDimension
- AcDbDiametricDimension
- AcDbOrdinateDimension
- AcDbRadialDimension
- AcDbRotatedDimension

FIGURE 20.1B: Detail of the entities hierarchy of the AutoCAD database. (Both Figures 20.1a and 20.1b ©1999 by Autodesk, Inc., reprinted with permission.)

OBJECT PROPERTIES

Every object is an instance of its class and therefore has an identity. Each object has its own set of methods and properties, as defined by its class. An object's methods define the actions the object is able to perform. Using its methods, a database object changes over time; it copies, exports, or explodes itself. Although this evolution is an interesting and complex topic, it is not our topic here. We look at the drawing database as it appears at a fixed time. In other words, we look at the static picture of a drawing database.

Different objects of the same type (class) always differ in one or more properties. Even if two lines are completely identical, they have a different handle. Otherwise, they would not be two lines, but only one.

Every class defines a certain set of properties, which describe this special instance of the class. Properties are often called attributes, but in the context of an AutoCAD drawing database, the term *attributes* is reserved for attribute objects—objects of the class AcDbAttribute. The phrase *member variables* is also often used to describe properties available to objects within a class.

The properties of each object form a set of definitions that should define the object completely. I said "should" because not in all cases does the database contain all the information needed to describe an object completely. Some objects rely on data external to the drawing database.

Every object needs its own set of properties to describe its mathematical definition. It's up to the author of a class to decide which properties objects of each class need to completely define their appearance.

Defined versus Calculated Properties

The decision of which properties to choose as the properties needed to completely define an object is not necessarily obvious. Think of how you would define a circle's size. By its radius? Diameter? Area? All these are equivalent; in other words, if you know one, you can calculate the others.

Usually the drawing database stores only one of these equivalents. This is called the *defining property*. In some cases, the class author decided to store two or more of these equivalents in the drawing database even though they could be calculated easily. You should avoid such a redundancy! Not only does it create drawing files that consume more space than necessary, but more important, it creates the possibility of inconsistent drawing data. How do you expect a computer to handle a circle whose radius you define as 5 and whose diameter you define as 7?

Even though in most cases the AutoCAD drawing database contains only the minimum set of defining properties, some access methods automatically allow you to read or even write calculated properties as well. When using such an access method, you cannot tell which property is the defining property. However, by looking at the drawing database file itself, you can distinguish between the two. When there are useful calculated properties, I will list them as well.

Part iv

Missing Properties

You would expect that the drawing database contains all the data needed to completely construct the drawing used to create the database. This is not the case. An AutoCAD drawing database is not complete.

Some information is missing from the drawing database, and some of this information is obvious, and some isn't. Among the more obvious missing details is font information. To display a line of text, you need to know which characters to draw and how these characters look. The drawing database contains the information about which characters to draw, but it does not contain the information about how these characters look.

Character definition is saved in a different file of type SHX or TTF. The drawing database contains only the name of this file. To completely generate a drawing, you need access to this secondary file as well. Like fonts, a drawing can also reference bitmap files, shape files, and, by use of externally referenced drawings, even other drawing databases. By embedding filenames, database key fields, and other referencing information, any drawing object can point to a large number of additional properties that are known only to the creator of this object.

Does This Book Completely Document the AutoCAD Drawing Database?

Will you find an explanation here for every property of every object you might encounter in an AutoCAD drawing database? The simple answer is: No!

Until 1994, it was possible to document every class found in an AutoCAD drawing database, because there was a fixed set of classes. But then came AutoCAD Release 13 and a completely redesigned drawing database.

One of the big advantages (or disadvantages, depending on your point of view) of this redesigned drawing database is that it no longer contains only a fixed set of predefined classes. Instead, everyone is able to extend the AutoCAD database classes and create his or her own.

Since Release 13, you may find wheel objects in a drawing database, or you may find tires, walls, doors, or authors. How these objects are defined is totally up to the authors of the objects. And even worse, it's also totally up to the object's author to decide if and how these objects will be accessible. Unfortunately, it's possible for a class author to make his object available only in ObjectARX while omitting DXF, AutoLISP, and ActiveX. Finally, it's of course totally up to the author whether to document such custom objects.

Which Objects Are Covered?

Which objects are important enough to be described here and to what level of detail? This question is much more difficult to answer than it seems, because you may encounter a large number of different objects in an AutoCAD drawing.

If a third-party sheet metal application saves its bending-tool objects in the drawing database, you'll probably want to know their definitions. But you won't be able to do so unless they have been documented by the objects' authors, and they can only be documented by the objects' authors. So I have to exclude discussion of all third-party objects.

What about third-party objects made by Autodesk? Their architectural add-on creates a number of useful objects, including walls, doors, and windows. What's the difference between third-party add-ons written by Autodesk and those written by others? There is none.

So, I'll concentrate on the so-called *core objects*. AutoCAD creates these without the help of third-party applications. Right? Wrong. Even the core AutoCAD program is just a set of different add-ons (if you can call it that). With AutoCAD, "bonus" routines, such as Wipeout, create custom, undocumented objects, and an integrated application, such as a rendering module, creates its own custom, undocumented objects.

Because I had to decide about coverage from object to object, I selected those objects that I found most important and most often used, and I concentrated on the basic concepts of the drawing database. If you understand these concepts, you'll find it easy to read or evaluate other objects not listed here from your drawing's database—as long as you find them documented by their author, of course.

What's Next?

This chapter introduced the general structure of the drawing database. You learned that the drawing database consists of blocks, symbol tables, dictionaries, and drawing-specific settings. The next chapter will teach you how to access the drawing database via DXF files, AutoLISP, Active X Automation, and ObjectARX.

Part iv

Chapter 21

ACCESSING THE DRAWING DATABASE

I n this chapter, you'll learn how to access the drawing database using various methods. You'll see a few code samples
and follow a demonstration of the basic process to read a drawing's database. This overview is not intended to teach you programming. To use one of the methods presented here, you'll
need additional information about the specific development
environment you want to use.

Adapted from *Mastering™ AutoCAD® 2000 Objects*
by Dietmar Rudolph
ISBN 0-7821-2562-X   448 pages $49.99

The first access method I'll discuss is the oldest and most common way to access an AutoCAD drawing file: using the DXF® file format. I'll start with this method because you don't need to master any programming language to use it. You can read and edit a DXF file using almost any text editor. But DXF is based on a long line of versions, in which Autodesk always tried to minimize the changes from one version to the next. As a result, DXF is full of historic burdens and often successfully hides the almost clean database structure I described in Chapter 20.

The second access method involves using AutoLISP functions. You will see that the drawing database looks slightly different when reading it from AutoLISP, but you'll also see that the differences are minor. The contents of the drawing database are always the same, no matter how you look at it.

The third access method uses ActiveX Automation. ActiveX Automation is not directly linked to a specific programming language. Instead, it is a set of interfaces that programs written in different languages can use to access an automation server's methods and properties. These interfaces are defined in a *type library* (.tlb). You'll see a demonstration using the ActiveX Automation interface to the drawing database from a couple of programming environments.

The fourth access method uses ObjectARX/ObjectDBX. Because this is the foundation on which AutoCAD itself is built, it should provide the most useful way to access the drawing data. Unfortunately, it doesn't. In ObjectARX, the database access is hidden in a set of C++ libraries, which means that C++ is the only supported development environment for ObjectARX. Unfortunately, C++ is not necessarily a language that makes programming easy and reliable.

At the end of this chapter, I'll briefly discuss other ways to interact with an AutoCAD drawing database, such as DWG libraries.

This chapter concentrates on *reading* a drawing database. Everything said here also applies to *writing* drawing data. But writing a drawing database is usually a bit more complex than reading it, because writing also means to properly initialize all data and to correctly create all database links that the object is supposed to honor.

THE SERIALIZED WAY — DXF

DXF is an abbreviation for Drawing Interchange Format. DXF is a registered trademark of Autodesk, which is now trying to replace the name with ObjectDXF. Despite this naming confusion, most people who deal with computer graphics claim to know what DXF is. And few really do.

The origins of DXF date from 1982 and the development of the first version of AutoCAD, at that time code-named MicroCAD. Autodesk founder and long-time president John Walker (at that time) set the specifications: "All versions of MicroCAD should be able to write an *entity interchange format* file. All versions of MicroCAD, regardless of internal file representation, will be able to interchange drawing[s] this way" (John Walker, *The Autodesk File*, New Riders Publishing, 1989, p. 474).

To understand this statement, you need to remember the microcomputer world of 1982. Hundreds of companies were developing custom microcomputers, all of them incompatible with one another and often using their own operating systems, file systems, and even different representations of floating-point numbers. MicroCAD was supposed to run on various machines, always using a drawing file format specifically optimized for the target computer. To transfer a drawing from one platform to another, Walker suggested copying the *complete* contents of the drawing database into a file that could be read on every computer: an ASCII text file. The recipient of the interchange file could then convert it back into a MicroCAD drawing file. Because the contents of the interchange file would completely represent the original drawing, the resulting drawing would resemble the original in every detail.

An *entity interchange file* is "a complete representation of the contents of an AutoCAD drawing database." Only the naming seemed to create problems. Walker's notes again: "Changed the extension and nomenclature for interchange files. Previously they were *entity interchange files, EIF*. Now they are *drawing interchange files, DIF*. There's a hundred people who know what a drawing is for every one who knows what an *entity* is" (*ibid.*, p. 480). So true, John. And how many know what an *object* is?

Finally, on September 18, 1982, John Walker logged: "Mike Riddle points out that *.DIF* is used for VisiCalc interchange files. Changed drawing interchange file extension to *.DXF* to keep some gonzo from trying to load one into VisiCalc" (*ibid.*, p. 486). Thus, the DXF file was born. Anyone remember VisiCalc?

Part iv

Because other users and third parties found the DXF file useful, Autodesk included a brief documentation of the file format with every release of AutoCAD. This led to an incredible number of applications based on DXF, including programs that automatically create or modify drawings, and import and export filters for almost every graphics program in the world.

Some Myths about DXF

Because of the way that DXF files are used in the industry, the origins and the initial meaning of the file format are often forgotten. Many people think of DXF as an international standard, because it's so common. But it's not! DXF was invented and is maintained by Autodesk, and the company changes the format at will.

Some people see DXF as a static format. But it's not! Because DXF is a complete representation of the AutoCAD drawing database, the specifications change as soon as the drawing database contents change. And this is the case with almost every release of a new AutoCAD version.

Some people think of DXF as a plot file format. In fact, when I wrote my first book on DXF, the desktop publisher wondered why I sent him HP/GL files for the illustrations. His publishing system was able to read DXF, so he expected the DXF images to display in his system just as I wanted them to display. But DXF is only the drawing database. It is not the visualization of the database on-screen or on paper. You can't tell from a DXF file whether an image of a 3D object is to be seen shaded, rendered, or with hidden lines removed.

A typical myth left over from older versions of the format is that a DXF file can define only a handful of geometric elements. But that is not the case! As you saw in Chapter 20, a drawing database can contain arbitrary objects. Consequently, a DXF file can hold arbitrary information. It's not difficult to create a DXF file representing an Excel spreadsheet. The only question is whether doing so makes sense.

Some Criticisms of DXF

More recent critics concentrate on the question of whether a DXF file is a *complete* representation of the drawing database. The myth is that DXF omits a huge amount of information contained in the AutoCAD drawing database as it would be saved in a DWG file. Again, this is not the case.

But there is a problem with DXF. The criticisms are valid. It is possible that a DXF file does not contain the complete drawing database. A drawing database can contain arbitrary objects, and, unfortunately, Autodesk left it to the authors of individual custom objects to decide whether they want their objects saved in DXF. If a developer was too lazy to implement the DXF output routines for his objects, they will be missing from the DXF file, and constructing the drawing database from the DXF file will create a different drawing. To try to control this inconsistency, Autodesk demands that applications qualified for the "Designed with ObjectARX" logo implement DXF filing functions that are logically equivalent in contents to their DWG filing counterparts.

A second, even more important criticism is the historic burden of DXF. Remember, a DXF file is a representation of the drawing database, and this changes with every version of AutoCAD. Therefore, it is to be expected that the most current DXF specification closely resembles the database structure, as explained in the previous section. But it doesn't.

Over the years of AutoCAD development, the programmers at Autodesk tried to minimize the changes in DXF. Although the goal was to break as few existing DXF applications as possible, the final result is a mess. The DXF file often successfully hides even an almost clean database structure.

Serializing Drawing Data

The AutoCAD drawing database is a multidimensional object: a container of containers of containers, and so on.

For filing purposes—that is, for writing the drawing database to a disk file—you need to flatten this multidimensional structure to a sequential structure. This procedure is called *serialization*. Reading a drawing file back into AutoCAD restores the hierarchical structure. This is true for both DXF and AutoCAD's own DWG file format.

You can serialize a multidimensional data structure in various ways. Within a DXF file, you'll find three serialization methods used:

▶ Bracketing

▶ Tagging

▶ Sequencing

Part iv

Brackets in a DXF file indicate the beginning and end of containers: for example, SECTION/ENDSEC, TABLE/ENDTAB, and BLOCK/ENDBLK. When you read a DXF file, these brackets look like objects, but they don't belong to the database structure and are inserted only for filing purposes.

Within a DXF file, every bit of information saved is tagged with a group code. The group code is a 16-bit positive integer and indicates both the information's data type and its meaning in the current context. For example, a tag code of 40 indicates a single 64-bit floating-point number, usually a length or scale factor. In the context of an AcDbCircle entity (that is, a circle), the meaning of group 40's value is the circle radius. In the context of an AcDbText entity (that is, a single line of text), the meaning of group 40's value is the text height.

Sequencing is used to organize database data in the serialized file. Thus in certain areas of the DXF file, the sequence of information bits is relevant for their interpretation. It is obvious that the placement of an object between brackets (that is, the sequence of brackets and objects) defines the container in which an object belongs. But also, within a single object, the sequence of information bits may or may not be relevant. In an AcDbLine (that is, a line), the endpoints are tagged differently, thus making the sequence in which they are stored irrelevant. In an AcDbSpline, all control points are tagged with the same group code, thus making the sequence very important.

ASCII and Binary DXF

A DXF file follows a very simple file structure. With one exception (the binary DXF sentinel string), all data in a DXF file comes in pairs. The first part of the pair is the group code (tag) discussed earlier. The second part, immediately following the tag, is the corresponding information bit, the group value.

DXF files come in two variants: as ASCII text files or as binary files. ASCII DXF files consist of printable characters only. You can print them out or look at them with your favorite text editor. In an ASCII DXF file, all numbers are written as you would type them. The number 100, for instance, is written as three characters: a "1" and two "0"s.

In a binary DXF file, the number 100 is compressed to a single byte with the value 100. If you look at a binary DXF file with a text editor, you won't be able to recognize the "100" byte. Whenever I list the contents of a binary file, I use the hexadecimal representation of each byte. A byte consists of 8 bits; some are set, and some are not. The hexadecimal representation of the "100" byte is 64h (h is for hexadecimal, and 64 means 100 because 100 = 6 * 16 + 4), which means that the corresponding bit sequences are 0110 and 0100.

Again with one exception (comments are allowed only in ASCII DXF files), both the ASCII and the binary DXF versions of a drawing database contain identical information. ASCII DXF files are easier to read and edit, and binary DXF files are more compact and faster to process.

In an ASCII DXF file, group code and group value are separated by line feeds, which means that when you print the file, each appears on a separate line. Because the only supported platform for AutoCAD is some form of Microsoft Windows, DXF files use the Windows line feed sequence CR/LF (0D0Ah).

NOTE

Old DXF files may also use Macintosh, VMS, or Unix line separators (0Dh, 0A0Dh, 0Ah).

In a binary DXF file, group codes and group values don't need a separator because the group code is always 16 bit—that is, 2 bytes. Also, most group values have a fixed length and therefore don't need a termination. Group values that have differing lengths are strings and binary chunks.

String values in binary DXF are terminated with a zero byte (00h)—that is, a byte in which all bits are zero. Binary chunks cannot be terminated by a zero byte because it may be part of the value and you don't want AutoCAD to stop reading the binary data simply because it contains a zero byte. Instead, binary chunks of data are preceded by an additional byte that contains the number of bytes in the chunk that follows. (For more information on how the different data types are saved in DXF and how they appear in the other environments, see Chapter 22.)

NOTE

In versions of AutoCAD prior to Release 13, binary DXF files used a group code value that consisted of either 1 or 3 bytes instead of the 2 bytes used today. Check the DXF file version to determine how to interpret group codes in binary DXF files; otherwise, your program may crash.

Differences between ASCII and Binary DXF

Even though they look very different, ASCII and binary DXF files carry the same amount of information taken from the AutoCAD drawing database used to create them. They also list the exact same data in the exact same sequence. There are only two differences in the contents of ASCII and binary DXF files:

- ASCII DXF files can contain comments, but binary DXF files cannot.

- A binary DXF file contains a sentinel string that is not in ASCII DXF files.

Comments are strings tagged with a 999 group code. AutoCAD does not add comment strings to a DXF file, but users editing the file can use the 999 group to comment their changes. Because you are not expected to edit a binary DXF file by hand, there are no comments in a binary DXF file.

Binary DXF files contain a sentinel string of 22 bytes. This string opens the DXF file to indicate the file type. It is *not* tagged information (in other words, it is not preceded by a group code). The sentinel string consists of the following:

- The string "AutoCAD Binary DXF"

- A line-feed sequence CR/LF (0D0Ah)

- An end-of-file character EOF (1Ah)

- A zero byte (00h)

The end-of-file character allows you to inadvertently print or output a binary DXF file without sending binary data to the screen or to the printer.

The Structure of a DXF File

As you already know, any information in a DXF file is a pair consisting of a group code and a group value. The only exception is the sentinel string that starts a binary DXF file.

A DXF file always ends with the end-of-file information, which is a group of code 0 and string *EOF*. In an ASCII DXF file, the last two lines are always the following:

```
0
EOF
```

In a binary DXF file, the last significant bytes are always the following:

00h 00h 69h 79h 70h 00h

The body of the DXF file is divided into seven sections, and each section is bracketed with a start-section bracket and an end-section bracket. The start-section bracket contains two groups: the first group is the string *SECTION* (group code 0), and the second group lists the section name string (group code 2). The end-section bracket is just the string *ENDSEC* (code 0). Let's look at what goes between the start and end brackets:

▶ The HEADER section contains drawing-specific settings saved with the database; I refer to these settings as the non-objects. The HEADER section is a sequential list of the setting name (a string in group 9) and the corresponding setting value (varying group codes).

▶ The CLASSES section provides auxiliary information regarding application-defined objects in the drawing database. It lists the class names in DXF and their corresponding C++ counterparts as well as printable information about the origin and use of the class. The information listed in this section does not represent database objects.

▶ The TABLES section contains the symbol tables and symbol table records. Each symbol table is enclosed between a start-table bracket and an end-table bracket. The start-table bracket contains various groups. Most important are the string *TABLE* (code 0) and the table name string (code 2). The end-table bracket consists of only the string *ENDTAB* (code 0).

▶ The BLOCKS section contains entities, which are all objects with a graphical representation. To maintain compatibility with older DXF versions, entities of the *MODEL_SPACE and *PAPER_SPACE container blocks are *not* listed in the BLOCKS section. Instead, they appear in their own section titled ENTITIES. Following the same pattern as the sections themselves, each block is bracketed by a start-block bracket and an end-block bracket. The start-block bracket contains the string *BLOCK* (code 0), the block name (code 2), and a number of additional groups. The end-block bracket contains the string *ENDBLK* (code 0) and some other groups.

Part iv

▶ The ENTITIES section should logically be part of the BLOCKS section. Again, for compatibility reasons, the entities from the *MODEL_SPACE and *PAPER_SPACE blocks are listed in this special section. Entities that reside in the *PAPER_SPACE block are listed in the ENTITIES section with a special group 67 code 1.

▶ The OBJECTS section contains all database objects that don't have a visual representation. This section does not use any bracketing. Instead, it's just a sequence of objects starting with the root directory.

▶ The THUMBNAILIMAGE section contains a small bitmap that can be used to provide a graphical visualization of the DXF file or the drawing as a whole.

The individual structures, group codes, and details associated with the various objects will be covered specifically in the discussion of these containers.

Objects in DXF

Each object in a DXF file starts with the object's class DXF name. This is a string, and the associated group code is 0. The group code 0 is not used inside objects. Thus, whenever a program that is reading this DXF file encounters group code 0, it recognizes the mark as the beginning of a new object.

To parse a given container into individual objects, it is necessary to split the container's contents at every group 0. It is also possible to split the whole DXF file at every group 0. Doing so provides the brackets used to represent the multidimensional structure of the database and auxiliary data, such as the thumbnail image bitmap.

If an object is directly embedded into another object, making the object itself into a container, the group code 0 cannot be used to indicate the embedded object's start. In such a case, the group code 101 is used to start an embedded object. The value of group code 101 is not the DXF class name of the embedded object; it is the string *Embedded Object*.

Following the object's start code (group 0 or 101) are the multiple data elements associated with this object, known as its properties. Here is a sample DXF excerpt defining an AcDbLine entity—that is, a straight line:

```
0
LINE
```

```
    5
   67
  330
   19
  100
AcDbEntity
    8
    0
  100
AcDbLine
   10
10.15197093840249
   20
5.593329978383998
   30
  0.0
   11
19.86617617830376
   21
9.915398417065873
   31
  0.0
```

You can see the various group pairs following the string *LINE* (code 0). The codes, number, and meaning of the groups describing the object are different from object type to object type. They result from the object's class definition.

A DXF file does not necessarily contain all the properties of a given object. To save file space, certain specific properties can be omitted and will default to standard values. In the previous example, you won't find a linetype (which would be tagged with group code 6) associated with the object, which means that the standard linetype is to be used. The standard linetype has the name CONTINUOUS and is a single continuous line without any gaps.

When you are writing a DXF file, I recommend that you don't rely solely on any defaults the reading program may use. Always fill in *all* the group codes. Unfortunately, AutoCAD itself does not follow this simple rule. When discussing the various object properties, I'll also list the default values to be used when a property is omitted from DXF if the default is not clear.

AutoLISP— DXF by Another Name

When AutoCAD introduced access to the drawing database through its built-in programming language, AutoLISP, the developers reused the DXF file format. DXF already allowed access to all database objects, and this was documented.

Today, when you access a drawing database from AutoLISP, you get a very DXF-like result. It is not exactly DXF, but the differences are minimal.

NOTE
Newer versions of AutoLISP, called VisualLISP, provide additional database access through ActiveX Automation, which I'll discuss in the next section.

If the DXF excerpt defining an AcDbLine entity from the previous section is to be evaluated in AutoLISP, the AutoLISP programmer will retrieve the following data list (formatted for clarity):

```
(
    (-1 . <Entity name: 2570520>)
    (0 . "LINE")
    (5 . "67")
    (330 . "19")
    (100 . "AcDbEntity")
    (67 . 0)
    (8 . "0")
    (100 . "AcDbLine")
    (10 10.1520 5.5933 0.0)
    (11 19.8662 9.9154 0.0)
    (210 0.0 0.0 1.0)
)
```

If you ignore the LISP-typical parentheses, you'll immediately recognize the familiar group code and value sequence. The main difference is that AutoLISP can work with coordinate lists such as this line's endpoints. So the group 10 in AutoLISP contains all three coordinates of the line's start point. In contrast, DXF can save only one coordinate per group. In DXF, group 10 contains only the start point's x coordinate; the y coordinate is in group 20, and the z coordinate is in group 30.

Another difference between DXF and AutoLISP is that AutoLISP returns *some* groups even if they have been given a default value. So you'll see the 67 and 210 groups listed in the AutoLISP file that were omitted from the DXF file, because they are standard (default) values. Other groups, such as the linetype (group 6), are still omitted if they have their default value.

Finally, you'll see the AutoLISP-internal *Entity name,* which is used to identify the object even if multiple databases are handled. The drawing-specific object handle is the string in group 5, by the way.

NOTE

Comparing the DXF and AutoLISP output of an entity seems to show a reduced precision in AutoLISP. This rounding occurs only in the printout of an AutoLISP expression. The internal values used in calculations are as exact as in the drawing database.

Database Access from AutoLISP

To extract any information about a database object, you use the AutoLISP entget function. The entget function takes one argument, which is the session-specific entity name. An optional second argument filters information belonging to specific add-ons. To get the complete database contents associated with an object, you first get the object's entity name. You can do this in several ways: for instance, by using the AutoLISP function ssget or entsel. Once you save the entity name to a variable (in this case, the symbol AnEntity), you can enter this AutoLISP expression at the command line:

```
(entget AnEntity '("*"))
=>
(
    (-1 . <Entity name: 2570520>)
```

```
      (0 . "LINE")
      (5 . "67")
      (330 . "19")
      (100 . "AcDbEntity")
      (67 . 0)
      (8 . "0")
      (100 . "AcDbLine")
      (10 10.1520 5.5933 0.0)
      (11 19.8662 9.9154 0.0)
      (210 0.0 0.0 1.0)

    )
```

Although the AutoLISP term is *entity name* and although the database access function is called entget, the function works on all kinds of database objects, with or without a graphical representation.

The entget function always returns a list containing the corresponding object's database information. This list is often called the *entity association list*. Each element of this list is one database field or property. This sublist (that is, list within a list) is either a dotted pair (two atoms separated by a dot) or a complete list. If it's a dotted pair, the first atom is the group code integer, and the second atom is the group value. If it's a complete list, the group code is the first element. In any case, you can retrieve the group code of each sublist using the standard AutoLISP car function, which retrieves the first element from a dotted pair or a list. You'll get the group value using the standard AutoLISP cdr function, which returns the second element of a dotted pair or a list without its first element. Here are two examples that you can type at the command line:

```
(car '(5 . "67"))
=> 5
(cdr '(5 . "67"))
=> "67"
(car '(10 10.1520 5.5933 0.0))
=> 10
(cdr '(10 10.1520 5.5933 0.0))
=> (10.1520 5.5933 0.0)
```

If you look back at the return value of the entget function, you'll see among the various sublists a dotted pair starting with the code −1. The −1 group provides this object's entity name just like any other group. Keep in mind that this group is temporary and not part of the drawing database.

As long as a group code is unique within an object's properties, you can use the assoc function to directly retrieve one group by using its group code. If the group code is not unique, like the 100 code in the AcDbLine example, you need to traverse the groups using AutoLISP's standard list-processing functions car and cdr, foreach and mapcar.

If an object in a drawing database is deleted, the corresponding entity name is still valid until the database is written to a disk file (saved). Deleted objects that are requested using the entget function return the AutoLISP equivalent of "not available": nil.

Getting Entity Names

As you've already learned, the drawing database consists of three kinds of object containers (symbol tables, dictionaries, and block containers) plus the settings (or non-objects). The method you use to retrieve the entity names of all objects in a container depends on the container type.

If the container is a symbol table, you retrieve an object's entity name using the tblobjname function. This function takes two arguments: the DXF class name of the symbol table and the key value string of the symbol table record you're looking for. To look at the properties of layer "0", enter this expression at the command line:

```
(entget (tblobjname "LAYER" "0") '("*"))
=>
(
   (-1 . <Entity name: 2570478>)
   (0 . "LAYER")
   (5 . "F")
   (100 . "AcDbSymbolTableRecord")
   (100 . "AcDbLayerTableRecord")
   (2 . "0")
   (70 . 0)
```

```
        (62 . 7)
        (6 . "CONTINUOUS")
  )
```

To get the entity name, you need to know the symbol record's key string. There is no built-in function to extract all key strings from a symbol table, but you can use the following function inside your program:

```
(defun SymbolTableContents
         (SymbolTableDXFName / SymbolTableRecord ReturnValue)
     (while (setq SymbolTableRecord
              (tblnext SymbolTableDXFName (not ReturnValue))
            )
       (setq ReturnValue
         (cons (cdr (assoc 2 SymbolTableRecord)) ReturnValue)
       )
     )
     (reverse ReturnValue)
  )
```

The tblnext function in the preceding routine steps through a symbol table and, with every call, returns some information about the next symbol table record. The data returned by tblnext is similar to the database information returned by entget, but the data is incomplete because several groups are missing. You should, therefore, always use entget to retrieve an object's properties.

The tblobjname function provides no access to symbol table records with duplicate keys. These types of records are allowed in the AcDbViewPortTable (VPORT). Therefore, it is not possible to retrieve the complete database information of viewport configurations using AutoLISP.

Retrieving Entities with AutoLISP

You will remember that entities (that is, objects that have a visual representation) are always contained in exactly one Block container. In the discussion on DXF sections at the beginning of this chapter, you also saw that the blocks *MODEL_SPACE and *PAPER_SPACE in a DXF file have undergone a special handling as they appear in a section on their own. When using AutoLISP, you have to keep both in mind: Basically, each entity goes to a single block container, but the *MODEL_SPACE and *PAPER_SPACE blocks are mixed up.

To access a block container, you again use the tblobjname function, this time providing the string "BLOCK" and the block name. Assuming there is a block named "SOMEBLOCK" in your drawing, enter this expression at the command line:

```
(entget (tblobjname "BLOCK" "SOMEBLOCK") '("*"))
=>
(
    (-1 . <Entity name: 2570578>)
    (0 . "BLOCK")
    (5 . "57")
    (100 . "AcDbEntity")
    (67 . 0)
    (8 . "0")
    (100 . "AcDbBlockBegin")
    (70 . 0)
    (10 0.0 0.0 0.0)
    (-2 . <Entity name: 2570580>)
    (2 . "SOMEBLOCK")
    (3 . "")
)
```

In addition to the usual −1 group, which reports the block object's entity name, you will recognize a second entity name (group −2) in the preceding bit of code. This entity name points to the first entity in the corresponding block container.

You can now retrieve the entity name from the −2 group and then use entget to extract this object's database information. To access the second object in the block container, you use the entnext function. The entity name of the current object (in this case, the first object) is taken by the entnext as an argument and returns the entity name of the following object. At the end of the block container, entnext returns nil.

WARNING

If you use entnext to traverse the *MODEL_SPACE* block, it will not stop at the container's last entity. Instead, entnext continues with the contents of the *PAPER_SPACE* block.

The tblnext function omits the *MODEL_SPACE* and all *PAPER_SPACE* blocks when traversing the blocks in the database. The only way to get a list of *all* blocks in the drawing is to use the ActiveX Automation interface from AutoLISP. Here's a function you could incorporate into your program:

```
(defun AllBlocks (/ ReturnValue)
   (vlax-for b (vla-get-blocks
                    (vla-get-activedocument
                     (vlax-get-acad-object)))
       (setq ReturnValue (cons (vla-get-name b) ReturnValue))
   )
)
```

Dictionary Access in AutoLISP

Database objects that don't have a graphical representation and that aren't symbol tables or symbol table records go to the third kind of container: a dictionary.

Accessing dictionaries through AutoLISP is similar to accessing symbol tables. There are a few differences, however.

If you know the dictionary's entity name and the key string of the object, you use the dictsearch function. This function is similar to the tblobjname function, but differs in two areas. First, the tblobjname function needs the DXF name of the symbol table, and dictsearch needs the entity name of the parent dictionary. This is the case because there can be an unlimited number of dictionaries and because dictionaries can contain other dictionaries.

The second difference is that dictsearch directly returns the database information, and tblobjname returns only the entity name that is to be used in entget. To get the entity name of an object contained in a dictionary, you extract the −1 group value from the list returned by dictsearch. You will need this entity name to extract application-specific data (xdata) attached to the object. Suppose you are looking for the properties of the

AcDbGroup object describing the AutoCAD group named AGROUP, and suppose you already retrieved the entity name of the group dictionary. Typing the following expression at the command line returns the data you want:

```
(dictsearch EntityNameOfGroupDictionary "AGROUP")
=>
(
    (-1 . <Entity name: 2570560>)
    (0 . "GROUP")
    (5 . "54")
    (102 . "{ACAD_REACTORS")
    (330 . <Entity name: 2570468>)
    (102 . "}")
    (100 . "AcDbGroup")
    (300 . "Testgroup comment")
    (70 . 0)
    (71 . 1)
    (340 . <Entity name: 2570530>)
    (340 . <Entity name: 2570528>)
)
```

Like symbol tables, you need to know the key with which an object has been stored if you want to access it through dictsearch. As an alternative, you can use the dictnext function, which traverses all objects in a dictionary. The dictnext function is like entnext and tblnext, but returns the complete database information for each object.

To get a list of all keys used in a dictionary, you might integrate a routine similar to this in your program:

```
(defun DictionaryKeys (DictionaryEntityName)
  (mapcar 'cdr
    (vl-remove-if-not
      '(lambda (x) (= (car x) 3))
      (entget DictionaryEntityName)
    )
  )
)
```

A last question on dictionaries remains: How do you get the dictionary's entity name? This depends on which object owns the dictionary. A dictionary can be owned by any other non-dictionary object, or it can be included in another dictionary.

If a dictionary is owned by a non-dictionary object, it's called that object's *extension dictionary*. You'll find the extension dictionary's entity name in the object's group code list. Here's an example:

```
(
    (-1 . <Entity name: 2570578>)
    (0 . "BLOCK")
    (5 . "57")
    (102 . "{ACAD_XDICTIONARY")
    (-1 . <Entity name: 2579843>)
    (102 . "}")
    (100 . "AcDbEntity")
    (67 . 0)
    ...
```

All dictionaries other than extension dictionaries are nested and form a hierarchical tree structure, as explained in Chapter 20. Every dictionary by itself is included in a parent dictionary. Only one dictionary has no such parent: the "root" of the tree. It contains the top dictionaries, which may contain objects or other dictionaries. This root dictionary is called the *named objects dictionary*. Its entity name is returned by the namedobjdict function, which takes no arguments.

Modifying and Making Objects in AutoLISP

You can delete, alter, or create database objects using AutoLISP. To delete an object, you use the entdel function and pass the entity name as an argument.

To modify an object, you'll use the entmod function. This function needs one argument, which is an entity association list similar to the one returned by entget. This list must contain the −1 group with the entity name of the object to modify. And it must contain any groups you want to modify, for example:

```
(entmod
    '(
```

```
            (-1 . <Entity name: 2570520>)
            (10 10.0 5.0 0.0)
    )
)
```

To make an object from scratch, you pass the new object's entity association list to the entmake or entmakex command. The entity association list must not contain an entity name or a handle. You need to provide a minimum amount of information to create the entity; if you don't, your attempt will fail. For instance, to create a circle, you need to supply at least the object type, the radius, and the center point. Additional properties can be added during entmake or later. This input from the command line creates a circle:

```
(entmake
    '(
            (0 . "CIRCLE")
            (10 10.0 5.0 0.0)
            (40 . 5.0)
    )
)
```

Any group not included in the entity association list will be set to its default value.

The exact procedure that you use to create objects depends on the container in which they are supposed to land:

Symbol Tables   You can make symbol table *records*, but you cannot create new symbol tables.

Blocks   You cannot create an individual entity and attach it to an arbitrary block container. You can create a new block container, which opens the container for writing; then all newly created entities are attached to this block. To close the block container, you need to use the entmake function to create an ENDBLK object. This is not a true object but the same pseudo-object used as the end-block bracket in a DXF file.

Layout Blocks   If you create entities without opening a specific block container, they are automatically appended to the *MODEL_SPACE block if their group 67 value is 0 or omitted. If the group 67 value is 1, entities go to the *PAPER_SPACE block. In addition, you can provide a group 410 containing a layout name. In this case, the created object goes into the block container associated with the group 410 layout.

Dictionaries   You can create dictionaries, but you cannot manipulate them directly using entmod. To add an object to a dictionary, you first create it with entmakex (not entmake) and then use dictadd to connect the new object to its parent. The dictadd function takes three arguments: the dictionary's entity name, the new key string, and the new object's entity name. The function dictrename and dictremove modify a dictionary object. Using entmod you can attach and/or modify xdata to a dictionary object, but you cannot modify the object's primary groups.

Creation and modification of objects and entities will fail if the supplied entity association list contradicts certain rules. The main rules are that you need to include all mandatory groups and that you are not allowed to change critical groups such as the entity name or the handle. AutoLISP also checks that objects only go into a container in which they will fit. If you reference other objects implicitly or explicitly, AutoLISP verifies that the referenced object exists and is of the correct type.

Reading and Writing Drawing Settings

AutoLISP provides full support for reading and writing drawing-specific settings that are saved inside the drawing database.

Every setting has a name or a key string. You use the getvar function to read a setting, and you use the setvar function to write it. Try this at the command line to read and write the PDMODE setting, which controls the display of AcDbPoint objects:

```
(getvar "PDMODE")
=> 0
(setvar "PDMODE" 3)
=> 3
```

A number of settings, such as the database version ACADVER (which in AutoLISP is *not* the database version but the AutoCAD version you work in) cannot be modified through AutoLISP.

In AutoLISP, you use the getvar and setvar functions not only for database-specific settings, but also to operate on a number of additional settings that are session specific or configuration specific.

THE SAME DATA WITH NAMES — ACTIVEX AUTOMATION

As you have learned, all the methods described in this chapter access the same drawing database contents. Only the access methods differ. In DXF and AutoLISP, properties are referenced by group codes—that is, by numbers. Using ActiveX Automation, the same properties are referenced by a name.

ActiveX Automation (also known as COM Automation) is not directly linked with a specific programming language. Instead, it is a set of interfaces that programs written in different languages can use to access an automation server's methods and properties. These interfaces are defined in a type library (.tlb). You can use this type library from many programming environments.

Here's an example of how the same database access in a program's code looks when using different programming languages:

Visual Basic ADatabaseCircle.Radius = 3.0

Visual LISP (vla-put-Radius AdatabaseCircle 3.0)

Delphi   ADatabaseCircle.Radius := 3.0;

Java   ADatabaseCircle.Radius(3.0);

ActiveX Automation or, more precisely, the dispatch interface to AutoCAD's COM objects as declared in the type library, defines Circle objects that have a Radius property that can be changed. How this change is performed is internal to the automation server, in this case AutoCAD. How the communication takes place is defined in COM (Microsoft's Component Object Model), the underlying architecture of ActiveX Automation. How you access the interface in a certain environment depends on the programming language and its syntax rules. Describing these rules is beyond the scope of this book because a large number of programming languages are available to choose from. See the documentation for your favorite development platform to learn how ActiveX Automation works within that specific environment.

Part iv

Most people use Visual Basic to write programs using ActiveX Automation. This can be done through the Visual Basic (VB) development system that creates stand-alone executables or through the Visual Basic for Applications (VBA) dialect included in products such as Microsoft Word, Microsoft Excel, or AutoCAD. Because VB(A) is the environment preferred for use with ActiveX Automation, I'll demonstrate this variant of drawing database access using VB(A) code. Please translate the examples to your favorite programming language.

NOTE

If you use VisualLISP to access AutoCAD's ActiveX Automation objects, you need to initialize the COM interface using the vl-load-com function.

Accessing the AutoCAD Database

An ActiveX Automation client (that is, the software you are writing to access AutoCAD objects) and an ActiveX Automation server (that is, AutoCAD) are two unrelated programs. They don't have to share the same address space and can even run on different computers. They communicate by means of a set of standard interfaces.

To open an ActiveX communication with AutoCAD, you need to *get* the AutoCAD object running in memory, or you need to *create* a new AutoCAD object. In a Visual Basic program this segment looks like this:

```
Dim AutoCADObject As AcadApplication
Set AutoCADObject = GetObject(, "AutoCAD.Application")
If Err.Number Then
  Set AutoCADObject = CreateObject("AutoCAD.Application")
End If
```

Once you connect your application to AutoCAD, you can access the drawings already opened by AutoCAD, or you can create or open another.

One service that the AutoCAD ActiveX Automation server provides to your application program is the Documents collection. The Documents collection contains all documents (which is the name ActiveX Automation uses for drawing databases) currently open in the AutoCAD to which you're connected. AutoCADObject.Documents .Item(0) is the first available database, if any are available. AutoCADObject.Documents .New creates a new drawing database from a template drawing, and AutoCADObject .Documents.Open opens another drawing file.

Using `AutoCADObject.Documents.Item(Index)`, you can select the drawing database with which you want your program to work. Alternatively, `AutoCADObject.ActiveDocument` is the drawing database currently active in AutoCAD.

Each of these calls returns an object of the type `AcadDocument`. By traversing this document object, you can access all segments of the drawing database. A bit of confusion often exists about the difference between a document and a database in AutoCAD's ActiveX interfaces. A document is a database loaded into the current AutoCAD session for editing. In addition to the database resident information, the document object also contains temporary information, such as selection sets, and methods to plot or interactively query information.

TIP

An `AcadDocument` is a database loaded into the current AutoCAD session for editing through the ActiveX Automation interface.

The next section describes how to use ActiveX Automation to retrieve and modify information from the database portion of the document.

Of Collections, Objects, and Interfaces

You already know that the objects in a drawing database follow a strict hierarchy. Every object is contained in exactly one container, which in turn may be a member of another container, and so on.

In Visual Basic, the equivalent of a container is a *collection*. If you query the symbol table containing all layers, you use the `.Layers` property of the document object. The `.Layers` property returns a collection containing all layers from the drawing database.

Collections have a `.Count` property that returns the number of objects in the collection. Using the `.Item` method, you can access every object in the collection. Collection indices start from zero:

```
With Collection
  For Index = 0 To .Count - 1
  DoSomethingWith .Item(Index)
  Next Index
End With
```

As I discussed in Chapter 20, symbol table records in the AutoCAD drawing database always have a unique key within the symbol table. This key can be used to directly access a member of a symbol table collection; for example:

```
TheDrawingDocument.Layers("ALAYERNAME")
```

The document object provides collections for every symbol table in the drawing database: `.DimStyles`, `.Layers`, `.Linetypes`, `.Registered-Applications`, `.TextStyles`, `.UserCoordinateSystems`, `.Viewports`, and `.Views`. In addition, the document object provides other collections that do not correspond to symbol tables.

Once you reach a symbol table record, you can access all related database fields using the object's properties. For instance, `ALayerObject.Handle` returns the layer's handle, and you can retrieve the layer's name using `ALayerObject.Name`. This series of properties and methods (as well as events) forms the *automation interface* to the layer object. Every database object has its own interface available through ActiveX Automation.

Accessing Entities via ActiveX Automation

As you remember, within the drawing database, entities (objects that have a graphical representation) belong to exactly one block container. Access to these containers and their contents is quite easy and logical if you work with ActiveX Automation.

The drawing database (the document object) contains a `.Blocks` collection. This collection contains all block containers. You can iterate through them using the collection index or by directly using the block name; for example, `TheDrawingDatabase .Blocks("SOMEBLOCK")`.

Unlike in AutoLISP, access to the *MODEL_SPACE and *PAPER_SPACE blocks is the same as access to any other block using ActiveX Automation. As a shortcut, you can also use the `.ModelSpace` and `.PaperSpace` properties of the document object to access these blocks. These properties are just aliases for the longer forms.

Any block container is a collection of the entities contained in the block. You can easily iterate through them using a routine such as this:

```
With TheDrawingDatabase.Blocks("SOMEBLOCK")

  For Index = 0 To .Count - 1

    DoSomethingWith .Item(Index)
```

```
Next Index
End With
```

Because entities don't have key strings, you need to iterate sequentially through the block container. Of course, there are other ways to find an item, such as by means of links from other objects, or you can find an item interactively. For more information, see the "VBA and ActiveX Automation" topic in AutoCAD's help system.

As soon as you reach an entity (an item in the block container), you can retrieve its database contents by simply using the corresponding properties. If you know that the entity is an AcDbLine, you can, for instance, query the start and end point using the .StartPoint and .EndPoint properties.

To access a property, you don't need the group code used in AutoLISP and DXF. You simply use the property name. Which property names are available depends on the type of object. For instance, a circle has a radius, and a line doesn't. Before using a property, it is wise to check the exact object type or to otherwise ensure that the property is available for the object in question. You'll find the object type using the .ObjectName property, which is the AutoCAD class name string; for example, "AcDbLine".

AutoLISP and DXF deliver only raw database contents; ActiveX Automation provides calculated properties that are not saved in the drawing database. Typical examples are the length of a line or the start point of an arc. Although you can modify defining properties, calculated properties are usually read-only.

Some complex database items are not available as properties of the object. This is the case when the property itself is not a simple data structure, such as a point or a string. If the data structure is a collection or even a more complex object, in order to retrieve the data, you need to call a method of the object that returns the information. This is true, for instance, for application-defined add-on information (xdata) or for the list of objects that make a hatch boundary. Therefore, you cannot write TheDatabaseItem.XData to retrieve or modify the object's data. Instead, you use:

```
Dim TheItemsXdataTypes As Variant
Dim TheItemsXdataValues As Variant
TheDatabaseItem.GetXData "", _
    TheItemsXdataTypes, TheItemsXdataValues
```

Part iv

The two variants in this method call will be filled by AutoCAD with the corresponding database contents. You need to use similar methods when writing complex data structures.

In contrast to AutoLISP and DXF, ActiveX Automation sometimes provides only a limited view of the drawing entities. One example is the DXF class name of an object, which is available through DXF, AutoLISP, and ObjectDBX, but not available through the ActiveX Automation interface.

Creating Entities via ActiveX Automation

The ActiveX Automation interface does not provide a general entity creation method such as AutoLISP's entmake. Instead, there is a separate creation method for each entity type.

As in AutoLISP, you need to supply an entity-specific set of minimum properties to create a valid object. Thus, to create a circle, you need to supply a radius and a center point. Unlike in AutoLISP, you cannot supply additional properties when creating the object. Properties such as layer and color must be set later.

Because block containers are just collections in ActiveX Automation, you create a new object by simply adding it to the collection using the correct add method. The collection you add the object to may be any block. Unlike in AutoLISP, you can easily add objects to existing blocks.

The various add methods are named according to the object they generate; for example, .AddLine, .AddCircle, or .AddArc. Note that not every database object has an add method. For instance, to add an arbitrary solid model, you can't use an .Add3dSolid method. In contrast, some add methods do not correspond directly to a database object. For instance, .AddBox and .AddCone both create an AcDb3dSolid object, but from different parameters.

Working with Dictionaries in ActiveX Automation

The document object's .Dictionaries collection in ActiveX Automation corresponds to the namedobjdict in AutoLISP. This collection is the root dictionary that contains the top dictionaries of the database container for objects without a graphical representation. In addition, any object's

`.GetExtensionDictionary` method returns this object's extension dictionary.

Every object in the `.Dictionaries` collection is a dictionary object, but not all dictionaries are members of the `.Dictionaries` collection. The `.Dictionaries` collection contains only the top-level dictionaries. If a dictionary is contained within another dictionary, it won't appear in the `.Dictionaries` collection. Instead, you will find it by traversing the hierarchical dictionary tree.

Any object in a dictionary is either another dictionary or an arbitrary object. The dictionary object provides methods to retrieve, rename, or delete a certain member object. Because every dictionary is a table of (similar or not) database objects, the dictionary owns methods for adding arbitrary objects to the collection.

Like AutoLISP, ActiveX Automation provides no functionality to define your own object classes, but you can use objects defined by AutoCAD or by add-ons written in ObjectARX as long as the objects themselves provide an ActiveX Automation interface. To add a custom object to a dictionary, you call the dictionary's `.AddObject` method with the new key string and the class name of the object to add.

AutoCAD's ActiveX Automation interface offers a number of shortcuts for AutoCAD-defined objects. For instance, you'll find the ACAD_GROUP dictionary as a separate `Groups` collection. But this is only an alias to simplify your code. It doesn't tell you anything about the database structure or contents. Other such shortcuts are the `PlotConfigurations` collection and `ADictionary.AddXRecord`.

Custom Objects in ActiveX Automation

An `AcDbLine` object is an AutoCAD entity. Thus, the `AcDbLine` class is derived from the `AcDbEntity` class, and every entity is an AutoCAD object or, in other words, is derived from `AcDbObject`. Translated to ActiveX Automation and COM, this means that the `AcadLine` object not only supports its own interface (`IAcadLine`) but also the `IACADEntity` and `IAcadObject` interfaces. Although the line's start point comes from the `IAcadLine` interface, its layer comes from the `IAcadEntity` interface, and its handle comes from the `IAcadObject` interface.

For standard AutoCAD objects, it does not matter which interface delivers the properties and methods you want to use. You're transparently calling the appropriate function, and the underlying interfaces are hidden.

However, non-standard (that is, custom) objects may not expose an automation interface if the object's author was too lazy to implement one.

NOTE

For ObjectARX logo compliance, a basic ActiveX implementation for every custom object is required.

If an object omits a complete interface, the hidden interfaces are still there and can be used. Because every custom object is derived from AcDbObject, you can still use some property, such as the .Handle property, of the object. If the custom object has a visual representation (that is, if it is derived from AcDbEntity), it automatically has a .Layer property and more. Also, the .AddCustomObject method creates a custom object if the corresponding class definition is available.

Non-objects in ActiveX Automation

Like AutoLISP, in ActiveX Automation, you can query the current value of certain settings saved in the drawing. In ActiveX Automation, you'll find these settings are part of the document object, not part of the database object.

The method to retrieve a setting is called GetVariable, which needs one argument: the setting's name. The counterpart is the SetVariable method, which takes the name and the new value as arguments.

As in AutoLISP, you can query all settings from the drawing database plus many more.

THE OBJECT-ORIENTED WAY — OBJECTARX

In ActiveX Automation, you deal with objects that have properties, methods, and, in some cases, events. Here, all we're interested in are the properties (although you have to use methods to get more complex properties as we did in the xdata discussion earlier).

Using ObjectARX and ObjectDBX, you get access to these same properties, but you access them using member functions of predefined C++ classes. Because we are still dealing with the same data, the differences are much less than one could expect.

ObjectDBX is the database part of ObjectARX. Because ObjectDBX is the foundation on which AutoCAD itself is built, it provides the most complete way to access a drawing's database. There can't be anything in an AutoCAD database that you cannot access using ObjectDBX. Object-DBX is extensible (in fact, the X is for *extensions*). You can load additional modules into ObjectDBX that define additional objects in the database. Thus, in a given database you may not be able to understand certain objects if the corresponding extension module is not available.

The only supported environment for ObjectDBX is Microsoft Visual C++. The complete functionality for database access is hidden in a set of C++ libraries, which you need to link to your application code. I won't go into the complex technical details of writing, compiling, and linking a complete ObjectDBX application, but I will describe how the AutoCAD database looks when you access it from within an ObjectDBX application. Compared with the three access methods I've already discussed (DXF, AutoLISP, and ActiveX Automation), this is remarkably simple to understand.

Accessing the AutoCAD Database

In any C++ program, if you want to use an object of a certain class, you *instantiate* it. You do so by calling the class's constructor, which then returns a pointer to the new object. In C++ code, this looks like the following:

```
AcDbDatabase *pDatabase = new AcDbDatabase(Adesk::kFalse);
```

The constructor for an AcDbDatabase object takes one argument, buildDefaultDatabase, which is Boolean (that is, of type Adesk::Boolean) and can be either Adesk::kTrue or Adesk::kFalse. This parameter defines how AutoCAD creates the drawing database. It must be Adesk::kTrue if you want to start with a plain blank database, and it must be Adesk::kFalse if you want to load an existing drawing file into this database.

Once you create the database object, you can use all associated member functions; for instance, readDwgFile(). In code, this is similar to ActiveX Automation. Depending on whether you work with references or pointers, you write either a dot or a pointing arrow:

```
pDatabase->readDwgFile("aDrawing.dwg");
aDatabase.readDwgFile("aDrawing.dwg");
```

You can create as many database objects as you like, and you can use them concurrently. Before using any database-related code, you need to have at least one drawing database to work on.

Although you can interact with all database objects you opened, there is always one *current* drawing database. If your application is running inside AutoCAD, you can access the database current to AutoCAD using the acdbHostApplicationServices()->workingDatabase() function.

Because instantiating a new database allocates all the memory needed to interact with the database object, you need to explicitly delete any object you created when you're done with it. (And, of course, you should file out— that is, write to a disk file—any changes before deleting the object.)

Opening and Closing Objects in a Database

ObjectDBX is the foundation that AutoCAD itself uses. When working in AutoLISP and ActiveX Automation, you use a friendly wrapper around the low-level AutoCAD functions. But when you work with ObjectDBX, you have to deal with the raw AutoCAD core functionality. This requirement becomes most obvious when opening and closing objects in a database.

Up to now, you assumed that your application was the only one to access a drawing database at a particular time, but this is not necessarily the case. Applications running inside AutoCAD share a drawing database with AutoCAD and among themselves. In almost all cases, ActiveX Automation and AutoLISP make you believe you are the only one working with the database by shielding the necessary actions to take for multiple access.

ObjectDBX operates differently. As you do when working with disk files in a multitasking environment, you need to explicitly open and close the objects you want to work with. You also need to tell AutoCAD how you are going to use the object. You can open an object for read-only or for write. (You can also open an object for notification, which means that your program is notified whenever the object changes. We're looking here at the properties of AutoCAD objects, not at their ability to change over time. Therefore, I won't discuss notification.) As you will expect, an object can be opened for read-only by multiple applications. Only one application at a time, however, can open an object for write.

To open an object, you pass four parameters to the `acdbOpenObject()` function:

▶ The memory address of a pointer to the object's location in memory

▶ The object's identification

▶ The open mode

▶ A flag indicating if you want to open erased objects as well

The function template looks like this:

```
extern Acad::ErrorStatus
acdbOpenObject(
  AcDbObject*& pObj,
  AcDbObjectId objId,
  AcDb::OpenMode mode,
  Adesk::Boolean openErasedObject = Adesk::kFalse);
```

The open mode is one of the following: `AcDb::kForRead`, `AcDb::kForWrite`, or `AcDb::kForNotify`. Open an object for read-only if you only want to extract information, and open it for write if you want to change information. As I said earlier, opening an object for notification is beyond our scope here.

NOTE
The `acdbOpenObject` function is just a shortcut to either `acdbOpenAcDb-Object()` or `acdbOpenAcDbEntity()`, depending on the type of object that is to be opened. If the `acdbOpenObject()` function does not exist for a certain class, you need to call `acdbOpenAcDbObject()` directly (or `acdbOpenAcD-bEntity()`, if the object is an entity).

Every object you open must be closed as soon as access to it is no longer needed. Don't delay closing an object; other applications may need it. To close an object, you call the `close()` method of the opened object like this:

```
pointerToOpenedObject->close();
```

ObjectARX and ObjectDBX provide hundreds of functions to access the drawing database. Many of them open objects implicitly. For instance, the `getBlockTable()` function not only returns a pointer to the block table, it also opens the block table object. This is why you have to provide an open mode for getBlockTable() as well. Consequently, you need to explicitly close the block table object as soon as you finish using it. Many get functions implicitly open objects, as do all object constructors. Thus, if you create a new AcDbLine object, don't forget to close it.

All ObjectDBX functions return an error code, which you should check, of course. After both acdbOpenObject() and close(), you have to look at the returned error code. If everything went smoothly, you will get Acad::eOk. See the ObjectDBX documentation for other error codes that a specific function can return.

Iterating through Containers

If you already know an object's key field string, perhaps a linetype's name, you can directly access the corresponding symbol table record by using the getAt() function:

```
Acad::ErrorStatus
AcDbLinetypeTable::getAt(
  const char* entryName,
  AcDbLinetypeTableRecord*& pRecord,
  AcDb::OpenMode openMode,
  Adesk::Boolean openErasedRecord = Adesk::kFalse) const;
```

You pass the object's key field string and the open mode. In return, you'll get a pointer to the corresponding symbol table record. The object will be opened, and you are responsible for closing it later.

If you don't want to open the symbol table record, you can use a variant of the getAt() function. It returns only the object's identification, which can be used in a later call to acdbOpenObject():

```
Acad::ErrorStatus
AcDbLinetypeTable::getAt(
  const char* entryName,
  AcDbObjectId& recordId,
  Adesk::Boolean getErasedRecord = Adesk::kFalse) const;
```

The error code returned by getAt() indicates whether the symbol table record was found (Adesk::eOk). If no object is using the specified key, you'll receive an error code of Adesk::eKeyNotFound.

If you don't know a symbol table record's key field string, you need to iterate through the symbol table to find the records contained therein. To do this, each symbol table object provides a `newIterator()` function that creates an iterator object for the symbol table. The function returns a pointer to the newly created iterator. Two optional arguments allow you to position the iterator at the container's beginning or end and to skip or include deleted objects:

```
Acad::ErrorStatus
newIterator(
    AcDbLinetypeTableIterator*& pIterator,
    Adesk::Boolean atBeginning = Adesk::kTrue,
    Adesk::Boolean skipDeleted = Adesk::kTrue) const;
```

You can use the iterator's `step()` function to step through the container's contents, or you can use the iterator's `seek()` function to position the iterator at a specific record. If you use `step()`, you need to call the iterator's `done()` function to recognize the end of the container.

At any time, you can use the iterator's `getRecord()` function to open the corresponding symbol table record object. As soon as the iterator is no longer needed, you must delete it. Here is a code segment showing how to iterate through the linetype table:

```
AcDbLinetypeTableIterator *pointerToIterator;
pointerToLinetypeTable->newIterator(pointerToIterator)
for (; !pointerToIterator->done(); pointerToIterator->step())
    {
    pointerToIterator->getRecord(pointerToRecord, AcDb::kForRead);
    doSomething(pointerToRecord);
    pointerToRecord->close();
    }
delete pointerToIterator;
```

To add additional records to a symbol table, you first create the corresponding object and then add it to the symbol table. If you don't add it to the container object, the newly created record will not become part of the database. The `add()` function for symbol tables comes in two variants, depending on whether you want the object identification back:

```
Acad::ErrorStatus
add(
    AcDbLinetypeTableRecord* pRecord);
```

or

```
Acad::ErrorStatus
add(
    AcDbObjectId& recordId,
    AcDbLinetypeTableRecord* pRecord);
```

Entity Handling in ObjectDBX

Using entities in ObjectDBX is similar to symbol record handling as discussed earlier. Every entity is a member of exactly one block container (unless it's a temporary object without an owner). You access the block containers using the block table records, which you get just like you get any other symbol table record.

Every block table record is a container for entities. Once you receive a pointer to the corresponding block table record (for example, by using the block table's getAt() function), you can iterate through the block contents. To do this, you once again use the newIterator() function. But this time you call the newIterator() function of the AcDbBlock-TableRecord object, not the function of the block table.

NOTE

Do not confuse AcDbBlockTableRecord::newIterator() with AcDb-BlockTable-Record::newBlockReferenceIdIterator(). The first function iterates through the contents of a block container referenced by the block table record. The second function iterates through all references to this block throughout the complete database.

While iterating through the contents of a block container, you will not get to the AcDbBlockBegin and AcDbBlockEnd objects of the block. These objects are supplied for compatibility reasons only. They exist in ObjectDBX only because old applications might have attached application-specific data (xdata) to them and there needs to be an access route to this data. If you ever need to access the two objects, use the block table record's openBlockBegin() and openBlockEnd() functions.

Because entities in a block container do not have a key string, no getAt() function exists to directly access one object without iteration. But because every database object (entity or not) has a unique handle, you can use this function to directly access a specific object no matter where it resides:

```
Acad::ErrorStatus
AcDbDatabase::getAcDbObjectId(
  AcDbObjectId& retId,
  Adesk::Boolean createIfNotFound,
  const AcDbHandle& objHandle,
  Adesk::UInt32 xRefId = 0);
```

If the object you find is an entity, you can use its `blockId()` function to find the block table record of the container to which it belongs.

Once you have a pointer to a specific entity, you can use all its member functions to set and retrieve the individual data associated with it. Typical member functions for retrieval are `color()` and `linetype()`. Typical member functions for setting are `setColor()` and `setLinetype()`.

You can use an entity's member functions to access all database-resident data associated with the object. In addition, you can use many member functions that simplify object handling (such as transformations).

Finally, ObjectDBX provides you with access to data elements not saved in the drawing database but taken directly from the class definition. One example is the location of grip points that AutoCAD displays for an object of a certain class. In ObjectDBX, you can query an object's grip points using the `getGripPoints()` function. This type of information is not available to ActiveX Automation, AutoLISP, or DXF.

To add another object to a block container, you use the block table record's `append-AcDbEntity()` function. Like the `add()` function for symbol tables, this function comes in two variants, depending on whether you want the database-internal identification of the object returned:

```
Acad::ErrorStatus
AcDbBlockTableRecord::appendAcDbEntity(
  AcDbObjectId& outputId,
  AcDbEntity* pEntity);
```

or

```
Acad::ErrorStatus
AcDbBlockTableRecord::appendAcDbEntity(
  AcDbEntity* pEntity);
```

Part iv

Working with Dictionaries in ObjectDBX

As you know, dictionaries either belong to a specific object or form a hierarchical tree with a root dictionary containing other dictionaries. To get a pointer to this root dictionary, you use the getNamedObjectsDictionary() function of the database.

To retrieve an object's extension dictionary, you use the extensionDictionary() function. Check the return value against isNull() to see if there is no extension dictionary for the object.

Once you get to this or any other dictionary, you can iterate through its objects using the newIterator() function discussed in the previous section. But the newIterator() function for dictionaries needs an additional parameter that defines the iterating sequence. If you supply AcRx::kDictSorted, you'll get the dictionary objects according to the alphabetic sequence of their keys. If you supply AcRx::kDictCollated, you'll iterate according to the sequence in which the objects were inserted in the dictionary.

Every object you'll find during iteration is either an object or another dictionary, through which you can also iterate.

If you know an entry's key field string, you can directly retrieve it using the dictionary's getAt() function.

Dictionaries don't have an add() or an append() function as symbol tables or block containers do, because they don't support simple adding of objects. Every object you add to a dictionary must have a search key string that will be used to retrieve the object later. Therefore, the corresponding function is called setAt():

```
Acad::ErrorStatus
AcDbDictionary::setAt(
  const char* srchKey,
  AcDbObject* newValue,
  AcDbObjectId& retObjId);
```

To add an object to a dictionary, both the dictionary and the object must be opened for write.

As is the case with ActiveX Automation, a couple of shortcuts are defined for the AutoCAD-specific dictionaries in ObjectARX. An example is getGroupDictionary(), which is short for a getAt() of the ACAD_GROUP dictionary in the root dictionary.

Database Settings and Result Buffers

ObjectDBX also contains shortcuts to the database settings. For example, the CECOLOR setting defines the default color for newly created database entities. You can access this setting using the AcDbDatabase::cecolor() and AcDbDatabase::setCecolor() functions.

For every setting, there is a function that retrieves the current value of the setting, and there is a correspondent set function to modify the value.

In addition, there is a generic function to read and write system variables, and it can access both the database settings and other temporary or configuration-dependent settings like those you get through the AutoLISP and ActiveX Automation functions. These functions are called acedGet-Var() and acedSetVar(). As the aced prefix demonstrates, these are not database functions but editor functions.

Using the acedGetVar() function is quite complicated, because it uses a special structure to return the setting's value. This value may be an integer, a real number, a point, or a string. Therefore, the result buffer (resbuf) structure contains a type field indicating the data type returned along with the true value. And to allow really complex return values, result buffers include a pointer to another result buffer. This allows result buffers to be linked and to return large lists of points, numbers, or strings.

OTHER WAYS TO ACCESS THE DRAWING DATABASE

DXF, AutoLISP, ActiveX Automation, and ObjectDBX/ObjectARX are four methods you can use to access the contents of an AutoCAD drawing database. Each has some disadvantages.

DXF is not AutoCAD's native file format. Although AutoCAD reads and writes DXF files transparently, users most often save their drawings in AutoCAD's DWG file format, which needs an additional user action to create a copy in DXF format.

AutoLISP and ActiveX Automation both rely on the presence of Auto-CAD when evaluating or modifying a drawing. Without AutoCAD, they can't be used to access drawings.

Routines based on ObjectDBX can run both inside AutoCAD and inside other programs. This allows you to create external programs that use native AutoCAD drawing files to save drawing databases. However, ObjectDBX is limited to one specific platform (Microsoft's 32-bit Windows) and to one specific development environment (Microsoft Visual C++). Although Visual C++ is the language of connection for AutoCAD programmers using ObjectDBX, Delphi and other object-oriented programs have occasionally broken through the barrier. Visual C++ is the only supported and tested environment to create ObjectDBX applications for the current version of AutoCAD.

A final problem with ObjectDBX is that you need to license its use from Autodesk. This licensing involves not only royalties, but also restrictions on marketing and use of your ObjectDBX-based programs. For instance, Autodesk does not allow you to create a program that directly competes with AutoCAD.

Due to these disadvantages, a number of alternatives are available to read and write a drawing's database. The most obvious alternative is to directly read an AutoCAD DWG drawing file without going through ObjectDBX. By doing this, you are free to select your development and target platforms as you are for DXF, but your users don't have to remember to use DXF instead of DWG.

Because Autodesk considers the DWG file format a trade secret and will not disclose it, you'll need to decipher the bits and pieces of a DWG file by yourself. But you're not alone. An organization called the Open-DWG Alliance was formed in 1998; its goal is to force Autodesk to document the structure and contents of AutoCAD drawing files. Until this happens, the alliance provides its members with tools and documents that help them to read and write DWG files directly. The Web page you'll find at http://www.opendwg.org documents the file format as the alliance has succeeded in reengineering it so far.

Before the formation of OpenDWG, some developers found out how DWG files are made up and sold their knowledge in the form of programming: Linowes of Sirlin, Gary Rohrabaugh of SoftSource, and Matt Richards of MarComp. Sirlin was acquired by Autodesk, and MarComp was acquired by Visio Corp. The MarComp libraries became the foundation of the OpenDWG libraries. The SoftSource libraries are called Drawing eXchange Engine (DXE).

Using the DWG file format directly or using the OpenDWG libraries (or other, similar libraries) also has disadvantages, as you might suspect. One disadvantage is that it's a lot like trying to hit a moving target. During the AutoCAD Release 14 lifetime (and after the formation of

OpenDWG), Autodesk introduced a slight change in the file format. You wouldn't have noticed this while using any of the methods described in this chapter, but programs based on third-party libraries suddenly didn't accept these files. You might wonder *why* Autodesk introduced this change other than to demonstrate the imperfection of the strategy to rely on reengineered libraries, but I'll leave the conclusions to you.

A second, even more severe disadvantage is the delay span. As soon as Autodesk releases a new version of AutoCAD and its accompanying new database format, you can be sure that the four main access methods discussed in this chapter will be updated. This means you can start adjusting your applications to the new database format immediately (or even earlier if you have access to alpha or beta versions). If you use a third-party library or your own direct-access routines, it will take some time until the changed file format has been reengineered and you can start porting your applications.

WHAT'S NEXT?

This chapter has illustrated the four main methods to access the drawing database: stand-alone programs use the DXF file format or the ObjectDBX libraries; add-ons use AutoLISP, ActiveX Automation, or ObjectDBX as well. You have learned how to programmatically retrieve, manipulate, and even create database objects. The next chapter will discuss the different data types that are used to describe AutoCAD database objects.

Chapter 22

DATA TYPES IN A DRAWING DATABASE

S o far, you have seen the drawing database as a series of objects collected into different containers. An object in this context is typically a line, an arc, or a circle. As you've learned, each object has its own set of properties that define this special instance of its class. For example, the defining properties of a circle are its center point and its radius.

Adapted from *Mastering™ AutoCAD® 2000 Objects* by Dietmar Rudolph

ISBN 0-7821-2562-X   448 pages $49.99

Within the drawing database, only the defining properties are saved and filed out (saved to a disk file). All other aspects of the object, such as its graphical appearance or any calculated properties, are not part of the drawing database. These aspects are subject to the program that is evaluating the database, which could be AutoCAD itself, a third-party application running inside AutoCAD, or a stand-alone program talking to AutoCAD or directly accessing a drawing database saved to a DXF or a DWG file.

If you look at the defining properties of any database object, you'll see that you need only a small number of data types to describe them. In the case of a circle, it's clear that the radius is a positive real number and that the center is a point in 3D. (The AutoCAD drawing database is 3D. Even if you draw a simple circle in 2D, the center point has three coordinates, as the List command in AutoCAD will tell you.)

This chapter discusses the basic data types used in the database objects. Let's start with simple numbers and look at how simple numbers appear in the various access methods. You will also see some typical properties that are saved as simple numbers to the drawing database.

INTEGERS IN THE DRAWING DATABASE

An integer stores a whole number in the drawing database—that is, a number that doesn't have a decimal part or a fraction. The most common integer is the *signed 16-bit integer* (an integer that takes up 16 bits [which equals 2 bytes] of storage space and contains a sign to indicate either a positive or negative number).

Many properties of objects in the drawing database are saved as signed 16-bit integers. One example is the number of faces in a polyface mesh object, which, for instance, may have 18 faces. How your program sees the number of faces depends on how you access the drawing database (using DXF, AutoLISP, ActiveX Automation, or ObjectDBX). This is also true for other types of integers, for real numbers, for strings, and for every other type of information in the drawing database.

This chapter explains how the same data (such as the 18 saved as the polyface object's number of faces) appears in different environments. Within the application program you write to extract or modify a property, you need to declare your variables accordingly. In some cases, you even need to perform certain conversions to correctly work with the data that the drawing database returns to you.

Signed 16-Bit Integer

A signed 16-bit integer (AcDb::kDwgInt16) is a whole number in the range −32768 through 32767. Where do these odd numbers come from? Using 16 bits, you can set individual bits in 65536 different combinations. This means that using a 16-bit integer you can store exactly one of 65536 numbers. Because your integer is signed, you need 1 bit to indicate whether the value is positive or negative. If the sign bit is not set, the number is positive. With 15 bits left, you can store 32768 different positive numbers ranging from 0 (no bit set) through 32767 (all 15 bits set). The remaining 32768 bit combinations are used to express negative numbers (from −1 through −32768).

In ASCII DXF, AutoCAD saves a signed 16-bit integer by writing the individual digits of the number to the DXF file. ASCII, the American Standard Code for Information Interchange, defines which combination of bits is to be used to represent a certain digit or character. For instance, the numeral 1 is represented by the bit code 0011 0001. In ASCII DXF, a signed 16-bit integer is right-justified to the sixth column and padded with leading spaces. Thus, integer 18 is saved to an ASCII DXF file with four leading spaces.

····18

(For clarity, nonprinting characters have been shown to indicate spaces.)

If you look at the individual bytes of the DXF file, you will see four space characters (whose hexadecimal representation is 20h), the numeral 1 (31h), and the numeral 8 (38h). The program you write to evaluate the ASCII DXF file needs to read the individual characters and translate them back to the number 18 that you want to use in your code. Fortunately, in most programming languages, built-in functions do this conversion for you.

There are two flavors of DXF: ASCII DXF, in which all numbers are saved digit by digit, and binary DXF, in which numbers are saved in their compressed binary form. When writing a 16-bit (or 2-byte) integer to a binary DXF file, AutoCAD simply writes the 2 bytes of which the number is made.

Part iv

When evaluating a DXF file from within your program, you need to read the 2 bytes and convert them back to a 16-bit integer. To do so, you need to know the order in which the bytes appear in the file. For instance, if the first byte you read is 12h (0001 0010) and the second byte is 00h (0000 0000), is the resulting integer calculated from the sequence 0001 0010 0000 0000 or from the sequence 0000 0000 0001 0010? The first sequence gives you the number 4608 (4096 + 512), and the second sequence gives you the number 18 (16 + 2). In binary DXF, 16-bit integers are always saved with their least-significant byte (the lower-value bits) first. Thus, the DXF sequence 12h 00h indeed means the number 18. You need to take this into account if your DXF reading program is supposed to run on a computer that uses a different byte order.

Negative numbers are saved using their binary complement. Thus, when converting the 2 bytes back to an integer, you need to first check whether the number is negative. You do so by looking at the sign (highest-value) bit. Because 16-bit integers are saved with the least-significant byte first, the sign bit is the first bit in the second byte. If the sign bit is set, you calculate the resulting number by first complementing each bit (that is, if it's 0, make it 1 and vice versa), add 1, and take the result as negative. Again, in most programming languages, standard functions do all this for you.

If you are not reading a drawing database byte by byte as you do when working with DXF, you don't have to worry about the internal formatting of a 16-bit integer. If you are working in AutoLISP, ActiveX Automation, or ObjectDBX, to retrieve the value of any property of an object in the drawing database, all you have to do is declare your variable so that it fits the data type that AutoCAD will return to you. If the data type does not fit, your program will probably crash or display unexpected results.

In AutoLISP, you don't declare variables. Instead, AutoLISP automatically creates an atom of a correct type. If you query an AutoCAD database object using entget, any property whose value is a 16-bit integer is returned as an atom of type integer.

If you query the value of a database object's property in ActiveX Automation, signed 16-bit integers are returned as numbers of type long. You need to declare your internal variables accordingly. When writing to a property, be aware that the ActiveX Automation data type long allows you to use numbers larger than 32767. Because the drawing database will only take a 16-bit portion of the number you pass, results may be different from what you expect.

In ObjectDBX, the corresponding data type is `Adesk::Int16`. Thus, whenever your program asks ObjectDBX to give you the value of a database object's property that is documented as a 16-bit integer, you need to declare the return value as `Adesk::Int16`.

Signed 32-Bit Integer

A signed 32-bit integer (`AcDb::kDwgInt32`) is a whole number in the range −2147483648 through 2147483647. Again, this comes from the maximum number of combinations (numbers) that can be expressed using 32 bits, one of them used as a sign bit. AutoCAD uses 32-bit integers when it needs to save to the drawing database those integers whose values exceed the 16-bit range. Only a few properties save their value as a 32-bit integer.

In ASCII DXF, you'll find a left-justified, signed 32-bit integer. Thus, the integer 18 is saved to an ASCII DXF file as 31h 38h.

NOTE
With 32-bit integers, there is no padding with space characters as there is with 16-bit integers.

In binary DXF, a signed 32-bit integer is saved within 4 bytes, with the least significant byte first. Thus, the integer 18 is saved as 12h 00h 00h 00h. Negative numbers are saved using their binary complement.

In AutoLISP, you receive an atom of type integer. In ActiveX Automation, signed 32-bit integers are returned as numbers of type long. In ObjectDBX, the corresponding data type is `Adesk::Int32`. You see that, in AutoLISP and ActiveX Automation, 16-bit integers and 32-bit integers are handled identically.

Signed 8-Bit Integer

A signed 8-bit integer (`AcDb::kDwgInt8`) is a whole number in the range −128 through 127, which is what combinations of 8 bits allow. Until Release 13 of AutoCAD, 8-bit integers were not used in the drawing database, and even today very few properties use 8-bit values.

In ASCII DXF, a signed 8-bit integer is left-justified. Thus, the integer 18 is saved to an ASCII DXF file as 31h 38h. You can't tell whether a number you see is supposed to be an 8-bit integer or a 32-bit integer (or even a string) just by looking at a DXF file. You need to know which data type is associated with the group code for the specific object.

In binary DXF, a signed 8-bit integer is saved as a single byte. Thus, the integer 18 is saved as 12h. Negative numbers are saved using their binary complement.

As is the case with 16-bit and 32-bit integers, neither AutoLISP nor ActiveX Automation distinguishes precision between 8-bit integers and 16-bit integers. Again you'll receive an atom of type integer in AutoLISP or a number of type long in ActiveX Automation. In ObjectDBX, the corresponding data type is Adesk::Int8.

DISGUISED INTEGERS

Signed integers of 16-bit length are used to store many of the properties of objects in the drawing database. You would expect that the value of such a property could be any number in the range −32768 through 32767, but this is not always the case.

Take, for instance, the property of a dimension style that specifies whether the first extension line is to be suppressed. This property is allowed to have only two values: yes and no. In most programming languages, you would use the Boolean data type, or yes/no, for such a setting.

The drawing database has no such data type. Instead, AutoCAD uses a signed 16-bit integer to save the setting to the drawing database. It simply declares that if the 16-bit integer is zero (0), the setting is "no", and if it's one (1), the setting is "yes". Other values are invalid.

In this property, the signed 16-bit integer type is abused to represent a completely different data type, the Boolean type. Depending on the object and property and depending on the programming environment, AutoCAD is sometimes friendly enough to convert the integer into the correct data type for you. In other cases, you need to do this conversion within the program you write.

In many places in the drawing database, integers represent a different, more specialized data type. If the environment you work in is friendly enough, you are working with database integers without knowing that they are integers. This section discusses these integers in disguise.

Enumerations As Integers

A typical example of data elements saved as an integer in a drawing database are *enumerations*. If a data type is an enumeration, it carries exactly one of a very limited set of values. The Boolean data type listed above, for instance, is an enumeration with only two possible values: yes (or true) and no (or false).

Let's look at the LUNITS database setting, which defines how to display linear units. In the drawing database, this setting is saved as a signed 16-bit integer and, as such, could take any value up to 32767. But if you look at the AutoCAD documentation, you will see that the only possible values for this setting are 1, 2, 3, 4, and 5. In DXF, AutoLISP, and ObjectDBX, the LUNITS setting looks like any other signed 16-bit integer, so you really can't tell that it is limited to the values 1 through 5. In ActiveX Automation, you can use the integer 1 if you want exponential (scientific) format, but you probably won't. Usually, you use the predefined constant acScientific to set the LUNITS value.

Predefined constants for the values of an integer are used when the value range is very small, as in the LUNITS example in which only five values are possible. It is wise to use predefined constants instead of the corresponding numbers in your code because your code is then more readable. Using predefined constants also allows a value of a constant to change with a new database version without breaking your code, although it is unlikely that constants change in this way from AutoCAD version to AutoCAD version.

Group Codes

Of the disguised integers that represent enumerations you may use in a program to access the AutoCAD drawing database, the DXF group code needs special consideration. The group code is invisible to ActiveX Automation and will be filled in by AutoCAD automatically when you create new objects or change the value of properties.

In ObjectDBX, you can use the many predefined constants of the enumerated type AcDb::DxfCode to fill in a DXF group code when writing certain properties of an object or to compare information you retrieved from the drawing database with a certain group code. In binary DXF, the group code is handled exactly the same as a signed 16-bit integer, but in ASCII DXF, the group code is saved right-justified to the third column (not the sixth, as is usual) with leading spaces. Group codes larger than 999 are left-justified.

WARNING

Older specifications of binary DXF used a combination of 1-byte and 3-byte group codes. Therefore, do not assume that the group code is 2-byte (16-bit) in every DXF file your program may need to read. If you do, your program will probably crash on old-style DXF files. Always check the second byte of the very first group code in the file. If this byte is zero (00h), it's a DXF file with all group codes saved as 16-bit integers. If the second byte is not zero, it's an old-style DXF file with 1-byte and 3-byte group codes.

Colors and Lineweights

A number of database fields define a color or lineweight property. In the drawing database, this information is stored as an ordinary signed 16-bit integer. Depending on the environment used to talk to the database, the value of a color or lineweight property may be automatically converted to a much friendlier data type and look quite different from an integer.

Colors in DXF and AutoLISP are integers associated with group code 62. In ActiveX Automation, a color is an object of type ACAD_COLOR with predefined constants for the most often used colors. In ObjectDBX, a color is an object of type AcCmColor with a lot of member functions.

Lineweights in DXF and AutoLISP are integers associated with group code 370. In ActiveX Automation, you'll get an object of type ACAD_LWEIGHT with predefined constants for the lineweights allowed. In ObjectDBX, the lineweight is a member of the enumeration AcDb::LineWeight; for example, kAcLnWt005.

Booleans as Integers

Even though a drawing database contains many settings of data type Boolean, there is no such type in the drawing database. A Boolean property (also known as a *flag*) can take only two values: yes or no, or true or false. Ordinarily, you would need only a single bit to save the value of such a property. Instead, even a simple flag such as Visibility is saved to the drawing database as a signed 16-bit integer and takes up 16 bits of storage space instead of only 1 bit.

When looking for the Visibility property of an object in either DXF or AutoLISP, you will find only the 16-bit integer. You then need to check whether this integer is 0 (visible) or 1 (invisible). In ObjectDBX, you can use an enumerated type called AcDb::Visibility to check whether the corresponding object is visible. The property value is either AcDb::kVisible or AcDb::kInvisible. (This is an exception. In ObjectDBX, most other Booleans are of type Adesk::Boolean.)

In ActiveX Automation, this data element is a true Boolean entity, as it should be. You can simply use true and false to set the Visibility property.

To save space in the database, you will find database objects to which several independent Boolean flags have been saved for what looks like a single property. If you look at the AcDbAttribute object in ActiveX Automation (AcadAttribute), you will find the following four Boolean flags:

▸ Constant

▸ Invisible

▸ Preset

▸ Verify

Similarly, in ObjectDBX you will find four member functions of AcDbAttribute, each to set or query the four flags of type Adesk::Boolean; for example, isConstant(), isInvisible(), and so on.

In both DXF and AutoLISP, you will get one single integer describing all four flags. Each flag has a numeric value of 0 (false) or 1 (true). These numeric values are combined into a single integer by factoring with 2, that is, by packing each value into one bit of the resulting integer.

Thus, if in the program you write to interact with the drawing database you want to verify that an attribute is preset, you need to extract the corresponding bit from the integer. This extraction is usually done through a logical and function (logand in AutoLISP). In this case, the preset property is saved in the fourth bit of the attribute's group 70 value. This means you need to and the integer with 2(4-1) and then check the result against zero to find out whether the property is set.

Part iv

Real Numbers in the Drawing Database

A *real number* (or simply *real*) is a number that has a decimal part. Most numeric values in an AutoCAD drawing database are not integers. All coordinates, lengths, or angle values are real numbers. (Even if they accidentally have no decimal or fractional part, they are still real numbers.)

In theory, a real number can have an indefinite number of significant digits. However, in data processing we're used to limiting real numbers to a finite range and precision because we don't really care what the 356th digit of a calculated number is and because we don't have the time to wait until the computer calculates such a precise result.

The AutoCAD drawing database uses 64-bit floating-point numbers to store real values (`AcDb::kDwgReal`). Of these numbers, 52 bits make up the mantissa, and the remaining 12 bits are used for the exponent.

NOTE

A *mantissa*, if you'll remember your high school math, is the part of a logarithm to the right of the decimal point. Real numbers in a computer are logarithms based on the number 2.

The mantissa defines the maximum precision of numbers. Using 52 bits, the precision is limited to approximately 4,500,000,000,000,000 numbers. This is precise enough to locate every object of the solar system within a single centimeter and should be sufficient for all technical drawings in the near future.

The 12-bit exponent defines the range in which the real numbers you will work with lie. Using different exponents, you can place the numbers in the range $\pm10^{-308}$ through $\pm10^{308}$, which should be sufficient. (Although the AutoCAD drawing editor does not allow you to input values that exceed $\pm10^{-99}$ to $\pm10^{99}$, the calculated numbers inside the drawing database may be larger or smaller than that.)

In AutoLISP, whenever you query the value of an object's property, you'll get real numbers as atoms of type real. In ActiveX Automation, this data type is called double. ObjectDBX defines a type called `ads_real`.

In binary DXF, a real number is saved as an 8-byte double-float, according to IEEE Standard 754-1985, with the least significant byte first. Thus, the real number 10.0 is saved to binary DXF as the following sequence of bytes: 00h 00h 00h 00h 00h 00h 24h 40h.

NOTE

The Institute of Electrical and Electronics Engineers (IEEE) is an organization that coordinates computing and communications standards. For more information on the IEEE, go to its website at www.ieee.org.

In ASCII DXF, saving a real number is both simple and complicated. It's simple because you write the number digit by digit just as you would in any programming language. It's complicated because you need to follow a few rules to create valid numbers:

▶ Any real number in ASCII DXF must have at least one digit before and one digit after the decimal delimiter.

▶ The decimal delimiter is always a decimal point, regardless of the local standard, which may be a comma in some geographic areas.

▶ The maximum number of digits is 16 because this is the maximum precision of a 52-bit mantissa. Thus, if you have 10 digits in front of the decimal point, you can't have more than 6 digits following it.

▶ You can append an exponent to the number if necessary. The exponent always starts with the letter E, followed by the sign of the exponent (+ or −), followed by a maximum of three digits.

Examples of properly formatted reals are 1.0, 0.56, and 0.7E+2. The following examples are not valid, and AutoCAD or another DXF-reading program may refuse to load the drawing file: 25., .12, 1 3/4, and 0.9E2.

TIP

When writing an ASCII DXF file in AutoCAD, you can set the precision. In fact, you set the number of digits to follow the decimal point. If you keep the default of 16 digits, the accuracy of numbers in the DXF file equals the accuracy within the database. Rounding errors are in the range you normally expect with finite-length real numbers.

WARNING

If you select fewer than 16 digits when setting the precision during DXF creation, you alter the database contents! The database in DXF now differs from the original database. Under extreme circumstances (using 0 digits), this may render the database information invalid, perhaps by introducing scale factors of zero.

Length Units

Although integers often define quantities (and are therefore considered unit-less), real numbers in a technical drawing usually have an associated unit. Most real numbers define lengths. To define a length completely, you need to add a unit of measurement.

Unfortunately, the AutoCAD drawing database is unit-less. The eye of the user of a drawing interprets its lengths. You can't tell just from looking at the coordinates in a drawing database whether the drawing uses millimeters, inches, or parsecs.

A unit of measurement is associated with blocks, which means that you can tell whether a block is designed to use millimeters or inches. However, AutoCAD itself does not honor these units. Only the Design Center application, which is shipped with AutoCAD, honors them. The unit assigned to blocks can be found as xdata attached to the block's symbol table record. For the *MODEL_SPACE block, such information is saved in the INSUNITS drawing setting.

Angle Units

Unlike length units, which are nonexistent, the unit of measurement for angles and directions in a drawing database is implicit. Unfortunately, the angle unit that is used depends on how you look at the drawing database.

In DXF (ASCII and binary), angles are measured in decimal degrees and are between but excluding $-360°$ and $360°$. In AutoLISP, ActiveX Automation, and ObjectDBX, angles are measured in radians and range from $-\pi$ to π.

Date and Time Values

In addition to lengths, angles, and just plain simple real numbers (such as scale factors), the drawing database uses real numbers to save date and time values.

The value of a couple of timers represents the number of days since the timer started. The fractional part of the real number is the fractional part of a day. An example of this is the cumulative editing time you can retrieve from the TDINDWG setting.

Date and time values, like the last save, are also saved within a real number. The AutoCAD drawing database uses Julian dates, which are calculated by the number of days since January 1, 4713 B.C. Again, the fractional part defines the hours, minutes, and so on.

In ObjectDBX, you'll get dates as instances of AcDbDate, a class containing several member functions that provide a more comfortable access to date values.

STRINGS IN THE DRAWING DATABASE

Besides numbers, a drawing database also contains several text strings— that is, combinations of text characters such as annotations, layer names, and so on. These strings fall into two categories: strings that will be displayed as part of the drawing (for example, text, multiline text, attributes, and so on) and strings that work as references (for example, layer names, filenames, and hyperlinks).

Database strings (AcDb::kDwgText) can be of any length. When working with properties of database objects that have string values, in AutoLISP and ActiveX Automation, you'll see the strings as string type objects. In ObjectDBX, the correspondent type is char*. In ASCII DXF, a string is simply a line of characters. In binary DXF, a string is also a sequence of characters, but terminated by a zero byte (00h).

Character Sets

Until recently, computers, operating systems, and application programs were limited in the number of different characters they could display and use. Some systems, such as Windows 95/98, are still limited in this way. On such systems, the user must select (typically during installation of the operating system) a certain set of characters to work with. For example, if your system is set to use Latin characters, you won't be able to type Japanese or Greek characters.

The AutoCAD drawing database is independent of the character set that a specific machine uses. The database supports the Unicode character set, which is a superset of all national character sets. Character sets are also called *code pages*.

Depending on the platform used to run the database access program, the full Unicode character set may not be available. For instance, although Windows NT allows you to work with the full Unicode range of characters, Windows 95/98 allows you to use only a small 256-character set.

If the full Unicode character set is not available, you will see database strings translated to the local character set. All characters in the local code page will be seen as is, whereas all Unicode characters not in the local set will be translated into a control code sequence. This sequence consists of a Unicode escape sequence followed by a 4-digit hexadecimal representation of the Unicode character. Whenever the program you write to access the drawing database retrieves a string from an object's property, you should expect that it may contain Unicode control codes, at least if you cannot guarantee that your program runs only on systems that support the full Unicode range of characters.

For example, look at the string *This is angle* α. Because the alpha character is usually not part of a Windows 95/98 code page, you will see this text represented as *This is angle \U+03b1*. Depending on your programming language, you might also see the backslash doubled.

If your program runs inside AutoCAD, you can query the non–database-resident global setting SYSCODEPAGE for the local code page name. The AutoLISP, ActiveX Automation, and ObjectDBX functions for retrieving the drawing settings also allow you to retrieve temporary and configuration-dependent settings from AutoCAD that are not saved to a drawing database. See the AutoCAD documentation on system variables for a complete list of the settings. If your program runs on its own using ObjectDBX, it must ask the operating system about the current code page.

If you are working with DXF, you need to use the code page that was active when the DXF file was written. You'll find the name of this code page in the HEADER section under the heading DWGCODEPAGE.

Character Range

Depending on what a string will represent in the drawing database, the number and range of characters that can be used may be limited. For example, symbol table record keys are not allowed to use the following characters:

<>/\":?*,='

Characters in the range 00h through 1Fh are unprintable control characters and are not allowed in any string in a drawing database.

HANDLES IN THE DRAWING DATABASE

The database-unique object handle (AcDb::kDwgHandle) is a 64-bit integer value. However, it is never seen as such.

In ObjectDBX, the handle is represented by its own class, AcDbHandle. In DXF, AutoLISP, and ActiveX Automation, the handle is shown to any program requesting it as a string containing the hexadecimal representation of the 64-bit integer. Thus, the handle 18 is represented by the string "12" (18 = 1 * 16 + 2).

If you're working in ObjectDBX, you can get the string representation of a handle using the function AcDbHandle::getIntoAsciiBuffer().

OBJECT POINTERS

There are four different types of inter-object links:

- ▶ AcDb::kDwgHardOwnershipId
- ▶ AcDb::kDwgSoftOwnershipId
- ▶ AcDb::kDwgHardPointerId
- ▶ AcDb::kDwgSoftPointerId

Object links require that one object point to the other object to which it is linked. How you see the other object's reference in the database depends on the method you use to evaluate it.

In DXF, you will find the referenced object's handle (again, in its string representation). When working with AutoLISP, the reference is the other object's Entity name. In ObjectDBX you will get an ObjectID.

In ActiveX Automation, you will not get a pointer to the referenced object at all. Instead, you will transparently get the object itself, which you can use directly.

Points in the Drawing Database

Every entity in a DXF file has at least one set of coordinates that define the object's position within the model. Depending on the object type, you need one or more points (AcDb::kDwg3Real) to describe the location and size of the entity. A *point* is an exact location in space defined by its x, y, and z coordinates.

Points in an AutoCAD drawing database always have three coordinates. Every model in the database is three-dimensional. Even a simple 2D draft has z coordinates; they're just all the same (0.0).

Even though coordinates are lengths that should each have a unit of measurement, the AutoCAD drawing database is unit-less. Each coordinate is just a unit-less 64-bit real number.

Points, Coordinates, and Point Lists

How object properties that are points are returned to your application program depends on the access method you use to read the drawing database.

ObjectDBX uses a special data type called AcGePoint3d to pass points as parameters to and from routines. The AcGePoint3d is an array of ads_real indexed by 0, 1, and 2. Predefined constants x, y, and z allow you to query a point's x coordinate by SomePoint[X].

In AutoLISP, a point is handled as a list of three real numbers. You can extract the three coordinates using the standard AutoLISP functions car, cadr, and caddr respectively.

ActiveX Automation has no predefined data type suited for points. Therefore, you use variants to read and write points. A single point is passed as an array of double indexed by 0, 1, and 2. Several objects are defined by a list of points. In this case, you also use an array of double, but it now needs to have more components (three doubles per point).

In DXF, the storage of points is a bit strange. For some reason, a point was not considered as a separate data type to fit into a single group value.

Instead, the three coordinates making the point are three individual groups. To read a point's coordinates, you need to read three group values. With every point, the group code for the y coordinate is calculated from the x coordinate's group code by adding 10, and for the z coordinate, by adding 20. Thus, if a point's group code in AutoLISP is 14, in DXF you'll find the x coordinate in group 14, the y coordinate in group 24, and the z coordinate in group 34.

Points, Vectors, and Offsets

A point exactly defines a location in 3D space; for example, the point with the x coordinate 10.0, the y coordinate 20.0, and the z coordinate 30.0. A *vector* exactly defines a bearing in 3D space, like from *here* 15.0 units along *this* direction. Another way to express a vector is to say: from *here* 5.0 units parallel to the x-axis, then 10.0 units parallel to the y-axis, and finally 10.0 units parallel to the z-axis. Both variants describe the exact same vector. Vectors are independent of their starting point (the *here* in the previous sentences). Wherever you move the vector around in space, it is always the same vector (because the vector is just the direction and the distance, not the location of *here*).

Both points and vectors have three coordinates, and so, both mathematically and in the AutoCAD database, there is no apparent difference between the two. Whether you see a coordinate set as a point or as a vector depends on the context in which you use it.

What I just explained and what is known mathematically as a vector is called an *offset* in all Autodesk documentation. Whenever the documentation uses the term *vector*, it is referring to a (mathematical) vector that has an additional special property: a length (distance) of one (1.0). Such a vector is usually called a *unit vector* or a *normalized* vector. Because the distance part of a normalized vector is always 1.0, an (Autodesk) vector just expresses a direction in 3D space.

When accessing a drawing database using ObjectDBX, you retrieve (Autodesk) vectors as objects of class AcGeVector3d, which is a structure (not an array) of three real numbers. You access a vector's y coordinate by writing SomeVector.y, in which SomeVector represents the vector you would name in your bit of code

If an object contains point, vector, and offset type properties, you will also notice a difference in the way these properties change while the object is modified. No matter whether the object is moved, scaled, rotated, stretched, or mirrored, point properties of this object usually change accordingly. Vector properties change only when the object is rotated or mirrored—they are independent of move, scale, or stretch operations. Offset properties work the same as vectors as they change with rotations and mirroring operations, but also change their length if the object is scaled.

Coordinate Systems

AutoCAD uses only three-dimensional, Cartesian coordinate systems. A Cartesian coordinate system is defined by its origin point and three axes. The three axes are perpendicular to one another and right-oriented, which means that they follow the right-hand rule:

> If the thumb, the index finger, and the middle finger of your right hand build 90° angles to one another and if the thumb points along the x-axis and the index finger points along the y-axis, the middle finger points along the z-axis.

Coordinate systems differ in their origin points and in the direction of their axes. When working with the AutoCAD drawing database, you will have to use various coordinate systems.

The complete drawing database is based on a global, arbitrary coordinate system called the World Coordinate System (WCS). The WCS origin is the point (0,0,0), where the x-axis goes from the WCS origin through the point (1,0,0), the y-axis through the point (0,1,0), and the z-axis through (0,0,1). A model or drawing can be oriented arbitrarily within the WCS, which means that there is nothing special about the WCS. If your model is a house, you don't say that the elevation is parallel to the WCS z-axis. Nothing will hinder you from drawing the house with the elevation parallel to the WCS x-axis. Thus, in relationship to the model, the WCS is just one arbitrary coordinate system.

While working in AutoCAD, a user can create his or her own Cartesian coordinate systems. These User Coordinate Systems (UCS) have their own origin and axis orientation. Although the database objects do not reflect in which UCS they were drawn, the drawing database contains a list of named UCS definitions that a user can recall. The UCS symbol table is the list of all named UCS definitions within the drawing database. When working interactively in AutoCAD, the drawing editor transparently converts an object's coordinates to the current coordinate system and vice versa. When working with the drawing database directly, your program eventually needs to do these conversions.

Another coordinate system you will encounter in the drawing database is the Screen Coordinate System (SCS), which is used to define window locations on the AutoCAD graphical user interface. The SCS defines coordinates starting from the lower-left corner of the screen's drawing display area, with the x-axis pointing to the right. The SCS is a two-dimensional coordinate system with the point (1,1) located at the upper-right corner of the screen's drawing display area. Thus, any point within the drawing display area has an x and/or y coordinate between 0.0 and 1.0.

Entity Coordinates

Every entity in the drawing database has an associated Entity Coordinate System (ECS), which may or may not be equal to the WCS. The Autodesk documentation has introduced the term Object Coordinate System (OCS) as an alternative to ECS. Because only entities (that is, objects with a graphical representation) have an ECS, this change in terminology does not represent a functional change. Because the term *Entity Coordinate System* is both more known and more correct, I'll stay with the abbreviation ECS.

For most entities, the ECS corresponds to the WCS, especially when you think of three-dimensional objects. But it makes sense to give two-dimensional planar (that is, flat) objects their own coordinate system. For example, consider a circular arc. Because the arc can be arbitrarily oriented in 3D space, you must first define a coordinate system (ECS) with its xy plane parallel to the plane on which the arc is drawn. All points on the arc curve have the same z coordinate in ECS. Also this coordinate system simplifies the storage of the arc's start and end parameters. Instead of using points or vectors, you can simply store the start and end angles relative to the x-axis of the ECS.

When accessing the drawing database, some point properties will be WCS points, and others will be ECS points. Whether a returned point is in WCS or ECS sometimes depends on the access method. The arc center, for instance, will be returned in WCS coordinates by ObjectDBX and the ActiveX Automation interface, but the same point property will be returned in ECS coordinates by AutoLISP and DXF.

Even though multiple coordinate systems are in use, the arc center point is still the arc center point; however, its coordinate values depend on the coordinate system in which you locate it. It's often necessary to translate an object's coordinates into another coordinate system. Because ObjectDBX returns points in WCS, you may want to know the coordinate values of a point if you used the ECS instead. To do this translation, ObjectDBX contains the `acdbWcs2Ecs()` transformation function, which takes a WCS point and returns the coordinate values within the ECS.

On the other hand, many point properties of objects are returned to AutoLISP in ECS coordinates. There is no built-in function to translate such an ECS point into the WCS, but you can easily create your own, for instance, by copying these lines to your program's code:

```
(defun PointInWCS (Entity PointInECS)
  (trans PointInECS Entity 0)
)
```

The Arbitrary Axis Algorithm

If you work with a DXF file, no predefined function is available to transform coordinates because there is only a data file in this format. When you're working in ActiveX Automation, there's also no predefined function.

Thus, for these two applications, you need to know how an object's ECS is defined and how you can calculate the ECS definition from the data you find in the drawing database.

To define a plane in space, you usually need a point and two vectors. At the time the drawing database was enhanced to 3D memory, disk space was still very expensive. Consequently, the AutoCAD drawing database uses only a single vector to fully define the ECS. How does this work?

The ECS is valid for planar entities only. A *planar entity* is any entity that has a two-dimensional nature: for example, a circle, an arc, an annotation object, or a hatch pattern. Even though you can orient such a planar entity anywhere in 3D space, you always need to first define the plane on which you draw the object (like placing a sheet of paper onto your drawing board and then moving, tilting, and rotating the drawing board). The sheet of paper on the drawing board defines the plane in space where the object should appear. The direction perpendicular to the drawing board's surface is called the *normal* (also known as *normal vector*) of the plane on which the object is drawn (or simply the normal of the object).

Because the normal is just a direction (and, if you remember the earlier discussion on vectors, therefore expressed as a normalized or unit vector—that is, a vector of length 1.0), it does not matter at which point we place our normal vector. It is always the same. When calculating the

ECS of a planar entity, you start with this normal vector and go back to the plane (or sheet) on which the object was drawn.

WHEN NORMALS DIFFER

In the drawing board example, I said that the normal is the direction perpendicular to the drawing board surface. If you think about this for a moment, you will recognize that *two* directions are perpendicular to the plane: one pointing toward you and the other pointing toward the drawing board. This is the reason for a typical problem in AutoCAD.

It is possible to draw two planar objects, maybe arcs, next to each other that have the same radius and, therefore, generate a similar outline. But one of these arcs may have its normal pointing "up," and the other may have its normal pointing "down." You will not notice the different normals during most AutoCAD operations. But if you try to fillet the two arcs, you'll get an error message because AutoCAD only fillets objects whose normals are parallel. Or, if you add a thickness to the arcs, they will extrude in different directions. The normal direction is also important during the generation of rendered images, because computer programs usually render only one side of a surface: the side to which the normal vector points.

The normal vector of a planar entity defines the ECS z direction, but the direction alone defines only the orientation of the drawing board surface, not its location. An unlimited number of parallel planes still share the same normal. As an arbitrary but valid prerequisite, the ECS origin is therefore set so that it is always equal to the WCS origin. You, therefore, eliminate all the parallel planes and are left with only one of them. It may not necessarily pass through your drawing board's surface, but the z coordinate of any point of your planar object tells you the location of the "drawing board surface."

Now, all that is left to find out is the direction of the remaining axes, x and y, within the plane you just calculated. And because the three axes are perpendicular to one another, you can easily calculate the ECS y-axis once you identify the ECS x-axis.

But how do you calculate the ECS x-axis? AutoCAD uses a trick called the *arbitrary axis algorithm*. This is not an arbitrary algorithm, but an algorithm to calculate an arbitrary axis. Because the sole input is the ECS z direction (the normal), it doesn't really matter which x-axis AutoCAD calculates; it is only important to always calculate the *same* x-axis from a given normal. Thus, your axis may be arbitrary, and you'll use this calculation:

```
ECS_X = WCS_Z × ECS_Z
```

In this formula, WCS_Z is the z-axis of the WCS, (0,0,1). But there is a small problem: What if the normal (ECS_Z) is equal or very close to the WCS z-axis (WCS_Z)? Because this proximity gives an undefined result, you must add one more check and one alternative, in which WCS_Y is (0,1,0):

```
if ECS_Z is close to WCS_Z
  then
    ECS_X = WCS_Y × ECS_Z
  else
    ECS_X = WCS_Z × ECS_Z
```

Now you only have to define what is meant by *is close to*. The arbitrary axis algorithm defines this as

$$(-\varepsilon < ECS\_Z[x] < \varepsilon) \; \partial \; (-\varepsilon < ECS\_Z[y] < \varepsilon)$$

which means that you call the axes *close* if both the normal's x and y components are smaller than ε, a threshold value. The value of ε is defined as 0.015625 = 1.0/64.0, a value you can display exactly in both decimal and binary forms, thus giving you a fast and exact calculation no matter type the of computer on which the algorithm is supposed to run.

Once you know the axes and origin, you can easily translate coordinates between the two coordinate systems. Most development environments come with routines that use transformation matrices to translate coordinates between coordinate systems.

BINARY DATA IN THE DRAWING DATABASE

All the information in a drawing database should consist of numbers and/or strings, but there are exceptions. It is possible to store other sorts of information inside a drawing database, such as a true-color animation of the designed part or the sound an engine is supposed to make.

Although you could divide the information into numbers and strings, it makes sense to keep this information in its binary form. Therefore, the drawing database allows another data type called a *binary chunk* (AcDb::kDwgBChunk). This chunk of binary data can hold everything that does not easily fit into numbers or strings. Any object in the drawing database can have one or more properties that hold binary data.

If you retrieve a binary chunk of data from the drawing database using AutoLISP or if you look into an ASCII DXF file, a binary chunk is seen as a string containing the hexadecimal representation of the binary data. To use it, you need to convert the hexadecimal codes back to binary data. In binary DXF, you'll simply see the binary data. But, because there is no end-of-data character, as is the case with strings (because in a binary chunk, any character might be a valid data byte), the binary chunk is preceded by length information.

The length information is a single unsigned 8-bit integer. Because the maximum number you can represent using 8 bits (without a sign bit) is 255, the maximum length of a binary chunk is 255 bytes (plus the 1 length byte). If you read a group value from a binary DXF file and the group value is supposed to be a binary chunk, you read the first byte (the length information), and then you read as many data bytes as this length of byte indicates.

In ObjectDBX, a binary chunk is seen as data of type ads_binary. This structure (struct) consists of length information called .clen and a pointer to the binary data. Even though the length information .clen is defined as a short, remember that the maximum length for binary chunks is 255 bytes.

In ActiveX Automation, a binary chunk is returned as a *safearray*, which is an array in which all elements are of the same type. In the case of binary chunks, the individual array elements are bytes.

What's Next?

This concludes the discussion of data types you may encounter in an AutoCAD drawing database. Even though a drawing can have many different objects, the objects' individual properties are made from only a few basic primitives. If the program you write to access the drawing database knows how to handle the three types of integers, real numbers, points and vectors, handles, pointers, strings, and binary chunks, all that is left to do is to read the individual objects from the drawing database and decode their properties.

Appendix A

3D RENDERING IN AutoCAD

Just a few years ago, it took the power of a workstation to create the kind of images you will create in this chapter. Today, you can render not just a single image, but several hundred images to build computer animations. And with the explosion of game software, the Internet, and virtual reality, real-time walkthrough sessions of 3D computer models are nearly as commonplace as word processors.

Adapted from *Mastering™ AutoCAD® 2000 Premium Edition* by George Omura

ISBN 0-7821-2499-2   1,664 pages $59.99

In this appendix, you'll learn how you can use rendering tools in Auto-CAD to produce rendered still images of your 3D models. With these tools, you can add materials, control lighting, and even add landscaping and people to your models. You also have control over the reflectance and transparency of objects, and you can add bitmap backgrounds to help set the mood.

Things to Do Before You Start

You will want to take certain steps before you begin working with the rendering tools so you won't run into problems later. First, make sure you have a lot of free disk space on the drive where Windows is installed. Having 100MB of free disk space will ensure that you won't exceed your RAM capacity while rendering. This may sound like a lot, but remember, you are attempting to do with your desktop computer what only workstations were capable of a few years ago. Also, make sure you have plenty of free disk space on the drive where your AutoCAD files are kept.

Creating a Quick Study Rendering

Throughout this appendix, you will work with a 3D model that was created using AutoCAD's solid modeling tools. The model is of two buildings on a street corner. You'll begin by creating a basic rendering using the default settings in the Render dialog box.

NOTE
You can download files for this book from Sybex's website at http://www.sybex.com. Search for "AutoCAD 2002 Complete" to locate the files.

1. Download the Facade.dwg file from the Sybex website and open it.

2. Open the Render toolbar from the Toolbar dialog box.

3. Choose View ≻ Render ≻ Render, or click the Render tool in the Render toolbar.

The Render dialog box appears. In time, you will become intimately familiar with this dialog box.

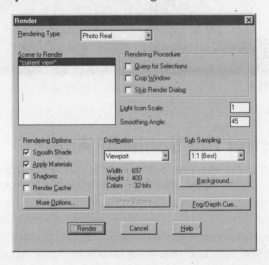

4. Click the Render button. AutoCAD takes a minute or two to render the current view. While it's working, you will see messages in the Command window showing you the progress of the rendering. When AutoCAD is done, the model appears as a surface-shaded model (see Figure A.1).

When you render a model without any special settings, you get what is called a *Z buffer shaded model*. The surfaces are shaded in their color and the light source is, by default, from the camera location. This view is much like a Hidden-Line view with color added to help distinguish surface orientation. You can actually get a similar view using the Flat Shade tool on the Shade toolbar.

FIGURE A.1: The Facade model rendered using all the default settings

Simulating the Sunlight Angle

The ability to add a sunlight source to a drawing is one of AutoCAD's key features. This tool is used frequently in the design of buildings in urban and suburban settings. Neighboring building owners will want to know if your project will cast darkening shadows over their homes or workplaces. The Sun option lets you accurately simulate the sun's location in relation to a model and its surrounding buildings. AutoCAD also lets you set up multiple light sources other than the sun.

Let's add the sun to your model to give a better sense of the building's form and relationship to its site.

1. Choose View ➤ Render ➤ Lights, or click Lights on the Render toolbar.

TIP

Whenever you are creating a new light or other object with the Rendering tool, you usually have to give it a name first, before you can do anything else.

2. In the Lights dialog box, choose Distant Light from the drop-down list next to the New button toward the bottom left.

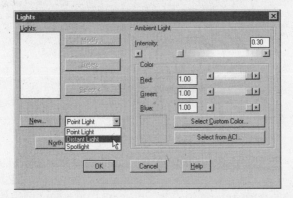

3. Click the New button. The New Distant Light dialog box appears.

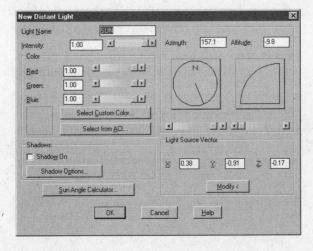

4. This dialog box lets you control various aspects of the light source, such as color and location. Type **SUN** in the Light Name input box.

5. Because you want to simulate the sun in this example, click the button labeled Sun Angle Calculator. The Sun Angle Calculator dialog box appears.

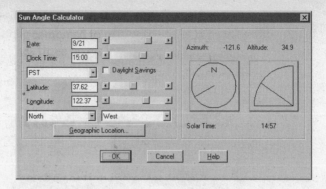

Notice that you have options for setting the date and time to determine the exact location of the sun. In addition, you have the option to indicate where true polar north is in relation to your model. AutoCAD assumes polar north is at the 90° position in the WCS.

6. One important factor for calculating the sun angle is finding your location on the earth. Click the Geographic Location button. The Geographic Location dialog box appears.

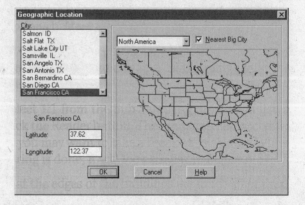

Here you can tell AutoCAD where your building is located in the world.

7. For the sake of this tutorial, suppose the Facade model is a building in San Francisco, California, USA. Select North America from the drop-down list above the map.

8. Locate and select San Francisco CA in the scrolling list to the left of the map. Notice that the Latitude and Longitude input boxes below the list change to reflect the location of San Francisco. For locations not listed, you can enter values manually in those input boxes.

9. Click OK to return to the Sun Angle Calculator dialog box. Set the Date value to **9/21** and the Clock Time value to **14:00**. Notice that the graphic to the right in the dialog box adjusts to show the altitude and azimuth angle of the sun for the time you enter.

10. Click OK in the Sun Angle Calculator dialog box and the New Distant Light dialog box, and then click OK again in the Lights dialog box.

11. Choose View ➢ Render ➢ Render, or click Render on the Render toolbar. Then, click the Render button in the Render dialog box. Your model will be shaded to reflect the sun's location (see Figure A.2).

FIGURE A.2: The Facade model with the sun light source added

Notice that the building itself looks darker than before, and that the ground plane is lighter. Remember that in the first rendering, the light source was the same as the camera location, so the wall facing you received more direct light. In this last rendering, the light source is at a glancing angle, so the surface appears darker.

This section mentioned that you can set the direction of polar north. You do so by clicking the North Location button in the Lights dialog box to open the North Location dialog box, shown in Figure A.3. With this dialog box, you can set true north in any of the following three ways:

▶ Click the graphic to point to the direction.

▶ Use the slide bar at the bottom to move the arrow of the graphic and adjust the value in the input box.

▶ Enter a value directly into the input box.

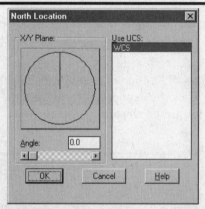

FIGURE A.3: The North Location dialog box

You also have the option to indicate which UCS is used to set the north direction. For example, you may have already set a UCS to point to the true north direction. You only need to select the UCS from the list and leave the angle at 0.

IMPROVING THE SMOOTHNESS OF CIRCLES AND ARCS

You might notice that at times when you're using the Render, Hide, or Shade tool, solid or region arcs appear segmented rather than curved. This appearance may be fine for producing layouts or back-grounds for hand-rendered drawings, but for final plots, you will want arcs and circles to appear as smooth curves. You can adjust the accuracy of arcs in your hidden, rendered, or shaded views through a setting in the Options dialog box.

CONTINUED ➡

The Rendered Object Smoothness setting in the Display tab of the Options dialog box can be modified to improve the smoothness of arcs. Its default setting is .5, but you can increase the value to as high as 10 to smooth faceted curves. In the Facade.dwd model, you can set Rendered Object Smoothness to 1.5 to render the arch in the entry as a smooth arc instead of a series of flat segments. This setting can also be adjusted using the Facetres system variable.

Adding Shadows

There is nothing like adding shadows to a 3D rendering to give the model a sense of realism. AutoCAD offers three methods for casting shadows. The default method is called Volumetric Shadows; this method takes a considerable amount of time to render more complex scenes. When you're using AutoCAD's Ray Trace option (described later in this appendix), shadows will be generated using the Ray Trace method. The third method, called Shadow Map, offers the best speed but requires some adjustment to get good results. Shadow Map offers a soft-edge shadow. Although shadow maps are generally less accurate than the other two methods, the soft-edge option offers a level of realism not available in either of the other methods.

In the following exercise, you will use the Shadow Map method. It requires the most adjustments and yields a faster rendering.

1. Choose View ➢ Render ➢ Lights, or click Lights on the Render toolbar.

2. In the Lights dialog box, make sure SUN is highlighted, and then click Modify. The Modify Distant Light dialog box appears.

TIP

When adding shadows, remember that you must turn on the Shadow option for both the Render dialog box *and* each light that is to cast a shadow.

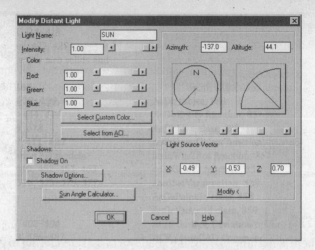

3. Click the Shadow On check box, and then click the Shadow Options button. The Shadow Options dialog box appears.

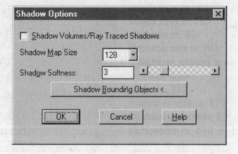

4. In the Shadow Map Size input box, select 512 from the drop-down list. This is the actual number of pixels used to create the shadow map.

5. Click the Shadow Bounding Objects button. The dialog box temporarily disappears to allow you to select objects from the screen. This option lets you select the objects you want to cast shadows.

6. Select the entire Facade building. Don't select any of the building next to it. When you are done, press Enter. The Shadow Options dialog box reappears.

7.   Click OK to close the Shadow Options dialog box, and then click OK in the Modify Distant Light dialog box. It may take several seconds before the dialog box closes.

8.   When you get to the Lights dialog box, click OK to close it.

9.   Click the Render button on the Render toolbar.

10. In the Render dialog box, click the Shadows check box, and then click the Render button. After a minute or two, the model appears rendered with shadows (see Figure A.4).

FIGURE A.4: The Facade model rendered with shadows using the Shadow Map method

Don't panic if the shadows don't appear correct. The Shadow Map method needs some adjustment before it will give the proper shadows. The default settings are appropriate for views of objects from a greater distance than your current view. The following exercise will show you what to do for close-up views:

1.   Open the Render dialog box again and click the More Options button. The Photo Real Render Options dialog box appears.

2. In the Depth Map Shadow Controls group, change the Minimum Bias value from 2 to **.1**.

3. In the same group, change the Maximum Bias value from 4 to **.2**.

4. Click OK to close the Photo Real Render Options dialog box, and then click Render. Your next rendering will show more accurately drawn shadows (see Figure A.5).

FIGURE A.5: The rendered view with the Shadow Bias settings revised

The shadows still look a bit rough. You can further refine the shadows' appearance by increasing the Shadow Map Size to greater than 512. This setting can be found in the Shadow Options dialog box in step 4 of the exercise just before the last one. Figure A.6 shows the same rendering with the Shadow Map Size set to 1024. As you increase the map size, you also increase render time and the amount of RAM required to render the view. If you don't have enough free disk space, you may find that Auto-CAD will refuse to render the model. You will then either have to free up some disk space or decrease the map size.

FIGURE A.6: The rendered view with the Shadow Map Size set to 1024

Notice that the shadow has a soft edge. You can control the softness of the shadow edge using the Shadow Options dialog box you saw in the exercise before the last one. The Shadow Softness input box and slide bar let you sharpen the shadow edge by decreasing the value or soften it by increasing the value. The soft shadow is especially effective for renderings of building interiors or scenes where you are simulating artificial light.

Adding Materials

The rendering methods you've learned so far can be extremely useful in your design efforts. Simply being able to see how the sun affects your design can be of enormous help in selling your ideas or helping get plans through a tough planning board review. But the look of the building is still somewhat cartoonish. You can further enhance the rendering by adding materials to the objects in your model.

Let's suppose you want a granite-like finish to appear on the Facade model. You also want the building next to the Facade model to appear as a glass tower. The first step to adding materials is to acquire the materials from AutoCAD's materials library.

1. Choose View ➤ Render ➤ Materials or click Materials on the Render toolbar.

The Materials dialog box appears.

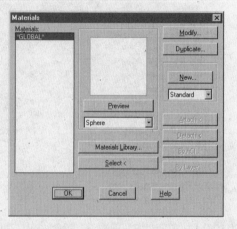

2. Click the Materials Library button in the middle of the dialog box. The Materials Library dialog box appears.

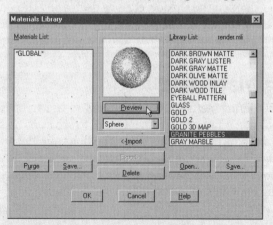

3. In the Library List box, find and select Granite Pebbles so it is highlighted. You will assign this material to the facade.

4. Click the Preview button in the middle of the dialog box. A view of the material appears on a sphere, giving you an idea of what the material looks like.

5. Click the Import button. Notice that Granite Pebbles now appears in the Materials List box to the left. This list box shows the materials you've transferred to your drawing.

6. Locate Glass in the Library List to the right and select it. Click the Preview button again to see what it looks like. Notice that the preview displays a transparent sphere showing some reflected light. You may notice a textured effect caused by the low color resolution of the AutoCAD display.

7. Click the Import button again to make Glass available in the drawing; then click OK to exit the Materials Library dialog box.

Once you've acquired the materials, you must assign them to objects in your drawing.

1. In the Materials dialog box, highlight the Granite Pebbles item in the list to the left, and then click the Attach button in the right half of the dialog box. The dialog box temporarily disappears, allowing you to select the objects you want to appear as Granite Pebbles.

2. Click the Facade model, including the steps, columns, and arched entrance, and then press Enter. After a moment, the Materials dialog box appears again.

3. Click Glass in the Materials list box.

4. This time you'll assign a material based on its layer. Click the By Layer button at right in the dialog box. The Attach by Layer dialog box appears.

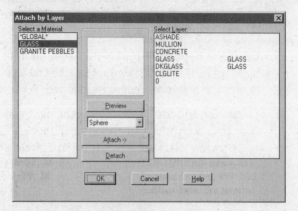

5. Shift+click Glass and Dkglass from the Select Layer list to the right, and then click the Attach button. Notice that the word *Glass* now appears next to the layer names you selected, indicating that the Glass material is associated with those layers.

6. Click OK to exit the Attach by Layer dialog box; then, click OK again to exit the Materials dialog box.

7. Render your model. You may want to take a break at this point, because the rendering will take a few minutes. When AutoCAD is done, your rendering will look like Figure A.7.

FIGURE A.7: The Facade model with the Glass and Granite Pebbles materials added

Adjusting the Materials' Appearance

The Facade model looks more like it has an Army camouflage paint job instead of a granite finish. Also, the glass of the office tower is a bit too transparent. Fortunately, you can make several adjustments to the materials. You will reduce the scale of the Granite Pebbles material so it is in line with the scale of the model. You will also darken the Glass material so it looks more like the tinted glass used in modern office buildings. You'll start with the Granite Pebbles.

1. Choose View ➢ Render ➢ Materials.

2. In the Materials dialog box, select Granite Pebbles from the Materials list, and then click the Modify button. The Modify Granite Material dialog box appears.

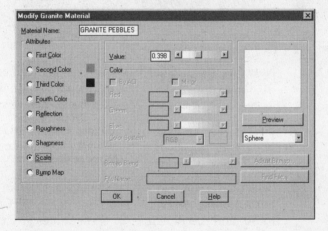

3. Click the Scale radio button in the Attributes button group at left in the dialog box.

4. Change the Value input box near the top of the dialog box from .398 to **.010**. This setting reduces the scale of the material.

5. Click OK to return to the Materials dialog box.

The Modify Granite Material dialog box offers a variety of options that let you control reflectivity, roughness, color, transparency, and, of course, scale. The Help button in the Modify Granite Material dialog box provides a brief description of these options. As you'll see when you continue with the next exercise, not all materials have the same options.

1. Select Glass from the Materials list, and then click the Modify button. The Modify Standard Material dialog box appears.

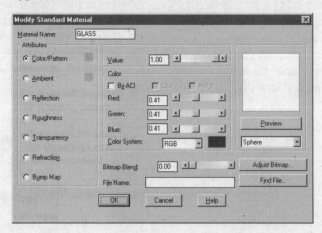

Notice that this dialog box offers a slightly different set of Attributes options than those offered in the Modify Granite Material dialog box you edited in the previous exercise.

2. Select the Transparency radio button in the Attributes button group, and then adjust the Value option downward to **.55**. This value has the effect of darkening the glass.

3. Select the Color/Pattern radio button; then, in the Color button group, adjust the Red value to **69**, the Green value to **60**, and the Blue to **.58**. These values give the glass a bronze tint.

4. Select Cube from the drop-down list just below the Preview button, and then click the Preview button to get a preview of the color settings.

5. Click OK in both the Modify Standard Material and Materials dialog boxes to exit them.

6. Render the view with the new material settings. After a few minutes, your view will look something like Figure A.8.

FIGURE A.8: The Facade model after modifying the material settings

There are four basic types of materials: Standard, Marble, Granite, and Wood. Each type has its own set of characteristics that you can adjust. You can even create new materials based on one of the four primary types of materials. Now let's continue by making another adjustment to the material settings.

The granite surface of the Facade is a bit too strong. You can reduce the graininess of the granite with further editing in the Modify Granite Material dialog box.

1. Click the Materials tool on the Render toolbar, select Granite Pebbles from the Materials list, and choose Modify.

2. In the Modify Granite Material dialog box, click the Sharpness Attribute radio button. Then, set the Value input box to **.20**.

3. Click OK, and then click OK again in the Materials dialog box.

4. Choose View ➤ Render ➤ Render, and then click the Render button of the Render dialog box. Your rendering appears after a few minutes with a softer granite surface (see Figure A.9).

FIGURE A.9: The rendered image with a softer granite surface

ADDING A BACKGROUND SCENE

You could continue by adding materials to the other parts of the model and adjusting them, but try dressing up your view by including a sky. To do so, you need to set up the background.

1. Open the Render dialog box, and then click the button labeled Background. The Background dialog box appears.

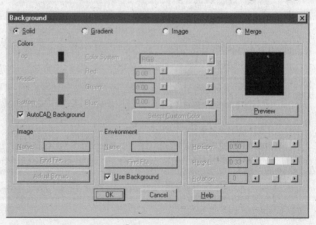

2. In the row of radio buttons across the top, click Image. Notice that several of the options near the bottom of the dialog box are now available.

3. Click the Find File button at lower left in the dialog box. The Background Image dialog box appears. This is a typical Auto-CAD file dialog box.

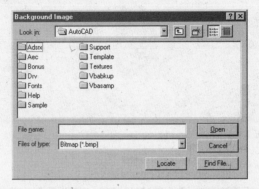

4. Use the Background Image dialog box to locate the Sky.tga file. It can be found in the \Textures\ subdirectory of the \AutoCAD 2002\ directory.

5. Back in the Background dialog box, click Preview to see what the file looks like. Sky.tga is a bitmap image of a blue sky with clouds.

6. Click OK. In the Render dialog box, click Render. The background appears behind the model, as shown in Figure A.10.

This example added a bitmap image for a background, but you can use other methods to generate a background. For example, you might prefer to use a gradient shade or color for the background. Doing so can help give a sense of depth to the image (see Figure A.11). You can, of course, add a single color to the background if you prefer.

To create a gradient background, select the Gradient radio button at the top of the Background dialog box. You can then adjust the color for the top, middle, and bottom third of the background. AutoCAD automatically blends the three colors from top to bottom to create the gradient colors.

FIGURE A.10: The Facade model rendered with a sky bitmap image for a background

FIGURE A.11: The Facade model with a gradient color background

EFFECTS WITH LIGHTING

Up to now, you've used only one light source, called a distant light, to create a sun. Two other light sources are available to help simulate light: point-light sources and spotlights. This section will show you some examples of how you can use these types of light sources, along with some imagination, to perform any number of visual tricks.

Simulating the Interior Lighting of an Office Building

Your current rendering shows a lifeless-looking office building. It's missing a sense of activity. You might notice that when you look at glass office buildings, you can frequently see the ceiling lights from the exterior of the building—provided the glass isn't too dark. In a subtle way, those lights lend a sense of life to a building.

To help improve the image, you'll add some ceiling lights to the office building. You've already supplied the lights in the form of square 3D Faces arrayed just at the ceiling level of each floor, as shown in Figure A.12.

In this section, you will learn how to make the ceiling lights appear illuminated.

1. Assign a reflective material to the squares. Choose View ➤ Render ➤ Materials and then click the Materials Library button.

2. In the Materials Library dialog box, locate and select White Plastic from the Library List at right, and then click Import.

3. Click OK to exit the Materials Library dialog box. In the Materials dialog box, highlight White Plastic in the list to the left and click the By Layer button.

4. In the Attach by Layer dialog box, make sure White Plastic is highlighted in the Select a Material list to the left; then, click the Clglite layer in the Select Layer list to the right.

5. Click the Attach button. The words *White Plastic* appear next to the Clglite layer name in the Select Layer list.

6. Click OK to exit the Attach by Layer dialog box, and then click OK to exit the Materials dialog box.

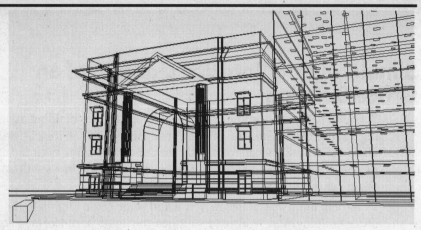

FIGURE A.12: The 3D Face squares representing ceiling light fixtures

You now have a reflective, white material assigned to the ceiling fixtures, but the reflective material alone will not give the effect of illuminated lights. You need a light source that can be reflected by the fixtures, giving the impression of illumination. For this, you'll use a point-light source.

1. Choose View ➢ 3D Viewpoint ➢ SE Isometric to get an Isometric view of the model.

2. Zoom in to the base of the office building so your view is similar to Figure A.13.

3. Choose View ➢ Render ➢ Lights. In the Lights dialog box, select Point Light from the New drop-down list; then, click the New button. The New Point Light dialog box appears.

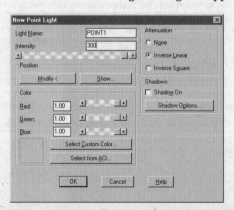

4. Enter **Point1** for the light name and **300** in the Intensity input box.

5. Click the Modify button, and then select a point at the very center of the office building base, as shown in Figure A.13.

6. Click OK to exit the New Point Light dialog box, and then click OK in the Lights dialog box.

7. Choose View ➤ Named Views. In the Named Views dialog box, select 3DFront and click the Restore button.

8. Click OK to exit the Named Views dialog box.

9. Render the view. After a minute, you will have a rendered view similar to Figure A.14.

The new point light in conjunction with the 3D Face light fixture adds a sense of life and depth to the office building. Notice that despite the fact that the light is located inside the box representing the office core, the light manages to strike all the lights of all the floors as if the floors and core were transparent. Because you didn't turn on the Shadow feature for the point-light source, its light passes through all the objects in the model.

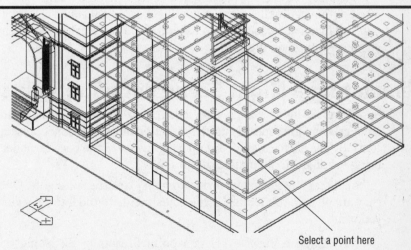

Select a point here

FIGURE A.13: Selecting the point-light source location in the SW Isometric view

FIGURE A.14: The rendered view with ceiling lights

Light is even falling on the granite facade building, illuminating the inside of the arched entrance. This result shows that with careful use of lighting, you can bring out some of the detail in the Facade model that might otherwise get lost with the distant light source.

Of course, you can use point-light sources in a more traditional way, representing lightbulbs or other nondirectional light sources. But by playing with light source location and shadow, you can create effects to help enhance your rendering.

Simulating a Night Scene with Spotlights

Spotlights are lights that are directed. They are frequently used to provide emphasis and are generally used for interior views or product presentations. In this exercise, you'll set up a night view of the Facade model using spotlights to illuminate the facade.

You'll start by setting up a view to help place the spotlights. Once they are placed, you'll make some adjustments to them to get a view you want.

1. Choose View ➢ 3D Viewpoint Presets ➢ SE Isometric; then, zoom in to the facade so your view looks similar to Figure A.15.

2. Choose View ➤ Render ➤ Lights. In the Lights dialog box, select Spotlight from the New drop-down list.

3. Click New. In the New Spotlight dialog box, enter **Spot-L** to designate a spotlight you will place on the left side of the facade.

4. Enter **400** in the Intensity input box. Click the Modify button.

5. At the `Enter Target Location:` prompt, use the Nearest Osnap and select the point on the window, as indicated in Figure A.15.

6. At the `Enter Light Location:` prompt, select the point indicated in Figure A.15. Once you've selected the light location, you return to the New Spotlight dialog box. You can, in the future, adjust the light location if you choose.

7. Click OK. In the Lights dialog box, click New again to create another spotlight.

8. This time, enter **Spot-R** for the name. Enter **400** for the intensity as before.

9. Click the Modify button and select the target and light locations indicated in Figure A.16.

10. Click OK to exit the New Spotlight dialog box, and then click OK again in the Lights dialog box. You now have two spotlights on your building.

11. Choose View ➤ Named Views and restore the 3DFront view.

12. Render the model (you should know how this is done by now). Your view will look similar to Figure A.17.

The rendered view has a number of problems. First, the sunlight source needs to be turned off. Second, the spotlights are too harsh. You can also see that the spotlights don't illuminate the center of the building, so you'll need to add some lighting at the entrance. These problems will be solved in the next section.

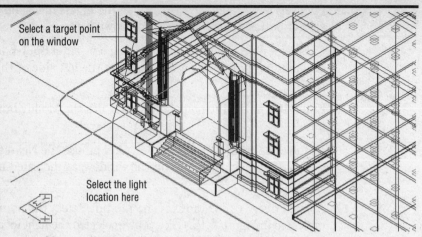

FIGURE A.15: Selecting the points for the first spotlight

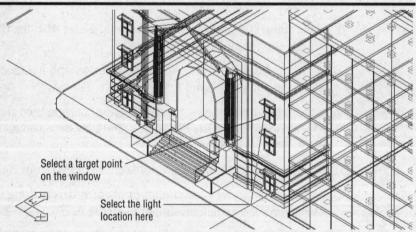

FIGURE A.16: Selecting the points for the second spotlight

FIGURE A.17: The rendered view of the model with the spotlights

Controlling Lights with Scenes

The first problem is how to turn off the sun. You can set the sunlight intensity value to 0 using the Modify Distant Light dialog box. Another way is to set up a scene. AutoCAD lets you combine different lights and views into named scenes. These scenes can then be quickly selected at render time so you don't have to adjust lighting or views every time you want a specific setup. Here's how it works.

1. Choose View ➤ Render ➤ Scenes, or click the Scenes tool on the Render toolbar.

The Scenes dialog box appears.

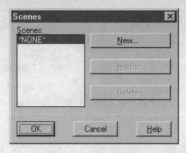

2. Click New. The New Scene dialog box appears.

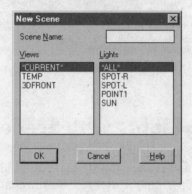

3. Enter **NIGHT** in the Scene Name input box.

4. Select 3DFront from the Views list and then Shift+click Spot-L, Spot-R, and Point1 in the Lights list.

5. Click OK. Notice that now you have Night listed in the Scenes list in the Scenes dialog box.

6. Click New again, and then type **DAY**.

7. Select 3DFront from the Views list, and Sun and Point1 from the Lights list. Click OK. You now have two scenes set up.

8. Click OK, and then open the Render dialog box. Notice that Day and Night are listed in the Scene to Render list box at upper left in the Render dialog box.

9. Select Night, and then click the Render button. Your view will look like Figure A.18.

FIGURE A.18: Rendering the night scene

Notice that without the sunlight source, your view is considerably darker. You will now add a few more light sources and adjust some existing ones.

1. Choose View ➤ 3D Viewpoint Presets ➤ SE Isometric, and then zoom in to the office building so your view looks similar to Figure A.19.

2. Open the Lights dialog box, select Point Light from the New drop-down list, and click New.

3. Enter the name **Point2**, and give this new point light an intensity value of **500**.

4. Click the Modify button and place the Point2 light in the center of the office building in the same location as Point1.

5. Click OK; then, create another point-light source and enter the name **Point3**. Enter an intensity of **150**.

6. Click the Modify button, adjust your view so it looks similar to Figure A.20, and then place the light in the facade entrance, as shown in Figure A.20. Use the .X, .Y, and .Z point filters to select the location of the light.

7. Click OK. In the Lights dialog box, select Spot-L from the list and click Modify.

8. In the Modify Spotlight dialog box, change the Falloff value at upper right to **80**.

9. Click OK, and then repeat steps 7 and 8 for the Spot-R spotlight.

10. Click OK in the Modify Spotlight dialog box.

11. In the Lights dialog box, increase the ambient light intensity to **50**, and then click OK.

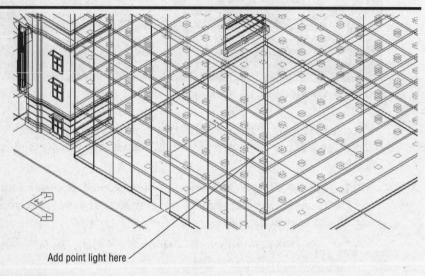

Add point light here

FIGURE A.19: Adding another point-light source to the office building

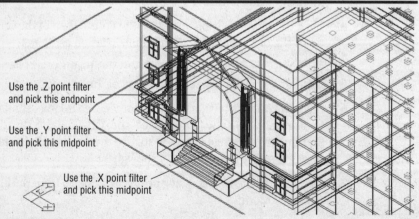

Use the .Z point filter and pick this endpoint

Use the .Y point filter and pick this midpoint

Use the .X point filter and pick this midpoint

FIGURE A.20: Adding a point-light source for the entrance to the facade

You've got the new lights installed and the spotlights adjusted. Before you render your scene, you need to include the new lights in the scene you set up for the night rendering.

1. Choose View ➤ Render ➤ Scene.

2. Highlight Night in the Scenes list, and then click the Modify button.

3. Shift+click Point2 and Point3 in the Lights list, and then Alt+click Point1 to deselect it.

4. Click OK in both the Modify Scene and Scenes dialog boxes.

5. Choose Render and make sure Night is selected in the Scene to Render list.

6. Click the Render button. Your view will look similar to Figure A.21.

The new rendering is brighter. You can also see the effects of an increased falloff for the spotlights. They don't have the sharp edge they had in the first night rendering, and the light is spread in a wider radius, illuminating more of the lower portion of the facade.

You also see another by-product of using the Scenes tool. You didn't have to return to the 3DFront view to render the model. Because the 3DFront view is included in the scene information, AutoCAD automatically rendered the model from that view when the Night scene was selected. If you were to issue the Regen command now, you would see that AutoCAD still maintains the SE Isometric view.

FIGURE A.21: The night rendering with added lights and an increased falloff area for the spotlights

ADDING REFLECTIONS AND DETAIL WITH RAY TRACING

You've been gradually building up the detail and realism in your renderings by adding light and materials. In this section, you'll learn how using a different rendering method can further enhance your 3D models. Up until now, you've been using the standard AutoCAD rendering method. Ray Tracing can add interest to a rendering, especially where reflective surfaces are prominent in a model. In this section, you'll use the Ray Tracing method to render your model after making a few adjustments to the glass material.

WHAT IS RAY TRACING?

To make a long, complicated story short, Ray Tracing simulates the way light works. It does so in somewhat of a reverse way. Ray Tracing analyzes the light path to each pixel of your display, tracing the light or "ray" from the pixel to the light origin as it bounces off objects in your model. Ray Tracing takes into account the reflectivity and, in the case of glass, the refraction of light as it is affected by objects in the model. Because more objects in a model offer more surfaces to reflect light, Ray Tracing becomes more time-consuming as the number of objects increases. Also, because each pixel is analyzed, a greater image size increases the render time geometrically. For example, by doubling the width and height of the view size, you are essentially increasing the number of pixels by four times.

AutoCAD offers Ray Tracing as an option for rendering both shadows and the entire scene. The Ray Trace options offer greater accuracy in exchange for slow rendering time. If you choose to select ray-traced shadows, for example, you can expect at least a fourfold increase in rendering time. Rendering an entire scene can increase rendering time by an order of magnitude.

Needless to say, if you are in a time crunch, you will want to save Ray Tracing just for the essential final renderings. Use the Photo Real or other rendering type options in the Render dialog box for study rendering or for situations that don't require the accuracy of Ray Tracing.

Assigning a Mirror Attribute to Glass

Glass is a complex material to model in computer renderings. The Auto-CAD standard rendering method simply gives glass a transparency with some highlight reflection. But glass has both refractive and reflective attributes that make it difficult to model. Because Ray Tracing models the way light works, it is especially well suited to rendering views that contain large areas of glass.

To demonstrate what Ray Tracing can do, you'll use it to render the Facade model, which happens to contain an office building with a typical glass exterior. You'll start by making an adjustment to the Glass material to make it appear more reflective.

1. Choose View ➢ Render ➢ Materials. In the Materials dialog box, highlight Glass in the list box and click the Modify button.

2. Click the Reflection radio button in the Attributes button group.

3. Click the Mirror check box in the Color button group, and then click OK to close the Modify Standard Material dialog box.

4. Click OK again in the Materials dialog box, and then open the Render dialog box.

5. Choose Photo Raytrace from the Rendering Type list box at the top of the dialog box.

6. Click the More Options button. The Photo Raytrace Render Options dialog box appears.

7. Set the Minimum Bias setting to **.1** and the Maximum Bias setting to **.2**. Whenever you change the rendering type, you must reset these settings. AutoCAD does not automatically transfer these settings to different rendering types.

8. Click OK, and then select Day from the Scene to Render list. Click the Background button.

9. In the Background dialog box, make sure the Use Background check box is checked in the Environment button group; then, click the OK button. This setting tells AutoCAD to reflect the background image in the glass.

10. Click the Render button. Your view will look similar to Figure A.22.

FIGURE A.22: The Facade model rendered with the Ray Tracing method

The sky bitmap used as a background is faintly reflected in the glass of the office building. The office building has also become brighter from the reflection. Also notice the secondary reflection of the interior ceiling on the west interior wall of the office.

The brightness of the office building is a bit overwhelming, so you will want to adjust the Glass material to tone it down.

1. Choose View ➤ Render ➤ Materials. With the Glass material highlighted, select Modify.

2. In the Modify Standard Material dialog box, make sure the Color/Pattern radio button is selected. Set the Value setting above the Color button group to **.20** to help darken the office building.

3. Click OK to close the Modify Standard Material dialog box, and then click OK in the Materials dialog box.

4. Render the scene again. Your view will look something like Figure A.23.

FIGURE A.23: The rendering with a lower Color/Pattern setting for the Glass material

You can further reduce the brightness of the office building by lowering the intensity value of the point-light source you added earlier.

Getting a Sharp, Accurate Shadow with Ray Tracing

In the beginning of this appendix, you learned how to use the Shadow Map method for casting shadows. Shadow maps allow a soft-edge shadow in exchange for accuracy. For exterior views, you may prefer a sharper shadow. The Facade example loses some detail using the Shadow Map method; in particular, the grooves in the base of the building disappear. By switching to the Ray Tracing method for casting shadows, you can recover some of this detail.

1. Choose View ➤ Render ➤ Lights. Select Sun from the Lights list and click Modify.

2. In the Modify Distant Light dialog box, click the Shadow Options button.

3. In the Shadow Options dialog box, click the Shadow Volumes/Ray Traced Shadows check box to place a check mark there.

4. Click OK in all the dialog boxes to exit them and return to the AutoCAD view.

5. Render the view using the Photo Ray Trace rendering type. Your view will look like Figure A.24.

FIGURE A.24: The Facade model using the Shadow Volumes/Ray Traced Shadows option

Notice that you can now see the rusticated base clearly. The shadows also appear sharper, especially around the surface detail of the Facade model.

CREATING AND ADJUSTING TEXTURE MAPS

You've already seen how you can assign a material to an object by adding the Granite Pebbles and Glass materials to the buildings in the Facade.dwg file. Many of these materials use bitmap image files to simulate textures. You can create your own surface textures or use bitmaps in other ways to help enhance your rendering. For example, you can include a photograph of buildings that may exist within the scene you are rendering.

Figure A.25 shows a bitmap image that was scanned into the computer and edited using a popular paint program. Now imagine that this building is across the street from the Facade model, and you want to include it in the scene to show its relationship to your building.

FIGURE A.25: A photographic image of a building that was scanned into a computer and saved as a bitmap file

The following exercise will show you how it's done:

1. Click Redraw on the Standard toolbar, and then adjust your view so it looks like the top image of Figure A.26.

2. Draw a line 133 feet long, as shown in the top image of Figure A.26.

3. Change the thickness of the line to 80 using the Properties tool.

4. Choose View ➣ Render ➣ Materials. In the Materials dialog box, click New. Notice that the New Standard Material dialog box is the same as the dialog box for the Glass material. The settings are not the same, however.

5. Enter **Build1** for the material name.

6. Make sure the Color/Pattern radio button is selected, and then click the Find File button in the lower-right corner of the dialog box.

7. Click the List Files of Type drop-down list. Notice that you have several file types from which to choose.

8. Choose GIF from the list, and then locate the Market2.gif file.

9. Choose Open to exit this dialog box. Then, click OK in the New Standard Material dialog box.

10. In the Materials dialog box, make sure Build1 is selected in the Materials list, and then click the Attach button.

11. Select the line you added in step 2 and press Enter.

12. Click OK to exit the Materials dialog box, and then render the scene. Your view will look like the bottom image of Figure A.26.

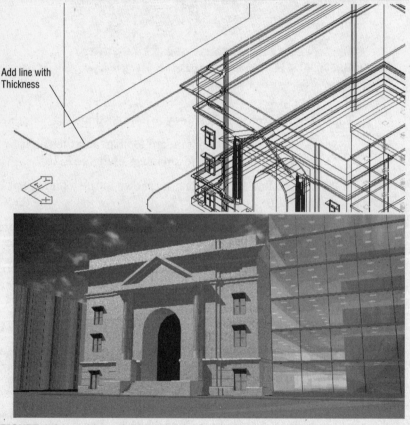

Add line with Thickness

FIGURE A.26: Adding a bitmap image of a building to your rendering

The bitmap image does not appear properly in the rendered view. Instead, it looks like a vertical streak of colors. When you see this streaking, you know your bitmap image or material is not properly aligned with the object to which it is attached. The following exercise introduces you to the tools you need to properly align a bitmap image to an object:

1. Redraw the screen. Then, choose View ➤ Render ➤ Mapping, or click Mapping on the Render toolbar.

2. At the Select objects: prompt, select the extruded line you created in the last exercise. The Mapping dialog box appears.

3. Click the Adjust Coordinates button. The Adjust Planar Coordinates dialog box appears.

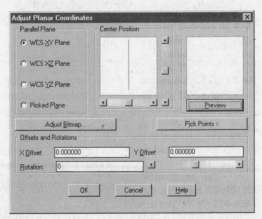

Notice the rectangle in the area labeled Center Position. It shows the relationship of the bitmap image to the object to which it has been assigned. All you can see is a vertical line.

4. Click the WCS YZ Plane radio button. The plane defined by the y- and z-axes is parallel to the surface on which you want the bitmap to appear.

5. Click the Preview button to see how the bitmap will appear on the vertical surface. You need to adjust the positioning of the bitmap.

6. To increase the size of the bitmap in relation to the surface so the image of the building completely covers the surface, you need one other dialog box. Click the Adjust Bitmap button. The Adjust Object Bitmap Placement dialog box appears (see the top image of Figure A.27).

7. Enter **.95** in the Scale input box to the left of the U, and then enter **.76** in the Scale input box to the left of the V. The U is the horizontal direction scale and the V is the vertical direction scale.

8. Click the Preview button to view the effect of the scaling. Notice that the image is larger but still not centered vertically.

9. Use the vertical Offset sliders to move the outer rectangle in the graphic upward so it looks like the bottom image of Figure A.27, and then click the Preview button again. Now the image fits within the rectangle.

10. Click OK in each of the dialog boxes to close them, and then render the model. Your view will look like Figure A.28.

Notice that the image of the building across the street now appears correctly and no longer looks like vertical streaks. Neither are there any odd blank spaces on the building. As you have seen in the previous exercise, the Adjust Object Bitmap Placement dialog box allows you to stretch the image vertically or horizontally in case the image is distorted and needs to be fitted to an accurately drawn object.

Another option is to use a paint program to refine the bitmap image before it is used in AutoCAD. AutoCAD attempts to place the bitmap accurately on a surface, so if the bitmap is fairly clean and doesn't have any extra blank space around the edges, you can usually place it on an object without having to make any adjustments other than its orientation.

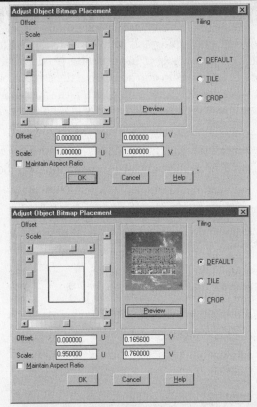

FIGURE A.27: The Adjust Object Bitmap Placement dialog box

FIGURE A.28: The rendered view with the bitmap image adjusted

Adding Landscaping and People

There's nothing like adding landscaping and people to a rendering to add a sense of life and scale. Computer images, in particular, need landscape props because they tend to appear cold and somewhat lifeless. AutoCAD offers a set of pre-built landscape objects to help soften the appearance of your rendering. Let's see how you can add a few trees and people to the Facade model.

1. Choose View ➤ Redraw, and then choose View ➤ Render ➤ Landscape New. You can also click the Landscape New tool on the Render toolbar.

The Landscape New dialog box appears.

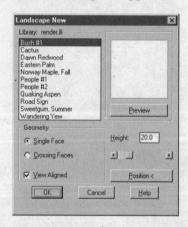

2. Click Quaking Aspen in the Library list, and then click Preview to view the item.

3. Use the slider below the Preview button to change the Height value from 20 to 100, the highest setting.

4. Click the Position button, and then click the point indicated in the top image of Figure A.29 to place the tree in front of the buildings. You may have to adjust your view.

5. Click the View Aligned check box to deselect this option. This option is explained later in this section.

6. Click OK. The tree appears as a rectangle with a text label telling you what it is, as shown in the bottom image of Figure A.29.

7. Copy the tree to the positions indicated in the bottom image of Figure A.29.

8. Render the view. You will see a view similar to Figure A.30.

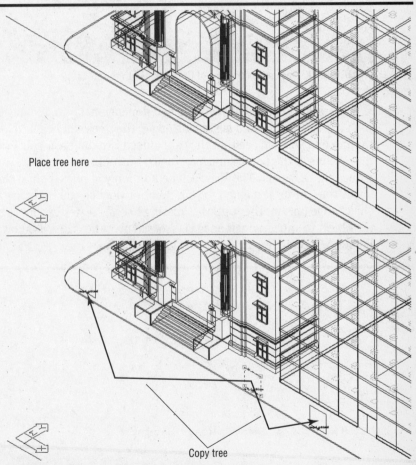

FIGURE A.29: Placing the trees in the Facade model

FIGURE A.30: The rendered view of the model with the trees

The trees you added are actually two-dimensional bitmap images. If you view the model from a glancing angle, the trees will begin to look thinner and you will see that they are indeed two-dimensional. Two of the options in the Landscape New dialog box offer some options to reduce the 2D effect. The View Aligned option you turned off in step 5 forces the tree to be aligned to your point of view, so you never see the object edge-on. Another option, Crossing Faces, creates two images of the object to appear. Each image is crossed over the other, as shown in Figure A.31, creating an almost 3D look.

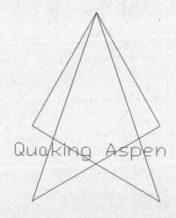

FIGURE A.31: The Crossing Faces option used with a landscape object

NEW OBJECT TYPES IN AUTOCAD

If you were to use the List tool to find out what the landscape objects were, you would discover that they are called Plant or People. Does AutoCAD 2000 have some new object types you don't know about? The answer is maybe.

AutoCAD 2000 allows third-party developers to add new object types that aren't native to the program. This is a fairly revolutionary idea. AutoCAD uses this capability by adding Plant and People objects. However, there is a problem with adding new object types: You need the third-party application to view and edit the objects you create. When the application is not present, the new objects become what AutoDesk calls *proxies*. Proxies allow themselves to be edited with a limited set of editing tools. The level of "editability" of proxies is determined by the application that created them. Where AutoCAD's rendering tools are concerned, the application is always present, so you are always able to edit the trees and people.

The ability to add new object types to an AutoCAD drawing has some far-reaching implications. The possibilities for third-party developers are enormous, and you, the end user, will benefit in many ways. The Landscape tool in AutoCAD is an example of what can be done.

A few things are wrong with this rendering. The trees are too small, and they appear to be shaded on the wrong side. The shadows on the trees don't reflect the location of the Distant Light setting in the model. The street is also unusually empty for a daytime scene. The trees are easily fixed using standard AutoCAD editing tools. You can also add some people using the Landscape New tool in the Render toolbar.

1. Redraw the screen, and then click one of the trees to expose its grips.

2. Click the grip at the base of the tree, right-click the mouse, and select Rotate from the pop-up menu.

3. Type **180** and press Enter to rotate the tree 180 degrees.

4. Click the grip again, right-click the mouse, and this time select Scale.

5. Type **2.4** and press Enter to increase the size of the tree by 2.4 times.

6. Repeat steps 1 through 5 for each of the other trees.

7. Open the Landscape New dialog box again and select People #1 from the list.

8. Enter a Height value of **66**, and then use the Position button to place the people at the entrance of the Facade building (see Figure A.32). The people will appear as triangles in the Wireframe view. (Make sure you use the Nearest Osnap override to place the people.)

9. Click OK. Repeat steps 7 and 8 to place People #2 in front of the office building between the trees (see Figure A.32).

10. Render the view. Your view will look similar to Figure A.33.

The shadows of the trees now match the sun's location, and they are a size better suited to the model. However, notice that the people are not lit very well, because when you placed them, you did not turn off the View Align option. They are facing your view tilted slightly away from the sun, which has the effect of darkening their image.

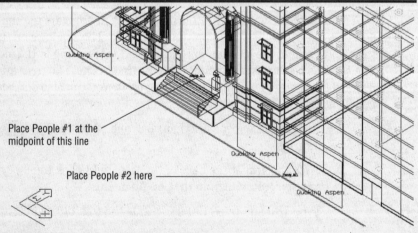

FIGURE A.32: Placing people in the scene

FIGURE A.33: The view after rendering, with the trees adjusted and people added

You can use View ➤ Render Landscape Edit to change the settings for landscape objects. You will be prompted to select an object. Once you do, the Landscape Edit dialog box appears, which is identical to the Landscape New dialog box. From there, you can make changes to the settings for the selected landscape object.

OTHER RENDERING OUTPUT OPTIONS

Throughout this appendix, you have been rendering to the AutoCAD drawing area. You can also render to a file, which enables you to recall the image at any time in any application, or render to the Render window. From there, you have a number of options in dealing with the rendered image.

Rendering to the Render Window

The Render window lets you control the resolution and color depth of your image. It also lets you save the images that you render in the Windows .bmp format. Another advantage of the Render window is that you can render several views and then compare them before you decide which ones to save.

1. Open the Render dialog box, and then select Render Window from the Destination drop-down list near the bottom of the dialog box.

2. Click Render. After a moment the Render window appears. It then takes a minute or two before the image finishes rendering and appears in the window.

Notice that the image is within its own window. If you render another view, that view will also appear in its own window, leaving the previous renderings undisturbed. You can use File ➣ Save in the Render window to save the file as a .bmp file for later editing or printing, or you can print directly from the Render window. You can also use the Render window to cut and paste the image to another application or to view other files in the .bmp format.

To set the size of renderings, you use the File ➣ Option tool in the Render window. This option opens the Windows Render Options dialog box (see Figure A.34). Here, you can choose from two standard sizes or enter a custom size for your rendering. You can also choose between 8-bit (256 colors) and 24-bit (16 million colors) color depth. Changes to these settings don't take effect until you render another view.

FIGURE A.34: The Windows Render Options dialog box

Rendering Directly to a File

Rendering to the Render window allows you to view and compare your views before you save them. However, you can only save your views in the .bmp format. If you plan to further edit the image in an image-processing program, this limitation may not be a problem. But if you want to use your image file with a program that requires a specific file format, you may want to render directly to a file. Here's how it's done.

1. Open the Render dialog box, and then select File in the Destination button group in the lower middle of the dialog box.

2. Choose More Options at the bottom of the Destination button group. The File Output Configuration dialog box appears.

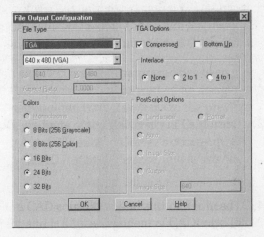

3. Click the File Type drop-down list to see the options. You can save your image in .gif, .tga, .tif, .pcx, or even PostScript format. Several other formats are also available. Notice the other options available in the dialog box, such as color depth, resolution, and compression. Not all these options are available for all the file types. For example, .gif is limited to 256 colors, so the other color options will not apply to .gif files.

4. Click OK to return to the Render dialog box, and then click the Render button. The Rendering File dialog box appears, prompting you for a filename for your image.

5. Enter **Facade1**. AutoCAD adds the filename extension for you.

6. Click OK, and AutoCAD proceeds to render to the file.

As AutoCAD renders to the file, it tells you in the command line how much of the image has been rendered.

IMPROVING YOUR IMAGE AND EDITING

Sometimes you will be rushing to get a rendering done and won't want to wait for each trial rendering to become visible. AutoCAD offers several tools that can save you time by limiting the resolution or area being rendered. Suppose you just want to render the area where you've added a tree to make sure it is in the right location. The following exercise will show you how this is done:

1. Choose View ➤ Named Views, and then restore the 3DFront view.

2. Open the Render dialog box and set the Destination option to Viewport.

3. Click the Crop Window check box to activate this option, and then click the Render button.

4. The prompt `Pick Crop Window to Render:` appears. Select the area shown in Figure A.35, indicated by the rubber-banding square. Once you select the window, AutoCAD renders only the area you selected.

The Crop Window option is a working tool and is not available when File or Render Window is selected as a destination.

You can also select specific objects to be included in the rendering by checking the Query for Selections check box in the Render dialog box. This option asks you to select a set of objects before it proceeds to render. You can render to all three destination options with Query for Selections turned on.

Crop window —————————————————

FIGURE A.35: Selecting the crop window

If you want to get a quick rendering with a reduced resolution to check composition, you can use the Sub Sampling drop-down list. Try the following exercise to see how it works:

1. Open the Render dialog box, and then open the Sub Sampling drop-down list.

2. Choose 3:1 from the list, make sure the Crop Window option is unchecked, and then click the Render button. Your view will render faster, but will look a bit crude (see Figure A.36).

FIGURE A.36: A rendered view with the Sub Sampling option set to 3:1

The different ratios in the Sub Sampling option tell you how many pixels are being combined to reduce the resolution of the image. For example, 3:1 combines three pixels into one to reduce the resolution to a third of the original.

SMOOTHING OUT THE ROUGH EDGES

The Sub Sampling option increases the jagged appearance of your rendering because of the reduced resolution. For your final rendering, you can improve the smoothness of edges and thereby increase the apparent resolution by using the Anti-Aliasing option in the Render dialog box. This option performs a kind of computer trick that reduces the jagged appearance of object edges. Anti-Aliasing blends the color of two adjacent contrasting colors, giving the effect of smoothing out the "stairstep" appearance of a computer-generated image. The improvement to your rendering can be striking. Try the following exercise to see firsthand what Anti-Aliasing can do:

1. Open the Render dialog box, and then click the More Options button.

2. In the Raytrace Rendering Options dialog box, click the Medium radio button in the Anti-Aliasing button group, and then click OK.

3. Select 1:1 from the Sub Sampling drop-down list, and then click the Render button. The rendering takes several minutes, so you may want to take a break at this point. When the rendering is done, it will look similar to Figure A.37.

Notice that the edges of the buildings are much smoother. You can also see that the vertical mullions of the office building are more clearly defined. One negative point is that the texture effect of the Facade model has been reduced. You may have to increase the scale value for the Granite Pebbles material setting to bring the texture back.

FIGURE A.37: A rendering with the Anti-Aliasing setting set to Medium

As you can see from this exercise, you trade rendering speed for a cleaner image. You will want to save the higher Anti-Aliasing settings for your final output.

IF YOU WANT TO EXPERIMENT...

In this appendix, you've participated in a guided tour of AutoCAD's rendering tools and have seen the main features of this product. Because of space considerations, this appendix didn't go into the finer details of many features, but you now have the basic knowledge from which to build your rendering skills. Without too much effort, you can adapt much of what you've learned here to your own projects. If you need more detailed information, use the Help button found in all the Render dialog boxes.

Computer rendering of 3D models is a craft that takes some time to master. Experiment with these rendering tools to see firsthand the types of results you can expect. You might want to try different types of views like an Isometric or Elevation view, the latter of which is shown in Figure A.38. With a bit more detail added, this rendered elevation could fit nicely into a set of renderings for a presentation.

FIGURE A.38: An Elevation view of the Facade model

INDEX

Note to the Reader: Throughout this index **boldfaced** page numbers indicate primary discussions of a topic. *Italicized* page numbers indicate illustrations.

Symbols

& (ampersands), 698
* (asterisks)
  in Diesel, 641
  as wildcard characters, 746
@ (at signs), 48, 50
\ (backslashes)
  in menus, 630–631
  for spaces, 321
[] <> (brackets)
  for default options, 56
  for line types, 647–648
  for menu items, 633–635
^ (carets), 629–630
: (colons), 753
, (commas)
  in Cartesian coordinates, 50
  for constants, 742
  in Dim statements, 735
  in hatch patterns, 651
  in line type patterns, 644–645
  for parameters, 782
$ (dollar signs), 636–638
" (double quotes), 604
= (equal signs)
  in comparison operators, 755
  in Diesel, 641
  in expressions, 732
! (exclamation points)
  in Diesel, 641
  for member references, 761
> (greater-than symbols)
  in comparison operators, 753, 755
  in Diesel, 641
  in pull-down menus, 631
  for text, 213–214
< (less-than symbols)
  for angles, 48
  in comparison operators, 753, 755
  in Diesel, 641

in pull-down menus, 631
  for text, 213–214
– (minus signs)
  in Diesel, 641
  in distance formats, 119
  in line type patterns, 644–645
  in pull-down menus, 631–632
(number signs), 746
() (parentheses)
  for arrays, 738
  in Diesel, 636–637
  for functions, 604
  for methods, 774
. (periods), 50, 853
+ (plus signs)
  in Diesel, 636, 641
  in menus, 631
? (question marks)
  for linked files, 532
  as wildcard characters, 746
; (semicolons), 630
' (single quotes)
  in distance formats, 119
  in VBA, 688
/ (slashes)
  in Diesel, 636, 641
  for options, 56
~ (tildes), 632
_ (underscores)
  for commands, 31
  in line type patterns, 644–645
  in names, 775

Numbers

0 layer, 252
2D drawings and objects, converting
  from 3D models, **485**
  from solids, **488–489**
<2points> option, 410

3 Point UCS tool, 390, *390*
3D Adjust Distance tool, 418, *418*
3D Continuous Orbit tool, 427, *427*
3D drawings and models. *See also* solids and
   solid modeling
   2D drawings from, **485**
   aligning objects in, **408–409**, *409*
   hidden lines in, 443–444, *444*
   importing, **477–479**, *478*
   perspective views for, **411–427**
   rendering. *See* rendering 3D models
   rotating objects in, **410**, 452–453, *453*
   viewports for, **371–376**, *373–375*, *377*
3D Faces, 378–379
3D forms
   extruded, **401–405**, *402–404*
   laying out, **385–388**, *386–387*
3D Meshes
   editing, **405–408**, *406*
   settings for, **397–398**, *397*
3D Orbit command, 411
3D Orbit tool, 411–412, *412*, 417
3D Orbit toolbar, 412, *412*
3D Pan tool, 416, *416*
3D polylines, **388**, *389*
3D Rotate tool, 408
3D Swivel tool, 422, *423*
3DMesh command, 398
3DPoly command, 388
3points slice option, 456
19wipe.dwg file, 578

A

a command, 139
About option, 83
ac prefix, 743
Acad.lin file, 642, 644, 646, 648
Acad.mnc file, 624
Acad.mnr file, 625
Acad.mns file, 614, 625
Acad.mnu file, 624
Acad.pat file, 649
Acad.pgp file, 588–590
AcadDocument object, 684, *684*, 825
accelerator keys, **634–635**
Access program, extracting data for, 333
accessing databases, **333–345**, **801–802**
   with ActiveX Automation. *See* ActiveX
      Automation

with AutoLISP. *See* AutoLISP language
with DXF. *See* DXF (Drawing Interchange
   Format) files
miscellaneous methods for, **839–841**
with ObjectARX. *See* ObjectARX environment; ObjectDBX environment
AcDb tables, 788
AcDbEntity function, 837
AcDbLine class, 829
acdbOpenObject function, 833–834
acdbWcs2Ecs function, 862
acedGetVar function, 839
acedSetVar function, 839
AcGePoint3d class, 858
AcGeVector3d class, 859
ACIS Surface Deviation option, 540
ACR (AutoCAD Command Reference), 81
Active Assistance option, 82
active styles, 160
ActiveDocument property, 763
ActiveX Automation, **823–824**
   angles in, 854
   binary data in, 865
   Booleans in, 851
   character sets in, 856
   collections, objects, and interfaces in,
      825–826
   colors in, 850
   custom objects in, **829–830**
   for database access, **824–825**
   dictionaries in, **828–829**
   entities in
      access to, **826–828**
      creating, **828**
   enumerations in, 849
   handles in, 857
   integers in, 845–848
   non-objects in, **830**
   pointers in, 858
   points in, 858
   strings in, 855
Add File To Startup Suite dialog box, 701, *702*
add function, 835
Add Layers command, 293
Add prefix, 762
Add Zone option, 508
AddArc method, 828
AddCircle method, 828
AddCustomObject method, 830
addition in Diesel, 636

AddLine method, 828
AddObject method, 829
AddText method, 694, 697, *697*
AddXRecord method, 829
Adjust Back Clipping tool, 426, *426*
Adjust Clipping Planes dialog box, 423–426, *424–426*
Adjust Front Clipping tool, 424, *424*
Adjust Object Bitmap Placement dialog box, 908, *909*
Adjust Planar Coordinates dialog box, 907–908, *907*
ads_binary type, 865
Advanced tab, **184–186**, *184*
AEC (Architecture/Engineering/Construction) tools, 540
AI command, 408
aliases, editing, **588–590**, *588–589*
Align tool, 408
Align Lefts tool, 720
Aligned Dimension tool, 236
Aligned with Dimension Line option, 201
aligning
    code lines, 723–724
    dimensions, 236–237, *237*
    objects, **408–409**, *409*
All options for selecting objects, 66
Alphabetic tab, 671, *671*
alt.cad.autocad newsgroup, 607
alternate dimensions, **232–233**
alternate units, **204–206**, *205*
Alternate Units tab, 204–206, *205*, 232
Alternate View button, 330
Always Ask Before Opening Projects With Macros option, 700
Always Left Justify option, 242
America Online service, 608
ampersands (&), 698
Angle Constraints leader option, 243
angles
    for arcs, 56, *57*, 139, 146
    in databases, **854**
    for dimension lines, 237, *238*, 244–245, *245*
    for dimension text, 215, 221–222
    dimensions for, **237–239**, *238*
    for extrusions, 404
    for hatch patterns, 175, 651, *652*
    for line types, 648
    in moving objects, 65
    for revolving polylines, 452–453

for rotating
    blocks, 258, 272–273
    doors, 137
    specifying, **48–49**, *49*
    for sun, 271, **870–874**, *871–874*
    for text, 162–163
Angular Dimension tool, 237
animation, **427**
Annotation tab, **242**
Anti-Aliasing option, 920–921
apostrophes (')
    in distance formats, 119
    in VBA, 688
appearance of windows, 271
Appearance tab, 670
Application object, **762**
applications, 658, **782–783**. *See also* VBA (Visual Basic for Applications)
    running, **678–679**, *679*
    saving, **679–680**, *679–680*
    starting from macros, **703–704**
Apply to All Active Viewports option, 370
Apply to Layout Dimensions Only option, 486
Ar command, 308
arbitrary axis algorithm, **862–864**
Arc tool, 38–39, 56
Arc Rotate tool, 547
ArcAlignedText tool, 574
ArcAlignedText Workshop dialog box, 574, *574*
arcballs, **413–415**, *413–415*
arcd macro, 605
Architectural units, 10, 120
Architecture/Engineering/Construction (AEC) tools, 540
arcs
    dimensions for, **237–239**
    macro for, 605
    moving, 68–69
    options for, 55–56, *57*, 58–59, **139**
    properties for, **84–85**, *85*
    smoothness of, **874–875**
    start points for, 139, 146
    for swinging doors, 133, *133*
    with UCS, 379
Area dialog box, 43, *43*
argument lists, 604
arguments, **782**
    in Diesel, 636
    for functions, 604
Array dialog box, 308, *308*

Array tool, 39, *39*, 308
arrays (objects), 308
arrays (programming), **738-740**
  accessing, **739-740**
  creating, **738-739**
  declaring, 689-690, 738-739
Arrowhead leader option, 243
arrows
  notes with, **240-244**, *243-244*
  options for, **242-243**, *243*
  styles for, **201-204**, *202-203*
arrows keys in accelerator keys, 635
ASCII code
  for integers, 845
  in strings, 735
ASCII files, DXF, **806-808**
Ask Me tab, **80-81**, *81*
assoc function, 815
Associate New Dimensions with Objects
  option, 227
association lists, 814-815, 821
associative dimensioning, 194, **227-232**, *227-230*
Associative hatch patterns, **179-180**, **189**
asterisks (*)
  in Diesel, 641
  as wildcard characters, 746
At command, 306
at signs (@), 48, 50
Ate command, 317
Attach by Layer dialog box, 882, *882*, 889
Attach option, **533**
Attach tab, 529, *529*, **535-537**, *536*
Attachment tab, **244**, *244*
Attdisp command, 322
Attedit command, 320
Attredef command, 326
Attribute Definition dialog box, 306-308, *306*,
  311-312
Attribute Extraction - Export dialog box,
  332-333, *332*
Attribute Extraction - Save Template dialog
  box, 332
Attribute Extraction - Select Attributes dialog
  box, 328-330, *329*
Attribute Extraction - Select Drawing dialog box,
  328, *328*
Attribute Extraction - Settings dialog box, 328
Attribute Extraction - User Template dialog
  box, 328

Attribute Extraction - View Output dialog box,
  330-331, *330-331*
Attribute tab
  in Edit Attribute, 324, *324*
  in Enhanced Attribute Editor, 319, *319*
attributes, 797
  adding to blocks, **304-308**, *305*
  creating, **304-308**
  definitions for, **305-308**
  editing, **316-327**, *317-319*, *323-325*
  extracting and exporting, **327-333**
  global changes to, **319-326**, *323-325*
  inserting blocks with, **312-315**, *313*,
    315-316
  invisible, **322**, *323*
  prompts for, 304, 306, 310
  redefining blocks with, **326-327**
  specifications for, **308-312**, *308-310*
  with UCS, 379
  uses for, **327**
AUG (AutoCAD User Guide), 81
Auto Data Tips option, 713, *713*
Auto Indent option, 714, *714*
Auto List Members feature, 690, *690*, 712, *713*
Auto Quick Info option, 713
Auto selection option, 68
Auto-smooth option, 537
Auto Syntax Check option, **711-712**, *711-712*
AutoCAD 2002 Help dialog box
  Contents tab, **78-83**, *79*
  for context-sensitive help, **82**
  Search tab, **80-82**, *80-81*
AutoCAD 2002 Today dialog box, 42, *42*
AutoCAD Alias Editor dialog box, 588-589, *588*
AutoCAD Command Reference (ACR), 81
AutoCAD Text Window, **83-84**, *84*
AutoCAD User Guide (AUG), 81
AutoDesk Resource Guide, 607
Autodesk User Group International option, 83
AutoLISP language, **601-602**, **812-813**
  angles in, 854
  binary data in, 865
  Booleans in, 851
  character sets in, 856
  colors in, 850
  coordinate systems in, 861-862
  database access from, **813-815**
  dictionary access in, **818-820**
  drawing settings in, **822-823**

entities in
  names for, **815–816**
  retrieving, **816–818**
enumerations in, 849
handles in, 857
integers in, 845–848
keyboard macros in, **602–605**, *603*
objects in, **820–822**
pointers in, 857
points in, 858
real numbers in, 852
strings in, 855
for submenus, **632**
automating
  label updating, **572–574**, *573*
  tasks. *See* macros
automation interface, 826
Autoselect feature, **69–71**
AutoView Linked Objects in Drawing tool, 352
axes
  for 3D rotating, 410
  UCS for, 19

B

b command, 255
Back Clipping On/Off tool, 426, *426*
Back UCS orientation, 364, *364*
BackColor property, 768
Background Compile option, 714
Background dialog box, 886–887, *886*, 901
background grids for icons, 621
Background Image dialog box, 887, *887*
background scenes and images, **886–887**,
  886–888
backgrounds
  color for, 15, *16*, 670, 768
  for text, **566–569**, *568*
backslashes (\)
  in menus, 630–631
  for spaces, 321
Backspace key, 47
BackStyle property, 770
Base Point option, 297
base points
  in copying, 141
  in inserting blocks, 297
  in selecting, **62–66**
  in stretching, 75

Baseline tool, 211
Baseline Dimension tool, 212–213
baselines, dimensions from, **211–213**, *212*
Batting line type, *647*
Beside the Dimension Line option, 204
binary data in databases, **864–865**
binary files, DXF, **806–808**
Bind option, 533
bitmap images
  in 3D models, **904–908**, *905–907*, *909*
  for icons, 621
  saving rendered views as, 916–917
Blend to Color Above option, 508
blipmode command, 278–279, 285
blips, 53
  with point filters, **277–280**, *279*
  turning off, 285
Block Attribute Manager dialog box,
  323–326, *323*
Block Definition dialog box, 254–255, *254*, 263
Block Edit menu, Edit Reference command, 284
Block Reference option, 242
block references, 255
block table, 788
blocks, **251–252**
  with associative dimensioning, 228
  with attributes, **304–308**, *305*, **312–315**,
    313, *315–316*, **326–327**
  in AutoLISP, 821
  blips with point filters for, **277–280**, *279*
  clipping, 590–591
  combining entities into, **790–791**
  defining, 252
  for doors, **252–263**, *253–254*, *256–258*,
    260–261, *263*
  extracting information from, **329–331**,
    330–331
  finding, **264–267**, *265*
  flipping, **259–260**, *260*
  guidelines for, **274–275**, *274*, *276*
  inserting, **256–258**, *256–258*, **312–315**
  for leader text, 242
  previewing, 293–294, *294*
  revising, **283–285**, *284–285*
  rotating, 258, *258*, **271–273**, *272–273*, 283
  shapes as alternative to, **594–596**, *595*
  for sharing information
    Design Center for, **289–295**, *291–296*
    dragging and dropping for, **286–289**,
      287–288

inserting drawings, **298–299**
Wblock for, **296–298**, *297*
in Symbol Tables container, 788
tools for, **575**
tracking for, **276–277**
with UCS, 379
ungrouping, 283
VIZblocks, **534–538**
window
creating, **267–270**, *268–270*
inserting, **271–283**, *272–274*, *276*,
279, *282*
Blocks collection, 826
BLOCKS sections in DXF files, 809
bold text, 161
boolean operations, 80, 430–433, *433*
Booleans as integers, 848, **850–851**
BORDER linetypes, *643*
borders
for active controls, 667
for Wipeout objects, 579–580
Bottom UCS orientation, 364, *364*
Boundary Creation dialog box, 509–514
boundary edges in extending, 104
Boundary Hatch dialog box, 174–176, 178,
183–184
advanced options for, **184–186**, *184*
tips for, **187**
Boundary Set options, **186**
BOX command, 435
Box tool, 435
boxes, *432*, 435–436
drawing, **95**
coordinates in, **95–97**, *96*
extending lines in, **104–105**, *105*
Fillet command for, **100–102**, *101*
Offset command for, **97–100**, *98–99*
openings in, **102–103**, *103*
trimming lines in, **105–109**, *106–109*
bracketing in DXF files, 806, 809
brackets ([] <>)
for default options, 56
for line types, 647–648
for menu items, 633–635
Break tool, 39, *39*
Break at Point tool, 39, *39*
breakat macro, **603–604**, *603*
breaking, keyboard macro for, **603–604**, *603*
breakpoints, 713, 724–725, 728

buffers in ObjectDBX, **839**
building elevations in VIZ, **527–528**
built-in constants, **742–746**, *742–745*
built-in keywords and types, icons for, 692, *692*
Button Editor dialog box, 620–621, *621*
Button Properties dialog box, 618–619, *619*, 622
buttons, 104
creating, **618–620**
editing, 624
icons for, **620–622**

C

Cadalyst, 601, 608
Cadence, 601, 608
calculated properties, **797**, 827
Camera tool, 411, *411*, 414–415
cameras, 411–415, *412*
adjusting, **418–423**, *419–423*
distance to target, **418–419**, *419*
canceling
commands, **47**, 99, 132
project loading, **703**
Cap Closed Objects option, 538
Cap End option, 538
Cap Start option, 538
capitalization in VBA, 689–690
Caption property, 671–672
captions, **671–673**, *671*
car function, 815
carets (^), 629–630
Cartesian coordinate systems, **50–52**, *50–52*, **95**,
96, 860
cascading menus, 12, **631**, 710
Case Else clause, 757
case of VBA names, 689–690
categories for toolbars, 615
Categorized tab, 266, 671, *671*
cdr function, 814–815
cecolor function, 839
CENTER linetypes, *643*
Center Mark tool, 239
Center options
for arcs, 56, 139–140, 146
for Osnaps, 307
Cha command, 458
Chamfer tool, 40, *40*, 458, *458*
chamfering, **458–459**, *458–459*
Change to Current Layer tool, 565

changes
    property values, **767–773**, *768–772*
    in VIZ, **502–504**, *502–504*
character ranges in databases, **856–857**
character sets in databases, **855–856**
Character tab, 353
CheckBox controls, 663
CheckNumericKey Procedure, 777–779
chords, 56
chunks, 865
Circle tool, 39, *39*
circles
    smoothness of, **874–875**
    with UCS, 379
circular stairs, **543–545**, *544*
circular surfaces, extruding objects along,
    403–405, *404*
circumscribe polygon option, 235
classes
    in databases, **794–796**, *795–796*
    icons for, 692, *692*
    of objects, **760–761**
CLASSES sections, 809
Clean tool, 474
cleaning up
    lines, **121–122**, *121–122*
    screen, **53**
Clear option for icons, 621
Click event procedures, 676
clicking, 30
climate considerations for windows, 271
clipping, extended, **590–591**, *591*
clipping planes, **423–426**, *424–426*
Clone Options dialog box, 518–519, 545
close method, 833–834
closing
    lines, 51
    ObjectARX objects, **832–834**
    shapes, 95
code pages, 856
Code window, 661–662, **673**, *673*, 686, *686*
    displaying, **673–674**, *674*
    event procedures in, **674–678**, *675*
    keyword color in, **689**
coding in VBA, **731–732**
    aligning, 723–724
    applications in, **782–783**
    conditions in, **753–757**
    constructs in, **775–779**
    debugging, **724**

    editing, **723–724**
    events in, **774–775**
    functions in, **781**
    indenting, 714, 723–724
    loops in, **757–759**
    methods in, **773–774**
    objects in, **760–766**, *765*
    parameters and arguments in, **781–782**
    programs in, **782**
    properties in, **767–773**, *768–772*
    running, **725**
    tab order in, **779–781**
    user-defined types in, **752**
Collapse All Hidden Text On This Page
    option, 79
collections
    in ActiveX Automation, **825–826**
    in VBA, 759, **761–762**
colons (:), 753
Color by Elevation rollout, **507–508**, *507*
Color Faces tool, 474
color function, 837
Color option, 536
Color Options dialog box, 12, 16, *16*
Color Selector dialog box, 502, *502*
Color, Thickness option, 536
colors
    for 3D surfaces, *473*, 474–475
    background, 15, *16*, 670, 768
    of cursor, **32–33**, *32–33*
    for grips, 73
    as integers, **850**
    of keywords, **689**
    for materials, 883–884
    in ObjectDBX, 837
    in rendering 3D models, 917
    for syntax errors, 711
    for terrains, **507–508**, *507*
    for title bars, 670
    in Viz, **534–536**, *535*
columns, database, 334
COM Automation. *See* ActiveX Automation
combining entities into blocks, **790–791**
ComboBox controls, 663
comma delimited format files, 333
Command AutoLISP function, 604
command line
    opening toolbars from, **616–617**
    for solids editing, **471–472**
Command: prompt, 94

Command window, **17–18**, *17–18*, 27, 53
CommandButton controls, 664
CommandButton1_Click procedure, 676–677
CommandButton2_Click procedure, 676–677
commands, **25**, **91–92**, *92*
   aliases for, **588–590**, *588–589*
   canceling, **47**, 99, 132
   cursor color in, **32–33**, *32–33*
   ending, **33–35**, *34*
   help for, **78–83**, *79–81*
   history of, 83–84, *84*
   keyboard for, **30**
   in menus, **29–30**, *29*, **629–630**, 660
   prompts for, **30–32**, *31–32*
   restarting, 102
   toolbar buttons for, **26–27**, *26–27*
   toolbar flyouts for, **28–29**, *28*
   transparent, 143
   in VBA, 660
commas (,)
   in Cartesian coordinates, 50
   for constants, 742
   in Dim statements, 735
   in hatch patterns, 651
   in line type patterns, 644–645
   for parameters, 782
Comment Block button, 717
comments
   in DXF files, 808
   in VBA, 688, 693, 717
common base extension lines, **211–213**, *212*
comp.cad.autocad newsgroup, 607
Compass tool, 417, *418*
Compile ACADProject command, 724
Compile On Demand option, 714
compiled menus, 625
compiler and compilation, 714, 732
Complete Word feature, 690–692, *690–691*
complex line types, **647–648**, *647*
composite solids, 431
compound trims, 129, *129*
concatenating strings, 698
conditions
   for database searches, **342**
   for If...Then... blocks, **753–754**
   for If...Then...Else... blocks, **755–756**
   for Select Case statements, **756–757**
Cone tool, 438
cones, 430, *432*, 438, *438*
configuring Data Link files, **336–339**, *337–338*

Constant attribute option, 312
constants, **740–741**
   built-in, **742–746**, *742–745*
   declaring, **741–742**
   icons for, 692, *692*
   scope of, **746–752**, *749*
Construction Line tool, 39, *39*
constructors, 831
containers, 805
   in databases, **787–789**
   iterating through, **834–836**
Contents tab, **78–79**, *79*, 765
context-sensitive help, **82**, 728
Continue Dimension tool, 210–211
continuing dimensions, **210–211**, 213
CONTINUOUS name, 811
Contour.dwg file, 499–500, 502–503
contour lines. *See* terrains
Contour Lines Per Surface option, 445
control structures
   If...Then... blocks, **753–754**
   If...Then...Else... blocks, **755–756**
   Select Case statements, **756–757**
controls, **662–665**, *662*
   dimensions and position of, **666–667**
   placing, **665–667**
   tab order of, **779–781**
Controls collection, 761, **766**
Convert button, 772
Convert Drawing Layers to Design Layers option,
   528, 530, 535, **538**
Convert to Block option, 263
converting
   2D polylines to 3D solids, **436–440**,
     437–440
   units. *See* Metric-Imperial Converter applica-
     tion
Cookie Cutter Trim command, 577
coordinates
   for 3D meshes, 398
   in AutoLISP, 813
   in databases, **858–864**
   for distances, **48–52**, *49–52*
   in hatch patterns, 651–653, *652–653*
   for points, 92–93, 858–859
   spherical and cylindrical, **387–388**
   in status bar, 18
Copy an Object option, 242
Copy button, 142
Copy tool, 289

Copy Edges tool, 471, *471*
Copy Faces tool, 470–471, *471*
Copy Nested Entities tool, 575
Copy Object tool, 39, *39*
copying, 723, 727
  blocks, 283, 575
  faces and edges, **470–471**
  with grips, 72, 76–77, *77*
  leader text, 242
  Move Copy Rotate tool for, **576–577**
  objects, **141–143**, *142–143*
  Wipeout objects, 579
cords, 56
core objects, 799
corner macro, 605
corners
  chamfering, **458–459**, *458–459*
  rounding, **100–102**, *101*, **456–457**, *457*
Count property, 825
Counter variables in For loops, 757–758
cp command, 142
Create Attached Labels option, 354
Create Defaults option, 501, *501*
Create Freestanding Label tool, 351, *351*, 353
Create Icon From Block Geometry option, 255
Create Instances of Blocks option, 538
Create New Data Source dialog box, 338, *338*
Create New Drawing dialog box, 93, 476, *476*
Create or Append Linetype File dialog box, 644
Create Slice tool, 426, *426*
Create tab, 500, 541–542
criteria for databases, **342**
Crop Window option, 918–919, *919*
cross sections, **487**, *488*
crosshair cursor, **20**, *20*, 33, *33*, 54
Crosshair Size setting, 20
Crossing Faces option, 912, *912*
Crossing Polygon selection option, 66
Crossing Polygon windows, 226
Crossing selection option, 66
crossing windows, 66, **69–71**, *70–71*
  for cutting edges, 151–152, *152*
  for stretching, 224–226, *224*
Ctrl key in accelerator keys, 634–635
current drawing database, 832
Current Module option, 722
current text style, **162**
Current Viewport option, 186
cursor color, **32–33**, *32–33*
cursor modes, 53–54, *54*

curved 3D surfaces, **389–396**, *391*, *393–395*, *397*
curved arrows for linked files, 532
Curved Steps option, 538
curves
  extrusions on, **447–449**, *448*, *450*
  vertices for, 548–550, *549–551*
Custom Components dialog box, 562
custom objects, **829–830**
Customize Toolbars dialog box, 614–615, *615*, 622
customizing AutoCAD
  hatch patterns, **649–653**
  line types, **642–648**
  menus, **625–635**
  toolbars, **612–625**
Customltype.dwg file, 592
Cut command, 723
cutting edges
  selecting, 151–152, *152*
  in trimming, 105
cutting wall openings, **126–132**, *127–131*
Cylinder command, 442
Cylinder tool, 442
cylinders, 430, *432*
cylindrical coordinate format, **387–388**

D

D command, 196, 232
Dal command, 236
Dan command, 237
DASHDOT linetypes, *643*
DASHED linetypes, *643*
Data Link dialog box, 335
Data Link files, 335
  configuring, **336–339**, *337–338*
  creating, **336**
Data Link Properties dialog box, 336–337, *337*, 339
Data Type Summary Help window, 733, *733*
data types
  in databases, **843–844**
    binary, **864–865**
    handles, **857**
    integers, **844–851**
    pointers, **857–858**
    points, **858–864**
    real numbers, **852–855**
    strings, **855–857**
  in VBA, **733–735**, *733*
    for arrays, 690, 738–739

defining, **752**
  memory for, 734, 737
Data Types Keyword Summary option, 734
Data View dialog box, 340–341, *341*, 345,
  . 347–354
database managers, 334
databases, **785–786**
  accessing, **333–345**, **801–802**
    with ActiveX Automation. *See* ActiveX
      Automation
    with AutoLISP. *See* AutoLISP language
    with DXF. *See* DXF (Drawing Interchange
      Format) files
    miscellaneous methods for, **839–841**
    with ObjectARX. *See* ObjectARX environ-
      ment; ObjectDBX environment
  adding rows to, **344–345**
  classes in, **794–796**, *795–796*
  containers in, **787–788**
  data types in. *See* data types
  dictionaries in, **789–790**
  entities and blocks in, **790–791**
  finding records in, **341–344**
  linking objects to, **345–355**
  locating objects in, **349–351**, *349–350*
  non-objects in, **791–792**
  objects in. *See* objects
  opening, **340–341**
  selecting graphics through, **350–351**
  symbol tables in, **788–789**
Date function, 698–699
dates
  in databases, **854–855**
  retrieving, 698–699
  for sun angle calculator, 872
db-mastersample.mdb file, 335, *335*, 339
Dba command, 212
dbConnect menu
  Data Sources command, 339
  Links command, 355
dbConnect tool, 340
dbConnect window, 340–341, *340*
dbConnectManager
  for accessing external databases, **333–345**
  for linking external databases, **345–355**
  setting up for, **335–339**, *337–338*
Dco command, 210
Ddi command, 239
Debug menu, Toggle Breakpoint command, 728
Debug toolbar, **718**, *718*

debugging, **724**
decimal form for distances, 120
decimal points, 50, 853
Decimal Separator option, 198
Decimal units, 10
declaring
  arrays, 689–690, 738–739
  constants, **741–742**
  procedures, 677
  variables, 712, **734–738**
Ded command, 215, 244
Default Settings area, 7
defaults, 6
  for attributes, 312
  icons for, 692, *692*
  for new drawings, 43
  for options and settings, 56
  for VBA GUI, **670**
defined properties, **797**
defining
  attributes, **305–308**
  data types, **752**
  surfaces, **398–399**, *400–401*
  UCS, **361–365**, *362*, *364*
definition points for dimensions, **216**
Defpoints layer, 216
Defun AutoLISP function, 603–604
degrees for angles, 854
Del key in accelerator keys, 635
Delete Faces tool, 463, *463*
Delete Labels command, 354
Delete option for layer states, 564
Delete source objects?: prompt, 145
Delete Zone option, 508
deleting. *See also* erasing
  alternate dimensions, **232–233**
  blocks, 263
  color zones, 508
  icons, 623
  layer states, 564
  layers, **566**
  links, 355
  sliced objects, 455
  surfaces, **463–464**, *464*
  toolbars from list, 613
delimiters, 332
Description button, 290
deselecting objects, 61
Design Center application, **289–295**,
  291–296, 854

design time vs. run time, **767**
Desktop button, 290
Desmooth option, 407
Detach option, 533
detail in rendering 3D models, **900–904**, *902–904*
Developer Help option, 82
di command, 281
dialog boxes, **770–772**, *771–772*
Diameter Dimension tool, 239
diameters, dimensions for, **239**, *240*
dictadd function, 822
dictionaries
    in ActiveX Automation, **828–829**
    in AutoLISP, **818–820**, 822
    in databases, **789–790**
    in ObjectDBX, **838**
Dictionaries collection, 828–829
dictnext function, 819
dictremove function, 822
dictrename function, 822
dictsearch function, 818–819
Diesel programming language, 573, **636–637**
    for menu option labels, **639–641**
    for menus, **638**
.dim extension, 599
Dim statement, 689–690, **735–736**
Dimension Edit tool, 215, 221, 244
dimension lines, 194, *194*
Dimension menu
    Align Text command, 222
    Aligned command, 236
    Angular command, 237
    Continue command, 210
    Leader command, 240
    Linear command, 209, 227
    Oblique command, 244
    Override command, 222
    Qdim command, 231
    Reassociate Dimensions command, 229
    Style command, 232
    Styles command, 486
    Tolerance command, 247
Dimension Style Export dialog box, 599, *599*
Dimension Style Import dialog box, 600, *600*
Dimension Style Manager dialog box, 196, *196*, 220, 486
    for alternate dimensions, 232
    for current dimension style, 206
    for editing dimension style, 206

dimension style table, 788
Dimension Text Edit tool, **222–223**
Dimension toolbar, **208**, *208*
Dimension Update tool, 221
dimensioned objects, editing, **224–226**, *224*
dimensions, **193–194**
    aligning, 236–237, *237*
    alternate, **232–233**
    alternate units for, **204–206**, *205*
    for angles, **237–239**, *238*
    for arrays, 740
    arrows for, **201–204**, *202–203*, **240–244**, *243–244*
    associative, 194, **227–232**, *227–230*
    components of, **194–195**, *194*
    continuing, **210–211**, 213
    definition points for, **216**
    editing, **213–234**
    extension lines for, 194, *194*, 209, **211–213**, *212*
    grids in, **207**, *207*
    Grips feature for, **216–218**, *217*
    horizontal and vertical, **209–210**, *210*
    leaders for, 220, **240–244**, *243–244*, 247
    for nonorthogonal objects, **234–239**, *236–238*, *240*
    notes for, **240–244**, *243–244*
    ordinate, **245–247**, *246*
    Osnap overrides with, **233–234**
    in Paper Space, **485–487**
    for radii, diameters, and arcs, **237–239**, *238*, *240*
    rotating, 226, 237, *237*
    skewing, **244–245**, *245*
    string of, **231–232**, *232*
    styles for, **194–207**, **218–223**, **599–600**, *599–600*, 788
    text for, 194, *194*
        appending data to, **213–214**
        height of, **199–200**, *200*
        location and orientation of, **200–201**, *201*
        moving, **200–201**, *201*, **219–221**, *219*, *221*
        rotating, **221–222**
        styles for, **218**
        tool for, **223**
    toolbar for, **208**, *208*
    of toolbox controls, **666–667**
    with UCS, 379
    units for, **197–199**, **204–206**, *205*
Dimfit dimension variable, 222–223

Dimim command, 600
Dimlinear command, 209
dimmed menu items, 632, 710
Dimoverride command, 223
Dimregen command, 228
Dimscale dimension variable, 234
DimStyles collection, 826
Dimtad dimension variable, 234
Dimtedit command, 222
Dimtih dimension variable, 234
Dimtix dimension variable, 239
Dimtofl dimension variable, 239
Direct Distance method, 52
directions
    for arcs, 146
    with extrusions, 405
    in moving objects, 65
disguised integers, **848–851**
displacement maps, 498
Display All Hidden Text On This Page option, 79
Display Alternate Units option, 205, 232
Display at UCS Origin Point option, 370
display order with overlapping objects,
    189–191, *190*
Display Properties dialog box, 670
display schemes, 670
Display Scroll Bars in Drawing Window
    option, 17
Display tab
    for background color, 15, *16*
    for command window, 17–18
    for crosshair cursor, 20, *20*
    for isolines, 445
    for scrollbars, 17
    for smoothness, 875
Display UCS Dialog UCS tool, 363, *363*, 365, 390
Distance command, 281
distances. *See also* dimensions
    in Architectural units, 120
    camera to target, **418–419**, *419*
    coordinates for, **48–52**, *49–52*
    formats for, 119
    in moving objects, 65
    between objects, 281
    with Offset command, **100**, 119
    rubber banding for, 52
DIVIDE linetypes, *643*
divided solids, separating, **474**, *474*
dividing lines on menus, 632
division in Diesel, 636

Dli command, 209, 211
Do loops, 759
docked items
    Design Center, 291, *291*
    Properties window, 267
    toolbars, **13–15**, *14–15*, 93, *93*, 708, *709*
documentation in VBA, 688, 693
Documents collection, **763–764**, 824
dollar signs ($), 636–638
done function, 835
donuts, 430, *432*, 439, *439*
door type symbols, 304
doors, **133**, *133*
    blocks for, **252–263**, *253–254*, *256–258*,
        260–261, *263*
    copying, **141–143**, *142–143*
    finishing, **145–146**, *147*
    mirroring, **143–145**, *144*
    rotating, **137–138**, *138*
    sliding glass doors, **147–155**, *147–154*
    swinging, **133–141**, *135–136*, *138*, *140*
Dor command, 246
DOT linetypes, *643*
dotted windows, 69–71, *70–71*
Double hatch pattern option, 175
double quotes ("), 604
doughnuts, 430, *432*, 439, *439*
Drafting Settings dialog box, 133–134, *134*, 233
dragging and dropping, **286–289**, *287–288*
Draw menu, 12, *13*
    3D Polyline command, 388
    Arc command, 139
    Block menu
        Base command, 311
        Define Attributes command, 306
        Make command, 255
    Hatch command, 174
    Line command, 94
    Rectangle command, 134
    Solids menu
        Box command, 435
        Cylinder command, 442
        Setup menu, Profile command, 483
        Setup menu, View command, 478
    Surfaces menu
        3D Face command, 369
        Ruled Surface command, 399
        Tabulated Surface command, 401
    Text command, 162
Draw toolbar, **38–41**, 93, *93*

drawing
  boxes, **95**
    coordinates in, **95–97**, *96*
    extending lines in, **104–105**, *105*
    Fillet command for, **100–102**, *101*
    Offset command for, **97–100**, *98–99*
    openings in, **102–103**, *103*
    trimming lines in, **105–109**, *106–109*
  lines, **44–46**, *45*, **92–94**, *92–93*
  views, **475–479**
drawing area, **15–17**, *16*
Drawing Exchange Engine (DXE) libraries, 840
Drawing Interchange Format. *See* DXF (Drawing
  Interchange Format) files
drawing objects, 673, **762**, *763*
  Application object, **762**
  Documents collection, **763–764**
drawings
  AutoLISP settings for, **822–823**
  components of, **786–787**
  creating, **42–47**
  inserting, **298–299**
  names of, **22**
  opening, **4–5**, *4–6*
  saving, **21–22**, *21–22*
  starting, 6–11, *6–11*
Draworder command, 191
DrawText macro
  code for, **687–694**
  running, **696–697**, *696–697*
  saving, **694–695**, *695*
  updating, **698–699**
drop-down lists, 686–687
.dvb extension, 680, 694, 716
Dview command, **421–422**
.dwg files, 115, 694, 840
DWG Import dialog box, 515, 525
DWG Linking tab, 528, *529*, **538–548**, *538–539*
Dwgname system variable, 574
Dwgprefix system variable, 574
DXE (Drawing Exchange Engine) libraries, 840
DXF (Drawing Interchange Format) files,
  802–804
  angles in, 854
  ASCII and binary, **806–808**
  and AutoLISP. *See* AutoLISP language
  binary data in, 865
  Booleans in, 851
  character sets in, 856
  colors in, 850
  coordinate systems in, 861
  criticisms of, **804–805**
  enumerations in, 849
  group codes in, 849
  handles in, 857
  for integers, 845–848
  myths about, **804**
  objects in, **810–812**
  pointers in, 857
  points in, 858–859
  real numbers in, 853
  serializing data with, **805–806**
  strings in, 855
  structure of, **808–810**
Dynamic Reload Group option, 533

E

ECS (Entity Coordinate System), 861–864
Edge Surface tool, 389, 396, *396*
edgemode command, 152
Edgemode variable, 152
edges
  boundary, 104
  copying, **470–471**
  cutting, 105, 151–152, *152*
  for surfaces, 389–390, **396**
Edit Attribute dialog box, 324–325, *324*
Edit Attributes dialog box, 313–314, *313*, 317
Edit menu
  Clone command, 519
  Complete Word command, 690
  Indent command, 728
  Paste command, 727
Edit option
  for layer states, 564
  for vertices, 407
Edit Polyline tool, 408
Edit Table tool, 340
Edit Text dialog box, 165, *165*
Edit toolbar, **717**, *718*
editing
  3D Meshes, **405–408**, *406*
  attributes, **316–327**, *317–319*, *323–325*
  AutoLISP objects, **820–822**
  blocks, **283–285**, *284–285*
  buttons, 624
  code commands for, **723–724**
  command aliases, **588–590**, *588–589*

dimension styles, 206
dimensioned objects, **224–226**, *224*
dimensions, **213–234**
with Grips, **72–78**
hatch patterns, **181–183**, *181*, *183*
layer states, 564
links, **354–355**, *355*, **530–532**, *531*
solids, **454**
  chamfering corners, **458–459**, *458–459*
  command line for, **471–472**
  copying faces and edges, **470–471**
  deleting surfaces, **463–464**, *464*
  extruding surfaces, **467–469**, *468*
  moving surfaces, **460–462**, *461–462*
  offsetting surfaces, **462**, *463*
  rotating surfaces, **464–465**, *465*
  rounding corners, **456–457**, *457*
  separating divided solids, **474**, *474*
  splitting solids, **454–456**, *455*
  surface features for, **472–474**, *473*
  tapering surfaces, **466**, *466–467*
  turning solids into shells, **469**, *470*
text, **566–574**
Editor tab, **711–714**, 738
Editor Format tab, 689, *689*
EIFs (entity interchange files), 803
Elevation view, 921, *922*
Ellipse tool, 39, *39*
Ellipse Arc tool, 39, *39*
Ellipse cone option, 438
ellipses (...), 30, 723
Else blocks, 677–678
ElseIf clause, 756
embedded objects, **794**, 810
empty strings, 678
Enable Grips within Blocks option, 264
Enable Macro Virus Protection option, 700
Enable Macros option, 700
End Function statement, 781
End If statement, 753–754
end-of-file information, 808
end-section brackets, 809
End statement, 678
End Sub statement, 677–678, 688, 776
End Type statement, 752
ENDBLK string, 809
ending commands, **33–35**, *34*
Endpoint button, 135
Endpoint Object Snap, 135
EndPoint property, 827

endpoints
  for arcs, 56, 139–140
  for base points, 63–64
  in copying, 141
ENDSEC bracket, 809
ENDTAB string, 809
Enhanced Attribute Editor dialog box, 317–319, *317–319*
Enter key, **34**, 102
Enter X scale factor: prompt, 257
entget function, 813–816
Entire Drawing option, 298
entities. *See also* objects
  in ActiveX Automation
    accessing, **826–828**
    creating, **828**
  in AutoLISP
    names of, **815–816**
    retrieving, **816–818**
  combining into blocks, **790–791**
  coordinates for, **861–862**
  in ObjectDBX, **836–837**
ENTITIES sections, 810
entity association lists, 814–815, 821
Entity Coordinate System (ECS), 861–864
entity interchange files (EIFs), 803
entity interchange format files, 803
Entity option with 3D rotating, 410
entmake function, 821
entmakex function, 821
entmod function, 820
entnext function, 817–818
entsel function, 813
Enumerated types, 767, 770, *770*
enumerations
  icons for, 692, *692*
  as integers, **849**
environment, VBA, **659–660**, *660*
  IDE. *See* IDE (Integrated Development Environment)
  toolbox, **662–667**, *662*
  UserForm modules, **661–662**, *661*
EOF string, 808
eq code, 641
equal signs (=)
  in comparison operators, 755
  in Diesel, 641
  in expressions, 732
Erase command, 96
Erase tool, 39, *39*

erasing. *See also* deleting
  blips, 53
  blocks, 283
  icons, 621
  lines, **95**
  Wipeout objects, 579
Esc (Escape) key, 35, 47, 99, 102, 132, 635
eval code, 641
event-driven processing, 774
event procedures, 662, **674–678**, *675*, 774–775
events, 692, *692*, **774–775**
ex command, 104
Excel files and programming, extracted data
  for, 333
exchanging data. *See also* exporting; importing
  accessing databases for, **333–345**
  Design Center for, **289–295**, *291–296*
  dragging and dropping for, **286–289**, *287–288*
  inserting drawings, **298–299**
  linking databases for, **345–355**
  Wblock for, **296–298**, *297*
exclamation points (!)
  in Diesel, 641
  for member references, 761
Exclude Objects by Layer option, 539
Exclude Selection tool, 598
Existing Set option, 186
exiting, 109
Explode Attributes to Text tool, 575
Explode tool, 40, *40*
Explode Text tool, 574
exploding
  attribute blocks, 326
  blocks, 283
  regions, 489
exponents for real numbers, 852–853
Export dialog box, 493
Export options for layer states, 565
exporting
  attribute information, **327–333**
  dimension styles, **599–600**, *599*
  layer states, 565
Express menu, Tools menu
  Dimstyle Export command, 599
  Dimstyle Import command, 600
Express toolbar, **561**
Express Standard toolbar, **576–587**
Express tools, **561**
  for blocks, **575**
  for command aliases, **588–590**

for dimensions, **599–600**
for extended clips, **590–591**, *591*
for external references, **582–584**
for filleting polylines, **596–597**, *597*
for full screen, **590**
for hatch patterns, **584–587**, *586–587*
for labels, **572–574**, *573*
for layers, **562–566**, *563–564*
for line types, **592–594**, *592–593*
for linked text documents, **571–572**
loading, **562**
for masking areas, **578–580**, *579–581*
for moving, copying, and rotating objects,
  576–577
for polyline properties, **577–578**
for revision clouds, **581–582**, *582*
for selection, **598–600**
for shapes, **594–596**, *595*
for stretching objects, **576**
for text, **566–574**
for trimming objects, **577**
expressions, **732–733**
  in Diesel, 636
  in Select case, 756–757
Ext command, 436, 446
Extend Beyond Dim Lines option, 202
Extend Beyond Ticks option, 202
Extend button, 104
Extend command, **104–105**, *105*, 132
Extend tool, 39, *39*
Extend to Block Entities tool, 575
Extended Clip tool, **590–591**, *591*
Extended Trim tool, 577, *577*
extending
  in block objects, 575
  lines, **104–105**, *105*
extension dictionaries, 820
extension lines, 194, *194*, 209, **211–213**, *212*
extensionDictionary function, 838
extents, zooming to, 121
exterior walls
  lines for, **115–118**, *116–117*
  openings for, **127–132**, *127–131*
external databases
  accessing, **333–345**
  linking objects to, **345–355**
external references
  with associative dimensioning, 228
  clipping, 590–591
  Pack 'n Go feature for, **582–584**, *583–584*

extracting attributes, **327–333**
Extrude tool, 436, *436*, 446
Extrude Faces tool, 467, *467*
extruding
   3D forms, **401–405**, *402–404*
   polylines, **436–437**, **445–449**,
     446–448, *450*
   surfaces, **467–469**, *468*
extrusions
   on curved paths, **447–449**, *448*, *450*
   tapering, **445–446**, *446–447*

F

f command, 100
F1 function key, 82, 635, 728
faces, copying, **470–471**
Facetres system variable, 875
False values, 755
Favorites button, 290
feature control symbols, **247–248**
Fenceline line types, 647, *647*
fences for selections, 67
File Link Manager, 503–504, *503*, **528–530**, *529*
   editing in, **530–532**, *531*
   options in, **532–534**
File Link Settings dialog box, 499, *499*, 504,
   528, *529*, 531, **534**
   Attach tab, **535–537**, *536*
   for color, **534–535**, *535*
   DWG Linking tab, **538–548**, *538–539*
   Geometry tab, **537–538**, *537*
   for layers, **535**
File menu
   Close command, 42, 95
   Close and Return to AutoCAD command,
     680, 704
   Exit command, 109
   New command, 42, 93, 476
   Open command, 115
   Print command, 722
   Reset command, 528
   Save command, 71, 680, 694, 916
   Save As command, 44
   Save Global1 command, 680
File Output Configuration dialog box, 917, *917*
files
   in Design Center, 291–293, *292–293*
   linking, **345–355**

names for, 44
project, **699–703**, *700–702*
rendering 3D models to, **917–918**
saving, 71
types of, 917
Files tab, 339
Fillet command, **100–102**, *101*, 456
   vs. Offset, 118
   vs. Trim, 122
Fillet tool, 40, *40*, 456
filleting
   macro for, 605
   polylines, **596–597**, *597*
   rounding corners with, **456–457**, *457*
Find and Replace dialog box, 569–571, *570*
Find and Replace Options dialog box, 571, *571*
Find and Replace tool, 569, *569*
Find button, 290
Find command, 723
Find Whole Word Only option, 745
finding. *See* searching
FindMax function, 753–754
Fit options, 219–220
Fit tab, 203, *203*
fixed-length strings, 735
flags, 850–851
flat trusses, 552, *552*
flipping blocks, **259–260**, *260*
floating items
   Design Center, 291
   Properties window, 267
   toolbars, 14
Flood option, 186
floors with openings, **522–527**, *523–526*
Flyout Properties dialog box, 623, *623*
flyouts, 40–41, *40*, **622–624**
fmBackStyleOpaque value, 770
fmBorders library, 743–744, *744*
folders in Design Center, 291–293, *292–293*
Font dialog box, 771, *771*
Font property, 771
fonts, 160–161
   for line types, 647–648
   in VBA, 771, *771*
foot signs (') in distance formats, 119
For loops, **757–759**
For Each loops, 759
foreach function, 815
Form Image option, 722

Format menu
    Align command, 720
    Dimension Style command, 196
    Make Same Size command, 720
    Text Style command, 160, 162
    Units command, 287
    Vertical Spacing command, 720
Forms collection, 761
Forms object model, **764–766**, *765*
fractions
    for dimensions, 199
    in distance formats, 119
    in VBA, 692
Frame controls, 664
Frame Text option, 242
Freeze Object Layer tool, 565
Front UCS orientation, 364, *364*
front views, drawing, **475–479**
Full Screen AutoCAD tool, **590**
function keys in accelerator keys, 635
functions, **781**
    in Diesel, 636
    parameter help for, 713, *713*

G

garage addition, **156–157**, *156*
Gas_line line type, 647, *647*
General Declarations section, 747, 752
General object, 684, *684*
General properties for text, 167
General tab
    options on, **714**, *714*
    for ToolTips, 716
Generate Mapping Coord. option, 534
Geographic Location dialog box, 872, *872*
geometric tolerance annotations, 794
Geometric Tolerance dialog box, 247–248, *247*
Geometry tab, **537–538**, *537*
Get Selection Set tool, 598, 600
GetAngle method, 774
getAt function, 834, 836, 838
getBlockTable function, 833–834
GetExtensionDictionary method, 829
getGripPoints function, 837
getGroupDictionary function, 838
getIntoAsciiBuffer function, 857
getNamedObjectsDictionary function, 838

getRecord function, 835
getvar function, 637–638, 641, 822–823
GetVariable method, 830
ghosting, 96
.gif files, 917
glass, mirror attribute for, **901–903**, *902–903*
glass doors, **147–155**, *147–154*
glazing, 269
Global Attribute Edit tool, 575
global changes to attributes, **319–326**, *323–325*
global objects, icons for, 692, *692*
Global1 project name, 717
Graded Solid option, 506
Graded Surface option, 506
graphics
    databases for, **350–351**
    in line types, 647–648
grayed menu items, 632, 710
grayed-out pages, 532
greater-than symbols (>)
    in comparison operators, 753, 755
    in Diesel, 641
    in pull-down menus, 631
    for text, 213–214
grids and gridlines
    in dimensions, **207**, *207*
    for icons, 621
    options for, 714
    in perspective views, 417, *418*
Grips feature, 69
    for block detection, **264**
    for copying objects, 76–77, 77
    for dimensions, **216–218**, *217*
    for editing objects, **72–78**
    for moving objects, **75–76**
    in ObjectDBX, 837
    for rotating objects, **76–77**, 77
    for stretching objects, **73–75**, *74*
    summary of, **77–78**
    for text, 166, 170, *170*
    for UCS, **366–367**
group codes
    in DXF files, 806–807
    as integers, **849–850**
guidelines for blocks, **274–275**, *274, 276*
GUIs
    creating, **668–670**, *668*
    screen. *See* screen

H

Handle property, 830
handles
    for active controls, 667, 720
    in databases, **857**
    for objects, 792
hard owners, 793
hard pointers, 793
Hatch Edit dialog box, 182
Hatch Pattern Palette dialog box, 178, *178*,
    181–182, *181*
hatch patterns, **173–174**
    adding, **174–176**, *175*
    advanced options for, **184–186**, *184*
    creating, **584–587**, *586–587*, **649–653**,
        650–653
    layers for, 174, 187
    matching, **187–188**
    modifying, **181–183**, *181*, *183*
    position of, **176–179**, *177–178*
    predefined, 178–179
    size of, **179–180**
    and space planning, **188–191**, *190*
    standard, *650*
    tips for using, **187**
Hatch tool, 40, *40*, 174
HEADER sections, 809
height
    of dimension text, **199–200**
    of text, 161, 307
    of UserForms, 767
Height property, 767
help
    for buttons, 619
    for commands, **78–83**, *79–81*
    context-sensitive, **82**
    for Diesel, 640–641
    for icons, 621
    sources of, **82–83**
    for toolbars, 613
    for VBA, 712, **725–728**, *726–728*
Help menu
    AutoCAD Help Topics command, 82
    Help command, 78
    Microsoft Visual Basic Help command,
        726, 734
help messages for menus, **632–634**
Help Topics dialog box, 640

Help window, 726, *726*
hexagons, dimensioning, **235–239**, *236–238*, *240*
hidden lines
    in 3D models, 443–444, *444*
    in viewports, **482–484**, *484*
HIDDEN linetypes, *643*
Hide command, 444
Hide Labels command, 354
Hide Origin Point Helper option, 537
hiding labels, **354**
highlighting, 60, *61*, 96
History button, 290
history of commands, 83–84, *84*
Home dimension text option, 215
horizontal dimensions, **209–210**, *210*
horizontal lines, 46
hot grips, 73–75, *74*, 77
Hot_water_supply line type, *647*
hotkeys, 30
hyphens (-)
    in Diesel, 641
    in distance formats, 119
    in line type patterns, 644–645
    in pull-down menus, 631–632

I

i command, 257, 313
IACADEntity interface, 829
IAcadObject interface, 829
Icon Editor tool, 619
icons, 104
    creating, **620–622**
    deleting, 623
    for UCS, **19**, *19*, 360, **370–371**
    in VBA, 692, *692*
ID names for menu items, 633–634
IDE (Integrated Development Environment),
    659–660, **707–708**, *709*
    code commands in
        for debugging, **724**
        for editing, **723–724**
        for running code, **725**
    help in, **725–728**, *726–728*
    menu bar in, **708–710**, *709*
    options in, **710–711**, *711*
        Editor, **711–714**
        General, **714**, *714*, 716
    Print command in, **721–722**, *722*

running macros from, **696**
toolbars in, **715**
   Debug, **718**, *718*
   Edit, **717**, *718*
   standard, **715–716**, *715*
   UserForm, **719–721**, *719*
identifiers in symbol tables, 789
identifying objects, **792–793**
IEEE Standard 754–1985, 853
If statements
   in Diesel, 641
   in VBA, 677–678
If...Then... blocks, **753–754**
If...Then...Else... blocks, **755–756**
Ignore options, 185
Image control, 665
implicit links, **793–794**
Import AutoCAD DWG File dialog box, 515, *515*,
   525–526, *525*, 537, 553, *554*
Import menu, AutoCAD DWG command, 537
Import options for layer states, 565
importing
   3D models, **477–479**, *478*
   dimension styles, **600**, *600*
   layer states, 565
   for VIZ
      plans, **514–521**, *515–522*
      trusses, **552–555**, *552–555*
Imprint tool, 473
inches, 119
Indent command, 723–724
indenting code lines, 714, 723–724
index entries in help, 726
Index tab, 82, 726, *726*
index values
   for arrays, 739–740
   for collections, 762
Inherit Properties option, 184
input with menus, **630–631**
Inquiry toolbar, 14–15, *14*
Ins key in accelerator keys, 635
Insert Block tool, 39, *39*, 256, 313
Insert button, face of, **715–716**
Insert command, 257
Insert dialog box, 473, 477
   for attributes, 313
   for blocks, 256–257, *256*, 259
Insert menu
   Block command, 257, 472, 477

File Link Manager command, 503, 528
   Linked DWG command, 499
   Module command, 685, 727
   UserForm command, 661, 668
Insert Units drop-down list, 297
inserting
   blocks, **256–258**, *256–258*, **312–315**
   drawings, **298–299**
Insertion cursor, 688
insertion points for blocks, 253, 258
instances of classes, 761
instantiation in ObjectARX, 831
integers in databases, **844–845**
   disguised, **848–851**
   signed, **845–848**
Integrated Development Environment. *See* IDE
   (Integrated Development Environment)
interfaces in ActiveX Automation, **825–826**
interference with primitives, 431
interior lighting, **889–892**, *890–892*
interior walls
   lines for, **118–126**, *119–126*
   openings for, **130–131**, *130–131*
Interpolate Points options, 507
Intersection Osnap option, 63
intersections
   for base points, 63
   cleaning up, 122
   of primitives, 430, *433*
intrinsic constants, **742–746**, *742–745*
invisible attributes, 311, **322**, *323*
"is a kind of" relationships, 795
isConstant function, 851
isInvisible function, 851
Island Detection
   method for, 186
   styles for, **185**
isNull function, 838
ISO format and standards for dimensions,
   234–235
ISO-25 style, 195, 234–235
Isolate Objects Layer tool, 565
isolines, **444–445**
Isolines system variable, 445
isometric views, **481–482**, *482*
italic text, 161
Item method, 825
iterating through containers, **834–836**

J

jambs, 126
joining primitives, **440–444**, *441–444*
Julian dates, 855
Just_G line type, *647*
Justification option, 164
justification points, **164–165**, *164–165*
Justify option, 163

K

Keep Dim Line With Text option, 220
keyboard for commands, **30**
keyboard macros, **602–605**, *603*
Keycad.LSP file, 604–605, *605*
keys
    in dictionaries, 790
    in symbol tables, 789
keyword color, **689**

L

L command, 94
Label controls, 663
Label Fields tab, 352–353, *352*
Label Template dialog box, 352–353, *352*
labels. *See also* text
    Diesel for, **639–641**
    hiding, **354**
    with links, **351–354**
    updating, **572–574**, *573*
landscape, **910–915**, *911–912*, *914–915*
Landscape Edit dialog box, 915
Landscape New dialog box, 910–911, *910*, 913
Landscape New tool, 910, *910*
large toolbar buttons, 613
last objects, selecting, 67
Last options
    with 3D rotating, 410
    in selecting, 67
Layer, Thickness option, 536
Layer, Thickness, Color option, 536
Layer Delete tool, 566
Layer Manager tool, 563–565, *563*
Layer Merge tool, 566
Layer option, 536

Layer Properties Manager dialog box, 562
    for hidden lines, 483
    for layer states, 562–563
Layer property, 830
Layer State Name dialog box, 563
layer table, 788
Layered Solid option, *504*, 505–506
layers
    for blocks, 252
    deleting, **566**
    for hatch patterns, 174, 187
    for materials, 882
    names for, 563
    objects for controlling, **565–566**
    saving and recalling settings for, **562–565**,
        563–564
    with Setup Drawing tool, 485
    in Symbol Tables container, 788
    in Viz, **535–536**
Layers collection, 826
Layers property, 825
layout blocks, 821–822
Layouts collection, 764
Le command, 240
Leader Line & Arrow tab, **242–243**
Leader Line option, 243
Leader Settings dialog box, 241, *241*
    Annotation tab, **242**
    Attachment tab, **244**, *244*
    Leader Line & Arrow tab, **242–243**
leaders for dimensions, 220, **240–244**,
    243–244, 247
leading zeros, 50
Learning Assistance option, 83
Left UCS orientation, 364, *364*
length of chords, 56
length units in databases, **854**
Lengthen tool, 39, *39*
less-than symbols (<)
    for angles, 48
    in comparison operators, 753, 755
    in Diesel, 641
    in pull-down menus, 631
    for text, 213–214
libraries
    constants in, 743–744
    icons for, 692, *692*
    for materials, 880–881, *880*
    for ObjectARX, 831

lifetime of variables, **748–752**
lighting effects, **888–889**
  interior lighting, **889–892**, *890–892*
  night scene lighting, **892–893**, *894–895*
  scenes for, **895–899**, *896–899*
Lights dialog box, 871, *871*, 874–875, 890, 893
Lights tool, 870, *870*, 875
.lin extension, 644
Line button, 93
Line command, 44, **92–94**, *92–93*, 132
line feeds, 807
line groups, **649–653**
LINE string, 811
Line tool, 39, *39*, 44, *44*
line types
  creating, **592–594**, *592–593*, **644–648**,
    645–647
  in ObjectDBX, 837
  in Symbol Tables container, 788
  viewing, **642**, *643*
Linear Dimension tool, 209, 211, 237
LineDetails type, 752
lines
  cleaning up, **121–122**, *121–122*
  closing, 51
  for dimensions, 209, *210*
  drawing, **44–46**, *45*, **92–94**, *92–93*
  erasing, **95**
  extending, **104–105**, *105*
  extruding objects along, **401–402**, *402–403*
  offsetting, **102–103**, *103*
  stretching, **73–75**, *74*
  trimming, **105–109**, *106–109*
  with UCS, 379
  for walls
    exterior, **115–118**, *116–117*
    interior, **118–126**, *119–126*
Lines And Arrows tab, 201–204, *202*
lines of text in command window, **17–18**, *17–18*
Linetype command, 642, 644
linetype function, 837
Linetype Manager, 593
linetype table, 788
Linetypes collection, 826
lineweights as integers, **850**
Link and Label Settings tool, 348, 351, 354
Link Manager dialog box, 354–355, *355*
Link Select dialog box, 349–350, *349*
Link Template dialog box, 346–347, *346*

link templates, **346–347**, *346*
Linked Files list box, **532**
linked text documents, **571–572**
linking objects, **793–794**
links
  creating, **345–348**, *346*, *348*
  editing, **354–355**, *355*, **530–532**, *531*
  File Link Manager for. *See* File Link Manager
  finding objects through, **349–351**, *349–350*
  labels with, **351–354**
list boxes of objects and procedures,
    673–675, *675*
List command, **264–267**, *265*
List tool, 83–84
List Entity Xdata tool, 601
List Xref/Block Entities tool, 575
ListBox controls, 663
Load button in Design Center, 290
Load/Unload Applications dialog box, 701, 703
loading
  Express tools, **562**
  menus, **626–629**, *627–628*
  project files, **699–703**, *700–702*
local character sets, 856
local variables, 747
location of hatch patterns, **176–179**, *177–178*
Lock Objects Layer tool, 566
logarithms for real numbers, 852
logical operators in help searches, 80
long lines in menus, 632
loop counters, 759
loops, **757**
  For, **757–759**
  While, **759**
.lsp extension, 604
LUNITS setting, 849

M

macros, 659–660, **683–684**, **775–776**
  with AutoLISP, **602–605**, *603*
  for buttons, 619–620
  code for, **687–694**
  Diesel language for, **636–641**
  for menus, 626, **632**
  running, **696–697**, *696–697*
  saving, **604–605**, **694–695**, *695*
  standard modules in, **685–687**, *685–686*
  starting applications from, **703–704**

Macros dialog box, 685–686, *685*, 696–697, *696*
Make Block command, 252
Make Block tool, 39, *39*, 254
Make Linetype tool, **592–594**, *592–593*
MakeShape.dwg file, 594
mantissas, 852–853
mapcar function, 815
Mapping dialog box, 907, *907*
Mapping tool, 907, *907*
masking
    text backgrounds, **566–569**, *568*
    Wipeout tool for, **578–580**, *579–581*
mass of solids, 491–492, *492*
Mass Properties tool, 491–492
Massprop command, 491
Match Objects Layer tool, 565
Match Properties tool, 187–188
matching hatch patterns, **187–188**
Materials dialog box, 880–883, *880*, 901,
    905–906
materials for rendering, **879–885**, *880–886*
Materials Library dialog box, 880–881, *880*, 889
Materials tool, 880, *880*
matrices, two-dimensional arrays for, 740
Maximize icon, 289
Maximum Elev. option, 507
Mclose option, 407
measurement units, 10–11, *10*
    in databases, **854**
    default setting for, 43
    for dimensions, **197–199**, **204–206**, *205*
members of classes, 761, 797
memory
    for data types, 734, 737
    for string types, **735**
    for variables, 747
Menu Bar tab, 627–628, *628*
Menu Customization dialog box, 627–629,
    627–628
Menu Groups tab, 627, *627*
menu option labels, **639–641**
menus
    accelerator keys in, **634–635**
    cascading, **631**, **710**
    for commands, **29–30**, *29*, **629–630**, 660
    creating, **626**
    Diesel for, **638**
    dividing lines on, 632
    files for, **624–625**

help messages for, **632–634**
loading, **626–629**, *627–628*
long lines in, 632
operation of, **629–635**
pull-down, **12–13**, *12–13*, **29–30**, *29*
right-click, **58–59**, *58–59*
submenus, **632**
    in VBA, 660, **708–710**, *709*
Merge Object with Current Design option,
    515, 525
meshes
    editing, **405–408**, *406*
    settings for, **397–398**, *397*
methods
    icons for, 692, *692*
    of objects, **773–774**, 796
Metric-Imperial Converter application
    captions in, **671–673**, *671*
    code window for, **673–678**, *673–675*
    GUI for, **668–670**, *668*
    running, **678–679**, *679*
    saving, **679–680**, *679–680*
mi command, 144
MicroCAD, 803
Microsoft Form objects, **764–766**, *765*
Microsoft Forms collection, **765**
Middle justification option, 164
Minimum Elev. options, 507
minus signs (-)
    in Diesel, 641
    in distance formats, 119
    in line type patterns, 644–645
    in pull-down menus, 631–632
mirror attribute for glass, **901–903**, *902–903*
Mirror command, 76, **143–145**, *144*, 226
mirror lines, 144
Mirror tool, 39, *39*, 144
mirroring
    objects, **143–145**, *144*
    with UCS, 394, *394*
missing properties, **798**
mistakes, correcting, 47, **132**
MKLTYPE dialog box, 592, *592*
MKSHAPE dialog box, 594
.mns extension, 625
.mnu extension, 624
*MODEL_SPACE block, 790–791, 816–818
ModelSpace collection, 761, 764
ModelSpace property, 826

Modemacro system variable, 636–637
Modify Dimension Style dialog box, 206, 486
Modify Distant Light dialog box, 875, *876*, 903
Modify Granite Material dialog box, 883, *883*, 885
Modify menu
   3D Operation menu
      Align command, 408
      Rotate 3D command, 410, 452
   Boolean menu
      Subtract command, 489
      Union command, 489
   Clip menu
      Image command, 591
      Xref command, 591
   Copy command, 142
   Erase command, 96
   Extend command, 104
   Fillet command, 100
   In-place Xref command, 284
   Mirror command, 144
   Object menu
      Attribute menu, Block Attribute Manager
         command, 323
      Attribute menu, Global command, 320
      Attribute menu, Single command, 317
      Polyline command, 407
      Text menu, Edit command, 213
   Offset command, 98, 116
   Polyline command, 375
   Rotate command, 137
   Solids Editing menu
      Subtract command, 443
      Union command, 441
   Text command, 165–167, 171
   Trim command, 105
Modify Spotlight dialog box, 898
Modify Standard Material dialog box, 884–885,
   884, 901–902
Modify tab, 548
Modify toolbar, **38–40**, 93, *93*
Modify Zones option, 508
modifying. *See* editing
module-level scope, **748**
modules
   icons for, 692, *692*
   VBA, 661
More menu
   Adjust command, 418
   Adjust Clipping Planes command, 423
   Swivel Camera command, 422

More Options dialog box, 901
Move Copy Rotate tool, 576
Move Down option, 325–326
Move Faces tool, 460–461, *460*
Move Text, Add Leader option, 220
Move Text, No Leader option, 220
Move tool, 39, *39*, 60, 69–71
Move Transform Type-in dialog box, 517
Move UCS origin tool, 395
Move Up option, 325–326
moving
   arcs, 68–69
   blocks, 283
   dimension text, **200–201**, *201*, **219–221**,
      219, *221*
   with grips, 72, **75–76**
   Move Copy Rotate tool for, **576–577**
   objects, **65**, *66*, **75–76**
   surfaces, **460–462**, *461–462*
   in UCS, **366–367**, *367–368*, *380*
   vertices, 226
   Wipeout objects, 579
mtext, **168–171**, *168–170*
mullions, 555
multidimensional arrays, **740**
multiline text, **168–171**, *168–170*
Multiline Text Editor, 168–171, *169*, 214, *214*
Multiline tool, 39, *39*
Multiline Text tool, 40, *40*
MultiPage controls, 664–665
multiple dimensions, editing, **215**
Multiple Entity Stretch tool, 576, *576*
Multiple Pedit tool, 578–579, *579*
Multiple selection option, 67

N

Name property for controls, 668, 672
named objects, 286
named objects dictionary, 820
Named UCSs tab, 365, *366*
Named View tab, 385
Named Viewports tab, 372–373, *373*
namedobjdict function, 820
names
   attributes, 326
   buttons, 619
   controls, 665, 668, 672
   drawings, **22**

entities, **815–816**
event procedures, 775
files, 44
icons, 621
layers, 563
line types, 644
macros, 686
objects, 659
text styles, 161
toolbars, 613–614
UCS, 365–366
in VBA, **736**
    capitalization of, 689–690
    constants, 741
Nclose option, 407
Nearest Osnap button, 268
negative numbers
    for arcs, 146
    integers, 845–846
nesting
    If statements, 754
    VIZblocks, 536
New Command Alias dialog box, 589, *589*
New Dimension Style dialog box, 196, *196–197*
    Alternate Units tab, 204–206, *205*
    Fit tab, 203, *203*
    Lines And Arrows tab, 201–204, *202*
    Primary Units tab, 197–199, *198*
    Text tab, 199–201, *200*
New Distant Light dialog box, 871, *871*
new drawings, **42–47**
New Label Template command, 353
New Label Template dialog box, 353
New Label Template tool, 351–353, *351*
New Link Template command, 346
New Link Template dialog box, 346, *346*
New Link Template tool, 346
New menu, Text Document command, 336
New options
    for boundary sets, 186
    for toolbars, 613
New Point Light dialog box, 890–891, *890*
New Query dialog box, 342, *342*
New Record command, 344
New Scene dialog box, 896, *896*
New Spotlight dialog box, 893
New Standard Materials dialog box, 906
New Text Style dialog box, 161, *161*
New Toolbar dialog box, 614, *614*
New View dialog box, 385

New Viewports tab, 371, 372
newBlockReferenceIdIterator method, 836
newIterator function, 835–836, 838
newsgroups, 607–608
Next clauses, 758
night scene lighting, **892–893**, *894–895*
non command, 281
nonorthogonal objects, dimensions for,
    234–239, *236–238*, *240*
Normal hatch pattern style, 185
normal vectors, **862–863**
normalized vectors, 859
normals, 538
North Location dialog box, 874, *874*
not equal to operator (<>), 753, 755
notes
    for arrows and dimensions, **240–244**,
        243–244
    linked text documents for, **571–572**
    in Paper Space, **485–487**
noun/verb selection method, **68–72**
Number of Points leader option, 243
Number of Sides polygon prompt, 235
number signs (#), 746

O

o command, 98, 116
Object Browser, **742–746**, *742–745*
Object Coordinate System (OCS), 861
Object lists, 673
Object options for slices, 456
object-oriented programming. *See* ObjectARX
    environment; ObjectDBX environment
Object Osnap tab, 233–234
Object Selection cursor, 54, *54*
Object-Selection mode, 60
Object Snap flyout, 135
Object Snap tab, 133–134, *134*
Object Snap toolbar, 147–148
Object Snaps (Osnaps). *See* Osnap Tracking and
    overrides
Object Type rollout, 541
object types
    adding, **913**
    for hatch patterns, **185**
Object UCS tool, 377, *378*
ObjectARX environment, 602, **830–831**
    container iteration in, **834–836**

for database access, **831–832**
objects in, **832–834**
ObjectDBX environment
  angles in, 854
  binary data in, 865
  Booleans in, 851
  character sets in, 856
  colors in, 850
  coordinate systems in, 861–862
  database settings in, **839**
  dates in, 855
  dictionaries in, **838**
  entity handling in, **836–837**
  enumerations in, 849
  group codes in, 849
  handles in, 857
  integers in, 845–848
  pointers in, 857
  points in, 858
  real numbers in, 852
  result buffers in, **839**
  strings in, 855
ObjectIDs, 792
ObjectName property, 827
objects, **760**. *See also* entities
  in ActiveX Automation, **825–826**
  aligning, **408–409**, *409*
  associating dimensions with, **228–231**,
    229–230
  in AutoLISP, **820–822**
  blocked. *See* blocks
  classes of, **760–761**
  collections of, **761–762**
  converted to blocks, 263
  copying, **141–143**, *142–143*
  covered, **798–799**
  in databases, **787–788**
    combining into blocks, **790–791**
    dictionaries, **789–790**
    embedding, **794**
    identifying, **792–793**
    linking, **793–794**
    pointers for, **857–858**
    symbol tables, **788–789**
  for defining surfaces, **398–399**, *400–401*
  deselecting, 61
  drawing, 673, **762**, *763*
    Application object, **762**
    Documents collection, **763–764**

in DXF, **810–812**
editing, **72–78**, **224–226**, *224*
extruding
  along circular surface, **403–405**, *404*
  along straight lines, **401–402**,
    402–403
finding, **349–350**, *349*
for layer control, **565–566**
Microsoft Forms, **764–766**, *765*
mirroring, **143–145**, *144*
moving, **65**, *66*, **75–76**
named, 286
names of, 659
nonorthogonal, dimensions for, **234–239**,
  236–238, 240
in ObjectARX, **832–834**
overlapping, 92, *92*, **189–191**, *190*
properties of, **84–85**, *85*, **796–798**
rotating. *See* rotating
selecting, **59–62**, *61–62*
  base points for, **62–66**
  noun/verb method, **68–72**
  options for, **66–68**
stretching, **73–75**, *74*, **576**
trimming, **577**
unblocking, 283
Objects option, 297
OBJECTS sections, 810
oblique angle for dimension text, 215
Oblique Angle option, 162
oblique dimension lines, *245*
Oblique options, 215
OCS (Object Coordinate System), 861
ODBC (Open Database Connectivity), **334**,
  338–339, *338*
ODBC Microsoft Access Setup dialog box,
  338–339, *338*
Offset command, **97–100**, *98–99*, 116
  distance with, **100**, 119
  errors with, 132
  vs. Fillet, 118
Offset Faces tool, 462, *462*
Offset from Dim Line option, 201, *201*
Offset From Origin option, 202
Offset tool, 39, *39*
offsets
  in databases, **859–860**
  for dimensions, 194, *194*
  for lines, **102–103**, *103*

for surfaces, **462**, *463*
for UCS orientation, **379–380**, *380*
One Object option, 536
One-to-One option, 536
online Help facility, 712
online services, **607–608**
Open a Drawing option, 4, 115
Open Database Connectivity (ODBC), **334**, 338–339, *338*
Open Drawings button, 290
Open-DWG Alliance, 840–841
open mode, 833
Open VBA Project dialog box, 700, *700–702*
Open Visual Basic Editor option, 700
openBlockBegin function, 836
openBlockEnd function, 836
opening
    bitmap files for icons, 621
    databases, **340–341**
    drawings, **4–5**, *4–6*
    objects, **701**, **832–834**
    toolbars, **616–617**
openings
    floors with, **522–527**, *523–526*
    marking, **102–103**, *103*
    walls, **126–132**, *127–131*
operands in VIZ, 505
operators in Diesel, 636
Option Base statement, **740**
Option Explicit statement, **737–738**
OptionButton controls, 664
options, choosing, **55–59**, *57*
Options dialog box
    for associative dimensions, 227
    for background color, 15, *16*
    for command windows, 17–18
    for crosshair cursor, 20, *20*
    for Data Link files, 339
    for grips, 264
    for isolines, 445
    for keyword color, 689, *689*
    for right-clicking, 34
    for scrollbars, 17
    for smoothness, 875
    for VBA, **711**, *711*
        Editor tab, **711–714**
        General tab, **714**, *714*, 716
        for Option Explicit, 738
Or command, 245
order of controls, **779–781**

Ordinate Dimension tool, 246, *246*
ordinate dimensions, **245–247**, *246*
orientation
    of dimension text, 201
    with UCS, **377–381**, *378*, *380*, *382*, **383–384**, *384*
    of VIZblocks, 537
Origin UCS tool, 364, *364*, 380
origins
    for dimensions, 194, *194*
    for hatch patterns, 177
    for line groups, 651, *652*
    in ordinate dimensions, 245–246
    for UCS, 245–246, 365, *365*, 370, **378–381**, *380*
    in WCS, 860
Ortho button, 138
orthogonal projections, 475
Orthogonal views, **478–479**, *480*, 515
Orthographic UCSs tab, 363–365, *363*
Osnap Flyout toolbar, 147–148
Osnap marker, 54, *54*
Osnap menu, 63–65
Osnap Tracking and overrides, 54, 135
    for base points, 63–64, *64*
    for center of circles, 307
    for dimensions, **233–234**
    disabling, 60
    for polylines, 388, *389*
    in UCS, 367
Other Predefined tab, 181–182, *181*
Outdent command, 724
Outer hatch pattern style, 185
Over the Dimension Line, with a Leader option, 204
Over the Dimension Line, without a Leader option, 204
overlapping objects
    display order with, **189–191**, *190*
    lines, 92, *92*
Override option, 505
ownership for links, 793

P

p-code, 732
    in debugging, 724
    options for, 714
Pack & Go dialog box, 582–583, *583*

Pack 'n Go feature, **582–584**, *583–584*
Pack 'n Go tool, 582, *582*
Palette tab, 769, *769*
Pan button, 276–277
panning in perspective views, **416–417**
paper clip symbols for linked files, 532
Paper Space, dimensions in, **485–487**
*PAPER_SPACE block, 791, 816–818
PaperSpace property, 826
Parameter Info feature, 773, *773*
parameters, **781–782**
    help for, 713, *713*
    for methods, 773, *773*
    for terrains, **505–506**, *505*
Parameters rollout, **505–506**, *505*
parentheses ()
    for arrays, 738
    in Diesel, 636–637
    for functions, 604
    for methods, 774
Parquet tile pattern, 178
Paste command, 723
Paste tool, 289
patterns
    hatch. *See* hatch patterns
    for line types, 644
pause function, 604
pausing
    in AutoLISP programs, 605
    for input in menus, **630–631**
PCX files, 917
people in 3D models, **913–915**, *914–915*
periods (.), 50, 853
Perpendicular Osnap, 154
perspective views, **411–415**
    animation in, **427**
    camera in, **418–423**, *419–423*
    clipping planes in, **423–426**, *424–426*
    turning on, **416–417**, *416*
    visual aids in, **417**, *418*
    zooming in, 419, *420*
PHANTOM linetypes, *643*
Photo Raytrace Render Options dialog box, 901
Photo Real Render Options dialog box,
    877–878, *878*
Pick Operand rollout, **505**, *505*
Pick Point setting, 255
pick points
    with attributes, 307
    with hatch patterns, 178, 187

pickboxes, 32–33, *32–33*, 96
picking. *See* selecting
Pin Riser Count setting, 542–544
plan views, 48
planar entities, 862
plans for VIZ
    importing, **514–521**, *515–522*
    setting up, **508–514**, *509–513*
Pljoin command, 597
Pljoin.dwg file, 597
PlotConfigurations collection, 829
plus signs (+)
    in Diesel, 636, 641
    in menus, 631
point filters, blips with, **277–280**, *279*
point lists, **858–859**
Point Selection cursor, 54, *54*
point selection mode, 47
point style, macro for, 605
Point tool, 39, *39*
pointer arrow, 26
pointers
    in databases, **857–858**
    for links, 793
points
    coordinates for, 92–93, 858–859
    in databases, **858–864**
    for dimensions, **216**
    indicating, **62–66**
    selecting, 44–45
    with UCS, 379
Pol command, 235
Polar button, 46
polar coordinates, **48–49**, *49*, **97**
Polar Tracking feature, 46, 54, *54*
Polygon tool, 39, *39*, 235
polygons, dimensioning, **235–239**, *236–238*, *240*
Polyline tool, 39, *39*, 436
Polyline Join tool, **596–597**
polylines
    for 3D views, 375–376, *377*
    extruding, **436–437**, **445–449**,
        446–448, *450*
    filleting, **596–597**, *597*
    for hatch patterns, 186
    for meshes, **388**, *389*
    properties of, **577–578**
    revolving, **450–454**, *451–454*
    for solid modeling, **436–440**, *437–440*
    with UCS, 379

position
    arcs, 139
    hatch patterns, **176–179**, *177–178*
    menu bar and toolbar, 708
    text boxes, 719
    toolbox controls, **666–667**
PostScript files, 917
pound signs (#), 746
precision of real numbers, 852
Precision option, 198
predefined hatch patterns, 178–179
Preferences dialog box, 54
prefixes for constants, 743
Preserve Access to Individual Objects option,
    535–536
Preset attribute option, 312
preset values, changing properties with,
    767–770, *768–770*
Preview button, 290, 293
previewing
    blocks, 293–294, *294*
    images, 5, *5*
Previous options
    for selections, 65, 67
    in zooming, 125
Primary Units tab, 197–199, *198*
primitives, 430–432, *432*, **438–440**, *438–440*
    boolean operations with, 430–433, *433*
    creating, **434–436**, *435–436*
    extruding polylines for, **445–449**,
        446–448, 450
    joining, **440–444**, *441–444*
    revolving polylines for, **450–454**, *451–454*
Print-ACADProject dialog box, 722, *722*
Print Setup dialog box, 722, *722*
printing UserForms, **721–722**, *722*
private scope, **747**
private-module level scope, **748**
procedure level scope, **747**
Procedure lists, 673–675, *675*
procedures, **776–779**, *776*
    declaring, 677
    event, 662, **674–678**, *675*, 774–775
    static, 748
processTwoValues procedure, 782
Product Support on Point A option, 82
Profiles tool, 12
program statements, **732**
programs, **782**

Project Explorer window, **716–717**, *717*
project files
    icons for, 692, *692*
    loading, **699–703**, *700–702*
Projection menu, Perspective command, 416
Prompt for Width option, 242
Prompt Only If File Cannot Be Found
    option, 539
prompts, 27
    for attributes, 304, 306, 310
    for commands, **30–32**, *31–32*
    responding to, **55–59**
properties and Properties dialog box, **767**
    for attributes, 309–310, *309–310*, 318–319,
        318, **323–326**, *323–325*
    for block detection, **266–267**, *267*
    for captions, 671–672, *671*
    changing values of, **767–773**, *768–772*
    defined vs. calculated, **797**
    for dimension text, 219–220
    for flyouts, **622–624**
    for hatch patterns, **182–183**, *183*
    icons for, 692, *692*
    missing, **798**
    for objects, **84–85**, *85*, **796–798**
    for polylines, 375, **577–578**
    for solids, **491–492**, *492*
    for text, **166–168**, *166–167*, 171
    for toolbars, 612–613
Properties tool
    for dimensions, 213
    importance of, **248**
Property Settings dialog box, 188, *188*
proxies, 913
ptx macro, 605
public scope, **747**
public-module level scope, **748**
pull-down menus, **12–13**, *12–13*, **29–30**, *29*
purging drawings, 298

Q

Qdim command, 231
Query Editor dialog box, 342–343, *342*
Query for Selections option, 918
Query tool, 342
question marks (?)
    for linked files, 532
    as wildcard characters, 746

Quick Dimension tool, 231
Quick Leader tool, 240
Quick Query tab, 342–343, *342*
Quick Setup Wizard, **9–11**, *9–11*, 42–43, *43*
quotation marks (' ")
    in distance formats, 119
    in macros, 604
    in VBA, 688

R

r command, 282
radians for angles, 854
radii
    for arcs, 139
    dimensions for, **239**, *240*
    with Fillet, 100–101
Radius Dimension tool, 239
Radius of Circle prompt, 235
Range frame, 722
ranges
    of characters in databases, **856–857**
    of real numbers, 852
raster images, clipping, 590–591
Ray Casting option, 185
Ray Trace shadow method, 875
Ray Tracing, **900–904**, *902–904*
Raytrace Rendering Options dialog box, 920
real numbers, **852–855**
rec command, 134
recalling layer settings, **562–565**, *563–564*
records
    in databases, **341–344**
    in dictionaries, 789–790
Rectangle command, 134–135
Rectangle tool, 39, *39*
redefining blocks, **326–327**
Redo command, 47, 723
Redo tool, 47
Redraw command, 280, 282
Redraw tool, 53, 905
Refedit toolbar, 285
Reference Edit dialog box, 284, *284*
Reference Elev. option, 507
reflections in 3D models, **900–904**, *902–904*
reflectivity for materials, 883
Reg command, 489
reg flags, 532
Regen command, 53

regeneration, controlling, 53
Region.dwg drawing, **489**, *490–491*
Region tool, 40, *40*, 489
Region Zoom tool, 519
regions, 470–471, **488–489**, *490–491*
registered application table, 788
RegisteredApplications collection, 826
relative coordinates, **48–52**, *49–52*, **95–97**, *96*
Reload button, **533**
Remote Text objects, 572–574
Remove Islands option, 184
Rename options
    for attributes, 326
    for UCS, 366
renaming
    attributes, 326
    drawings, **22**
    toolbars, 613
    UCS, 366
Render dialog box, 869, 873, 916–919
Render tool, 869, *869*, 873
Render toolbar, 868
Render window, **916–917**, *916*
Renderable option, 554
Rendered Object Smoothness setting, 875
rendering 3D models, **867–868**
    background scenes for, **886–887**, *886–888*
    Elevation view in, 921, *922*
    to files, **917–918**
    landscape and people in, **910–915**, *911–912,*
        914–915
    lighting effects for, **888–899**, *890–892,*
        894–899
    materials for, **879–885**, *880–886*
    Ray Tracing in, **900–904**, *902–904*
    to Render window, **916–917**, *916*
    resolution settings in, **919–920**, *919*
    setting up for, **868–869**, *869–870*
    shadows in, **875–879**, *876–879*
    smoothing images in, **920–921**, *921*
    sunlight angle for, **870–874**, *871–874*
    texture maps for, **904–908**, *905–907, 909*
Repeat command, 102
repeating code, loops for, **757**
    For, **757–759**
    While, **759**
repetitive tasks. *See* macros
Replace command, 723
replacing text, **569–571**, *570–571*

Report dialog box, 584, *584*
Require Variable Declaration option, 712, 738
Rescale to Match Units option, 537
Reset command, 725
resizing
    text boxes, **719–721**
    windows, 708
resolution in rendering 3D models, **919–920**, *919*
Resolve External Reference File dialog box,
    539, *539*
Resolve External References (Xrefs) option, 539
resource files, 625
Restart List command, 265
restarting commands, 102
result buffers, **839**
Retain option, 263
Retain Boundaries option, 185
Retriangulate option, 506
returning to AutoCAD, **680–681**
Reuse Current annotation option, 242
Reuse Next annotation option, 242
Rev command, 451
revising. *See* editing
Revision Cloud tool, 581, *581*
revision clouds, **581–582**, *582*
Revolve tool, 451, *451*
Revolved Surface tool, 403, *403*
revolving polylines, **450–454**, *451–454*
Right-Click Customization option, 34
right-clicking, 30
    for ending commands, **34**
    menu options in, **58–59**, *58–59*
right-hand rule, 860
right-side views, **475–479**
Right UCS orientation, 364, *364*
Riser Ht setting, 542, 544
ro command, 137
root dictionaries, 789–790
Rotate command, 76, 137, 226
Rotate Faces tool, 464–465, *465*
Rotate method, 773, *773*
Rotate option, 215
Rotate tool, 39, *39*, 137
rotating
    in 3D space, **410**, 452–453, *453*
    blocks, 258, *258*, **271–273**, *272–273*, 283
    dimension text, 215, **221–222**
    dimensions, 226, 237, *237*
    doors, **137–138**, *138*

with grips, **76–77**, *77*
line types, 648
Move Copy Rotate tool for, **576–577**
perspective views, 414, *414*
stairs, 544
surfaces, **464–465**, *465*
text, 163, 165
UCS, **366–367**, *367–368*, **381–383**, *382*, 448
Rotation option, 163, 165
roughness for materials, 883
rounding corners, **100–102**, *101*, **456–457**, *457*
rounding numbers, 813, 853
rows, database, 334, **341–344**
Rtext command, 572–573
rubber banding, **44–45**, *45*, 52
Ruled Surface tool, 399, *399*
ruled surfaces, **398–399**, *400–401*
Run menu, Sub/UserForm command,
    678, 725, 728
Run Sub/UserForm tool, 696
run time vs. design time, **767**
RunMetricToImperialConverter procedure,
    703–704
running
    applications, **678–679**, *679*
    code, **725**
    macros, **696–697**, *696–697*
Running Osnaps, 60

S

Save As dialog box
    for attribute data, 332
    in VBA, 680, *680*, 695, *695*
Save button, 21, *21*
Save Drawing As dialog box, 21–22, *21*, 44
Save/Save As option, 533
Save UCS with Viewport option, 371, 385
saving
    applications, **679–680**, *679–680*
    attribute data, **332–333**, *332*
    drawings, **21–22**, *21–22*
    files, 71
    icons, 621
    layer settings, **562–565**, *563–564*
    macros, **604–605**, **694–695**, *695*
    rendered views, 916–917
    UCS, **365–366**, *366*

Savoye-ground.dwg file, 508
Scale command, 76
Scale tool, 39, *39*
scaling
    blocks, 257, 283
    dimensions, 234, 486
    with inserting, 313
    materials, 883
Scene tool, 895, *895*
Scenes dialog box, 895, *896*, 899
scenes for lighting, **895–899**, *896–899*
scope, **746**
    procedure level, **747**
    public vs. private, **747**
    Static keyword in, **748–751**, *749*
    UserForm and module-level, **747–748**
screen, **11–12**
    cleaning up, **53**
    command window, **17–18**, *17–18*
    crosshair cursor, **20**, *20*
    drawing area, **15–17**, *16*
    scrollbars, **17**
    status bars, **18–19**, *18–19*
    title bars and pull-down menus, **12–13**, *12–13*
    toolbars, **13–15**, *14–15*
    UCS icon, **19**, *19*
Screen Coordinate System (SCS), 861
ScrollBar controls, 665
scrollbars
    turning off, **17**
    on UserForms, 665
SCS (Screen Coordinate System), 861
Search Results pane, 745
Search tab, **80–82**, *80–81*
Search the Web For option, 81
searching
    for blocks, **264–267**, *265*
    for database records, **341–344**
    for files, 290
    in help system, **80–82**, *80–81*
    with Object Browser, **744–746**
    for objects, **349–350**, *349*
    for text, **569–571**, *570–571*
Second Point option, 140
SECTION string, 809
Section tool, 487, *487*
sections
    drawing, **487**, *488*
    in DXF files, 809

seek function, 835
Select All command, 727
Select and Move tool, 517–519, 544, 550
Select and Rotate tool, 544
Select by Name tool, 500, 516
Select Case statement, **756–757**
Select Color dialog box, *473*, 474
Select Data Source dialog box, 337–338, *337*
Select Drawing File dialog box, 477
Select File dialog box, 5, *5*, 115
Select File to Import dialog box, 514, 525
Select Layers dialog box, 539, *539*
Select Menu File dialog box, 627
Select Object dialog box, 500
Select object to offset: prompt, 98, 116
Select Object tool, 520, 526
Select Objects control, 663
Select Objects dialog box, 516–519, 530
Select Objects: prompt, 104–105
Select Project dialog box, 686
Select Shape File dialog box, 594
Select Text File dialog box, 572
selecting
    cutting edges, 151–152, *152*
    Express tools for, **598–600**
    menus, 627
    objects, **59–62**, *61–62*
        base points for, **62–66**
        noun/verb method, **68–72**
        options for, **66–68**
    points, 44–45
    previous selections, 65
    right-click menu options, **58–59**, *58–59*
    with subtraction, **598–599**
Selection tab, 264
Selection Tools menu, Get Selection Set command, 600
semicolons (;), 630
sentinel strings, 808
Separate tool, 474
separating divided solids, **474**, *474*
sequencing in DXF files, 806
serialization with DXF. *See* DXF (Drawing Interchange Format) files
setAt function, 838
setCecolor function, 839
setColor function, 837
setLinetype function, 837
Settings dialog box, 325, *325*

Setup Choices dialog box, 562
Setup Drawing tool, 485
Setup option, 722
Setup Profile tool, 482–484
Setup View tool, 478–482
setvar function, 822–823
SetVariable method, 830
shading in perspectives, 417, *418*
Shading Modes menu
   Gouraud Shaded command, 427
   Hidden command, 417
Shadow Map method, **875–879**, *876–879*
Shadow Options dialog box, 876–877, *876*,
   879, 903
Shadow Volumes/Ray Trace Shadows
   option, 903
shadows
   adding, **875–879**, *876–879*
   Ray Tracing for, **903–904**, *904*
shape definitions, 594
shapes
   closing, 95
   creating, **594–596**, *595*
   grips for editing, 72
   for line types, 648, *649*
   with UCS, 379
sharing information. *See also* exporting; importing
   accessing databases for, **333–345**
   Design Center for, **289–295**, *291–296*
   dragging and dropping for, **286–289**,
      287–288
   inserting drawings, **298–299**
   linking databases for, **345–355**
   Wblock for, **296–298**, *297*
sharpness of materials, 885
Shelf Specification application, 776–779, *776*
Shell tool, 469, *469*
shells, turning solids into, **469**, *470*
Shift key
   in accelerator keys, 634–635
   for base points, 63
shortcut menus, 34, 58–59, *59*
Show Labels command, 354
Show Options option, 533
Show ToolTips option, 613, 716
.shx extension, 648, 798
sides of openings, 127
signed integers in databases, **845–848**
Simplification rollout, **506–507**, *506*

single-line text
   inserting, **162–164**, *163*
   justification points for, **164–165**, *164–165*
   properties of, **166–168**, *166–167*
   wording of, **165–166**, *165*
single quotes (')
   in distance formats, 119
   in VBA, 688
Single selection option, 68
size
   arcs, 139
   crosshair cursor, **20**, *20*, 54
   drawings, 10–11
   grips, 73
   hatch patterns, **179–180**
   shadow maps, 876, 878–879, *879*
   text, 161
   text boxes, **719–721**
   toolbox controls, **666–667**
   windows, 708
skeleton procedures, 775
skewing
   dimension lines, **244–245**, *245*
   UCS, 382–383
Skip Hatches and Points option, 539
slashes (/)
   in Diesel, 636, 641
   for options, 56
Slice command, 454
Slice tool, 454, *454*
sliding glass doors, **147–155**, *147–154*
Smooth surface option, 407
smoothness
   in 3D models, **920–921**, *921*
   of arcs and circles, **874–875**
Snapbase system variable, 177, 179
soft owners, 793
soft pointers, 793
softness of shadows, 879
Solid command, 179
Solid hatch pattern, 179
Solid to Top of Zone option, 508
Solidedit command, **471–472**
solids and solid modeling, **430–432**
   for 2D drawings, **488–489**, *490–491*
   chamfering in, **458–459**, *458–459*
   command line for, **471–472**
   copying faces and edges on, **470–471**
   creating primitives for, **434–436**, *435–436*

deleting surfaces, **463–464**, *464*
extruding surfaces, **467–469**, *468*
moving surfaces, **460–462**, *461–462*
offsetting surfaces, **462**, *463*
polylines for, **436–440**, *437–440*
properties of, **491–492**, *492*
with regions, **488–489**, *490–491*
rotating surfaces, **464–465**, *465*
rounding corners on, **456–457**, *457*
separating divided solids, **474**, *474*
splitting, **454–456**, *455*
stereolithography in, **492–493**
surface features for, **472–474**, *473*
tapering surfaces, **466**, *466–467*
turning solids into shells, **469**, *470*
with UCS, 379
Solids toolbar, 434, *434*
Solids Editing toolbar, 440, *440*
source text files, 625
space planning and hatch patterns,
  188–191, *190*
spaces
  in attribute values, **321**
  in distances, 119
  in fixed-length strings, 735
  in hatch patterns, 175
special characters, 171
Specify base point or displacement: prompt, 142
Specify first corner point: prompt for rect-
  angles, 134
Specify first part of mirror line: prompt, 144
Specify first point: prompt, 94
Specify insertion point: prompt, 277–278
Specify next point: prompt, 94
Specify offset distance: prompt, 97, 100
Specify On Screen option, 257, 477
Specify other corner point: prompt, 136
Specify point on side to offset: prompt, 98
Specify rotation angle: prompt, 137, 258
Specify second part of mirror line: prompt, 144
Specify second point of arc: prompt, 140
Specify second point of displacement: prompt, 142
Specify start point of arc: prompt, 139
Sphere tool, 439
spheres, 430, *432*, 439, *439*
spherical coordinate format, **387–388**
SpinButton controls, 665
Spiral Stair option, 543
spiral stairs, **543–545**, *544*

Spline option, 549
Spline Rendering Group option, 534
Spline tool, 39, *39*
splines for topography, **498–502**, *498–502*
splitting solids, **454–456**, *455*
spotlights, **892–893**, *894–895*, 898, *898–899*
spreadsheet files, extracting data for, 333
square brackets ([])
  for line types, 647–648
  for menu items, 633–635
ssget function, 813
STA (Stereolithograph Apparatus), 493
stairs
  circular, **543–545**, *544*
  finishing, **545–546**, *545–547*
  parameters for, **542–543**, *542*
  tracing over imported lines, **540–542**, *541*
  walls for, **547–552**, *548–551*
Standard cursor, 53, *54*
Standard dimension style, 195, *195*
standard hatch patterns, *650*
standard line types, **642**, *643*
standard modules, **685–687**, *685–686*
standard symbols, 55, *55*
Standard text style, 160
Standard toolbar, 14, 708, **715–716**, *715*
standard windows, 69–71, *70*
Start from Scratch option, 6
start-section brackets, 809
starting applications from macros, **703–704**
starting points for arcs, 139, 146
StartPoint property, 827
startup, loading projects at, **701–702**, *702*
Startup dialog box, **4**
  for new drawings, **6–8**, *6–9*
  opening drawings in, **4–5**, *4–6*
Startup Suite dialog box, 701–702, *702*
StartUpPosition property, 768, *768*
statements, **732**
Static keyword, **748–751**, *749*
status bars, **18–19**, *18–19*
step function, 835
Steps clause, 758
stereolithography, **492–493**
Stitch Border option, 506
.stl extension, 493
Stlout command, 493
Stretch command, **73–75**, **224–226**
Stretch tool, 39, *39*, 224–226

stretching
    dimensioned objects, **224-226**, *224*
    lines, **73-75**, *74*
    objects, **576**
strings
    in binary DXF files, 807
    concatenating, 698
    in databases, **855-857**
    of dimensions, **231-232**, *232*
    memory for, **735**
Style option, 163
styles
    for arrows, **201-204**, *202-203*
    for dimensions, **194-207**, **218-223**,
        599-600, *599-600*, 788
    for Island Detection, **185**
    for text, **160-162**, *160-161*, 788
Su command, 443
Sub-Object button, 552
Sub statement, 688, 776
submenus, **632**
Subtract tool, 443, *443*
subtraction
    of primitives, 430, *431*, *433*, **443-444**,
        444, 489
    selection with, **598-599**
Sun Angle Calculator dialog box, 871-873, *872*
sunlight angle
    for 3D models, **870-874**, *871-874*
    for windows, 271
Super Hatch tool, **584-587**, *585*
SuperHatch dialog box, 585-587, *585*
Support Assistance option, 83
surfaces, **385**
    adding features to, **472-474**, *473*
    curved, **389-396**, *391*, *393-395*, *397*
    defining, **398-399**, *400-401*
    deleting, **463-464**, *464*
    edges of, 389-390, **396**
    extruding, **467-469**, *468*
    laying out forms for, **385-388**, *386-387*
    mesh settings for, **397-398**, *397*
    modeling, **429-430**
    moving, **460-462**, *461-462*
    offsetting, **462**, *463*
    polylines for, **388**, *389*
    rotating, **464-465**, *465*
    tapering, **466**, *466-467*
Surfaces toolbar, 396, *396*
Surftab1 system variable, 397, 402, 405

Surftab2 system variable, 397, 405
Surftype system variable, 407
swinging doors, **133-141**, *135-136*, *138*, *140*
SwitchIt1 procedure, 749-751
SwitchIt2 procedure, 749-751
Symbol Tables container, **788-789**
symbolic constants, **741-742**
symbols and symbol tables, 171
    in AutoLISP, 821
    in databases, **788-789**
    in expressions, 732
    standard, 55, *55*
syntax errors, **711-712**, *711-712*, 732
SYSCODEPAGE setting, 856
System tab, 768-769, *769*

T

T intersections, cleaning up, 122
Tab Delimited File option, 332
tab order, **779-781**
Tab Width setting, 714
TabIndex property, 781
tables
    database, 334
    two-dimensional arrays for, 740
TABLES sections, 809
tabs, spaces for, 714
TabStrip controls, 664
Tabulated Surface tool, 401, *401*
tags
    for blocks, 306, 309, 320
    in DXF files, 806
Taper Faces tool, 466, *466*
tapering
    extrusions, **445-446**, *446-447*
    surfaces, **466**, *466-467*
Targa files, 917
tblnext function, 816, 818
tblobjname function, 815-817
TDINDWG setting, 855
Template folder, 7
templates
    for drawings, **7-8**, *8-9*
    link, **346-347**, *346*
temporary tracking points, 135
terrains
    options for, **504-505**, *504*
        Color by Elevation rollout, **507-508**, *507*

Parameters rollout, **505–506**, *505*
Pick Operand rollout, **505**, *505*
Simplification rollout, **506–507**, *506*
splines for, **498–502**, *498–502*
updating, **502–504**, *502–504*
text, **159**
  for attributes, 307
  backgrounds for, **566–569**, *568*
  for dimensions, 194, *194*
    appending data to, **213–214**
    height of, **199–200**, *200*
    location and orientation of,
      200–201, *201*
    moving, **219–221**, *219, 221*
    rotating, **221–222**
    styles for, **218**
    tool for, **223**
  editing, **566–574**
  finding and replacing, **569–571**, *570–571*
  height of, 307
  in line types, 647–648
  multiline, **168–171**, *168–170*
  single-line, **162–168**, *163–167*
  style for, **160–162**, *160–161*, 788
  in title bars, 672
  for ToolTips, 716
  with UCS, 379
text boxes and TextBox controls,
  663, **665–667**
  position of, 719
  size of, **719–721**
text documents, linked, **571–572**
Text Fit tool, 574
text justification points, 164
text lines in command window, **17–18**, *17–18*
Text Mask tool, 567, *567*
Text Options group, 307
Text Options tab, 318, *318*
Text Style dialog box, 160–162, *160*
text style table, 788
Text tab, 199–201, *200*
Text Window, **83–84**, *84*, 264–265, *265*
TextBox_KeyDown procedure, 675–676
TextBox1_KeyDown procedure, 675–676, 678
TextBox1_KeyPress procedure, 778
TextBox2_KeyDown procedure, 676
TextBox2_KeyPress procedure, 778
TextBox3_KeyPress procedure, 778
TextStyles collection, 826
texture. *See* hatch patterns

texture maps, **904–908**, *905–907, 909*
TGA format, 917
thickness
  for trusses, 554
  for VIZblocks, 536
Thickness setting, 554
third-party software, **605–607**
ThisDrawing object, 673, **684–685**, *684*, 764
three-dimensional arrays, 740
Through option, 100
THUMBNAILIMAGE sections, 810
.tif extension and tiff files, 917
tildes (~), 632
tiled viewports, 371
Time function, 698–699
timers, 855
times
  in databases, **854–855**
  retrieving, 698–699
title bars, **12–13**, *12–13*
  color of, 670
  text in, 672
  in VBA, 661, 708
title blocks, 476
titles, menu, 629
.tlb libraries, 802
Toggle Breakpoint buttons, 718
ToggleButton controls, 664
Tol command, 247
Tolerance dialog box, 242
tolerance symbols, **247–248**, *247*
Tolerance tool, 247
Toolbar command, 616
toolbar flyouts, **28–29**, *28*
Toolbar menu, Inquiry command, 14
Toolbar properties dialog box, 612–613, *613*
toolbars
  buttons on, **26–27**, *26–27*, **618–624**
  creating, **614–616**
  docking, **13–15**, *14–15*
  flyouts with, 40–41, *40*
  opening from command line, **616–617**
  options for, **612–614**, *612–613*
  in VBA, 708, *709*, **715**
    Debug, **718**, *718*
    Edit, **717**, *718*
    standard, **715–716**, *715*
    UserForm, **719–721**, *719*
  working with, 41
Toolbars dialog box, **561**, **612–614**, *612*

toolbox controls, **662–667**, *662*
  dimensions and position of, **666–667**
  placing in UserForms, **665–667**
Toolbox icon, 662
tools, 104
Tools menu
  Attribute Extraction command, 328
  Customize Menu command, 627
  dbConnect command, 340
  Display Order menu
    Bring to Front command, 189
    Send to Back command, 189, 191
  Drafting Settings command, 133, 233
  Inquiry command, 83, 264
  List Entity Xdata command, 601
  Load Application command, 701, 703
  Macro menu
    Load Project command, 700, 703
    Macros command, 685, 696
    VBA Manager command, 701
    Visual Basic Editor command, 660
  Move UCS command, 381
  Named UCS command, 365, 370
  New UCS menu
    Object command, 377
    Origin command, 380, 450
    View command, 481
    World command, 450, 487
    Y command, 448
    Z Axis Rotate command, 381
  Options command. *See* Options dialog box
  Orthographic UCS command, 447
  Preferences command, 54
  UCS menu
    3 Point command, 390
    Named UCS command, 390, 481
    Origin command, 245
    World command, 386
    Z Axis Vector command, 382
  in VBA, **710–711**
  Xdata Attachment command, 601
ToolTips, 4, 613
  for flyouts, 28, *28*
  options for, 714
  text for, 716
  for toolbars, 14, 26
  VBA, 725
Top UCS orientation, 364, *364*
top views, **475–479**
Topics Found dialog box, 734, *734*

topography
  options in, **504–508**, *504–507*
  splines for, **498–502**, *498–502*
  updating, **502–504**, *502–504*
tori, 430, *432*, 439, *439*
Torus tool, 439
tr command, 105
Trace UCS option, 379
tracing over imported lines, **540–542**, *541*
tracking for blocks, **276–277**
Tracks line type, *647*
trailing spaces, 735
Transform gizmo, 550
transparency of materials, 883–884
transparent commands, 143
Tree View, 290–291
trees in 3D models, **910–915**, *911–912*, *914–915*
Trim tool, 39, *39*
Trim to Block Entities tool, 575
trimming, 105
  in blocks, 575
  Edgemode variable for, 152
  errors with, 132
  vs. Fillet, 122
  lines, **105–109**, *106–109*
  objects, **577**
  picking lines with, 124
  zooming for, 122–124, *123*
True Associative Dimensioning, **227–232**,
  227–230
True values, 755
trusses, **552–555**, *552–555*
TTF files, 798
tubes, modeling, 430, *431–432*
tubular trusses, 553, *553*
Turn Objects Layer tool, 566
two-car garage, **156–157**, *156*
two-dimensional arrays, 740
Txtpath.lsp tool, 574
Type keyword, 752
type libraries, 802
Type option, 175
types. *See* data types

U

U command, 47, 515
  with grips, 75
  for selecting, 61, 102

UCS (user coordinate system), **360**, *360*, 860
   controlling, **377**
   defining, **361–365**, *362*, *364*
   icon for, **19**, *19*, 360, **370–371**
   mirroring with, 394, *394*
   moving in, **366–367**, *367–368*
   orientation of, **377–381**, *378*, *380*, *382*,
     383–384, *384*
   origins for, 245–246, 365, *365*, 370,
     378–381, *380*
   rotating, **366–367**, *367–368*, **381–383**,
     382, 448
   saving, **365–366**, *366*
   in Symbol Tables container, 788
   working in, **366–371**, *367–369*
UCS command, 245, 377, 380, 384
UCS Control dialog box, 481
UCS dialog box, 363–365, *363*, *366*, 370, *370*
UCS toolbar, 363, *363*
UCS II toolbar, **395**, *395*
unblocking objects, 283
Uncheck All button, 329
Uncomment Block button, 717
underscores (_)
   for commands, 31
   in line type patterns, 644–645
   in names, 775
Undo button and command, 723
   for icons, 621
   for lines, 102, 107
   for object selection, 67
   for Trim and Extend, 132
Undo tool, 47
   for grips, 75
   for selecting, 61
ungrouping blocks, 283
Uni command, 441
Unicode character set, 856
Unify Normals option, 515, 538
Union tool, 441, *441*
unions of primitives, 430, *433*, 441, *442*, 489
unit vectors, 859
Units dialog box, 42–43, *43*
units of measurement, 10–11, *10*
   in databases, **854**
   default setting for, 43
   for dimensions, **197–199**, **204–206**, *205*
Unlock Objects Layer tool, 566
Unnamed option, 365–366

Up button, 290
Update View to Plan When UCS is Changed
   option, 371
updating
   DrawText macro, **698–699**
   labels, **572–574**, *573*
   VIZ changes, **502–504**, *502–504*
Use 1/2 of Lines option, 507
Use 1/2 of Points option, 506
Use 1/4 of Lines option, 507
Use 1/4 of Points option, 506
Use a Template option, 476
Use a Wizard option, 9
Use Background option, 901
use first point as displacement option, 63–64
Use Overall Scale Of option, 203
User Coordinate System object, 537
user coordinate system table, 788
User Coordinate Systems. *See* UCS (user coordi-
   nate system)
user-defined hatch patterns, 175
User Defined options, 175
user-defined types, 692, *692*, **752**
user input in menus, **630–631**
User Preferences tab
   for associative dimensions, 227
   for right-clicking, 34
UserCoordinateSystems collection, 826
UserForm modules, **661–662**, *661*
UserForm scope, **747–748**
UserForm toolbar, **719–721**, *719*
UserForms, 661, *661*
   placing toolbox controls in, **665–667**
   printing, **721–722**, *722*

V

values
   displaying, 713
   in expressions, 732–733
variables, **733–735**, *733*
   arrays of, **738–740**
   declaring, 712, **734–738**
   displaying values of, 713
   lifetime of, **748–752**
   scope of, **746–752**, *749*
   static, 748
Variant type, 735–736
vb prefix, 743

VBA (Visual Basic for Applications)
   for ActiveX Automation, 824
   applications in, 658, **782–783**
      running, **678–679**, *679*
      saving, **679–680**, *679–680*
      starting from macros, **703–704**
   captions in, **671–673**, *671*
   code window for, **673–678**, *673–675*
   coding in. *See* coding in VBA
   constants in, **740–746**, *742–745*
   data types in, **733–735**, *733*
      for arrays, 690, **738–739**
      defining, **752**
      memory for, 734, 737
   environment for, **659–660**, *660*
      IDE. *See* IDE (Integrated Development
         Environment)
      toolbox, **662–667**, *662*
      UserForm modules, **661–662**, *661*
   expressions in, **732–733**
   GUIs, creating, **668–670**, *668*
   macros in. *See* macros
   project files in, **699–703**, *700–702*
   returning to AutoCAD, **680–681**, **697**
   statements in, **732**
   variables in
      arrays of, **738–740**
      declaring, **734–738**
      scope in, **746–752**, *749*
VBA Manager dialog box, 701
vbaide command, 660
vectors in databases, **859–860**
Verify option, 312
verifying attributes, 307, 312
Vertex option, 548
vertical dimensions, 200, **209–210**, *210*
vertical lines, 46
vertices
   for 3D meshes, 407
   for curves, 548–550, *549–551*
   moving, 226
View Aligned option, 912
View AutoCAD button, 680, *680*
View Control dialog box, 319
View Linked Objects in Drawing tool, 350
View Linked Record in Table tool, 349
View menu
   3D Views menu
      Front command, 477

      Plan View command, 385
      SE Isometric command, 481
      Select command, 435
      SW Isometric command, 362
   Camera command, 411
   Code command, 661
   Display command, 19, *19*
   Hide command, 443
   Named View command, 312, 385
   Object command, 661, 674
   Object Browser command, 743
   Paper Space command, 477, 481
   Project Explorer command, 688, 704, 717
   Properties Window command, 671
   Redraw command, 280, 910
   Redraw View command, 53
   Render menu
      Landscape Edit command, 915
      Landscape New command, 910
      Lights command, 870, 875, 890,
         893, 903
      Mapping command, 907
      Materials command, 880, 883,
         901–902, 905
      Render command, 869, 873
      Scene command, 895, 899
   Set UCS command, 384
   Shade menu
      2D Wireframe command, 369
      Hidden command, 369
   Toolbars command, 715
   Toolbox command, 662
   User command, 515
   Viewports command, 371–372
   Views command, 515
   Zoom command, 361
View Selections hatch pattern option, 184
View slice option, 456
view table, 788
View UCS tool, 384, *384*
viewing
   built-in constants, **742–746**, *742–745*
   line types, *642*, *643*
Viewpoint Presets dialog box, 435, *435*
viewpoints, 435
viewport table, 788
viewports
   for 3D drawings, **371–376**, *373–375*, *377*
   hidden lines in, **482–484**, *484*

for standard views, **477–479**, *478*
in Symbol Tables container, 788
Viewports collection, 826
Viewports dialog box, 371–372, *371*, *373*
views
with 3D rotating, 410
perspective. *See* perspective views
for solid modeling, 435
standard, **475–479**
in Symbol Tables container, 788
Views button, 290
Views collection, 826
visibility of attributes, **322**, *323*
Visibility property, 850–851
Visible property, 767
Visual Aids menu
Compass command, 417
Grid command, 417
Visual Basic for Applications. *See* VBA (Visual
Basic for Applications)
Visual Basic Reference dialog box, 726, *726*, 734,
765, *765*
Visual C++ language, 831
visualization of blocks, 790
VisualLISP language, 812
VIZ, **497–498**
elevations and wall profiles in, **527–528**
File Link Manager in. *See* File Link
Manager
floors with openings in, **522–527**, *523–526*
options in, **504–508**, *504–507*
plans for
importing, **514–521**, *515–522*
setting up, **508–514**, *509–513*
stairs in
circular, **543–545**, *544*
finishing, **545–546**, *545–547*
parameters for, **542–543**, *542*
tracing over imported lines,
540–542, *541*
walls for, **547–552**, *548–551*
for topography, **498–502**, *498–502*
trusses in, **552–555**, *552–555*
updating changes in, **502–504**, *502–504*
VIZblocks, **534–538**
vl-load-com function, 824
Volumetric Shadows, 875
Vpoint command, 435

W

W command, 226
Walker, John, 803
walls
exterior, **115–118**, *116–117*
interior, **118–126**, *119–126*
laying out, **114**, *115*
openings for, **126–132**, *127–131*
in VIZ
profiles for, **527–528**
for stairs, **547–552**, *548–551*
Wblock command, **296–298**, *297*
WCS (world coordinate system), 360, *360*,
860–864
Wedge tool, 439–440
wedges, 430, *432*, 439–440, *440*
Weld option, 537
Wend clause, 759
What's New option, 83
When Rendering option, 506
While loops, **759**
width
of polylines, 578
of text, 161
Width Factor setting, 161
Width property, 767
wildcard characters, **746**
window blocks
creating, **267–270**, *268–270*
inserting, **271–283**, *272–274*, *276*, *279*, *282*
Window menu
open drawings on, 289
Tile Vertically command, 286
Window options, 67
Window Polygon option, 67
Window Polygons, 67, 226
windows
appearance of, 271
crossing, **69–71**, 224–226, *224*
for cutting edges, 151–152, *152*
mullions for, 555
resizing, 708
for selecting objects, 61–62, *62*, 67, **69–71**,
70–71
Windows Render Options dialog box, 916, *916*
Wipeout object, **567–569**
Wipeout tool, **578–580**, *579*

Wizards for new drawings, **9–11**, *9–11*
Wizards option, 42
word-wrap, 162
wording of single-line text, **165–166**, *165*
world coordinate system (WCS), 360, *360*, 860–864
World Wide Web (WWW) sites, **607–608**
WP command, 226
Write Block dialog box, 296–298, *297*
www.autodesk.com site, 606–607
www.cadence.com site, 608
www.omura.com site, 608
www.sybex.com site, 608

X

x axes, UCS for, 19
X Axis Rotate option, 381
x coordinates
    for points, 92, 858–859
    in status bar, 18
X scale factor for blocks, 258
Xaxis option, 410
Xdata Attachment tool, 601
Xdatum option, 246
XY/YZ/ZX slice option, 456

Y

y axes, UCS for, 19
Y Axis Rotate option, 381
y coordinates
    for points, 92, 858–859
    in status bar, 18
Y scale factor for blocks, 258

Y scale factor: prompt, 257
Yaxis option, 410
Ydatum option, 246

Z

Z Axis Rotate UCS tool, 381, *381*
Z Axis Vector UCS tool, 382–383, *383*
Z buffer shaded models, 869
z command, 123
z coordinates
    for points, 858–859
    in status bar, 18
Z factor for blocks, 258
Zaxis option
    with 3D rotating, 410
    with slicing, 456
zeros
    in dimension text, 199
    with fractions, 692
    leading, 50
Zigzag line type, *647*
Zones by Base Elevation list, 501–502, 508
Zoom command and zooming
    with hatch patterns, 187
    in perspective views, 419, *420*
    for trimming, 122–124, *123*
    Zoom Extents, 121
    Zoom Previous, 125, 259–260
Zoom Extent tool, 549
Zoom Extents tool, 40–41, *40*, 540
Zoom Extents All tool, 543, 545
Zoom Window flyout, *40*
Zoom Window option, 123, 259
zoom windows, 123, *123*, 259–260

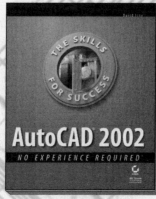

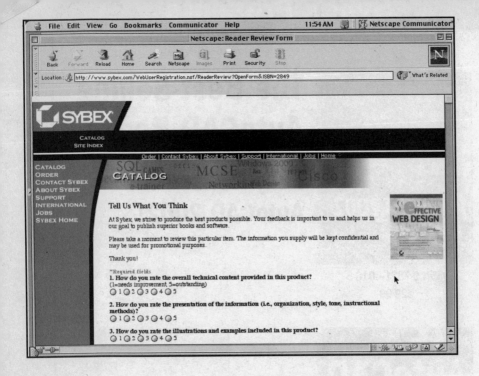

Your feedback is critical to our efforts to provide you with the best books and software on the market. Tell us what you think about the products you've purchased. It's simple:

1. Visit the Sybex website
2. Go to the product page
3. Click on **Submit a Review**
4. Fill out the questionnaire and comments
5. Click **Submit**

With your feedback, we can continue to publish the highest quality computer books and software products that today's busy IT professionals deserve.

www.sybex.com

SYBEX Inc. • 1151 Marina Village Parkway, Alameda, CA 94501 • 510-523-8233

About the Contributors

Some of the best—and bestselling—Sybex authors have contributed from their books to *AutoCAD 2002 Complete*.

Marion Cottingham, Ph.D., is the author of *Excel 2000 Developer's Handbook*, from Sybex. She is a Senior Lecturer in the Department of Computer Science and Software Engineering at the University of Western Australia and has been programming computers for twenty-four years. She has been developing applications with Microsoft Visual Basic since 1992 and runs professional development training courses for both industry and the general public.

David Frey has been teaching AutoCAD to architects, engineers, and high school students for the last eight years. His books for Sybex include *AutoCAD 2000: No Experience Required* and *AutoCAD 14: No Experience Required*. David holds a master's degree in architecture from the University of California at Berkeley.

George Omura is an architect and illustrator who has been using AutoCAD for fifteen years. As a CAD specialist, he has worked on design projects ranging from resort hotels to metropolitan transit systems to the prestigious San Francisco Library project. A graduate of the University of California at Berkeley, he is the all-time bestselling AutoCAD author. George's other AutoCAD books, all from Sybex, include *AutoCAD Instant Reference*, and *Mastering AutoCAD for Mechanical Engineers.*

Dietmar Rudolph is a CAD consultant and author. He heads CR/LF Corporation in Essen, Germany, and is a Vice-President of CADLock, Inc., in Fredericksburg, OH. Since 1986 he has written, translated, and published more than 50 books and hundreds of articles about CAD and AutoCAD.

MASTERING™
3D STUDIO VIZ® 3
GEORGE OMURA

ISBN 0-7821-2775-4
1,152 pages
$49.99

3D Studio VIZ 3 is a powerful real-time 3D design and modeling tool from Autodesk and Discreet, the makers of AutoCAD and 3D Studio MAX. This is the most comprehensive guide to VIZ available—it shows architects, mechanical and civil engineers, planners, interior designers, and other design professionals how to create 3D models quickly and intuitively. From bestselling *Mastering Auto-CAD* author George Omura, this book describes the full range of 3D Studio VIZ's capabilities, such as lighting and environmental effects, photo-realistic rendering, presentation options, and interoperability with other Autodesk products. The accompanying CD is filled with design examples, animated walkthroughs, and routines.

MASTERING™
AutoCAD® VBA
MARION COTTINGHAM

ISBN: 0-7821-2871-8
704 pages
$49.99

You can do more with AutoCAD VBA, and you can learn to do it with *Mastering AutoCAD VBA*. Perfect for AutoCAD users who want to improve their productivity and workflow. AutoCAD with VBA allows users to link to other applications, create macros and use common libraries and VBA management tools. The book is also packed with valuable tutorials to have you up-to-speed quickly with AutoCAD VBA's unique features. The companion CD includes all the code in the book!